A Practi
Canadian Extradition

Elaine F. Krivel, Q.C.

Counsellor, International Criminal Operations
at the Canadian Mission to the European Union (Brussels)
(formerly Director, Federal Prosecution Service
Ontario Regional Office
Department of Justice)

Thomas Beveridge

General Counsel
Director
International Assistance Group, Department of Justice

John W. Hayward

Former counsel with the Department of Justice

CARSWELL

A THOMSON COMPANY

♾ The paper used in this publication meets the minimum requirements of American National Standard for Information Sciences — Permanence of Paper for Printed Library Materials, ANSI Z39.49-1984.

National Library of Canada Cataloguing in Publication Data

Krivel, Elaine
  A practical guide to Canadian extradition

Includes index.
ISBN 0-459-26026-X

1. Canada. Extradition Act.   2. Extradition — Canada.   I. Beveridge, Thomas, 1957.
II. Title.

KE9275.K74 2002   345.71'052   C2001-930531-1
KF9635.K74 2002

CARSWELL

A THOMSON COMPANY

One Corporate Plaza	Customer Relations
2075 Kennedy Road	Toronto 1-416-609-3800
Toronto, Ontario	Elswhere in Canada/U.S. 1-800-387-5164
M1T 3V4	Fax 1-416-298-5094
	World Wide Web: http://www.carswell.com
	E-mail: orders@carswell.com

In loving memory of my parents,
Saul and Sadie Krivel,
and for the future,
to my nieces, Julia and Susannah

Elaine F. Krivel, Q.C.

For my mother and Harshi

John W. Hayward

Acknowledgments

We would like to thank the Law Foundation of Ontario for their grant in support of this project.

We would like to thank the following for their encouragement and their comments: Daniel Bellemare, Q.C., William Corbett, Q.C., Paul Evraire, Q.C., Robert Prior, Donald MacIntosh, Jacques Lemire.

We would also like to thank Kim Gray, Tina Antonangelli and Nasim Kassam, for their assistance in the preparation and organization of the manuscript.

We would like to note that the views expressed in this book are those of the authors and are not to be attributed to the Department of Justice.

Elaine F. Krivel, Q.C.
Thomas Beveridge
John W. Hayward
December 2001

TABLE OF CONTENTS

Escape of Person Sought While in Custody and Arrest (s. 61)

Delay Before Surrender and Waiver of Time Period (s. 62)

Place of Surrender (s. 63)

Postponement of Surrender (s. 64)

Return to Canada (s. 65)

Temporary Surrender (ss. 66–68)

APPENDIX A

LETTERS ROGATORY

APPENDIX B

THE *MUTUAL LEGAL ASSISTANCE IN CRIMINAL MATTERS ACT* AND MUTUAL LEGAL ASSISTANCE AGREEMENTS

INTRODUCTION

§1.0 OBJECTIVES OF EXTRADITION LAW

Extradition law has various objectives. Firstly, given that crime and criminals frequently and increasingly cross national boundaries, extradition law is designed to enhance the investigation, prosecution, and suppression of crime. This point is made in the preamble to the *Treaty on Extradition Between Canada and the United States of America* (hereinafter *Canada–United States Extradition Treaty*):

> Canada and the United States of America, desiring to make more effective the co-operation of the two countries in the repression of crime by making provision for the reciprocal extradition of offenders, agree as follows . . . .

The point was also made by La Forest J. in the Supreme Court of Canada case of *United States v. Cotroni* (1989), 48 C.C.C. (3d) 193 (S.C.C.), at pp. 215–216:

> The investigation, prosecution and suppression of crime for the protection of the citizen and the maintenance of peace and public order is an important goal of all organized societies. The pursuit of that goal cannot realistically be confined within national boundaries. That has long been the case, but it is increasingly evident today. Modern communications have shrunk the world and made McLuhan's global village a reality. The only respect paid by the international criminal community to national boundaries is when these can serve as a means to frustrate the efforts of law enforcement and judicial authorities. The trafficking in drugs, with which we are here concerned, is an international enterprise and requires effective tools of international cooperation for its investigation, prosecution and suppression. Extradition is an important and well-established tool for effecting this cooperation.

Secondly, and following from the above passage, in providing more effective means for combating international criminal activity, extradition law is intended to afford greater protection to the Canadian public. As La Forest J. stated in *Cotroni*, at p. 216:

> The importance of extradition for the protection of the Canadian public against crime can scarcely be exaggerated. To afford that protection, there must be arrangements that ensure prosecution not only of those who commit crimes while they are physically in Canada and escape abroad, but also of those whose acts abroad have criminal effects in this country. This requires reciprocal arrangements with other states seeking similar objectives. As I noted in *Libman v. The Queen* (1985), 21 C.C.C. (3d) 206 at p. 231, 21 D.L.R. (4th) 174, [1985] 2 S.C.R. 178 (S.C.C.), it would be a sad commentary on our law if it was limited to the prosecution of minor offenders while permitting more seasoned criminals to operate on a world-wide scale.

1

La Forest J. in *Cotroni* indicated that the objectives of extradition include "bringing fugitives to justice for the proper determination of their guilt or innocence". In this way it "shares one of the basic objectives of all criminal prosecutions: to discover the truth in respect of the charges brought against the accused in a proper hearing." (p. 217)

What flows from the foregoing objectives is the principle that a state should extradite to a requesting state unless it can prosecute the offence itself, or there is a third country able and prepared to do so. The principle that crime should not go unpunished is captured by the Latin maxim "*Aut dedere, aut judicare*": extradite or prosecute.

§2.0 SOURCES OF EXTRADITION LAW: INTERNATIONAL ARRANGEMENTS AND DOMESTIC LEGISLATION

The two sources of Canada's extradition law — international arrangements and domestic law — were described by La Forest J. in his judgment in *United States v. McVey* (1992), 77 C.C.C. (3d) 1 (S.C.C.), at pp. 6–7:

> To begin with, it is important to remember that under customary international law states have no obligation to surrender fugitives from justice to other states; see *U.S.A. v. Allard* (1991), 64 C.C.C. (3d) 159 at p. 162, [1991] 1 S.C.R. 861, 40 Q.A.C. 274. To create such obligation, it is necessary to enter into treaties. So far as the international obligations of Canada (and for that matter other states) are concerned, therefore, they must be found within the confines of the treaties . . . .
>
> Equally these principles and rules do not exist at common law. At common law, the executive had no power to extradite criminals. Nor would a treaty obligation undertaken by Canada alone authorize the executive to do so. A treaty does not alter the law of the land. A statute is required to implement it. From the standpoint of domestic law, therefore, extradition is a creature of statute. The domestic law of this country is to be found in the *Extradition Act*; see also *Allard*, *supra*, at p. 162.

§2.1 International Agreements

Canada is currently bound by a number of bilateral and multilateral arrangements which concern extradition. As a member of the Commonwealth, Canada has also had historical obligations to return fugitives from justice to those countries which recognize the Queen as Head of State, even in the absence of a treaty.

Canada has extradition treaties with the following countries:

Country	Entered into Force	Country	Entered into Force
Albania	July 11, 1927	Argentina	February 9, 1894
Austria	August 30, 1969	Belgium	March 17, 1902
Bolivia	November 4, 1898	Chile	August 22, 1898
Colombia	December 16, 1899	Cuba	May 22, 1905

Czech Republic	December 15, 1926	Denmark	February 13, 1979
Ecuador	July 2, 1886	El Salvador	January 13, 1883
Estonia	September 18, 1928	Finland	February 16, 1985
France	December 1, 1989	Germany	September 30, 1979
Greece	February 26, 1912	Guatemala	December 13, 1886
Haiti	February 21, 1876	Hong Kong	June 13, 1997
Hungary	March 30, 1874	Iceland	July 7, 1873
India	February 10, 1987	Israel	December 19, 1969
Italy	June 27, 1985	Korea (South)	February 1, 1995
Latvia	September 18, 1928	Liberia	March 23, 1894
Lithuania	September 1928	Luxembourg	March 15, 1881
Mexico	October 21, 1990	Monaco	May 23, 1892
Netherlands	December 1, 1991	Nicaragua	August 24, 1906
Norway	October 17, 1873	Panama	August 26, 1907
Paraguay	July 17, 1911	Peru	May 20, 1907
Philippines	November 12, 1990	Portugal	March 19, 1894
Romania	May 21, 1894	San Marino	March 19, 1900
Spain	August 15, 1990	Slovak Republic	December 15, 1926
Switzerland	March 19, 1996	Sweden	October 30, 2001
Tonga	November 29, 1879	Thailand	November 24, 1911
Uruguay	March 20, 1885	United States	March 22, 1976

In addition to the bilateral treaties set out above, Canada is bound by the following multilateral instruments which provide for extradition and mutual legal assistance schemes in particular circumstances regardless of whether Canada has a bilateral agreement with a particular country:

- Convention for the Suppression of Unlawful Seizure of Aircraft, signed at The Hague on 16 December 1970 (entered into force on 14 October 1971)

- Convention for the Suppression of Unlawful Acts against the Safety of Civil Aviation, signed at Montreal on 23 September 1971 (entered into force on 26 January 1973)

- Convention on the Prevention and Punishment of Crimes against Internationally Protected Persons, including Diplomatic Agents, adopted by the General Assembly of the United Nations on 14 December 1973 (entered into force on 3 June 1983)

- Convention on the Physical Protection of Nuclear Material, adopted at Vienna on 26 October 1979 and opened for signature at Vienna and New York on 3 March 1980 (entered into force on 8 February 1987)

3

- Protocol for the Suppression of Unlawful Acts of Violence at Airports Serving International Civil Aviation, supplementary to the Convention for the Suppression of Unlawful Acts against the Safety of Civil Aviation, signed at Montreal on 24 February 1988 (entered into force on 6 August 1989)

- Convention for the Suppression of Unlawful Acts against the Safety of Maritime Navigation, done at Rome on 10 March 1988 (entered into force on 1 March 1992)

- Protocol for the Suppression of Unlawful Acts against the Safety of Fixed Platforms located on the Continental Shelf, done at Rome on 10 March 1988 (entered into force on 1 March 1992)

- Inter-American Convention on Mutual Assistance in Criminal Matters (in force for Canada July 3, 1996)

- UN Convention against Illicit Traffic in Narcotic Drugs and Psychotropic Substances (in force for Canada 11 November 1990)

- Convention against Torture and other Cruel, Inhuman or Degrading Treatment or Punishment (in force for Canada 24 July 1987)

Discretionary extradition provisions are provided by the following conventions:

- First Geneva Convention (1949) Wounded and Sick

- Second Geneva Convention (1949) Maritime

- Third Geneva Convention (1949) Prisoners of War

- Fourth Geneva Convention (1949) Civilians

- Protocol 1 Additional to the Geneva Conventions (1977)

- Convention on the Prevention and Punishment of the Crime of Genocide (1952)

Canada's historical position as a member of the Commonwealth gave rise to obligations to other Commonwealth countries to return fugitives from justice to those countries. Surrender was not made under treaty obligation but rather as a matter of courtesy to countries which recognized the Queen as Head of State (see *Argentina (Republic) v. Mellino* (1987), 33 C.C.C. (3d) 334 (S.C.C.), at p. 349). Rendition, as it was known, was governed prior to the new *Extradition Act* by the *Fugitive Offenders Act*, R.S.C. 1985, c. F-32. The new *Extradition Act* now designates most of these

4

states as extradition partners and Canada's obligations to them are thus continued. They are:

Antigua and Barbuda	Malaysia
Australia	Mauritius
The Bahamas	New Zealand
Barbados	Papua New Guinea
Belize	St. Kitts & Nevis
Britain	St. Lucia
*includes Colonies	St. Vincent & The Grenadines
Grenada	Solomon Islands
Jamaica	Tuvalu
Lesotho	

Many of the extradition treaties currently binding on Canada were entered into by the United Kingdom between 1870 and the Second World War, at a time when Canada as a member of the British Empire was subject to such Imperial treaties (see *United States v. McVey, supra,* at p. 7). More specifically, thirty-three of Canada's extradition treaties were entered into by Great Britain during this period: those with Albania, Argentina, Belgium, Bolivia, Chile, Colombia, Cuba, Czech Republic, Ecuador, El Salvador, Estonia, Greece, Guatemala, Haiti, Hungary, Iceland, Latvia, Liberia, Lithuania, Luxembourg, Monaco, Nicaragua, Norway, Panama, Paraguay, Peru, Portugal, Romania, San Marino, Thailand, Tonga, Uruguay, and Yugoslavia.

The remainder of the extradition treaties now binding on Canada were entered into by the Canadian government following the Second World War. More specifically, sixteen of Canada's bilateral extradition treaties were entered into by the Canadian government since the Second World War: those with Austria, Denmark, Finland, France, Germany, India, Israel, Italy, South Korea, Mexico, the Netherlands, the Philippines, Spain, Sweden, Switzerland, and the United States.

Historically, most treaties provided a list of offences for which extradition could be granted. Since the mid- to late 1980s, the trend has been for treaties to adopt a punishability standard, that is, extradition will be granted for any offence carrying a potential punishment equal to or greater than the standard specified in the treaty. See, for example, the extradition treaties with the following countries: Finland (both a list and a punishability standard) (in force on February 16, 1985); France (in force December 1, 1989); India (in force February 10, 1987); Italy (both a list and a punishability standard) (in force June 27, 1985); South Korea (in force February 1, 1995); Mexico (in force October 21, 1990); the Netherlands (in force December 1, 1991); the Philippines (in force November 12, 1990); Spain (in force August 15, 1990); Switzerland (in force March 19, 1996); and the United States (treaty as amended by Protocol in force November 26, 1991).

Until 1991, Article 2 of the *Canada–United States Extradition Treaty* provided that "[p]ersons shall be delivered up according to the provisions of this Treaty for any of the offenses listed in the Schedule annexed to this Treaty, which is an integral part of this Treaty, provided these offenses are punishable by the laws of both Contracting Parties by a term of imprisonment exceeding one year." Thus extradition between the two countries was limited to those offences listed in the schedule to the treaty. By contrast, in 1991, Article 2 of the *Canada–United States Extradition Treaty* was changed to a pure punishability standard: "[e]xtradition shall be granted for conduct which constitutes an offense punishable by the laws of both Contracting Parties by imprisonment or other form of detention for a term exceeding one year or any greater punishment." (This amendment was made by Protocol and came into force on November 26, 1991. The full history of the current extradition treaty between Canada and the United States is as follows: The treaty was signed in Washington, D.C., on December 3, 1971. The treaty was amended by an Exchange of Notes on June 28 and July 9, 1974. Instruments of Ratification were exchanged and the treaty came into force on March 22, 1976. The treaty was amended by Protocol on November 26, 1991.)

The shift from a list to a no-list approach has resulted in more offences becoming extraditable.

§2.2 Canadian Extradition Legislation

Prior to the enactment of the 1999 *Extradition Act* (S.C. 1999, c. 18), Canada's international extradition obligations were implemented by two pieces of federal legislation. The first was the *Fugitive Offenders Act*, R.S.C. 1985, c. F-32. This Act applied to jurisdictions which, like Canada, recognized the Queen as Head of State. Because they recognized the same sovereign, an extradition treaty was not required. As La Forest J. stated in *Argentina (Republic) v. Mellino* (1987), 33 C.C.C. (3d) 334 (S.C.C.), at p. 349: "Surrender under that Act [*Fugitive Offenders Act*] is not made under treaty obligation but as a matter of courtesy to Commonwealth countries." This process was referred to as "rendition" rather than extradition. In all other cases, the governing legislation was the *Extradition Act*, R.S.C. 1985, c. E-23. Generally, a treaty applied in conjunction with the *Extradition Act*. However, in exceptional circumstances under Part II of the former *Extradition Act*, extradition could be accomplished irrespective of treaty.

Section 130 of the new *Extradition Act* expressly repeals the *Fugitive Offenders Act*. Rendition is henceforth provided for in the *Extradition Act*. More specifically, s. 9(1) of the new Act provides that, "[t]he names of members of the Commonwealth or other States or entities that appear in the schedule are designated as extradition partners." Section 2 defines an "extradition partner" as "a State or entity with which Canada is party to an extradition agreement, with which Canada has entered into a specific agreement or whose name appears in the schedule." As extradition partners designated under the Act, the states to whom the former *Fugitive Offenders Act* applied are now provided with full rights to make extradition requests under the new Act, notwithstanding the absence of an extradition treaty with Canada.

The assimilation of rendition within the new *Extradition Act* is significant because rendition will now be governed by the same rules and procedures as extradition to non-Commonwealth jurisdictions. The former *Extradition Act* had a number of important differences from the *Fugitive Offenders Act*. The test for committal is one example. Under s. 18 of the former *Extradition Act*, the requesting state was required to meet the same sufficiency of evidence standard that applies at a preliminary hearing in Canada (which is also the same test required to be met under the new Act). Under s. 11 of the *Fugitive Offenders Act*, the requesting jurisdiction was required to produce evidence that raised a "strong or probable presumption" that the fugitive committed the offence in question.

(a) Origins of Canadian *Extradition Act*

Part I of the former Act had its roots in the British *Extradition Act*, 1870 (U.K.), 1870, c. 52. The approach adopted by the British *Extradition Act* was to set out a general procedure for the surrender of fugitives under any treaty then in force or subsequently entered into by the United Kingdom. Prior to the 1870 legislation, a separate Act was required to implement each treaty (see *Hansard*, Parliamentary Debates, June 16, 1870, at p. 301 (House of Commons), and August 1, 1870, at p. 1268 (House of Lords)). In 1877, following the British example, Canada passed legislation which created a general procedure for the surrender of fugitives to any country with which the Imperial Government had entered or would thereafter enter a treaty (*Extradition Act*, S.C. 1877, c. 25). The inception of the Canadian *Extradition Act* was discussed by La Forest J. in his judgment in *United States v. McVey, supra*, at p. 7:

> The genesis of the present Act may be traced to the first British statute of general application on the subject, the *Extradition Act*, 1870 (U.K.), c. 52. The Act was made applicable to Canada pursuant to s. 17, but because s. 27 retained previous Canadian legislation, it led to great confusion in Canada, and Canada took steps to provide for its own extradition procedure, the *Extradition Act*, S.C. 1877, c. 25 . . . .

The 1877 Canadian Act was modeled on the 1870 British Act, with only a few minor differences in order and language. This point was made by La Forest J. in *United States v. McVey, supra*, at p. 7:

> The Canadian Act of 1877 was very closely modelled on the British Act of 1870. The changes for the most part were to the order in which the provisions appear and some inconsequential verbal changes . . . .

The Canadian *Extradition Act* of 1877 formed the nucleus of Part I of the Canadian *Extradition Act* as it existed until the passing of the 1999 Act. Until 1992, only a few minor amendments were made to the 1877 Act (see the following: S.C. 1882, c. 20;

R.S.C. 1886, c. 142; S.C. 1909, c. 14; R.S.C. 1985, c. E-23; and R.S.C. 1985, c. 27 (1st Supp.)).

(b) 1992 Amendments to *Extradition Act*

In 1992, two important aspects of Part I of the *Extradition Act* underwent substantial amendments (*An Act to amend the Extradition Act*, S.C. 1992, c. 13; the 1992 amendments came into force on December 1, 1992 (SI/92-99, Order Fixing December 1, 1992 as the Date of the Coming into Force of the Act, Canada Gazette, Part II, v. 126:24, p. 4503). Firstly, s. 9(3) was added to the Act with the intention of clarifying the *Charter* jurisdiction of judges under the Act (*Act to amend the Extradition Act*, *supra*, s. 2). This subsection provided that, "[f]or the purposes of the *Constitution Act, 1982*, a judge who is a superior court judge or a county court judge has, with respect to the functions that that judge is required to perform in applying this Act, the same competence that that judge possesses by virtue of being a superior court judge or a county court judge." Prior to the addition of s. 9(3) to the Act, an extradition judge was not a "court of competent jurisdiction" for the purpose of s. 24 of the *Charter* (see *R. v. Schmidt* (1987), 33 C.C.C. (3d) 193 (S.C.C.); *Argentina (Republic) v. Mellino, supra*). *Charter* issues could only be dealt with by a superior court judge on a *habeas corpus* application to review the committal decision of the extradition judge. As a superior court judge, the *habeas corpus* judge was the court of competent jurisdiction for the purposes of s. 24 of the *Charter* (see *Mellino*, p. 352). Within the limits of the extradition judge's role, s. 9(3) provided *Charter* jurisdiction.

Section 9(3) is continued by s. 25 of the new Act, which provides that, "[f]or the purposes of the *Constitution Act, 1982*, a judge has, with respect to the functions that the judge is required to perform in applying this Act, the same competence that that judge possesses by virtue of being a superior court judge."

The second aspect of the 1992 amendments concerned the provisions of the former *Extradition Act* relating to appeals, that is, ss. 19, 23, 24, 25, and 28 (see *Act to Amend the Extradition Act*, *supra*, ss. 3–6).

The purpose of the 1992 appeal amendments was to streamline the appeal procedures under the Act, while at the same time ensuring adequate protections for the person sought. Minister of Justice Kim Campbell made the following comment on second reading (*Hansard*, November 7, 1991, at pp. 4777–4778):

> In developing a more streamlined appeal and review system, I have been guided by the following principles. First, the appeal and review process of extradition matters should resemble as nearly as possible the remedies available to those charged with criminal offences in Canada. Second, the person whose extradition is sought should enjoy the protections of the *Canadian Charter of Rights and Freedoms*. Third, to the extent possible, duplication of proceedings should be avoided.
>
> . . .

Nevertheless, the extradition judge can now know the recourse under the *Canadian Charter of Rights and Freedoms* that may apply to the duties he is required to perform in applying this law.

The changes made in 1992 to the appeals provisions have been incorporated into the new *Extradition Act*. In this respect, the new Act reflects the above-cited goals of streamlining the appeals procedure and avoiding duplication of proceedings.

Prior to these 1992 amendments, as noted above, review of an extradition judge's decision to commit a person for surrender was done through a *habeas corpus* application to a superior court of the province (see s. 19 of the *Extradition Act*, R.S.C. 1985, c. E-23; *Argentina (Republic) v. Mellino* (1987), 33 C.C.C. (3d) 334 (S.C.C.), at p. 352; and *United States v. St. Gelais* (1994), 90 C.C.C. (3d) 83 (Que. C.A.), at p. 87, leave to appeal refused (1994), 90 C.C.C. (3d) vi (note) (S.C.C.). The fugitive then had a right of appeal to the provincial court of appeal (see s. 784(3)–(5) of the *Criminal Code*, R.S.C. 1985, c. C-46; *Germany (Federal Republic) v. Rauca* (1983), 4 C.C.C. (3d) 385 (Ont. C.A.), at p. 396; *Argentina (Republic) v. Mellino, supra,* and *United States v. St. Gelais, supra*). A further appeal could be made, with leave, to the Supreme Court of Canada (see also *R. v. Schmidt, supra,* at pp. 206–208).

After this process had been completed, the case was then referred to the Minister of Justice for a decision regarding the actual surrender of the person sought (s. 25 of the *Extradition Act*, R.S.C. 1985, c. E-23). A review of the Minister's decision could then be made by way of *habeas corpus* application either to the superior court of the province (*Idziak v. Canada (Minister of Justice)* (1989), 53 C.C.C. (3d) 385 (Ont. H.C.), at pp. 401–402, affirmed (1990), 72 O.R. (2d) 480 (Ont. C.A.), affirmed (1992), 77 C.C.C. (3d) 65 (S.C.C.), reconsideration refused (1992), 9 Admin. L.R. (2d) 1n (S.C.C.)) or the Federal Court. The jurisdiction of the Federal Court came from the fact that the decision of the Minister was within the Federal Court's jurisdiction to review the decision of a "federal board, commission or other tribunal" as defined by s. 2 of the *Federal Court Act*, R.S.C. 1985, c. F-7. In *Kindler v. Canada (Minister of Justice)* (1986), 69 N.R. 227 (Fed. C.A.), at pp. 227–228, the Federal Court of Appeal held the Federal Court — Trial Division had jurisdiction to undertake reviews of the Minister's surrender decisions. As with the review of the extradition judge's decision, the person then had a right of appeal to the court of appeal, either federal or provincial, depending upon the court in which the review had been brought. A further appeal could be made, with leave, to the Supreme Court of Canada.

Under the 1992 amendments, the first recourse against either the extradition judge's decision or the Minister's decision was to the provincial court of appeal (see ss. 19.2 and 25.2 of the post-1992 Act; see also *United States v. St. Gelais, supra,* at p. 88; *United States v. Houslander* (1993), 13 O.R. (3d) 44 (Ont. Gen. Div.), at p. 53; and *United States v. Wong* (1995), 98 C.C.C. (3d) 332 (B.C. C.A.), at pp. 335, 339, leave to appeal to S.C.C. refused (1995), 101 C.C.C. (3d) vi (S.C.C.)). The amendments thus eliminated one level of review, that being the bringing of a *habeas corpus* application before the superior court of the province. This point was made by the Ontario Court of Appeal in *United States v. Vanasse* (1993), 67 O.A.C. 370 (Ont.

9

C.A.), at p. 371. The amendments also provided the court of appeal with the power to defer an appeal of the extradition judge's finding until after the Minister had made a decision with respect to surrender (see s. 19.4(2)). The amendments provided for a joint hearing of the appeal of the extradition judge's decision and the review of the Minister's surrender decision (see s. 25.2(9)).

In addition, the amendments ousted the jurisdiction of the Federal Court to deal with reviews of the Minister's surrender decision (see s. 25.2(1)).

(c) Extradition in Absence of International Agreement (Part II of former *Extradition Act*)

Under the former Act, extradition to a country which did not have a treaty with Canada was governed by Part II, ss. 35–40 of that Act, which enabled the Governor General to proclaim that extradition under the Act would be in force with respect to the named country on a date specified in the proclamation.

Such proclamations occurred on only three occasions. The first was for the Federal Republic of Germany in 1974 (SI/74-40, *Canada Gazette*, Part II, v. 108). The second was for Brazil in 1979 (SI/79-160, *Canada Gazette*, Part II, v. 113:20, p. 3658). The third was for India in 1985 (SI/85-190, *Canada Gazette*, Part II, v. 119:23, p. 4615). Canada subsequently signed extradition treaties with Germany and India.

This procedure had the significant disadvantage of applying only to offences which might occur after the date of the Part II proclamation (s. 36). As a result, extradition was not possible to a non-treaty country, even if the *Extradition Act* was made applicable to that country by the application of a Part II proclamation, if the offence took place before the proclamation. Extradition from Canada on a case-by-case basis was not an option under the former Act.

Both of these problems are now eliminated by the new *Extradition Act*, which effects significant improvement over the former legislative scheme by permitting Canada to make case-by-case extradition determinations with respect to requests from countries that are not otherwise extradition partners. More specifically, s. 10(1) provides that "[t]he Minister of Foreign Affairs may, with the agreement of the Minister, enter into a specific agreement with a State or entity for the purpose of giving effect to a request for extradition in a particular case." Section 2 defines "Minister" as the "Minister of Justice" and "specific agreement" as "an agreement referred to in section 10 that is in force."

§3.0 NEW *EXTRADITION ACT*

§3.1 Aims

The new *Extradition Act* came into force on June 17, 1999. The aim of the new Act is to modernize and streamline Canada's extradition procedure, thereby enabling Canada to more effectively meet its international extradition obligations. The new

Act springs from the recognition that Canada's prior extradition legislation — the *Extradition Act* (R.S.C. 1985, c. E-23) and the *Fugitive Offenders Act* (R.S.C. 1985, c. F-32), both of which remained largely unchanged from their inception in the late nineteenth century until their repeal by the new Act — was not designed to cope with modern criminal activity, which has taken advantage of modern technology and communication systems to become increasingly transnational in character. These points were made by Ms. Eleni Bakopanos, Parliamentary Secretary to the Minister of Justice and Attorney General of Canada, while introducing Bill C-40 (now the *Extradition Act*) to the House of Commons on second reading (*House of Commons Debates*, October 8, 1998, 1st Session, 36th Parliament, v. 135, pp. 9003–9004):

> The bill overhauls extradition laws in Canada and creates a modern, effective system for extradition appropriate for the 21st century. It will help us to better meet our international commitments and ensure that Canada is not a safe haven for criminals seeking to avoid justice.

> The *Extradition Act*, which is of general application, and the *Fugitive Offenders Act*, which applies to the extradition process between Commonwealth countries referred to as rendition, both date from the late 1800s.

> Aside from amendments to the extradition appeal process enacted in 1992, these statutes have remained essentially unchanged from the last century.
> [Translation.]

> Extradition laws as they now stand cause serious problems, as we are unable to turn over criminals to countries with which we do not have extradition agreements or treaties; to entities other than a state, such as United Nations tribunals for war crimes; or to countries where extradition treaties are in force but where an outdated list of offences does not include modern offences like drug trafficking, money laundering and computer crimes.

> The current extradition process places onerous evidentiary requirements on foreign states and the legislation does not set out clear and adequate procedural and human rights safeguards for persons whose extradition is being sought.

> Given the increasing ease of international travel, the advancement of technology and the global economy, major crime and criminals are no longer local in nature.

> Transnational crime and criminals are now the norm, not the exception. Canada's laws must be modernized in recognition of that reality.

Parliamentary Secretary Bakopanos drew particular attention to the difficulty many foreign states had under the former extradition regime in complying with Canadian evidentiary rules, at p. 9004:

> In the case of a number of requests from countries other than the United States extradition proceedings cannot be instituted. In other instances states are so discouraged by the

different hurdles imposed by our current extradition law that they do not even initiate an extradition request. The primary problem is that the current legislation mandates that the foreign states submit evidence in support of their request in a form which meets the complicated requirements of Canadian evidentiary rules.

For countries which do not have a common law system, and for which concepts such as hearsay are unknown, this requirement makes the preparation of a request for extradition a tremendously difficult task, and in some instances an impossible one. Even with countries with a similar legal tradition such as the United States, we have heard on numerous occasions how difficult it is to obtain extradition from Canada. In the context of our other common law jurisdictions such as Great Britain and Australia, Canada's system is viewed as one fraught with difficulties due to the antiquity of our legislation.

§3.2 Broadened Scope of New *Extradition Act*

There were a number of frailties inherent in the former legislation which the new Act has attempted to remedy, including:

(a) The evidentiary process. Under the old Act, as indicated in the speech of Eleni Bakopanos above, subject to treaty, evidence was required to be provided through the use of first person affidavits devoid of hearsay. This was considered to impede extradition to countries unfamiliar with the requirements of our legal system, most notably those with civil law traditions. The introduction of the record of the case in s. 32(1) of the new Act will permit summaries of the evidence to be provided in a form more compatible with the evidence gathering procedures of the requesting state.

(b) Even for other common law countries, the requirement for affidavit evidence made extradition more difficult in complex cases or cases with a large number of witnesses or victims, because affidavit evidence would have to have been obtained from all of them. Under the former Act there was often no reciprocity because Canada's first-hand affidavit requirement often imposed higher evidentiary burdens on the other country than that country did on Canada. For example, the United States accepts materials containing hearsay whereas under the former Act Canada did not. The record of the case enables reference to be made to the witnesses' evidence without the necessity of a first person affidavit.

(c) There was no mechanism for extraditing to entities other than states, such as the United Nations War Crimes Tribunals. These entities are now named as extradition partners.

(d) Other than the somewhat difficult proclamation procedures of Part II of the former Act, there was no provision for extradition from Canada to countries with which we had no treaty or rendition obligation. Under s. 10 of the new Act, specific agreements for extradition can be made on a case-by-case basis with non-extradition partners. Also, countries can be added to, or deleted from, the list of extradition partners in accordance with s. 9(2) of the new Act.

(e) Extradition to commonwealth countries formerly governed by the *Fugitive Offenders Act*, and to other states governed by the former *Extradition Act*, created two separate extradition regimes. The new Act replaces the two former statutes and creates one uniform code of procedure.

(f) Neither the *Fugitive Offenders Act* nor the former *Extradition Act* provided for a code of procedure with respect to such matters as arrest, bail and conduct of the hearing. The new Act sets out a complete code of procedure.

(g) In the former Act, the Minister's authority to refuse surrender was only dealt with in reference to political offence situations (s. 22) (although treaties often gave direction respecting refusal to extradite.) The new Act gives greater guidance in this regard in that it enumerates specific grounds upon which the Minister's discretion to refuse to surrender may be exercised. The new Act similarly specifies the authority of the Minister to make surrender conditional on or subject to assurances. There are also specified grounds which require the Minister to refuse surrender (ss. 40–47).

(h) Although a practice had developed under the former system whereby a fugitive could waive the requirements of the formal extradition process, or consent to committal or surrender in order to expedite his or her return to the requesting state, these procedures were not referred to in the legislation. They are now codified in the new Act (ss. 70–72), and certain safeguards are addressed, such as requiring the judge to inform the person of the protections relinquished by resorting to the waiver procedure.

(i) The former legislation had no provision for the temporary surrender of a person to another state. The new Act permits, in s. 66, for the temporary surrender of a person who is serving a sentence in Canada, so that the trial in the foreign state can proceed in a timely fashion, and the person subsequently returned to Canada for the completion of the Canadian sentence.

(j) In addition to modernizing the extradition process, the new Act also makes important modifications to the *Canada Evidence Act*, R.S.C. 1985, c. C-5, *Criminal Code*, R.S.C. 1985, c. C-46, and *Mutual Legal Assistance in Criminal Matters Act*, R.S.C. 1985, c. 30 (4th Supp.), allowing Canadian courts to use video and audio link technology to obtain "virtual" testimony from witnesses abroad or elsewhere in Canada, in proceedings under those Acts (see ss. 89–90, ss. 92–95 and 113).

(k) The new Act also takes account of the interaction between the extradition and refugee processes, given that conflicts can arise when someone subject to an extradition request makes a claim for refugee status. The Act modifies the *Extradition Act* and *Immigration Act* to avoid a duplication in decision making and to limit delay in the extradition process (see ss. 40(2), 48(2), 75 and 96).

§3.3 Extradition Process

The extradition process is comprised of distinct ministerial and judicial functions. It is the Minister of Justice's function at the outset of the process to receive the extradition request from the extradition partner and to be satisfied that the preconditions with respect to punishment, as set out in s. 3(1)(a) and 3(3) of the Act, have been met. If the Minister is so satisfied, then pursuant to s. 15, an authority to proceed will be issued in which the Minister identifies the equivalent Canadian offence or offences established by the alleged conduct of the person sought. After the authority to proceed is issued, the judicial phase of the extradition process is engaged. The extradition judge at the hearing will assess the evidence provided by the extradition partner against the crimes described by the Minister in the authority to proceed. If it is found that there is sufficient evidence to commit the person sought for surrender, the Minister then determines whether the person sought should actually be surrendered to the extradition partner. This is the second part of the ministerial phase, the first being the Minister's issuance of an authority to proceed.

Any discussion of the respective roles of the extradition judge and the Minister of Justice under the new Act must take into account the jurisprudence decided under the former *Extradition Act*. The judicial and ministerial roles which existed under the former Act have been maintained, and in fact further delineated, in the new Act as a result of the detailed directions the new Act sets out with respect to the exercise of ministerial functions. The case law decided under the former Act will continue to be looked to in this regard when interpreting the new legislation. The ministerial role under the new Act has been expanded as a result of the introduction of the requirement for an authority to proceed to be issued before the judicial proceedings can be held. Under the former Act, the ministerial phase followed upon the judicial phase and, for that reason, the case law referred to extradition as a two-phase process.

The distinction between the judicial and the ministerial phases of the extradition process under the former *Extradition Act* was succinctly described by Cory J. in the Supreme Court of Canada decision of *Idziak v. Canada (Minister of Justice)* (1992), 77 C.C.C. (3d) 65 (S.C.C.), at p. 86, reconsideration refused (1992), 9 Admin. L.R. (2d) 1n (S.C.C.):

> It has been seen that the extradition process has two distinct phases. The first, the judicial phase, encompasses the court proceedings which determine whether a factual and legal basis for extradition exists. If that process results in the issuance of a warrant of committal, then the second phase is activated. There, the Minister of Justice exercises his or her discretion in determining whether to issue a warrant of surrender. The first decision-

making phase is certainly judicial in its nature and warrants the application of the full panoply of procedural safeguards. By contrast, the second decision-making process is political in its nature. The Minister must weigh the representations of the fugitive against Canada's international treaty obligations.

The distinction between the judicial and ministerial roles in the extradition process as described by Cory J. is equally applicable to the new *Extradition Act*. The new Act maintains the dual structure comprised of a judicial decision-making phase and a ministerial discretionary phase, the latter involving a process that is largely political in nature.

The case law under the former *Extradition Act* was clear that the extradition hearing judge did not have the authority to order the actual surrender of the person sought to the extradition partner. The situation remains the same under the new Act, the function assigned to the extradition hearing judge and the test to be applied at the hearing being substantially the same as before. The extradition judge determines if there is sufficient evidence to commit the person sought for surrender, that is, to issue an order of committal. In *Philippines (Republic) v. Pacificador* (1993), 83 C.C.C. (3d) 210 (Ont. C.A.), at p. 222 (leave to appeal to S.C.C. refused (1994), 87 C.C.C. (3d) vi (S.C.C.)), Doherty J.A. for the Ontario Court of Appeal described the role of the extradition judge in the context of the extradition process:

> Extradition is primarily a function of the executive and a product of international agreements made between states. The ultimate guilt or innocence of the fugitive is not the concern of the Canadian executive or judiciary: *R. v. Schmidt* (1987), 333 C.C.C. (3d) 193 at p. 208, 39 D.L.R. (4th) 18, [1987] 1 S.C.R. 500. The judicial phase of the extradition process is but part of that entire process and is preliminary to the Minister's ultimate determination concerning the surrender of the fugitive.

In sum, the new Act retains the distinct roles that were assigned to the extradition judge and the Minister under the former *Extradition Act*. More specifically, at the extradition hearing the judge will assess the sufficiency of the evidence for committal. It is still the Minister's responsibility, subsequent to an order of committal being issued by the extradition judge, to determine if surrender should take place. In the new Act the Minister is also given the responsibility, at the beginning of the process, to decide whether an authority to proceed should be issued permitting the extradition to go forward to the judicial phase. This requires the Minister to determine whether the punishability requirements set out in s. 3 of the Act have been complied with and to determine what Canadian offences are established by the alleged foreign criminal conduct.

The new Act establishes a complete code of procedure for extradition. The process is summarized in the chart below:

THE EXTRADITION PROCESS*

Provisional arrest

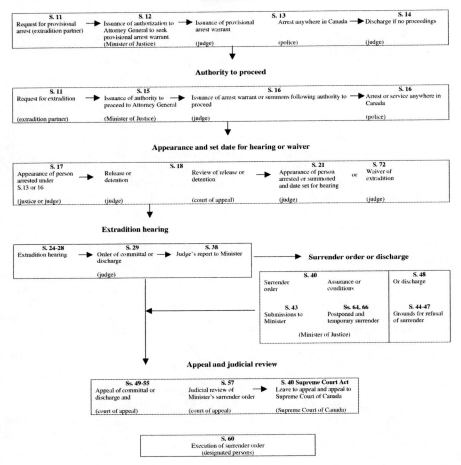

S. 11	S. 12	S. 13	S. 14
Request for provisional arrest (extradition partner)	Issuance of authorization to Attorney General to seek provisional arrest warrant (Minister of Justice)	Issuance of provisional arrest warrant (judge)	Arrest anywhere in Canada → Discharge if no proceedings (police) (judge)

Authority to proceed

S. 11	S. 15	S. 16	S. 16
Request for extradition (extradition partner)	Issuance of authority to proceed to Attorney General (Minister of Justice)	Issuance of arrest warrant or summons following authority to proceed (judge)	Arrest or service anywhere in Canada (police)

Appearance and set date for hearing or waiver

S. 17	S. 18	S. 21	S. 72
Appearance of person arrested under S.13 or 16 (justice or judge)	Release or detention (judge) → Review of release or detention (court of appeal)	Appearance of person arrested or summoned and date set for hearing (judge)	or Waiver of extradition (judge)

Extradition hearing

S. 24-28	S. 29	S. 38
Extradition hearing	Order of committal or discharge (judge)	Judge's report to Minister

Surrender order or discharge

S. 40		S. 48
Surrender order	Assurance or conditions	Or discharge
S. 43 Submissions to Minister	**Ss. 64, 66** Postponed and temporary surrender	**S. 44-47** Grounds for refusal of surrender
	(Minister of Justice)	

Appeal and judicial review

Ss. 49-55	S. 57	S. 40 Supreme Court Act
Appeal of committal or discharge and (court of appeal)	Judicial review of Minister's surrender order (court of appeal)	Leave to appeal and appeal to Supreme Court of Canada (Supreme Court of Canada)

S. 60
Execution of surrender order (designated persons)

EXTRADITION ACT

An Act respecting extradition, to amend the *Canada Evidence Act*, the *Criminal Code*, the *Immigration Act* and the *Mutual Legal Assistance in Criminal Matters Act* and to amend and repeal other Acts in consequence

S.C. 1999, c. 18,
as am. S.C. 2000, c. 24, ss. 47-53 (in force October 23, 2000)

Short Title (s. 1)

1. This Act may be cited as the *Extradition Act*.

Interpretation (s. 2)

§1.0 DESCRIPTION

Section 2 of the *Extradition Act* provides:

DEFINITIONS
    2. The definitions in this section apply in this Act.

"**Attorney General**" means the Attorney General of Canada.

"**court**" means

    (a) in Ontario, the Ontario Court (General Division);*
    (b) in Quebec, the Superior Court;
    (c) in New Brunswick, Manitoba, Alberta and Saskatchewan, the Court of Queen's Bench;
    (d) in Nova Scotia, British Columbia, the Northwest Territories, the Yukon Territory and Nunavut, the Supreme Court; and
    (e) in Prince Edward Island and Newfoundland, the Trial Division of the Supreme Court.

"**court of appeal**" means

    (a) in the Province of Prince Edward Island, the Appeal Division of the Supreme Court; and
    (b) in all other provinces, the Court of Appeal.

---

* The Ontario Court (General Division) was renamed the Ontario Superior Court of Justice by S.O. 1996, c. 25, s. 8, which came into force April 19, 1999.

17

"**extradition agreement**" **means an agreement that is in force, to which Canada is a party and that contains a provision respecting the extradition of persons, other than a specific agreement.**

"**extradition partner**" **means a State or entity with which Canada is party to an extradition agreement, with which Canada has entered into a specific agreement or whose name appears in the schedule.**

"**International Criminal Court**" **means the International Criminal Court as defined in subsection 2(1) of the** *Crimes Against Humanity and War Crimes Act***. [en. S.C. 2000, c. 24, s. 47]**

"**judge**" **means a judge of the court.**

"**justice**" **has the same meaning as in section 2 of the** *Criminal Code***.**

"**Minister**" **means the Minister of Justice.**

"**specific agreement**" **means an agreement referred to in section 10 that is in force.**

"**State or entity**" **means**

    (a) **a State other than Canada;**
    (b) **a province, state or other political subdivision of a State other than Canada;**
    (c) **a colony, dependency, possession, protectorate, condominium, trust territory or any territory falling under the jurisdiction of a State other than Canada;**
    (d) **an international criminal court or tribunal; or**
    (e) **a territory.**

The terms "court" and "court of appeal" are defined to refer to the superior court of each province and the appellate court of each province, respectively.

"International Criminal Court," as defined in the *Crimes Against Humanity and War Crimes Act*, S.C. 2000, c. 24, s. 2(1), "means the International Criminal Court established by the *Rome Statute*." This court has jurisdiction to prosecute and try individuals for genocide, crimes against humanity and war crimes. The *Rome Statute* will enter into force once sixty countries have ratified it.

A "judge" is defined as a "judge of the *court*" (emphasis added), and hence the term "judge" for the purposes of the Act refers to a judge of the superior court of the applicable province.

A "justice" is defined as having the same meaning as that term has in s. 2 of the *Criminal Code*, which defines a "justice" as a justice of the peace or provincial court judge. The role of "justices" in the new Act is restricted to first appearances of arrested persons. Section 17 anticipates that a person arrested under s. 13 or 16 of the Act must be brought before a judge or justice within 24 hours of the arrest.

The term "extradition agreement" is defined to encompass an agreement possessing the following elements: the agreement is in force; Canada is a party to it; the agreement contains a provision respecting the extradition of persons; the agreement is not a "specific agreement."

A "specific agreement" is defined as an agreement referred to in s. 10 of the Act that is in force. Section 10 provides that the Minister of Foreign Affairs, with the agreement of the "Minister" (defined in this section as the Minister of Justice), may enter into an agreement with a "State or entity" to give effect to a specific extradition request. This is in contrast to the typical international extradition agreement which provides rules governing all requests from a given jurisdiction made under the agreement during the period in which the agreement is in force.

A "State or entity" is defined to include the following: a State other than Canada (including any subdivision of that State or territory falling under the jurisdiction of that State); an international tribunal; or a territory.

An "extradition partner" is defined as a "State or entity" falling within any of the following three categories: Canada is party to an extradition agreement with the State or entity; Canada has entered into a specific agreement with the State or entity; the State or entity is listed in the schedule to the Act.

§2.0 COMPARISON WITH FORMER ACT

The definitions section of the new Act makes a number of changes, updates, and/ or clarifications *vis-à-vis* the former *Extradition Act*. In terms of jurisdictional matters, at the appellate level, both the new and old Acts contain the same definition of "court of appeal." However, the new Act clarifies the issue of jurisdiction during the judicial phase of the extradition process. The former Act defined a "judge" as a "person authorized to act judicially in extradition matters." It was then necessary to turn to s. 9 to determine which persons were so authorized, the answer being judges of the superior courts and county courts of a province, as well as commissioners appointed for the purpose of adjudicating extradition matters. The new Act is clearer, providing definitions of "court" and "judge" that establish that the authority to act judicially in extradition matters is reserved for judges of the superior court of the province. The term "justice" was not defined or utilized in the former Act.

The terms "Attorney General" and "Minister" were not defined in the former *Extradition Act*. Under that Act, the Attorney General was not assigned a role in the extradition process. In the new *Extradition Act*, the Attorney General has assumed the role of taking carriage of the proceedings during the judicial phase of the process.

With respect to the scope of Canada's international obligations, the new and former Acts contain a number of differences. The former Act defined an "extradition arrangement" or "arrangement" to encompass a "treaty, convention or arrangement" between Canada and a "foreign state." The former Act then defined a "foreign state" to include colonies and dependencies of a state.

19

By contrast, the new Act has adopted a broader approach. The new Act applies not merely to states in the conventional sense of a sovereign country, but also to "entities," such as international criminal tribunals, and to "territories."

Moreover, the term "extradition partner" is defined to include not only states and entities with which Canada has entered an agreement, but also those appearing in the schedule to the Act. The schedule lists most of the Commonwealth jurisdictions as well as two specific international criminal tribunals dealing with crimes alleged to have been committed in Rwanda and Yugoslavia. The inclusion of Commonwealth jurisdictions in the schedule has the effect, when read in conjunction with s. 9 of the new Act, of absorbing the field of rendition (extradition between Commonwealth jurisdictions, formerly governed by the *Fugitive Offenders Act*) within the scheme of the *Extradition Act*.

The former Act contained a definition of the term "extradition crime," specifically any crime listed in the schedule to the Act or in the applicable extradition arrangement. Section 18 of the former Act then provided that the extradition judge should commit the person sought for surrender if sufficient evidence of the extradition crime was adduced as would justify the person's committal for trial had the offence been committed in Canada. The definition of "extradition crime," in tandem with s. 18, gave rise to certain issues regarding the extradition judge's determination. In particular, the question arose as to whether the determination focused on the person's conduct or on a comparison of the characterization of that conduct in the requesting and requested jurisdiction (see the "double criminality" issue discussed under s. 3, §2.0). Section 2 of the new Act does not define the term "extradition crime." However, s. 3 of the new Act provides an extended definition of "extraditable conduct," which seeks to clarify some of the ambiguities of the former Act. Section 3(1) does not refer to a specific list of offences for which extradition may be granted. Rather, it employs a punishability standard, that is, a person may be committed for surrender if his or her conduct, had it occurred in Canada, constituted an offence carrying certain minimum punishments.

The former Act (as well as the now-repealed *Fugitive Offenders Act*) defined, and used throughout the Act, the term "fugitive." The new Act does not use this term. Rather, the new Act utilizes the word "person." Unlike the term "fugitive," the term "person" does not imply any prejudgment of the person sought.

Section 2 of the now-repealed *Fugitive Offenders Act* provided a definition of the term "provincial court judge": "any justice of the peace or any person having authority to issue a warrant for the apprehension of persons accused of offences and to commit those persons for trial." Section 11 of that Act provided a "provincial court judge" with the authority to hold a committal hearing. Therefore, under the scheme of the *Fugitive Offenders Act*, provincial court judges had jurisdiction over s. 11 hearings. By contrast, the new *Extradition Act*, which now exclusively governs rendition, reserves jursidiction over committal hearings to judges of the superior court of the province.

§3.0 SIGNIFICANCE OF CHANGE

Apart from clarifying and updating certain points, the changes to the definitions in the new Act are significant for the following reasons. Firstly, the definition of "State or entity" extends the range of "extradition partners" to international tribunals and "territories." Secondly, the definition of "extradition partner," when read in conjunction with s. 9 of the Act, absorbs the field of rendition within the scheme of the Act. Thirdly, in absorbing rendition, the new Act, through the definitions of "court" and "judge," shifts the jurisdiction over rendition hearings from provincial court to superior court judges.

§4.0 ANALYSIS

The definitions in the new Act are clearer and more up-to-date. For instance, the definitions of "court" and "judge" eliminate the reference to county court judges. Moreover, the definitions reflect contemporary realities and sensibilities. For instance, enabling international tribunals to make extradition requests reflects Canada's obligations to these bodies and the increasing internationalism of criminal law, particularly in the area of crimes against humanity such as torture and genocide. Finally, the definitions reflect the federal government's goal of harmonizing and streamlining the extradition process. This is most evident in the new Act's absorption of rendition. Henceforth, extradition to both Commonwealth and non-Commonwealth jurisdictions, not to mention extradition pursuant to specific agreements (i.e., in the absence of an international agreement or for an offence not listed in the agreement), will be governed by the same rules and procedures.

§5.0 RELATED SECTIONS

s. 6.1 — No Immunity from Request for Surrender by International Criminal Court
s. 9 — Designated States and Entities
s. 10 — Specific Agreements

Extraditable Conduct (s. 3)

§1.0 DESCRIPTION

Section 3 of the *Extradition Act* provides as follows:

GENERAL PRINCIPLE
3. (1) A person may be extradited from Canada in accordance with this Act and a relevant extradition agreement on the request of an extradition partner for the purpose of prosecuting the person or imposing a sentence on — or enforcing a sentence imposed on — the person if

    (a) subject to a relevant extradition agreement, the offence in respect of which the extradition is requested is punishable by the extradition partner, by imprisoning or otherwise depriving the person of their liberty for a maximum term of two years or more, or by a more severe punishment; and

    (b) the conduct of the person, had it occurred in Canada, would have constituted an offence that is punishable in Canada,

        (i) in the case of a request based on a specific agreement, by imprisonment for a maximum term of five years or more, or by a more severe punishment, and

        (ii) in any other case, by imprisonment for a maximum term of two years or more, or by a more severe punishment, subject to a relevant extradition agreement.

CONDUCT DETERMINATIVE

    (2) For greater certainty, it is not relevant whether the conduct referred to in subsection (1) is named, defined or characterized by the extradition partner in the same way as it is in Canada.

EXTRADITION OF A PERSON WHO HAS BEEN SENTENCED

    (3) Subject to a relevant extradition agreement, the extradition of a person who has been sentenced to imprisonment or another deprivation of liberty may only be granted if the portion of the term remaining is at least six months long or a more severe punishment remains to be carried out.

This section defines, by the nature of the penalty and conduct, the offences for which a person may be extradited from Canada. Section 3(1) describes the penalties in the jurisdiction making the extradition request that must pertain to the offence for which the person is sought. Section 3(1) also describes the penalties that would have to apply in Canada to the conduct had it occurred here.

For both accused and convicted persons sought for extradition, s. 3(1)(a) requires that, subject to a relevant extradition agreement, the offence be punishable by the extradition partner by imprisonment for two years or more, or by a more severe punishment. The equivalent offence in Canada, based on the conduct alleged by the extradition partner, must be punishable in accordance with s. 3(1)(b)(i) and (ii). Section 3(1)(b)(i) applies to extradition pursuant to a specific agreement, requiring in such a case that the crime be punishable in Canada by five years or more in prison, or by a more severe punishment. Section 3(1)(b)(ii) applies to all other cases, requiring, subject to the terms of any applicable extradition treaty, that the crime be punishable in Canada by imprisonment for two years or more, or by a more severe punishment.

In considering whether the conduct for which the extradition partner seeks extradition amounts to an offence in Canada, s. 3(2) directs that it is not necessary that the two jurisdictions name, define, or characterize the offence in the same fashion.

Section 3(3) is an additional requirement that applies in the case of requests for persons who have been convicted and sentenced in the requesting state. In such cases, extradition may only be granted if there remains to be served at least six months of the sentence, or a more severe punishment remains to be carried out.

For an offence to be extraditable, the following penalty criteria in s. 3 must be met:

1. *Extradition Partner with Extradition Agreement:*

   • Extradition partner: As described in the extradition agreement.

   • Canada: Same.

2. *Extradition Partner with No Extradition Agreement:*

   • Extradition partner: Imprisonment for two years or more, or more severe punishment.

   • Canada: Same.

3. *Extradition Partner with Specific Agreement:*

   • Extradition partner: Imprisonment for two years or more, or more severe punishment.

   • Canada: Imprisonment for five years or more, or more severe punishment.

As can be seen, a five-year penalty requirement applies to the equivalent Canadian offence in the case of extradition under specific agreement (s. 10). This appears to indicate that Canada will not consider it worthwhile to enter into these special arrangements for extradition unless the offence underlying the request is considered to be sufficiently serious so as to justify entering into a case-specific agreement with a country with which Canada has not otherwise negotiated general extradition treaty arrangements.

§2.0 COMPARISON WITH FORMER ACT

§2.1 Treaty Terms and Definitions of "Fugitive" and "Extradition Crime" in Former Act

There was no provision in the former *Extradition Act* that described extraditable conduct in relation to the penalty an offence attracted in the respective countries. However, in defining extraditable conduct, the definition of "fugitive" and "extradition crime" dealt with matters comparable to those in s. 3 of the new Act. The former Act applied to "fugitives" who had committed or had been convicted of an "extradition crime." Only an individual who fit within these defined concepts could be committed for surrender at an extradition hearing under s. 18 of the former Act. Furthermore, only a person so committed could be subject to the Minister's order of surrender under s. 25 of the former Act.

Section 2 of the former Act defined "fugitive" or "fugitive criminal" as follows:

[A] person being or suspected of being in Canada, who is accused or convicted of an extradition crime committed within the jurisdiction of a foreign state;

"[E]xtradition crime" was defined in the following manner:

(a) any crime that, if committed in Canada, or within Canadian jurisdiction, would be one of the crimes described in Schedule I, and

(b) in the application of this Act to the case of an extradition arrangement, any crime described in the arrangement, whether or not it is included in that Schedule;

The two definitions together constituted the principle of double criminality, which required the conduct for which extradition was sought to be recognized as criminal in both jurisdictions.

Schedule I of the former Act provided a list of offences in generic terms which were crimes for which extradition could be granted, such as murder, manslaughter, abduction, larceny or theft, and fraud, to name a few. Section 3 of the former Act incorporated treaty provisions by making the operation of the Act subject to the terms of a treaty.

If the applicable treaty contained no provisions describing extraditable crimes, then Schedule I of the Act would have applied, and extradition would have been possible only for the crimes listed therein. However, the Schedule dated from the late nineteenth century, and thus it did not encompass important areas of contemporary criminal activity. For instance, narcotics trafficking was not listed in the Schedule. Accordingly, under the former regime, extradition for offences not included in the Schedule depended upon the terms of the applicable treaty or convention.

Like the former Act, some of Canada's extradition treaties, particularly the older ones, contain a list of extraditable crimes, and when they do they are referred to as "list treaties." Canada's other treaties, in particular the more recent ones, have opted for a punishability standard. In such treaties, extradition may be granted for any conduct which constitutes an offence in the requesting and requested jurisdictions carrying a potential punishment equal to or greater than the standard specified in the treaty. These are known as "no list" treaties. See, for example, the extradition treaties with the following countries: Finland (both a list and a punishability standard) (in force on February 16, 1985); France (in force December 1, 1989); India (in force February 10, 1987); Italy (both a list and a punishability standard) (in force June 27, 1985); Korea (in force February 1, 1995); Mexico (in force October 21, 1990); the Netherlands (in force December 1, 1991); the Philippines (in force November 12, 1990); Spain (in force August 15, 1990); Switzerland (in force March 19, 1996); and the United States (treaty as amended by protocol in force November 26, 1991).

Thus, under the former Act, an American request could have been honoured with respect to any conduct which amounted to an offence in both jurisdictions and which attracted a term of imprisonment in each jurisdiction of more than one year or any greater punishment as that is the standard prescribed by the *Canada–United States Extradition Treaty*. Under the new Act this will still be the operating requirement. Section 3 of the new Act is clear that the punishability standards set out in that section for extradition partners and for Canada are "subject to a relevant extradition agreement." Thus the terms of an existing extradition agreement will always operate in lieu of the penalties otherwise described in s. 3. With respect to list treaties possessing no punishment criteria, it would appear that the penalty provisions of s. 3 of the new Act will be displaced in their entirety.

§3.0 SIGNIFICANCE OF CHANGE

§3.1 Minister's Role Under S. 3 Concerning Extraditable Conduct

The role of the Minister under s. 3 of the new Act must be considered alongside s. 15 of the Act. Section 15 deals with the issuance, by the Minister of Justice, of the authority to proceed. Together, these sections provide the Minister with the duty to receive extradition requests and assess them with regard to certain specified preconditions of approval. More specifically, the Minister must be satisfied that the conditions set out in ss. 3(1)(a) and 3(3) are met before authorizing the Attorney General, on behalf of the extradition partner, to seek an order for committal at the extradition hearing under s. 29 of the Act.

Watt J. in *Germany (Federal Republic) v. Schreiber* (July 6, 2000), [2000] O.J. No. 2618 (Ont. S.C.J.), described the role of the Minister in dealing with the requirements of these sections as follows:

> [61] To decide whether to seek a provisional arrest warrant or issue an authority to proceed, the Minister is required to consider whether the provisions of s. 3(1)(a) of

the Act have been met. Section 3(1)(a) deals with extraditable conduct. It does so by making reference to the punishment provided for the offence in the jurisdiction of the extradition partner. But the section also mentions the *purpose* of the request of the extradition partner. It may be for *any* of three (3) purposes:

    i. *prosecuting* the person;
    ii. *imposing a sentence* on the person; or,
    iii. *enforcing a sentence* earlier imposed on the person in the requesting state

for an offence described in paragraph 3(1)(a).

[62] It is inevitable, as it seems to me, that the Minister will be obliged to consider the *purpose* of the extradition request in determining whether the requirements of s. 3(1)(a) of the Act have been met. It is an integral part of administering the Act and dealing with requests for extradition made under it and any applicable treaty. This element of *purpose* is central to our extradition scheme: we do *not* extradite without reason. We extradite in order for the extradition partner

    i. to *prosecute*;
    ii. to *sentence*; or,
    iii. to *enforce* an existing *sentence*.

Unless the materials submitted by the extradition partner reveal one of these purposes, the Minister is *not* entitled to authorize the Attorney General to apply for a provisional arrest warrant under s. 12 of the Act, because the person is *not* arrestable. Nor could the Minister issue an authority to the Attorney General to proceed under s. 15 of the Act with an application for committal. The necessary foundation would *not* have been put in place.

[63] More to the point, however, is that the decision-maker on this issue is the *Minister, not* the extradition hearing *judge*. This authority follows not only from the responsibilities assigned to the Minister *generally* under s. 7 of the Act, but also from the *specific* obligations imposed in connection with provisional arrest warrants and the authority to proceed.

Section 3(1)(a) infers that the Minister determines whether the conduct for which extradition is sought is in fact an offence in the other country. This is a codification of a ministerial responsibility which was recognized in the jurisprudence under the former Act.

Under the former Act, the aspect of double criminality which required the crime to be a crime in the foreign country was considered a task for the Minister and for the requesting state and not for the extradition judge. The new Act codifies this aspect of the Minister's responsibilities in s. 3. La Forest J. in *United States v. McVey* (1992), 77 C.C.C. (3d) 1 (S.C.C.), at pp. 37–38, stated:

In the courts below, considerable attention was devoted to broad, comprehensive definitions of double criminality and extradition crimes by specialists in the field. Essentially, these definitions say that for a person to be extradited the act charged must be a crime in the requesting state and be listed or described in the treaty and fall within the name or description in the treaty as understood in the requesting state, and it must also be a crime in the requested state that falls within the name or description of a listed crime in the requested state. These broad definitions (descriptions would be a better word) are not directed solely at the role of the extradition judge, but constitute attempted descriptions of the general theory behind the whole process — prosecutorial, diplomatic and judicial. Viewed from that perspective, the definitions are basically sound and are useful as expository tools. Thus the act must be a crime in the requesting country. Why would it prosecute otherwise? That originally is a matter for the prosecuting authorities and ultimately for the courts of the demanding state, here the United States. Similarly, officials in the state department in the United States must conclude that the act charged falls within the treaty according to the laws of that country. They are unfamiliar with our laws. The requested state will naturally wish to monitor the treaty to ensure that its obligations are engaged, and for that purpose the requesting state is required by the treaty to supply documentation enabling the requested state to do so.

Just as the extradition judge under the former Act was not required to consider whether the conduct alleged against the fugitive was a crime in the requesting country, the extradition judge under the new Act is not directed to consider whether the provisions of s. 3(1)(a) or 3(3) have been satisfied. The possible exception to this may be if an application to amend the authority to proceed is made at the extradition hearing pursuant to s. 23. In that case, it is arguable that the extradition judge, like the Minister, would have to be satisfied that the conditions in s. 3(1)(a) and 3(3) are met with respect to the added or amended offences.

§3.2 Extradition Judge's Role Under S. 3 Concerning Extraditable Conduct

Under the former Act, the jurisprudence made it the responsibility of the extradition judge to identify which Canadian offence was disclosed by the conduct in question and to determine whether the conduct alleged amounted to a crime in Canada which was listed in the Act or treaty. The new Act reduces the role of the extradition judge in this regard. No longer is the extradition judge required to determine which Canadian crime the conduct discloses. The equivalent Canadian crime disclosed by the conduct is now identified by the Minister in the authority to proceed when it is issued pursuant to s. 15. The authority to proceed then governs the proceedings throughout both the judicial hearing phase and the subsequent ministerial phase.

As a result of this change, the extradition judge's role is simply to assess the conduct alleged in order to determine whether it accords with the crime identified by the Minister in the authority to proceed.

This task is directed towards the requirements of s. 3(1)(b), which specify that in order to be extraditable, the conduct of the person would also have to have constituted a punishable offence in Canada had the conduct taken place in Canada. The requirements of s. 3(1)(b) are therefore linked with responsibilities of the extradition judge in applying the test for committal under s. 29 of the Act. The extradition judge's role with respect to the determination of whether conduct is extraditable under s. 3 of the

Act was contrasted with the role of the Minister in that regard in *United States v. Drysdale* (2000), 32 C.R. (5th) 163 (Ont. S.C.J.). Dambrot J. commented, at p. 190:

> [78] It is the task of the Minister, by virtue of s. 15(1), after receiving an extradition request, to determine compliance with s. 3(1)(a), or s. 3(3) where applicable, and then to determine what offences under Canadian law correspond to the conduct alleged against the person in the requesting state, as distinct from the question of the sufficiency of the evidence. Sections 32 and 33 of the *Act* then contemplate that evidence, which is available for use in the foreign prosecution, will be placed before the extradition judge in the form of affidavits or a record of the case. The judge then determines whether the conduct of the person sought, as disclosed in the evidence placed before him or her, satisfies the requirement of s. 3(1)(b). Finally, armed with the judge's order of committal and report under s. 38, the Minister must decide, subject to review by the Court of Appeal of the relevant province pursuant to s. 57, whether surrender should be ordered. As will be seen, while the rule of double criminality is preserved by the new *Act*, the extradition judge is not its sole guardian. The extradition judge has but a modest role to play in ensuring that the rule is respected. The Minister has a significant role. In the end, the appellate courts have the final word.

The principle of double criminality, which requires the conduct for which extradition is sought to be recognized as criminal in both jurisdictions is, as Dambrot J. observed, enshrined in the provisions of s. 3 of the new Act. The extradition judge's function in making this determination involves an assessment of the evidence supplied by the extradition partner to decide whether it meets the test for committal under s. 29 of the Act and therefore satisfies the requirements of s. 3(1)(b).

§4.0 ANALYSIS

§4.1 Meaning of "a more severe punishment" in Penalty Criteria Under S. 3 of New Act

The reference in s. 3 to "a more severe punishment" in place of the stated terms of imprisonment appears to encompass the possibility that an extradition request may be made for which the penalty is not one of imprisonment but of death. This might be the case with certain American states.

Similar wording appears in Article 2(1) of the *Canada–United States Extradition Treaty*, which refers to punishment of "imprisonment or other form of detention for a term exceeding one year *or any greater punishment*" (emphasis added). In this respect, the treaty includes the possibility that the penalty criteria may be met by a sentence of a more severe nature than imprisonment.

A death penalty case would satisfy the punishability requirements of s. 3 so as to be extraditable. However, as a result of the decision of the Supreme Court of Canada in *United States v. Burns* (2001), 151 C.C.C. (3d) 97 (S.C.C.), except in exceptional cases, it would be incumbent upon the Minister to seek assurances that the death penalty would not be carried out, before the person could be lawfully extradited from Canada.

§4.2 Status of Person Under Foreign Law

Subsection 3(1) of the new Act provides that a person may be extradited *"for the purpose of prosecuting the person* or imposing a sentence on — or enforcing a sentence imposed on — the person" (emphasis added). This is a broader description of the target of the extradition request than the term "fugitive" used under the former Act. Section 2 of the former Act defined a "fugitive" or "fugitive criminal" as someone "accused" or "convicted" in the "foreign state."

This definition restricted the interpretation of the subject of the request in terms of the status of the person before the court in the requesting jurisdiction. More specifically, the definition required that the person be an "accused" (if he or she was not already convicted). This was occasionally problematic when applied to the continental legal systems. In the United Kingdom case of in *Re Ismail*, [1999] 1 A.C. 320 (U.K. H.L.), the House of Lords held that the word "accused" in their Act should be interpreted in a broad and generous manner. Lord Steyn stated, at p. 327:

> It is not always easy for an English court to decide when in a civil law jurisdiction, a suspect becomes an "accused person". All one can say with confidence is that a purposive interpretation of "accused" ought to be adopted in order to accommodate the differences between legal systems. In other words, it is necessary for our courts to adopt a cosmopolitan approach to the question whether as a matter of substance rather than form the requirement of there being an "accused" person is satisfied.

(See also *Germany (Federal Republic) v. Kretz* (May 19, 1998), 1998 CarswellOnt 1999, [1998] O.J. No. 2062, where the Ontario Court of Appeal endorsement referred to the treaty requirement of being subject to prosecution rather than the Act requirement of being an accused; and *France (Republic) v. De Havilland Aircraft of Canada Ltd.* (1991), 65 C.C.C. (3d) 449 (Ont. C.A.), and *R. v. Zingre* (1981), 61 C.C.C. (3d) 465 (S.C.C.), for descriptions of the continental systems of criminal justice.)

Section 3(1) of the new Act is directed towards eliminating any dispute over the issue of whether the person sought is an accused in the sense understood in Canada. It requires only that the request be made *"for the purpose of prosecuting the person* or imposing a sentence on — or enforcing a sentence imposed on — the person" (emphasis added). However, the issue was raised under the new Act in *Germany (Federal Republic) v. Schreiber, supra*, when counsel for Schreiber sought an order for further disclosure in order to assert that Schreiber was not yet an accused under German law. The request was denied on the basis that consideration of the status of the person under the foreign law is a ministerial function under s. 3(1)(a).

§4.3 Jurisdiction and Territoriality

Section 2 of the former Act defined a "fugitive" as a person who "is accused or convicted of an extradition crime *committed within the jurisdiction of a foreign state*" (emphasis added). This wording gave rise to litigation over the extradition judge's authority to inquire into the jurisdiction of the requesting state to prosecute the offence for which the fugitive's extradition was sought. In *United States v. Lépine* (1993), 163 N.R. 1 (S.C.C.), the Supreme Court of Canada appeared to decide that the jurisdiction of the requesting jurisdiction was a matter for the Minister of Justice rather than the extradition judge. In that case the extradition judge had questioned the jurisdiction of the State of Pennsylvania over drug offences resulting from the seizure of an airplane loaded with a cargo of cocaine which made a refueling stop in Pennsylvania on its way to its destination in Nova Scotia. La Forest J. found that the extradition judge had been wrong to concern himself with the jurisdiction of the requesting state over the offence. Noting that nothing in the test for committal in s. 18 of the former Act required the judge to consider where the acts charged took place, La Forest J. held as follows, at pp. 8, 14–15:

> [10] I state immediately that I am fully in agreement with counsel's submission that an extradition judge is not vested with the function of considering the jurisdiction of the requesting state to prosecute the offence.
>
> . . .
>
> [17] To conclude, I am of the view that the judge should not have considered the issue of territoriality or jurisdiction at all. That is a matter for the executive, as contemplated by the *Treaty*. There is nothing in the *Extradition Act* that gives the extradition judge any power to deal with the matter, his sole authority being to consider whether there is sufficient evidence (which he held there was here) to constitute the crime if it had been committed in Canada.

Although this appeared to be a clear pronouncement on the part of the Supreme Court of Canada, the issue came up again in the case of *Romania (State) v. Cheng* (1997), 114 C.C.C. (3d) 289 (N.S. S.C.). The officers of a Taiwanese freighter were sought for extradition by Romania for allegedly throwing overboard three Romanian stowaways on the high seas while the ship was on the way to Canada. MacDonald J. of the Nova Scotia Supreme Court discharged these individuals on the basis that they could not be fugitives as defined in the Act.

MacDonald J. held that the crew members were not "fugitives" as defined under the former Act because the acts had not occurred within the territory of the state of Romania. He held that the term "jurisdiction" as contained in the definition of "fugitive" meant territorial jurisdiction. Significant reliance was placed on Article 1 of the *Canada–Romania Extradition Treaty*, which provides that the contracting parties agree to extradite those persons accused or convicted of an offence committed in the territory of the requesting party. Read together with the definition of "fugitive" in the

Extradition Act, MacDonald J. concluded that Canada was only obliged to extradite with respect to crimes committed within the geographical boundaries of the requesting state.

The Nova Scotia Court of Appeal refused to hear an appeal on the merits from the decision of MacDonald J. on the basis that the appeal was moot, the alleged fugitives having by then left Canada. Hallett J.A., in the decision reported at (1997), 119 C.C.C. (3d) 561, stated as follows, at p. 565:

> The issue raised on this appeal does not raise an important question that needs to be answered by this Court. MacDonald J.'s decision does not have widespread implications. This Court's decision would not have the effect of finalizing the law on the meaning of the word jurisdiction as it appears within the definition of "fugitive" in the *Extradition Act*; that would require a decision of the Supreme Court of Canada.

The structure of the new Act would appear to eliminate any further debate on this point. Section 3 is concerned with requests for extradition for the purpose of prosecuting or imposing a sentence upon — or enforcing a sentence imposed on — the person sought. Territoriality is not a component of s. 3. The territorial considerations that arose from the definition of "fugitive" in the former Act have been eliminated by the new description of extraditable conduct set out in s. 3.

Section 5 of the new Act has specifically addressed the issue of territoriality by providing that a person may be extradited whether or not the conduct occurred in the territory of the extradition partner and whether or not Canada could exercise jurisdiction in similar circumstances. However, territorial considerations may give rise to a discretionary ground of refusal at the ministerial phase, since s. 47(*e*) of the new Act provides the Minister with the discretion to refuse surrender if none of the conduct occurred in the territory over which the extradition partner has jurisdiction.

§4.4 Section 3(2): Crime May Bear Different Name in Two Jurisdictions

Section 3(2) gives statutory effect to a principle that had developed in the jurisprudence under the former Act, which is, that exact correspondence is not required in the characterizing or naming of the offence in the requesting and requested jurisdictions for the conduct to be extraditable. In *United States v. Smith* (1984), 15 C.C.C. (3d) 16 (Ont. Co. Ct.), affirmed (1984), 16 C.C.C. (3d) 10 (Ont. H.C.), for instance, Borins Co. Ct. J. (as he then was) stressed that what mattered was not the correspondence of the description of the charges in the two countries but rather that the underlying conduct was criminal in both jurisdictions. In that case, the United States had requested extradition on a charge of murder for conduct which in Canada amounted to manslaughter. It was held that the conduct amounted to an extradition crime although differently characterized or named in the two countries. Borins Co. Ct. J. made the point as follows, at pp. 30–31:

31

Therefore, the question is not whether the conduct alleged against Catherine Smith and constituting murder contrary to s. 187 of the California Penal Code would also constitute murder had it taken place in Canada. The question is whether the conduct alleged against Catherine Smith would have constituted *any* criminal offence pursuant to Canadian law had it occurred in Canada.

The Supreme Court of Canada referred to and approved of Borins Co. Ct. J.'s approach in *United States v. McVey, supra*, at p. 10. With respect to the specific facts in *United States v. McVey* that alleged the exportation of high technology equipment to the U.S.S.R., which offences were unknown to Canadian law but which involved fraudulent documents, La Forest J. nonetheless concluded that the conduct was extraditable. He wrote that the conduct amounted to forgery and conspiracy in Canadian law, *supra*, at p. 39:

> The issue is not whether the crime charged is called forgery or not in either country, but whether the conduct charged can fairly be said to fall within the expressions "forgery" and "conspiracy" in the treaty. In considering this issue, it must be remembered that the crimes listed in the treaty are not to be interpreted according to the niceties of the applicable legislation of either country. Rather, they are described in compendious terms to catch broad categories of conduct: see *La Forest's Extradition*, 3rd ed., at p. 76, and the cases there cited. In other words, extradition crimes are described in a comprehensive and generic sense.

More recently, in *United States v. Commisso* (2000), 47 O.R. (3d) 257 (Ont. C.A.), O'Connor J.A. observed, at p. 268:

> [44] It is not necessary that the Canadian offence established by the conduct be described by the same name or that it have the same legal elements as the offence charged in the requesting state. The protection afforded by the double criminality rule is ensured if the conduct that underlies the foreign charge constitutes any extradition crime under the laws of Canada . . . .

To the same effect, see the recent British Columbia Court of Appeal case of *Stewart v. Canada (Minister of Justice)* (1998), 131 C.C.C. (3d) 423 (B.C. C.A.).

Section 3(2) expressly provides that the name, definition, or characterization of the conduct by the extradition partner is not relevant. In this way, s. 3(2) constitutes an acknowledgment of the continued applicability of the principles developed in the jurisprudence under the former Act concerning this issue. Moreover, s. 3(2) reflects the principle that extradition is conduct-based.

§4.5 Minimum Sentence Remaining to be Carried Out in Case of Convicted Persons

Section 3(3) provides that, before extradition may be granted, a convicted person must have at least six months remaining to be served on his or her sentence or a more severe punishment remains to be carried out. This provision, like those in s. 3(1)(a) and 3(1)(b) concerning the penalty requirements for the offence, is subject to override by the terms of an extradition agreement.

Once again, the former Act contained no such stipulations, and the extradition of convicted fugitives was not restricted to those with a particular length of the sentence remaining to be served. Notwithstanding the lack of specific provisions in this respect, at least one court was willing to read such a requirement into the former Act. In *Reutcke v. R.* (1984), 11 C.C.C. (3d) 386 (B.C. C.A.), no evidence had been presented with respect to how much of the sentence imposed upon the fugitive by the requesting state remained to be served. Seaton J.A., on behalf of the British Columbia Court of Appeal, noted that according to the definition in s. 2 of the former Act, a "fugitive" included a "person convicted of an extradition crime committed within the jurisdiction of a foreign state." He went on to note, at p. 387:

> The Act seems to make everyone who has ever been convicted a fugitive for life. That cannot be. The Act must contemplate that there is sentence left to be served.

In the absence of evidence that there was a sentence remaining to be served, the court ordered the discharge of the fugitive in that case. Although there was no minimum amount of sentence necessary to be served, it was clear that something had to be left to be served.

Because it is subject to the terms of an extradition treaty, the requirement of s. 3(3) that a sentence of at least six months remains to be served will, in the case of the *Canada–United States Extradition Treaty*, be displaced by Article 9(4) of the treaty. This Article requires only that a statement of the sentence still to be served be provided. There is no condition in the treaty that a minimum sentence must remain in order for an individual to be subject to the extradition process. Some of Canada's extradition treaties do, however, provide specific time limits. The treaties with Finland (1985) and Korea (1995) set the sentence remaining to be served at four months. Those with Spain (1990) and the Netherlands (1991), like the Act, set it at six months.

Section 3(3) indicates that Canada does not wish to deal with extradition requests when only a trivial amount of a sentence remains to be served by a person sought. In the absence of an obligation undertaken by treaty, the domestic law thus sets the bar in this regard at six months.

§5.0 CASE LAW

France (Republic) v. De Havilland Aircraft of Canada Ltd. (1991), 65 C.C.C. (3d) 449 (Ont. C.A.).
Germany (Federal Republic) v. Kretz (May 19, 1998), 1998 CarswellOnt 1999, [1998] O.J. No. 2062 (C.A.).
Germany (Federal Republic) v. Schreiber (July 6, 2000), [2000] O.J. No. 2618, Watt J. (Ont. S.C.J.).

Ismail, Re, [1999] 1 A.C. 320 (U.K.H.L.).
Reutcke v. R. (1984), 11 C.C.C. (3d) 386 (B.C.C.A.).
R. v. Zingre (1981), 61 C.C.C. (3d) 465 (S.C.C.).
Romania (State) v. Cheng (1997), 114 C.C.C. (3d) 289 (N.S.S.C.), dismissed as moot (1997), 119 C.C.C. (3d) 561 (N.S.C.A.).
Stewart v. Canada (Minister of Justice) (1998), 131 C.C.C. (3d) 423 (B.C.C.A.).
United States v. Burns (2001), 151 C.C.C. (3d) 97 (S.C.C.).
United States v. Commisso (2000), 47 O.R. (3d) 257 (C.A.).
United States v. Drysdale (2000), 32 C.R. (5th) 163 (Ont. S.C.J.).
United States v. Lépine (1993), 163 N.R. 1 (S.C.C.).
United States v. McVey (1992), 77 C.C.C. (3d) 1 (S.C.C.)
United States v. Smith (1984), 15 C.C.C. (3d) 16 (Ont. Co. Ct.), affirmed (1984), 16 C.C.C. (3d) 10 (Ont. H.C.).

§6.0 RELATED SECTIONS

s. 5 — Jurisdiction
s. 10 — Specific Agreements
s. 15 — Power of Minister to Issue Authority to Proceed
s. 29 — Order of Committal by Extradition Judge

Reinstitution of Proceedings (s. 4)

§1.0 DESCRIPTION

Section 4 of the *Extradition Act* provides as follows:

> **FURTHER PROCEEDINGS**
> **4. For greater certainty, the discharge of a person under this Act or an Act repealed by section 129 or 130 does not preclude further proceedings, whether or not they are based on the same conduct, with a view to extraditing the person under this Act unless the judge is of the opinion that those further proceedings would be an abuse of process.**

Section 4 codifies the right to reinstitute proceedings. This right applies even after a previous discharge and even when the previous discharge was based on the same conduct.

§2.0 COMPARISON WITH FORMER ACT

There was no similar provision under the former *Extradition Act*. However, some treaties addressed this issue. The treaties did so by providing for the reinstitution of proceedings in cases where there had been a previous discharge due to required documentation for the extradition hearing not being provided within the time period following provisional arrest (see the following provisions from Canada's extradition treaties: Article 11(3) of the United States treaty, Article 9 of the Philippines treaty, Article 11 of the Indian treaty, and Article 10 of the Spanish treaty).

Additionally, the jurisprudence that developed under the former Act held that the discharge of a fugitive after an extradition hearing was not a bar to the recommencement of proceedings. In the case of *Piperno v. Italy (Republic)* (1982), 68 C.C.C. (2d) 236 (Fed. T.D.), the Federal Court — Trial Division held that a previous discharge did not prevent a second hearing on the same facts. Walsh J. held that this alone was not an abuse of process requiring intervention by the courts, at pp. 240–241:

> In Canada the jurisprudence is clear to the effect that more than one preliminary inquiry can be held on the same charge: see *Lavigne v. The Queen* (1979), 13 C.R. (3d) 91; *Re White and The Queen* (1981), 61 C.C.C. (2d) 329; *Re Coutts and The Queen* (1978), 45 C.C.C. (2d) 125, 12 C.R. (3d) 277, 22 A.R. 356; *R. v. Ewanchuk* (1974), 16 C.C.C. (2d) 517, [1974] 4 W.W.R. 230. While it is true that these cases were all based on interpretation of provisions of our *Criminal Code*, it is apparent that there is nothing contrary to the duty to act fairly or to natural justice in such a duplication of proceedings.

Section 13 of the former Act directed that the extradition hearing be conducted "as nearly as may be" to a domestic preliminary inquiry. On this basis, the domestic jurisprudence dealing with the recommencement of proceedings after discharges at preliminary inquiries was relevant to the same issue in the extradition context.

In *Argentina (Republic) v. Mellino* (1987), 33 C.C.C. (3d) 334 (S.C.C.), at p. 348, La Forest J., made the following comment:

> Since a discharge at an extradition hearing for lack of evidence, like that at a preliminary hearing, is not final, it has long been recognized that new proceedings may be instituted on new, or even on the same evidence before the judge at the original hearing or another judge: see, for example, *A.-G. Hong Kong v. Kwok-a-Sing* (1873), L.R. 5 P.C. 179; *Re Harsha (No. 2)* (1906), 11 C.C.C. 62, 11 O.L.R. 457 (Ont. H.C.); *Re State of Wisconsin and Armstrong* (1972), 8 C.C.C. (2d) 452, 30 D.L.R. (3d) 727, [1972] F.C. 1228 (C.A.). This was recognized by the judge and the parties, who acted on that basis.

The jurisprudence under the former Act has now been codified by s. 4.

§3.0 SIGNIFICANCE OF CHANGE

Section 4 of the new Act precludes double jeopardy or *res judicata* principles from being applicable at extradition hearings. The section incorporates the case law concerning reinstitution of proceedings. However, it includes the safeguard that a judge may terminate the reinstituted proceeding if it amounts to an abuse of process. The codification of this safeguard makes it clear that this remedy is available in the extradition context.

§4.0 ANALYSIS

The domestic test for abuse of process pronounced in *R. v. Power*, [1994] 1 S.C.R. 601, that is, that only in the clearest of cases should the courts terminate proceedings on the basis of abuse of process, would be the operative test in the extradition context. (See also *United States v. Cobb* (2001), 152 C.C.C. (3d) 270 (S.C.C.), reconsideration refused (June 14, 2001), Docs. 26912, 27610, 27774 (S.C.C.)). Given the international context of extradition, reaching the abuse of process threshold may be even more difficult than it is in the domestic prosecutorial context. In *Argentina (Republic) v. Mellino, supra*, the Supreme Court of Canada considered whether the reinstitution of extradition proceedings 17 months after a discharge due to evidentiary difficulties at the first proceedings constituted an abuse of process. La Forest J., in his majority judgment, found that there was no abuse of process. In coming to this conclusion, he made the following comment, at p. 348:

> In assessing the issue, a court must not overlook that extradition proceedings must be approached with a view to conform with Canada's international obligations. The courts have on many occasions reiterated that the requirements and technicalities of the criminal law apply only to a limited extent in extradition proceedings. One cannot view delay resulting from the complexity involved in dealing with activities that reach across national boundaries and involve different systems of law and several levels of bureaucracies in the same way as that in local prosecutions.

The remedy for an abuse of process is directed at a situation that offends against the community's notions of justice and fair play. Deschênes J. engaged in a lengthy discussion of this point in *R. v. Rumbaut* (1998), 125 C.C.C. (3d) 368 (N.B. Q.B.). This was a case in which Rumbaut had been extradited from Switzerland to stand trial in New Brunswick on drug importing charges. Rumbaut alleged that to continue the proceedings would be abusive given that the Canadian authorities had not disclosed to the Swiss authorities that Rumbaut had previously been the subject of an extradition request to Spain. The Spanish request had been refused on the basis that Rumbaut was a Spanish national and as a result Canada then requested that Spain refer the matter to its competent authorities for prosecution there. In finding that there was no abuse of process, Deschênes J. made the following comment, at pp. 376–377:

> I simply do not believe that to refuse a stay of proceedings on the basis of the evidence before me would damage the integrity of the Court nor do I believe that it has been shown that the impugned conduct was violative of those fundamental principles of justice which underlie a community's sense of fair play and decency to such an extent as to outweigh the societal interest in the effective prosecution of a criminal case.
>
> In my view, this is not the "extremely rare" case or "clearest of cases" where (to use the words of L'Heureux-Dubé, J. in *R. v. Power* (1994), 89 C.C.C. (3d) 1 (S.C.C.) at p. 10) "there is conspicuous evidence of improper motives or bad faith or of an act so wrong that it violates the conscience of the community such that it would genuinely be unfair and indecent to proceed."

In arriving at this decision, Deschênes J. also referred to the common law legal principles relating to staying proceedings for abuse of process outlined by Brien Prov. J. in *R. v. Cheverie* (1995), 164 N.B.R. (2d) 62, 421 A.P.R. 62 (N.B. Prov. Ct.), at pp. 70–73.

In *United States v. Cobb* (2001), 152 C.C.C. (3d) 270 (S.C.C.) (heard together and released concurrently with *United States v. Shulman* (2001), 152 C.C.C. (3d) 294 S.C.C.), *United States of America v. Tsioubris* (2001), 152 C.C.C. (3d) 292 (S.C.C.) and *United States v. Kwok* (2001), 152 C.C.C. (3d) 225 (S.C.C.), reconsideration refused in *Cobb, Shulman* and *Tsioubris* (June 14, 2001), Docs. 26912, 27610, 27774 (S.C.C.), the Supreme Court of Canada upheld a stay of proceedings based upon abuse of process. The extradition judge in *Cobb* found that the United States had made out a *prima facie* case for extradition but refused to order committal because of extra-judicial comments made by the American judge and prosecutor, which had been publicly reported. The American judge had stated that people who were extradited to face charges would receive the maximum jail sentence the law permitted him to give. The prosecutor, in an interview shown on Canadian television, had stated that any accused who chose to fight extradition would serve a longer sentence under more stringent conditions, including conditions involving homosexual rape. The extradition judge, Hawkins J., imposed the stay, holding that it would shock the Canadian conscience to commit individuals for surrender in light of threats to intimidate the fugitives into abandoning their rights to resist extradition ((1997), 11 C.R. (5th) 310 (Ont. Gen. Div.)).

Arbour J. in the Supreme Court of Canada upheld the stay of proceedings, holding that it was justified either as a remedy based on s. 7 of the *Charter* or on the basis of the court's inherent powers at common law to control its own process and prevent abuse. The abuse, as she saw it, was the attempted intimidation of one party by the other. She stated, at pp. 291–292:

> [52] By placing undue pressure on Canadian citizens to forego due legal process in Canada, the foreign State has disentitled itself from pursuing its recourse before the courts and attempting to show why extradition should legally proceed. The intimidation bore directly upon the very proceedings before the extradition judge, thus engaging the appellants' right to fundamental justice at common law, under the doctrine of abuse of process, and as also reflected in s. 7 of the *Charter*. The extradition judge did not need to await a ministerial decision in the circumstances, as the breach of the principles of fundamental justice was directly and inextricably tied to the committal hearing.

> [53] In my view, the extradition judge had the jurisdiction to control the integrity of the proceedings before him, and to grant a remedy, both at common law and under the *Charter*, for the abuse of process. He was also correct in concluding as he did that this was one of the clearest of cases where to proceed further with the extradition hearing would violate "those fundamental principles of justice which underlie the community's sense of fair play and decency" (*Keyowski, supra*, at pp. 658–59), since the Requesting State in the proceedings, represented by the Attorney General of Canada, had not

repudiated the statements of some of its officials that an unconscionable price would be paid by the appellants for having insisted on exercising their rights under Canadian law.

The reasoning in *Cobb* applied equally to Tsioubris, whose extradition hearing had also been stayed by Hawkins J. for the same reasons. In *United States v. Shulman, supra,* the comments of the American judge and prosecutor had come to light only after the committal hearing had concluded. Arbour J. held that on the basis of the reasoning in *Cobb,* the Court of Appeal at the time of the appeal from the committal had the jurisdiction to consider fresh evidence concerning the abuse of process and to enter a stay of proceedings at that time.

While these were not cases concerning s. 4 of the new Act, the principles set out in *Cobb, Tsioubris* and *Shulman,* and the tests enunciated in them, will be looked to in any consideration of whether an abuse of process has occurred as a result of reinstitution of proceedings after a discharge.

§5.0 CASE LAW

Argentina (Republic) v. Mellino (1987), 33 C.C.C. (3d) 334 (S.C.C.).
Piperno v. Italy (Republic) (1982), 68 C.C.C. (2d) 236 (Fed. T.D.).
R. v. Cheverie (1995), 164 N.B.R. (2d) 62, 421 A.P.R. 62 (N.B. Prov. Ct.).
R. v. Power, [1994] 1 S.C.R. 601.
R. v. Rumbaut (1998), 125 C.C.C. (3d) 368 (N.B. Q.B.).
United States v. Cobb (2001), 152 C.C.C. (3d) 270 (S.C.C.), reconsideration refused (June 14, 2001), Docs. 26912, 27610, 27774 (S.C.C.).
United States v. Kwok (2001), 152 C.C.C. (3d) 225 (S.C.C.).
United States v. Shulman (2001), 152 C.C.C. (3d) 294 (S.C.C.), reconsideration refused (June 14, 2001), Docs. 26912, 27610, 27774 (S.C.C.).
United States of America v. Tsioubris (2001), 152 C.C.C. (3d) 292 (S.C.C.), reconsideration refused (June 14, 2001), Docs. 26912, 27610, 27774 (S.C.C.).

§6.0 RELATED SECTIONS

s. 14 — Discharge of Person Sought If No Proceedings Instituted

Jurisdiction (s. 5)

§1.0 DESCRIPTION

Section 5 of the *Extradition Act* provides as follows:

JURISDICTION
5. A person may be extradited

(a) **whether or not the conduct on which the extradition partner bases its request occurred in the territory over which it has jurisdiction; and**

(b) **whether or not Canada could exercise jurisdiction in similar circumstances.**

Section 5(a) establishes that a person may be extradited regardless of whether the conduct underlying the request occurred within territory over which the extradition partner has jurisdiction. Section 5(b) adds that a person may be extradited whether or not Canada could exercise similar extraterritorial jurisdiction over the offence.

§2.0 COMPARISON WITH FORMER ACT

The definition of "fugitive" in s. 2 of the former *Extradition Act* gave rise to questions about whether the offence for which extradition was sought had to have a territorial connection with the requesting state. A "fugitive" was defined as a person accused or convicted of an extradition crime "committed within the jurisdiction of a foreign state." In *United States v. Lépine* (1993), 163 N.R. 1 (S.C.C.), the Supreme Court of Canada held that the jurisdiction of the requesting state to prosecute was not a matter for the consideration of the extradition judge. In this respect, La Forest J. made the following comment, at pp. 8–9:

> There is nothing in the Act that requires the judge to consider where the acts charged took place or the jurisdiction of the requesting state. The issue of jurisdiction of the requesting state and its organs to prosecute a crime is essentially a matter governed by the law of that state.

Although this appeared to be a clear pronouncement on the part of the Supreme Court of Canada, the issue came up again in the case of *Romania (State) v. Cheng* (1997), 114 C.C.C. (3d) 289 (N.S. S.C.), dismissed as moot (1997), 119 C.C.C. (3d) 561 (N.S. C.A.). The officers of a Taiwanese freighter were sought for extradition by Romania for allegedly throwing overboard three Romanian stowaways on the high seas while the ship was on the way to Canada. MacDonald J. of the Nova Scotia Supreme Court held that the crew members were not "fugitives" as defined under s. 2 of the former Act because the acts had not occurred within the territory of the state of Romania. MacDonald J. decided that the term "jurisdiction" as contained in the definition of "fugitive" meant territorial jurisdiction. MacDonald J. placed significant reliance on Article 1 of the *Canada–Romania Extradition Treaty* which defined the obligation to extradite as being with respect to offences committed in the territory of the requesting party. Reading the treaty and the Act together, MacDonald J. concluded as follows, at p. 324:

Thus according to the treaty, I find that Canada is obliged to extradite only those individuals alleged to have committed a crime within the geographical boundaries of the Requesting State.

Furthermore I conclude that the reference to "jurisdiction" in the definition of "fugitive" as contained in the *Extradition Act* means "territorial jurisdiction". It follows that in order to be "fugitives" under the *Extradition Act*, it must be alleged that the Detainees committed crimes within the geographical boundaries of the State of Romania. There are no such allegations. It follows that the Detainees are not "fugitives" under the *Extradition Act* and as such I have no jurisdiction to commit them for extradition.

The Nova Scotia Court of Appeal dismissed an appeal from this decision on the basis that it was moot because the fugitives had left the country by the date the appeal was heard. The court did observe, however, that MacDonald J.'s decision turned on the provisions of the *Canada–Romania Extradition Treaty* and that the principles set out by the Supreme Court of Canada in *United States v. Lépine, supra,* were not displaced by MacDonald J.'s decision.

Section 5 of the new *Extradition Act* has statutorily clarified the situation by making it clear that the territorial location of the offence is not a factor in determining whether a person may be extradited from Canada. Nor is Canadian jurisdiction in similar circumstances an issue for consideration.

§3.0 SIGNIFICANCE OF CHANGE

Section 5(a) of the new Act addresses the arguments that were presented in *Romania (State) v. Cheng, supra.* If a similar fact situation arises in the future, s. 5 establishes that the issuance of an order of committal by the extradition judge will not be precluded by the fact that the conduct occurred outside the territory of the extradition partner. However, this section should be considered in connection with s. 47(e). In the latter provision, the Minister of Justice is provided with the discretionary right to refuse surrender in cases in which the conduct occurred entirely outside the territory of the extradition partner.

Section 5(b) addresses one of the arguments made in *United States v. Lépine, supra,* namely, that an extradition judge could refuse to commit if the conduct which was said to have taken place in the requesting state, had it occurred in Canada, would not have justified the exercise of criminal jurisdiction over the offence under Canadian law. This was essentially a reverse image approach to the issue of jurisdiction. If Canada would not take jurisdiction in similar circumstances, then, it was argued, the extradition judge could refuse to commit for surrender to the requesting state. The Supreme Court of Canada held in *United States v. Lépine, supra,* that the extradition judge had no jurisdiction to consider this issue. Section 5(b) appears to be a codification of the principles enunciated in that case.

The inclusion of s. 5(b) also avoids the complicated legal arguments advanced before the House of Lords in *R. v. Bartle, Ex parte Pinochet Ugarte (No. 3), (sub nom. R. v. Bow Street Metropolitan Stipendiary Magistrate)* [1999] 2 All E.R. 97. In that case, Spain asserted extraterritorial jurisdiction over alleged acts of torture committed in Chile against Spanish nationals. The House of Lords determined that a number of the offences for which extradition was sought by Spain could not succeed because at the time of the commission of the offences, British law did not assert extraterritorial jurisdiction over this category of offence. If such a situation were to arise in Canada under the new Act, it would not be necessary to establish dual jurisdiction in Canada and the extradition partner in order for the extradition request to proceed. The legal arguments that succeeded in the *Pinochet* case would not succeed in Canada.

§4.0 ANALYSIS

Section 5 has to be considered together with s. 47(e). The latter provision sets out that the Minister of Justice may refuse to make a surrender order if the Minister is satisfied that "none of the conduct on which the extradition partner bases its request occurred in the territory over which the extradition partner has jurisdiction."

Section 5 eliminates territorial jurisdiction as an issue for the extradition judge. Section 47(e) of the Act makes it a matter for the concern of the Minister of Justice when the conduct occurred entirely outside the requesting state's territory. As a result, it is no impediment to extradition that the conduct occurred entirely outside the requesting state's territory. This is not a basis on which the extradition judge can refuse to order committal. However, it is a basis upon which the Minister may refuse to order surrender in the exercise of the Minister's discretion under s. 47(e).

In this regard the Minister's discretion is limited to situations where the conduct in question is entirely extraterritorial. This is distinguishable from situations where part of the conduct takes place in the requesting state and part in other foreign states, or in the requested state. When some of the offensive conduct takes place in the requesting state, the assertion of jurisdiction by the extradition partner is logical. The question of jurisdiction is only clearly raised when none of the conduct takes place in the territory of the requesting state.

The reason for the residual discretion in these circumstances may be that political considerations could come into play if conduct occurs completely outside the territory of the extradition partner making the request. In such cases, another foreign jurisdiction's interests may have to be taken into account in considering the request or the Canadian authorities may simply consider that the extradition partner is proceeding on too broad a basis with respect to a particular prosecution (see *United States v. McVey* (1992), 77 C.C.C. (3d) 1 (S.C.C.), at p. 39).

§5.0 CASE LAW

R. v. Bartle, Ex parte Pinochet Ugarte (No. 3), *(sub nom. R. v. Bow Street Metropolitan Stipendiary Magistrate)* [1999] 2 All E.R. 97 (H.L.).

Romania (State) v. Cheng (1997), 114 C.C.C. (3d) 289 (N.S.S.C.), dismissed as moot (1997), 119 C.C.C. (3d) 561 (N.S.C.A.).
United States v. McVey (1992), 77 C.C.C. (3d) 1 (S.C.C.).
United States v. Lépine (1993), 163 N.R. 1 (S.C.C.).

§6.0 RELATED SECTIONS

s. 47(e) — Minister May Refuse to Make Surrender Order When None of Conduct Occurred in Requesting Jursidiction

Retrospectivity (s. 6)

§1.0 DESCRIPTION

Section 6 of the *Extradition Act* provides as follows:

> **RETROSPECTIVITY**
> **6. Subject to a relevant extradition agreement, extradition may be granted under this Act whether the conduct or conviction in respect of which the extradition is requested occurred before or after this Act or the relevant extradition agreement or specific agreement came into force.**

Section 6 allows for retrospectivity, that is, a person may be extradited under the Act regardless of whether the conduct or conviction in question occurred before or after the coming into force of the Act, the applicable extradition agreement, or the applicable specific agreement.

§2.0 COMPARISON WITH FORMER ACT

The only relevant provision concerning retrospectivity in the former *Extradition Act* was found in Part II, dealing with the exceptional situation of extradition in the absence of a treaty or for a crime not listed in the treaty. More specifically, s. 36 in Part II expressly prohibited retrospectivity: "This Part applies to any crime mentioned in Schedule III that is committed after the coming into force of this Part with respect to any foreign state to which this Part has, by proclamation pursuant to subsection 35(1), been declared to apply."

The former Act did not contain any retrospectivity provision with respect to the more common situation of extradition pursuant to an international agreement. The now-repealed *Fugitive Offenders Act* also did not contain any such provision. However, retrospectivity provisions were, and are, commonly found in extradition treaties. The *Canada–Belgium Extradition Treaty*, for instance, provides in Article 15 that the Treaty applies to all crimes listed in the Treaty whether or not they were committed before or after the Treaty came into force. Similar provision is made in Article 18(2) of the *Canada–United States Extradition Treaty*. See also Article 21 of the *Canada–Netherlands Extradition Treaty* and Article VI of the *Canada–Germany Extradition Treaty*.

§3.0 SIGNIFICANCE OF CHANGE

Section 6 makes it clear that the new *Extradition Act* applies to conduct or convictions that occurred prior to the coming into force of the Act, the applicable extradition agreement, or the applicable specific agreement. It gives domestic force to principles already enunciated in many of Canada's extradition treaties.

§4.0 ANALYSIS

Section 6 ensures that a person will not be able to avoid extradition by arguing that the conduct or conviction occurred before the coming into force of the Act, the applicable international agreement, or the applicable specific agreement.

§5.0 RELATED SECTIONS

Canada–Belgium Extradition Treaty, Article 15
Canada–Germany Extradition Treaty, Article VI
Canada–Netherlands Extradition Treaty, Article 21
Canada–United States Extradition Treaty, Article 18(2)

No Immunity (s. 6.1)

§1.0 DESCRIPTION

Section 6.1 of the *Extradition Act* provides as follows:

NO IMMUNITY

6.1 Despite any other Act or law, no person who is the subject of a request for surrender by the International Criminal Court or by any international criminal tribunal that is established by resolution of the Security Council of the United Nations and whose name appears in the schedule, may claim immunity under common law or by statute from arrest or extradition under this Act.

§2.0 COMPARISON WITH FORMER ACT

There was no similar provision in the former Act. Section 6.1 was enacted by the *Crimes Against Humanity and War Crimes Act*, S.C. 2000, c. 24, s. 48, which contained a number of consequential amendments to the *Extradition Act* (and to the *Mutual Legal Assistance in Criminal Matters Act*).

§3.0 SIGNIFICANCE OF CHANGE

The purpose of the amendments made by the *Crimes Against Humanity and War Crimes Act*, of which the addition of s. 6.1 to the *Extradition Act* is one, is to enable Canada to provide to the International Criminal Court the full measure of co-operation allowed by the *Extradition Act* and the *Mutual Legal Assistance in Criminal Matters Act* in the investigation and prosecution of offences under the International Criminal Court's jurisdiction. The amendments accordingly would implement the responsibilities undertaken towards the International Criminal Court when Canada ratified the *Rome Statute* in June 2000. The *Rome Statute* establishes an International Criminal Court with jurisdiction to prosecute and try individuals for genocide, crimes against humanity and war crimes, and it will enter into force once 60 countries have ratified it.

§4.0 ANALYSIS

Section 6.1 would deny diplomatic immunity to persons sought by the International Criminal Court or by any international criminal tribunal that is established by resolution of the Security Council of the United Nations and whose name appears in the schedule to the *Extradition Act* (currently the Yugoslavia and Rwanda tribunals). In this respect, a person's current or former status as a member of a foreign government could not be raised as an objection to the extradition request. Domestic exclusion of any immunity based on the official position of the person sought accords with the principles set out in Article 27 of the *Rome Statute*, which reads as follows:

> This Statute shall apply equally to all persons without any distinction based on official capacity. In particular, official capacity as a Head of State or Government, a member of a Government or parliament, an elected representative or a government official shall in no case exempt a person from criminal responsibility . . . .

§5.0 RELATED SECTIONS

Rome Statute, Article 27.

Responsibilities of Minister of Justice (s. 7)

§1.0 DESCRIPTION

Section 7 of the *Extradition Act* provides as follows:

FUNCTIONS OF THE MINISTER
7. The Minister is responsible for the implementation of extradition agreements, the administration of this Act and dealing with requests for extradition made under them.

This section broadly defines the responsibilities of the Minister of Justice, which are specifically dealt with in other sections of the Act. It provides that the implementation of extradition agreements and the administration and handling of extradition requests are primarily the responsibility of the Minister.

§2.0 COMPARISON WITH FORMER ACT

There was no equivalent section in the former *Extradition Act*. Whether a matter was appropriately raised at the extradition hearing or should await the consideration of the Minister was often in issue. The courts were therefore called upon repeatedly to delineate judicial and ministerial responsibilities.

In *United States v. Dynar* (1997), 115 C.C.C. (3d) 481 (S.C.C.), Cory and Iacobucci JJ. described the phases of the extradition process and the corresponding responsibilities of the extradition judge and the Minister of Justice, at pp. 520–521:

> [118] The first step, the committal hearing, is the judicial phase of the process in which the fugitive is brought before a judge who determines whether the evidence justifies surrender of the fugitive. If the Requesting State has made out its case, the fugitive is committed. If not, the fugitive is discharged. If the fugitive is committed for surrender, the warrant of committal, as well as any report from the judge presiding over the committal hearing, is forwarded to the Minister of Justice, who then makes the final decision whether the fugitive should be surrendered. This second phase of the process is political in nature and is not in issue in the cross-appeal.
>
> . . .
>
> [120] The jurisdiction of the extradition judge is derived entirely from the statute and the relevant treaty. Pursuant to s. 3 of the Act, the statute must be interpreted as giving effect to the terms of the applicable treaty. La Forest J., writing for the majority in *McVey*, *supra*, at p. 519, stated that courts must find a statutory source for attributing a particular function to the extradition judge, and that "courts should not reach out to bring within their jurisdictional ambit matters that the Act has not assigned to them". In particular, it was held in *Republic of Argentina v. Mellino*, [1987] 1 S.C.R. 536, at p. 553, 33 C.C.C. (3d) 334, 40 D.L.R. (4th) 74, that

> . . . *absent express statutory or treaty authorization,* the sole purpose of an extradition hearing is to ensure that the evidence establishes a *prima facie* case that the extradition crime has been committed. [Emphasis added.]

> As a result, the role of the extradition judge has been held to be a "modest one", limited to the determination of whether or not the evidence is sufficient to justify committing the fugitive for surrender: see, for example, *United States of America v. Lépine,* [1994] 1 S.C.R. 286 at p. 296, 87 C.C.C. (3d) 385, 111 D.L.R. (4th) 31; *Mellino, supra,* at p. 553; *McVey, supra,* at p. 526.

As a result of the modest role assigned by statute, the Supreme Court of Canada emphatically rejected any role for the courts in monitoring treaty compliance. Thus, in *United States v. Lépine* (1993), 163 N.R. 1 (S.C.C.) and *United States v. McVey* (1992), 77 C.C.C. (3d) 1 (S.C.C.), the court held that attempts by the courts to monitor treaty compliance were a usurpation of a function of the executive.

The larger role played by the Minister of Justice in the extradition process was described by Cory J. in *Idziak v. Canada (Minister of Justice)* (1992), 77 C.C.C. (3d) 65 (S.C.C.), reconsideration refused (1992), 9 Admin. L.R. (2d) 1n (S.C.C.), in his discussion of the two-stage process, at p. 86:

> The first decision-making phase is certainly judicial in its nature and warrants the application of the full panoply of procedural safeguards. By contrast, the second decision-making process is political in its nature. The Minister must weigh the representations of the fugitive against Canada's international treaty obligations.
>
> . . .
>
> Parliament chose to give discretionary authority to the Minister of Justice. It is the Minister who must consider the good faith and honour of this country in its relations with other states. It is the Minister who has the expert knowledge of the political ramifications of an extradition decision.

Section 7 of the new Act gives legislative force to the line of cases recognizing the primacy of the Minister in extradition matters.

§3.0 SIGNIFICANCE OF CHANGE

The inclusion of s. 7 in the new Act is an assertion by Parliament that extradition continues to be primarily an executive matter. Section 7 may be considered as an interpretative aid insofar as the interpretation of the new Act should be guided by the principle that extradition is primarily a function of the executive and that the jurisdiction of the extradition judge is strictly circumscribed. This section would appear to function as a direction to avoid the blurring of judicial and ministerial roles that had to be remedied by the Supreme Court of Canada in decisions such as *United States v. McVey, supra,* and *United States v. Lépine, supra.* Under the new Act, when a dispute arises over whether a function belongs to the Minister or the extradition judge, s. 7 may operate in favour of the Minister.

The role of the Minister in dealing with extradition requests and implementing extradition agreements seems clear enough. In the cases of *United States v. McVey, supra,* and *United States v. Lépine, supra,* the Supreme Court of Canada established the principle that the Minister is responsible for monitoring treaty compliance. This principle has been incorporated into the new Act through s. 7, which provides that the "Minister is responsible for the implementation of extradition agreements" and for "dealing with requests for extradition made under them."

Section 7 also assigns responsibility for "the administration of this Act" to the Minister of Justice. This is intended to recognize the following powers assigned to the Minister under the Act: the initiation of the extradition process through the issuance of an authority to proceed (s. 15); the ability to terminate the proceedings at any time (s. 23); the authority to amend the authority to proceed (s. 23); and the responsibility for ultimately determining in accordance with the provisions of the Act whether to order surrender (s. 40).

§4.0 ANALYSIS

Section 7 of the Act is a statement of general authority recognizing the primacy of the Minister in the extradition process. The specific responsibilities of the Minister, however, are detailed elsewhere in the Act. Watt J., in *Germany (Federal Republic) v. Schreiber* (July 6, 2000), [2000] O.J. No. 2618 (Ont. S.C.J.), commented upon the significance of s. 7 in the following terms:

> [40] The Minister of Justice is responsible for the *implementation* of extradition agreements, the administration of the Act and, of greater significance here, dealing with requests for extradition under the Act or an applicable agreement. The language of this enabling authority, s. 7 of the Act, is unconfined, at least in terms. Specific authority is given in other sections of the Act and articles of the Treaty.

Watt J. enumerated some of the Minister's s. 7 responsibilities, which are taken up in other sections of the Act as including the authority to receive requests (s. 11), the authority to approve an application to the court by the Attorney General of Canada for a provisional arrest warrant (s. 12), and the authority to issue an authority to proceed with an extradition hearing (s. 15). These examples deal with the functions of the Minister prior to the holding of an extradition hearing. After the extradition hearing, if there has been a committal, the Minister has the authority and the discretion to determine whether the person will, in fact, be ordered surrendered to the extradition partner. As Watt J. described it:

> [60] In a temporal sense, the involvement of the Minister brackets that of the superior court judge. The Minister *receives* the request from the extradition partner. It is the Minister's statutory responsibility under s. 7 of the Act to *deal* with the request. It is for the Minister to decide whether she or he will authorize the Attorney General to apply for a provisional arrest warrant. Further, it is for the Minister to say whether she

or he will issue an authority to proceed that authorizes the Attorney General to seek, on behalf of the extradition partner, a judicial order of committal under s. 29 of the Act. . . .

[65] The Minister of Justice is the guardian of Canadian sovereignty interests. At the front end of the process, it is his or her function to ensure that the request of the extradition partner is compliant with the Act and the applicable treaty. Her decision, albeit of a political nature, may well involve considerations of foreign law that are beyond the scope of the extradition hearing judge's authority.

The Minister's involvement at the end of the process is contingent upon a judicial order for committal. At that point, it is in the discretion of the Minister to surrender or not surrender the individual. This is the ultimate responsibility for dealing with requests for extradition provided for by s. 7 of the Act.

§5.0 CASE LAW

Germany (Federal Republic) v. Schreiber (July 6, 2000), [2000] O.J. No. 2618, Watt J. (Ont. S.C.J.).
Idziak v. Canada (Minister of Justice) (1992), 77 C.C.C. (3d) 65 (S.C.C.), reconsideration refused (1992), 9 Admin. L.R. (2d) 1n (S.C.C.).
United States v. Dynar (1997), 115 C.C.C. (3d) 481 (S.C.C.).
United States v. Lépine (1993), 163 N.R. 1 (S.C.C.).
United States v. McVey (1992), 77 C.C.C. (3d) 1 (S.C.C.).

§6.0   RELATED SECTIONS

s. 11 — Minister's Power to Receive Provisional Arrest or Extradition Requests
s. 15 — Power of Minister to Issue Authority to Proceed
s. 23 — Substitution and Amendment of Authority to Proceed
s. 40–42 — Powers of Minister

Publication of Extradition Agreements (s. 8)

§1.0 DESCRIPTION

Section 8 of the *Extradition Act* provides as follows:

PUBLICATION IN *CANADA GAZETTE*
   8. (1) Unless the extradition agreement has been published under subsection (2), an extradition agreement — or the provisions respecting extradition contained in a multilateral extradition agreement — must be published in the *Canada Gazette* no later than 60 days after it comes into force.

(2) **An extradition agreement — or the provisions respecting extradition contained in a multilateral extradition agreement — may be published in the *Canada Treaty Series* and, if so published, the publication must be no later than 60 days after it comes into force.**

JUDICIAL NOTICE
(3) **Agreements and provisions published in the *Canada Gazette* or the *Canada Treaty Series* are to be judicially noticed.**

Section 8 requires that an extradition agreement, or the provisions of a multilateral agreement dealing with extradition, be published in either the *Canada Gazette* or the *Canada Treaty Series* no later than sixty days after the agreement comes into force. Once published in accordance with this section, an extradition agreement (or the extradition provisions of a multilateral agreement) shall be judicially noticed.

§2.0 COMPARISON WITH FORMER ACT

Sections 7 and 8 of the former *Extradition Act* read as follows:

> **7.** Any order of Her Majesty in Council referred to in section 4, any order of the Governor in Council made under section 4 or 5 and any extradition arrangement shall, as soon as possible, be published in the *Canada Gazette* and laid before both Houses of Parliament.

> **8.** The publication in the *Canada Gazette* of an extradition arrangement or an order in council is evidence of the arrangement or order, of the terms thereof and of the application of this Part pursuant and subject thereto, any court or judge shall without proof take judicial notice of the arrangement or order, and the validity of the order and the application of this Part pursuant and subject thereto shall not be questioned.

In general, ss. 7 and 8 of the former Act are similar to s. 8 of the new Act. There are, however, certain differences. Section 8 of the new Act allows for publication in the *Canada Treaty Series* as well as the *Canada Gazette*. The new s. 8 also specifies a precise time frame (60 days) for publication, whereas the former Act was less precise, requiring publication "as soon as possible." Finally, the new Act eliminates the requirement that the agreement be laid before both Houses of Parliament.

§3.0 SIGNIFICANCE OF CHANGE

The new Act is more precise than the former Act in terms of the time frame for the publication of extradition agreements. The new Act also provides for a higher degree of flexibility in allowing for publication in both the *Canada Gazette* and the *Canada Treaty Series*. With respect to multilateral agreements, the new Act specifies that only those parts of the agreement concerning extradition need to be published.

Finally, the new Act is more expeditious in eliminating the requirement that the agreement be presented before both Houses of Parliament.

§4.0 ANALYSIS

Under the former *Extradition Act*, the issue was raised as to whether the judicial notice requirement of ss. 7 and 8 was unconstitutional in infringing on the exclusive power of the judiciary. In *R. v. Waddell* (1992), 18 W.C.B. (2d) 183 (B.C. S.C.), affirmed on other grounds (1993), 87 C.C.C. (3d) 555 (B.C. C.A.), leave to appeal refused (1994), 88 C.C.C. (3d) vi (S.C.C.), the court upheld the provision.

§5.0 CASE LAW

R. v. Waddell (1992), 18 W.C.B. (2d) 183 (B.C. S.C.), affirmed on other grounds (1993), 87 C.C.C. (3d) 555 (B.C. C.A.), leave to appeal refused (1994), 88 C.C.C. (3d) vi (S.C.C.).

Designated States and Entities (s. 9)

§1.0 DESCRIPTION

Section 9 of the *Extradition Act* provides as follows:

DESIGNATED EXTRADITION PARTNERS
9. (1) The names of members of the Commonwealth or other States or entities that appear in the schedule are designated as extradition partners.

AMENDMENTS TO THE SCHEDULE
(2) The Minister of Foreign Affairs, with the agreement of the Minister, may, by order, add to or delete from the schedule the names of members of the Commonwealth or other States or entities.

Section 9(1) designates as extradition partners for the purposes of the Act those states or entities appearing in the schedule to the Act. In particular, the schedule lists various Commonwealth jurisdictions, two non-Commonwealth jurisdictions, Costa Rica and Japan, two international tribunals dealing with violations of international law in Rwanda and Yugoslavia, and as a result of amendments contained in the *Crimes Against Humanity and War Crimes Act*, the International Criminal Court.
Section 9(2) allows the Minister of Foreign Affairs, with the agreement of the "Minister" (defined in s. 2 of the Act as the Minister of Justice), to add to, or delete from, the schedule the names of Commonwealth jurisdictions and other states and

entities. The terms "extradition partner" and "State or entity" are defined in s. 2 of the Act.

§2.0 COMPARISON WITH FORMER ACT

Prior to the coming into force of the new *Extradition Act*, extradition to non-Commonwealth jurisdictions was governed by the former *Extradition Act*, and extradition to Commonwealth jurisdictions which recognized the Queen as head of state (known as "rendition") was governed by the now-repealed *Fugitive Offenders Act*.

A treaty was not required in the case of rendition under the *Fugitive Offenders Act*. By contrast, under the former *Extradition Act*, as most extraditions were dealt with under Part I of that legislation (titled "Extradition Under Treaty"), an extradition treaty was generally required. Part II of the former *Extradition Act* provided a mechanism for extradition in the absence of a treaty, but it was narrow in scope and seldom used. Section 35 of the former *Extradition Act* established how and when extradition was possible under Part II. It provided that Part II "does not come into force, with respect to fugitive offenders from any foreign state, until it has been declared by proclamation of the Governor General to be in force and effect with respect to that foreign state after a day to be named in the proclamation." Part II was only proclaimed on three occasions. The first was for the Federal Republic of Germany in 1974 (SI/74-40, *Canada Gazette*, Part II, v. 108). The second was for Brazil in 1979 (SI/79-160, *Canada Gazette*, Part II, v. 113:20, p. 3658). The third was for India in 1985 (SI/85-190, *Canada Gazette*, Part II, v. 119:23, p. 4615). Canada subsequently signed extradition treaties with Germany and India (see the list of Canada's extradition treaties in the Introduction, §2.1).

Section 9 of the new Act, read in conjunction with the definition of "extradition partner" in s. 2, incorporates rendition within the scheme of the new Act. In addition, s. 9, read together with the definition of "State or entity" in s. 2, broadens the range of actors who may request extradition of persons from Canada to include international criminal tribunals.

§3.0 SIGNIFICANCE OF CHANGE

Section 9 of the new Act makes extradition possible to any state or entity appearing in the schedule to the Act. An extradition agreement is not required. Indeed, Canada has no extradition agreement with a number of the states that appear in the schedule, such as countries with which Canada shares the Queen as Head of State and in respect of which extradition was formerly dealt with pursuant to the *Fugitive Offenders Act*. The new *Extradition Act* also allows for extradition in the absence of a treaty with Commonwealth countries that do not recognize the Queen as Head of State. As well, the schedule names non-Commonwealth states, Costa Rica and Japan, with which Canada has no extradition treaty, thereby making possible extradition with these countries. Section 9 also provides for the designation of international criminal tribunals as extradition partners. The schedule to the Act currently names two United Nations tribunals as extradition partners: those dealing with violations of international law in Rwanda and Yugoslavia, as well as the International Criminal Court. This will permit Canada to receive and act upon requests for extradition from those entities.

§4.0 ANALYSIS

The naming of extradition partners is an executive decision to be determined by the agreement of the Minister of Justice and the Minister of Foreign Affairs. Considerations informing such a determination may be expected to include whether the foreign judicial system is considered to be sufficiently compatible with that of Canada in respect of due process and fairness, and, as well, the willingness of the state or entity to reciprocate extradition requests made by Canada. See *R. v. Schmidt* (1987), 33 C.C.C. (3d) 193 (S.C.C.), at p. 215.

§5.0 CASE LAW

R. v. Schmidt (1987), 33 C.C.C. (3d) 193 (S.C.C.).

§6.0 RELATED SECTIONS

s. 2 — Interpretation — Definitions of "extradition partner," "Minister," and "State or entity"
Schedule to the Act

Specific Agreements (s. 10)

§1.0 DESCRIPTION

Section 10 of the *Extradition Act* provides as follows:

SPECIFIC AGREEMENTS
10. (1) The Minister of Foreign Affairs may, with the agreement of the Minister, enter into a specific agreement with a State or entity for the purpose of giving effect to a request for extradition in a particular case.

INCONSISTENCY
(2) For greater certainty, if there is an inconsistency between this Act and a specific agreement, this Act prevails to the extent of the inconsistency.

EVIDENCE

(3) A certificate issued by or under the authority of the Minister of Foreign Affairs to which is attached a copy of a specific agreement entered into by Canada and a State or entity is conclusive evidence of the agreement and its contents without proof of the signature or official character of the person appearing to have signed the certificate or agreement.

Section 10(1) enables the Minister of Foreign Affairs, with the agreement of the "Minister" (defined in s. 2 as the Minister of Justice) to enter into a specific agreement with a state or entity for the purpose of giving effect to a specific extradition request. In other words, it is now possible to enter into an *ad hoc* extradition agreement applying to one particular case. The term "State or entity" is defined in s. 2 to include a state other than Canada (including any subdivision of that state or territory falling under the jurisdiction of that state), an international tribunal, or a territory. Therefore, Canada may enter into a specific agreement with any of these actors. The term "specific agreement" is defined in s. 2 as "an agreement referred to in section 10 that is in force." This provision allows for extradition from Canada when the requesting jurisdiction is neither named in the schedule to the Act pursuant to s. 9 nor party to an extradition agreement with Canada. By entering into a specific agreement, the requesting state is thereby deemed to be an "extradition partner" for the purposes of the Act. More specifically, s. 2 defines an "extradition partner" as "a State or entity with which Canada is party to an extradition agreement, with which Canada has entered into a specific agreement or whose name appears in the schedule."

Section 10(2) addresses situations of inconsistency between the Act and a specific agreement, providing that the Act shall prevail to the extent of any inconsistency.

Section 10(3) deals with an evidentiary issue. It establishes that a certificate issued by the Minister of Foreign Affairs with a copy of the specific agreement attached is "conclusive evidence" of the agreement and its contents. The requesting state, through the Attorney General of Canada, need not prove the signature or official character of the person appearing to have signed the certificate or agreement.

Section 10 is located within Part II of the Act setting out the general rules and procedures governing extradition from Canada. Therefore, specific agreements are governed entirely by the rules set out in the Act.

§2.0 COMPARISON WITH FORMER ACT

The precursor to s. 10 is Part II (ss. 35–40) of the former *Extradition Act*. Part II dealt with extradition to non-Commonwealth countries "irrespective of treaty." (Extradition to countries that recognized the Queen as Head of State, known as rendition, has historically taken place in the absence of international agreements. Prior to being incorporated within the scheme of the new *Extradition Act*, rendition from Canada was governed by the *Fugitive Offenders Act*.)

The meaning of the phrase "irrespective of treaty" was provided by s. 37(1) of the former *Extradition Act*, which stated that extradition under Part II was lawful — assuming the other requirements of Part II were met — notwithstanding that no extradition agreement existed between Canada and the requesting state or that the extradition agreement did not include the crime in question.

Section 35 of the former Act established how and when extradition was possible under Part II. It provided that Part II "does not come into force, with respect to fugitive offenders from any foreign state, until it has been declared by proclamation of the Governor General to be in force and effect with respect to that foreign state after a day to be named in the proclamation." Part II was only proclaimed on three occasions. The first was for the Federal Republic of Germany in 1974 (SI/74-40, *Canada Gazette*, Part II, v. 108). The second was for Brazil in 1979 (SI/79-160, *Canada Gazette*, Part II, v. 113:20, p. 3658). The third was for India in 1985 (SI/85-190, *Canada Gazette*, Part II, v. 119:23, p. 4615). Canada subsequently signed extradition treaties with Germany and India.

Section 36 of the former Act restricted Part II to crimes listed in Schedule III of the Act and committed after the coming into force of Part II (the issue of retrospectivity under the new and former Acts — *i.e.*, the application of the Act in question to conduct or convictions occurring before the coming into force of the Act — is discussed in the commentary under "Retrospectivity" (s. 6)).

Section 39 of the former Act provided that the list of crimes in Schedule III was to be interpreted according to Canadian law as it existed on the date of the commission of the alleged offence. Section 39 also established that the list in Schedule III was deemed to include only those crimes that were indictable offences under Canadian law.

Section 40 of the former Act provided that extradition under Part II could not be made to a foreign jurisdiction if the law in that jurisdiction permitted the fugitive to be tried for offences other than those for which the fugitive was extradited, unless the executive authority of the foreign state gave an assurance that the fugitive would only be tried for the offences for which extradition was granted.

Section 37(2) of the former Act provided that the procedure outlined in Part I of the Act (*i.e.*, extradition under treaty) for the arrest, committal, detention, surrender, and conveyance of fugitives applied to extraditions under Part II.

Section 38 of the former Act stipulated that all expenses connected with the extradition of a fugitive from Canada to a foreign state under Part II were to be borne by the requesting state.

One can see a number of changes in the way the new and former *Extradition Acts* addressed the issue of extradition in the absence of an extradition agreement or for a crime not listed in the agreement. To begin with, at a structural level, the former Act dealt with extradition irrespective of treaty in an entirely separate part of the Act. This part was governed, in light of s. 37(2), by the rules of Part I ("Extradition Under Treaty"). However, it contained certain features that were distinct from Part I. For example, it contained a separate list of crimes (Schedule III) that did not contain many of the offences appearing in the list governing Part I. By contrast, s. 10 of the new

Act is fully integrated into the general rules and procedures governing extradition from Canada. Therefore, by way of example, s. 3 of the new Act, setting out the range of conduct for which extradition may be granted under the Act, applies to extradition pursuant to extradition agreement or specific agreement (s. 3 replaces the list approach of the former Act with a general punishability standard — see the discussion in the commentary under "Extraditable Conduct" (s. 3)).

Another difference between the schemes of the new and former Acts is that the mechanism for triggering an extradition irrespective of an extradition agreement is no longer a proclamation by the Governor General, but rather an agreement entered into by the Minister of Foreign Affairs with the approval of the Minister of Justice. The involvement of the Governor General in Part II of the former Act reflected the constitutional principle that foreign affairs are the prerogative of the Crown. For the limited purpose of entering into specific agreements, this function has now been given to the Minister of Foreign Affairs and the Minister of Justice.

A further difference is that extraditions pursuant to specific agreement (as well as all other extraditions under the new Act) apply retrospectively. Section 6 of the new Act provides that "extradition may be granted under this Act whether the conduct or conviction in respect of which the extradition is requested occurred before or after this Act or the relevant extradition agreement or specific agreement came into force" (note, however, that ss. 84 and 85 limit extradition under the new Act to matters with respect to which an extradition hearing has not yet commenced). By contrast, s. 36 of the former Act prohibited retrospectivity: "[Part II] applies to any crime mentioned in Schedule III that is committed after the coming into force of this Part with respect to any foreign state to which this Part has, by proclamation pursuant to subsection 35(1), been declared to apply."

Finally, it is worth noting that the new Act has added express inconsistency and evidentiary provisions (s. 10(2) and 10(3)) that were not present in Part II of the former Act. Section 10(2) provides that, in the event of an inconsistency between the provisions of the Act and the specific agreement, the Act shall prevail to the extent of any inconsistency. Subsection 10(3) establishes that a certificate issued by the Minister of Foreign Affairs with a copy of the specific agreement attached is "conclusive evidence" of the agreement and its contents. The requesting state, through the Attorney General of Canada, need not prove the signature or official character of the person appearing to have signed the certificate or agreement.

§3.0 SIGNIFICANCE OF CHANGE

This is an innovative addition to the new Act which will permit Canada to consider extradition requests on a case-by-case basis from countries that are not otherwise extradition partners. There was no similar authority under the former Act. Although extradition was possible under the former Act to countries Canada was not bound to by treaty, this required the rather cumbersome procedure of obtaining a proclamation from the Governor General under Part II of the former Act, permitting extradition to that state. However, even in cases in which the proclamation was made, it did not apply retrospectively and so offences alleged to have occurred prior to the proclamation date were not extraditable. Section 10 of the new Act does, of course, have retrospective application, and thereby effects a significant improvement in Canada's ability to do justice in any particular case.

§4.0 ANALYSIS

See the previous sections.

§5.0 RELATED SECTIONS

s. 2 — Interpretation
s. 3 — Extraditable Conduct
s. 6 — Retrospectivity

Minister's Power to Receive Provisional Arrest or Extradition Requests (s. 11)

§1.0 DESCRIPTION

Section 11 of the *Extradition Act* provides as follows:

REQUEST TO GO TO MINISTER
11. (1) A request by an extradition partner for the provisional arrest or extradition of a person shall be made to the Minister.

PROVISIONAL ARREST REQUEST TO GO TO MINISTER
(2) A request by an extradition partner for the provisional arrest of a person may also be made to the Minister through Interpol.

Section 11 describes the procedure to be followed by an extradition partner when making a request to Canada for the extradition or provisional arrest of a person. Section 11(1) sets out the general rule that all such requests are to be made to the Minister of Justice by the extradition partner. The term "extradition partner" is defined in s. 2 of the Act as "a State or entity with which Canada is party to an extradition agreement, with which Canada has entered into a specific agreement or whose name appears in the schedule" (this term is discussed in more detail in the commentary under "Interpretation" (s. 2).

In the case of requests for provisional arrest, s. 11(2) provides that the request can be made to the Minister through the intermediary of Interpol. Provisional arrest is an arrest procedure permitted in the Act and in most of Canada's extradition treaties. It enables the apprehension of the person sought prior to receipt of the formal request for extradition and supporting documentation required for the extradition hearing. Provisional arrest may be resorted to in any situation in which the public interest in effecting the arrest of the person is engaged. The risk of flight is one such example.

Interpol stands for the International Criminal Police Organization. This is an international organization coordinating police activities among member countries.

§2.0 COMPARISON WITH FORMER ACT

The comparable section of the former *Extradition Act* was s. 20. This section dealt with the requisitioning of the fugitive by the foreign state. Section 20 provided as follows:

> **20.** (1) A requisition for the surrender of a fugitive criminal of a foreign state who is, or is suspected to be, in Canada, may be made to the Minister of Justice
>
> (a) by any person recognized by the Minister of Justice as a consular officer of that state resident at Ottawa; or
>
> (b) by any minister of that state communicating with the Minister of Justice through the diplomatic representative of Her Majesty in that state.
>
> (2) If neither of the modes referred to in subsection (1) is convenient, the requisition shall be made in such other mode as is settled by arrangement.

The former Act was more specific in s. 20(1) about identifying the agents of the foreign state who could be recognized as having the authority to make a request for extradition from Canada. It included a recognized consular official of that state resident in Ottawa or a Minister of the foreign state communicating to a Canadian consular official in that state. However, it is notable that the wording of s. 20(1) was permissive and not mandatory with respect to the enumerated lines of communication. Moreover, s. 20(2) made it clear that, as a matter of convenience, the two countries were free to make other arrangements respecting the transmission of requests.

In practice, currently, as under the former regime, the treaties provide for the means of communication. Requests for the arrest and extradition of fugitives may be received through the channels prescribed by the relevant treaty. In the case of the *Canada–United States Extradition Treaty*, the request is made through the diplomatic channel. Some extradition treaties, such as that with the Netherlands, provide for the request to be made between Justice Departments or, in some situations, through Interpol.

Currently, as under the former regime, requests from the United States take the form of a numbered and dated diplomatic note from the Embassy of the United States of America in Ottawa to the Department of Foreign Affairs and International Trade requesting the apprehension and return of a fugitive. The diplomatic note engages the assistance of the Canadian authorities and typically provides a description of the accused, a brief overview of the facts, and a brief statement of the law applicable in the requesting jurisdiction.

Even though American requests are made to the Department of Foreign Affairs and International Trade, responsibility for honouring the request still falls to the Department of Justice. In order to assist in carrying out the functions assigned by the *Extradition Act* to the Minister of Justice, a special department exists to carry out functions exercised by the Minister as the central authority for Canada. This section is called the International Assistance Group (IAG). Located at 284 Wellington Street in Ottawa, K1A 0H8, it forms part of the Federal Prosecution Service of the Department of Justice. All requests for extradition made to Canada are coordinated by the IAG. Once a request for extradition is received, it and the documentary evidence provided in support of the request are considered by the IAG with a view to determining whether there has been compliance with the Act and the provisions of the applicable treaty. The IAG may ask for clarification or further information or details before proceeding further with a request. The execution of the request before the court is handled by the regional office of the Department of Justice where the person sought for extradition is located.

Under the former regime there was no authority for a province of Canada or state of the United States to make an extradition request directly, the treaty partners being the national entities. This will not change under the new Act. Section 11 requires that requests be made by an "extradition partner." This term is defined in s. 2 as "a State or entity with which Canada is party to an extradition agreement, with which Canada has entered into a specific agreement or whose name appears in the schedule." Section 2 defines a "State or entity" to include a province, state, or political subdivision of a state other than Canada. However, Canada's existing extradition agreements are between two countries, not between states and provinces or other political subdivisions.

Unlike the new *Extradition Act*, the former Act made no provision for the communication of requests for provisional arrests. Under the former regime such requests were governed entirely by treaty provisions.

§3.0 SIGNIFICANCE OF CHANGE

Although the new *Extradition Act* directs extradition requests to the Minister of Justice, treaties and established practices may provide for other avenues of communication. Other than the reference to the extradition partner there is no attempt to narrow the range of persons who might qualify to make the request on behalf of the extradition partner. The wording of the section seems to recognize that communications between Canada and foreign states are matters of diplomatic arrangement, and that there is no need for legislated provisions in the Act concerning how, or through whom, the foreign state should communicate.

Section 11(2) permits Interpol to communicate the request for a provisional arrest. This appears to recognize the modern reality that criminals can move rapidly over international borders and the cooperative nature of law enforcement in the international community. Permitting urgent requests for provisional arrests to be communicated through Interpol recognizes that the time required for the observance of the usual diplomatic niceties may not be available if the individual is to be apprehended. In other words, the slower diplomatic channels will not be insisted upon if there is a need to move swiftly to apprehend the person.

§4.0 ANALYSIS

The simplified provisions of s. 11 of the new Act with respect to communicating requests for extradition are reflective of the language used in the more modern extradition treaties. For instance, Article 9(1) of the *Canada–United States Extradition Treaty* states simply that "[t]he request for extradition shall be made through the diplomatic channel." Article VII of the treaty with Mexico, as another example, states that requests shall "be transmitted through diplomatic channels." Section 11 of the Act states only that the request of the extradition partner should be made to the Minister of Justice. The actual method of communication is left to be determined according to the diplomatic arrangements established by the two countries.

Section 11(2) is also a simplified provision for the communication of provisional arrest requests. Requests for provisional arrest have also been covered by the terms of the modern treaties, and a number of the treaties have made provision for these requests to be communicated through Interpol. Domestic law is now in accord with international practice as negotiated in such treaties.

§5.0 RELATED SECTIONS

s. 2 — Interpretation — Definition of "extradition partner"
s. 7 — Responsibilities of Minister of Justice
s. 12 — Minister's Approval of Request for Provisional Arrest Warrant
s. 13 — Issuance of Provisional Arrest Warrant
s. 14 — Discharge of Person Sought If No Proceedings Instituted
s. 15 — Power of Minister to Issue Authority to Proceed

Warrant for Provisional Arrest (ss. 12-14)

§1.0 INTRODUCTION

Sections 12, 13, and 14 of the *Extradition Act* appear under the heading "Warrant for Provisional Arrest." These sections deal with the prerequisites and procedures for obtaining a provisional arrest warrant. Provisional arrest is an arrest procedure, permitted not only under the Act but also in most treaties, enabling the apprehension of the person sought prior to the receipt of the formal request for extradition and the documentation required for the extradition hearing. This is in contrast to the situation in which an extradition request is presented with the required accompanying documentation and an arrest of the person sought is then effected. The latter situation is sometimes colloquially referred to as a "straight arrest." Straight arrest generally occurs when the location of the person sought is known and there is no urgency. This allows for the proper preparation in due course of the documentation required by s. 33 of the Act that will be used at the extradition hearing in Canada.

The provisional arrest situation arises when the presence of a person sought in Canada becomes known suddenly and unexpectedly or in circumstances which do not provide sufficient time for the extradition partner to prepare the documentation required for an extradition hearing. For instance, the person sought may be passing through Canada on the way to another jurisdiction. The new Act addresses such urgent situations by allowing for the provisional arrest of a person.

Minister's Approval of Request for Provisional Arrest Warrant (s. 12)

§1.0 DESCRIPTION

Section 12 of the *Extradition Act* provides as follows:

MINISTER'S APPROVAL OF REQUEST FOR PROVISIONAL ARREST

12. The Minister may, after receiving a request by an extradition partner for the provisional arrest of a person, authorize the Attorney General to apply for a provisional arrest warrant, if the Minister is satisfied that

(a) **the offence in respect of which the provisional arrest is requested is punishable in accordance with paragraph 3(1)(a); and**

(b) **the extradition partner will make a request for the extradition of the person.**

Section 12 describes the authority of the Minister of Justice to authorize the Attorney General of Canada to apply for the provisional arrest of a person. In order to do so, the Minister of Justice must be satisfied that two conditions have been met. Firstly, pursuant to s. 12(a), the Minister must be satisfied that the offence in question is punishable in accordance with the provisions of s. 3(1)(a) of the Act. Section 3(1)(a) requires that, in order to be extradited, the offence for which a person is sought must be punishable by imprisonment for a maximum period of two years or more in the requesting state. Section 3(1)(a) is, however, subject to the provisions of the relevant extradition agreement. Secondly, pursuant to s. 12(b), the Minister must be satisfied that the extradition partner will make a formal request for extradition as provided for in s. 11(1) of the Act.

§2.0 COMPARISON WITH FORMER ACT

The former *Extradition Act* contained no provisions relating to requests for the provisional arrest of persons sought. Under the former regime, such requests were entirely governed by treaty provisions in combination with s. 10 of the former Act. Section 10 provided as follows:

> **10.** (1) Whenever this Part applies, a judge may issue a warrant for the apprehension of a fugitive on a foreign warrant of arrest, or an information or a complaint laid before the judge, and on such evidence or after such proceedings as in the opinion of the judge would, subject to this Part, justify the issue of the warrant if the crime of which the fugitive is accused or is alleged to have been convicted had been committed in Canada.

Article 11 of the *Canada–United States Extradition Treaty* is an example of provisional arrest being provided for by treaty. Article 11 provides that in cases of urgency the requesting state may seek the apprehension of the fugitive pending the presentation of the formal extradition request. Article 11 requires that the request for provisional arrest include the following: a description of the person sought; an indication that the extradition of this person will be sought; a statement that a warrant of arrest or judgment of conviction against this person exists; and information, usually a brief outline of the facts, that would justify the issuance of a warrant in Canada if the offence had occurred in Canada.

Accordingly, under the former Act, through a provisional arrest provision in the applicable treaty, together with s. 10, a requesting state was able to obtain the provisional arrest of a fugitive. This provided the requesting state with the time necessary to prepare the documentation required under the Act and the applicable treaty for the extradition hearing.

§3.0 SIGNIFICANCE OF CHANGE

Under s. 12 of the new *Extradition Act*, the Minister of Justice may authorize an application for the provisional arrest of a person sought for extradition. Under the former regime, there was no requirement for this type of ministerial authorization of a request for provisional arrest. The request under the old regime was made to the central authority, in practice the International Assistance Group (IAG) of the Department of Justice, and from there the request was forwarded to the regional office of the Department, which would handle the application. The IAG would monitor the request for compliance with the treaty and determine whether to proceed with arrest. However, as long as the treaty provisions were met, no specific approval was required. In practical terms, the same criteria that had to be satisfied in monitoring the treaty will have to be met under s. 12 of the Act. Under the new Act, monitoring compliance with the requirements of s. 12 will be undertaken by the IAG on behalf of the Minister of Justice.

Under the former regime, prior to a provisional arrest matter commencing, the requirements of Article 2(1) of the *Canada–United States Extradition Treaty* would have been addressed. Article 2(1) provides as follows:

> Extradition shall be granted for conduct which constitutes an offense punishable by the laws of both Contracting Parties by imprisonment or other form of detention for a term exceeding one year or any greater punishment.

Article 2(1) and other similar treaty provisions will still govern the punishment criteria required to be established in order to proceed by way of provisional arrest. Section 12(a) of the new Act provides that the offence in question must be punishable in accordance with s. 3(1)(a) of the Act. However, s. 3(1)(a) sets out explicitly that the punishment criteria in that provision are "subject to a relevant extradition agreement." Accordingly, in the case of requests from the United States, the punishment criteria provided in Article 2(1) will continue to prevail over the Act.

§4.0 ANALYSIS

Sections 11 and 12 of the new *Extradition Act*, taken together, keep the provisional arrest process within ministerial control. Section 11 requires that the request for provisional arrest be directed to the Minister of Justice. Section 12 permits the Minister to authorize the Attorney General of Canada to apply for a provisional arrest warrant, if the Minister is satisfied that the stipulated criteria have been met. In addition to being satisfied that the requesting state will make a formal extradition request (s. 12(b)), the Minister, when considering a provisional arrest request, needs to be satisfied that the penalty requirements of s. 3(1)(a) are met (s. 12(a)). Therefore, under s. 3(1)(a), for both accused and convicted persons, the Minister must be satisfied that the offence is punishable by a maximum of two years' imprisonment or more, subject to a relevant extradition agreement. This contrasts with the requirements to be met before the Minister can issue an authority to proceed under s. 15. Section 15 permits the Attorney General to seek a committal of the person sought under s. 29 of the Act. Under s. 15, the Minister must be satisfied that the requirements of both s. 3(1)(a) and 3(3) are met. Section 3(3) applies to convicted persons, providing, subject to the terms of an extradition agreement, that extradition may only be granted if there remains to be served at least six months of the sentence, or a more severe punishment remains to be carried out. Accordingly, with respect to accused persons, the punishment requirements for the issuance of an authority to proceed under s. 15 are the same as those that would have to be met to authorize a provisional arrest. By contrast, in the case of convicted persons, the authority to proceed would only issue if, in addition to the punishment criteria of s. 3(1)(a), the Minster is also satisfied pursuant to s. 3(3) that there remains to be served at least six months of the sentence imposed (subject to the terms of a treaty).

Therefore, in the case of convicted persons, there are more stringent requirements to be met in order to authorize the authority to proceed to seek a committal under s. 29 of the Act than there are to provisionally arrest the person. It is thus possible that a person may be provisionally arrested who would not subsequently be proceeded against because the sentence remaining to be served was less than the six months set out in s. 3(3). The less stringent standards may be explainable by virtue of the fact that in situations of urgency the requesting state may not have detailed information concerning the time outstanding on the sentence to be served. The request for provisional arrest may also be made through Interpol. A police force may become aware that a person who is an escaped convict from their jurisdiction is in Canada. However, at that point in time, the police force may not have access to the records of correctional facilities or other organizations in the requesting state. For this reason, the police force may be unable to obtain information about the length of time outstanding on the sentence. In such cases, the person could be arrested provisionally and the sentencing information obtained subsequent to the arrest for the purposes of the authority to proceed under s. 15.

Once the Minister of Justice is satisfied that the preconditions of s. 12 have been met, that section requires that the Minister authorize the Attorney General of Canada to apply for a provisional arrest warrant. Section 12 does not specify the form that the authorization is to take. Therefore, the authorization presumably may be provided by the Minister's counsel either orally or in writing. Section 24(2) of the *Interpretation Act* permits counsel for the Minister of Justice to approve or authorize matters requiring the approval of the Minister. Section 24(2) provides as follows:

> Words directing or empowering a minister of the Crown to do an act or thing, regardless of whether the act or thing is administrative, legislative or judicial, or otherwise applying to that minister as the holder of the office, include
>
> . . .
>
> (d) notwithstanding paragraph (c), a person appointed to serve, in the department or ministry of state over which the minister presides, in a capacity appropriate to the doing of the act or thing, or to the words so applying.

§5.0 RELATED SECTIONS

s. 3 — Extraditable Conduct
s. 7 — Reponsibilities of Minister of Justice
s. 11 — Minister's Power to Receive Provisional Arrest or Extradition Requests
s. 13 — Issuance of Provisional Arrest Warrant
s. 14 — Discharge of Person Sought If No Proceedings Instituted
s. 15 — Power of Minister to Issue Authority to Proceed

Issuance of Provisional Arrest Warrant (s. 13)

§1.0 DESCRIPTION

Section 13 of the *Extradition Act* provides as follows:

PROVISIONAL ARREST WARRANT
13. (1) A judge may, on *ex parte* application of the Attorney General, issue a warrant for the provisional arrest of a person, if satisfied that there are reasonable grounds to believe that

(a) **it is necessary in the public interest to arrest the person, including to prevent the person from escaping or committing an offence;**
(b) **the person is ordinarily resident in Canada, is in Canada, or is on the way to Canada; and**
(c) **a warrant for the person's arrest or an order of a similar nature has been issued or the person has been convicted.**

CONTENTS OF THE WARRANT
(2) A provisional arrest warrant must

(a) **name or describe the person to be arrested;**
(b) **set out briefly the offence in respect of which the provisional arrest was requested; and**
(c) **order that the person be arrested without delay and brought before the judge who issued the warrant or before another judge in Canada.**

EXECUTION THROUGHOUT CANADA
(3) A provisional arrest warrant may be executed anywhere in Canada without being endorsed.

Section 13(1) sets out the procedure to be followed by the Attorney General of Canada when applying for a warrant of provisional arrest. It also provides the criteria for the issuance of a provisional arrest warrant by the judge. It establishes that the application can be *ex parte* and that the requirement for the judge to issue the warrant is based on reasonable grounds existing that the specified three criteria are satisfied. The three criteria are as follows: that the warrant be necessary in the public interest; that the person sought have a connection to Canada; and that the judge be satisfied that a warrant or order exists for the person's arrest or that the person has been convicted in the requesting jurisdiction.

Section 13(2) specifies the information that the provisional arrest warrant must contain, namely the identity of the person to be arrested, the offence in question, and that the person be arrested without delay and brought before a Canadian judge.

Section 13(3) indicates that a provisional arrest warrant may be executed Canada-wide.

§2.0 COMPARISON WITH FORMER ACT

The former *Extradition Act* contained no provision dealing specifically with provisional arrest procedures. Under that Act, s. 10 gave the judge the same authority to issue an extradition arrest warrant as a justice would have to issue a warrant in domestic circumstances. Provisional arrest warrants issued under the former Act were issued under the authority of s. 10 together with any treaty provision dealing with provisional arrest, such as Article 11 of the *Canada–United States Extradition Treaty*. By contrast, s. 13(1) of the new Act specifically provides a basis for the issuance of provisional arrest warrants. The first two requirements for the issuance of a provisional arrest warrant, set out in s. 13(1)(a) and 13(1)(b) (that it would be in the public interest, and that the person is in, on the way to, or ordinarily resident in Canada), are similar to domestic warrant requirements, although they are written in terms of the extradition context. The third requirement, set out in s. 13(1)(c) (that a warrant of arrest has been issued, or the person has been convicted in the requesting jurisdiction), is unique to extradition. The power to issue a provisional arrest warrant is no longer analogized to the authority to issue a warrant in similar domestic circumstances. Once the Minister has authorized an application pursuant to s. 12, s. 13(1) sets out three specific grounds required to be established before a provisional arrest warrant may issue.

Section 13(1) provides for the application to be made *ex parte*. Although s. 10 of the former Act did not specify that applications for arrest warrants were to be made *ex parte*, in practice they were. This was the case because giving notice to a fugitive who was most likely a flight risk would have been counterproductive. The provision for the application to be made *ex parte* under the new Act removes any debate about this issue. There may be circumstances when a person sought for extradition is aware that an arrest warrant is to be obtained and would like his or her counsel present at the application proceedings to make submissions against the issuance of the warrant. The specific indication in s. 13(1) that the application is to be *ex parte* would appear to militate against such an attendance.

Section 13(2), unlike any provision in the former Act, specifies the information which the warrant for arrest must contain. In practice, however, warrants issued under the former regime for the most part contained the same information as is required by s. 13(2).

A procedural difference between the s. 13 of the new Act and s. 10 of the former Act is that the latter required that the Minister be notified of the issuance of a warrant and be provided with the supporting material. By contrast, s. 13 does not have the same ministerial notice requirement. Presumably, this is because it is the Minister under s. 12 of the new Act who authorizes the application for the provisional arrest warrant, and therefore the Minister already has knowledge of the proceedings.

Under the former regime, there was no authority for a police officer to arrest a fugitive without a warrant, unless the fugitive had committed an offence contrary to Canadian law. The foreign warrant itself was not enough to justify an arrest in Canada. This remains the situation under the new Act.

Section 13(3), which enables a provisional arrest warrant to be executed anywhere in Canada without being endorsed, is comparable to s. 11 of the former Act.

§3.0 SIGNIFICANCE OF CHANGE

Although the three criteria in s. 13(1) are specific, they are very broad in nature. It appears that the public interest criteria referred to in s. 13(1)(a) mirrors s. 507(4) of the *Criminal Code*. The latter provides that a justice may issue a warrant for the arrest of an accused if there are reasonable grounds to believe that it is necessary in the public interest to do so. With respect to the public interest criteria referred to in s. 13(1)(a), a number of situations could be included in this category. One situation is urgency, which was always a requirement for provisional arrest requests under Article 11 of the *Canada–United States Extradition Treaty*. Urgency generally concerned flight risk situations, and s. 13(1)(a) now specifically provides for this as a ground for the issuance of a provisional arrest warrant. In addition, under s. 13(1)(a), the likelihood that the person will commit other offences is also a ground justifying the issuance of a provisional arrest warrant. The examples given in the Act are not exhaustive of what might fall under the public interest umbrella. Security of the public generally or the risk of the person being deported to a third country could each be considered public interest issues justifying the issuance of a provisional arrest warrant.

Section 13(1)(b) of the new Act does not require the person sought actually to be in Canada. Under the former regime, provisional arrest warrants were only obtained when there were grounds to believe that the person sought was physically in this country (see *Re McVey and The Queen* (1987), 37 C.C.C. (3d) 444 (B.C. S.C.), at p. 448). It is now clear that the issuance of a warrant is not confined to situations where the person is actually within the territorial jurisdiction of Canada. Rather, it extends to situations where the person is ordinarily resident in Canada or is believed to be on the way to Canada.

Section 13(1)(c) requires that "a warrant for the person's arrest or an order of a similar nature has been issued or the person has been convicted." The words "order of a similar nature" recognize the potentially different methods of compelling attendance that exist in other countries. Moreover, from the wording of s. 13(1)(c), it is clear that the judge has only to be satisfied of the existence of a warrant for the person's arrest or an order of a similar nature or that the person has been convicted. There is no requirement that a copy of the warrant or order or conviction be produced. A statement of the existence of the document would appear to suffice. In essence, this was the same situation under the former regime, at least with respect to American requests. Article 11(1) of the *Canada–United States Extradition Treaty* provides that in cases of urgency a request for provisional arrest has to be accompanied by "a statement of the existence of a warrant of arrest or a judgment of conviction against the person." Article 11(1) does not require a copy of these documents.

Section 13(2) of the Act now mandates what information is required in a provisional arrest warrant. This is similar to what is required by Form 7 of the *Criminal Code* for domestic arrest warrants.

§4.0 ANALYSIS

§4.1 Public Interest Component (s. 13(1)(a))

Provisional arrest was not addressed in the former *Extradition Act*. Under the treaties, it was generally provided for with respect to situations of urgency involving flight risk. The new *Extradition Act* does not require urgency to justify provisional arrest. However, it clearly contemplates that urgency will justify a provisional arrest by including in s. 13(1)(a) prevention of the person from escaping as an instance in which "public interest" is engaged. Section 13(1)(a) refers to two instances in which a provisional arrest would be in the public interest. In addition to the prevention of escape, it also mentions the prevention of further offences. However, the concept of public interest is a broad one and may encompass any number of circumstances.

§4.2 Connection to Canada (s. 13(1)(b))

Section 13(1)(b) requires that the person sought "is ordinarily resident in Canada, is in Canada, or is on the way to Canada." This provision makes the provisional arrest procedure more efficient by enabling provisional arrest warrants to be obtained without the person sought actually being in Canada. Therefore, a warrant can be ready to be executed upon the arrival of the person in Canada. This will diminish the opportunity for the person to evade apprehension because the warrant will already have been obtained when the presence of the person in Canada is confirmed. See §4.5 "Contents of Supporting Material" below.

§4.3 Procedure to Obtain *Ex Parte* Warrant

The practice for obtaining a warrant of provisional arrest under the former regime was for Department of Justice counsel to appear on behalf of the requesting state before the extradition judge with a police officer who would swear a document titled "Information and Complaint." Under the new Act, Department of Justice counsel will continue to appear on applications for provisional arrest warrants. However, in accordance with the provisions of s. 13, counsel will appear as a representative of the Attorney General of Canada. The document "Information and Complaint" originated from s. 10 of the former Act. Section 10 provided that a judge could issue a warrant for the apprehension of a fugitive on an information or a complaint laid before the judge. Section 13(1) of the new Act does not specify what kind of documentation should be placed before the judge on an application for a provisional arrest warrant, simply that the judge must be satisfied on reasonable grounds that the criteria set out in s. 13(1) are met.

Applications under s. 10 of the former Act would have been supported with sworn evidence. Section 13(1) of the new Act does not indicate a requirement for the supporting evidence to be under oath. Obviously, sworn affidavit evidence will continue to be acceptable. However, it may now be permissible to obtain a provisional arrest warrant based upon unsworn material. Provisional arrest warrants are frequently sought under urgent circumstances, for instance, when there is a risk of imminent flight. Often, applications for provisional arrest warrants will be made on evenings, weekends, holidays, and after normal business hours. In urgent situations the representative of the Attorney General of Canada may appear alone before the judge relying upon the information faxed by the requesting state or Interpol setting out the particulars of the request. The section therefore accommodates urgent situations where it may not be possible to prepare more formal material in the form of a sworn affidavit.

§4.4 Documentation Required By Treaty

The contents of the supporting material to obtain a provisional arrest warrant will have to take into account the requirements of s. 13(1) of the Act. It can be expected that requesting countries will continue to be guided in their requests by the terms of the applicable extradition treaty. The terms of the treaties may require the provision of information that would be in addition to the information required by s. 13(1).

For instance, Article 11 of the *Canada–United States Extradition Treaty* provides that in cases of urgency the requesting state may seek the apprehension of the fugitive pending the presentation of the formal extradition request through the diplomatic channel. A request for provisional arrest under Article 11(1) of the Treaty requires the following information: a description of the person sought, an indication that the extradition of the person will be sought, a statement that a warrant of arrest or judgment of conviction against this person exists, and information (usually a brief outline of the facts) that would justify the issuance of a warrant in Canada had the offence occurred in Canada. Compliance with the treaty provisions should meet the public interest and warrant requirements of s. 13(1)(a) and 13(1)(c) of the Act.

§4.5 Contents of Supporting Material

The material relied on in support of the Attorney General's application for a provisional arrest warrant should address the three pre-conditions set out in s. 13(1) of the Act, namely, the public interest component, the connection to Canada and that a warrant or order of a similar nature is outstanding for the person's arrest in the requesting jurisdiction. In the case of an American request, a document entitled

"Provisional Arrest Request" is usually provided which sets out the information required by Article 11 of the *Canada–United States Extradition Treaty* (described in the previous section). This document can be referred to or included in the material in support of the application. Other countries provide similar information when provisional arrest is requested. This should satisfy the public interest requirement of s. 13(1)(a) and the existence of a warrant requirement of s. 13(1)(c).

It is inferred in s. 13 of the Act and in the treaty provisions dealing with provisional arrest that prior to a provisional arrest warrant being obtained there will be sufficient information confirming the identity of the person. It will still be necessary for domestic police to provide identification information indicating that the person sought for extradition is ordinarily resident in Canada, is in Canada, or is on the way to Canada pursuant to s. 13(1)(b). This information will have to be incorporated into the supporting material placed before the extradition judge on the application.

Under the former regime, the identity of a fugitive was generally concerned with providing information that the person was in Canada and that this person was the individual sought by the requesting state. As a result of s. 13(1)(b) of the Act, the focus on providing identification information will not only encompass whether the person is in Canada, but will also extend to whether the person sought is ordinarily resident in Canada or is on the way to Canada.

Under s. 13 of the new Act, providing sufficient information regarding identity for the purposes of obtaining a provisional arrest warrant will not differ from the procedure used under the former Act. Under the latter regime, the information and complaint typically included the report of the police officer with respect to the identification of the fugitive. Often this took the form of a report indicating how the fugitive had been located and confirming that the person located appeared to be the same person sought by the foreign jurisdiction. The police generally had a photograph of the person sought provided by the requesting jurisdiction or in some cases fingerprints of the person taken by the foreign authorities. The photographs or fingerprints were usually attached as exhibits to the information and complaint of the police officer.

The issue of identity under the new Act can be addressed in a similar fashion. If the person sought has had fingerprints taken in Canada, then identity can easily be confirmed by a comparison of the Canadian fingerprints with the fingerprints provided by the foreign jurisdiction. For persons sought who are in Canada or ordinarily resident in Canada, the police usually confirm the presence of the individual in this country after conducting surveillance on the target and with reference to photographs provided by the requesting state or by showing the photographs to people who might know the person.

In the case of a person who is believed to be on the way to Canada, the basis of this belief, and a description of the person, including any photographs or fingerprints, should be contained in the supporting material.

§4.6 Contents of Provisional Arrest Warrant

Section 13(2) itemizes the information that must be included in the provisional arrest warrant. Section 13(2)(a) states that the provisional arrest warrant must "name or describe" the person to be arrested. The ability to describe rather than name the person is important because in some cases the name of the person may not yet have been ascertained. Section 13(2)(b) requires that the warrant "set out briefly the offence in respect of which the provisional arrest was requested." The plain reading of this section seems to contemplate that it is the foreign offence that is to be set out in the warrant, the foreign offence being the offence in respect of which the provisional arrest was requested. Support for this interpretation can be found in comparing s. 13(2)(b) with s. 15(3)(c). The latter section requires that the authority to proceed, issued by the Minister of Justice, contain "the name of the offence or offences under Canadian law that correspond to the alleged conduct" of the person sought. Section 13(2)(b), by contrast, does not specify that the equivalent Canadian offence be set out in the warrant. Indeed, at the provisional arrest stage of the proceedings, this makes good sense given that the Minister may not at that point be in possession of sufficient information to make such a determination.

Either practice may be valid, as in fact was the case under the previous Act. La Forest J., in his judgment for a majority of the Supreme Court of Canada in *United States v. McVey* (1992), 72 C.C.C. (3d) 1, at pp. 10–11, held that it was appropriate to name either the Canadian offence or the foreign offence in the warrant of apprehension:

> This does not ordinarily pose any problem because most Canadian extradition cases are with the United States and as a general rule the same criminal act or conduct falls within an offence of the same name in both countries. There is, however, much to be said for Blanchflower's view (*ibid.*, pp. 171-4) that the information in support of the warrant of arrest should set forth the name of the Canadian offence in the first place; it would be a better practice and avoid confusion. But s. 10(1) is not explicit on the point and either practice is valid. Consistent with the general principle that extradition laws should be liberally construed so as to achieve the purposes of the treaty, a much less technical approach to extradition matters than to common law warrants has been adopted: see *La Forest's Extradition*, 3rd ed., at pp. 128-9.

§5.0 CASE LAW

McVey and The Queen, Re (1987), 37 C.C.C. (3d) 444 (B.C.S.C.).
United States v. McVey (1992), 72 C.C.C. (3d) 1 (S.C.C.) .

§6.0 RELATED SECTIONS

s. 11 — Minister's Power to Receive Provisional Arrest or Extradition Requests
s. 12 — Minister's Approval of Request for Provisional Arrest Warrant

s. 14 — Discharge of Person Sought If No Proceedings Instituted
s. 15(3) — Contents of Authority to Proceed
s. 16(2) — Summons or Warrant Not Required for Person Provisionally Arrested
Canada–United States Extradition Treaty, Article 11 — Provisional Arrest Warrants
Criminal Code, s. 507(4) — Summons to be Issued Except in Certain Cases
Criminal Code, Form 7 — Warrant for Arrest

Discharge of Person Sought If No Proceedings Instituted (s. 14)

§1.0 DESCRIPTION

Section 14 of the *Extradition Act* provides as follows:

DISCHARGE IF NO PROCEEDINGS
14. (1) A person who has been provisionally arrested, whether detained or released on judicial interim release, must be discharged

> **(a) when the Minister notifies the court that an authority to proceed will not be issued under section 15;**
>
> **(b) if the provisional arrest was made pursuant to a request made under an extradition agreement that contains a period within which a request for extradition must be made and the supporting documents provided,**
>
>> **(i) when the period has expired and the extradition partner has not made the request or provided the documents, or**
>>
>> **(ii) when the request for extradition has been made and the documents provided within the period but the Minister has not issued an authority to proceed before the expiry of 30 days after the expiry of that period; or**
>
> **(c) if the provisional arrest was not made pursuant to a request made under an extradition agreement or was made pursuant to an extradition agreement that does not contain a period within which a request for extradition must be made and the supporting documents provided,**
>
>> **(i) when 60 days have expired after the provisional arrest and the extradition partner has not made the request or provided the documents, or**
>>
>> **(ii) when the request for extradition has been made and the documents provided within 60 days but the Minister has not issued an authority to proceed before the expiry of 30 additional days.**

EXTENSION

(2) On application of the Attorney General, a judge

(a) may extend a period referred to in subsection (1); or

(b) shall, in the case of a person arrested on the request of the International Criminal Court, extend a period referred to in subsection (1) for the period specified by the Attorney General, not to exceed 30 days.

RELEASE OF PERSON

(3) In extending a period under subsection (2), the judge may also grant the person judicial interim release or vary the conditions of their judicial interim release.

Section 14(1) requires the discharge of a person sought in the following circumstances:

• When the Minister of Justice has made a positive determination not to issue an authority to proceed under s. 15 (s. 14(1)(a)).

• In the case of a treaty request: when the formal extradition request and the documents required for the extradition hearing have not been provided within the time limit set out in the treaty (s. 14(1)(b)(i)).

• Again in the case of a treaty request: when the formal request and supporting documents have been provided within the time limits prescribed by the treaty but the Minister has not issued an authority to proceed within 30 days after the expiry of this time period (s. 14(1)(b)(ii)).

• In the case of a treaty that contains no prescribed time periods and in the case of non-treaty requests: when the formal request and supporting documentation for the extradition hearing have not been received within 60 days of the date of the arrest (s. 14(1)(c)(i)).

• Again in the case of a treaty that contains no prescribed time periods and in the case of non-treaty requests: when the formal request for extradition and supporting documentation has been provided within 60 days but the Minister has not issued the authority to proceed before the expiry of 30 additional days (s. 14(1)(c)(ii)).

Section 14(2), as re-enacted by the *Crimes Against Humanity and War Crimes Act*, S.C. 2000, c. 24, s. 49, provides that, upon the application of the Attorney General, a judge has the discretion to extend the time periods in s. 14(1). However, if the person were sought on the request of the International Criminal Court, the extension would be mandatory for the period specified by the Attorney General to a maximum of 30 days.

Section 14(3) allows the judge, when extending a time period under s. 14(2), to grant or vary judicial interim release orders.

§2.0 COMPARISON WITH FORMER ACT

As previously discussed in connection with s. 13, the former *Extradition Act* had no specific provisions dealing with provisional arrest. Therefore, the former Act had nothing comparable to s. 14, that is, it did not contain any provisions allowing for the discharge of a person sought in the event that the formal extradition request and supporting materials were not received within specified time limits. Accordingly, under the former regime, the provisions of the treaties in this respect governed completely. The bilateral treaties that provide for provisional arrest set out time periods within which the formal request and supporting documentation must be supplied, failing which the person is to be discharged. Article 11(3) of the *Canada–United States Extradition Treaty* is typical of this kind of provision:

> A person arrested shall be set at liberty upon the expiration of sixty days from the date of arrest pursuant to such application [for provisional arrest] if a request for extradition and the documents specified in Article 9 have not been received. This stipulation shall not prevent the institution of proceedings with a view to extraditing the person sought if the request and documents are subsequently received.

There are similar provisions in Article 9 of the *Canada–Philippines Extradition Treaty*, Article 11 of the *Canada–India Extradition Treaty*, and Article 10 of the *Canada–Spain Extradition Treaty*, among others. The time periods set out in the different treaties may differ but the effect of the provisions is the same: to set free the person sought if the formal request and documentation required is not provided within the specified time period.

§3.0 SIGNIFICANCE OF CHANGE

The negotiated terms of the treaties with respect to the time periods within which the formal request and supporting materials are to be provided continue to apply. However, the Act has modified the operation of the treaty terms by providing that the time periods may be extended on the order of a judge.

In conjunction with the time periods stipulated for the provision of the formal request and supporting documents, s. 14 also sets out the time periods within which the Minister of Justice must issue the authority to proceed. The time periods established for the Minister follow upon the expiry of the time periods within which the formal request and the supporting documentation must be supplied.

In the case of a treaty request, s. 14(1)(b)(ii) entitles the Minister to 30 days following the time period in the treaty. In the *Canada–United States Extradition Treaty*, for example, the time period for making the formal request and providing the supporting documentation is 60 days. Therefore, assuming this time period is complied with, the Minister has 30 days in addition to the 60 days in which to issue the authority to proceed, that is, 90 days after the provisional arrest of the person.

Section 14(1)(c)(ii) is the comparable provision for non-treaty requests or treaty requests where the treaty does not provide for time limits. It provides that the formal request and supporting documentation must be received within 60 days. The Minister is provided with an additional 30 days in which to issue the authority to proceed. The section could be read as providing the Minister with 30 days from the date on which the Minister receives the request and the documents. However, it would be more consistent with s. 14(1)(b)(ii) to view the time period as being 30 days after the 60-day period has expired, for a total of 90 days.

§4.0 ANALYSIS

The purpose of s. 14 is to implement safeguards and impose time limits on the duration of provisional arrest given its exceptional nature. Provisional arrest is exceptional because it allows for the arrest of a person in urgent or other pressing circumstances without Canada actually having received the extradition request from the requesting state. As well, the application for the provisional arrest is made without having the benefit of the complete record which will be supplied in support of the extradition request. Section 14 places limits upon the length of time that a person can remain subject to extradition proceedings prior to receipt of the formal extradition request, the documentation for use at the hearing, and the authority to proceed. The section is flexible, however, in that it permits the time periods to be extended by a judge. The authority to extend the time periods in favour of the requesting state is balanced by the provision that allows the judge to grant or vary judicial interim release orders.

An extension of any of the time periods in s. 14(1) may be obtained under s. 14(2), upon application by the Attorney General to a judge. In *Germany (Federal Republic) v. Schreiber* (October 25, 1999), unreported (Ont. S.C.J.), *per* Hamilton J., *Germany (Federal Republic) v. Oeffner* (December 1, 2000), unreported (Ont. S.C.J.), *per* Dunnet J. and *Hungary (Republic) v. Kocsis* (October 7, 1999), unreported (Ont. S.C.J.), *per* Ewaschuk J., orders extending the time periods were made after the periods in s. 14(1) had already expired. In *Kocsis, supra*, Ewaschuk J. stated, at p. 3 of the ruling:

> I decline to accept Mr. Wilson's argument that merely because other provisions in the Act refer to the extension of time before or after the expiry of the requisite time period mandates that I have power to extend the period only before it has expired. I do so on the basis that s. 14(2) of the new *Extradition Act* must be interpreted in a remedial fashion as required by s. 12 of the federal *Interpretation Act*.

Section 14(2) was amended to provide for a mandatory extension of time for a period specified by the Attorney General not to exceed 30 days for requests made by the International Criminal Court.

This amendment provides flexibility to the application of the time periods in the interests of justice. The mandatory extension of time for requests by the International Criminal Court reflects the gravity of the offences that fall within the jurisdiction of that court—war crimes, crimes against humanity, and genocide—and recognizes that the strict application of limitation periods should not be used to prevent individuals suspected of such crimes from being brought to justice.

The safeguards provided by the time limits set out in s. 14 are more fully discussed in the commentary under "Power of Minister to Issue Authority to Proceed" (s. 15), §4.2 "Time Limits for Issuance of Authority to Proceed."

§5.0   CASE LAW

Germany (Federal Republic) v. Oeffner (December 1, 2000), Dunnet J. (Ont. S.C.J.).
Germany (Federal Republic) v. Schreiber (October 25, 1999), Hamilton J. (Ont. S.C.J.).
Hungary (Republic) v. Kocsis (October 7, 1999), Ewaschuk J. (Ont. S.C.J.).

§6.0 RELATED SECTIONS

s. 4 — Reinstitution of Proceedings
s. 12 — Minister's Approval of Request for Provisional Arrest Warrant
s. 13 — Issuance of Provisional Arrest Warrant
s. 15 — Power of Minister to Issue Authority to Proceed
s. 18 — Judicial Interim Release

Power of Minister to Issue Authority to Proceed (s. 15)

§1.0 DESCRIPTION

§1.1 Minister's Power to Issue Authority to Proceed (s. 15(1))

Section 15(1) of the *Extradition Act* provides as follows:

MINISTER'S POWER TO ISSUE
15. (1) The Minister may, after receiving a request for extradition and being satisfied that the conditions set out in paragraph 3(1)(a) and subsection 3(3) are met in respect of one or more offences mentioned in the request, issue an authority to proceed that authorizes the Attorney General to seek, on behalf of the extradition partner, an order of a court for the committal of the person under section 29.

Section 15(1) describes the procedure by which requests for extradition made to Canada are reviewed and approved. The Minister of Justice is given the duty of receiving extradition requests and assessing them with regard to certain specified preconditions for approval. The Minister must be satisfied that the conditions set out in s. 3(1)(a) and 3(3) of the Act are met. Section 3(1)(a) provides that, in order to be extradited, the offence for which a person is sought must be punishable in the requesting state by imprisonment for a maximum period of two years or more, subject to the terms of a relevant extradition agreement. Section 3(3) provides that, with respect to a person already convicted and sentenced to imprisonment, there must be at least six months of the sentence remaining to be served in order for the person to be extradited, again subject to a relevant extradition agreement. These preconditions must be met with respect to one or more of the offences mentioned in the request. If the conditions are met, the Minister of Justice may authorize the Attorney General of Canada on behalf of the extradition partner to seek an order of committal under s. 29 of the Act.

§1.2 Competing Requests (s. 15(2))

Section 15(2) of the *Extradition Act* provides as follows:

COMPETING REQUESTS
(2) If requests from two or more extradition partners are received by the Minister for the extradition of a person, the Minister shall determine the order in which the requests will be authorized to proceed.

This subsection gives the Minister of Justice the discretion to determine which extradition request will be given priority in the event that the Minister receives more than one request for the same person.

§1.3 Contents of Authority to Proceed (s. 15(3))

Section 15(3) of the *Extradition Act* provides as follows:

CONTENTS OF AUTHORITY TO PROCEED
(3) The authority to proceed must contain

(a) the name or description of the person whose extradition is sought;
(b) the name of the extradition partner; and
(c) the name of the offence or offences under Canadian law that correspond to the alleged conduct of the person or the conduct in respect of which the person was convicted, as long as one of the offences would be punishable in accordance with paragraph 3(1)(b).

Section 15(3) sets out the information that the authority to proceed must contain, namely: the identity of the person sought; the foreign state or entity seeking extradition; and the names of the equivalent Canadian offences for which extradition is sought, provided that at least one of the offences meets the punishment criteria set out in s. 3(1)(b) of the Act. Section 3(1)(b), subject to a relevant extradition agreement, requires the following: in the case of a request based on a "specific agreement" (defined in ss. 2 and 10 of the Act), the equivalent Canadian offence is punishable by imprisonment for five years or more; in the case of a request under an extradition agreement, the equivalent Canadian offence is punishable by imprisonment for two years or more.

§1.4 Copy of Authority to Proceed (s. 15(4))

Section 15(4) of the *Extradition Act* provides as follows:

COPY OF AUTHORITY TO PROCEED
     (4) A copy of an authority to proceed produced by a means of telecommunication that produces a writing has the same probative force as the original for the purposes of this Part.

Section 15(4) permits the use of a copy of the authority to proceed for any purpose under the Act.

§2.0 COMPARISON WITH FORMER ACT

The former *Extradition Act* had nothing comparable to s. 15 of the new Act. Extradition proceedings under the previous scheme were less structured than under the new Act and did not depend upon the issuance of an authority to proceed from the Minister. Under the former regime, the request for extradition was made through the diplomatic channels, by way of a diplomatic note, to the Department of Foreign Affairs and International Trade. The diplomatic note usually made the request for extradition, specified the offences for which extradition was sought, and provided a brief outline of the allegations. In practice, the request was acted upon by counsel for the Minister of Justice at the International Assistance Group (IAG) in Ottawa because the Minister was responsible for deciding whether or not a fugitive would in fact be surrendered. Therefore, after receiving the diplomatic note, the Minister's counsel would review the request and the supporting material in order to determine if the request complied with the terms of the Act and the applicable treaty. If it did comply, the request and the supporting materials were forwarded to counsel in the regional office of the Department of Justice who then took carriage of the proceedings. In this sense, the Minister's office controlled, or at least was closely involved with, the extradition proceedings from the outset.

The new Act legislates the early involvement of the Minister and formally requires specific documentation to be issued by the Minister to initiate the proceedings. Whereas the former Act involved a loose scheme, requiring that a great deal be inferred regarding the procedure to be followed, the new Act is much clearer, providing a defined procedure and a commencing document which sets out the Canadian equivalent charge.

Section 15(2), which authorizes the Minister to determine the order in which competing requests for the same individual will proceed, also had no counterpart in the former *Extradition Act*. However, many of the treaties made provision for how the requested state was to determine the issue of competing requests for the same person (see, for example, Article 13 of the *Canada–United States Extradition Treaty*). The inclusion of s. 15(2) is a natural recognition in domestic law of the Minister's control over matters concerning requests from two or more countries for the same person.

§3.0 SIGNIFICANCE OF CHANGE

The loose structure that existed under the former Act has been replaced in the new Act by a highly formalized process. This stems from the legislated role of the Minister of Justice under s. 7 of the Act, which confers upon the Minister responsibility for the implementation of extradition agreements, the administration of the Act, and the handling of extradition requests. In the exercise of these responsibilities, s. 15 imposes certain duties upon the Minister: under s. 15(1), the Minister must be satisfied that certain specified criteria have been met concerning the penalties obtaining in the requesting state with respect to the conduct for which the individual is sought; and under s. 15(2), the Minister must determine the order in which competing extradition requests will proceed. Once these subsections have been satisfied, the Minister is required to formally issue an authorization to proceed before the extradition proceedings can go forward.

Under the former Act, the Minister's power to extradite was exercised only after an extradition judge had determined through a judicial hearing that a *prima facie* case had been established by the requesting state. Under the new Act, ministerial authority over the process has been extended to the commencement of the proceedings. As set out in s. 15, an extradition request cannot proceed through the courts without the Minister's authorization. The Minister's authority to proceed is a precondition to the adjudication of the courts on the issue of the sufficiency of the evidence for committal.

Under the former Act, the diplomatic note containing the extradition request was filed at the commencement of the extradition hearing in some provinces. It is now clear that the diplomatic note does not have to be produced at any stage of the extradition proceedings. It will only be of concern to the Minister when reviewing the request for extradition. There were competing cases under the former regime with respect to the role of the diplomatic note in governing the proceedings. For instance, in *Von Einem v. Germany (Federal Republic)* (1984), 14 C.C.C. (3d) 440 (B.C. C.A.), at p. 442, the British Columbia Court of Appeal held that proceedings in the courts were not initiated by the diplomatic request for extradition. Rather, they were commenced by a foreign warrant of arrest or information and complaint as provided for in s. 10 of the former Act. By contrast, in *United States v. Pitman* (December 18, 1985), Doc. CA 701/85, the Ontario Court of Appeal was of the opinion that the diplomatic note was the foundation of the extradition proceedings. Accordingly, in Ontario, the practice was to file the diplomatic note at the commencement of the extradition hearing and to include it as an exhibit in the application for a warrant of apprehension when available.

Under the new Act, the foundation of the extradition proceedings is clearly the authority to proceed. The only actions which can be undertaken prior to the issuance of an authority to proceed are those concerning provisional arrest under ss. 11 and 12, which are themselves subject to ministerial control. In *United States v. Drysdale* (2000), 32 C.R. (5th) 163 (Ont. S.C.J.), Dambrot J. observed two functions for the authority to proceed, one as a mechanism to ensure that the Minister's decision to authorize the seeking of committal proceeds in a timely fashion, since its issuance is subject to the time periods set out under s. 14, and the other as the equivalent to a domestic charging document. He stated, at p. 180:

> [51] It appears to me that the authority to proceed has two functions in the extradition process. First, it is analogous to the information or indictment in a domestic prosecution, and thus gives notice to the person sought of what is alleged against him or her, and forms the basis of an order committing the person for extradition where such an order is made. Second, the authority to proceed ensures that the Minister's decision to authorize the seeking of committal on behalf of the requesting state is made in a timely way, in order to ensure that a person arrested provisionally does not languish in custody, or continue to have his or her liberty constrained by a judicial release order for an unnecessarily prolonged period of time. . . .
>
> [52] The "indictment" function of the authority to proceed arises from a number of provisions of the new *Act*. Section 24(1) provides that upon receipt of an authority to proceed, the judge shall hold an extradition hearing. Section 23(2) permits the judge hearing the request, upon the application of the Attorney General, to amend the authority to proceed in accordance with the evidence. Section 29(1) authorizes a judge to commit a person sought to await surrender if there is evidence of conduct which, if it had occurred in Canada, would justify committal for trial in Canada on the offence set out in the authority to proceed. Section 29(2)(b) requires that the order of committal contain the offence set out in the authority to proceed for which the committal is ordered. Section 58(b) provides that if the Minister makes an order of surrender, it shall include a description of the offence for which committal was ordered, or the conduct for which the person is being surrendered. Accordingly, the committal order will have a role to play in the application of the rule of speciality. It does not require a detailed analysis of the provisions in the *Criminal Code* governing criminal pleadings to appreciate the similarity of purpose of an information or indictment on the one hand, and the authority to proceed on the other. Of course, having regard to the differences between a domestic prosecution and an extradition proceeding, these purposes cannot be identical.

The conduct of the extradition proceedings is now the responsibility of the Attorney General of Canada. The former *Extradition Act* was not specific about the manner in which the requesting state was to pursue its request. With respect to who should represent the requesting state at the extradition hearing, it was the practice up until the 1970s for the requesting state to hire private counsel (see, for example, *Wisconsin (State) v. Armstrong* (1973), 10 C.C.C. (2d) 271 (Fed. C.A.), in which Mr. Austin Cooper Q.C. was retained to represent the State of Wisconsin on a review of the issuance of a warrant of committal after an extradition hearing). From the 1970s onward, the practice was for counsel with the Federal Prosecution Service in the regional office of the Department of Justice in the jurisdiction where the fugitive was located to represent the requesting state at the hearing. When counsel from the Department of Justice appeared, they appeared as counsel for the requesting state. (See *United States v. Cobb* (2001), 152 C.C.C. (3d) 270 (S.C.C.), reconsideration refused (June 14, 2001), Docs. 26912, 27610, 27774 (S.C.C.).)

Under s. 15 of the new Act, the Minister of Justice authorizes counsel for the Attorney General of Canada to appear for the extradition partner at the extradition hearing and seek an order of committal. In practice, this will still be counsel from the regional office in the jurisdiction where the extradition proceedings are to be held.

The new Act clearly delineates the respective roles of the Attorney General of Canada and the Minister of Justice. The Attorney General conducts the extradition hearing in court and, subsequently, the Minister considers the merits of surrender. Under the former Act, it was argued that the executive discretion to refuse surrender and the duty to present extradition requests in court both fell within the responsibilities of the Minister of Justice, thus creating an unacceptable conflict in the roles of the Minister. In *United States v. Cotroni* (1989), 48 C.C.C. (3d) 193 (S.C.C.), and *Idziak v. Canada (Minister of Justice)* (1992), 77 C.C.C. (3d) 65 (S.C.C.), at p. 87 (reconsideration refused (1992), 9 Admin. L.R. (2d) 1n (S.C.C.)), the Supreme Court of Canada rejected the argument that there was an unacceptable conflict in the Minister performing the dual roles of prosecutor during the judicial phase and adjudicator during the ministerial phase. Accordingly, by clearly delineating the dual roles, the new Act addresses arguments of conflict of interest and apprehension of bias that were raised under the former extradition regime.

In providing that a copy of the authority to proceed produced by means of telecommunication has the same force as the original, s. 15(4) recognizes the modern technological reality that there exists various ways in which writing may be electronically communicated. The subsection eliminates any confusion that might otherwise have arisen over the probative force of copies of the authority to proceed for the purposes of this part of the Act.

§4.0 ANALYSIS

As part of the Minister's statutory authority to administer the *Extradition Act* and deal with requests for extradition, the Minister is authorized to issue an authority to proceed under s. 15(1) of the Act. This statutory discretion is engaged once the Minister receives a request for extradition and is satisfied, in relation to at least one of the offences set out in the request, that the requirements of s. 3(1)(a) and 3(3) of the Act have been satisfied.

In *Germany (Federal Republic) v. Schreiber* (July 6, 2000), [2000] O.J. No. 2618 (Onmt. S.C.J.), Watt J. described the Minister's function under these sections as follows:

[60] In a temporal sense, the involvement of the Minister brackets that of the superior court judge. The Minister *receives* the request from the extradition partner. It is the Minister's statutory responsibility under s. 7 of the Act to *deal* with the request. It is for the Minister to decide whether she or he will authorize the Attorney General to apply for a provisional arrest warrant. Further, it is for the Minister to say whether she or he will issue an authority to proceed that authorizes the Attorney General to seek, on behalf of the extradition partner, a judicial order of committal under s. 29 of the Act.

[61] To decide whether to seek a provisional arrest warrant or issue an authority to proceed, the Minister is required to consider whether the provisions of s. 3(1)(a) of the Act have been met. Section 3(1)(a) deals with extraditable conduct. It does so by making reference to the punishment provided for the offence in the jurisdiction of the extradition partner. But the section also mentions the *purpose* of the request of the extradition partner. It may be for *any* of three (3) purposes:

    i. *prosecuting* the person;
    ii. *imposing a sentence* on the person; or,
    iii. *enforcing a sentence* earlier imposed on the person in the requesting state

for an offence described in paragraph 3(1)(a).

[62] It is inevitable, as it seems to me, that the Minister will be obliged to consider the *purpose* of the extradition request in determining whether the requirements of s. 3(1)(a) of the Act have been met. It is an integral part of administering the Act and dealing with requests for extradition made under it and any applicable treaty. This element of *purpose* is central to our extradition scheme: we do *not* extradite without reason. We extradite in order for the extradition partner

    i. to *prosecute*;
    ii. to *sentence*; or,
    iii. to *enforce* an existing *sentence*.

Unless the materials submitted by the extradition partner reveal one of these purposes, the Minister is *not* entitled to authorize the Attorney General to apply for a provisional arrest warrant under s. 12 of the Act, because the person is *not* arrestable. Nor could the Minister issue an authority to the Attorney General to proceed under s. 15 of the Act with an application for committal. The necessary foundation would *not* have been put in place.

. . .

[87] . . . The requests for provisional arrest or extradition are made to the Minister. It is for the Minister to review the materials offered by the extradition partner in support of the request to determine whether it is in order. This determination involves, amongst other things, a consideration of foreign law. It is the Minister who must be satisfied that the requirements of s. 3(1)(a) of the Act have been met before she or he is entitled to instruct the Attorney General to apply for a provisional warrant of arrest under s. 12 or issue an authority to the Attorney General to proceed under s. 15(1) of the Act. Section 3(1)(a) of the Act defines extraditable conduct. It also makes it clear that the *purpose* of the extradition partner in requesting extradition must be any of

    i. *prosecuting* the fugitive;
    ii. *imposing a sentence*; or,
    iii. *enforcing a sentence* already imposed in the foreign jurisdiction.

Inherent in the exercise of this discretion is a determination by the Minister that the person is "sought for the purpose of prosecution" in the requesting jurisdiction, which is one of the prerequisites for extraditability under section 3. Watt J. held that the extradition hearing judge has no authority to review the Minister's determination in this regard.

§4.1 Determination of Canadian Equivalent Offence

Section 15(3)(c) mandates that the Minister of Justice shall name in the authority to proceed the Canadian offence that corresponds to the conduct for which the person is sought. In this way, the Minister frames the inquiry which will take place before the extradition judge. The extradition judge under s. 29(1)(a) is required to assess whether the evidence of the conduct constitutes the offence described in the authority to proceed. The new Act involves the Minister directly in the judicial proceedings in this respect. In one of the few decisions to comment on this aspect of the new Act, in *United States v. Drysdale* (2000), 32 C.R. (5th) 163 (Ont. S.C.J.), the extradition judge stated, at p. 191:

[82] . . . I consider the authority to proceed to be a document of fundamental importance in an extradition hearing. The offences listed in it will provide the focus of the determination to be made. The thoughtful selection of offences, and their careful drafting, will be essential to the conduct of the proceeding.

Since the committal, if it occurs, will be made with respect to the offence or offences set out in the authority to proceed, it is apparent that the authority to proceed performs a function at the extradition hearing which is similar to that performed by an information or an indictment in domestic criminal proceedings. As a result of the indictment function performed by the authority to proceed, the new Act does not require that the foreign charging document be placed before the extradition judge. In the former scheme, the foreign indictment was looked to by the extradition judge in order to orient the inquiry at the hearing. That is, the first step in applying the committal test under s. 18(1)(b) of the former Act was to determine what conduct underlay the foreign charges. As O'Connor J.A. stated, at p. 168, in *United States v. Commisso* (2000), 143 C.C.C. (3d) 158 (Ont. C.A.), leave to appeal to S.C.C. refused (2000), 261 N.R. 197 (note) (S.C.C.):

> [33] . . . [I]t has been held that the court should consider only the conduct that underlies the foreign charge for which extradition is being sought. The extradition judge is concerned with whether that conduct would *prima facie* constitute an extradition crime under the laws of Canada had it taken place in Canada: *McVey* at p. 21; *United States of America v. Manno* (1996), 112 C.C.C. (3d) 544 (Que. C.A.) at p. 558. Put another way, the double criminality rule does not permit an extradition judge to base the committal decision on evidence of conduct that "has nothing to do" with the conduct charged in the foreign jurisdiction: *U.S.A. v. Tavormina* (1996), 112 C.C.C. (3d) 563 (Que. C.A.) at p. 569.
>
> [34] I interpret this requirement, that the court should only look to the conduct underlying the foreign charge to mean that the conduct to be considered in the s. 18(1)(*b*) assessment must have some connection to the foreign charge or must constitute some evidence of that charge.
>
> [35] The extradition judge may look to the foreign indictment, but only for the purpose of determining what conduct is to be included in the assessment under s. 18(1)(*b*). The foreign indictment enables the extradition judge to identify the conduct with which a fugitive is charged in the requesting jurisdiction. In referring to the foreign indictment however, the court must not be concerned with whether the conduct establishes the commission of the foreign charge nor with whether the foreign court has jurisdiction to try the charge: *Manno*, at pp. 558-59.

As the passage above indicates, having reference to the foreign indictment sometimes led hearing judges to impermissibly consider foreign law, or to go further than the former Act mandated by considering whether the foreign charges had been made out rather than simply determining whether there was conduct disclosed which amounted to any Canadian offence. As a result of the introduction of the authority to proceed, the extradition hearing judge will now have no occasion to refer to the foreign indictment and as a result the focus of the inquiry will be directly related to an assessment of the evidence in relation to the Canadian offences identified by the Minister in the authority to proceed. This should result in a more expeditious proceeding.

§4.2 Time Limits for Issuance of Authority to Proceed

The provisions of s. 14 of the Act contemplate that the documentary material in support of the request will be in hand before the authority to proceed is issued. Section 14 deals with the discharge of a person who has been provisionally arrested when the request for extradition, supporting documentation, and authority to proceed have not been received within certain time limits. In both s. 14(1)(b) and 14(1)(c), the time periods within which the authority to proceed must be forthcoming start to run only after both the formal request and the supporting documents have been provided. Under s. 14(1)(b), if the provisional arrest request was pursuant to treaty then the person must be discharged if the request and supporting materials are not received within the time period specified in the treaty. If the extradition partner has met the time requirements of the treaty, the Minister has 30 days after the period specified in the treaty in order to issue the authority to proceed. If the applicable treaty does not contain a specified time period for making the request and providing the supporting documentation or if the provisional arrest was not made pursuant to a treaty request, then the extradition partner has 60 days after arrest to provide the documentation and the Minister has a further 30 days in which to issue an authority to proceed.

These discharge provisions indicate that the new authority to proceed operates as a safeguard to ensure that the extradition proceedings are commenced expeditiously and that a person provisionally arrested will not be in custody or restrained by bail terms for an unwarranted period of time. In *United States v. Drysdale, supra,* the extradition judge described the "liberty function" of the authority to proceed as follows, at pp. 181–182:

[53] The "liberty" function arises from the time limits placed by s. 14 of the *Act* on the issuance of the authority to proceed in cases involving provisional arrest. A full understanding of this provision requires an appreciation of the way extradition proceedings are commenced.

[54] Traditionally, the process began with a request for extradition being made from state to state through diplomatic channels. The request was accompanied by a description of the person sought, a statement of the facts of the case, the text of the foreign offence, information regarding any limitation period, a warrant of arrest and the requisite evidence to justify arrest and committal. Little of this is found in the text of the former *Act*, but that is exactly what is contemplated, for example, by Article 9 of the Canada-United States treaty. Section 10 of the former *Act*, however, then authorized a judge to issue a warrant for the apprehension of a fugitive based on the foreign warrant of arrest, or on an information or a complaint laid before the judge, accompanied by such evidence as would justify the issuance of a warrant if the crime had been committed in Canada.

[55] It often transpired, however, that the whereabouts of a fugitive in a requested state became known before a request for extradition had been made. In many of these cases, there was reason to fear that the delay necessary to permit the extradition request to be processed through diplomatic channels would place in jeopardy the possibility of effecting an arrest. For this reason, many treaties provided for provisional arrest on a less formal basis pending the presentation of the request for extradition through formal channels. Article 11(1) of the Canada-United States treaty, for example, authorizes provisional arrest in cases of urgency. In order to ensure that a person does not languish in custody pending the arrival of a formal request, Article 11(3) provides that the arrested person shall be set at liberty if the request and the accompanying documents required by Article 9 are not received within sixty days of an arrest.

[56] The new *Act* places much of the foregoing in the statute for the first time, and augments it with time limits relating to the authority to proceed. As I have already noted, s. 15 permits the Minister to issue an authority to proceed after receiving a request for extradition. Section 16 permits the Attorney General to apply to a judge for an arrest warrant after an authority to proceed is issued. Section 14, however, permits the Minister, after receiving a request for a provisional arrest warrant from an extradition partner, to authorize the Attorney General to apply to a judge for such a warrant. Section 13 permits a judge to issue a provisional arrest warrant if the judge is satisfied that it is necessary in the public interest. Section 14(1) then compels a provisionally arrested person to be discharged if: (a) the Minister notifies the court that no authority to proceed will be issued; (b) if any time limit in a treaty for the receipt of an extradition request and supporting documents (such as the sixty day time limit in Article 11(3) of the Canada-United States treaty) has passed and (i) the request has not been made or the documents not received; or (ii) the request has been made and the documents received within the time limit in a treaty, but the Minister has not issued an authority to proceed within thirty days after the expiry of the period; or (c) in cases where there is no such time limit, (i) if sixty days after the provisional arrest have passed and no extradition request has been made or documents provided; or (ii) where a request was made and the documents provided within sixty days, but the Minister has not issued an authority to proceed within an additional thirty days.

[57] As is apparent, the new authority to proceed has been used as a safeguard to ensure that proceedings are commenced expeditiously in respect of persons who are provisionally arrested, in addition to the narrower safeguard respecting the time for receiving a request that may exist in a particular treaty.

§4.3 Competing Requests

Section 15(2), which gives the Minister of Justice the power to determine the order in which competing requests for the same person will proceed, removes the issue of competing requests from judicial consideration. Once again, it is made clear that the Minister has control over the proceedings in the courts. Thus it would not be open for a judge to adjourn a proceeding in respect of one request in favour of awaiting the outcome of a competing request. The court must deal with the requests in the order decided by the Minister. Deciding the priority to be given to competing requests is clearly a political decision involving Canada's international obligations. The authority to determine the order in which requests will be authorized to proceed recognizes the Minister's authority to make determination affecting "the good faith and honour of this country in its relations with other states" (*R. v. Schmidt* (1987), 33 C.C.C. (3d) 193 (S.C.C.), at p. 215).

Many treaties address the manner in which competing requests for the same individual should be resolved. For example, Article 13 of the *Canada–United States Extradition Treaty* provides that the requested state shall determine to which of two or more competing states it will extradite the person, and it sets out the criteria by which this determination shall be made:

13. (1) A requested State upon receiving two or more requests for the extradition of the same person either for the same offense, or for different offenses, shall determine to which of the requesting States it will extradite the person sought.

(2) Among the matters which the requested State may take into consideration are the possibility of a later extradition between the requesting States, the seriousness of each offense, the place where the offense was committed, the dates upon which the requests were received, and the provisions of any extradition agreements between the requested State and the other requesting State or States.

By allowing the Minister of Justice to control the order of the proceedings in court, s. 15(2) is a natural companion to the Minister's authority to determine to which country the person will ultimately be extradited.

§5.0 CASE LAW

Germany (Federal Republic) v. Schreiber (July 6, 2000), [2000] O.J. No. 2618, Watt J. (Ont. S.C.J.).
Idziak v. Canada (Minister of Justice) (1992), 77 C.C.C. (3d) 65 (S.C.C.), reconsideration refused (1992), 9 Admin. L.R. (2d) 1n (S.C.C.).
R. v. Schmidt (1987), 33 C.C.C. (3d) 193 (S.C.C.).
United States v. Cobb (2001), 152 C.C.C. (3d) 270 (S.C.C.), reconsideration refused (June 14, 2001), Docs. 26912, 27610, 27774 (S.C.C.).
United States v. Commisso (2000), 47 O.R. (3d) 257 (Ont. C.A.).
United States v. Cotroni (*sub. nom. Cotroni c. Centre de Prévention de Montréal*) (1989), 48 C.C.C. (3d) 193 (S.C.C.).
United States v. Drysdale (2000), 32 C.R. (5th) 163 (Ont. S.C.J.).
United States v. Pitman (December 18, 1985), Doc. CA 701/85 (Ont. C.A.).
Von Einem v. Germany (Federal Republic) (1984), 14 C.C.C. (3d) 440 (B.C. C.A.).
Wisconsin (State) v. Armstrong (1973), 10 C.C.C. (2d) 271 (Fed. C.A.).

§6.0 RELATED SECTIONS

s. 3 — Extraditable Conduct
s. 14 — Discharge of Person Sought If No Proceedings Instituted
s. 29 — Order of Committal by Extradition Judge

Warrant of Arrest or Summons (s. 16)

§1.0 DESCRIPTION

§1.1 Application for Warrant of Arrest or Summons (s. 16(1))

Section 16(1) of the *Extradition Act* provides as follows:

> **WARRANT OF ARREST OR SUMMONS**
> **16. (1) The Attorney General may, after the Minister issues an authority to proceed, apply *ex parte* to a judge in the province in which the Attorney General believes the person is or to which the person is on their way, or was last known to be, for the issuance of a summons to the person or a warrant for the arrest of the person.**

This provision permits the Attorney General of Canada after an authority to proceed has been issued by the Minister of Justice, to apply *ex parte* to a judge for a summons or a warrant of arrest for the person sought. The application is made to a judge in the jurisdiction in which the Attorney General believes the person to be, or to be on the way to, or where the person was last known to be.

§1.2 When Provisionally Arrested (s. 16(2))

Section 16(2) of the *Extradition Act* provides as follows:

> **WHEN PROVISIONALLY ARRESTED**
> **(2) If the person has been arrested pursuant to a provisional arrest warrant issued under section 13, the Attorney General need not apply for a summons or warrant under subsection (1).**

When the person sought has already been arrested provisionally under s. 13 of the Act, the person does not have to be rearrested or summoned pursuant to s. 16(1).

§1.3 Issuance of Summons (s. 16(3))

Section 16(3) of the *Extradition Act* provides as follows:

> **ISSUANCE OF SUMMONS OR WARRANT OF ARREST**
> **(3) The judge to whom an application is made shall issue a summons to the person, or a warrant for the arrest of the person, in accordance with subsection 507(4) of the *Criminal Code*, with any modifications that the circumstances require.**

Section 16(3) describes the authority of the judge to issue a summons or a warrant of arrest for the person sought. The judge is directed to make the determination in accordance with s. 507(4) of the *Criminal Code*, modified to fit the circumstances of the *Extradition Act*. Section 507(4) of the *Criminal Code* reads as follows:

> **507.**(4) Where the justice considers that a case is made out for compelling an accused to attend before him to answer to a charge of an offence, he shall issue a summons to the accused unless the allegations of the informant or the evidence of any witness or witnesses taken in accordance with subsection (3) disclose reasonable grounds to believe that it is necessary in the public interest to issue a warrant for the arrest of the accused.

§1.4 Execution Throughout Canada (s. 16(4))

Section 16(4) of the *Extradition Act* provides as follows:

EXECUTION THROUGHOUT CANADA
(4) A warrant that is issued under this section may be executed, and a summons issued under this section may be served, anywhere in Canada without being endorsed.

Warrants and summonses issued under s. 16 operate Canada-wide without the necessity of being endorsed.

§1.5 Date of Hearing — Summons (s. 16(5))

Section 16(5) of the *Extradition Act* provides as follows:

DATE OF HEARING — SUMMONS
(5) A summons that is issued under this section must

(a) set a date for the appearance of the person before a judge that is not later than 15 days after its issuance; and
(b) require the person to appear at a time and place stated in it for the purposes of the *Identification of Criminals Act*.

Section 16(5) describes what a summons must contain. The summons must provide a date for the first appearance of the person sought before the court. The date must be no later than 15 days after the issuance of the summons. Section 16(5) also mandates that the summons set out a time and place for the person to appear for photographing and fingerprinting for the purposes of the *Identification of Criminals Act*.

§1.6 Effect of Appearance (s. 16(6))

Section 16(6) of the *Extradition Act* provides as follows:

EFFECT OF APPEARANCE
(6) A person appearing as required by subsection (5) is considered, for purposes only of the *Identification of Criminals Act*, to be in lawful custody charged with an indictable offence.

This subsection makes the provisions of the *Identification of Criminals Act* regarding fingerprinting and photographing applicable to a person who is the subject of a summons issued pursuant to s. 16(5).

§2.0 COMPARISON WITH FORMER ACT

§2.1 Straight Arrest

The governing provision of the former *Extradition Act* with respect to the issuance of process was s. 10, which authorized the issuance of a warrant for the arrest of a fugitive. Section 10 stipulated the following:

10. (1) Whenever this Part applies, a judge may issue a warrant for the apprehension of a fugitive on a foreign warrant of arrest, or an information or a complaint laid before the judge, and on such evidence or after such proceedings as in the opinion of the judge would, subject to this Part, justify the issue of the warrant if the crime of which the fugitive is accused or is alleged to have been convicted had been committed in Canada.

Section 16 of the new Act provides for the issuance of process in the situation that was referred to colloquially under the old Act as a "straight arrest." A straight arrest was distinguishable from the provisional arrest situation in that there was no element of urgency. The straight arrest was resorted to when the documentation required for the extradition hearing had been received. Since the requesting state was in a position to proceed with the hearing after receipt of the documentation, it made sense, then, to arrest the person.

Under the former Act, the judge was required to determine whether the criminal conduct alleged would justify the issuance of a warrant if the crime had been committed in Canada. One way that the judge could have been so satisfied was by a review of the documentation. In the practice followed in Ontario, these materials would have been attached to the information and complaint. Attaching the authenticated materials was not, however, the practice followed in all jurisdictions.

Under the new Act, the judge looks to s. 507(4) of the *Criminal Code* for the authority to issue a summons or a warrant for the arrest of the person sought. In either case (summons or warrant), s. 507(4) requires the judge to be satisfied that a case is made out for compelling the person to attend before the court to answer the charge. In order to satisfy this test, it may not be necessary to produce the evidence that will be filed at the hearing. A summary of the conduct alleged to have been committed by the person sought may suffice to meet the s. 507(4) test.

§2.2 *Ex Parte* Application

Section 16 of the new Act provides for the application to be made *ex parte*. Although s. 10 of the former Act did not specify that applications for arrest warrants were to be made *ex parte*, in practice they were. The justification for the practice of *ex parte* proceedings under the former Act was the concern that the person sought might flee if given notice that an arrest warrant would be obtained. This is still a valid concern and the new Act now specifically authorizes the application to be made *ex parte*.

§2.3 Application to Judge in Particular Province

Section 16(1) of the new Act does not require the person sought for extradition to actually be in Canada. What is required is that the Attorney General of Canada believes that the person is in or is on the way to a particular province or that the person was last known to be in a particular province. It is to a judge in that province that the Attorney General is authorized, after the issuance of the authority to proceed, to make the application for a warrant of arrest or a summons. By virtue of the definition of "province" in s. 35 of the *Interpretation Act*, the word "province" includes the Yukon Territory, the Northwest Territories, and Nunavut.

This contrasts with s. 13 of the new Act dealing with applications for provisional arrest warrants. Section 13 does not specify that the application for a provisional arrest warrant be made to a judge in a particular province. Section 13 is concerned with situations in which grounds exist to believe that the person sought is on the way to Canada, is in Canada, or is ordinarily resident in Canada. Section 13 is drafted in national rather than provincial terms and does not restrict an application for a provisional arrest warrant to a judge in any particular province.

The difference in the way ss. 13 and 16 of the new Act are drafted may be attributable to the following. In provisional arrest situations, the warrant is being applied for at a preliminary stage of the proceedings and the province in which the person sought will ultimately be located may not be known. In provisional arrest situations, urgency may dictate that the warrant be obtained without delay in order that the person not escape apprehension. It might be known that a person is coming to Canada without knowing exactly where the person will arrive. By contrast, the straight arrest situation envisaged by s. 16 comes after the Minister of Justice has considered the extradition request and issued the authority to proceed. At this stage, it is likely that there is definite information as to the province in which the person sought is located and, therefore, in which provincial jurisdiction the hearing will take place.

The requirement under s. 16(1) that the application for a warrant of arrest be made to a judge in the province where the person is, is on the way to, or was last known to be, accords with the practice under the former Act. The jurisprudence dealing with the former Act required that the application for a warrant of apprehension be made to a judge in the jurisdiction where the fugitive was suspected of being. The application of this rule was illustrated in the British Columbia Supreme Court case of *Re McVey and The Queen* (1987), 37 C.C.C. (3d) 444 (B.C. S.C.). In that case, an application for a warrant of apprehension was brought before a judge in Vancouver, British Columbia. The material in support of the application stated that the fugitive was believed to be in the Yukon Territory. The fugitive was then arrested in the Yukon Territory and transported to Vancouver. A *habeas corpus* application was brought before Toy J. in the British Columbia Supreme Court. Toy J. quashed the warrant upon which McVey had been arrested on the basis that a judge in the Yukon Territory would have had jurisdiction in the circumstances to issue a warrant of apprehension, but a judge in British Columbia did not have such jurisdiction (p. 448):

> It is accordingly my conclusion that legal representatives of foreign countries who choose to seek extradition of fugitives must select the appropriate jurisdiction where there is reason to believe a fugitive is or will be found in which to initiate extradition proceedings in Canadian courts . . . . The courts and commissioners in the Yukon Territory appointed under the *Extradition Act* had jurisdiction to hear an application for a warrant of apprehension against McVey on August 19, 1987; however, the courts and commissioners appointed within British Columbia did not.

§2.4 Summons

There was no authority under the former *Extradition Act* for a fugitive to be brought before the court by the issuance of a summons. Under the former Act, all fugitives were arrested by warrant. The provisions of the *Identification of Criminals Act* concerning fingerprinting and photographing applied to fugitives on the basis of s. 2(1)(b) of that Act, which extended those provisions to persons "apprehended under the *Extradition Act*." Under the new *Extradition Act*, a person sought for extradition may be required to attend court by the issuance of a summons. This might otherwise have raised the issue as to whether such persons are "apprehended" within the meaning of s. 2(1)(b) of the *Identification of Criminals Act*. However, s. 16(6) of the new *Extradition Act* addresses this issue by deeming a person who is summoned to be in custody charged with an indictable offence. In this way, s. 16(6) makes applicable s. 2(1)(a) of the *Identification of Criminals Act*, which permits the fingerprinting or photographing of any person who is in lawful custody charged with, or convicted of, an indictable offence.

§2.5 Warrant May Be Executed Canada-Wide

Section 16(4) provides for a warrant issued under this section to be executed anywhere in Canada without being endorsed, and for a summons issued under this section to be served anywhere in Canada without being endorsed. This is comparable to an arrest warrant issued under s. 10 of the former Act which was, by virtue of s. 11, enforceable anywhere in Canada.

§2.6 No Notification to Minister Required by New Act

Section 10(2) of the former *Extradition Act* required that the Minister of Justice be notified of the issuance of a warrant and be provided with the supporting material. Section 16 of the new Act does not have the same ministerial notice requirements as s. 10(2) of the former Act. Presumably, this is because it is the Minister who authorizes, by way of the authority to proceed, the application of the Attorney General of Canada for the issuance of a summons or warrant of arrest. Under the former Act, the concern was that the Minister of Justice be kept advised of extradition proceedings being taken in Canada. The structure of the new Act makes this unnecessary as the entire process involves the Minister from the outset.

§3.0 SIGNIFICANCE OF CHANGE

§3.1 Securing Appearance of Person Sought Before Court

Pursuant to s. 16(3) of the new *Extradition Act*, s. 507(4) of the *Criminal Code* now applies to extradition proceedings. It is thus open to the judge to whom an application is made under s. 16 to issue either a summons or a warrant for the arrest of the person sought. A summons was not an option under the former *Extradition Act*. By virtue of the incorporation of s. 507(4) of the Code, the process for securing the attendance in court of a person sought under the *Extradition Act* is now identical to the domestic process for securing the appearance of a person accused of a Canadian offence.

The additional option of issuing a summons would appear to recognize that, as in domestic circumstances, there may be individuals sought for extradition for whom arrest by warrant would be unnecessary. In many instances, persons sought will be Canadian citizens who have roots in the community and with respect to whom flight concerns will be slight. In those cases, a summons may appropriately be relied upon to secure the person's attendance before the court.

§3.2 Warrant in Anticipation of Person Sought Being Located

The new Act is explicit that the summons or warrant may be issued even if the location of the person sought is uncertain. The Attorney General of Canada is authorized to apply to a judge in the province where the Attorney General believes that the person is, is on the way to, or was last known to be. This is a significant change from the practice under the former Act which was to include in the information and complaint evidence that the person was actually in the jurisdiction at the time the application for a warrant of apprehension was made. This practice originated from treaty provisions stating that the obligation to extradite is engaged when the person sought is within the territory of the requested state. Section 3 of the former Act provided that an extradition treaty was to take precedence over the Act to the extent of any inconsistency between the two. Section 3 also provided that the Act was to be construed in such a manner as to provide for the execution of the treaty arrangements. Section 10 of the former Act did not, by its own terms, restrict the application for a warrant to circumstances in which the fugitive was physically present in Canada. However, the authority to issue a warrant for a fugitive was interpreted in light of the treaty provisions and the direction in s. 3 to interpret those provisions to give effect to the treaty.

§4.0 ANALYSIS

Under s. 16 of the new *Extradition Act*, through the adoption s. 507(4) of the *Criminal Code*, the procedure for compelling the attendance of a person sought for extradition has been brought into line with domestic procedures for securing attendance. Clearly, the legislators saw no need to maintain or establish a separate body of procedural rules for the same processes that are already familiar and well established in domestic criminal law.

Section 16 is, however, tailored to fit the context of extradition. Firstly, summonses issued under s. 509 of the *Criminal Code* "may" require an accused charged with committing an indictable offence to appear for the purposes of the *Identification of Criminals Act*. By contrast, s. 16(5) makes the requirement to appear for this purpose mandatory. This is understandable given the residual concern over flight risk that will be present in any extradition case. Secondly, s. 509 of the *Criminal Code* does not specify a time limit within which the person must appear. Section 16(5), on the other hand, provides that an appearance in court must take place within 15 days of the issuance of the summons. The 15-day requirement for a return date brings the person sought under the control of the court within a tighter time frame. It also acknowledges that international obligations are engaged and that, as such, the extradition should proceed with dispatch.

In the domestic application of s. 507(4), a summons is to be given priority unless the public interest necessitates the issuance of a warrant. Section 16(3), which makes s. 507(4) applicable to the extradition context, adds the caveat that s. 507(4) applies "with any modifications that the circumstances require." It may be that public interest concerns in the extradition context, which encompass honouring Canada's international obligations, will lead to greater reliance on warrants over summonses than might be the case in domestic proceedings.

As mentioned, to justify the issuance of a warrant under s. 507(4), there is a public interest component. In addition to considerations of Canada's international obligations, the examples of public interest specified in s. 13 of the Act regarding circumstances justifying the issuance of a provisional arrest warrant will be of assistance. Section 13(1)(a) refers to the public interest, including prevention of the person from escaping or committing an offence. These would seem to be equally cogent reasons justifying the issuance of a warrant under s. 16. Depending on the degree of concern regarding flight, a warrant will likely be sought in circumstances in which the Attorney General intends to seek a detention order or a release with conditions of bail.

Subsection 507(4) incorporates s. 507(3) of the *Criminal Code*, which specifies that the evidence in support of the application for a warrant or summons will be on oath. This accords with the practice under the former *Extradition Act*, as the information and complaint was always a sworn document.

The procedure which one would expect to be followed to obtain a summons or a warrant for the arrest of a person sought pursuant to s. 16 is as follows: Firstly, the Attorney General would submit a signed application document indicating what is being applied for, that is, a summons or a warrant. Section 16(1) indicates that the Attorney General may apply for a warrant or summons when the Minister has issued an authority to proceed. Accordingly, there should be either an indication in the application document that the Minister has issued the authority to proceed, with details describing its contents, or the authority to proceed (or a copy of it) should be attached to the application document. Accompanying the application document, there should be an affidavit-type document sworn under oath by the informant. Under the former Act, the document was known as an "Information and Complaint," which was the type of document referred to in s. 10 of the former Act as the relevant document required in order to obtain an arrest warrant. Under the new Act, since the arrest and summons procedure is governed by s. 507(4) of the *Criminal Code*, this document could be called an information, that being the document used in domestic situations. However, the name given to the document, be it "affidavit" or "information," would not appear to be a matter of great concern.

The document sworn in support of the application will have to contain information to satisfy the criteria set out in s. 16(1) that the person sought is in Canada, or on the way to Canada, or last known to have been in Canada. There should be identification evidence that connects the person to the person being sought. This might entail the inclusion of information concerning any surveillance conducted on the person by the police, or any photographic or fingerprint-matching evidence. If a warrant is being sought as opposed to a summons, the document should also contain grounds to justify the issuance of the warrant, such as flight risk or risk to the security of the public. If the documentary evidence being relied upon at the hearing is not available to be attached as an exhibit to this document, then a summary of the allegations should be included. When applications are made, counsel for the Attorney General of Canada will attend, with the assisting police officer in whose name the supporting material is drafted, on an *ex parte* basis and usually in the judge's chambers.

The application and supporting material can be the subject of a sealing order if they contain information that should not be disclosed to the public, such as informer information, information about ongoing investigations (either foreign or domestic), and information concerning investigative techniques. When the warrant or summons has been issued, the original application, information, and warrant or summons will be filed in the registrar's office of the court. A duplicate original of the warrant or summons will be taken by the police officer for execution purposes. The sealing order will usually indicate that the documents are not to be unsealed except by an order of a judge of the same court. The sealing order will remain public.

§4.1 Application of Part XVI of *Criminal Code*

Section 19 of the Act states that Part XVI of the *Criminal Code* ("Compelling Appearance of an Accused before a Justice and Interim Release") "applies, with any modifications that the circumstances require, in respect of a person arrested under section 13 or 16 or to whom a summons has been issued under section 16." Consequently, the *Criminal Code* sections dealing with the execution of summonses, the inability to serve a summons, non-attendance after being served with a summons, the execution of warrants, and the failure to attend court are applicable to extradition proceedings modified to fit the circumstances.

Since the provisions of Part XVI of the *Criminal Code* are applicable to the issuance of summonses and warrants of arrest, Form 6 for summonses and Form 7 for warrants of arrest under the *Criminal Code*, with any necessary modifications, should be used for extradition purposes. Section 511(1) specifies what a warrant of arrest must contain, namely, the name or description of the accused, a brief description of the offence in respect of which the accused is charged, and an order that the accused be arrested forthwith and brought before the court. In extradition warrants, the offence that will be described will be the equivalent Canadian crime for which the person is sought, as described by the Minister of Justice in the authority to proceed.

Section 511(3) provides the judge or justice with the discretion to postpone the execution of the warrant: "[n]otwithstanding paragraph (1)(*c*), a judge or justice who issues a warrant may specify in the warrant the period before which the warrant shall not be executed, to allow the accused to appear voluntarily before a judge or justice having jurisdiction in the territorial division in which the warrant was issued." Section 511(4) deems the warrant to be executed when the accused appears voluntarily. Section 511(3) and (4) seem at odds with the purpose of extradition in apprehending persons sought and having extradition proceedings proceed with dispatch in order to adhere to our international obligations. There may, however, be situations where the person sought is not a flight risk and is aware of the extradition request and has made it known that he or she wishes to voluntarily surrender. These provisions would most likely be resorted to when the foregoing circumstances exist and the Attorney General of Canada wishes to have the person sought released on conditions, and therefore a summons would not suffice.

The contents of a summons are set out in s. 509(1) of the *Criminal Code*. Section 509(1) requires that the summons be directed to the accused, set out briefly the offence in respect of which the accused is charged, and require the person to attend court at a time and place stated therein. The modification in the extradition context that will prevail in respect of the summons is again that the offence that will be described in the summons is that specified by the Minister of Justice in the authority to proceed. Section 16(5) of the new *Extradition Act* also mandates that the return appearance date be within 15 days after the issuance of the summons as opposed to the unspecified return date referred to in s. 509(1) of the *Criminal Code*. Furthermore, s. 16(5) of the new Act requires mandatory attendance for the purposes of fingerprinting and photographing pursuant to the *Identification of Criminals Act*. The comparable *Criminal Code* provision, s. 509(5), is discretionary.

§4.2 Inability to Serve Summons

Section 512(2)(c) of the *Criminal Code*, which applies by virtue of s. 19 of the Act, states that a warrant may be obtained when it appears that the summons cannot be served because an accused is evading service. It is thus clear that s. 512(2)(c) will apply to a person sought under the *Extradition Act* who is evading service of a summons.

If there is no basis to obtain a warrant in the case of difficulty in serving a summons, a fresh application for another summons for a further 15 days would be permitted by s. 512(1)(b). Section 512(1)(b) provides that where a justice has reasonable grounds to believe that it is necessary in the public interest to issue a summons or a warrant, he or she may do so even though a summons has been previously issued. Such might be the case, for instance, when the person sought has gone on holiday and will not be back in the country within the specified 15-day time limit to appear in court and there is no indication that the person is evading service.

It may be that s. 512(1)(b) may be resorted to for the issuance of a warrant in situations where a summons has been issued and there is difficulty locating the person. In that case, the summons has not proved to be effective, and a warrant would be desirable because, with a warrant in existence, the person may be apprehended as soon as his or her whereabouts is known.

The material to be relied upon in each of the situations described above could be a supplementary affidavit explaining the reasons the summons cannot be served, with the previous application material attached as an exhibit.

§4.3 Failure to Respond to Summons

Section 512(2)(a) of the *Criminal Code* provides that where service of a summons is proved and the accused fails to attend in court a warrant may be issued. This is available and will apply in the extradition context by virtue of s. 19 of the Act. Similarly, when the person sought fails to attend according to the summons for the purposes of the *Identification of Criminals Act*, s. 510 of the *Criminal Code* will allow the issuance of a warrant of arrest for the person.

§5.0 CASE LAW

McVey and The Queen, Re (1987), 37 C.C.C. (3d) 444 (B.C.S.C.).

§6.0 RELATED SECTIONS

s. 7 — Responsibilities of Minister of Justice
s. 11 — Minister's Power to Receive Provisional Arrest or Extradition Requests
s. 12 — Minister's Approval of Request for Provisional Arrest Warrant
s. 13 — Issuance of Provisional Arrest Warrant
s. 14 — Discharge of Person If No Proceedings Instituted
s. 15 — Power of Minister to Issue Authority to Proceed
s. 17 — Appearance
s. 19 — Applicability of Part XVI of *Criminal Code* to ss. 13 and 16 of *Extradition Act*
Criminal Code, Part XVI — Compelling Appearance of an Accused Before a Justice and Interim Release
Identification of Criminals Act, s. 2(1) — Fingerprints and Photographs
Interpretation Act, s. 35 — Definition of "province"

Appearance (s. 17)

§1.0 DESCRIPTION

§1.1 Appearance (s. 17(1))

Section 17(1) of the *Extradition Act* provides as follows:

APPEARANCE
17. (1) A person who is arrested under section 13 or 16 is to be brought before a judge or a justice within twenty-four hours after the person is arrested, but if no judge or no justice is available during this time, the person shall be brought before a judge or a justice as soon as possible.

Section 17(1) provides that a person sought who is arrested either provisionally (s. 13) or after an authority to proceed has been issued (s. 16) is to be brought before a judicial officer within 24 hours, or if that cannot be done, as soon as possible. The judicial officer may be either a judge or a justice. A "judge" is defined in s. 2 of the *Extradition Act* as "a judge of the court." "Court" is defined in the same section as the superior court of the province. The term "justice" is defined in s. 2 of the Act as having "the same meaning as in section 2 of the *Criminal Code*." In s. 2 of the *Criminal Code*, a "justice" is defined as "a justice of the peace or a provincial court judge."

§1.2 Appearance Before Justice (s. 17(2))

Section 17(2) of the *Extradition Act* provides as follows:

> **APPEARANCE BEFORE JUSTICE**
> **(2) The justice before whom a person is brought under subsection (1) shall order that the person be detained in custody and brought before a judge.**

Section 17(2) sets out the authority of the justice to remand the person sought, in custody, to be brought before a judge.

§2.0 COMPARISON WITH FORMER ACT

There was no similar provision under the former *Extradition Act*, either specific or general, setting out the time within which the person sought was to be brought before the court. The form of the warrant which was appended as Form 1 to the former Act required that the fugitive be apprehended forthwith and brought before a judge, although the form did not provide a time limit. Therefore, the form indicated the procedure, and in practice fugitives were brought to court without delay. Section 17 of the new Act specifically sets out the time limit for bringing the person before a judicial officer and the category of judicial officer before whom the person may be brought after being arrested.

In addition, the new Act expands the categories of judicial officers before whom the person may be brought. Under the new Act, the judicial officer may be a superior court judge, provincial court judge, or justice of the peace. Under the former Act, the applicable judicial officer was set out in s. 13:

> **13.** The fugitive referred to in section 12 shall be brought before a judge, who shall, subject to this part, hear the case, in the same manner, as nearly as may be, as if the fugitive was brought before a justice of the peace, charged with an indictable offence committed in Canada.

A "judge," as defined in s. 2 of the former Act, was limited to judges of the superior or county courts of the province. Therefore, even for a first appearance, the person could only be brought before one of those judges. By comparison, the new Act expands the categories of judicial officers before whom a first appearance can be made to include provincial court judges or justices of the peace. However, s. 17(2) limits the function of these judicial officers to ordering that the person sought be remanded, in custody, to be brought before a "judge," i.e., superior court judge.

§3.0 SIGNIFICANCE OF CHANGE

Section 17 of the new *Extradition Act* mirror-images s. 503(1) of the *Criminal Code*. In so doing, s. 17 introduces familiar domestic procedural requirements into the extradition context. Section 503(1) of the Code provides for a person arrested to be taken before a justice within 24 hours or as soon thereafter as possible. The difference between the *Criminal Code* regime and s. 17 is that, when a person is arrested on domestic charges and brought before a justice under s. 503(1), the justice has the authority to enter into a consideration of whether the person should be released or detained. By contrast, s. 17(2) of the Act limits the jurisdiction of the justice of the peace or provincial court judge to ordering that the person be detained in custody and be brought before a judge. Only a "judge," i.e., superior court judge, may consider the issue of release or detention.

§4.0 ANALYSIS

Section 17 of the new *Extradition Act* provides greater flexibility than did the former Act with respect to bringing the person sought to court. Section 17 also provides the person sought with greater protections, similar to those afforded to an accused in the domestic context, namely, the right to be brought before a judicial officer within 24 hours or as soon thereafter as possible.

Perhaps in response to the addition of a time limit within which the person is to be brought before a judicial officer, the category of judicial officers has been expanded, making it easier to comply with the specific time requirements of the section. Under the new Act, a person who cannot be taken before a superior court judge before the close of court on Friday will not have to wait until the opening of the superior court the following Monday to be brought under the authority of the courts. Rather, the person sought might be seen by a justice of the peace, many of whom are available during evenings and on weekends, and many of whom are willing to attend, or are in fact located, at the jails. Similarly, in communities which are served by a provincial court but which have no superior court, the person could be taken before a provincial court judge in order for arrangements to be made to transport him or her to a judge of the superior court. The only function assigned to a justice of the peace or a provincial court judge under s. 17(2) is to order that the person be detained in custody and brought before a judge. This provides the person sought with the protection of court supervision over his or her custody. In this respect, the person sought will not languish in jail or remain in the custody of the police longer than necessary. Pursuant to s. 17(1), judicial control over the custody of the person must take place within 24 hours or as soon as possible thereafter if the 24-hour time limit cannot be met.

§5.0 CASE LAW

§5.1 Non-Compliance with S. 17 and *Charter* Consequences

In *Argentina (Republic) v. Mellino* (1987), 33 C.C.C. (3d) 334 (S.C.C.), the Supreme Court of Canada held that the conduct of Canadian officials is subject to *Charter* scrutiny. Consequently, it could be argued that non-compliance with this section would be a violation of a person's *Charter* rights. In this regard, domestic cases may be applicable.

In *R. v. Charles* (1987), 36 C.C.C. (3d) 286 (Sask. C.A.), the Saskatchewan Court of Appeal held that non-compliance with the domestic time requirement in s. 503(1) of the *Criminal Code* was a violation of the accused's s. 9 *Charter* rights. In *R. v. Tam* (1995), 100 C.C.C. (3d) 196 (B.C.C.A.), the British Columbia Court of Appeal held that non-compliance with the time requirement, while unlawful, did not amount to arbitrary detention for the purposes of s. 9 of the *Charter*.

§6.0 RELATED SECTIONS

s. 2 — Interpretation
s. 13 — Issuance of Provisional Arrest Warrant
s. 16 — Warrant of Arrest or Summons
Criminal Code, s. 503(1) — Taking an Accused Person Before a Justice
Charter of Rights and Freedoms, s. 9 — Arbitrary Detention or Imprisonment

Judicial Interim Release (s. 18)

§1.0 DESCRIPTION

§1.1 Judicial Interim Release (s. 18(1)–(1.2))

Section 18(1) of the *Extradition Act* provides as follows:

DECISION OF JUDGE

18. (1) The judge before whom a person is brought following arrest under section 13 or 16 shall

> **(a) if the person has been arrested on the request of the International Criminal Court, order the detention in custody of the person unless**
> > **(i) the person shows cause, in accordance with subsection 522(2) of the *Criminal Code*, that their detention in custody is not justified, and**

     (ii) the judge is satisfied that, given the gravity of the alleged offence, there are urgent and exceptional circumstances that justify release — with or without conditions — and that the person will appear as required; or

  (b) in any other case, order the release, with or without conditions, or detention in custody of the person.

Section 18(1) of the Act provides the authority for the judge before whom a person sought is brought to order either the release or the detention of the person. In other words, the person sought is entitled to a bail hearing. The right to be considered for bail applies to persons who are arrested provisionally under s. 13 of the Act and to persons who are arrested or summoned under s. 16 following the issuance of an authority to proceed. A "judge" is defined in s. 2 of the Act as a superior court judge in the province or territory where the person sought is located.

In the case of bail for persons sought by the International Criminal Court, s. 18(1)(a) provides that there is a reverse onus on the person to show cause for his or her release. Furthermore, it must be demonstrated to the satisfaction of the judge that there are urgent and exceptional circumstances justifying the person's release and that the person will appear as required.

Section 18(1)(b) deals with requests other than requests from the International Criminal Court. When read together with s. 19, which incorporates Part XVI of the *Criminal Code*, which includes the domestic bail provisions, s. 18(1)(b) gives the extradition judge the authority to release or detain a person in accordance with domestic law.

Section 18(1.1) and (1.2) of the *Extradiction Act* provide as follows:

MANDATORY ADJOURNMENT

    (1.1) An application for judicial interim release in respect of a person referred to in paragraph (1)(a) shall, at the request of the Attorney General, be adjourned to await receipt of the recommendations of the Pre-Trial Chamber of the International Criminal Court. If the recommendations are not received within six days, the judge may proceed to hear the application.

RECOMMENDATIONS OF PRE-TRIAL CHAMBER

    (1.2) If the Pre-Trial Chamber of the International Criminal Court submits recommendations, the judge shall consider them before rendering a decision.

In the case of a person sought for extradition by the International Criminal Court, s. 18(1.1) requires the judge to adjourn the proceedings in respect of judicial interim release for seven days, if requested by the Attorney General, in order to obtain the recommendations of the Pre-Trial Chamber of the International Criminal Court. If recommendations are submitted by that body, then s. 18(1.2) provides that they must be considered by the Canadian court before a decision on judicial interim release is rendered.

§1.2 Review by Court of Appeal (s. 18(2))

Section 18(2) of the *Extradition Act* provides as follows:

REVIEW BY COURT OF APPEAL
(2) A decision respecting judicial interim release may be reviewed by a judge of the court of appeal and that judge may

(a) confirm the decision;
(b) vary the decision; or
(c) substitute any other decision that, in the judge's opinion, should have been made.

Section 18(2) provides the means by which an order made under s. 18(1) may be reviewed by a judge of the court of appeal. Wide latitude has been given to the reviewing judge, who may confirm or vary the original order or substitute any other decision for that of the judge who made the order under s. 18(1).

§2.0 COMPARISON WITH FORMER ACT

The issue of bail for fugitives was not specifically addressed in the former *Extradition Act*. Early case law cast doubt on whether the court could grant bail to a fugitive. In *Barnes v. Tennessee* (1972), 34 C.C.C. (2d) 122 (Ont. H.C.), Wright J. held that express provision would have been made for the application of the *Criminal Code* bail provisions to extradition matters had it been intended for these provisions to apply to fugitives. This was because of the special nature of extradition proceedings and the international obligations which rest upon them (pp. 129–130):

> I should add that the provisions and point of view of the *Bail Reform Act*, R.S.C. 1970, c. 2 (2nd Supp.); 1970-71-72 (Can.), c. 37, or Part XIV of the *Criminal Code*, R.S.C. 1970, c. C-34 (as it is variously known), do not apply to applications for bail of fugitives subject to extradition proceedings. They do not apply in their terms. If they did, they would represent a unilateral amendment of Canada's obligations under its extradition treaties and might, in large measure, defeat the paramount purpose of those treaties.

Nonetheless, Wright J. held that, independently of statute, a superior court judge had a common law jurisdiction to admit a fugitive to bail. However, he added the following comment, at p. 129:

> [I]t should be used sparingly and cautiously exercised, that great weight should be given to the mutual commitments of Canada and other states in extradition, that these should

be respected and assured, and that, in fine, bail should not be granted except in rare circumstances, and then when there is no serious risk, on the evidence, of the prisoner not surrendering for extradition, and the Court proceedings in connection with it.

Ultimately, the view developed that the authority to admit a fugitive to bail derived from the provisions of s. 13 of the former *Extradition Act*. Section 13 mandated treatment of the fugitive "as nearly as may be" to a person charged with an indictable offence in Canada.

In *United States v. Khan* (1982), 70 C.C.C. (2d) 5 (Man. C.A.), at p. 8, O'Sullivan J.A. of the Manitoba Court of Appeal made the following observations about the authority which flowed from s. 13 of the former Act with respect to the power to grant bail:

> I think the extradition judge derives his authority to remand from section 13 of the *Extradition Act* which reads:

>> 13. The fugitive shall be brought before a judge, who shall, subject to this Part, hear the case, in the same manner, as nearly as may be, as if the fugitive was brought before a justice of the peace, charged with an indictable offence committed in Canada.

> In England, it seems clear that an extradition judge has authority by virtue of a similar section to remand in custody but also to remand on bail. Thus, 18 Hals., 4th ed., p. 92, para. 224 says:

>> The magistrate hears the case in the same manner and has the same powers, as near as may be, as if the accused were before him charged with an indictable offence committed in England. In particular he may adjourn the hearing and remand the accused in custody or on bail.

> In my opinion, a judge under the *Extradition Act* has the same powers and duties to remand in custody or on bail as a justice dealing with a person accused of an indictable offence under the *Code*.

The issue of whether a fugitive could be granted bail was settled for Ontario in the case of *Global Communications Ltd. v. Canada (Attorney General)* (1984), 10 C.C.C. (3d) 97 (Ont. C.A.), in which Thorson J.A. speaking for the Court of Appeal held as follows, at pp. 104–105:

> In my opinion, therefore, there is no reason why, as a matter of either statutory construction or practicability, the *Bail Reform Act* provisions of the *Criminal Code* should not be held to apply "as nearly as may be" in extradition matters. However, I would go further. Looking at this issue from the viewpoint of the legislative policy sought to be implemented by Parliament when it enacted the *Bail Reform Act*, to hold that that Act has no application to proceedings under the *Extradition Act* would, in my opinion, be to frustrate altogether that policy as it would otherwise have application in this by no means unimportant area of our law.

Once the courts had determined that the bail provisions of the *Criminal Code* applied to persons being dealt with under the *Extradition Act*, it followed that the procedural provisions of the Code also applied. Consequently, the reverse onus provisions of s. 515(6) of the *Criminal Code* apply to extradition matters. Thus, for instance, fugitives who were not ordinarily resident in Canada or who were charged with an offence listed in that subsection bore the burden of demonstrating that their release was warranted.

The definition of "judge" in s. 2 of the new *Extradition Act* encompasses only superior court judges. By contrast, an "extradition judge" was defined under s. 9 of the former Act as a judge of the superior court or of the county court of a province as well as all commissioners who were appointed for the purpose by the Governor in Council under the Great Seal. The latter category fell early into desuetude, and in practice fugitives under the former Act were dealt with in the county or superior courts by a judge of those courts.

One consequence of having both superior and county court judges defined as extradition judges under the former Act was that the incorporation of the procedural provisions of the *Criminal Code* meant that county court judges were incompetent to consider bail with respect to certain offences. Section 522 of the Code reserves the consideration of bail with respect to s. 469 offences to judges of the superior court of criminal jurisdiction of the province. Consequently, fugitives under the former Act who were sought for offences that in Canada would have been s. 469 offences — including treason, mutiny, piracy, and murder — could only be released by order of the superior court. Accordingly, while a county court judge by virtue of s. 9 of the former *Extradition Act* was competent to preside over the extradition hearing of a fugitive wanted to stand trial for murder, he or she had no jurisdiction to consider the issue of bail for the same fugitive. This was confirmed by the Ontario Court of Appeal in *Canada v. Owens* (1987), 35 C.C.C. (3d) 574 (Ont. C.A.), in which a district court judge had purported to assume the authority to consider bail for a fugitive wanted for murder in California. Howland C.J.O. speaking for the Court of Appeal held that a district court judge had no such jurisdiction, that jurisdiction being reserved, as in the case of domestic murder charges, for a judge of the superior court of the province.

Pursuant to s. 13 of the former Act, the procedure for review of a bail or detention order under that Act was also governed by the provisions of the *Criminal Code*. Section 13 mandated that the fugitive be treated "as nearly as may be" to a person charged with an indictable offence in Canada. A "judge" acting under s. 13 with respect to bail, as with other matters governed by that section, exercised the authority of a justice of the peace (except in the case of offences reserved for a superior court judge as in the example of *Canada v. Owens, supra*). This meant that the review provisions of the Code applied to the decision of the extradition judge as if he or she had been a justice of the peace dealing with judicial interim release under s. 515 of the *Criminal Code*. A review of this decision could be applied for under s. 520 of the *Criminal Code* in the case of the fugitive or under s. 521 in the case of the requesting state. Both sections provide the mechanism for a judge to review a decision of a justice who has made an order under s. 515 of the Code. In the extradition context, this meant that rather than a judge reviewing the decision of a justice of the peace, as in the domestic context, the reviewing judge was a judge of the same court as the judge who made the original order. In practice, judicial deference to a fellow member of the court meant that an order was unlikely to be interfered with unless a significant change in circumstances could be demonstrated.

While the review provisions of the *Criminal Code* were generally invoked before a superior court judge, in the case of *Thailand (Kingdom) v. Saxena* (1998), 129 C.C.C. (3d) 528 (B.C. C.A. [In Chambers]), the requesting state brought a review of a release order to a single judge of the Court of Appeal. A superior court judge had revoked the fugitive's bail on the grounds that the fugitive had violated the terms of his judicial interim release order. The fugitive then applied for bail before the extradition judge who was conducting the hearing but this judge refused to hear the application so as not to hear evidence that might be inadmissible in the hearing. Another superior court judge heard the matter and granted bail. Esson J.A. held that he had jurisdiction as a judge of the Court of Appeal to hear the application. He noted the following, at pp. 530–531:

> [3] There is no doubt that judges of this court have concurrent jurisdiction with judges of the Supreme Court [of British Columbia] to deal with matters of bail in extradition proceedings in some circumstances. That somewhat unusual situation arises from the definition in the *Code* of the phrase "Superior Court of Criminal Jurisdiction". In this province, the phrase means "the Supreme Court or the Court of Appeal". There is now a similar provision for all other provinces except Quebec and Prince Edward Island where jurisdiction is conferred only on the superior trial court.
>
> [4] The only power of a Court of Appeal, as distinct from single judges of the court, to deal with bail matters is that conferred by s. 680 of the *Code*. That section is confined to cases involving charges listed in s. 469 which include murder and treason, but not offences of the kind alleged against the fugitive in this case, *i.e.*, charges of embezzling some $88 million from a Thai Bank.

Esson J.A. found that he had the jurisdiction under s. 521 to review the order of release made with respect to the fugitive.

As indicated above, the application of the bail provisions, and specifically of s. 522 of the *Criminal Code*, meant that offences described in s. 469 of the Code could only be heard by a superior court judge. These offences include murder, piracy, treason, mutiny, and the like. Section 522(4) specifically provides that an order made by a judge under this section is not subject to review except as provided in s. 680. Section 680 provides that, if directed by the Chief Justice of the Court of Appeal, an order under s. 522 of the *Criminal Code* can be reviewed by the Court of Appeal, and that the Court of Appeal may confirm the decision, vary it, or substitute such other decision that in the opinion of the Court of Appeal should have been made. The applicability of this review procedure to extradition requests under the former *Extradition Act* concerning s. 469 offences was confirmed by the Ontario Court of Appeal in *Canada v. Owens, supra*, and by the British Columbia Court of Appeal in *Thailand (Kingdom) v. Saxena, supra*.

It is clear that the powers of review given to the Court of Appeal under s. 18(2) of the new *Extradition Act* are in the same terms as those set out in s. 680 of the *Criminal Code*, but without the requirement that the Chief Justice direct the review, and with the specific provision that they be exercised by a single judge of the court of appeal rather than the full panel.

§3.0 SIGNIFICANCE OF CHANGE

The authority to order bail or detention is now explicit in the new *Extradition Act*, as is the authority and procedure for the review of an order of detention or order of judicial interim release.

By virtue of s. 19 of the new Act, Part XVI of the *Criminal Code*, which includes judicial interim release provisions, is applicable to extradition matters.

§4.0 ANALYSIS

§4.1 Requests Involving the International Criminal Court

Section 18(1)(a) provides that in the case of bail for persons sought by the International Criminal Court there is a reverse onus on the person whose extradition is sought to show cause for his or her release, and which requires that it be demonstrated to the satisfaction of the judge that there are urgent and exceptional circumstances justifying the person's release and that the person will appear as required.

The new provisions indicate that the issue of bail for persons sought by the International Criminal Court raises different concerns from other extradition requests. A separate regime has been provided for the consideration of the issue of bail for individuals sought by this court. Parliament has dictated that the gravity of the offences within the jurisdiction of the International Criminal Court — war crimes, crimes against humanity, and genocide — means that it would seldom be appropriate for individuals suspected of these offences to be granted bail.

Under s. 18(1.1) and (1.2), the Canadian court would be required to receive and consider recommendations from the Pre-Trial Chamber of the International Criminal Court concerning judicial interim release of persons sought by that body. The Attorney General may request a mandatory adjournment of up to six days in order to obtain these recommendations.

Article 59(4) of the *Rome Statute*, which established the International Criminal Court, appears to be the source of the more stringent provisions for bail of persons sought by the International Criminal Court. Article 59(4) reads as follows:

> In reaching a decision on any such application, the competent authority in the custodial State shall consider whether, given the gravity of the alleged crimes, there are urgent and exceptional circumstances to justify interim release and whether necessary safeguards exist to ensure that the custodial State can fulfil its duty to surrender the person

to the Court. It shall not be open to the competent authority of the custodial State to consider whether the warrant of arrest was properly issued in accordance with article 58, paragraph 1(a) and (b).

§4.2 Requests Other Than From the International Criminal Court

With respect to requests from states or entities other than the International Criminal Court, the effect of ss. 18(1)(b) and 19 of the new *Extradition Act* is to apply the domestic bail provisions to the extradition context.

Although the domestic standards apply, the question of whether there should be an order of judicial interim release made with respect to a person sought for extradition may give rise to different considerations than would arise in the context of domestic proceedings for a similar offence. In the early case of *Gaynor v. Greene* (1905), 9 C.C.C. 255 (Que. C.A.), at p. 263, it had been noted that the issue of extradition bail might best be approached with caution:

> In ordinary criminal cases, the Crown is dealing with its own rights, and may imperil these rights and afford opportunity of escape to prisoners by admitting to bail, or even to absolve them altogether.
>
> But in extradition cases, the sovereign power, as stated by Chief Justice Fuller in *Wrights' Case*, is under a grave international obligation, if a case is made out, to deliver over the prisoners to another nation whose laws have been violated and whose rights are being dealt with, and nothing should be done that might lead to the failure to carry out this international obligation.
>
> Another reason is, that in extradition cases, the prisoner is already a fugitive from justice. These considerations are obvious but important; and, in my opinion, justify the statement that while in ordinary criminal cases the rule is to accept bail, in extradition cases it is, or ought to be, just the reverse, and that it is only in exceptional cases and where great injustice will be done by refusal to bail, that bail ought at all to be accepted. I think a belief that an extradition commissioner is as free to accept bail in extradition cases as is a magistrate in ordinary criminal cases might lead, in many cases, to a failure on the part of this country to carry out its international obligations and bring great discredit on the administration of criminal justice.
>
> I do not understand that the other members of the Court differ in opinion on this point, but I have felt it my duty to emphasize, as it were, the view I have taken of the matter before us.

Even subsequent to the decision in *Global Communications, supra,* the applicability of the principle was still recognized in some of the jurisprudence. In *Canada v. Pitman* (April 28, 1986), Doc. RE 974/86, [1986] O.J. No. 273, Hollingworth J. of the Supreme Court of Ontario acknowledged that the honouring of Canada's international obligations was a factor to be considered with respect to whether bail would be appropriate for a person sought for extradition. In *United States v. Liebowitz* (May 27, 1987), Doc. York E4/87, [1987] O.J. No. 1505 (Dist. Ct.), and *United States v.*

Greco (February 27, 1986), [1986] 16 W.C.B. 297 (Ont. Dist. Ct.), Borins D.C.J. (as he then was) was similarly of the view that the court should not lose sight of the international obligations inherent in extradition proceedings when considering the matter of bail. In the *Greco* case the fact that the fugitive had fled from the United States after being convicted in that jurisdiction was considered a factor particularly adverse to the granting of bail. Borins D.C.J. noted as follows:

> To analogize to an application for bail pending appeal, I must take into consideration the fact that there is no longer a presumption of innocence. Mr Greco has already been convicted in the State of Florida, and, hence is not entitled to the benefit of being presumed innocent until proved guilty.

It may be expected that lacking the presumption of innocence, a convicted person will continue to find it more difficult to obtain bail than a person sought for prosecution.

§4.3 Review by Superior Court Judge

While s. 18(2) clearly confers jurisdiction to review extradition bail upon a judge of the court of appeal, such jurisdiction may not be exclusive. In *Germany (Federal Republic) v. Schreiber* (2000), 147 C.C.C. (3d) 404, Watt J. of the Ontario Superior Court of Justice, held that the permissive language of s. 18(2) foreclosed the argument that a judge of the court of appeal had exclusive review jurisdiction. Rather, in light of the referential incorporation of Part XVI of the *Criminal Code* through s. 19 of the *Extradition Act*, Watt J. was of the opinion that the variance provisions of the *Criminal Code* could still be exercised by a superior court judge. Watt J. held that s. 18(2) operates so as to permit review of judicial interim release for offences listed in s. 469 of the *Criminal Code* by a single judge of the court of appeal. In this way, s. 18(2) avoids the domestic requirement of a direction by the Chief Justice under s. 680 of the *Criminal Code*, which would, if given, require a hearing by a full panel of the court of appeal unless the parties agreed to a single judge. Save for the exclusive jurisdiction of a single judge of the court of appeal to review bail in matters of s. 469 offences, Watt J. concluded that a judge of a superior court of criminal jurisdiction has authority to vary or review any other bail order made by another judge of the same court.

§4.4 Review in Court of Appeal

Sharpe J.A. in *United States v. Chan* (2000), 144 C.C.C. (3d) 93 (Ont. C.A. [In Chambers]), observed, at pp. 94–95, with respect to the standard of review under s. 18(2):

> [2] This is a new provision and counsel for the United States was unable to provide me with any authority providing guidance as to the standard of review. It would appear

to me that by way of analogy to the review of judicial interim release or detention orders, there is an onus upon the applicant to demonstrate an error in principle to justify review: see Ewaschuk, *Criminal Pleadings and Practice in Canada*, 2nd ed., vol. I, para. 6:1400. The issue, accordingly, is not whether I would grant bail if the matter came before me at first instance, but rather, whether the applicant can demonstrate reviewable error on the part of LaForme J. [the judge at the bail hearing].

The dicta of Sharpe J.A. in *Chan* was adopted by Otis J.A. in *United States v. Palmucci* (January 11, 2001), Doc. 500-10-002027-017 (Que. C.A.).

§5.0 CASE LAW

Barnes v. Tennessee (1972), 34 C.C.C. (2d) 122 (Ont. H.C.).
Canada v. Owens (1987), 35 C.C.C. (3d) 574 (Ont. C.A.).
Canada v. Pitman (April 28, 1986), Doc. RE 974/86, [1986] O.J. No. 273, Hollingworth J. (Ont. S.C.).
Gaynor v. Greene (1905), 9 C.C.C. 255 (Que. C.A.).
Germany (Federal Republic) v. Schreiber (2000), 147 C.C.C. (3d) 404 (Ont. S.C.J.).
Global Communications Ltd. v. Canada (Attorney General) (1984), 10 C.C.C. (3d) 97 (Ont. C.A.).
Thailand (Kingdom) v. Saxena (1998), 129 C.C.C. (3d) 528 (B.C.C.A. [In Chambers]).
United States v. Chan (2000), 144 C.C.C. (3d) 93 (Ont. C.A. [In Chambers]).
United States v. Greco (February 27, 1986), [1986] 16 W.C.B. 297, Borins D.C.J. (Ont. Dist. Ct.).
United States v. Khan (1982), 70 C.C.C. (2d) 5 (Man. C.A.).
United States v. Liebowitz (May 27, 1987), Doc. York E4/87, [1987] O.J. No. 1505 (Ont. Dist. Ct.).
United States v. Palmucci (January 11, 2001), Doc. 500-10-002027-017, Otis J.A. (Que. C.A.).

§6.0 RELATED SECTIONS

s. 2 — Interpretation
s. 13 — Issuance of Provisional Arrest Warrant
s. 16 — Warrant of Arrest or Summons
s. 19 — Applicability of Part XVI of *Criminal Code* to ss. 13 and 16
s. 28 — Power to Compel Witnesses
Rome Statute, Article 59(4).

Applicability of Part XVI of *Criminal Code* to Ss. 13 and 16 of *Extradition Act* (s. 19)

§1.0 DESCRIPTION

Section 19 of the *Extradition Act* provides as follows:

CRIMINAL CODE
> **19. Part XVI of the *Criminal Code* applies, with any modifications that the circumstances require, in respect of a person arrested under section 13 or 16 or to whom a summons has been issued under section 16.**

Section 19 makes Part XVI of the *Criminal Code* ("Compelling Appearance of Accused Before a Justice and Interim Release") applicable to persons arrested under ss. 13 and 16 of the Act and persons summoned under s. 16 of the Act, with such modifications as are appropriate to the extradition context. Part XVI deals with bringing the accused before the court after the accused has been charged with an offence. The provisions in Part XVI include arrest with warrant, arrest without warrant, and the summons and promise to appear process. Part XVI deals with judicial interim release and detention orders, the review of such orders, and matters incidental to bail hearings such as publication bans. It also provides for the endorsement of warrants, the authority to enter dwelling houses with and without warrants, and the obtaining of telewarrants.

§2.0 COMPARISON WITH FORMER ACT

There was no express provision in the former *Extradition Act* providing for *Criminal Code* procedural provisions to apply. Section 19 of the new Act makes applicable Part XVI of the *Criminal Code* in its entirety, with appropriate modifications to suit the extradition context. Part XVI deals with bringing accused persons before the court once charged with an offence and with the issue of release or detention. The former Act did not deal with the process for bringing a fugitive before the court. However, Form 1 of the former Act ("Warrant of Apprehension") directed that the arrest was to be effected "forthwith." It also set out the judicial officer, a "judge," before whom the fugitive was to be brought following arrest.

The aspect of Part XVI of the *Criminal Code* dealing with judicial interim release was governed, under the former Act, by s. 13. Section 13 indicated that the fugitive was to be dealt with "in the same manner, as nearly as may be, as if the fugitive was brought before a justice of the peace, charged with an indictable offence committed in Canada." Section 13 had the effect of incorporating the judicial interim release sections of the *Criminal Code*. The Manitoba Court of Appeal in *United States v. Khan* (1982), 70 C.C.C. (2d) 5 (Man. C.A.), determined that s. 13 gave the extradition judge the same authority as a justice dealing with a person accused of an indictable offence in Canada, including the power to remand on bail. The Ontario Court of Appeal in *Global Communications Ltd. v. Canada (Attorney General)* (1984), 10 C.C.C. (3d) 97 (Ont. C.A.), confirmed that these *Criminal Code* provisions, including those dealing with publication bans on bail hearings, were applicable to extradition proceedings.

§3.0 SIGNIFICANCE OF CHANGE

As with other provisions of the new *Extradition Act* (such as s. 17), s. 19 is significant in that it incorporates domestic procedural mechanisms into the extradition context, with such modifications as are required. Section 19 explicitly incorporates Part XVI of the *Criminal Code*, thereby eliminating a source of ambiguity under the former Act that led to litigation. As discussed above, it was only after the *Khan* and *Global Communications* decisions that the scope of the incorporation of the *Criminal Code* interim release provisions into extradition proceedings, through s. 13 of the former Act, was determined.

§4.0 ANALYSIS

What is important to note in s. 19 of the new Act is that Part XVI of the *Criminal Code* is made applicable with "any modifications that the circumstances require." It is obvious when looking at ss. 16, 17, and 18 that the sections which deal with summons, arrest, appearance after arrest or summons, and judicial interim release have already modified certain procedures to accord with the extradition context. For instance, the promise to appear and arrest without warrant process which is referred to in Part XVI of the *Criminal Code* is not an option under s. 16. Section 16 requires judicial authorization for the issuance of a warrant or summons. As indicated in the discussion of s. 17(2), the authority of the justice, being a justice of the peace or provincial court judge, is limited to remanding into custody a person who has been arrested under the *Extradition Act* and ordering them to be brought before a judge of the superior court. This differs from the domestic authority of a justice who may conduct a bail hearing. By contrast, s. 18 of the new *Extradition Act* gives jurisdiction over bail for all extradition offences to the extradition judge (i.e., a judge of the superior court of the province — see s. 2 of the Act), regardless of whether the offences are s. 469 offences in domestic law. Moreover, s. 18(2) adds a single judge of the court of appeal as a venue for the review of extradition release and detention orders.

Section 16 of the Act also contains an explicit example of a modification made to adapt *Criminal Code* provisions to the extradition context. Section 16(5) provides that, when a person is summoned to appear in court, attending pursuant to the *Identification of Criminals Act* for the purposes of fingerprinting and photographing is a mandatory requirement. In contrast, it is a discretionary requirement in the domestic process.

There are certain provisions in Part XVI of the *Criminal Code* that are not dealt with in the *Extradition Act*, such as the authority to enter a dwelling house with or without a warrant. The sections dealing with the authority to enter a dwelling house were amendments to the Code made subsequent to the Supreme Court of Canada case of *R. v. Feeney* (1997), 115 C.C.C. (3d) 129. It is apparent that s. 19, when incorporating Part XVI of the Code, intends the incorporation of such provisions. There will, of course, be instances when a person sought will be arrested in a dwelling house. Under the former Act, subsequent to these Code amendments, it was sometimes necessary when seeking a warrant of apprehension to obtain, in the same document, a so-called "*Feeney* warrant" in the event that it became necessary to enter a dwelling house in the course of effecting the arrest. This practice will continue.

The provisions of Part XVI concerning telewarrants may also apply to extradition matters in appropriate circumstances. There is no reason that the directions of s. 19 of the new Act to apply the Part XVI Code provisions with any modifications that the circumstances require should not apply to telewarrants. Applying these provisions would require s. 529.5 of the Code to be interpreted so as to allow the Attorney General of Canada to have formed the opinion that obtaining a warrant directly would not be practicable and to make the application for a telewarrant in the same manner as would be required of a peace officer in domestic circumstances. Overall, s. 19 appears to make available to extradition matters the wide range of procedural options available in the domestic context, unless it is clear that circumstances peculiar to extradition require otherwise.

Other sections of the *Criminal Code*, while they may apply to extradition matters, may only be infrequently resorted to. For instance, s. 525 of the Code dealing with 90-day judicial reviews of an accused person's detention, while presumably equally applicable to extradition proceedings, is unlikely to be invoked given that extradition proceedings are expected to proceed with dispatch.

§5.0 CASE LAW

Global Communications Ltd. v. Canada (Attorney General) (1984), 10 C.C.C. (3d) 97 (Ont. C.A.).
R. v. Feeney (1997), 115 C.C.C. (3d) 129 (S.C.C.).
United States v. Khan (1982), 70 C.C.C. (2d) 5 (Man. C.A.).

§6.0 RELATED SECTIONS

s. 13 — Issuance of Provisional Arrest Warrant
s. 16 — Warrant of Arrest or Summons
s. 17 — Appearance
s. 18 — Judicial Interim Release

s. 20 — Bail Pending Appeal, Judicial Review, and Between Committal and Surrender

Criminal Code, Part XVI — Compelling Appearance of Accused Before a Justice and Interim Release

Application of s. 679 of *Criminal Code* to Judicial Interim Release (s. 20)

§1.0 DESCRIPTION

Section 20 of the *Extradition Act* provides as follows:

SECTION 679 OF THE *CRIMINAL CODE*
20. Section 679 of the *Criminal Code* applies, with any modifications that the circumstances require, to the judicial interim release of a person pending

(a) **a determination of an appeal from an order of committal made under section 29;**
(b) **the Minister's decision under section 40 respecting the surrender of the person; or**
(c) **a determination of a judicial review of the Minister's decision under section 40 to order the surrender of the person.**

Section 679 of the *Criminal Code* provides for the granting of bail pending an appeal to the court of appeal of the province or to the Supreme Court of Canada. Section 20 makes s. 679 applicable to appeals of the order of committal and applications for judicial review of the Minister's decision. Section 20 also makes s. 679 applicable to the period of time between the issuance of the committal order by the extradition hearing judge and the determination of the Minister concerning surrender. Section 20 adds the qualification that s. 679 applies "with any modifications that the circumstances require."

§2.0 COMPARISON WITH FORMER ACT

Section 19.5(1) was the provision of the former *Extradition Act* dealing with bail pending appeal. It provided as follows:

19.5 (1) Sections 677, 678.1, 679, 682 to 685 and 688 of the *Criminal Code* apply, with such modifications as the circumstances require, to appeals under this Act.

Subsection 19.5(1) has been split in the new Act into s. 20 and s. 52. Section 20, which appears in the new Act under the heading of "Appearance," is concerned only with the incorporation of the bail pending appeal provisions of s. 679 of the *Criminal Code*. All of the other Code provisions dealing with other aspects of appeals that were previously incorporated by s. 19.5(1) are now dealt with in s. 52 of the new Act under the heading of "Appeal," which commences at s. 49.

Section 20 sets out the three specific situations in which bail pursuant to s. 679 of the *Criminal Code* is available. The former Act stated simply that s. 679 of the Code applied to appeals under the Act. The two appeals available under the former Act were from the committal order of the extradition hearing judge and from the Minister's surrender decision. The former Act was silent with respect to whether judicial interim release was available for the period of time between the extradition judge's committal order and the Minister's surrender decision. Sections 20(a) and 20(c) of the new Act continue to provide for bail pending an appeal of the committal order and a judicial review of the Minister's surrender decision. In addition, s. 20(b) provides for bail during the time period between the issuance of the committal order and the Minister's determination concerning surrender.

§3.0 SIGNIFICANCE OF CHANGE

The omission from the former Act of bail pending the Minister's surrender decision was problematic. It created a gap in the scheme of extradition that required judicial intervention. In the absence of an appeal of the extradition judge's committal order, the former Act did not provide for bail pending the Minister's decision. However, in *Re Berladyn* (December 24, 1992), Doc. Vancouver CC880571 (B.C. S.C.), Hall J. of the British Columbia Supreme Court found that the inherent jurisdiction of the court enabled it to grant a fugitive bail pending the Minister's decision:

> . . . I am of the view that this court does have jurisdiction, in appropriate cases, to grant bail, even as late as the time that we are at here in these proceedings. By that, I mean at the stage where the court process is finished and the matter is before the Minister for final decision . . .
>
> I am satisfied that there is jurisdiction in this court to grant bail, based on the inherent jurisdiction of the court.

However, Hall J. added that this would only be done in limited circumstances:

> [W]hile there is jurisdiction in the court to grant bail, I would say that it would have to be a quite unusual case before the court, exercising that jurisdiction, would be justified in granting bail. I don't propose at this stage to list what those extraordinary or unusual circumstances might be, but I do think that they would be cases that would be very much out of the ordinary where there would be a real probability or possibility that something of substance could be urged before the Minister that could lead the Minister to exercise a discretion against making the order of extradition.

§4.0 ANALYSIS

Section 20 of the new Act provides that the bail pending appeal provision in s. 679 of the *Criminal Code* applies in the three following situations: appeal from the order of committal; judicial review of the Minister's surrender decision; and during the time period between the issuance of the committal order and the Minister's surrender decision. Section 20 adds the qualification that s. 679 applies "with any modifications that the circumstances require."

Cases decided under s. 19.5 of the former *Extradition Act* will continue to be of assistance since they were engaged in interpretation of s. 679 as adapted to the extradition context. For instance, in *United States v. Ross* (July 5, 1993), Doc. Vancouver CA017111 (B.C.C.A. [In Chambers]), the applicant argued that, under s. 19.5(1), the requesting state should bear the onus of proving the criteria set out in s. 679(3) of the Code. The applicant claimed that the phrase "with such modifications as the circumstances require" used in s. 19.5(1) permitted the court to make this adaptation to s. 679 in the specific context of an application for bail pending an appeal of an extradition judge's decision. Section 679(3) reads as follows:

> **679.** (3) In the case of an appeal referred to in paragraph 1(*a*) or (*c*), the judge of the court of appeal may order that the appellant be released pending the determination of his appeal if the appellant establishes that
>
> (a) the appeal or application for leave to appeal is not frivolous,
> (b) he will surrender himself into custody in accordance with the terms of the order, and
> (c) his detention is not necessary in the public interest.

Wood J.A. of the British Columbia Court of Appeal dismissed the argument. He held that the phrase "with such modifications as the circumstances require" does not permit the court to make fundamental changes to s. 679 of the Code:

> [4] In my view, the words "with such modifications as the circumstances require," found in s. 19.5(1) of the *Extradition Act*, do not permit me to re-write the explicit terms of s. 679(3), so as to enact fundamental changes to the substance of that provision, such as reversing the onus which the section places on an appellant/applicant. That phrase enables me, where necessary, to replace that wording of s. 679 which is inconsistent with an extradition application, with language more appropriate to such a proceeding. But it does not authorize me to legislate substantive changes to the section according to counsel's view of what the law should be in the circumstances. I am satisfied that the onus is on the applicant to establish that he can meet the criteria described in s. 679(3)(a) through (c).

Wood J.A. went on to hold that the requirement under s. 679(3)(a) of the Act that the appeal not be "frivolous" involves a very low threshold:

[6] . . . In my view, the term "frivolous" is a term of art in the criminal law. In the context of s. 679(3) it describes an appeal that has no hope of success, an appeal which can be said to be "unarguable." It presents a very low threshold which the applicant has to meet. Were it otherwise, the section would extend an invitation to a single judge of this court to pass an opinion on the likelihood of the appeal succeeding. I do not believe that was the intent of Parliament.

Wood J.A. also considered the criteria under s. 679(3)(b) that the appellant will surrender into custody as and when required. He observed that, given the principle in extradition law that states must strive to honour their international obligations, the risk of non-appearance must in the context of extradition proceedings be viewed in a more severe light than in domestic matters:

[15] But the courts of this country have long recognized that a correct approach to extradition proceedings is characterized by good faith in honouring Canada's international obligations; see: *Schmidt v. The Queen*, [1987] 1 S.C.R. 500. In my view, adherence to that principle requires a court considering a bail application such as this to limit the assumption of the risk of non-appearance more severely than might otherwise be acceptable in the case of domestic proceedings.

[16] After anxious consideration, I have reached the conclusion that the risk the applicant will not surrender himself into custody, as directed by any order I might make, is greater than that which is commensurate with the fulfilment of Canada's international obligations in matters of extradition. Accordingly he has failed to meet the onus required of him under s. 679(3)(b) of the *Criminal Code*.

Accordingly, the applicant did not meet the second criteria under s. 679(3) of the Code and Wood J.A. did not consider the third criteria.

§5.0 CASE LAW

Berladyn, Re (December 24, 1992), Doc. Vancouver CC880571 (B.C.S.C.).
United States v. Ross (July 5, 1993), Doc. Vancouver CA017111 (B.C.C.A. [In Chambers]).

§6.0 RELATED SECTIONS

s. 29 — Order of Committal by Extradition Judge
s. 40 — Surrender Order by Minister of Justice
Criminal Code, s. 679 — Release Pending Determination of Appeal

Date of Extradition Hearing (s. 21)

§1.0 DESCRIPTION

Section 21 of the *Extradition Act* provides as follows:

DATE OF HEARING — PROVISIONAL ARREST
21. (1) If a person has been provisionally arrested, the judge before whom the person is brought shall

- **(a) order the person to appear before the court from time to time during the period referred to in paragraph 14(1)(*b*) or (*c*); and**
- **(b) set a date for the extradition hearing if the Minister has issued an authority to proceed.**

DATE OF HEARING AFTER AUTHORITY TO PROCEED ISSUED
(2) If a person has been arrested or is a person to whom a summons has been issued under section 16, the judge before whom the person is brought shall set a date for the extradition hearing.

HEARING
(3) The judge shall set an early date for the extradition hearing, whether that date is in or out of the prescribed sessions of the court.

Section 21(1) deals with the setting of an extradition hearing date with respect to persons who have been provisionally arrested under s. 13 of the Act. Provisional arrest enables the apprehension of a person sought prior to the receipt of a formal request for extradition. Under s. 15 of the Act, the Minister of Justice may only issue an authority to proceed once an extradition request has been received, and the authority to proceed is the document upon which extradition proceedings are based. Since provisional arrests occur prior to the receipt of an extradition request, they also occur prior to the issuance of an authority to proceed.

Section 21(1)(a) provides the judge before whom a provisionally arrested person is brought with the power to remand the proceedings pending the issuance of an authority to proceed by the Minister of Justice. Specifically, it permits the judge to "order the person to appear before the court from time to time during the period referred to in paragraph 14(1)(*b*) or (*c*)." Section 14(1) mandates the discharge of a person sought if certain steps are not taken by the Minister of Justice or the extradition partner within the time periods set out in that provision. For the purposes of s. 21(1)(a), the relevant time periods set out in s. 14 are those during which the Minister of Justice must have issued an authority to proceed. Section 14(1)(b) deals with the situation in which the provisional arrest is made pursuant to the terms of an extradition agreement and the agreement contains a time period within which an extradition request must be made and supporting documents provided. In this situation, the maximum time

117

permitted to the Minister for issuing the authority to proceed is the time period set out in the extradition agreement for making the extradition request and supplying the supporting documents plus 30 days. Section 14(1)(c) deals with two situations: firstly, when the provisional arrest is not made pursuant to the terms of an extradition agreement; secondly, when the request is made pursuant to the terms of an extradition agreement and the agreement does not contain a time period within which an extradition request must be made and supporting documents provided. In either of these two situations, the maximum time permitted to the Minister for issuing the authority to proceed is 90 days.

Section 21(1)(b) provides that the judge must set a date for the extradition hearing if the Minister of Justice has issued an authority to proceed.

Section 21(2) deals with the setting of extradition hearing dates in respect of persons who have been arrested or summonsed under s. 16 of the Act. Section 16 deals with the apprehension of persons sought after the Minister of Justice has received an extradition request and issued an authority to proceed. For persons arrested or summonsed under s. 16 of the Act, s. 21(2) directs that the judge before whom the person is brought shall set the extradition hearing date.

Section 21(3) mandates the setting of an early date for the extradition hearing, regardless of the prescribed sitting dates of the court.

§2.0 COMPARISON WITH FORMER ACT

Section 21 of the *Extradition Act* deals with the power of the court to remand a person sought and to set a date for the extradition hearing. The former Act had no provision specifically detailing this authority. Rather, under s. 13 of the former Act, extradition proceedings were conducted in a manner analogous to domestic proceedings. Section 13 read as follows:

> **13.** The fugitive referred to in section 12 shall be brought before a judge, who shall, subject to this Part, hear the case, in the same manner, as nearly as may be, as if the fugitive was brought before a justice of the peace, charged with an indictable offence committed in Canada.

Accordingly, under the former Act, the extradition court had similar powers to a domestic court, including the power to remand the fugitive and to set hearing dates.

§3.0 SIGNIFICANCE OF CHANGE

Section 21 is a specific procedural provision requiring early dates to be scheduled for extradition hearings. Section 21 makes the setting of the hearing date mandatory once the authority to proceed has been issued by the Minister of Justice. Section 21 contemplates that extradition hearings are to take precedence over any other scheduling regarding the sittings of the court.

§4.0 ANALYSIS

Prior to the enactment of the new *Extradition Act*, the jurisprudence dictated that extradition matters were to proceed with dispatch (see *R. v. Schmidt* (1987), 33 C.C.C. (3d) 193 (S.C.C.) and *United States v. Dynar* (1997), 115 C.C.C. (3d) 481 (S.C.C.)). Section 19.4(1) of the former Act provided for this with respect to appeals:

> **19.4** (1) An appeal under this Act shall be scheduled for hearing by the court of appeal at an early date, whether that date is in or out of the prescribed sessions of that court.

Section 19.4(1) has been continued in s. 51(1) of the new *Extradition Act* with respect to appeals. Section 21(3) of the new Act extends this statutory requirement to the setting of early dates for the extradition hearing.

§5.0 CASE LAW

R. v. Schmidt (1987), 33 C.C.C. (3d) 193 (S.C.C.).
United States v. Dynar (1997), 115 C.C.C. (3d) 481 (S.C.C.).

§6.0 RELATED SECTIONS

ss. 12–14 — Warrant for Provisional Arrest
s. 14 — Discharge of Person Sought If No Proceedings Instituted
s. 15 — Authority to Proceed
s. 16 — Warrant of Arrest or Summons
s. 51(1) — Hearing of Appeal

Transfer of Proceedings to Another Place in Canada (s. 22)

§1.0 DESCRIPTION

Section 22 of the *Extradition Act* provides as follows:

APPLICATION FOR TRANSFER
22. (1) On application of the Attorney General or the person arrested or to whom a summons has been issued under section 16, the judge shall, if satisfied that the interests of justice so require, order that the proceedings be transferred to another place in Canada and that the person appear before a judge in that place, and

> **(a)** if the person is detained, that the person be conveyed by a peace officer to the place; and
> **(b)** if the person is not detained or has been released on judicial interim release, that the person be summoned to appear at the place.

EXECUTION THROUGHOUT CANADA
> **(2)** A summons issued under paragraph (1)(*b*) may be served anywhere in Canada without being endorsed.

ORDER RESPECTING EXPENSES
> **(3)** If the order under subsection (1) was made on the application of the Attorney General, the judge may order that the Attorney General pay the person's reasonable travel expenses incurred further to the order.

Section 22 enables a change of venue anywhere in Canada for extradition proceedings. It can be on the application of the Attorney General or the person sought. If it is on the application of the Attorney General, the Attorney General may be liable to pay travel expenses. If the judge orders the transfer of the proceedings and the person sought is in custody, a peace officer must convey the person to the new venue. If the person has been released on bail, the judge can order a summons for the person to attend at the new venue. The summons may be served anywhere in Canada.

§2.0 COMPARISON WITH FORMER ACT

There was no provision in the former *Extradition Act* dealing with the transfer of proceedings to another jurisdiction. Notwithstanding the lack of specific provisions in the former Act, from time to time judges would transfer proceedings to another court, usually in the same province. This was normally done in situations where the fugitive was arrested and resided in a jurisdiction other than that in which the warrant of apprehension was issued. On the application of the fugitive, or the court on its own motion, the judge would order that the proceedings and court record be transferred to the court of the other jurisdiction. The authority to transfer the proceedings stemmed from the inherent jurisdiction of the court to control its own process. It also perhaps stemmed from s. 9(1) of the former Act. This provision authorized the extradition judge "to act judicially in extradition matters under this Part within the province" and, for the purposes of Part I of the Act, gave the extradition judge "all the powers and jurisdiction of any judge or provincial court judge of the province." Part I of the former Act was concerned with the power to issue warrants for the apprehension of a fugitive to bring the fugitive under the control of the courts, and with the conduct of extradition proceedings after the person was brought before the court.

There are cases that have held that an extradition judge has the authority to transfer extradition proceedings from one province to another. In *United States v. Down* (1998), 124 C.C.C. (3d) 289 (Man. Q.B.), the fugitive was a Canadian citizen and had returned to British Columbia voluntarily in 1996 to deal with charges that he was facing in that province. An extradition warrant of apprehension was issued against him in Manitoba where he had been visiting. After being arrested in Saskatchewan he was returned to Manitoba to be dealt with under the *Extradition Act*. The fugitive brought an application for a change of venue before the Manitoba Court of Queen's Bench. Oliphant J. granted the application, relying on the decision in *Re Dejerkic* (1975), 24 C.C.C. (2d) 164 (Nfld. Dist. Ct.), wherein the Newfoundland District Court granted a similar application transferring proceedings from Newfoundland to Quebec. Oliphant J. made the following comment, at p. 296:

> [24] One of the factors considered by Murray D.C.J. was that in criminal matters, a judge may transfer an accused from one jurisdiction to another. A judge sitting as an extradition judge has all the powers of a judge sitting on a criminal matter.

Oliphant J. was of the view that s. 599 of the *Criminal Code* pertaining to change of venue had no application but that there was nothing in the Act which precluded him "from ordering that the extradition hearing for Mr. Down be conducted before a judge of the British Columbia Supreme Court in that province" (at p. 301).

In arriving at this result, Oliphant J. considered a number of factors: Mr. Down lived in British Columbia at the time of his arrest; he wished to call witnesses pursuant to s. 15 of the former Act; fugitive's counsel practised in British Columbia; and most of the other co-accused subject to the extradition request were located in British Columbia. In this regard, Oliphant J. stated as follows, at p. 301:

> [62] Mr. Down's ability to conduct his case would be seriously, if not fatally, impaired if the hearing were to be conducted in Manitoba. I need only mention the difficulty in compelling witnesses from British Columbia to come to Manitoba for these proceedings. If Mr. Down wanted to obtain production of documents in the hands of third parties resident in British Columbia, there is a serious question as to whether an order from this court for such production would have the desired effect.

Oliphant J. was required to "read in" the authority to transfer proceedings from one jurisdiction to another under the former *Extradition Act*. The new Act provides specifically for this authority.

§3.0 SIGNIFICANCE OF CHANGE

Section 22 of the Act is significant in that it provides specific statutory authority for the transfer of extradition proceedings anywhere in Canada.

§4.0 ANALYSIS

Section 22 has introduced greater flexibility to extradition by providing that extradition proceedings may be transferred to another jurisdiction anywhere in Canada if the judge is satisfied that "the interests of justice so require." Section 22 mirrors the domestic change of venue rules set out in s. 599 of the *Criminal Code*. Section 22, like s. 599, permits the application to be brought by either the person sought or the Attorney General. Moreover, both sections provide that, if a transfer is granted on the application of the Attorney General, the Attorney General may be ordered to cover the travelling expenses of the person sought, if that person is out of custody. Unlike s. 599, which only provides for a transfer to another jurisdiction within the same province, s. 22 allows for extradition proceedings to be transferred anywhere in Canada. In granting the authority to transfer proceedings Canada-wide, the new *Extradition Act* recognizes the often highly mobile character of individuals who may be fleeing apprehension. Since extradition by its nature is concerned with a foreign offence to be tried in a foreign country, there is no natural locus for the commencement of extradition proceedings in any particular Canadian jurisdiction. As in the *United States v. Down* case, *supra*, a basis should be shown by the applicant to justify the transfer of the proceedings to another jurisdiction.

The Attorney General may submit that it would be in the interests of justice to transfer the proceedings to another jurisdiction in the following circumstances:

• There are co-accused being sought, and they are in different provinces when apprehended.

• The proceedings are commenced and the arrest warrant is issued in one province. However, the investigating force which has jointly investigated with the foreign force — as well as witnesses or evidence that might be called at the hearing — is in another province.

The circumstances under which the court may view it to be in the interests of justice to consider the application of the person sought for a transfer of proceedings might include the following:

• The person resides or otherwise has roots in a jurisdiction other than the one in which the proceedings have been commenced.

• The person lives in a jurisdiction near or contiguous to the jurisdiction in which the proceedings have been commenced, but it is inconvenient or costly for the person sought to travel back and forth to that court.

• The person's sureties or counsel are in another jurisdiction.

Domestic cases under s. 599 of the *Criminal Code* are unlikely to be of assistance in interpreting the test to be met under s. 22 for transferring extradition proceedings, the test being "that the interests of justice so require." The focus in domestic applications for the transfer of proceedings to another jurisdiction is on the issue of the right to a fair trial. Fair trial issues are not engaged in extradition matters, which are akin to domestic preliminary inquiries. See *R. v. Schmidt* (1987), 33 C.C.C. (3d) 193

(S.C.C.) and *United States v. Smith* (1984), 15 C.C.C. (3d) 16 (Ont. Co. Ct.), affirmed (1984), 16 C.C.C. (3d) 10 (Ont. H.C.). Section 599 of the *Criminal Code* only applies to indicted accused. It would not permit the transfer of a preliminary inquiry to another jurisdiction. That the new Act provides for the transfer of extradition proceedings means that the test for transfer is related to circumstances which are uniquely applicable to extradition as opposed to the issue of fair adjudication of innocence or guilt. The *United States v. Down* case, *supra*, indicates the kind of criteria that a court may look to in determining the convenient forum in an application for change of venue.

§5.0 CASE LAW

Dejerkic, Re (1975), 24 C.C.C. (2d) 164 (Nfld. Dist. Ct.).
R. v. Schmidt (1987), 33 C.C.C. (3d) 193 (S.C.C.).
United States v. Down (1998), 124 C.C.C. (3d) 289 (Man. Q.B.).
United States v. Smith (1984), 15 C.C.C. (3d) 16 (Ont. Co. Ct.), affirmed (1984), 16 C.C.C. (3d) 10 (Ont. H.C.).

§6.0 RELATED SECTIONS

Criminal Code, s. 599 — Change of Venue

Substitution and Amendment of Authority to Proceed (s. 23)

§1.0 DESCRIPTION

Section 23 of the *Extradition Act* provides as follows:

SUBSTITUTION OF AUTHORITY TO PROCEED
23. (1) The Minister may substitute another authority to proceed at any time before the extradition hearing begins. All documents issued and orders made by the court apply in respect of the new authority to proceed, unless the court, on application of the person or the Attorney General, orders otherwise.

NEW DATE FOR HEARING
(1.1) Where the Minister substitutes another authority to proceed under subsection (1) and the person applies for another date to be set for the beginning of the extradition hearing in order to give the person an opportunity to examine the new authority, the judge may set another date for the hearing.

AMENDMENT OF AUTHORITY TO PROCEED

(2) The judge may, on application of the Attorney General, amend the authority to proceed after the hearing has begun in accordance with the evidence that is produced during the hearing.

WITHDRAWAL OF THE AUTHORITY TO PROCEED

(3) The Minister may at any time withdraw the authority to proceed and, if the Minister does so, the court shall discharge the person and set aside any order made respecting their judicial interim release or detention.

Section 23(1) sets out the authority of the Minister of Justice to substitute a new authority to proceed prior to the commencement of the extradition hearing. When this occurs, s. 23(1.1) provides the judge with the authority, on the application of the person sought, to reschedule the extradition hearing to provide the person with the opportunity to examine the new authority to proceed.

Section 23(2) establishes that, after the extradition hearing has begun, the Attorney General may apply to the judge to have the authority to proceed amended to accord with the evidence produced at the hearing.

Section 23(3) authorizes the Minister of Justice to withdraw the authority to proceed at any time. When this occurs, the court is mandated to discharge the person sought and set aside any judicial interim release or detention order.

§2.0 COMPARISON WITH FORMER ACT

The authority to proceed has already been discussed in the commentary to s. 15 of the Act. Section 23 deals with the substitution, amendment and withdrawal of the authority to proceed. The authority to proceed was not part of the former *Extradition Act*.

§3.0 SIGNIFICANCE OF CHANGE

The discussion under s. 15 of the Act considers the effect of the introduction of the authority to proceed on extradition proceedings. The authority to proceed is the document that enables the extradition hearing to go forward and which describes the equivalent Canadian offences for which the person is sought. Section 23(1) is designed to avoid a duplication of the court processes that have occurred in a matter — such as arrest, summons, bail hearing, and the scheduling of court dates — when there is a substitution of the original authority to proceed. Other than for the correction of errors, a substitution of the authority to proceed will likely occur when different or additional offences are to be reflected in the authority to proceed as a result of a change in the offences for which extradition is sought by the extradition partner. For example, in the case of the United States, there may be superseding indictments filed in the American court containing different or additional charges resulting from continuing grand jury proceedings. Another situation may be that the person sought has fled from the requesting state during an ongoing investigation and all charges which the person is facing have not been finalized at the time the person is apprehended. This could result in an expansion of the request to reflect the newly determined charges; for instance, the person was originally sought for the offence of wounding but the subsequent death of the victim results in the substituted authority to proceed setting out a murder offence.

Under the former *Extradition Act*, changes in the offences for which the request for extradition was sought would have necessitated a recommencing of the court proceedings, in the sense that the person would have had to be rearrested under a fresh warrant. This would have necessitated a new bail hearing. It may also have required rescheduling of the hearing. The former Act, as well as most of Canada's extradition treaties, was silent about the consequences of a change in the offence for which extradition was requested. Since there were no provisions similar to s. 23 of the new Act, the practice developed of rearresting the person. The uncertainty that existed under the former Act about whether the particular proceedings had to be recommenced by the rearrest of the fugitive owing to a change in the extradition request has been eliminated by s. 23. In applying the existing orders and documents in a matter to the substituted authority to proceed, s. 23 eliminates the delay that resulted under the former Act from the need to rearrest the person and hold a new bail hearing. As with other sections of the new Act, such as s. 21(3) which mandates the judge to set an early date for the extradition hearing, s. 23 reflects the focus of the new Act upon ensuring that extradition proceedings are handled with dispatch.

§4.0 ANALYSIS

Section 23 of the *Extradition Act* continues where s. 15 of the Act leaves off. Section 15 is concerned with the power of the Minister of Justice to issue an authority to proceed. The authority to proceed is a document issued by the Minister that enables the extradition proceedings, including the extradition hearing, to move forward. In the process of issuing the authority to proceed, the Minister of Justice must ascertain and incorporate into the authority to proceed the Canadian offence(s) that correspond to the conduct alleged by the extradition partner. The substitution, amendment, and withdrawal of the authority to proceed are dealt with under s. 23 of the Act rather than s. 15. It is apparent from the structure of the Act that the sections are arranged according to the order in which procedures would be expected to unfold in the course of extradition proceedings. Section 23 is placed in the Act so as to dovetail with the provisions governing the extradition hearing because it concerns the ability to take certain actions affecting the authority to proceed either before or during the hearing.

§4.1 Substitution of Authority to Proceed Before Hearing

In most circumstances, the Minister of Justice will have the record of the case, or documents submitted in conformity with the terms of an extradition agreement, before him or her when determining whether to issue the authority to proceed. The record of the case is a compilation of documents which, pursuant to s. 32 of the Act, will be admitted as evidence at the extradition hearing. In the case of a person sought for trial, the record of the case will contain a summary of the evidence available to the extradition partner for use in the prosecution. In the case of a person sought who has already been convicted by the extradition partner and whose extradition is requested for the imposition or enforcement of a sentence, the record of the case will include reference to the conviction and conduct for which the person was convicted. The record of the case may include other relevant documents such as evidence regarding identification. A review of the record would give the Minister of Justice the opportunity to consider which Canadian offence would be constituted by the alleged conduct. However, as a result of proceedings in the requesting state, there may arise charges in addition to, or different from, those that the person sought was facing when the extradition request was made. The extradition partner may change its request to incorporate these additional or different charges. If it does so, the extradition partner may be expected to send supplementary materials to reflect the additional or different charges. As is contemplated by s. 33(5) of the Act, supplementary material can be included in the record of the case. Consequently, if supplementary material reflects additional or different offences, it would be appropriate for the Minister of Justice to substitute a new authority to proceed prior to the commencement of the extradition hearing.

The substitution may also be done in order to correct an error or oversight in the original authority to proceed. The error or oversight could be in connection with the name or description of the person sought, the name of the extradition partner, or the name of the equivalent Canadian offence(s), all of which is required under s. 15 to be included in the authority to proceed.

§4.2 Documents and Orders Continue to Apply to Substituted Authority to Proceed

Section 23(1) of the *Extradition Act* provides that "[a]ll documents issued and orders made by the court apply in respect of the new authority to proceed, unless the court, on application of the person or the Attorney General, orders otherwise." At this point in the proceedings, the documents issued and orders made by a court are likely to include the following: arrest warrant(s), summons(es), judicial interim release order(s), detention order(s), and orders dealing with the scheduling of the hearing. It is likely that the Attorney General will make an application that the existing documents and orders not apply to the new authority to proceed when the new authority sets forth a more serious offence or more numerous offences than did the original authority to proceed. This is because the Attorney General may not wish the original bail to apply to the more serious or more numerous charges. In the case of a person who was served with a summons to appear in court pursuant to the original authority to proceed, the Attorney General may be of the view that detention or release on terms is more appropriate given the charges described in the substituted authority to proceed. In such a case, the Attorney General would seek an order of the court preventing the automatic application of the existing orders or processes.

It would be expected that an application to the court in this situation would comply with the rules of the court in the particular province in which the application is brought. Depending upon the circumstances, the application may or may not be on notice to the person sought. The giving of notice might be envisaged when the person has already been granted judicial interim release but a more onerous form of release is desirable in light of the substituted authority to proceed. For example, the Attorney General may seek to have a surety bail substituted with respect to a person who has been released on his or her own recognizance. The Attorney General may be expected to bring the application *ex parte* if notifying the person would involve the risk of flight.

In the inverse situation, that is, where the substituted authority to proceed sets out less serious offences, the person sought might be expected to apply to have the previous orders and documents not apply to the substituted authority to proceed. More specifically, the person may apply to vary an existing bail to less onerous terms or, if the person has been detained, he or she may apply for a judicial interim release order.

§4.3 Application Procedures in Different Scenarios

(a) Situation 1 — Both parties are content that documents and orders continue to apply

If neither party makes an application under s. 23(1), the existing orders and documents will automatically be applied to the substituted authority to proceed. In this scenario, the Attorney General will have disclosed the substituted authority to proceed to counsel for the person sought and will have advised counsel that the Attorney General will not be seeking an order preventing the existing documents and orders from applying to the substituted authority to proceed. After counsel for the person sought has received and reviewed the substituted authority to proceed and is content that the existing documents and orders apply, counsel will communicate this position to the Attorney General and no attendance will be required in court prior to the next return date. Proceedings in court from that point forward will be governed by the substituted authority to proceed. There would be no reason to file the original authority to proceed at the hearing as it will have been superseded by the substituted authority to proceed.

(b) Situation 2 — Person sought applies for new date for hearing under s. 23(1.1) or any other relief under s. 23(1)

Section 23(1.1) allows the person sought to apply for another date to be set for the beginning of the extradition hearing in order to give the person an opportunity to examine the new authority to proceed. In this sense, s. 23(1.1) provides for an application to have one type of order covered by s. 23, namely the hearing date, not apply. After the substituted authority to proceed is disclosed by the Attorney General to counsel for the person sought and if the extradition hearing has already been scheduled, counsel will have to bring an application before the court to adjourn the hearing date if the person sought would like an opportunity to consider the effect of the substituted authority to proceed. Depending on the procedural rules of each province, such an application would necessitate the Attorney General being served with a notice of application and perhaps a supporting affidavit indicating the reasons for the request to adjourn the hearing and attaching copies of the original and substituted authorities to proceed. In the event that the substituted authority is provided shortly before the hearing date, it would be reasonable to expect that counsel for the person sought would apply for an abridgment of time for the application. On extremely short notice of a substituted authority to proceed, it may be necessary for the person sought to make the application for an adjournment on the date of the hearing itself. If an adjournment is granted to the person sought, and after having had time to consider the effect of the substituted authority to proceed, there would be nothing to preclude further applications under s. 23(1) concerning previous orders. For instance, the person sought may apply for an order that, in light of the new authority to proceed, an existing bail be varied to more lenient terms or a release order be replaced by a summons. The material required in support of such applications will be the notice of application and supporting affidavit to which will be annexed any relevant documentation. The material will explain the reasons for the order sought. The Attorney General will be served with the material.

(c) Situation 3 — Attorney General's application for existing orders not to apply

There are two procedures that may ensue when the Attorney General seeks an order that the existing documents and orders not apply to a substituted authority to proceed. The first procedure concerns *ex parte* applications. The second concerns situations in which counsel for the Attorney General will give notice of the application to counsel for the person sought.

(i) Ex parte *applications*

The substituted authority to proceed may reflect more serious or more numerous offences than the original authority to proceed. In some of these cases, the Attorney

General may have concerns of a risk of flight if the person sought is notified that the Attorney General intends to seek an order that the existing documents and orders should not apply to the substituted authority to proceed. The documents and orders which it is likely that the Attorney General would seek not to have apply are judicial interim release orders or summonses which may no longer be appropriate in light of the offences reflected in the substituted authority to proceed. Notwithstanding the more serious nature of the substituted authority to proceed, a plain reading of s. 23 indicates that the existing documents and orders automatically continue to apply to the new authority to proceed unless the court makes an order to the contrary.

In terms of the procedure that must be followed, a two-stage application process appears to be necessary. Firstly, the Attorney General applies under s. 23 with an application and a supporting affidavit attaching the original and substituted authorities to proceed and explaining the necessity for *ex parte* proceedings. The Attorney General requests an order that the existing documents and orders not apply to the person sought with respect to the offences disclosed in the substituted authority to proceed. The Attorney General must also set out the reasons in support of this position. If the Attorney General is successful at this first stage of the application and the judge grants an order preventing the existing documents and orders from applying in respect of the substituted authority to proceed, the matter of bringing the person back before the court will have to be addressed. This is because if the existing orders such as a judicial interim release order or a summons have been vacated, it will be necessary to bring the person sought back to court to consider these matters anew. As a result, the application under s. 23 will likely be joined with an application for a warrant under s. 16 of the Act for the arrest of the person sought on the new charges as disclosed in the substituted authority to proceed. Since the applications under ss. 23 and 16 are joined, the same material may be relied upon in support of each application. If the warrant for the arrest of the person sought is granted, the person will be apprehended and brought before the court and a new bail hearing will take place.

Section 23(1) does not state whether the application is to be *ex parte* or on notice. However, s. 16 provides for warrants of arrest and summonses to be obtained *ex parte*. If the Attorney General makes an application that the existing release order or summons should not apply because detention or a more stringent form of release is warranted, it follows that the s. 23 application should also be *ex parte*.

(ii) *Applications of Attorney General brought on notice*

Unless a warrant is being sought as described in the previous section, it may be expected that applications by the Attorney General under s. 23(1) will be on notice to the person sought. These applications will concern situations where, for instance, the Attorney General wishes to seek a more stringent form of release in respect of the substituted authority to proceed, yet flight risk is not an issue. The Attorney General may also apply for an adjournment of the scheduled hearing date. This may arise in situations where the substituted authority to proceed necessitates additional preparation or perhaps requires obtaining additional witnesses.

Applications under s. 23 will be served and filed according to the rules applicable in the particular province. It can be expected that the Attorney General will serve counsel for the person sought with the following: (1) an application document setting out the return date for the hearing of the application; (2) supporting material in the form of an affidavit annexing the original and substituted authorities to proceed and outlining the reasons why the new release order is being sought.

§4.4 Amendment of Authority to Proceed During Hearing (s. 23(2))

Section 23(2) establishes that the judge may, on application by the Attorney General, amend the authority to proceed after the extradition hearing has begun to accord with the evidence adduced at the hearing. There are several observations to be made about the operation of this provision:

1. The application to amend the authority to proceed can only be made by the Attorney General. The subsection does not authorize an application for amendment to be made by the person sought or by the judge on his or her own motion.

2. By providing the judge with the ability to "amend" the authority to proceed, the judge has been given a broad power to add to, or subtract from, the charges set out in the authority to proceed.

3. Any amendment regarding the offences named in the authority to proceed must be made in accordance with the evidence introduced at the extradition hearing.

4. The power to amend is in the discretion of the judge.

(a) Application for amendment to authority to proceed can only be made by Attorney General

The procedure outlined in s. 23(2) is somewhat analogous to domestic procedures outlined in the *Criminal Code*. However, unlike the domestic procedures, in the extradition context only the Attorney General can apply for the court to exercise the power to amend. The authority to proceed serves the function at the extradition hearing that an information or indictment serves in domestic proceedings. It is the equivalent to a charging document. The analogous domestic procedures are found in ss. 548 and 601(4) of the *Criminal Code*. The former permits a judge at a preliminary inquiry to commit an accused to stand trial on any offence disclosed by the evidence. The latter allows a court to amend an indictment to accord with the evidence taken at trial. Sections 548 and 601(4) do not depend upon an application by either party for the exercise of the power and the court may do so on its own initiative. However, it is generally as a result of submissions by one of the parties that a court will exercise the authority.

In contrast to the Code provisions, s. 23(2) of the *Extradition Act* provides that the judge's determination of whether the authority to proceed should be amended can only be triggered by an application from the Attorney General. Section 23(2) makes no provision for defence counsel to make a request for an amendment or for the judge to make an amendment on the court's own motion. The judge has the discretion to refuse the Attorney General's application, but amendment only becomes a matter for the consideration of the court upon the application of the Attorney General. In this respect, the Attorney General has a significant degree of control over the framework of the inquiry at the extradition hearing. In other words, the inquiry that is initially framed by the Minister of Justice via the crimes set out in the authority to proceed can only be altered upon the application of the Attorney General.

(b) By providing judge with ability to "amend" authority to proceed, judge given broad power to add to, or subtract from, charges set out in authority to proceed

Section 23(2) establishes that the judge has the power, on application by the Attorney General, to amend the authority to proceed after the extradition hearing has begun to accord with the evidence adduced at the hearing. The granting of this power to the extradition judge indicates that the extradition hearing is intended to be a flexible inquiry, measuring the evidence against the crimes defined by the Minister of Justice in the authority to proceed. This flexibility means that defence counsel will gain little by arguing that a different offence than the offence set out in the authority to proceed has been proven. Faced with this argument, counsel for the Attorney General may choose to accept defence counsel's characterization of the evidence and move to amend the authority to proceed to reflect the different offence. In this respect, the scope for technical arguments about the evidence is greatly reduced.

(c) Any amendment regarding offences named in authority to proceed must be made in accordance with evidence produced at extradition hearing

It is likely that a request by the Attorney General for an amendment to the authority to proceed will frequently come about in the course of submissions pertaining to the sufficiency of the evidence for an order of committal under s. 29 of the *Extradition Act*. By way of example, it may develop in the course of argument and in the opinion of the extradition judge that the evidence is more supportive of trafficking in a drug as opposed to importing it. In such a case, the Attorney General may choose to ask the judge to amend the authority to proceed to reflect trafficking in a drug as the comparable Canadian offence for the conduct disclosed by the evidence.

It is also possible, particularly if *viva voce* evidence is adduced, that additional offences to those set out in the authority to proceed may be revealed. In that case, too, the Attorney General may request that the new offences be added to the offences already set out by the Minister of Justice in the authority to proceed. The scope of amendment is not restricted by the terms of s. 23(2) but rather is broad and general. It appears to be open to the extradition judge, if the Attorney General so applies, to delete one offence and substitute another, or to add new offences to those already existing in the authority to proceed.

(d) Power to amend is in discretion of judge

The power to amend the authority to proceed in the course of the extradition hearing is triggered by the request of the Attorney General. However, once triggered, the power to amend remains within the discretion of the extradition judge. For that reason, if other or different offences are disclosed by the extradition partner's evidence, and this is recognized prior to the hearing, the safer course of conduct would be for the Minister of Justice to issue a substitute authority to proceed. It would not be prudent for the Attorney General to be complacent and wait to ask the judge at the hearing to amend the authority to proceed since this request might be refused. The judge may refuse the amendment if it could not be made without prejudicing the rights of the person sought. For instance, in the course of the hearing the evidence might disclose a crime unrelated to, or more serious than, the crime for which the person sought had prepared. In this case, the judge may think it unfair to amend the authority to proceed. Of course, even in those circumstances, it might be argued that any prejudice occasioned by an amendment could be cured by an adjournment of the hearing to allow the person sought to prepare to meet the request as framed in the amended authority to proceed.

It is expected that defence counsel will take issue with requests for an amendment to the authority to proceed. If defence counsel submits that the evidence disclosed does not support the offence described in the authority to proceed, and the judge agrees, a discharge will follow unless the judge accedes to a request by counsel for the Attorney General to amend the authority to proceed to accord with the evidence.

§4.5 Withdrawal of Authority to Proceed (s. 23(3))

Section 23(3) gives the Minister the discretion to withdraw the authority to proceed at any time. If this occurs, it has the effect of requiring the court to immediately discharge the person sought and to set aside any existing detention or bail orders. Such a discharge will not have the effect of preventing further proceedings from being instituted against the person sought at a subsequent time. This is because s. 4 of the new Act specifically provides for the reinstitution of proceedings unless the further proceedings would amount to an abuse of process (for further analysis of the reinstitution of proceedings, see the commentary to s. 4).

§4.6 Fair and Liberal Interpretation

Section 23 creates a large degree of flexibility in relation to the amendment of the authority to proceed. This flexibility reflects the many pronouncements of the courts to the effect that a "fair and liberal" interpretation should be given the law pertaining to extradition so as to give effect to the purpose of the legislative scheme.

§5.0 RELATED SECTIONS

s. 4 — Reinstitution of Proceedings
s. 7 — Responsibilities of Minister of Justice
s. 15 — Power of Minister to Issue Authority to Proceed
s. 16 — Warrant of Arrest or Summons
s. 29 — Order of Committal by Extradition Judge
s. 32 — Admissibility of Evidence at Extradition Hearing
s. 33 — Record of the Case

Extradition Hearing (s. 24)

§1.0 DESCRIPTION

Section 24 of the *Extradition Act* provides as follows:

EXTRADITION HEARING
24. (1) The judge shall, on receipt of an authority to proceed from the Attorney General, hold an extradition hearing.

APPLICATION OF PART XVIII OF THE *CRIMINAL CODE*
(2) For the purposes of the hearing, the judge has, subject to this Act, the powers of a justice under Part XVIII of the *Criminal Code*, with any modifications that the circumstances require.

Section 24(1) requires the judge to hold an extradition hearing upon receipt of an authority to proceed. The authority to proceed, which is the foundation of extradition proceedings, is issued by the Minister of Justice pursuant to s. 15 of the Act. A "judge" is defined in s. 2 of the Act as "a judge of the court." The term "court" is defined in s. 2 as the superior court of the province.

Section 24(2) makes Part XVIII of the *Criminal Code*, dealing with preliminary hearings, applicable to the extradition hearings.

§2.0 COMPARISON WITH FORMER ACT

Section 24 is comparable to s. 13 of the former *Extradition Act*. Section 13 directed the extradition judge to "hear the case, in the same manner, as nearly as may be, as if the fugitive was brought before a justice of the peace, charged with an indictable offence in Canada." The effect of both sections is to make the provisions of the *Criminal Code* dealing with domestic preliminary hearings applicable to extradition hearings. The former *Extradition Act* did not, however, have the same condition precedent to the holding of the extradition hearing that exists under s. 24 of the new Act. Under s. 24, prior to the holding of an extradition hearing, the authority to proceed issued by the Minister of Justice, which is a new requirement, must have been filed with the court by the Attorney General.

§3.0 SIGNIFICANCE OF CHANGE

The major change is the introduction of the authority to proceed. The receipt by the judge of the authority to proceed under s. 24(1) is a condition precedent to the commencement of an extradition hearing, otherwise the role of the extradition judge has not changed from that which was set out under s. 13 of the former Act, which was a function analogous to that performed by a justice at a preliminary hearing.

The authority to proceed is an innovative document which is now the foundation of the extradition hearing, and which performs a function analogous, but not identical, to a domestic information or indictment. Dambrot J. described the function of the authority to proceed in *United States v. Drysdale* (2000), 32 C.R. (5th) 163 (Ont. S.C.J.), at p. 180:

> [52] The "indictment" function of the authority to proceed arises from a number of provisions of the new *Act*. Section 24(1) provides that upon receipt of an authority to proceed, the judge shall hold an extradition hearing. Section 23(2) permits the judge hearing the request, upon the application of the Attorney General, to amend the authority to proceed in accordance with the evidence. Section 29(1) authorizes a judge to commit a person sought to await surrender if there is evidence of conduct which, if it had occurred in Canada, would justify committal for trial in Canada on the offence set out in the authority to proceed. Section 29(2)(b) requires that the order of committal contain the offence set out in the authority to proceed for which committal is ordered. Section 58(b) provides that if the Minister makes an order of surrender, it shall include a description of the offence for which committal was ordered, or the conduct for which the person is being surrendered. Accordingly, the committal order will have a role to play in the application of the rule of speciality. It does not require a detailed analysis of the provisions in the *Criminal Code* governing criminal pleadings to appreciate the similarity of purpose of an information or indictment on the one hand, and the authority to proceed on the other. Of course, having regard to the differences between a domestic prosecution and an extradition proceeding, these purposes cannot be identical.

§4.0 ANALYSIS

§4.1 Two-Step Process

Under the former regime, the extradition process consisted of two distinct phases, each phase having a different function. The first or judicial phase involved judicial proceedings before an extradition judge to determine if there was sufficient evidence to commit the fugitive for surrender to the requesting state. If it was found at the judicial stage that there was sufficient evidence to commit the fugitive for surrender, the process moved to the ministerial or executive stage. This stage involved the exercise of executive discretion by the Minister of Justice regarding whether the fugitive should actually be surrendered to the requesting state. As Arbour J. described it in the recent decision of *United States v. Kwok* (2001), 152 C.C.C. (3d) 225 (S.C.C.), at pp. 245-246:

> [33] The two steps of the extradition process are thus distinct and separate. The extradition judge does not have the authority to order the actual surrender of the fugitive to the foreign State; that is the exclusive responsibility of the executive pursuant to s. 25 . . . . Conversely, the Minister cannot exercise the power to surrender a fugitive until he or she has been committed for that purpose by a judge.

There was a fundamental distinction in the nature of the two phases. The decision in the first phase was clearly judicial in nature and warranted the application of the complete range of procedural rights. By contrast, the ministerial phase of the extradition process required the Minister of Justice to make a decision that was largely political in nature. The Minister was required to balance the position of the fugitive against Canada's international treaty obligations. As put by La Forest J. in *R. v. Schmidt* (1987), 33 C.C.C. (3d) 193 (S.C.C.), at p. 215, the Minister's decision involved "the good faith and honour of this country in its relations with other states."

The distinction between the judicial and the ministerial phases of the extradition process was explained by Cory J. in *Idziak v. Canada (Minister of Justice)* (1992), 77 C.C.C. (3d) 65 (S.C.C.), reconsideration refused (1992), 9 Admin. L.R. (2d) 1n (S.C.C.), at p. 86:

> It has been seen that the extradition process has two distinct phases. The first, the judicial phase, encompasses the court proceedings which determine whether a factual and legal basis for extradition exists. If that process results in the issuance of a warrant of committal, then the second phase is activated. There, the Minister of Justice exercises his or her discretion in determining whether to issue a warrant of surrender. The first decision-making phase is certainly judicial in its nature and warrants the application of the full panoply of procedural safeguards. By contrast, the second decision-making process is political in its nature. The Minister must weigh the representations of the fugitive against Canada's international treaty obligations.

Cory J. rejected any conflict in the exercise of the dual roles assigned to the Minister of Justice under the former Act, at p. 87:

> The appellant contends that a dual role has been allotted to the Minister of Justice by the *Extradition Act*. The Act requires the Minister to conduct the prosecution of the extradition hearing at the judicial phase and then to act as adjudicator in the ministerial phase. These roles are said to be mutually incompatible and to raise an apprehension of bias on their face. This contention fails to recognize either the clear division that lies between the phases of the extradition process, each of which serves a distinct function, or to take into account the separation of personnel involved in the two phases.
>
> It is correct that the Minister of Justice has the responsibility to ensure the prosecution of the extradition proceedings and that to do so the Minister must appoint agents to act in the interest of the requesting state. However, the decision to issue a warrant of surrender involves completely different considerations from those reached by a court in an extradition hearing. The extradition hearing is clearly judicial in its nature while the actions of the Minister of Justice in considering whether to issue a warrant of surrender are primarily political in nature. This is certainly not a case of a single official acting as both judge and prosecutor in the same case. At the judicial phase the fugitive possesses the full panoply of procedural protection available in a court of law. At the ministerial phase, there is no longer a *lis* in existence. The fugitive has by then been judicially committed for extradition. The Act simply grants to the Minister a discretion as to whether to execute the judicially approved extradition by issuing a warrant of surrender.
>
> It is significant that the appellant's argument has already been rejected by this court in *United States of America v. Cotroni* (1989), 48 C.C.C. (3d) 193, [1989] 1 S.C.R. 1469, 42 C.R.R. 101. At p. 226, La Forest J. noted:
>
>> . . . I find the argument that the mere fact that the executive discretion to refuse surrender and the duty to present requests for extradition in court, both fall within the responsibilities of the Minister of Justice, somehow create an unacceptable conflict to have no merit.
>
> I agree with this comment. Certainly, the arrangement could not raise apprehension of bias in a fully informed observer. The appellant's allegation of institutional bias must fail.

More recently, Dambrot J. applied the reasoning of *Idziak v. Canada (Minister of Justice)* to *habeas corpus* proceedings in the case of *Pacificador v. Canada (Minister of Justice)* (1999), 60 C.R.R. (2d) 126 (Ont. Gen. Div.), at pp. 149–151. Based on this reasoning, he held that departmental staff can assist the Minister in performing both roles without creating an apprehension of bias.

That the new Act gives the Minister the responsibility to issue an authority to proceed which is the foundation of extradition proceedings in the courts does not change the essential nature of the two-step process. What the new Act does do is legislate the procedure to be followed in initiating the extradition proceedings. As explained above, the former Act did not explicitly give a review or coordinating role to the Minister with respect to the receipt of requests and the initiation of proceedings, even though this role was in practice performed through the Minister's counsel in the International Assistance Group (IAG). Section 15 makes this responsibility explicit.

§4.2 Modest Role of Extradition Judge

The Supreme Court of Canada has repeatedly indicated that the role of the extradition judge is a modest one and that attempts to expand the function of the extradition hearing or to undertake investigations in court that are not strictly assigned to the extradition judge are to be avoided.

In *Argentina (Republic) v. Mellino* (1987), 33 C.C.C. (3d) 334 (S.C.C.), at p. 349, the court made the following statement about the narrow role of the extradition judge:

> [T]the role of the extradition judge is a modest one; absent express statutory or treaty authorization, the sole purpose of an extradition hearing is to ensure that the evidence establishes a *prima facie* case that the extradition crime has been committed.

This statement was reiterated by the Supreme Court in *United States v. McVey* (1992), 77 C.C.C. (3d) 1 (S.C.C.); *United States v. Lépine* (1993), 163 N.R. 1 (S.C.C.); and *United States v. Dynar* (1997), 115 C.C.C. (3d) 481 (S.C.C.).

In *United States v. Dynar, supra,* at pp. 524–525, the court described the statutory powers of an extradition judge as being "limited." Cory and Iacobucci JJ. were clear that the simple function of the extradition hearing should not be complicated by considerations extraneous to the functions assigned by the legislation:

> [131] Procedures at the extradition hearing are of necessity less complex and extensive than those in domestic preliminary inquiries or trials. Earlier decisions have wisely avoided imposing procedural requirements on the committal hearing that would render it very difficult for Canada to honour its international obligations. Thus, in *Mellino, supra,* at p. 548, reservations were expressed about procedures that would permit an extradition hearing to become the forum for lengthy examinations of the reasons for delay in either seeking or undertaking extradition proceedings. La Forest J., for the majority, held that this would be "wholly out of keeping with extradition proceedings".
>
> [132] The statutory powers of an extradition judge are limited. The hearing judge may receive sworn evidence offered to show the truth of the charge or conviction (s. 14), receive evidence to show that the particular crime is not an extradition crime (s. 15), and take into account sworn, duly authenticated depositions or statements taken in a foreign state (s.16). The obligation on the Requesting State is simply to establish a *prima facie* case for the surrender of the fugitive and it is not required to go further than this. The committal hearing is neither intended nor designed to provide the discovery function of a domestic preliminary inquiry. See *Philippines (Republic of) v. Pacificador* (1993), 14 O.R. (3d) 321 (C.A.), at pp. 328-39, 83 C.C.C. (3d) 210, leave to appeal refused, [1994] 1 S.C.R. x, 87 C.C.C. (3d) vi. Specifically, disclosure of the relationship between United States and Canadian authorities in an investigation is not a requirement imposed on the Requesting State under either the Act or the treaty.

§4.3 Purpose of Extradition Hearing

Section 24(2) of the new *Extradition Act* clearly provides that an extradition judge has the same powers at an extradition hearing that the judge had under s. 13 of the former Act. More specifically, under both sections, the judge has the same powers as a justice under Part XVIII of the *Criminal Code* presiding at a preliminary hearing. However, although an extradition hearing is analogous to a preliminary inquiry, in many respects it is not a mirror image. This is due to the different purposes of the two proceedings. The extradition hearing, unlike a preliminary inquiry, is not a hearing that precedes a person's trial in this country. The innocence or guilt of the person sought will be determined in the requesting state and not in Canada.

The purpose of the extradition hearing is to establish that there is sufficient evidence that the alleged conduct of the person sought, if committed in Canada, would constitute a crime. This is a significant component of the process as Canada will not extradite an individual for conduct that would not constitute a crime in Canada. In La Forest J.'s words in *R. v. Schmidt* (1987), 33 C.C.C. (3d) 193 (S.C.C.), at p. 209:

> The hearing thus protects the individual in this country from being surrendered for trial for a crime in a foreign country unless *prima facie* evidence is produced that he or she has done something there that would constitute a crime mentioned in the treaty if committed here. It must be emphasized that this hearing is not a trial and no attempt should be made to make it one. The trial, when held, will be in the foreign country according to its laws for an alleged crime committed there, and it should require no demonstration that such a prosecution is wholly within the competence of that country. A judge at an extradition hearing has no jurisdiction to deal with defences that could be raised at trial unless, of course, the Act or the treaty otherwise provides.

Although analogous to a domestic preliminary inquiry, the distinctions of an extradition hearing were pointed out by Doherty J.A. in *Philippines (Republic of) v. Pacificador* (1993), 83 C.C.C. (3d) 210 (Ont. C.A.), leave to appeal to S.C.C. refused (1994), 87 C.C.C. (3d) vi (S.C.C.). He noted that the counterpart to s. 24 in the former Act (s. 13) was directed to procedure and did not equate the purpose of the extradition hearing with the purpose of a domestic preliminary inquiry. He observed at p. 218:

> The preliminary inquiry serves a discovery purpose in our domestic criminal law. This purpose dictates that the evidentiary scope of the hearing be expanded beyond evidence needed to establish a *prima facie* case to evidence which may assist the accused in making full answer and defence at trial. Extradition is a creature of statute. The purpose underlying the judicial phase of the extradition process must be found in the Act. The sole purpose, as set out in s. 18(1)(*b*) of the Act, is to determine whether the evidence adduced establishes a *prima facie* case against the fugitive: *McVey v. United States of America* (1992), 77 C.C.C. (3d) 1 at p. 20, 97 D.L.R. (4th) 193, [1992] 3 S.C.R. 475. Nothing in the statute speaks to a discovery function akin to that played by the preliminary inquiry.

Nor can that function be read into the Act. The extradition court cannot be concerned with the ultimate merits of the charge or the fairness of the adjudicative process to which the fugitive will be subject in the foreign court: *United States of America v. Allard* (1987), 33 C.C.C. (3d) 501 at p. 507, 40 D.L.R. (4th) 102, [1987] 1 S.C.R. 564. Equally, the extradition court cannot oversee a discovery process relating to some potential future proceeding in a foreign country when that proceeding will be conducted according to foreign laws and possibly to different notions of concepts such as "full answer and defence". The extradition judge could not possibly determine whether certain evidence offered at the extradition hearing is relevant to a fugitive's right to make full answer and defence at some subsequent proceeding, when the extradition judge has no knowledge of what full answer and defence means in the context of the foreign proceeding, and no knowledge of the legal matrix in which the ultimate adjudication of the merits of the charge would occur? The extradition judge could no more decide these issues than he or she could decide the merits of the allegation.

In *Germany (Federal Republic) v. Schreiber* (July 6, 2000), [2000] O.J. No. 2618 (Ont. S.C.J.), Watt J. referred to s. 24(2) of the new Act as reinforcement for the principle that the role of the extradition judge is a modest one. In *Schreiber*, Watt J. declined to order certain disclosure that had been requested on the basis that he had no jurisdiction to hear the applications with respect to which the disclosure was said to be relevant. He also held that having been assigned by the Act an authority analogous to that of a preliminary inquiry justice, he had no jurisdiction to order disclosure. He stated:

[84] A further observation about disclosure is in order. Section 24(2) of the Act assimilates the powers of the extradition hearing judge to those of a justice conducting a preliminary inquiry in domestic proceedings under Part XVIII of the *Criminal Code*. It is settled law, in this province at least, that a justice at preliminary inquiry has *no* authority to review Crown disclosure decisions, including the extent and timing of this disclosure. See, for example, *R. v. Girimonte* (1997), 121 C.C.C. (3d) 33, 44-5 (Ont. C.A.), per Doherty J.A.

[85] No useful purpose would be served by a further parade of the governing authorities. They yield a common result. An extradition hearing judge has a modest function to perform. The boundaries are marked out by the enabling statute and applicable treaty. Neither grants to the judge the authority she or he has over prosecutorial disclosure decisions in domestic trial proceedings. The incorporation by s. 24(2) of the Act of the powers of a justice at a preliminary inquiry does *not* advance the case for disclosure. Nor does the enactment of s. 25. The *Charter* jurisdiction that it confers is firmly tethered to the functions that the superior court judge is empowered to perform under the Act.

The nature and purpose of the extradition hearing has not changed under the new Act and the principles developed in the cases under the former Act are still applicable.

§5.0 CASE LAW

Argentina (Republic) v. Mellino (1987), 33 C.C.C. (3d) 334 (S.C.C.).
Germany (Federal Republic) v. Schreiber (July 6, 2000), [2000] O.J. No. 2618, Watt J. (Ont.S.C.J.).
Idziak v. Canada (Minister of Justice) (1992), 77 C.C.C. (3d) 65 (S.C.C.), reconsideration refused (1992), 9 Admin. L.R. (2d) 1n (S.C.C.).
Pacificador v. Canada (Minister of Justice) (1999), 60 C.R.R. (2d) 126 (Ont. Gen. Div.).
Philippines (Republic) v. Pacificador (1993), 83 C.C.C. (3d) 210 (Ont. C.A.), leave to appeal to S.C.C. refused (1994), 87 C.C.C. (3d) vi (S.C.C.).
R. v. Schmidt (1987), 33 C.C.C. (3d) 193 (S.C.C.).
United States v. Drysdale (2000), 32 C.R. (5th) 163 (Ont. S.C.J.).
United States v. Dynar (1997), 115 C.C.C. (3d) 481 (S.C.C.).
United States v. Kwok (2001), 152 C.C.C. (3d) 225 (S.C.C.).
United States v. Lépine (1993), 163 N.R. 1 (S.C.C.).
United States v. McVey (1992), 77 C.C.C. (3d) 1 (S.C.C.).

§6.0 RELATED SECTIONS

s. 7 — Responsibilities of Minister of Justice
s. 15(1) — Minister's Power to Issue Authority to Proceed
s. 15(4) — Copy of Authority to Proceed
s. 25 — Charter Jurisdiction of Extradition Judges
s. 26 — Orders Restricting Publication of Evidence
s. 27 — Exclusion of Person From Hearing
s. 28 — Power to Compel Witnesses
s. 29 — Order of Committal
s. 30 — Authority to Keep Person Sought in Custody Following Order of Committal and Duration of Order
ss. 31–37 — Rules of Evidence
ss. 40–48 — Powers of Minister
Criminal Code, Part XVIII — Procedure on Preliminary Inquiry

Charter Jurisdiction of Extradition Judges (s. 25)

§1.0 DESCRIPTION

Section 25 of the *Extradition Act* provides as follows:

COMPETENCE
25. For the purposes of the *Constitution Act, 1982*, a judge has, with respect to the functions that the judge is required to perform in applying this Act, the same competence that that judge possesses by virtue of being a superior court judge.

§2.0 COMPARISON WITH FORMER ACT

The comparable provision under the former *Extradition Act* was s. 9(3), which read as follows:

9. (3) For the purposes of the *Constitution Act, 1982*, a judge who is a superior court judge or a county court judge has, with respect to the functions that that judge is required to perform in applying this Act, the same competence that that judge possesses by virtue of being a superior court judge or a county court judge.

Section 25 of the new *Extradition Act* is identical to s. 9(3) of the former Act (see *United States v. Kwok* (2001), 152 C.C.C. (3d) 225 (S.C.C.), p. 242, para. 24, per Arbour J.). Section 25 does not specify that the judge is a superior or county court judge. This is unnecessary in the new Act because "judge" is defined in s. 2 of the Act as a "judge of the court" and "court" is defined under s. 2 as the superior court of the particular province.

Section 9(3) was a relatively recent addition to the former Act. It was added by amendment to the Act in 1992 (*An Act to Amend the Extradition Act*, S.C. 1992, c. 13, s. 3). Prior to the addition of s. 9(3), the Act made no provision for the exercise of *Charter* jurisdiction by an extradition judge. *Charter* relief could be obtained, however, by a *habeas corpus* review of the committal decision of the extradition judge. This was confirmed by the Supreme Court of Canada in *Argentina (Republic) v. Mellino* (1987), 33 C.C.C. (3d) 334. Most recently the Supreme Court of Canada in *United States v. Kwok* (2001), 152 C.C.C. (3d) 225 (S.C.C.), described the regime prior to the 1992 amendments as follows, at pp. 246-247:

[35] Prior to the 1992 amendments, review of the committal decision was provided for in s. 19(*a*) of the *Extradition Act*, R.S.C. 1970, c. E-21, which provided that the

fugitive who had been ordered committed for surrender had a right to apply for a writ of *habeas corpus*. In the same way, *Charter* jurisdiction lay not with the extradition judge but with the superior court judge sitting on *habeas corpus* review of the extradition judge's decision to commit: *Mellino, supra*, at p. 557. The *habeas corpus* judge was required to determine whether the extradition judge had jurisdiction to commit the fugitive. In determining the legality of the fugitive's detention and/or committal, the *habeas corpus* judge had jurisdiction to grant remedies under s. 24 of the *Charter: ibid.* In that decision, this Court determined that the extradition judge had no jurisdiction to determine whether there had been an unreasonable delay in requesting extradition, such as to constitute a violation of ss. 7 and 11 of the *Charter*. That competence belonged to the *habeas corpus* judge.

[36] In turn, this power of review by way of *habeas corpus* could not be used to pre-empt the ministerial decision whether to surrender, a subsequent stage of the extradition process. La Forest J. recognized in *Mellino, supra*, at p. 558, that there did exist, even at the *habeas corpus* stage, an exceptional power, under s. 7 of the *Charter*, to stay extradition proceedings in circumstances where "the decision to surrender a fugitive for trial in a foreign country would in the particular circumstances violate the principles of fundamental justice". La Forest J. went on to say:

> . . . a court must firmly keep in mind that it is in the executive that the discretion to surrender a fugitive is vested. Consequently, barring obvious or urgent circumstances, the executive should not be pre-empted. In cases where the feared wrong may be avoided by interstate arrangements, it may be doubted that the courts should ordinarily intervene before the executive has made an order of surrender.

Thus, barring obvious or urgent circumstances, a decision to stay the extradition process was only open to a judge of the Trial Division of the Federal Court, sitting in review of the Minister's decision to surrender the fugitive (*Federal Court Act*, R.S.C. 1970, c. 10 (2nd Supp.), s. 17(4)(*b*)). The need to await the exercise of executive discretion was stressed again in *Schmidt, supra*, at p. 522, *per* La Forest J.

[37] Hence, even within the broad *habeas corpus* jurisdiction as it existed prior to the 1992 amendments, both the committal proceedings, and judicial review of these proceedings, were curtailed by the existence of the second, executive stage of the extradition process, which had to be allowed to follow its course. This dual track of judicial and executive decision-making, each accompanied by its own review process, was cumbersome and time-consuming. On the one hand, an appeal from the *habeas corpus* review of the committal decision could be taken as of right to the provincial court of appeal and, with subsequent leave, to this Court. On the other hand, the separate Ministerial decision concerning surrender could be judicially reviewed in the Trial Division of the Federal Court, with further potential appeals to the Federal Court of Appeal and to this Court: A.W. La Forest, *La Forest's Extradition To and From Canada* (3rd ed., 1991), at pp. 179-220.

The Supreme Court of Canada recognized in *Kwok, supra*, that the addition of s. 9(3) had the effect of collapsing into one the jurisdictions which previously had been separately exercised by the extradition judge and by the *habeas corpus* judge. Since

s. 25 of the new Act is identical to s. 9(3) of the former Act, this merged jurisdiction is the jurisdiction exercised by an extradition judge pursuant to the current Act.

§3.0 SIGNIFICANCE OF CHANGE

There is no change from the former *Extradition Act* (as amended in 1992) with respect to the forum for *Charter* relief during the judicial phase of extradition proceedings. The new *Extradition Act* maintains the structure of the former Act with respect to the routes of appeal and the exercise of *Charter* jurisdiction, and the philosophy underpinning the Act in this respect remains the same. The Minister of Justice in 1992, Kim Campbell, made the following comments about the 1992 amendments to the *Extradition Act* (*Hansard*, November 7, 1991, at pp. 4777–4778):

> In developing a more streamlined appeal and review system, I have been guided by the following principles. First, the appeal and review process of extradition matters should resemble as nearly as possible the remedies available to those charged with criminal offences in Canada. Second, the person whose extradition is sought should enjoy the protections of the *Canadian Charter of Rights and Freedoms*. Third, to the extent possible, duplication of proceedings should be avoided.
>
> . . .
>
> Nevertheless, the extradition judge can now know the recourse under the *Canadian Charter of Rights and Freedoms* that may apply to the duties he is required to perform in applying this law.

Arbour J. in *Kwok, supra*, in discussing the legislative intent underlying the 1992 amendments, made reference to the above comments of the then Minister of Justice.

§4.0 ANALYSIS

§4.1 *Charter* Arguments at Judicial Phase

Prior to the 1992 amendments to the former *Extradition Act*, *Charter* issues could not be raised at the extradition hearing, even in cases in which the *Charter* did apply in the extradition context. The extradition court was not a "court of competent jurisdiction" for the purposes of s. 24 of the *Charter*. The fugitive could, however, bring a *habeas corpus* application to review an extradition judge's committal order. In *Argentina (Republic) v. Mellino, supra*, La Forest J. found that the court in *habeas corpus* proceedings was a "court of competent jurisdiction" within the meaning of s. 24 of the *Charter*. However, the court's *Charter* jurisdiction only extended to the actions of Canadian officials in extradition proceedings, and not to those of officials of foreign states. Moreover, La Forest J. held that the need for *Charter* review of the actions of Canadian officials would only be present in "the rarest of cases." He stated, at p. 352:

> In the rare cases where the actions of Canadian executives or officials may give rise to the need for Charter review, I do not think the extradition judge has Charter jurisdiction. For reasons of efficiency, the Act and the treaty have strictly confined his role. Parliament has indicated how extradition proceedings are to be reviewed — by superior courts by means of the writ of *habeas corpus*. A court in *habeas corpus* proceedings is ordinarily confined to questions of jurisdiction, but as such proceedings are contemplated by Parliament as the sole means of review in extradition proceedings, and from which, moreover, it has provided appeals to the Court of Appeal and to this court, a court in *habeas corpus* proceedings is obviously a court of competent jurisdiction for the purposes of s. 24 of the Charter.

More generally, La Forest J. in *Argentina (Republic) v. Mellino* concluded that the reasoning of the Supreme Court of Canada in *R. v. Mills* (1986), 26 C.C.C. (3d) 481, regarding the lack of jurisdiction of preliminary hearing judges to grant *Charter* remedies, was even more applicable in the extradition context, at pp. 349–350:

> I repeat: the role of the extradition judge is a modest one; absent express statutory or treaty authorization, the sole purpose of an extradition hearing is to ensure that the evidence establishes a *prima facie* case that the extradition crime has been committed. The procedure bears a considerable affinity to a preliminary hearing, and the judge's powers have some similarity to those of a magistrate presiding at such a hearing, who, as this court held in *Mills v. The Queen* (1986), 26 C.C.C. (3d) 481, 29 D.L.R. (4th) 161, [1986] 1 S.C.R. 863, has no power to administer Charter remedies. Indeed, the reasoning in *Mills* appears to me to be even more applicable to an extradition judge.

Section 9(3) was added to the former *Extradition Act* in 1992 (*An Act to Amend the Extradition Act*, S.C. 1992, c. 13, s. 3). Section 9(3) read as follows:

> **9.** (3) For the purposes of the *Constitution Act, 1982*, a judge who is a superior court judge or a county court judge has, with respect to the functions that that judge is required to perform in applying this Act, the same competence that that judge possesses by virtue of being a superior court judge or a county court judge.

The intention of the amendment, evidenced in the wording of s. 9(3), was that the extradition judge was to be "a court of competent jurisdiction" for the purposes of granting *Charter* relief. The specific parameters of this jurisdiction were the subject of consideration in the post-amendment jurisprudence. More specifically, two competing interpretations emerged: the first held that s. 9(3) only conferred upon extradition judges jurisdiction to grant *Charter* relief in respect of the duties the judges were required to perform under the *Extradition Act*; the second was that extradition judges had a general *Charter* jurisdiction. The implication of the second interpretation was that extradition judges had jurisdiction to grant *Charter* relief in areas over which the *Extradition Act* conferred jurisdiction upon the Minister of Justice.

The first, and narrower, interpretation of s. 9(3) was favoured in the cases of *United States v. Leon* (April 7, 1994), Hayes J. (Ont. Gen. Div.), affirmed without ruling on the s. 9(3) issue (1995), 96 C.C.C. (3d) 568 (Ont. C.A.), affirmed (1996), 105 C.C.C. (3d) 385 (S.C.C.); *United States v. Garcia* (May 11, 1994), Doc. E16/92, [1994] O.J. No. 1027, Jarvis J. (Ont. Gen. Div.), affirmed (July 18, 1996), Doc. CA C21023 (Ont. C.A.), leave to appeal to S.C.C. refused (1997), 102 O.A.C. 318 (note) (S.C.C.); *United States v. Singh* (October 14, 1994), Doc. E-21, Ewaschuk J. [1994] O.J. No. 3941 (Ont. Gen. Div.); *United States v. Palmer* (January 23, 1996), Doc. E-20/94, Wein J. (Ont. Gen. Div.), appeal dismissed [1997] O.J. No. 608 (Ont. C.A.); *Re D'Agostino* (1997), (*sub nom. United States v. D'Agostino*) 41 C.R.R. (2d) 325 (Ont. Gen. Div.) (*per* Wilson J.); *Hong Kong v. Ma* (December 12, 1997), Ewaschuk J. (Ont. Gen. Div.); *United States v. Shulman* (September 13, 1995), Lyon J., [1995] O.J. No. 4497 (Ont. Gen. Div.), affirmed (1998), 128 C.C.C. (3d) 475 (Ont. C.A.) (*per* Carthy, Doherty and Charron JJ.A.) [reversed (2001), 152 C.C.C. (3d) 294 (S.C.C.), reconsideration refused (June 14, 2001), Docs. 26912, 27610, 27774 (S.C.C.)]; *United States v. Turenne* (1998), 133 Man. R. (2d) 131 (Q.B.) (*per* Steel J.); *Thailand (Kingdom) v. Saxena* (April 29, 1999), Doc. Vancouver CC960599, Maczko J., 1999 CarswellBC 922 (B.C. S.C.) and *Thailand (Kingdom) v. Saxena* (June 10, 1999), Doc. Vancouver CC960599, [1999] B.C.J. No. 1364 (B.C. S.C.) (*per* Maczko J.); *United States v. Cheema* (1999), 65 C.R.R. (2d) 234 (B.C.S.C.) (*per* Bennett J.), leave to appeal to S.C.C. refused (2001), 271 N.R. 193 (note) (S.C.C.).

The second and more expansive interpretation to s. 9(3) was favoured in the cases of *United States v. Tilley* (1996), 183 A.R. 158 (Q.B.), *United States v. Tilley* (1996), 183 A.R. 1 (Q.B.) (*per* Veit J.); *United States v. Kerslake* (1996), 142 Sask. R. 112 (Q.B.) (*per* Baynton J.).

The leading decision proposing an expansive jurisdiction for the extradition judge in *Charter* matters under s. 9(3) was the decision of the Quebec Court of Appeal in *United States v. Cazzetta* (1996), 108 C.C.C. (3d) 536, leave to appeal to S.C.C. refused (1996), 110 C.C.C. (3d) vi (S.C.C.). In that case, Chamberland J.A. held that a fugitive could bring a *Charter* challenge under ss. 6 and 7 at the extradition hearing based on allegations that a *Charter* breach would occur if the Minister were to ultimately order his or her surrender. Cazzetta alleged that he had been the target of a reverse sting drug operation (offering to sell drugs to a willing buyer), jointly conceived by American and Canadian law enforcement authorities, in which it was a condition of the operation that overt acts be committed in the United States as well as Canada for the sole purpose of ensuring that the buyers could be extradited to face the higher penalties in the United States. Chamberland J.A. held, at p. 546, that it was not necessary to await the Minister's decision on surrender before the challenge could be litigated:

> Section 9(3) of the Act gives a superior court judge or a county court judge presiding over an extradition hearing jurisdiction to hear the relevant evidence and determine a *Charter*-based challenge from the perspective of both section 24 and section 52. The extradition judge is now competent, therefore, to declare a principle of law incompatible

with the *Constitution Act, 1982* (section 52); he is also a court of competent jurisdiction to register a breach or denial of a *Charter* right and to grant an appropriate remedy (section 24(1)) or exclude evidence obtained, in such conditions (section 24(2)).

Chamberland J.A. added, at p. 552:

> He may, of course, put his submissions to the Minister of Justice, who is "duty bound to act in accordance with the dictates of the *Charter*" (*Operation Dismantle Inc.* v. *The Queen*, [1985] 1 S.C.R. 441 at p. 455, 18 D.L.R. (4th) 481 (S.C.C.), *per* Dickson J.), and there is no reason to assume that the Minister will overlook his "duty to obey constitutional norms by surrendering an individual to a foreign country under circumstances where doing so would be fundamentally unjust" (*Schmidt, supra, per* La Forest J., at page 552). However, where, as in the case at bar, the fugitive elects to present the extradition judge with a *Charter* challenge, the judge must exercise the jurisdiction now granted him by section 9(3) of the Act; he has jurisdiction over the parties, the subject-matter and the remedy sought (the three-pronged test proposed by Lamer J. (as he then was) in *Mills v. The Queen, supra*, and confirmed by a number of subsequent decisions of the Supreme Court of Canada, including the recent judgment in *Mooring* v. *Canada (National Parole Board)*, Court File No. 24436, February 8, 1996) [now reported 104 C.C.C. (3d) 97 (S.C.C.)].

The decision in *Cazzetta, supra*, was not followed in Ontario. (See *Re D'Agostino, supra* (*per* Wilson J.).) The Ontario Court of Appeal in *United States v. Kwok* (1998), 127 C.C.C. (3d) 353, came to the conclusion that *Cazzetta* had been wrongly decided. In that case, Kwok had been sought by the United States for his alleged involvement in a conspiracy to distribute, possess with intent to distribute, and import heroin into the United States. The evidence alleged that Kwok and the co-conspirators conducted these activities from within Canada. The evidence was comprised of communications intercepted by both the American and the Canadian authorities. Kwok sought additional disclosure before the extradition judge and again before the Minister of Justice. He claimed that the disclosure was relevant to his right to remain in Canada as guaranteed by s. 6(1) of the *Charter*. The s. 6 *Charter* argument alleging that extradition violates the fugitive's right to remain in Canada is referred to as the "*Cotroni* issue" because it was dealt with by the Supreme Court of Canada in *United States v. Cotroni* (*sub nom. Cotroni c. Centre de Prévention de Montréal*) (1989), 48 C.C.C. (3d) 193. The *Cotroni* issue involves the determination of whether domestic prosecution should be preferred to extradition when both states have jurisdiction to prosecute. The extradition judge and the Minister of Justice refused his request. Kwok appealed both the committal order of the extradition judge and the surrender order of the Minister of Justice. Only the appeal from the decision of the extradition judge is relevant to the present discussion concerning the scope of the jurisdiction conferred by s. 9(3).

Kwok argued that the extradition judge had erred in holding that any potential s. 6(1) *Charter* application was "either premature or beyond the purview of the extradition hearing." (p. 360) Kwok submitted that s. 9(3) of the Act did confer jurisdiction on the extradition judge and that the extradition hearing was the appropriate forum for determining all issues arising out of the extradition process. In support of this contention, he relied on the decision of the Quebec Court of Appeal in *United States v. Cazzetta, supra.*

Charron J.A., writing for the Ontario Court of Appeal, was of the opinion that *United States v. Cazzetta*, had been wrongly decided. In coming to this conclusion she was heavily influenced by the decision of the Supreme Court of Canada in *United States v. Dynar* (1997), 115 C.C.C. (3d) 481 (S.C.C.). *United States v. Dynar* was decided after the release of *United States v. Cazzetta.* Charron J.A. made the following comment, at pp. 362-363:

> [20] . . . With the greatest of respect, I believe *Cazzetta* was wrongly decided. The Supreme Court of Canada decision in *Dynar*, which was decided after *Cazzetta*, is instructive on this issue. While the Court in *Dynar* did not find it necessary to define the scope of the *Charter* jurisdiction conferred upon the extradition judge by s. 9(3), it is clear from the reasons in the majority judgment that the pre-amendment cases on the modest role of the judiciary in the extradition process are still applicable. Whatever *Charter* jurisdiction is conferred upon the extradition judge by s. 9(3) must be read in the light of this limited role.

Since s. 6(1) mobility rights are not engaged at the committal stage of extradition proceedings but only in the Minister's decision to surrender, the Court of Appeal concluded that there was no justiciable *Charter* issue raised at the extradition hearing.

On appeal to the Supreme Court of Canada, in *United States v. Kwok* (2001), 152 C.C.C. (3d) 225 (S.C.C.), the decision of the Ontario Court of Appeal was upheld, and the decision of the Quebec Court of Appeal in *Cazzetta* disapproved. Writing for the court, Arbour J. reviewed the competing lines of authority with respect to the scope of *Charter* jurisdiction conferred by s. 9(3) and concluded that the narrow approach was correct. She stated, at pp. 254-255:

> [54] In my view, the 1992 amendments did not confer unlimited *Charter* jurisdiction on the extradition judge and therefore do not render obsolete all previous extradition case law. Section 9(3) clearly confers *Charter* jurisdiction upon the extradition judge insofar as the issues are specific to the functions of the extradition hearing, and to the extent that the *Charter* remedies could have previously been granted by the *habeas corpus* judge. This is consistent with this Court's decision in *Dynar, supra*, which confirmed that the limited role of the extradition judge had not been substantially modified by the 1992 amendments. The added jurisdiction conferred upon the extradition judge must be understood in light of this governing principle. Through s. 9(3), the extradition judge acquired the jurisdiction formerly reserved to the *habeas corpus* judge, and nothing else.
>
> . . .
>
> [57] Given the legislative intent behind the 1992 amendments, the interpretation of s. 9(3) in the full context of the Act, in accordance with the principle of statutory construction endorsed by this Court in *Rizzo & Rizzo Shoes Ltd. (Re)*, [1998] 1 S.C.R.

27, 154 D.L.R. (4th) 193, and the still relevant pre-existing case law, I conclude that the amendments were not meant to alter the fundamental two-tiered structure of the Act. While s. 9(3) eliminates the *habeas corpus* stage, both the extradition judge and the Minister maintain their separate functions and jurisdictions within the process. Section 9(3) of the *Extradition Act* does not confer an expanded *Charter* jurisdiction upon the extradition judge. It simply permits the extradition judge to exercise the jurisdiction previously reserved for the *habeas corpus* judge, which includes remedies for the *Charter* breaches that pertain directly to the circumscribed issues relevant at the committal stage of the extradition process, and otherwise leaves the powers and functions of the committal court substantially unchanged.

The *Charter* jurisdiction of the extradition judge was further developed in the cases of *United States v. Cobb* (2001), 152 C.C.C. (3d) 270 (S.C.C.), reconsideration refused (June 14, 2001), Docs. 26912, 27610, 27774 (S.C.C.), *United States v. Tsioubris* (2001), 152 C.C.C. (3d) 292 (S.C.C.), reconsideration refused (June 14, 2001), Docs. 26912, 27610, 27774 (S.C.C.), and *United States v. Shulman* (2001), 152 C.C.C. (3d) 294 (S.C.C.), reconsideration refused (June 14, 2001), Docs. 26912, 27610, 27774 (S.C.C.), which were released at the same time as the decision in *Kwok*.

Cobb, Grossman, Tsioubris, and Shulman were among a number of individuals accused of wire and mail fraud in Pennsylvania. Prior to the extradition hearing in the case of Cobb and Tsioubris, but after Shulman had already been committed, it was learned that the judge assigned to the case in Pennsylvania had, during the sentencing of another accused, stated that those accused who fought extradition rather than cooperating would, if returned, receive the maximum sentence the law would allow. In addition, the Assistant U.S. Attorney on the case and whose affidavit had been submitted in the extradition materials, gave an interview to the Canadian television programme "The Fifth Estate" in which he stated that the individuals in Canada contesting extradition could, if returned to the United States, find themselves in jail as the "boyfriend of a very bad man."

Cobb, Grossman, and Tsioubris brought a motion before Hawkins J. of the Ontario Court (General Division), seeking relief under s. 24 of the *Charter* and s. 52 of the *Constitution Act* alleging that their *Charter* rights would be violated if they were extradited to the United States. They claimed that they would face cruel and unusual treatment in the state of Pennsylvania.

Hawkins J. ((1997), 11 C.R. (5th) 310) held that s. 9(3) of the *Extradition Act* provided him with jurisdiction to entertain the application. He held that the public statements made by the Pennsylvania judge and Assistant U.S. Attorney constituted a s. 7 *Charter* violation. He ruled that the statements made by these officials satisfied the test enunciated by the Supreme Court of Canada in *Kindler v. Canada (Minister of Justice)* (1991), 67 C.C.C. (3d) 1 (S.C.C.), that is, they "[shock] the Canadian conscience" and were "simply not acceptable." (p. 317) On this basis, Hawkins J. stayed the proceedings.

On appeal ((1999), 139 C.C.C. (3d) 283), Brooke J.A. for the Ontario Court of Appeal held that the stay should not have been entered. In the opinion of the Court of Appeal, the situation the fugitives might face in the foreign court was a matter for the Minister and not within the *Charter* competence of the extradition judge under s. 9(3).

The Supreme Court of Canada on appeal upheld the decision of the extradition judge and reimposed the stay of proceedings (*United States v. Cobb* (2001), 152 C.C.C. (3d) 270 (S.C.C.)). In the opinion of the court, the issue was not possible treatment of the fugitives in the U.S. court but rather whether their extradition hearing could be fair in the circumstances. In the opinion of Arbour J., s. 7 of the *Charter* as well as the common law gave the extradition judge the authority to control the integrity and fairness of the proceedings before him. As in *Kwok*, the court confirmed the limited role of the extradition judge and the necessity for *Charter* issues to relate to the initial phase of the extradition process in order to be justiciable before an extradition judge. However, the court held that this was such a case. Arbour J. stated, at pp. 285-286:

> [35] The Requesting State is a party to judicial proceedings before a Canadian court and is subject to the application of rules and remedies that serve to control the conduct of parties who turn to the courts for assistance. Even aside from any claim of *Charter* protection, litigants are protected from unfair, abusive proceedings through the doctrine of abuse of process, which bars litigants — and not only the State — from pursuing frivolous or vexatious proceedings, or otherwise abusing the process of the courts.
>
> . . .
>
> [39] This Court's observation in *Mellino, supra*, that a superior court judge sitting in extradition proceedings has no inherent jurisdiction to stay proceedings based on the common law doctrine of abuse of process must now be interpreted in light of the 1992 amendments to the *Extradition Act*. When *Mellino* was decided, the extradition judge had a narrow role to play and was subject to the supervisory authority of the superior court exercising *habeas corpus* jurisdiction. The jurisdiction to protect against abuse of process rested with the *habeas corpus* judge, as the extradition judge had no inherent jurisdiction either at common law or under the *Charter*: see *Mills v. The Queen*, [1986] 1 S.C.R. 863, 26 C.C.C. (3d) 481, 29 D.L.R. (4th) 161. The consolidation of the *habeas corpus* jurisdiction with that of the committal judge, confirmed in *Kwok, supra*, now vests the authority to apply the doctrine of abuse of process in the committal court.
>
> [40] The decision of Hawkins J. granting a stay of proceedings was therefore justified, in my opinion, either as a remedy based on s. 7 of the *Charter* or on the basis of the court's inherent powers at common law to control its own process and prevent its abuse. In this case, the abuse of process was directly and inextricably related to the committal hearing.

In the opinion of Arbour J. the concerns raised by the fugitives were properly part of judicial phase of the extradition process. She noted that nothing the Minister could have done would address the unfairness of a committal obtained in such tainted circumstances. In her view the extradition judge did not need to await a ministerial decision since the breach of fundamental justice was "directly and inextricably related to the committal hearing." (p. 287)

In *Shulman*, the Supreme Court ruled that notwithstanding the fact that the offending comments from the U.S. judge and prosecutor had occurred subsequent to his committal hearing, Shulman was entitled to apply for a stay before the Court of Appeal hearing his appeal from committal. Shulman had applied to introduce fresh evidence concerning the comments of the U.S. judge and prosecutor but the Court of Appeal had dismissed the application on the basis that the evidence related to matters that were for the Minister of Justice. With respect to the *Charter* jurisdiction of appellate courts in extradition proceedings, Arbour J. noted, at pp. 308-309:

> [31] The 1992 amendments simplified that process by abolishing the recourse to *habeas corpus* and vesting jurisdiction in the provincial courts of appeal over both the appeal from committal and the judicial review from the Minister's decision on surrender. The amendments allowed for the possibility of a combined hearing of both issues.
>
> [32] As some of the functions previously exercised by the *habeas corpus* judge are now within the competence of the superior court judge presiding over the committal hearing, the role of the Court of Appeal has also been significantly expanded, particularly with regard to alleged violations of constitutional rights. In the case of *Charter* issues arising at the ministerial stage, such as s. 6 mobility issues, the Court of Appeal is now the original judicial forum in which they can be raised. This unavoidably leads to an expanded role for the Courts of Appeal, including having to receive evidence relevant to the *Charter* challenges that neither the extradition judge nor the Minister had any obligation to receive.
>
> [33] Not only is the Court of Appeal a forum of original jurisdiction for *Charter* purposes under the *Extradition Act* as a result of the 1992 amendments, but it also has, like all courts, an implied, if not inherent, jurisdiction to control its own process, including through the application of the common law doctrine of abuse of process.

As a result, Arbour J. held that the evidence sought to be tendered before the Court of Appeal was not fresh evidence. In her view it was original evidence relevant to the claim that the requesting state, as a party to the litigation, had disentitled itself from the assistance of the Canadian courts through the behaviour of its officials. She stated, at p. 316:

> [60] The Court of Appeal erred in declining to receive the fresh evidence. Even if the U.S. Government did not endorse their views, by allowing its officials to place undue pressure on a Canadian citizen to forego due legal process in Canada, the Requesting State has disentitled itself from pursuing its extradition request before the courts. The intimidation bore upon the judicial phase of the extradition process in its entirety, thus engaging the appellant's right to fundamental justice under s. 7 of the *Charter* as well as by virtue of the doctrine of abuse of process.
>
> [61] This Court, just as the Court of Appeal did, has the requisite jurisdiction to control the integrity of the proceedings before it, and to grant a remedy, both at common law and under the *Charter*, for abuse of process. Since the Requesting State in these proceedings, represented by the Attorney General of Canada, has not repudiated the statements of one of its officials that an unconscionable price would be paid by the appellant for having insisted on exercising his rights under Canadian law, this is a clear

case where to proceed further with the extradition hearing would violate "those fundamental principles of justice which underlie the community's sense of fair play and
decency" (*R. v. Keyowski*, [1988] 1 S.C.R. 657, at pp. 658-59, 40 C.C.C. (3d) 481).

A second issue concerning the fairness of the hearing in *Shulman* was based upon
the assertion that the use of affidavit material provided by alleged co-conspirators
awaiting sentencing in the United States was an invitation to perjury, and that therefore
the quality of this evidence violated his rights under s. 7 of the *Charter*. Shulman
argued that the extradition judge had the authority under s. 24(2) of the *Charter* to
exclude this material from the hearing. Arbour J. dismissed this argument, noting that
the *Charter* applies only domestically and has no extraterritorial effect except to
Canadian authorities. She observed, at p. 315, that in an appropriate case an extradition
judge could exclude evidence gathered by foreign authorities if it had been obtained
"in such an abusive manner that its admission *per se* would be unfair under s. 7 of
the *Charter*: *United States v. Dynar*, [1997] 2 S.C.R. 462, 115 C.C.C. (3d) 481, 147
D.L.R. (4th) 399; *R. v. Harrer*, [1995] 3 S.C.R. 562, 101 C.C.C. (3d) 193, 128 D.L.R.
(4th) 98." However, Arbour J. observed that the fact that the affiants were awaiting
sentencing at the time they swore their evidence was a matter which went to weight.
The weighing of evidence and the assessment of credibility, she held, are not matters
within the jurisdiction of an extradition judge.

§4.2 Specific *Charter* Issues Raised at Judicial Phase Both Before and After 1992 Amendments to Former *Extradition Act*

In addition to the *Cotroni* issue discussed above in the Supreme Court of Canada
case of *Kwok*, and which had been previously litigated in the cases of *Leon, supra,
Palmer, supra, Swystun v. United States* (1987), 40 C.C.C. (3d) 222 (Man. Q.B.),
United States v. Iaquinto (March 26, 1991), (Ont. Gen. Div.) and (*sub nom. Canada
v. Iaquinto*) (June 27, 1991), Doc. CA 356/91 (Ont. C.A.), leave to appeal to S.C.C.
refused (1991), 137 N.R. 387 (note) (S.C.C.), *Cazzetta, supra*, and *D'Agostino, supra*,
there were other types of *Charter* issues frequently raised during the judicial phase
both before and after the addition of s. 9(3) to the former *Extradition Act* in 1992.
The courts generally declined to deal with these *Charter* issues on the basis that they
were premature as they concerned matters solely within the jurisdiction of the Minister
of Justice at the executive phase of the extradition process.

Issues raised in this regard included double jeopardy in the cases of *R. v. Schmidt*
(1987), 33 C.C.C. (3d) 193 (S.C.C.), and *United States v. Langlois* (1989), 50 C.C.C.
(3d) 445 (Ont. C.A.), the imposition of the death penalty in *United States v. Kindler*
(1985), 22 C.C.C. (3d) 90 (Que. S.C.), *Kindler v. Canada (Minister of Justice)* (1991),
67 C.C.C. (3d) 1 (S.C.C.), *Garcia, supra*, and *United States. v. Burns* (1997), 116
C.C.C. (3d) 524 (B.C.C.A.), affirmed (2001), 151 C.C.C. (3d) 97 (S.C.C.), the imposition of minimum penalties by the requesting state that would not be applicable in
Canada in the case of *United States v. Jamieson* (1991), 73 C.C.C. (3d) 460 (Que
C.A.), leave to appeal to S.C.C. refused (1992), 73 C.C.C. (3d) vi (note) (S.C.C.), the

fugitive's mental condition in *Larabie v. R.* (1998), 42 C.C.C. (3d) 385 (Ont. H.C.), and possible oppressive treatment by the requesting state in *Ma, supra.*

The inclusion in the new Act of specific factors requiring ministerial considera-tion when determining whether to surrender a person underscores that the issues referred to above are not matters for the determination of the extradition hearing judge. Section 44(1)(a) of the new Act mandates the Minister to refuse surrender if to do so would be unjust or oppressive. Section 44(2) gives the Minister discretion to refuse to surrender if the death penalty may ensue and section 47(a) indicates that the Minister may refuse to surrender if a double jeopardy situation exists.

Under the new Act, the double jeopardy issue was raised in the case of *United States v. Drysdale* (2000), 32 C.R. (5th) 163 (Ont. S.C.J.), in support of a *Charter* argument seeking a stay of proceedings before the extradition judge. The persons sought argued that they had already been convicted in Canada for the offences for which their extradition was requested and that to continue with the extradition hearing would infringe their rights under s. 7 of the Charter. Dambrot J. held that this was a matter which could be raised with the Minister of Justice. He stated, at p. 174:

> [24] I note that where a person sought advances a meritorious claim of double jeopardy, the Minister has ample jurisdiction to vindicate it. Section 44(1) of the *Act* compels the Minister to refuse to make a surrender order where surrender would be unjust or oppressive. Section 47 permits the Minister to refuse to make a surrender order where the person would be entitled, if charged in Canada, to be discharged because of a previous acquittal or conviction. In addition, article 4 of the *Treaty on Extradition Between Canada and the United States of America* provides that extradition shall not be granted when the person whose surrender is sought has been tried and discharged or punished in the territory of the requested state for the offence for which his extradition is requested. I do not presume the outcome of the application of any of these provisions. I simply point out that the Minister has responsibilities with respect to this issue. Her decision is subject to review in the Court of Appeal. I see no good reason for me to strain to usurp the function of the Minister or the Court of Appeal. It seems apparent that this application is premature.

The structure of the new Act indicates that ministerial matters are outside the jurisdiction of extradition judges.

§4.3 *Charter* Motions Concerning Evidence Gathered in Canada

In *United States v. Leon* (April 7, 1994) [affirmed (1995), 96 C.C.C. (3d) 568 (Ont. C.A.), affirmed (1996), 105 C.C.C. (3d) 385 (S.C.C.)], Hayes J. of the Ontario Court (General Division) held that the addition of s. 9(3) to the former *Extradition Act* in 1992 gave the extradition judge the authority to consider s. 8 *Charter* breaches in respect of evidence seized in Canada and sought to be adduced at the extradition hearing by the requesting state. In that case, eight kilograms of cocaine had been seized from a warehouse in Ontario. The requesting state sought to introduce the cocaine into evidence at the extradition hearing. It was relevant to the extradition hearing because it had allegedly been purchased in the United States contrary to the drug laws of that country. Hayes J. made the distinction between evidence gathered in Canada and that obtained in the requesting state.

Hayes J. referred to the decision of Corbett J. of the Ontario Court (General Division) in *R. v. Reid* (February 11, 1994), Corbett J. (Ont. Gen. Div.). In the latter case, the fugitive sought to invoke s. 8 of the *Charter* with respect to a blood sample taken pursuant to a search warrant issued in Pennsylvania. The sample was taken for the purpose of DNA testing. Relying on s. 32 of the *Charter*, which states that the *Charter* applies to all matters within the authority of Parliament and the provincial legislatures, Corbett J. held that the *Charter* did not apply where the evidence was obtained in the United States in accordance with apparently lawful procedures.

Hayes J. commented that in the case before him the requesting state had tendered *viva voce* evidence regarding the execution of the search warrant, the warrant having been executed in Canada by Canadian authorities. He then concluded as follows, at p. 20 of the judgment:

> The fugitive is entitled to have this extradition judge consider the facts as they relate to an alleged breach of s. 8. and such consideration is not prohibited by s. 32. By virtue of s. 9(3), this court is competent to consider a breach of s. 8 It is a function that I am required to perform when applying the *Extradition Act.*

On the merits, Hayes J. found that there was no breach of s. 8 of the *Charter.*

Hayes J.'s decision was appealed to the Ontario Court of Appeal, *supra.* The court appeared to acknowledge that Hayes J. was correct in holding that the extradition hearing judge had jurisdiction to consider *Charter* issues relating to evidence gathered in Canada and tendered at the hearing (at p. 573):

> With respect to the fourth ground, that the extradition judge ought to have assumed jurisdiction to deal with the alleged Charter violations, it is submitted that s. 9(3) of the *Extradition Act* which came into force in 1992 had clearly conferred jurisdiction on a superior court judge sitting on an extradition hearing to deal with Charter violations and to grant remedies accordingly. Here, Hayes J. recognized that he had jurisdiction to grant Charter remedies and he entered into and disposed of an application by the appellant alleging that the search of the warehouse in Toronto violated s. 8 of the Charter.

In *R. v. Barranca* (December 14, 1994), [1994] O.J. No. 3942 (Ont. Gen. Div.), Keenan J. ruled that the fugitives could have disclosure of intercepted communications and the corresponding authorizations which had been obtained in Canada. It was alleged that a U.S. agent had come to Canada to arrange a purchase of heroin from the fugitives. An authorization under Part VI of the *Criminal Code* was obtained in order for the agent to record conversations at meetings by means of a device secreted on his person. In support of the extradition request, the United States provided an affidavit from the agent deposing to the substance of his alleged conversations with the fugitives in respect of the drug deal. The affidavit from the U.S. agent was intended to be introduced as evidence at the extradition hearing. The United States did not provide copies or transcripts of the intercepted conversations. In a motion brought before Keenan J., the fugitives asked for, and received, the recorded interceptions as well as the authorizations and affidavits in support of the authorizations.

In terms of his jurisdiction, Keenan J. held that s. 9(3) of the former *Extradition Act* gave the extradition judge the power to grant *Charter* relief in appropriate cases. Keenan J. indicated that his order only encompassed those interceptions made under authorizations granted by Ontario justices and not those obtained pursuant to orders granted in the requesting state.

In *United States v. Ahluwalia* (*sub nom. United States v. Ahluwalia and Sohal*) (December 1, 1995), Doc. Toronto E-15/93 (Ont. Gen. Div.), counsel for Sohal argued that his client's rights under s. 8 of the *Charter* had been infringed by the use in the authenticated materials of intercepted communications which counsel alleged were unauthorized. It was counsel's position that there was no indication in the materials as to where the interceptions took place. Hoilett J. of the Ontario Court (General Division) dismissed this argument. More specifically, Hoilett J. found that the communications in question were intercepted in the United States through American interceptions, and thus the *Charter* did not apply to these communications:

> There is no merit in the *Charter* argument advanced. All the indications are that such electronic surveillance as took place was the result of U.S.A. interceptions conducted by DEA agent/s. It would be rank speculation, in my view, to suggest that there were any unauthorized interceptions by Canadian police authorities and it is common ground that the *Charter* has no extra-territorial application, concerning which reference may usefully be made to *R. v. Schmidt* (1987), 33 C.C.C. (3d) 193 (S.C.C.).

Although the fugitive's submission on this point was dismissed, the decision implicitly recognizes the jurisdiction of the extradition judge to deal with *Charter* breaches in connection with communications intercepted in Canada.

In *United States v. Dynar, supra*, the Supreme Court of Canada dealt with a factual situation in which there had been cross-border police cooperation, but in which the evidence tendered in support of the request included only evidence obtained in America. The material in support of the request made no mention of the extent or nature of Canadian involvement in the investigation. Dynar submitted that he was entitled to disclosure of the involvement of Canadian authorities to possibly support a *Charter* challenge in an attempt to exclude the evidence. The Supreme Court ruled that, in the circumstances of this case, disclosure of Canadian involvement in the investigation was not required. It was held that the fugitive had received full disclosure of the material to be relied upon by the requesting state at the hearing and that that was sufficient. The court was of the view that the disclosure of Canadian involvement in the case could not have been of any assistance to the fugitive in mounting a challenge to the sufficiency of the evidence relied upon by the United States in support of the request for extradition. Cory and Iacobucci JJ., in considering whether a *Charter* argument could have been made in an attempt to exclude the evidence, held that there was no justiciable *Charter* issue in the case, at pp. 527–528:

[141] Mr. Dynar contends that as a result of the Requesting State's non-disclosure, there is no evidentiary record on the basis of which he can even attempt to make a *Charter* argument. Yet the evidence presented by the Requesting State does disclose enough information to conclude that there is simply no "air of reality" to the contention that Mr. Dynar could establish a *Charter* violation by the Canadian officials in the gathering of the evidence. The evidence before Keenan J. included the affidavit of Agent Matthews. It clearly reveals that the FBI had been interested in the activities of Mr. Dynar for some time; that Matthews himself was aware of previous occasions on which Mr. Dynar had admitted to laundering large sums of money in the State of Nevada, and that he initiated the investigation on the basis of his suspicions regarding Mr. Dynar's telephone call to Lucky Simone. The affidavit provides a sufficient basis to conclude that the investigation, the evidence and the prosecution were essentially American. No amount of cooperation by the Canadian authorities could change that.

. . .

[143] It is true that the fugitive is entitled to be committed only on the basis of evidence that is legally admissible according to law of the province in which the committal hearing takes place: see *La Forest's Extradition, supra*, at p. 160. But it has been consistently and properly held that the *Charter* generally does not apply extraterritorially. As a result, Canadian courts cannot impose upon foreign evidence the standards of admissibility that have developed in the jurisprudence dealing with s. 24(2) of the *Charter*.

[144] Mr. Dynar was entitled to a fair hearing before the extradition judge, and in our opinion he received one. He was not entitled to disclosure from the Requesting State beyond the production of the evidence that it was relying upon to establish its *prima facie* case. In any event, the evidence provided by the Requesting State did contain sufficient information to conclude that the evidence was gathered entirely in the United States, by American officials, for an American trial. It follows that no justiciable *Charter* issue can arise in this case. In these circumstances, a new hearing is simply not justified.

(c) Disclosure of Materials in the Hands of the Canadian Authorities

[145] Mr. Dynar argued that even if he was not entitled to additional disclosure from the American authorities he was entitled to disclosure of the materials in the hands of the Canadian authorities. Since no justiciable *Charter* issue can arise from the potential involvement of the Canadian authorities in the gathering of evidence in this case, it is not necessary to consider the degree of disclosure that might be required in other circumstances.

It is clear from the decision of the Supreme Court in *United States v. Dynar* that if there is Canadian involvement in the obtaining of the evidence provided for use at the hearing, an application for disclosure of the Canadian involvement for the purposes of mounting a *Charter* challenge to exclude the evidence may be successful.

Dynar was relied upon by Bennett J. in *United States v. Cheema* (1999), 65 C.R.R. (2d) 234 (B.C.S.C.), leave to appeal to S.C.C. refused (2001), 271 N.R. 193 (note) (S.C.C.), in support of his ruling that the extradition judge's only new power resulting from the addition of s. 9(3) to the former Act in 1992 was the power to rule on search and seizure issues concerning evidence gathered in Canada. Arbour J. in *United States v. Kwok, supra,* referred approvingly to the decision of Bennett J. in *Cheema.*

§4.4   Early Cases Determining *Charter* Jurisdiction Under the Act

Prior to the release of the Supreme Court of Canada's decision in *United States v. Kwok,* there were decisions recognizing the limited *Charter* jurisdiction of the extradition judge under the new Act. Dambrot J., in *United States v. Quintin* (2000), 4 Imm. L.R. (3d) 255 (Ont. S.C.J.), was asked to exercise jurisdiction under s. 25 of the Act to grant a stay of proceedings on the basis that among other allegations, related immigration proceedings were a disguised form of extradition, the conduct of law enforcement officers, immigration officials and the Department of Justice, and the arrest and commencement of the extradition proceedings constituted an abuse of process, and that the extradition proceedings were oppressive, vexatious, and offended the fundamental principles of justice underlying the community's sense of fair play and decency. In dismissing the application for the stay, Dambrot J. relied upon the decisions of the Ontario Court of Appeal in *United States v. Cobb* (1999), 139 C.C.C. (3d) 283 (Ont. C.A.) [additional reasons at (1999), 139 C.C.C. (3d) 283 at 287 (Ont. C.A.), reversed (2001), 152 C.C.C. (3d) 270 (S.C.C.), reconsideration refused (June 14, 2001), Docs. 26912, 27610, 27774 (S.C.C.)] and of the Supreme Court of Canada in *Schmidt, Mellino* and *Dynar, supra,* and stated, at pp. 272–273:

> The claim made by the applicants that their immigration procedings were a disguised form of extradition, however meritorious, simply has nothing to do with the functions that I am required to perform in applying the *Extradition Act,* or the fairness of the proceedings before me. Their remedy, if any, lies elsewhere: in civil proceedings against the government; in proceedings attacking deportation; and perhaps even in submissions to the Minister.

In *United States v. Drysdale, supra,* Dambrot J. entertained an application brought by two of the persons sought for a stay of proceedings pursuant to s. 24(1) of the *Charter* on the basis that they had already been convicted in Canada of the offences for which their extradition was requested. Dambrot J. observed that the double jeopardy issue was a matter for the Minister of Justice under s. 47 of the Act. With respect to the jurisdictional basis for the *Charter* argument advanced by the persons sought, that their extradition hearing would be unfair and oppressive because it could lead to them being unfairly put on trial in the United States, Dambrot J. stated, at p. 174:

> [27] With respect to the second argument advanced by the applicants, it is sufficient to say that any time persons accused of a crime are in a position to complain that it would be oppressive to place them on trial, they could equally complain that the extradition hearing or preliminary hearing that would enable them to be placed on trial is also

oppressive. More than that is necessary to invoke the *Charter* jurisdiction of this Court. It must be established that there is something that makes the extradition proceeding unfair divorced from the alleged unfairness of the ultimate prosecution before a *Charter* remedy is justified.

Watt J. in *Germany (Federal Republic) v. Schreiber* (July 6, 2000), [2000] O.J. No. 2618 (Ont. S.C.J.), also recognized that the jurisdiction of an extradition judge in *Charter* matters under the new Act continues to be narrow. In that case, Schreiber was sought by Germany for offences alleging tax evasion, bribery, and aiding and abetting criminal breach of trust. A motion was brought before Watt J. sitting as an extradition judge, which sought disclosure of a variety of materials, including documentation in the hands of the foreign prosecution authorities, material obtained as a result of a domestic investigation involving the person sought (though unrelated to the German investigation) which had involved a Canadian request to Switzerland for banking information involving Schreiber and certain corporate entities said to be under his control, and communications and documentation passing between the political authorities in the two countries concerning the extradition request itself. Some of these materials were said to be relevant to the issue of whether the Minister or her officials were biased against Schreiber and whether the extradition proceedings constituted an abuse of process.

Watt J. denied the disclosure request. With reference to the proposed argument that ministerial conduct had rendered the extradition proceedings an abuse of process, Watt J. held that an extradition judge has no jurisdiction to entertain such an application. He recognized that the jurisdiction of an extradition judge continued to be a narrow one, and that the jurisprudence under the former Act continued to provide guidance in that regard. He observed, at para. 75:

> [75] The *Act* does *not* affirm or otherwise incorporate the plenary *Charter* authority otherwise enjoyed by the superior court. See, for example, *Mills v. R.* (1986), 26 C.C.C. (3d) 481, 494, per McIntyre J., and 517-8, per Lamer J.; and, *Rahey v. The Queen* (1987), 33 C.C.C. (3d) 289, 299, per Lamer J. Section 25, like its predecessor, s. 9(3), links the *Charter* jurisdiction of the extradition hearing judge to the functions that the judge is required to perform under the *Act*.

In regards to the function required to be performed by the extradition judge, Watt J. noted that s. 24(2) of the Act analogized the role of the extradition judge to that of a domestic justice conducting a preliminary inquiry. Watt J. further observed that a domestic preliminary inquiry justice has no *Charter* jurisdiction and no statutory or other authority to order disclosure from the Crown. Watt J. concluded that the tests he was required to apply by virtue of s. 29(1) of the Act did not extend to entertaining the proposed application for abuse of process on behalf of the Minister. He noted that no review of ministerial actions was assigned by the Act to the extradition judge and concluded that such "[r]eviews of an alleged abuse of process are for the Court of Appeal [under s. 57 of the Act], *not* the extradition hearing judge", at para. 88.

In a subsequent proceeding in the same case (*Germany (Federal Republic) v. Schreiber* (2001), 150 C.C.C. (3d) 523 (Ont. S.C.J.)), an application for declaratory *Charter* relief pursuant to the Ontario *Rules of Civil Procedure* was brought before the extradition judge in order to invoke his jurisdiction as a superior court judge. The application was quashed. Watt J. held that there was no justification for the invocation of civil rules of procedure in extradition proceedings, which are criminal in nature.

§4.5 Constitutional Attacks to *Extradition Act*

Prior to the 1992 amendments to the former *Extradition Act*, the extradition judge did not have jurisdiction to consider the constitutionality of the *Extradition Act* and its provisions. However, the court on a *habeas corpus* application did have such jurisdiction. These principles were set out by Doherty J.A. on behalf of the Ontario Court of Appeal in the pre-amendment case of *Pacificador v. Philippines (Republic)* (1993), 83 C.C.C. (3d) 210 (Ont. C.A.), leave to appeal to S.C.C. refused (1994), 87 C.C.C. (3d) vi, [1994] 1 S.C.R. x (S.C.C.). The fugitive in that case contended on the *habeas corpus* application that the *prima facie* case standard for committal contemplated by s. 18(1)(b) of the former *Extradition Act* was so low that it violated the fugitive's rights under s. 7 of the *Charter*. On the jurisdictional issue, Doherty J.A. held as follows, at pp. 221–222:

> Before turning to the merits of this submission, I must consider the respondent's argument that the *habeas corpus* judge did not have jurisdiction to address the Charter argument and that consequently, this court should not hear the merits of the Charter argument.
>
> Under the law as it stood when the hearing was conducted before Watt J., he [the extradition judge] had no jurisdiction to consider the constitutionality of the legislation. The *habeas corpus* judge was a court of competent jurisdiction in respect of Charter challenges to the validity of the extradition hearing before Watt J.
>
> . . .
>
> In oral argument, counsel for the appellant made a straightforward constitutional challenge to the legislative provision controlling the decision of the extradition judge. The *habeas corpus* judge had jurisdiction to determine that issue.

The Court of Appeal dismissed the argument on the merits. The addition of s. 9(3) to the former *Extradition Act* in 1992 had the effect of vesting the extradition judge with those powers exercised prior to 1992 by the *habeas corpus* judge. The following comment by then federal Minister of Justice Kim Campbell appears to confirm this point (*Hansard*, November 7, 1991, at p. 4778):

> Under the present law, *Charter* issues may only be raised before the judge, usually on the same court as the extradition judge who received the writ of *habeas corpus* pursuant to the extradition request.
>
> This results in needless duplication of administering evidence and wastes the courts' time. This change would allow *Charter*-based arguments concerning applications to be

considered at a later stage of the proceedings, without having to go before a different judge.

This statement was made with reference to *Charter* remedies rather than to remedies under s. 52 of the *Constitution Act, 1982*. However, the statement reflected a general intention on the part of Parliament that extradition judges — under s. 9(3) — assume the jurisdiction previously exercised by judges in *habeas corpus* applications to avoid "needless duplication" of court proceedings. This was recognized by Arbour J. in *United States v. Kwok, supra*. Accordingly, based on Doherty J.A.'s view in *Pacificador v. Philippines (Republic)* that the *habeas corpus* judge had jurisdiction to entertain constitutional attacks on the provisions of the *Extradition Act*, s. 9(3) conferred the same jurisdiction on extradition judges.

The jurisdiction conferred upon extradition judges by s. 9(3) has been continued in the new *Extradition Act* by s. 25. Accordingly, any challenges to the constitutionality of the new legislation will be appropriately made before the extradition judge. This has been recognized under the new Act by Ewaschuk J. in *Bourgeon v. Canada (Attorney General)* (2000), 35 C.R. (5th) 25 (Ont. S.C.J.), Dilks J. in *Canada v. Yang* (September 25, 2000), (Ont. S.C.J.) and Vertes J. in *Germany (Federal Republic) v. Ebke*, [2001] 6 W.W.R. 517 (N.W.T.S.C.), each of whom ruled upon constitutional challenges to the validity of the evidence provisions contained in ss. 32–34 of the new Act.

§5.0 CASE LAW

Argentina (Republic) v. Mellino (1987), 33 C.C.C. (3d) 334 (S.C.C.).

Bourgeon v. Canada (Attorney General) (2000), 35 C.R. (5th) 25 (Ont. S.C.J.).

Canada v. Iaquinto (June 27, 1991), Doc. CA 356/91 (Ont. C.A.), leave to appeal refused (1991), 137 N.R. 387 (note) (S.C.C.).

Canada v. Yang (September 25, 2000), Dilks J. (Ont. S.C.J.).

D'Agostino, Re (1997), (*sub nom. United States v. D'Agostino*) 41 C.R.R. (2d) 325 (Ont. Gen. Div.).

Germany (Federal Republic) v. Ebke, [2001] 6 W.W.R. 517 (N.W.T.S.C.).

Germany (Federal Republic) v. Schreiber (July 6, 2000), Watt J., [2000] O.J. No. 2618 (Ont. S.C.J.).

Germany (Federal Republic) v. Schreiber (2001), 150 C.C.C. (3d) 523 (Ont. S.C.J.).

Hong Kong v. Ma (December 12, 1997), Ewaschuk J. (Ont. Gen. Div.).

Kindler v. Canada (Minister of Justice) (1991), 67 C.C.C. (3d) 1 (S.C.C.).

Larabie v. R. (1998), 42 C.C.C. (3d) 385 (Ont. H.C.).

Pacificador v. Philippines (Republic) (1993), 83 C.C.C. (3d) 210 (Ont. C.A.), leave to appeal to S.C.C. refused (1994), 87 C.C.C. (3d) vi, [1994] 1 S.C.R. x (S.C.C.).

R. v. Barranca (December 14, 1994), [1994] O.J. No. 3942, Keenan J. (Ont. Gen. Div.).

R. v. Mills (1986), 26 C.C.C. (3d) 481 (S.C.C.).

R. v. Reid (February 11, 1994), Corbett J. (Ont. Gen. Div.).

R. v. Schmidt (1987), 33 C.C.C. (3d) 193 (S.C.C.).

Swystun v. United States (1987), 40 C.C.C. (3d) 222 (Man. Q.B.).

Thailand (Kingdom) v. Saxena (April 29, 1999), Doc. Vancouver CC960599, Maczko J., 1999 CarswellBC 922 (B.C. S.C.).

Thailand (Kingdom) v. Saxena (June 10, 1999), Doc. Vancouver CC960599, Maczko J., [1999] B.C.J. No. 1364 (B.C. S.C.).

United States v. Ahluwalia, (*sub nom. United States v. Ahluwalia and Sohal*) (December 1, 1995), Doc. Toronto E-15/93, Huilett J. (Ont. Gen. Div.).

United States v. Burns (1997), 116 C.C.C. (3d) 524 (B.C.C.A.), affirmed (2001), 151 C.C.C. (3d) 97 (S.C.C.).

United States v. Cazzetta (1996), 108 C.C.C. (3d) 536 (Que. C.A.), leave to appeal to S.C.C. refused (1996), 110 C.C.C. (3d) vi (S.C.C.).

United States v. Cheema (1999), 65 C.R.R. (2d) 234 (B.C.S.C.), leave to appeal to S.C.C. refused (2001), 271 N.R. 193 (note) (S.C.C.).

United States v. Cobb (1997), 11 C.R. (5th) 310 (Ont. Gen. Div.), reversed (1999), 139 C.C.C. (3d) 283 (Ont. C.A.), additional reasons (1999), 139 C.C.C. (3d) 283 at 287 (Ont. C.A.), reversed (2001), 152 C.C.C. (3d) 270 (S.C.C.), reconsideration refused (June 14, 2001), Docs. 26912, 27610, 27774 (S.C.C.).

United States v. Cotroni (1989), 48 C.C.C. (3d) 193 (S.C.C.).

United States v. Drysdale (2000), 32 C.R. (5th) 163 (Ont. S.C.J.).

United States v. Dynar (1997), 115 C.C.C. (3d) 481 (S.C.C.).

United States v. Garcia (May 11, 1994), Doc. E16/92, [1994] O.J. No. 1027, Jarvis J. (Ont. Gen. Div.), affirmed (July 18, 1996), Doc. CA C21023 (Ont. C.A.), leave to appeal to S.C.C. refused (1997), 102 O.A.C. 318 (note) (S.C.C.).

United States v. Iaquinto (March 26, 1991), (Ont. Gen. Div.), and (*sub nom. Canada v. Iaquinto*) (June 27, 1991), Doc. CA 356/91 (Ont. C.A.), leave to appeal to S.C.C. refused (1991), 137 N.R. 387 (note) (S.C.C.).

United States v. Jamieson (1991), 73 C.C.C. (3d) 460 (Que. C.A.), leave to appeal to S.C.C. refused (1992), 73 C.C.C. (3d) vi (note) (S.C.C.).

United States v. Kerslake (1996), 142 Sask. R. 112 (Q.B.).

United States v. Kindler (1985), 22 C.C.C. (3d) 90 (Que. S.C.).

United States v. Kwok (1998), 127 C.C.C. (3d) 353 (Ont. C.A.), affirmed (2001), 152 C.C.C. (3d) 225 (S.C.C.).

United States v. Langlois (1989), 50 C.C.C. (3d) 445 (Ont. C.A.).

United States v. Leon (April 7, 1994), Hayes J. (Ont. Gen. Div.), affirmed (1995), 96 C.C.C. (3d) 568 (Ont. C.A.), affirmed (1996), 105 C.C.C. (3d) 385 (S.C.C.).

United States v. Palmer (January 23, 1996), Doc. E-20/94, Wein J. (Ont. Gen. Div.), appeal dismissed [1997] O.J. No. 608 (Ont. C.A.).

United States v. Quintin (2000), 4 Imm. L.R. (3d) 255 (Ont. S.C.J.).

United States v. Shulman (September 13, 1995), Lyon J., [1995] O.J. No. 4497 (Ont. Gen. Div.), affirmed (1998), 128 C.C.C. (3d) 475 (Ont. C.A.), reversed (2001), 152

C.C.C. (3d) 294 (S.C.C.), reconsideration refused (June 14, 2001), Docs. 26912, 27610, 27774 (S.C.C.).
United States v. Singh (October 14, 1994), Doc. E-21, Ewaschuk J. [1994] O.J. No. 3941 (Ont. Gen. Div.).
United States v. Tilley (1996), 183 A.R. 158 (Q.B.).
United States v. Tilley (1996), 183 A.R. 1 (Q.B.).
United States v. Tsioubris (2001), 152 C.C.C. (3d) 292 (S.C.C.), reconsideration refused (June 14, 2001), Docs. 26912, 27610, 27774 (S.C.C.).
United States v. Turenne (1998), 133 Man. R. (2d) 131 (Q.B.).

§6.0 RELATED SECTIONS

s. 2 — Interpretation
Charter of Rights and Freedoms, s. 6 — Mobility Rights
Charter of Rights and Freedoms, s. 7 — Life, Liberty, and Security of the Person
Charter of Rights and Freedoms, s. 8 — Search and Seizure
Charter of Rights and Freedoms, s. 24 — Enforcement
Constitution Act, 1982, s. 52
Canada–United States Extradition Treaty, Article 6 — Death Penalty Cases
Canada-United States Extradition Treaty, Article 17 bis — Procedure When Requesting and Requested State Have Jurisdiction to Prosecute the Offence

Orders Restricting Publication of Evidence (s. 26)

§1.0 DESCRIPTION

Section 26 of the *Extradition Act* provides as follows:

ORDER RESTRICTING PUBLICATION OF EVIDENCE
    26. Before beginning a hearing in respect of a judicial interim release or an extradition hearing, a judge may, on application by the person or the Attorney General and on being satisfied that the publication or broadcasting of the evidence would constitute a risk to the holding of a fair trial by the extradition partner, make an order directing that the evidence taken not be published or broadcast before the time that the person is discharged or, if surrendered, the trial by the extradition partner has concluded.

Section 26 states that the extradition judge has the discretion to order a ban on publication or broadcasting of evidence taken at a judicial interim release hearing or an extradition hearing. Either the person sought or the Attorney General may bring the application for such an order. Section 26 further states that the judge should be satisfied that publishing or broadcasting the evidence would jeopardize the holding of a fair trial in the requesting jurisdiction.

If the order is made, it continues until such time as the person sought is either discharged or, if surrendered, the trial in the requesting jurisdiction is concluded.

§2.0 COMPARISON WITH FORMER ACT

Under the former *Extradition Act*, there was no specific provision that dealt with the authority of the court to order that evidence taken on a bail hearing or extradition hearing not be published or broadcast. However, ss. 517 and 539 of the *Criminal Code*, which apply to domestic bail hearings and preliminary inquiries and which provide for publication bans on evidence taken in those proceedings, were incorporated by reference into extradition proceedings through the operation of s. 13 of the former Act. Section 13 provided that extradition proceedings were to be conducted "in the same manner, as nearly as may be, as if the fugitive was brought before a justice of the peace, charged with an indictable offence committed in Canada." This had the effect of analogizing extradition proceedings to domestic bail and preliminary inquiry proceedings, and made the *Criminal Code* provisions applicable, including ss. 517 and 539 concerning banning the publication of evidence (see *United States v. Khan* (1982), 70 C.C.C. (2d) 5 (Man. C.A.), and *Global Communications Ltd. v. Canada (Attorney General)* (1984), 10 C.C.C. (3d) 97 (Ont. C.A.)).

Under the former *Extradition* Act, by virtue of ss. 517 and 539 of the *Criminal Code*, a ban on publication was mandatory if applied for by the accused/fugitive and discretionary if requested by the prosecutor/requesting state.

§3.0 SIGNIFICANCE OF CHANGE

As mentioned above, the sections of the *Criminal Code* concerning bans on the publication or broadcasting of evidence tendered at a bail hearing (s. 517) or preliminary hearing (s. 539) are mandatory when requested by an accused and discretionary when requested by the Crown. Under s. 13 of the former *Extradition Act*, these *Criminal Code* sections applied "as nearly as may be" to extradition bail hearings and extradition hearings, resulting in mandatory bans on publication when requested by the fugitive. The ban remained within the discretion of the court if it was applied for by the requesting state. Also, under ss. 517 and 539, there are no specific criteria required to be established for granting a publication ban, such as risk to holding a fair trial.

Section 26 of the new *Extradition Act* indicates that a judge has the discretionary authority to ban publication of the evidence tendered at an extradition bail hearing or extradition hearing regardless of which party brings the application. The discretion is only exercisable when the judge is satisfied that "the publication or broadcasting of the evidence would constitute a risk to the holding of a fair trial by the extradition partner." Section 26 provides that the order banning publication will remain in force until the person sought has been discharged or the trial in the extradition partner has concluded. This is the same as ss. 517 and 539 of the *Criminal Code* concerning the duration of a ban on the publication of evidence in domestic bail and preliminary inquiry proceedings.

Given the provisions of ss. 19 and 24(2) of the new Act, it is possible that the mandatory bans on publication for bail hearings and preliminary inquiries provided by the *Criminal Code* have application to extradition hearings. Section 19 of the new Act incorporates Part XVI of the Code, which includes s. 517. Section 24(2) of the new Act, for the purposes of extradition hearings, incorporates the powers of a justice under Part XVIII of the Code, which includes s. 539. It may be that there is no change from the former regime in the application of these *Criminal Code* provisions to bans on publication in the extradition context. In fact, in *Germany (Federal Republic) v. Ebke*, [2001] 6 W.W.R. 517 (N.W.T.S.C.), the judge presiding at an extradition bail hearing held that even though Ebke was in custody pursuant to the new *Extradition Act*, in the context of the bail hearing the provisions of s. 517 of the Code applied.

§4.0 ANALYSIS

Section 26 may simply be a statutory affirmation of the right to apply for bans on publication during the extradition process, an issue which had been the subject of judicial determination under the former Act (see *Global Communications, supra, Khan, supra*).

It could be argued that s. 26 is unnecessary considering ss. 19 and 24(2) of the new Act incorporate into the new Act certain *Criminal Code* procedural provisions, including the *Criminal Code* provisions for dealing with bans on publication of evidence at bail hearings (s. 517) and at preliminary hearings (s. 539). The continued applicability of these Code sections would be in keeping with the legislative policy expressed in the jurisprudence under the former Act for applying the domestic provisions pertaining to publication bans to extradition hearings. Thorson J.A. in *Global Communications, supra*, stated, at pp. 104–105:

> In my opinion, therefore, there is no reason why, as a matter of either statutory construction or practicability, the *Bail Reform Act* provisions of the *Criminal Code* should not be held to apply "as nearly as may be" in extradition matters. However, I would go further. Looking at this issue from the viewpoint of the legislative policy sought to be implemented by Parliament when it enacted the *Bail Reform Act*, to hold that that Act has no application to proceedings under the *Extradition Act* would, in my opinion, be to frustrate altogether that policy as it would otherwise have application in this by no means unimportant area of our law.

In addition, the scheme of the new Act is to adopt, insofar as they may be applicable, the domestic criminal procedures. This is reflected in the provisions dealing with arrest (s. 16(3) of the Act incorporating s. 507(4) of the *Criminal Code*), the identification of criminals (s. 16(5) and (6) incorporating the *Identification of Criminals Act*), bail pending appeal (s. 20 of the Act incorporating s. 679 of the *Criminal Code*), and appeals (s. 52 incorporating a number of *Criminal Code* appeal sections). The bail hearing and preliminary inquiry sections of the *Criminal Code* are similarly incorporated into the extradition scheme by ss. 19 and 24(2) of the *Extradition Act*. This lends support to the view that the Code provisions of s. 517 and s. 539, as incorporated through ss. 19 and 24(2) of the Act respectively, are applicable to ban the publication of evidence in the extradition context. The extradition judge at the bail hearing in the *Ebke* case ([2001] 6 W.W.R. 517 (N.W.T.S.C.)), did in fact resort to the *Criminal Code* provisions in this regard when granting a ban on publication under s. 517.

Two decisions under the new Act have resorted to the common-law power to ban the publication of evidence, holding that the provisions of s. 26 of the new Act are not exclusive. In *Germany (Federal Republic) v. Ebke* (2000), 150 C.C.C. (3d) 252, Vertes J. of the Northwest Territories Supreme Court considered an application for a ban on publication of evidence under the new Act. Ebke's extradition had been sought by Germany based on his alleged involvement in a German terrorist organization. Subsequent to being arrested on the extradition warrant he was charged with Canadian offences pursuant to the *Immigration Act*, on allegations that he had misrepresented material facts at the time of his admission to Canada. A ban on publication of the evidence at the extradition hearing was sought by counsel for Ebke on the basis that publication of allegations of terrorist activity would be so inflammatory as to prejudice Ebke's right to a fair trial on the Canadian charges. Vertes J. observed, at p. 257, that s. 26 of the new Act did not apply in the circumstances:

> [9] Ebke's counsel conceded that there are no grounds to support the issuance of a publication ban under this section. There is no evidence that the publication or broadcast of evidence from this hearing would constitute a risk to Ebke receiving a fair trial in Germany. I was told by counsel that a trial in Germany would not be conducted before a jury as we know it but before a panel of judges instead.

Nevertheless, Vertes J. allowed the application, holding that he had a common-law discretionary power to order a ban on publication in order to safeguard Ebke's fair trial rights on the domestic charges.

In *United States v. M. (D.J.)* (2001), 156 C.C.C. (3d) 276 (Ont. S.C.J.), leave to appeal to S.C.C. refused (November 15, 2001), Doc. 28688 (S.C.C.), the Sun Media Corporation brought an application before Grossi J. seeking an order rescinding previous court orders that had sealed the application record upon which the warrant of arrest had been obtained, and banned the publication of evidence taken during the judicial interim release hearing. These orders included a ban upon the publication of the identity of the person sought.

Grossi J. denied the application to reconsider these orders. With respect to the sealing of the court file, Grossi J. held that the provisions of s. 487.3(1) of the *Criminal*

Code are applicable to arrest warrants issued pursuant to the *Extradition Act* and accordingly that the court could rely upon this section to prohibit access to information presented in support of a request for a provisional arrest warrant under s. 13 of the *Extradition Act*. With respect to the publication ban, Grossi J. held that s. 26 of the *Extradition Act* did not oust the extradition judge's powers under the common law to order a publication ban in circumstances not covered by the terms of s. 26. He held that the common law in this case authorized the imposition of a ban in order to protect the identities of alleged victims. Finally, Grossi J. was of the opinion that the appropriate venue to challenge the access and publication ban orders was not by way of an application to the Superior Court to reconsider the orders but, since they were final orders rather than interim orders, by way of an application for leave to appeal to the Supreme Court of Canada pursuant to s. 40 of the *Supreme Court Act*.

§5.0 CASE LAW

Germany (Federal Republic) v. Ebke (2000), 150 C.C.C. (3d) 252 (N.W.T.S.C.).
Germany (Federal Republic) v. Ebke, [2001] 6 W.W.R. 517 (N.W.T.S.C.).
Global Communications Ltd. v. Canada (Attorney General) (1984), 10 C.C.C. (3d) 97 (Ont. C.A.).
United States v. Khan (1982), 70 C.C.C. (2d) 5 (Man. C.A.).
United States v. M. (D.J.) (2001), 156 C.C.C. (3d) 276 (Ont. S.C.J.), leave to appeal to S.C.C. refused (November 15, 2001), Doc. 28688 (S.C.C.).

§6.0 RELATED SECTIONS

s. 27 — Exclusion of Person From Hearing
Criminal Code, ss. 517, 539

Exclusion of Person from Hearing (s. 27)

§1.0 DESCRIPTION

Section 27 of the *Extradition Act* provides as follows:

EXCLUSION OF PERSON FROM HEARING
27. The presiding judge may make an order excluding any person from the court for all or part of an extradition hearing or hearing in respect of a judicial interim release if the judge is of the opinion that it is in the interest of public morals, the maintenance of order or the proper administration of justice to exclude the person.

Section 27 confers upon the extradition judge the authority to exclude "any person" from the court during all or part of a person's bail or committal hearing. The exclusion order may be based on any of three interests: public morals; the maintenance of order; or the proper administration of justice.

§2.0 COMPARISON WITH FORMER ACT

Section 13 of the former *Extradition Act* provided that the fugitive "shall be brought before a judge, who shall, subject to this Part, hear the case, in the same manner, as nearly as may be, as if the fugitive was brought before a justice of the peace, charged with an indictable offence committed in Canada." Section 13 meant that the extradition hearing was to be conducted "in the same manner, as nearly as may be" to a Canadian preliminary inquiry. Therefore, by implication, s. 13 imported into the extradition hearing the provisions relating to preliminary inquiries in Part XVIII of the Canadian *Criminal Code*. In particular, s. 537(1)(h) provides a justice at a preliminary inquiry with the power to "order that no person other than the prosecutor, the accused and their counsel shall have access to or remain in the room in which the inquiry is held, where it appears to him that the ends of justice will be best served by so doing."

However, s. 27 of the new Act is different from the former Act in the following respects. Firstly, s. 27 enables the exclusion of any person in bail hearings as well as extradition hearings. The former Act, in implicitly incorporating the preliminary inquiry provisions of Part XVIII of the *Criminal Code*, allowed for the exclusion of persons from extradition hearings. With respect to bail proceedings, the case law dealing with the former *Extradition Act* held that s. 13 of the former Act had the effect of incorporating the *Criminal Code* bail provisions into the extradition context (see *Global Communications Ltd. v. Canada (Attorney General)* (1983), 5 C.C.C. (3d) 346 (Ont. H.C.), affirmed (1984), 10 C.C.C. (3d) 97 (Ont. C.A.), and *United States v. Khan* (1982), 70 C.C.C. (2d) 5 (Man. C.A.). However, none of the bail provisions in the Code allow for the exclusion of persons from a bail hearing.

Secondly, s. 27 expressly outlines three separate bases for excluding persons: public morals, the maintenance of order, and the proper administration of justice. By contrast, in incorporating s. 537(1)(h) of the *Criminal Code*, the former Act provided for the exclusion of persons if "the ends of justice [would] be best served by so doing." Finally, s. 27 permits the extradition judge to exclude "any person," whereas the former Act, by reference to s. 537(1)(h), only allowed for a blanket order excluding all persons other than the prosecutor, the accused and his or her counsel from the court.

§3.0 SIGNIFICANCE OF CHANGE

Section 27 of the new Act is broader and more nuanced than the scheme existing in the former Act and it applies to bail hearings as well as extradition hearings. It appears to permit a more selective exclusion order ("any person"), rather than the *in camera* proceeding contemplated under s. 537(1)(h) of the *Criminal Code*, which was incorporated by reference into the former Act by s. 13. Section 27 is also clearer than the former Act, in that it provides an express delineation of the judge's power, rather than incorporating powers by an implicit reference to Part XVIII of the Code.

§4.0 ANALYSIS

Section 27 identifies three bases upon which would be appropriate to exclude members of the public from the courtroom at the bail hearing or the extradition hearing: public morals; the maintenance of order; and the proper administration of justice. An example of a situation where members of the public might be excluded due to concerns related to public morals might be when there is evidence of a shocking or graphic nature pertaining to violence or sexual matters. Maintaining order during the court proceedings may encompass excluding the public in situations where there are security concerns, or concerns over disruptive behaviour. With respect to excluding members of the public due to concerns for the proper administration of justice, this could encompass situations involving sensitive issues of state or issues attracting privilege such as informant issues, the use of investigative techniques, or ongoing investigations.

The issue of security concerns arose in *R v. Vaudrin* (1982), 2 C.C.C. (3d) 214 (B.C. S.C.). During the accused's preliminary inquiry on a charge of rape, Crown counsel was successful in an application to exclude the public from the courtroom. The accused was a large, bearded man. Seated in the courtroom, among other members of the public, were three large, bearded men to whom defence counsel intended to draw the complainant's attention in cross-examination to challenge her identification of the accused. Given the size of the three men and the alleged membership of one of them in a motorcycle gang with a reputation for intimidating witnesses, Crown counsel contended that their presence in court would inhibit the testimony of the Crown's witnesses. Crown counsel's application was not supported by any evidence. The accused brought an application before the British Columbia Supreme Court to have the provincial court judge's ruling quashed.

Spencer J. granted the application in light of the lack of evidence in support of Crown counsel's application, at pp. 219–220:

> Turning to the merits of the case before me, it is clear that there was no evidence at all upon which the learned provincial court judge might find that the presence of the three large men or of the public generally might lead to a breach of order in his court. Nor was there evidence upon which His Honour might conclude that the three men were intimidating to the witnesses. Whilst the provincial court judge in some circumstances is entitled to rely upon the representations of counsel, where those representations are challenged by opposing counsel and where it is clear that Crown counsel did not purport to speak of personal knowledge nor purport to convey instructions he had received on the matter, the representations are no more than speculation and not evidence upon which the learned judge was entitled to base an order for exclusion of the public generally or of the three individuals.

Spencer J.'s conclusion was based on the "strong inclination" in the jurisprudence in favor of the public's right of access to the courts (at p. 219). However, Spencer J. was dealing with a *Criminal Code* preliminary inquiry provision that only allowed for a blanket exclusion of the public rather than a selective exclusion of certain members of the public. As indicated above, s. 13 of the former *Extradition Act* implicitly incorporated by reference the preliminary inquiry provisions of the *Criminal Code*. Within those provisions, s. 537(1)(h) permits a justice to exclude the public from the proceedings at a preliminary inquiry. The case law considering this section held that the justice had no authority to exclude only certain individuals from the courtroom. Thus, in *R. v. Sayegh (No. 1)* (1982), 66 C.C.C. (2d) 430 (Ont. Prov. Ct.), and *R. v. Sayegh (No. 2)* (1982), 66 C.C.C. (2d) 432 (Ont. Prov. Ct.), it was held that the justice had no authority to exclude only members of the foreign press who had indicated an intention to publish details of the proceedings notwithstanding the ban on publication issued by the court. By contrast, the inclusion of s. 27 in the new *Extradition Act* allowing for the exclusion of "any person" under one of the three bases listed in the section, would appear to authorize just such a selective exclusion from the courtroom.

§5.0 CASE LAW

Global Communications Ltd. v. Canada (Attorney General) (1983), 5 C.C.C. (3d) 346 (Ont. H.C.), affirmed (1984), 10 C.C.C. (3d) 97 (Ont. C.A.).
United States v. Khan (1982), 70 C.C.C. (2d) 5 (Man. C.A.).
R. v. Sayegh (No. 1) (1982), 66 C.C.C. (2d) 430 (Ont. Prov. Ct.).
R. v. Sayegh (No. 2) (1982), 66 C.C.C. (2d) 432 (Ont. Prov. Ct.).
R. v. Vaudrin (1982), 2 C.C.C. (3d) 214 (B.C. S.C.).

§6.0 RELATED SECTIONS

Criminal Code, Part XVIII, s. 537(1)(h).

Power to Compel Witnesses (s. 28)

§1.0 DESCRIPTION

Section 28 of the *Extradition Act* provides as follows:

POWER TO COMPEL WITNESSES
28. A judge who presides over an extradition hearing or a hearing in respect of a judicial interim release may compel a witness to attend the hearing and sections 698 to 708 of the *Criminal Code* apply, with any modifications that the circumstances require.

Section 28 confers upon the extradition judge the power to compel a witness to attend the bail hearing and/or the extradition hearing. To assist the bail hearing or extradition hearing judge in compelling the attendance of witnesses, s. 28 expressly incorporates ss. 698 to 708 of the *Criminal Code*. Sections 698 to 708 are contained within the section of the *Code* on "Procuring Attendance." The sections deal with the following matters:

- ss. 698–700.1: Issuance and content of subpoenas

- ss. 701–703.2: Service and geographic scope of subpoenas

- ss. 704–708: Defaulting or absconding witnesses and contempt of court.

§2.0 COMPARISON WITH FORMER ACT

Section 13 of the former *Extradition Act* provided that the fugitive "shall be brought before a judge, who shall, subject to this Part, hear the case, in the same manner, as nearly as may be, as if the fugitive was brought before a justice of the peace, charged with an indictable offence committed in Canada." Section 13 meant that the extradition hearing was to be conducted "in the same manner, as nearly as may be" to a Canadian preliminary inquiry. Therefore, by implication, s. 13 imported into the extradition hearing the provisions relating to preliminary inquiries in Part XVIII of the Canadian *Criminal Code*. With respect to bail proceedings, the case law dealing with the former *Extradition Act* held that s. 13 had the effect of incorporating the *Criminal Code* bail provisions into the extradition context (see *Global Communications Ltd. v. Canada (Attorney General)* (1983), 5 C.C.C. (3d) 346 (Ont. H.C.), affirmed (1984), 10 C.C.C. (3d) 97 (Ont. C.A.) and *United States v. Khan* (1982), 70 C.C.C. (2d) 5 (Man. C.A.). Section 697 of the Code deals with the applicability of the "Procuring Attendance" provisions (i.e., ss. 698–708 of the Code). It states that "this Part applies where a person is required to attend to give evidence in a proceeding to which this Act applies." Accordingly, s. 13 of the former *Extradition Act*, in implicitly incorporating the preliminary inquiry and bail provisions of the Code, also incorporated ss. 698 to 708 of the Code.

§3.0 SIGNIFICANCE OF CHANGE

In light of the foregoing, s. 28 represents an express codification of the regime for procuring the attendance of witnesses that was implicitly understood to exist under the former Act.

§4.0 ANALYSIS

See above sections.

§5.0 CASE LAW

Global Communications Ltd. v. Canada (Attorney General) (1983), 5 C.C.C. (3d) 346 (Ont. H.C.), affirmed (1984), 10 C.C.C. (3d) 97 (Ont. C.A.).
United States v. Khan (1982), 70 C.C.C. (2d) 5 (Man. C.A.).

§6.0 RELATED SECTIONS

Criminal Code, ss. 698–708.

Order of Committal (s. 29)

§1.0 DESCRIPTION

§1.1 Test for Committal (s. 29(1))

Section 29(1) of the *Extradition Act* provides as follows:

ORDER OF COMMITTAL
    29. (1) A judge shall order the committal of the person into custody to await surrender if:

(a) **in the case of a person sought for prosecution, there is evidence admissible under this Act of conduct that, had it occurred in Canada, would justify committal for trial in Canada on the offence set out in the authority to proceed and the judge is satisfied that the person is the person sought by the extradition partner; and**

(b) **in the case of a person sought for the imposition or enforcement of a sentence, the judge is satisfied that the conviction was in respect of conduct that corresponds to the offence set out in the authority to proceed and that the person is the person who was convicted.**

Section 29(1) sets out the evidentiary standard required for an extradition judge to order the committal of a person sought into custody to await surrender. This is the same as the *Shephard* test (*United States v. Shephard* (1976), (*sub nom. United States v. Sheppard*) 30 C.C.C. (2d) 424 (S.C.C.)) for domestic preliminary inquiries. If the judge does not order the committal of the person, the judge must order his or her discharge (s. 29(3)).

In the case of persons who are accused but not convicted of an offence in the foreign jurisdiction, s. 29(1)(a) provides that the extradition judge must determine whether there is evidence of conduct that, had the conduct occurred in Canada, would justify the committal of the person for trial in Canada for the offence set out in the authority to proceed. The role of the extradition judge is analogous to that of a justice conducting a domestic preliminary inquiry.

In the case of persons who have been convicted by the extradition partner of a crime and who are sought for the enforcement or imposition of a sentence, s. 29(1)(b) requires that the extradition judge be satisfied that the person sought was convicted with respect to conduct that corresponds to the offence set out in the authority to proceed.

In either case, the extradition judge must be satisfied that the person before the court is identified as the person sought or convicted by the extradition partner.

§1.2 Contents of Order of Committal (s. 29(2))

Section 29(2) of the *Extradition Act* provides as follows:

ORDER OF COMMITTAL
   (2) The order of committal must contain

   (a) the name of the person;
   (b) the offence set out in the authority to proceed for which the committal is ordered;
   (c) the place at which the person is to be held in custody; and
   (d) the name of the extradition partner.

Section 29(2) describes the required contents of the order of committal. It must include the name of the person sought, the offence set in the authority to proceed for which the committal is ordered, the place where the person sought is to be detained in custody, and the name of the extradition partner.

§1.3 Discharge of Person Sought (s. 29(3))

Section 29(3) of the *Extradition Act* provides as follows:

DISCHARGE OF PERSON
   (3) A judge shall order the person discharged if the judge does not order their committal under subsection (1).

Under s. 29(3), if the extradition judge is not satisfied that the criteria in s. 29(1)(a) and (b) have been established, the judge is required to discharge the person.

§1.4 Relevant Date for Committal Determination (s. 29(4))

Section 29(4) of the *Extradition Act* provides as follows:

RELEVANT DATE
(4) The date of the authority to proceed is the relevant date for the purposes of subsection (1).

Under s. 29(4), when the extradition judge considers whether the offence, had it occurred in Canada, would justify committal for trial in Canada, the relevant date for that inquiry into Canadian law is the date of the authority to proceed.

§1.5 Extradition When Person Sought Is Not Present for Conviction (s. 29(5))

Section 29(5) of the *Extradition Act* provides as follows:

EXTRADITION WHEN PERSON NOT PRESENT AT CONVICTION
(5) Subject to a relevant extradition agreement, if a person has been tried and convicted without the person being present, the judge shall apply paragraph (1)(*a*).

In cases where a person sought has been tried and convicted by the extradition partner without the person being present, s. 29(5) directs that the test set out in s. 29(1)(a) for persons accused of offences is the one that must be met in order for the judge to issue an order of committal.

§2.0 COMPARISON WITH FORMER ACT

§2.1 Committal Test for Accused Persons (s. 29(1)(a))

Section 29(1)(a) sets out the standard to be met by the evidence at an extradition hearing in order to support an order of committal for an accused person to await surrender. The governing provision of the former *Extradition Act* for the issuance of a warrant of committal in the same circumstances was s. 18(1)(b), which O'Connor J.A. of the Ontario Court of Appeal described in *United States v. Commisso* (2000), 143 C.C.C. (3d) 158 (Ont. C.A.), as embodying the following test, at p. 170:

> [45] . . . the test under s. 18(1)(b) may be paraphrased as follows: the extradition judge shall commit a fugitive for surrender if satisfied that the conduct that underlies the foreign charge, wherever it took place, would if it occurred in Canada constitute a *prima facie* case of any of the offences listed in the *Extradition Act*, or described in the relevant extradition treaty.

The test set out in s. 29(1)(a) for committal is essentially the same as the test in the former Act (see, for instance, *Australia v. Ho* (December 11, 2000), Doc. Vancouver CC990288, [2000] B.C.J. No. 2651 (B.C.S.C.)).

The Supreme Court of Canada in *R. v. Schmidt* (1987), 33 C.C.C. (3d) 193 (S.C.C.), at p. 209; *United States v. McVey* (1992), 77 C.C.C. (3d) 1 (S.C.C.) at pp. 26–27; and most recently, *United States v. Dynar* (1997), 115 C.C.C. (3d) 481 (S.C.C.), at p. 520, discussed the purpose of an extradition hearing under s. 18(1)(b). In *United States v. Dynar*, Cory and Iacobucci JJ. (Lamer, La Forest, L'Heureux-Dubé and Gonthier JJ. concurring) commented as follows, at p. 521:

> [121] One of the most important functions of the extradition hearing is the protection of the liberty of the individual. It ensures that an individual will not be surrendered for trial in a foreign jurisdiction unless, as previously mentioned, the Requesting State presents evidence that demonstrates on a *prima facie* basis that the individual has committed acts in the foreign jurisdiction that would constitute criminal conduct in Canada. See *McVey, supra*, at p. 519; *Commonwealth of Puerto Rico v. Hernandez*, [1975] 1 S.C.R. 228 at p. 245, 14 C.C.C. (2d) 209, 41 D.L.R. (3d) 549, *per* Laskin J.; *Canada v. Schmidt*, [1987] 1 S.C.R. 500 at p. 515, 33 C.C.C. (3d) 193, 39 D.L.R. (4th) 18.

The purpose of s. 29(1)(a) of the new Act has not changed from that which was described by the Supreme Court of Canada in connection with s. 18(1)(b) of the former Act. As with s. 18(1)(b), s. 29(1)(a) ensures that no person will be ordered surrendered to an extradition partner unless there is sufficient evidence, such that in Canada, the person could be committed to stand trial for the offence set out in the authority to proceed.

A comparison of s. 29(1)(a) of the new Act and s. 18(1)(b) of the former Act yields the following observations:

1. Both sections analogize the extradition hearing to a domestic preliminary inquiry and consequently the evidentiary standard of proof is that of sufficient evidence to commit for trial had the alleged conduct occurred in Canada. Parliament clearly intended to keep the legal standard which prevailed under the former regime. This point was made by Ms. Eleni Bakopanos, Parliamentary Secretary to the Minister of Justice and Attorney General of Canada, while introducing Bill C-40 (the current *Extradition Act*) to the House of Commons on second reading (*House of Commons Debates*, October 8, 1998, 1st Session, 36th Parliament, v. 135):

    Under the new bill the legal standard for extradition would be retained. That is, a Canadian judge will still have to be satisfied that there is sufficient evidence before her or him of the conduct underlying the request for extradition which, if it occurred in Canada, would justify a trial for a criminal offence. Lawyers like to refer to this as the prima facie test.

    . . .

    Finally, as noted above, the extradition judge will order committal of the person into custody to await surrender only if evidence would justify committal for trial in Canada if the offence was committed here in Canada.

2. Section 29(1)(a) is clear that the inquiry is conduct-focused. It expressly states that the "conduct" must correspond to the offence set out in the authority to proceed. By contrast, s. 18(1)(b) of the former Act did not speak expressly of a conduct-based test for committal. However, since the extradition proceeding was analogous to a domestic preliminary inquiry, conduct was clearly the focus that developed in the jurisprudence (*United States v. Dynar, supra*; *United States v. McVey, supra*). Article 2 of the *Canada–United States Treaty* is also indicative of the conduct-based approach to extradition.

3. The former *Extradition Act* had no document analogous to the authority to proceed. As described in the commentary to s. 15, the authority to proceed is now the foundation of the extradition hearing. Section 29(1)(a) requires the judge to determine if the conduct disclosed by the evidence amounts to the offence or offences specified in the authority to proceed. The question to be answered under the former regime was whether the conduct disclosed by the evidence constituted a crime in Canada which was also an extradition crime. An extradition crime under the former Act meant an act that, if committed in Canada, would constitute a crime described in the Act or the treaty. For this purpose, it was more often the treaty which was resorted to (*United States v. McVey, supra*, at p. 8).

4. The new *Extradition Act* specifies the need to prove that the person before the court is the person sought by the extradition partner. By contrast, s. 18(1)(b) of the former Act did not specifically refer to the identity issue. However, it was inferred to be a proof requirement from the reference to "fugitive" in the section and from the definition of "fugitive" in s. 2 of the former Act. Section 2 of the former *Extradition Act* provided as follows:

    "fugitive" or "fugitive criminal" means a person being or suspected of being in Canada, who is accused or convicted of an extradition crime committed within the jurisdiction of a foreign state;

5. Section 19.1(2) of the former *Extradition Act* required that the extradition judge, at the commencement of the hearing, inform the fugitive of his or her right to make submissions to the Minister of Justice. This has not been included in the new Act. Therefore, this is a matter that the extradition judge no longer has to deal with. Section 19(a) of the former Act also required that the extradition judge, upon committal of the fugitive, inform the fugitive that he or she would not be surrendered until after the expiration of 30 days and that he or she has the right to appeal the committal order. This has been maintained in the new Act under s. 38(2) with the additional requirement that the judge also advise the person sought of the right to apply for judicial interim release.

§2.2 Committal Test for Convicted Persons (s. 29(1)(b))

Section 29(1)(b) of the new *Extradition Act* sets out the standard to be met at an extradition hearing in order to support an order of committal for a convicted person to await surrender. The governing provision of the former Act for the issuance of a warrant of committal in the same circumstances was s. 18(1)(a), which provided that the extradition judge should commit the fugitive for surrender if satisfied on the evidence that the fugitive had been convicted in the requesting state of an extradition crime.

Under s. 18(1)(a), there were two methods by which the requesting jurisdiction could prove the extradition crime aspect of this provision (see *Washington (State) v. Johnson* (1988), 40 C.C.C. (3d) 546 (S.C.C.)): firstly, by examining the text of the applicable foreign law (which was usually contained in the documentary evidence submitted by the requesting jurisdiction) and ascertaining whether the essential elements of that offence corresponded with any Canadian offence; secondly, if there was no correspondence between the elements, by examining the conduct of the fugitive as disclosed by the requesting jurisdiction's documentary evidence to ascertain if the conduct constituted a crime in Canada. This was the same test used in the case of accused persons.

In *United States v. Wong* (1995), 98 C.C.C. (3d) 332 (B.C. C.A.), leave to appeal to S.C.C. refused (1995), 101 C.C.C. (3d) vi (S.C.C.), the British Columbia Court of Appeal held that the choice of method of proof in *Washington (State) v. Johnson*, *supra*, was a real choice, and that it was not necessary to satisfy both methods of proof. In *Wong*, the extradition judge had discharged a convicted fugitive because he was not satisfied that the conduct of the fugitive would amount to an offence if committed in Canada. The British Columbia Court of Appeal reversed the decision and held as follows, at pp. 350–351:

> [O]nce the learned judge found that the evidence supported the conclusion that the respondent had been convicted of an offence containing all the elements of a Canadian extradition crime, the requirements of s. 18(1)(*a*) of the *Extradition Act* were met and there was no need for a further inquiry into the specific conduct underlying the conviction.

The new Act does not contemplate the availabilty of the first method of proof enunciated in *Washington (State) v. Johnson*. That is, it does not provide for a comparison of the text of the foreign law in order to determine if the essential elements of a Canadian offence are present. This is clear from the fact that s. 29(1)(b) speaks expressly of the extradition judge determining if "conduct" matches the offence in the authority to proceed. The fact that the record of the case in s. 33(1)(b)(ii) specifically requires inclusion of a document describing the conduct for which the person was convicted, is a clear indication that this is necessary in order for the extradition judge to perform the test under s. 29(1)(b). Also, under the new Act, there is no requirement in any case that the text of the foreign law or the foreign indictment (which would be required to apply the first branch of the *Washington (State) v. Johnson* tests) be put before the extradition court.

In *United States v. Persaud* (November 3, 1999), 1999 CarswellOnt 4263, [1999] O.J. No. 4992 (Ont. S.C.J.), Ewaschuk J. held that the new Act requires an express description of the conduct underlying the conviction. In *Persaud*, there was no summary of the conduct which had led to the conviction and Ewaschuk J. was asked to infer that the essential elements of the foreign offence were the same as the Canadian offence named in the authority to proceed, by looking at the offence set out in the foreign indictment which was before the court. This in effect invoked the first branch of the *Washington (State) v. Johnson* test. Ewaschuk J. observed that the former s. 18(1)(a) made no reference to conduct but only required proof that the person had been convicted of an extradition crime. He underscored that the new Act is concerned with proof that the person was convicted in respect of " 'conduct' that corresponds to the Canadian offences set out in the authority to proceed." (para. 13) He stated, at paras. 10, 12, 15:

> [10] In keeping with the modern principle that extradition must be conduct based, s. 29 has incorporated that principle in respect of both offence extraditions and convictions extraditions . . . .
>
> . . .
>
> [12] . . . I must accept the validity of the foreign convictions and must not be concerned with whether their essential elements correspond in a general sense to the Canadian offences set out in the Minister's authority to proceed. However, I must nonetheless be satisfied that the conduct underlying the foreign convictions corresponds in a general sense to the Canadian offences set out in the authority to proceed.
>
> . . .
>
> [15] What s. 29(1)(b) requires is merely a summary of the material facts underlying the foreign convictions. In this case, the documents filed in support of the application make no reference whatsoever to the factual conduct underlying the convictions which would permit me to determine whether that conduct corresponds to the Canadian offences set out in the authority to proceed.

In *United States v. Bonamie* (October 24, 2001), Doc. Edmonton Appeal 0003-0281-A3, 2001 ABCA 267 (Alta. C.A.), the extradition judge accepted copies of the American indictments as evidence, pursuant to s. 33(1)(b)(ii) of the Act, of the conduct for which the person sought was convicted. The Alberta Court of Appeal upheld the decision of the extradition judge on the basis that the indictments described the conduct sufficiently to satisfy the statutory requirements for committal.

Section 29(1)(b) requires only that the judge be "satisfied" that "the conviction was in respect of conduct that corresponds to the offence set out in the authority to proceed." When documents are provided for the extradition hearing in the form of a record of the case (see s. 32(1)(a)), s. 33(1)(b)(ii) requires that the record contain a document describing the conduct for which the person sought was convicted. A summary of the conduct would appear to suffice. An examination would then be required of the conduct described in this document in relation to the Canadian offence or offences cited in the authority to proceed. Evidence may still be introduced at the extradition hearing in reliance upon the terms of an extradition treaty (see s. 32(1)(b)). Article 9(2) of the *Canada–United States Extradition Treaty* requires that the request for extradition be accompanied by a statement of the facts of the case. This is similar to the requirements of the record of the case.

Under the former Act, if the conduct-based test was employed, the use of the word "evidence" in s. 18(1)(a) arguably meant that the requesting jurisdiction was required to provide admissible evidence of this conduct for use at the extradition hearing and could not have relied on a summary of the facts (see *Washington (State) v. Johnson, supra*).

Proof of the conviction was required to be put before the extradition judge under the former *Extradition Act* because s. 18(1)(a) of the former Act required evidence to prove "that the fugitive was so convicted." This was usually provided by way of an affidavit with the appropriate conviction documents appended. Section 29(1)(b) of the new Act requires the judge to be satisfied that "the conviction was in respect of conduct that corresponds to the offence set out in the authority to proceed." In the case of documentation presented by way of a record of the case, s. 33(1)(b)(i) of the new Act requires inclusion of a copy of the document that records the conviction of the person. With respect to documentation tendered pursuant to treaty (as per s. 32(1)(b) of the new Act), Article 9(4) of the *Canada–United States Extradition Treaty*, by way of example, requires the request for extradition to be accompanied, in the case of a convicted person, by the judgment of conviction and sentencing information.

Section 29(1)(b) of the new *Extradition Act* specifies that the extradition judge must be satisfied that the person before the court is the person convicted by the extradition partner. Section 18(1)(a) of the former Act did not specifically refer to the identity issue. However, the need to establish identity was inferred from the reference to "fugitive" in s. 18(1)(a) and the definition of "fugitive" in s. 2 of the Act. The new Act goes further and specifies methods of establishing identity. Section 33(2) of the new Act indicates that the record of the case may include documentation regarding identification. Presumably, this documentation would be comprised of a photograph or fingerprint evidence. In addition, s. 37 of the new Act specifically provides that comparison of the name and physical characteristics of the person before the court to the evidence in this regard provided by the extradition partner is evidence of identity.

§2.3 Contents of Order of Committal (s. 29(2))

Section 29(2) of the new *Extradition Act* specifies the required contents of the order of committal. In particular, the order must include the name of the person sought, the offence named in the authority to proceed to which the order of committal pertains, the place where the person is to be held in custody, and the name of the extradition partner making the request. There was no specific provision in the former Act specifying the required contents for warrants of committal. However, Form 2 appended to the former Act suggested that the warrant of committal should set out the name of the fugitive, the name of the crime of which the fugitive was accused or convicted, and the name of the place asserting jurisdiction over this crime. The form was directed to the keeper of the jail who was expected to detain the person.

With respect to setting out the name of the crime, in *United States v. McVey*, *supra*, §2.1 at p. 12, the Supreme Court of Canada held that this could be the name of the crime as it was known in the foreign jurisdiction or the name that the offence would bear in Canada. Either practice was considered valid. This is no longer the case. Section 29(2)(b) requires that the order of committal set out the offence named in the authority to proceed to which the committal pertains, and s. 15(3)(c) of the new Act requires that the authority to proceed name the equivalent Canadian offence.

§2.4 Discharge of Person Sought (s. 29(3))

Section 29(3) of the new *Extradition Act* requires the extradition judge to discharge the person sought if an order of committal is not issued under s. 29(1). Section 29(3) had its counterpart in s. 18(2) of the former Act, which read as follows:

> **18.** (2) If the evidence referred to in subsection (1) is not produced, the judge shall order the fugitive to be discharged.

Accordingly, s. 18(2), like s. 29(3), mandated the discharge of the person sought if the requirements for committal were not met.

§2.5 Relevant Date for Committal Determination (s. 29(4))

Section 29(4) of the new *Extradition Act* establishes as the relevant date for the s. 29(1) committal determination the date of the authority to proceed. This means that the inquiry under s. 29(1)(a) into whether the conduct disclosed by the evidence would justify committal for trial in Canada for the crime described in the authority to proceed will be determined according to the law of Canada as of the date of the authority to proceed. In the case of an inquiry under s. 29(1)(b) with respect to a convicted person, the judge must be satisfied that the person sought was convicted with respect to conduct that as of the date set out in the authority to proceed was a crime in Canada.

Section 29(4) effects a change from the rule which prevailed under the previous legislation. Section 34 of the former Act provided as follows:

> **34.** The list of crimes set out in Schedule I shall be construed according to the law existing in Canada at the date of the commission of the alleged crime, whether by common law or by statute, and as including only such crimes, of the description comprised in the list, as are indictable offences under that law.

The effect of s. 34 was to make the date of the commission of the offence the relevant date for the determination of whether the alleged conduct would have amounted to a crime under Canadian law had it occurred in Canada. Section 34 was directed by its terms to crimes listed in the schedule to the former Act. However, the rule was also applied to crimes defined by treaty. This was one of the issues raised before the Supreme Court of Canada in *United States v. Allard* (1991), 64 C.C.C. (3d) 159 (S.C.C.), reconsideration refused (July 11, 1991), Doc. 20626 (S.C.C.). The request for extradition concerned an airplane hijacking when hijacking was not a crime under Canadian law. La Forest J., in analyzing the treaty provisions, determined that, although hijacking was an extradition crime according to treaty, it was fatal to the request that hijacking was not a crime in Canadian law at the time of the commission of the offence. He stated, at p. 164:

> It is true that s. 34 applies in terms only to crimes listed in Sch. I of the Act, but it must not be forgotten that when s. 34 came into force, these crimes were the only extradition crimes. The Canadian Act was closely modelled on the British statute except that, unlike the latter, it provided for the addition of crimes without adding to the Schedule. While the section was drafted in a rather clumsy manner, the general principle is clearly apparent. It would be odd if a different rule were applied to crimes listed in Sch. I than to those mentioned in the treaty only.
>
> The foregoing seems consistent with s. 18(1)(*b*) of the Act, which provides for the issue of a warrant for the committal of the fugitive until surrendered to the foreign state. This section reads:
>
> > 18(1) The judge shall issue a warrant for the committal of the fugitive to the nearest convenient prison, there to remain until surrendered to the foreign state, or discharged according to law,
> >
> > . . .
> >
> > (*b*) in the case of a fugitive accused of an extradition crime, *if such evidence is produced as would, according to the law of Canada*, subject to this Part, *justify the committal of the fugitive for trial, if the crime had been committed in Canada.*

(Emphasis added.)
> I am, therefore, of the view that a fugitive may only be extradited if the act of which he is charged was a crime recognized in Canada at the time it was committed.

This is no longer the rule under the new *Extradition Act*. The relevant date for the s. 29(1) committal determination is the date of the authority to proceed.

§2.6 Extradition When Person Sought Has Been Tried and Convicted Without Being Present

Section 29(5) provides that, subject to a relevant extradition agreement, a person who has been tried and convicted by the extradition partner without the person being present is to be treated in Canada, for the purposes of the extradition hearing, as an accused person. Consequently, the procedure outlined in s. 29(1)(a) applies to such a person. Section 29(5) is expressly limited to persons who have been "tried and convicted without the person being present." Absconding during the trial will likely disallow application of this section since the person will have been present for at least part of the trial, and will be convicted without being present only because of having absconded. Case law under the former Act recognized that a person who absconds during his or her trial is differently situated than a person convicted by a foreign state in proceedings of which the person had no notice and in which the person had no opportunity to participate (see *Re Whipple* (1972), 6 C.C.C. (2d) 517 (B.C. S.C.), and *United States v. Wagner* (1995), 104 C.C.C. (3d) 66 (B.C. C.A.), leave to appeal to S.C.C. refused (1996), 106 C.C.C. (3d) vi (note) (S.C.C.)).

The former Act did not have a provision similar to s. 29(5). However, it did distinguish between persons who were convicted generally and persons who were convicted by reason of contumacy. Section 2 of the former Act contained the following definition:

> "conviction" or "convicted" does not include the case of a condemnation under foreign law by reason of contumacy, but "accused person" includes a person so condemned;

A conviction in contumacy was generally understood to be a conviction entered in the absence of the accused which would be set aside, and the trial itself held in the event the person was arrested or surrendered (see *R. v. Brixton Prison Governor, Ex parte Kotronis*, [1969] 3 All E.R. 304 (U.K.), at p. 312; *Athanassiadis v. Greece (Government)*, [1969] 3 All E.R. 293 (U.K. H.L.); *Re Coppin* (1866), 2 Ch. App. 47 (U.K.); *Yugoslavia (Republic) v. Rajovic (No. 3)* (1981), 62 C.C.C. (2d) 544 (Ont. Co. Ct.)). Accordingly, the former Act required a person convicted by reason of contumacy to be subject to the same test for commital as applied in the case of an accused person since a conviction in contumacy was not final.

The meaning of the term "contumacy" may vary somewhat from country to country. Article 4(f) of the *Canada–Israel Extradition Treaty* provides that a person convicted *in contumacium* shall not be extradited. This suggests that, in that treaty, the term is not being used to describe an individual who will be given a trial if and when returned. Article 12 of the *Canada–Germany Extradition Treaty* provides that the requested state may refuse extradition in the case of a conviction for contumacy unless the requesting state gives assurances that the person sought will be entitled to have the conviction reviewed by a court in points of fact and law. This indicates that in Germany a person is not entitled to an automatic retrial.

In any event, it is clear that while all convictions in contumacy are convictions for which the accused was not present, not all convictions in the absence of the accused are convictions in contumacy. The new *Extradition Act* has eliminated the distinction, and all those tried and convicted without being present are now treated in the same manner, that is, as persons accused of a crime in the foreign jurisdiction. Consequently, subject to the provisions of a treaty, such a person is dealt with in accordance with s. 29(1)(a) rather than s. 29(1)(b).

§3.0 SIGNIFICANCE OF CHANGE

§3.1 Changes Effected by S. 29(1)(a)

Section 29(1)(a) of the new *Extradition Act* has changed the extradition hearing and the role of the extradition judge in the following respects:

- the extradition judge is no longer required to consider whether the offence for which the person is sought is an "extradition crime" which was a requirement under the former Act;

- the introduction of the authority to proceed (s. 15) now requires the judge to assess the sufficiency of the extradition partner's evidence against the Canadian crimes set out therein by the Minister;

- the extradition judge is no longer required by the Act to receive evidence that an offence is a political crime;

- the circumstances under which the extradition judge may receive evidence tendered by the person sought for extradition is specifically provided for.

(a) "Extradition crime" no longer issue for hearing judge because of introduction of authority to proceed

Section 18(1)(b) of the former Act required the extradition hearing judge to determine in the case of a fugitive accused of an "extradition crime" that the evidence produced was sufficient to justify committal for trial if the crime had been committed in Canada. Thus the judge was required to make a determination that the crime in question was an "extradition crime." Section 2 of the former Act defined an "extradition crime" as either a crime referred to in the schedule to the *Extradition Act* or referred to in a treaty. Section 3 of the former Act provided that extradition treaties took precedence over the Act to the extent of any inconsistency between the two. Thus a treaty would prevail over the list of extradition crimes in Schedule I of the Act in circumstances where the treaty provided an expanded definition or list of extradition crimes.

The first criteria for determining whether the offence was an extradition crime — that is, the conduct in question constituted an offence in the requesting and requested states — came to be known as the "double criminality" requirement. Then, as now, the assessment of double criminality was focused on the conduct of the fugitive. It was the alleged conduct of the fugitive that had to constitute an offence in the requesting and requested jurisdictions. It did not matter that both jurisdictions referred to the offence by a different name (see *United States v. Smith* (1984), 15 C.C.C. (3d) 16 (Ont. Co. Ct.), at pp. 27–28, affirmed (1984), 16 C.C.C. (3d) 10 (Ont. H.C.)). It was for the Minister of Justice to be satisfied that the conduct alleged constituted an offence in the requesting state (*United States v. McVey, supra*, §2.1, at p. 41). The jurisdiction of the extradition judge was to determine whether the alleged conduct of the fugitive constituted an offence in Canada which was listed in the schedule to the former Act or which was referred to in the applicable treaty.

La Forest J., on behalf of a majority of the Supreme Court of Canada in *United States v. McVey*, at pp. 26–27, pointed out that the reason for ensuring that the alleged conduct constituted an offence in Canada is to ensure that no one is extradited to a foreign country for an offence which is not a crime in Canada:

> As I noted earlier, "extradition crime" for the purposes of the Act means an act committed in the requesting state that would constitute a crime described in the treaty if committed in this country. This definition undergirds the reasoning in a number of passages in *R. v. Schmidt, supra*, including the passage quoted above to elucidate the purpose of the procedure, namely (at p. 209 C.C.C., p. 34 D.L.R.):
>
>> The hearing thus protects the individual in this country from being surrendered for trial for a crime in a foreign country unless *prima facie* evidence is produced that he or she has done something there that would constitute a crime mentioned in the treaty if committed here.

When the judge was making the determination as to whether the crime disclosed by the conduct was referred to in an extradition treaty, the judge's determination in this regard depended upon the type of treaty involved. The older treaties contain a list of crimes for which extradition can be sought ("list" treaties). The modern trend is for treaties to refer to extraditable crimes in terms of penalty criteria ("no-list" treaties). For instance, Article 2 of the Canada–United States treaty provides for extradition in cases involving conduct punishable by both parties by imprisonment for one year or more.

Under the new *Extradition Act*, the extradition judge is no longer concerned with determining whether the crime is covered by the treaty either by way of a list of extradition crimes or through a penalty-based criteria. Rather, this is one of the matters that must be considered by the Minister of Justice when the Minister is deciding whether to issue an authority to proceed pursuant to s. 15 of the Act (see *Germany (Federal Republic) v. Schreiber* (July 6, 2000), [2000] O.J. No. 2618, Watt J. (Ont. S.C.J.)). Section 15 requires that the Minister, in deciding whether to issue an authority to proceed, determine whether the penalty criteria set out in s. 3(1)(a) and 3(3) of the Act have been met (s. 3(1)(a) and 3(3) are "subject to a relevant extradition agreement," and thus the Minister must also consider the penalty criteria in the applicable treaty). When the authority to proceed is issued under s. 15, the Minister will have identified the equivalent Canadian offence described by the alleged conduct. Under s. 29(1)(a), the judge need only assess the evidence against the offence described in the authority to proceed. The double criminality assessment by the extradition judge under the former *Extradition Act* has been diluted. In the new Act, the extradition judge only measures the alleged conduct against the already defined offence which is set out in the authority to proceed. The judge does not determine what Canadian offence the conduct constitutes or whether the offence is described or listed in the relevant treaty.

(b) Function of authority to proceed at hearing

The extradition judge must look at the crime named in the authority to proceed and the conduct alleged by the extradition partner and determine if the evidence submitted is sufficient for committal. This task makes the authority to proceed analogous to a charging document in a domestic proceeding. This point was noted in *United States v. Drysdale* (2000), 32 C.R. (5th) 163 (Ont. S.C.J.), where Dambrot J. observed, at p. 180:

> [51] It appears to me that the authority to proceed . . . is analogous to the information or indictment in a domestic prosecution, and thus gives notice to the person sought of what is alleged against him or her, and forms the basis of an order committing the person for extradition where such an order is made . . . .
>
> [52] The "indictment" function of the authority to proceed arises from a number of provisions of the new Act. Section 24(1) provides that upon receipt of an authority to proceed, the judge shall hold an extradition hearing. Section 23(2) permits the judge hearing the request, upon the application of the Attorney General, to amend the authority to proceed in accordance with the evidence. Section 29(1) authorizes a judge to commit a person sought to await surrender if there is evidence of conduct which, if it had occurred in Canada, would justify committal for trial in Canada on the offence set out in the authority to proceed. Section 29(2)(b) requires that the order of committal contain the offence set out in the authority to proceed for which the committal is ordered. Section 58(b) provides that if the Minister makes an order of surrender, it shall include a description of the offence for which committal was ordered, or the conduct for which the person is being surrendered. Accordingly, the committal order will have a role to play in the application of the rule of speciality. It does not require a detailed analysis of the provisions in the *Criminal Code* governing criminal pleadings to appreciate the similarity of purpose of an information or indictment on the one hand, and the authority to proceed on the other. Of course, having regard to the differences between a domestic prosecution and an extradition proceeding, these purposes cannot be identical.

(c) Political crime evidence not admissible at hearing

Under s. 15 of the former *Extradition Act*, the extradition judge was mandated to receive evidence when the issue raised was that the crime was a political crime or otherwise not an extradition crime. The new Act completely eliminates the function of receiving this evidence at the extradition hearing. The receipt of political evidence under s. 15 of the former Act was for the purpose of assisting the Minister of Justice under s. 22 of the former Act in ascertaining whether surrender should be refused owing to the political character of the offence. Under the former Act, in *United States v. Kwok* (2001), 152 C.C.C. (3d) 225 (S.C.C.), a discretion to receive evidence generally, directed for use before the Minister, was also recognized.

Under the new Act, there is no provision involving the extradition judge in the consideration of political crimes. The issue has been made an entirely ministerial matter under s. 46 of the new Act. Any evidence to be submitted to the Minister of Justice in this respect would follow the usual practice for making submissions to the Minister, i.e., by way of writing or through an application for an oral hearing (the right of the person sought to make submissions is set out in s. 43).

(d) Effect of s. 32(1)(c) upon application of test for committal in s. 29(1)(a)

There is one area under the new *Extradition Act* in which the role of the extradition judge may be expanded. Section 32(1)(c) indicates that the extradition judge is entitled to admit evidence adduced by the person sought that is relevant to the tests to be applied under s. 29(1), if the extradition judge considers the evidence to be reliable. Under s. 15 of the former Act, the fugitive was permitted to call evidence relating to the political character of the offence or to whether the offence was an extradition crime. There was no statutory provision allowing the calling of any other evidence by the fugitive, although there was some recognition in the case law of a right on the part of a fugitive to testify at the hearing (see *United States v. Adam* (1999), 120 O.A.C. 271 (Ont. C.A.)). Under s. 14 of the former Act, the evidence of a witness was admissible on oath or solemn affirmation to establish the truth of the charge or the fact of the conviction. Because s. 14 referred to the "truth of the charge or the fact of the conviction," it was interpreted as indicating the requesting state's right to call *viva voce* evidence in support of its request. It was supplementary to, or in lieu of, the requesting state's right to present evidence in the form of authenticated documents under ss. 16 and 17.

What has changed in the conduct of the hearing is the statutory recognition of the ability of the person sought to call evidence that is relevant to the standard set out by s. 29(1)(a) with respect to committal if the extradition judge deems it to be reliable.

Nothing in s. 32(1)(c) speaks to an automatic right on the part of a person sought to call evidence at an extradition hearing. On the contrary, the wording of the provision indicates that the extradition judge may be required to consider two preliminary factors as preconditions to admissibility. The first is a consideration of whether the proposed evidence is relevant to the extradition judge's function under s. 29(1). The second is an assessment of whether the proposed evidence is reliable. These considerations may require a determination by way of a *voir dire*. If the proposed evidence is determined to be both relevant to the tests in s. 29(1) and reliable, it may be admitted. The use to which the extradition judge may put this evidence, once admitted, will be governed by the principles of the *Shephard* test (see §1.1, *supra*), which was recently considered by the Supreme Court of Canada in *R. v. Arcuri* (2001), 157 C.C.C. (3d) 21 (S.C.C.).

The Supreme Court of Canada in *Arcuri* recognized that exculpatory evidence led by an accused on a domestic preliminary inquiry could be considered by the preliminary inquiry judge in determining whether, on the whole of the evidence, there was a sufficient case for committal for trial. This limited weighing of the whole of the evidence, the court stated, would be appropriate when the Crown relies on circumstantial evidence. The same logic would apply to extradition requests when the evidence is circumstantial in light of s. 32(1), which permits the reception of evidence tendered by the person sought that would be relevant to the test for committal to be applied by the extradition judge.

Section 32(1)(c) must contemplate reliable and relevant evidence which establishes that there is an insufficient case for committal. Anything less would violate the principles of the *Shephard* test by taking the ultimate determination of guilt or innocence from the jury. This is because if there is any evidence upon which the trier of fact might convict, the case must be left to the trier of fact. Section 29(1)(a) clearly indicates that the *Shephard* test will remain the standard for committal under the new Act.

With specific reference to the right of the person to call evidence, in *United States v. Akrami*, 2000 BCSC 1438, Romilly J. of the British Columbia Supreme Court ruled that the inclusion of s. 32(1)(c) was simply a codification of the previously acknowledged right of a fugitive to adduce evidence at a hearing. In Romilly J.'s view, s. 32(1)(c) did not permit the extradition judge to consider challenges to the reliability of the extradition partner's evidence and he rejected an application for further disclosure which was said to be required in order to mount such a challenge.

See the commentary to ss. 31–36, §2.4, "Evidence Adduced by Person Sought."

(e) Effect of s. 32(1)(c) upon issue of identity in s. 29(1)(a)

Section 29(1)(a) requires that the extradition hearing judge be satisfied that the person before the court is the person sought by the extradition partner. (This is to be distinguished from the ultimate issue of the identity of the accused as the person who committed the offence.) There may be some issue as to the extent to which s. 32(1)(c) applies to this issue since s. 32(1)(c) refers to the person sought being allowed to call evidence with respect to the "tests set out in subsection 29(1)." Firstly, it is probably inaccurate to speak of the matter of identity of the person as being a test. Rather, it is an issue for the judge to consider. Secondly, the right conferred by s. 32(1)(c) is given to "the person sought for extradition." However, s. 29(1)(a) requires that the extradition judge be satisfied that the person before the court is, in fact, the "person sought by the extradition partner." Since only a person sought can rely on s. 32(1)(c), it would appear that the identity issue would need to be settled by the extradition judge as a preliminary matter before s. 32(1)(c) comes into play. As a consequence, it could be argued that a person seeking to challenge his or her identity as the person sought would not be required to have this evidence introduced through recourse to s. 32(1)(c). Therefore, the most convincing view is that the extradition judge should hear the person's identity evidence and weigh it as he or she sees fit in determining whether the judge is satisfied, as s. 29(1) requires, that the person before the court is the person sought. Since the identity determination is clearly a function given to the extradition judge, there can be no objection to the weighing of evidence or the assessment of credibility with respect to evidence in this regard.

With respect to the issue of identity in terms of whether it was the person sought who actually committed the crime in question, it would appear that the opportunity to give evidence under s. 32(1)(c) could not be invoked because such evidence would most likely be in the nature of alibi evidence or a defence.

§3.2 Test for Committal of Convicted Persons (s. 29(1)(b))

Section 29(1)(b) only requires the extradition judge to determine if the conduct which led to the conviction constitutes the Canadian offence described in the authority to proceed. Section 29(1)(b) eliminates the optional method of proof set out in *Washington (State) v. Johnson, supra,* §2.2, of comparing the elements of the foreign and domestic offences for the purpose of ensuring correspondence between the two. Under the former *Extradition Act,* this method of satisfying the test in s. 18(1)(a) left open the possibility that the requesting jurisdiction would be required to prove foreign law and, in order to do so, call expert evidence. Requiring the extradition judge to consider foreign law was frowned upon by the Supreme Court of Canada in other contexts within the extradition process. In connection with the idea of considering defences at an extradition hearing, La Forest J. in *R. v. Schmidt, supra,* §2.1, at pp. 209–210, commented upon the fact that this would require the consideration of expert evidence of foreign law and that it would seriously interfere with the "efficient working of a salutory system devised by states for the mutual surrender of suspected wrongdoers."

The disapproval of introducing foreign law at the hearing was voiced with even more force by La Forest J. in *United States v. McVey, supra,* §2.1, at pp. 38–39:

> But extradition is today very frequently sought. And with the exponential growth of international crime that has since taken place, it would now be an easy task for criminal enterprises to frustrate the operation of the extradition laws, mutually set up by states to combat criminal activities, by flying in a battery of experts on foreign law whenever one of the entrepreneurs in these unsavoury operations was in danger of being brought to justice. Sopinka J. suggests that proof of foreign law is made in many trials involving transnational activities. But extradition proceedings are not trials. They are intended to

be expeditious procedures to determine whether a trial should be held; even the evidence against the fugitive is presented in writing without the benefit of cross-examination.

In addition to eliminating any consideration of foreign law with respect to the extradition of convicted persons, s. 29(1)(b) endorses an expeditious approach to the conduct-based test set out in that provision. The extradition judge simply has to be satisfied from a description of the conduct that the conviction corresponds to the offence(s) set out in the authority to proceed. Ewaschuk J. had occasion to consider this in *United States v. Persaud, supra*, §2.2, at paras. 12–13:

> [12] . . . However, I must nonetheless be satisfied that the conduct underlying the foreign convictions corresponds in a general sense to the Canadian offences set out in the authority to proceed.
>
> [13] It is the federal Minister of Justice's responsibility, pursuant to s. 15(3)(c) of the *Extradition Act*, to determine the name of the Canadian offences which correspond to the conduct in respect of which the fugitive was convicted, and to set out those offences in the authority to proceed. However, it is the extradition judge's responsibility, pursuant to s. 29(1)(b), to determine if the foreign convictions were in respect of "conduct" that corresponds to the Canadian offences set out in the authority to proceed. It is the fugitive's "conduct," not his foreign convictions, which must correspond to the Canadian offences set out in the authority to proceed. Obviously, the validity of the foreign convictions is immaterial to the judge's statutory responsibilities.

§3.3 Contents of Order of Committal (s. 29(2))

Section 29(2) of the new *Extradition Act* details the required contents of the committal order. Section 29(2) requires that the committal order include the name of the person sought, the offence set in the authority to proceed for which the committal is ordered, the place where the person sought is to be detained in custody, and the name of the extradition partner.

§3.4 Discharge of Person Sought (s. 29(3))

As discussed above under §2.4, s. 29(3) mirrors s. 18(2) of the former Act. Accordingly, s. 29(3) does not effect any change with respect to when persons sought are to be discharged.

§3.5 Relevant Date for Committal Determination (s. 29(4))

Section 29(4) of the new *Extradition Act* provides that the date of the authority to proceed is the relevant date for the purposes of determining whether the conduct underlying the extradition request amounts to the Canadian crime set out in the authority to proceed. This is a major change from what was required under the former Act. Under the former regime, if the conduct did not constitute a crime in Canada at the time that it was committed, extradition was not possible unless a treaty specifically provided otherwise. Under the new Act it is irrelevant whether the conduct was an offence in Canada when it was committed. What is important is that the conduct constitutes a Canadian offence at the time that the authority to proceed is issued. This is not subject to treaty override; therefore, the Act will prevail in the event of a conflicting provision in a treaty.

§3.6 Extradition When Person Sought Has Been Tried and Convicted Without Being Present (s. 29(5))

Subject to provisions in an extradition treaty, s. 29(5) of the new *Extradition Act* addresses the conduct of extradition hearings in the case of persons sought who were tried and convicted in the requesting jurisdiction without being present. In such circumstances, s. 29(5) provides that the hearing is to be conducted pursuant to s. 29(1)(a), that is, that the person sought be treated as an accused rather than a convicted person for the purposes of the extradition hearing. The former Act made no such distinction. Fugitives who had been tried and convicted without being present were treated as convicted fugitives, and thus dealt with according to s. 18(1)(a), unless the conviction was in contumacy (i.e., the conviction was not final and would be set aside on return) as defined under s. 2 of the former Act.

The new Act makes no distinction between contumacy convictions and final convictions. So long as the person was tried and convicted without being present the test applied at the extradition hearing will be that for accused persons under s. 29(1)(a), unless an applicable treaty provides otherwise.

§4.0 ANALYSIS

§4.1 Extradition Hearing When Person Sought for Purpose of Prosecution (s. 29(1)(a))

(a) Pre-hearing issues — Disclosure

Disclosure decisions under the former Act will continue to be relevant to matters proceeding under the new Act. The Supreme Court of Canada in *United States v. Dynar* (1997), 115 C.C.C. (3d) 481, and in *United States v. Kwok* (2001), 152 C.C.C. (3d) 225, cases decided under the former Act, indicated that the extent of disclosure required in extradition was less than in domestic prosecutions given the limited nature and purpose of the hearing. Since this has not changed under the new Act, disclosure obligations will be determined according to the same principles.

(i) General disclosure for purposes of extradition hearing

In *R. v. Stinchcombe*, [1991] 3 S.C.R. 326, the Supreme Court of Canada held that in domestic criminal cases the defence is entitled to receive disclosure of all relevant evidence whether or not the prosecution intends to rely upon it. This exacting standard, based as it is on an accused's constitutionally entrenched right to make full answer and defence, does not apply with the same vigour in the extradition context. The level of disclosure required in extradition is defined by the nature of the proceeding. The definitive statement of principle in this area was set out by the Supreme Court of Canada in *United States v. Dynar, supra*.

In *United States v. Dynar*, the fugitive had been charged in the United States with attempt and conspiracy to launder money. He was a Canadian citizen who had been the subject of a sting operation involving numerous calls between an FBI agent in the United States and the fugitive in Canada, as a result of which the fugitive agreed to launder what he believed to be the proceeds of crime. At the extradition hearing, the United States relied upon affidavits from investigating officers as well as transcripts of the incriminating conversations. Dynar was committed for surrender. Subsequent to the hearing, and subsequent to the decision of the Minister of Justice to surrender Dynar, it was learned that Canadian authorities had been involved with the Americans in the investigation. A formal co-operative arrangement had been in place in which information had been exchanged between the American and Canadian authorities regarding Dynar's activities. On appeal, Dynar argued that he should have received disclosure of the Canadian involvement in the case. Dynar's main argument was described as follows, at p. 519:

> He argues that he did not receive adequate disclosure of the involvement of the Canadian investigating authorities in the gathering of the evidence that was the basis for the committal order. This lack of disclosure, he submits, justifies a new hearing at which full disclosure should be given, which in turn may provide him with the basis for arguing that a stay of proceedings is warranted.

The Supreme Court found, at pp. 524–525, that there had been no breach of fundamental justice concerning the disclosure that had been provided to Dynar:

> [133] . . . Any requirement for disclosure that is read into the Act as a matter of fundamental justice under s. 7 of the *Charter* will therefore necessarily be constrained by the limited function of the extradition judge under the Act, and by the need to avoid imposing Canadian notions of procedural fairness on foreign authorities.
>
> [134] The Requesting State concedes that the fugitive is entitled to know the case against him. See *United States of America v. Whitley* (1994), 94 C.C.C. (3d) 99, 119 D.L.R. (4th) 693 (Ont. C.A.), affirmed [1996] 1 S.C.R. 467, 104 C.C.C. (3d) 447, 132 D.L.R. (4th) 575 (Ont. C.A.). In light of the purpose of the hearing, however, this would simply entitle him to disclosure of material on which the Requesting State is relying to establish its *prima facie* case.

. . .

[129] The context and purpose of the extradition hearing will shape the level of procedural protection that is available to a fugitive. In *Kindler v. Canada (Minister of Justice),* [1991] 2 S.C.R. 779, at p. 844, 67 C.C.C. (3d) 1, 84 D.L.R. (4th) 438, the position was put by the majority in this way:

> While the extradition process is an important part of our system of criminal justice, it would be wrong to equate it with the criminal trial process. It differs from the criminal process in purpose and procedure and, most importantly, in the factors which render it fair. Extradition procedure, unlike the criminal procedure, is founded on the concepts of reciprocity, comity and respect for differences in other jurisdictions.

See also *Mellino, supra* at p. 551.

[130] It follows that it is neither necessary nor appropriate to simply transplant into the extradition process all the disclosure requirements referred to in *Stinchcombe*, [*R. v. Stinchcombe* (1991), 68 C.C.C. (3d) 1 (S.C.C.)], *supra*, *Chaplin*, [*R. v. Chaplin* (1995), 96 C.C.C. (3d) 225 (S.C.C.)], *supra*, and *O'Connor* [*R. v. O'Connor* (1995), 103 C.C.C. (3d) 1 (S.C.C.)], *supra*. Those concepts apply to domestic criminal proceedings, where onerous duties are properly imposed on the Crown to disclose to the defence all relevant material in its possession or control. This is a function of an accused's right to full answer and defence in a Canadian trial. However, the extradition proceeding is governed by treaty and by statute. The role of the extradition judge is limited and the level of procedural safeguards required, including disclosure, must be considered within this framework.

That *R. v. Stinchcombe* is only applicable in full force to a Canadian trial where the concept of full answer and defence is in issue was again confirmed by the Supreme Court of Canada in *United States v. Kwok* (2001), 152 C.C.C. (3d) 225. In *Kwok*, the fugitive was a Canadian citizen who sought disclosure of (1) the fruits of a Canadian investigation that had paralleled the American investigation for which his extradition on drug charges was sought; (2) all discussions between Canadian and American police; and (3) all discussions between Canadian and American authorities concerning the decision to proceed with a prosecution in the United States rather than in Canada. Arbour J. held, at pp. 266-267, that the requested disclosure was not required and that *Stinchcombe* did not apply:

> [99] *Stinchcombe, supra*, dealt with disclosure in a criminal trial context where the right to make full answer and defence is directly engaged on issues of guilt or innocence. Extradition proceedings are not concerned with issues of guilt or innocence. Rather, they are in some ways akin to preliminary inquiries. . . .

> . . .

> [101] In this case, the appellant was entitled to know the case against him, including

the materials upon which the United States relied upon to establish a *prima facie* case. Since the Requesting State was not relying upon materials in the possession of Canadian authorities, and in the absence of any indication of bad faith or improper motives on the part of prosecuting authorities, there was no obligation to provide further disclosure of materials requested.

Accordingly, only material that is relevant to the function of the extradition hearing judge must be disclosed. This includes material that will be relied upon by the extradition partner in support of the extradition request. Some specific disclosure issues are discussed below.

(ii) *Disclosure of additional material held by requesting state*

In *United States v. Dynar, supra,* and in *United States v. Kwok, supra,* the Supreme Court of Canada held that there is no right to the disclosure of Canadian-held material relating to the investigation of a person sought that is not relied on at the extradition hearing. In light of this holding, it appears that there is similarly no right for a person sought to gain disclosure of unused evidence in the hands of the extradition partner. This issue arose in England in *R. v. Governor of Pentonville Prison,* [1993] 3 All E.R. 504 (Q.B.). The fugitive in that case asked the Divisional Court for access to material in the possession of the requesting state that had not been provided for use at the hearing. Apart from the practical impossibility of such an order, the court considered it to be contrary to the structure of the extradition scheme, at p. 508:

> The requesting state must be the sole arbiter of such material as it chooses to place before the court in support of its application and in purported compliance with the relevant domestic extradition legislation. It alone will decide what material in support of its allegations it places before . . . the court . . . . If it furnishes inadequate evidence, then it takes the risk that its request will be refused; in which event, it will be up to the requesting state to determine whether it starts fresh proceedings or not. Neither principles of comity nor the express terms of the Act afford the court in this country any right, still less power, to request further material from the requesting state as a condition precedent to committal. For that reason, the submission that the magistrate should, at the very least, have requested of the Hong Kong government a sight of any unused material is of no substance, and we reject it.

A similar situation arose before Lyon J. of the Ontario Court (General Division) in *United States v. Shulman* (September 13, 1995), [1995] O.J. No. 4497 (Ont. Gen. Div.), appeal allowed on other grounds (1998), 128 C.C.C. (3d) 475 (Ont. C.A.), reversed (2001), 152 C.C.C. (3d) 294 (S.C.C.), reconsideration refused (June 14 2001), Docs. 26912, 27610, 27774 (S.C.C.), in which a disclosure request was made concerning material in the hands of the requesting state. The fugitive, a Canadian, faced extradition in connection with charges alleging that, while in Canada, he and others made illegal sales of gemstones to residents of the United States through telephone conversations originating in Canada. All of the affidavit evidence concerning the unlawful business activities of the fugitive was provided by alleged co-conspirators who, at the time the affidavits were prepared, had pleaded guilty but had not been sentenced. The fugitive sought complete disclosure of plea negotiations between the alleged co-conspirators, whose affidavits comprised the case in support of the extradition request. Lyon J. denied the request. In language similar to that subsequently used by the Supreme Court of Canada in *United States v. Dynar, supra,* Lyon J. stated, at paras. 21 and 27):

> [21] The applicant submits that the request for disclosure is relevant to the issue of admissibility of the co-conspirators' affidavits in the extradition hearing itself on the basis that the [affiants], or some of them, have pleaded guilty and have not been sentenced at the time of swearing of the affidavits.
>
> . . .
>
> [27] . . . [T]his request is not in relation to matters which have relevance to any issue which the extradition judge is called on to consider. Such information may no doubt be capable of affecting the weight to be given to such affidavits but would not affect their admissibility before this Court. The extradition judge does not have the responsibility nor the right to weigh evidence or to assess credibility.

In *Germany (Federal Republic) v. Krapohl* (1995), 79 O.A.C. 77 (Ont. C.A.), the extradition judge had discharged the fugitive on charges of fraud and theft because the requesting state had failed to disclose in its evidence some potentially exculpatory evidence. The Ontario Court of Appeal held that the judge had erred in discharging the fugitive. The Ontario Court of Appeal had occasion to consider this issue again when the judicial review of the Minister of Justice's surrender decision came before it (*Germany (Federal Republic) v. Krapohl* (1998), 110 O.A.C. 129 (Ont. C.A.). It had been argued that the Minister at the second phase of the proceedings should have addressed the alleged non-disclosure. In holding that there was no obligation on the part of the Minister to disclose the material, the court made the following observation about disclosure obligations in the circumstances of this case, at p. 133:

> [16] In my view he was correct in law. The Extradition Treaty between Canada and Germany requires no more of the requesting state than that it provide the extradition process with evidence to support a prima facie case. Beyond this, the Treaty imposes no obligation of disclosure on the requesting state. Nor does the *Act* or the *Charter of Rights and Freedoms*: see *United States of America et al. v. Dynar,* [1997] 2 S.C.R. 462; 213 N.R. 321; 101 O.A.C. 321.

Also, in *Thailand (Kingdom) v. Saxena* (April 29, 1999), Doc. Vancouver CC960599, 1999 CarswellBC 922 (B.C.S.C.), it was argued on behalf of the fugitive that the requesting state had not produced all of the documents relating to a transaction. Maczko J. ruled that it was unnecessary for the requesting state to submit all of the evidence available to it. However, he added one qualification, noting that there was a distinction to be drawn between tendering only part of a document and choosing not to tender a document at all. He ruled that, in keeping with the principles of fundamental justice, if the requesting state chose to rely upon a document at the extradition hearing it had to produce the entire document.

In *Germany (Federal Republic) v. Schreiber* (July 6, 2000), [2000] O.J. No. 2618, 2000 CarswellOnt 5257 (Ont. S.C.J.), a case decided under the new Act, a number of items of additional disclosure had been sought from the extradition judge including documentary material in the hands of the German prosecutorial authorities which had been referred to in the evidence summarized in the record of the case but which had not, itself, been provided. Watt J. described the basis upon which this disclosure was sought as follows:

> [23] According to Mr. Schreiber, these documents are relevant as well on the hearing before the extradition judge. He wants them because he (Schreiber) has a right to adduce evidence to show that the test for committal under s. 29(1)(a) of the Act has *not* been met. This evidence would be admissible, he submits, under s. 32(1)(c) of the *Act*. Disclosure of it is necessary for Mr. Schreiber to make full answer and defence at the hearing. [Emphasis in original.]

Watt J. denied the application for the requested disclosure, and held that since the evidence to be relied upon at the hearing had been provided, no further disclosure was required. However, he also acknowledged his jurisdictional incapacity to make the disclosure order requested in any event. He noted that having been given by s. 24(2) of the Act a jurisdiction analogous to that of a preliminary inquiry justice, he had no authority to order disclosure. He stated as follows:

> [84] A further observation about disclosure is in order. Section 24(2) of the *Act* assimilates the powers of the extradition hearing judge to those of a justice conducting a preliminary inquiry in domestic proceedings under Part XVIII of the *Criminal Code*. It is settled law, in this province at least, that a justice at a preliminary inquiry has *no* authority to review Crown disclosure decisions, including the extent and timing of this disclosure. See, for example, *R. v. Girimonte* (1997), 121 C.C.C. (3d) 33, 44-5 (Ont. C.A.), per Doherty J.A.

Watt J. also recognized that a Canadian order with respect to disclosure could have no operation as against a foreign country. He held as follows:

> [89] The Record of the Case has been disclosed to the applicant. It is quite detailed and identifies the source of the material on which its numerous statements of fact are said to be based. There is *no* warrant in the *Act* or treaty to require disclosure of the primary materials in the custody of the authorities in the Federal Republic. At all events, such an order would *not* be enforceable. Domestic disclosure commands do *not* extend to foreign jurisdictions. [Emphasis in original.]

Romilly J. agreed with Watt J. in *United States v. Akrami, supra*, §3.1(d). Romilly J. dismissed an application for disclosure in the hands of the extradition partner, which the person had requested in order to challenge the reliability of the evidence adduced in support of the request. Romilly J. held, at para. 22, that "requests to test the reliability and credibility of the Requesting State's evidence are not valid bases for disclosure." Additionally, relying upon the decision of Watt J. in *Schreiber*, Romilly J. held that an extradition judge had no jurisdiction in any event to order the disclosure of materials held by a foreign state.

(iii) Disclosure of material in hands of requesting state when evidence led at hearing is not documentary

At least one Canadian court has been prepared to order disclosure of evidence in the hands of the requesting state. In *Romania v. Cheng* (1996), 153 N.S.R. (2d) 271, 450 A.P.R. 271 (N.S.S.C. [In Chambers]), certain crew members of a Taiwanese ship made allegations to the R.C.M.P. in Halifax that the ship's officers had killed some Romanian stowaways by forcing them overboard at sea. Based on the crew members' statements, Romania requested the extradition of the officers to stand trial for the murder of the stowaways. Since the witnesses to the alleged crime were physically present in Canada, an unusual situation in extradition proceedings, the evidence in support of a *prima facie* case of murder was established by calling *viva voce* evidence. Both Canadian and Romanian authorities had interviewed the witnesses in Halifax. By the time of the hearing, the Romanian investigators had returned home. Because the evidence at the hearing was to be led *viva voce* and the witnesses were available for cross-examination, MacDonald J. ruled that any statements given by these witnesses should be disclosed, whether held by Canadian or by Romanian authorities. MacDonald J. commented as follows, at p. 276:

> [15] (1) As noted earlier, the evidence against these fugitives is based upon the alleged eye witness accounts of Filipino crewmen and perhaps one surviving remaining Romanian stowaway. This evidence will be fundamental to the case before me. The Crown will no doubt present evidence from some or all of these witnesses. The Crown should therefore disclose all and any statements whether obtained here or elsewhere given by its proposed *eye* witnesses. I acknowledge that it is not my function to assess weight and credibility. Yet, I expect that some or all of these witnesses will be cross-examined despite the expeditious nature of these proceedings.

MacDonald J. held that while there may be no right to cross-examine when the evidence was provided by affidavit, there was a right to cross-examine when the evidence was given orally. He concluded as follows, at p. 276:

> [16] A right to cross-examination should be an *effective* right to cross-examination. To be effective the defence should have all statements made by the aforesaid informants. In this case I have no way of knowing the evidence that will be presented before me. It

would not be practical for me at this stage to screen for disclosure purposes all such evidence. However for example, if one of the Crown's proposed aforesaid eyewitnesses has recanted, the defence should know this regardless of where and when this statement was made. This recantation could be used to challenge this witness during cross-examination. That would certainly have an impact on the sufficiency of evidence before me therefore making it relevant. [Emphasis in original.]

The soundness of this conclusion is doubtful given that it is not open to the extradition judge to resolve inconsistencies in the evidence or make findings of credibility (see the discussion earlier in this chapter). The better position seems to be that challenges to the veracity of evidence in support of a charge are more appropriately left to the court that will try the charge in the requesting jurisdiction.

(iv) Disclosure of evidence gathered in Canada pursuant to Canadian court orders

In *R. v. Barranca* (December 14, 1994), [1994] O.J. No. 3942 (Ont. Gen. Div.), Keenan J. (who was also the extradition judge in *United States v. Dynar, supra*) ordered disclosure of Canadian authorizations and intercepted communications which had been obtained in aid of an American investigation into alleged drug activities by Barranca and three co-accused, all of whom were based in Canada. The allegations were that an American agent had come to Canada to arrange a purchase of heroin from the fugitives. According to the evidence of the agent, he had led the fugitives to believe that he would distribute the heroin in the United States. The American agent's meetings with the fugitives were recorded by means of a device secreted on his person. An authorization under Part VI of the *Criminal Code* was obtained in order for the agent to lawfully record his meetings with the fugitives. In support of the extradition request, the United States provided an affidavit from the agent deposing to the substance of his conversations with the fugitives in respect of the alleged drug deal. The United States did not provide copies or transcripts of the taped conversations.

The fugitives sought disclosure of the recorded interceptions as well as the authorizations and affidavits in support of the authorizations. In granting the disclosure, Keenan J. commented as follows:

> The extradition judge has an obligation to examine the evidence that is submitted and pass on its sufficiency. The fugitive is entitled to be represented by counsel and is entitled to mount a challenge to the sufficiency of the evidence. It is axiomatic that the fugitive has a right to information which may assist him in challenging the validity or sufficiency of the evidence.
>
> In this case the evidence upon which the requesting state relies is the affidavit evidence of the FBI agent who participated in the intercepted communication. In order to successfully challenge the accuracy or the interpretation of those communications given by the author of the affidavit, the defence is entitled to examine the communication itself and to mount any challenge that there may be to its accuracy.

The fact that the requesting state presents as evidence only the content that it has collected from the conversations themselves does not disable this court from examining other evidence which may be pertinent. It does not disable the fugitive or his counsel from presenting other evidence of other parts of the conversation which may tend to call into question the sufficiency of the evidence relied upon.

Keenan J. was clear that his disclosure order applied only to Canadian-held evidence concerning the communications and not to anything in the possession of the American authorities. Notwithstanding this, his assertion that unused evidence not tendered by the requesting state may be admissible to challenge the accuracy of the affidavit evidence pertaining to the intercepted communications does not accord with the function assigned by the Act to an extradition judge as enunciated in Supreme Court of Canada cases such as *Argentina (Republic) v. Mellino* (1987), 33 C.C.C. (3d) 334, and *United States v. McVey* (1992), 77 C.C.C. (3d) 1, and most recently *Dynar*, and *Kwok, supra,* §4.1(a).

The Supreme Court held in *United States v. Dynar* that disclosure of Canadian involvement in that case was not required. The court found that the fugitive had received full disclosure of the material to be relied upon by the requesting state at the hearing, and that was enough. The court was of the view that the disclosure of Canadian involvement in the case could have been of no assistance to the fugitive in mounting a challenge to the sufficiency of the evidence relied upon by the United States in support of the request for extradition. Cory and Iacobucci JJ., in considering whether a *Charter* argument could have been made in an attempt to exclude the evidence, held that there was no justiciable *Charter* issue in the case, at pp. 527–528:

> [141] Mr. Dynar contends that as a result of the Requesting State's non-disclosure, there is no evidentiary record on the basis of which he can even attempt to make a *Charter* argument. Yet the evidence presented by the Requesting State does disclose enough information to conclude that there is simply no "air of reality" to the contention that Mr. Dynar could establish a *Charter* violation by the Canadian officials in the gathering of the evidence. The evidence before Keenan J. included the affidavit of Agent Matthews. It clearly reveals that the FBI had been interested in the activities of Mr. Dynar for some time; that Matthews himself was aware of previous occasions on which Mr. Dynar had admitted to laundering large sums of money in the State of Nevada, and that he initiated the investigation on the basis of his suspicions regarding Mr. Dynar's telephone call to Lucky Simone. The affidavit provides a sufficient basis to conclude that the investigation, the evidence and the prosecution were essentially American. No amount of cooperation by the Canadian authorities could change this.
>
> . . .
>
> [143] It is true that the fugitive is entitled to be committed only on the basis of evidence that is legally admissible according to law of the province in which the committal hearing takes place: see *La Forest's Extradition, supra,* at p. 160. But it has been consistently and properly held that the *Charter* generally does not apply extraterritorially. As a result, Canadian courts cannot impose upon foreign evidence the standards of

admissibility that have developed in the jurisprudence dealing with s. 24(2) of the *Charter*.

[144] Mr. Dynar was entitled to a fair hearing before the extradition judge, and in our opinion he received one. He was not entitled to disclosure from the Requesting State beyond the production of the evidence that it was relying on to establish its *prima facie* case. In any event, the evidence provided by the Requesting State did contain sufficient information to conclude that the evidence was gathered entirely in the United States, by American officials, for an American trial. It follows that no justiciable *Charter* issue can arise in this case.

In *United States v. Kwok*, *supra*, a similar situation arose. Kwok had been the subject of parallel Canadian and American investigations into his alleged drug trafficking activities. There had been both Canadian and U.S. authorization in effect for the interception of his communications and those of various co-conspirators.

Kwok requested complete disclosure of the Canadian investigation as well as of all discussions between the Canadian and American police and prosecuting authorities before both the extradition judge and the Minister on the grounds that he could not make effective representations on his s. 6(1) *Charter* rights without access to the requested material. His request was denied by both the extradition judge and the Minister, and their decisions in this regard were upheld by the Supreme Court of Canada. Arbour J. stated, at p. 267:

> [101] In this case, the appellant was entitled to know the case against him, including the materials upon which the United States relied upon to establish a *prima facie* case. Since the Requesting State was not relying upon materials in the possession of Canadian authorities, and in the absence of any indication of bad faith or improper motives on the part of prosecuting authorities, there was no obligation to provide further disclosure of materials requested.

Arbour J. held that *Dynar*, *supra*, was dispositive of the appeal and that only where a justiciable *Charter* issue can arise from the potential involvement of the Canadian authorities in the gathering of evidence is it necessary to consider the degree of additional disclosure that might be required.

(v) *Disclosure of other Canadian material for* Charter *challenge and ministerial purposes*

In *United States v. Cheema* (1999), 65 C.R.R. (2d) 234 (B.C. S.C.), leave to appeal to S.C.C. refused (2001), 271 N.R. 193 (note) (S.C.C.), Bennett J. of the Supreme Court of British Columbia ordered disclosure of certain material in the hands of Canadian authorities for use by the fugitive at the ministerial phase. He found that an air of reality had been established in that the material sought might establish a *Charter* breach on the part of the Canadian police who were alleged to have conducted an illegal drug importation with a police agent who had been involved with Cheema.

Leave to appeal from the decision of Bennett J. in *Cheema* was denied on April 5, 2001. On the same date, the Supreme Court's decision in *United States v. Kwok, supra*, was released. In *Kwok*, the Supreme Court held that there exists a discretionary authority for an extradition judge to hear evidence outside the ambit of his or her jurisdiction when it is expedient to do so. In connection with the discretion to accept otherwise inadmissible evidence for use in proceedings subsequent to the hearing (the ministerial phase or *Charter* challenge on appeal), Arbour J. also recognized the concomitant authority of the extradition judge to order disclosure for this purpose, at p. 267:

> [101] . . . Requests for disclosure of materials related to issues which properly belong to the executive phase of extradition, and to the judicial review thereof, have no independent relevance before the extradition judge and are subsumed in his or her discretion to hear evidence related to such issues.

Kwok was decided under the former Act, and whether there will continue to be a residual discretion for an extradition judge to allow evidence on matters unrelated to the hearing and to order disclosure accordingly might be questioned given the provisions of the new Act.

In *Germany (Federal Republic) v. Schreiber, supra*, §4.1(a)(ii), decided prior to the release of the Supreme Court's decision in *Kwok*, but decided under the provisions of the new Act, Watt J. made the observation that having been given by s. 24(2) of the new Act a jurisdiction akin to that of a judge at a preliminary inquiry, he had no jurisdiction to order disclosure. He stated:

> [84] A further observation about disclosure is in order. Section 24(2) of the *Act* assimilates the powers of the extradition hearing judge to those of a justice conducting a preliminary inquiry in domestic proceedings under Part XVIII of the *Criminal Code*. It is settled law, in this province at least, that a justice at preliminary inquiry has *no* authority to review Crown disclosure decisions, including the extent and timing of this disclosure. See, for example, *R. v. Girimonte* (1997), 121 C.C.C. (3d) 33, 44-5 (Ont. C.A.), per Doherty J.A. [Emphasis in original.]

In *Australia v. Ho* (January 26, 2000), Doc. Vancouver CC990288 (B.C.S.C.), also decided prior to the release of the decision in *Kwok*, but decided under the new Act, Romilly J. denied an application for disclosure of written reports and correspondence between Canadian and Australian authorities concerning the reason that the Australian request for extradition was made two years after the issuance of the arrest warrant for the person sought. The documents were sought in order to establish that the person's *Charter* rights had been infringed by the actions of the Canadian authorities and in order to make submissions on this point to the Minister of Justice. Romilly J. held that he had no jurisdiction to make the order that was sought.

(vi) *Inadvertent disclosure of confidential material*

In *United States v. Mokdad* (February 12, 1999), Doc. E-25/98 (Ont. Gen. Div.), the Crown erroneously disclosed to defence counsel confidential material relating to a cross-border investigation into heroin trafficking. The Crown argued that the defence should be ordered by the court to refrain from any wider dissemination of the material on the grounds that disclosure to the public at large, outside the limited group who had been exposed to the material, would be harmful to the interests of law enforcement by revealing their investigative procedures for these types of offences. Cusinato J. held that he had inherent jurisdiction to make the order requested by the Crown. On this basis, he ordered that the fugitive's counsel would be entitled to retain the material until the conclusion of the hearing but that counsel could not disseminate the material further and had to return the material to the police at the conclusion of the hearing. Counsel had argued that the material might be of assistance to the fugitive in the event that he had to face trial in the United States, and therefore the fugitive should be allowed to keep the material. Cusinato J. rejected this submission on the basis that the degree of disclosure required for a trial in the foreign state should be determined by the courts of that jurisdiction.

(b) Conduct of hearing

(i) *Tendering authority to proceed*

Under s. 24(1) of the *Extradition Act*, it is a condition precedent to the holding of the extradition hearing that the authority to proceed, issued by the Minister of Justice under s. 15, has been filed with the court by the Attorney General. It is not necessarily the original which needs to be filed as s. 15(4) makes it clear that copies will suffice. Section 15(4) provides that a copy of the authority to proceed has the same probative force as the original for the purposes of Part 2 of the Act. (Part 2 is titled "Extradition From Canada" and includes the provisions governing extradition hearings.)

Two cases under the new Act have indicated that the Minister may need to consider identifying the Canadian offences in the authority to proceed with some specificity rather than identifying a general offence. In *United States v. Drysdale* (2000), 32 C.R. (5th) 163 (Ont. S.C.J.), Dambrot J. was critical of the fact that the authority to proceed identified the Canadian offences in the rather compendious terms of "conspiracy to export hash," and "conspiracy to import hash." He commented, at p. 192:

> [83] With the greatest of respect to the drafter of these authorities to proceed, and taking into account the fact that the document is a very new innovation, I cannot avoid commenting that these lists are less than helpful. In a situation involving facts that give rise to numerous possible conspiracy offences, some broad, some narrow, some national, and some international, an effort ought to be made, in my view, to make clear what

conspiracies under Canadian law the Minister wants the extradition judge to consider. It should not be left to the extradition judge to conjure up all the possible conspiracies that might arise on the evidence, and then to consider which of these are supported by sufficient evidence to justify committal. The extradition judge ought not to be asked to play the additional role of prosecutor.

[84] Fortunately, in this case, counsel for the requesting state was prepared, at my instance, in the course of oral argument, to specify what offences were actually intended to be considered.

LaForme J., in *United States v. Debarros* (February 9, 2000), Doc. E-9/99 (Ont. S.C..J.), was of the same opinion, commenting, at para. 37, that "the authority to proceed ought to provide more detail as to the actual Canadian criminal offences that the Minister wishes the extradition judge to consider. This would be particularly helpful when dealing with multiple conspiracies as we are dealing with here."

(ii) *Establishing identity*

At the extradition hearing, the Attorney General of Canada, on behalf of the extradition partner, must satisfy the court that the person before the court is the individual wanted in the foreign jurisdiction. This requirement flows from the concluding sentence in s. 29(1)(a), which provides that the extradition judge must be "satisfied that the person is the person sought by the extradition partner." If this cannot be established, the person sought will be discharged.

If the person brought before the court is found to be the person sought by the extradition partner, the second question is whether there is sufficient evidence that this person committed an offence that would justify committal for trial in Canada. These are two distinct issues, although both relate to issues of identity. The first concerns "identity of the person." That is, it must be established that the person before the court is the person who is the subject of the extradition request. The second concerns proof that the person before the court is the author of the crime alleged. The evidence led on behalf of the extradition partner may apply so as to address both identity requirements. However, these are two distinct issues. Therefore, it is possible that the identity evidence will be sufficient with respect to the first issue but insufficient with respect to the second issue. Frailties in the evidence on the second aspect of identity go directly to the issue of whether a case for committal has been established.

On the first aspect of identity, many extradition treaties require the extradition partner to supply evidence relating to the identity of the person named in the foreign warrant of arrest. Section 32(1)(b) of the new *Extradition Act* permits the introduction of evidence in accordance with extradition agreements. Thus the identity provisions of treaties continue to have relevance under the new Act. For example, Article 9(3) of the *Canada–United States Extradition Treaty* provides as follows:

> **9.** (3) When the request relates to a person who has not yet been convicted, it must also be accompanied by a warrant of arrest issued by a judge or other judicial officer of

the requesting State and by such evidence as, according to the laws of the requested State, would justify his arrest and committal for trial if the offense had been committed there, *including evidence proving the person requested is the person to whom the warrant of arrest refers.* [Emphasis added.]

Section 32(1)(a) of the new Act provides for the admission of evidence pursuant to documents contained in a certified record of the case. Section 33(2) indicates that the record of the case may include "documents respecting the identification of the person sought for extradition."

Only one case at the appeal level — *Philippines (Republic) v. Pacificador* (1993), 83 C.C.C. (3d) 210 (Ont. C.A.), leave to appeal to S.C.C. refused (1994), 87 C.C.C. (3d) vi (S.C.C.) — appears to have addressed the standard of proof to be applied in satisfying the extradition court that the person before it is the person named in the warrant. The Ontario Court of Appeal held that identity must be established on a balance of probabilities. Doherty J.A., speaking for the court, described the issue as it had been presented to the court, at p. 214:

> The appellant submits that the requesting state must establish that the fugitive before the court is the person named in the warrant issued by the requesting state. The requesting state acknowledges that obligation and led evidence at the hearing to show that the appellant was the person referred to in the warrant. The evidence led Watt J. to conclude that identity had been "plainly established".
>
> The appellant submits that the requesting state must do more than "plainly establish" the identity of the person before the court as the person named in the warrant. He maintains that the burden of proof on the requesting state is some unarticulated standard short of proof beyond a reasonable doubt, but higher than proof on a balance of probabilities.
>
> I cannot accept this argument. Counsel's inability to articulate the applicable standard of proof demonstrates the defect in this argument. Absent applicable statutory language, a party who bears the ultimate burden of proof on a fact in issue, must meet one of two standards of proof. That party must prove the fact either beyond a reasonable doubt, or on the balance of probabilities: Sopinka, Lederman, and Bryant, *The Law of Evidence in Canada* (1992), p. 141.
>
> The appellant quite properly conceded in oral argument that proof beyond a reasonable doubt was not an appropriate standard. It must follow that the requesting state was required to establish identity on the balance of probabilities. The finding by Watt J. that the requesting state had "plainly established" that the appellant was the person named in the warrant issued by the requesting state constitutes a finding by him that identity had been established on the balance of probabilities. His use of the adjective "plainly" reflects an appreciation of the need to carefully scrutinize the evidence before concluding that the requesting state had established identity on the balance of probabilities.

The standard enunciated by the Ontario Court of Appeal, that is, proof on a balance of probabilities, will continue as the standard to be applied to the determination of whether the person sought is the person before the court.

If the person brought before the court is found to be the person sought by the extradition partner, the second question relating to identity is whether there is sufficient evidence that this person committed an offence that would justify committal for trial in Canada. This question concerns proof that the person before the court is the author of the alleged crime. This requires the application of the test enunciated by the Supreme Court of Canada in *United States v. Shephard, supra*, §1.1, namely, that there is "some evidence" upon which a jury, properly instructed, could convict.

A useful illustration of a case in which the identity evidence was insufficient and the test for a *prima facie* case was not met is *Puerto Rico (Commonwealth) v. Hernandez (No. 2)* (1973), 15 C.C.C. (2d) 56 (Fed. C.A.). The Federal Court of Appeal was called upon to review the decision of the extradition judge that the identity evidence in connection with a murder charge was insufficient to support the issuance of a warrant of committal. The identification evidence was given by a witness who did not previously know the fugitive, who made the identification one year after the event, and "whose only opportunity to observe him was a fleeting one from a distance of some 60 ft., if indeed he ever got that close," at p. 63. In upholding the discharge, Thurlow J.A. on behalf of the court stated as follows, at p. 64:

> It was submitted that the learned Judge erred in law in holding that the identification evidence of the witness Atilano was of no weight or value in the absence of supporting evidence and in holding that the evidence of Atilano was an opinion rather than a positive identification. I regard these, however, not as rulings on questions of law by the learned Judge but as his impression of the value or weight of the particular testimony. It seems perfectly obvious that on the facts the identification could be put no higher than an opinion which the witness had formed and that without further supportive material or corroboration it could not reasonably be taken seriously.

The *Puerto Rico (Commonwealth) v. Hernandez (No. 2)* decision predated the test set out by Ritchie J. of the Supreme Court of Canada in *United States v. Shephard, supra*, but was referred to by Ritchie J. in that case. Ritchie J. appeared to view the decision as a situation in which the evidence was such that a properly instructed jury could not convict. Commenting upon the decision, Ritchie J. commented as follows, at p. 434:

> It thus appears to me clear that in that case it was held that there was not enough evidence to support a *prima facie* case against the accused and in fact that it was "inconceivable that a person should be put on trial on such flimsy evidence". It was upon this ground that the extradition Judge in that case based his opinion as to insufficiency.

More recently, in *United States v. Wagner* (1995), 104 C.C.C. (3d) 66 (B.C. C.A.), leave to appeal to S.C.C. refused (1996), 106 C.C.C. (3d) vi (S.C.C.), the British Columbia Court of Appeal expressed the opinion that the decision in *Puerto Rico (Commonwealth) v. Hernandez* had been overtaken, and that it was not within the authority of an extradition judge or a preliminary inquiry judge to refuse to commit on the grounds that the identification evidence was flimsy or made under difficult conditions. The court noted that in England the trial judge might take the case from the jury if the judge was of the opinion that the quality of the evidence is poor "as for example when it depends solely on a fleeting glance or on a longer observation made in difficult conditions" (quoting Widgery C.J. in *R. v. Turnbull*, [1976] 3 All E.R. 549 (C.A.), at p. 553). The court observed that the English test had been rejected by a majority of the Supreme Court of Canada in *Mezzo v. R.*, [1986] 1 S.C.R. 802. After referring to the majority judgment (written by McIntyre J.) in *Mezzo v. R.*, Ryan J.A. for the British Columbia Court of Appeal in the *Wagner* case concluded as follows, at p. 73:

> [22] In my view, this passage demonstrates that the majority in *Mezzo* rejected the approach in *Hernandez*. The result then, is this — once the Crown has offered material which may be said to have attained the status of "evidence", that is, where the testimony or documentary material offered is relevant to and probative of the issue in question, the trial judge is not empowered to direct a verdict of acquittal, but must leave the question of weight to the jury.

It may still be open to argue that the material presented is so poor as to not attain the status of "evidence." As Watt J. stated in outlining the standard for a *prima facie* case in *Pacificador v. Philippines (Republic)* (July 27, 1992), (Ont. Gen. Div.), it may not achieve the "capacity" to sustain a conviction.

(iii) *Methods of establishing identity*

Under the former regime, the requesting state generally fulfilled its obligation to provide proof of the identity of the fugitive named in the warrant by including either a photograph or fingerprints of the person in the package of authenticated materials sent for use at the hearing. A comparison of the person before the court could then be made against the photograph or fingerprints. However, it was also possible to prove the issue of identity without reference to either fingerprints or photographs. Arrested fugitives frequently made statements acknowledging their status as the person sought for the crime alleged to have been committed in the foreign jurisdiction. These methods of addressing identity will continue to have application under the new Act.

Section 37 of the Act is a new provision which now deems that certain types of identity evidence are probative of the issue of whether the person sought is the person before the court: similarities between the name of the person before the court and that referred to in the documents submitted by the extradition partner; and similarities between the physical characteristics of the person before the court and those contained in a photograph, fingerprint, or other description of the person.

Under the new Act, as was the case under the old system, fingerprints, photographs, and statements made by the person sought may also be used in the determination of whether there is evidence that the person sought committed the offence.

(A) *Photographs*

With respect to establishing the identity of the person, in most cases, the documentary evidence provided by the extradition partner will contain a photograph of the individual who is charged with the offence. Whether the evidence in support of the request is provided in summary form by way of the record of the case provisions in s. 32(1)(a) or in accordance with the terms of an extradition agreement pursuant to s. 32(1)(b), it may be expected that the identity of the person in the photograph as the person sought and as the author of the crime will be established by the evidence of a person in the position to make this identification.

In order to establish identity as the person sought, at the extradition hearing, the Attorney General may call evidence to show that the person before the court is the person depicted in the photograph. As indicated above, s. 37(b) of the new *Extradition Act* states that a similarity between the physical characteristics of the person before the court and those of the person in the photograph is evidence that the person before the court is the person referred to in the order of arrest or any other document in support of the request.

A police officer's identification of the person sought from a photograph is admissible opinion evidence (*United States v. Garcia* (May 11, 1994), Doc. E16/92, [1994] O.J. No. 1027 (Ont. Gen. Div.), affirmed (July 18, 1996), Doc. CA C21023, 1996 CarswellOnt 2408 (Ont. C.A.), leave to appeal to S.C.C. refused (1997), 102 O.A.C. 318 (note) (S.C.C.)). In Ontario, establishing that the person before the court is the person named in the warrant of arrest was often done by way of *viva voce* evidence from one of the Canadian police officers responsible for locating and arresting the individual. The evidence of such a witness was normally to the effect that, having been provided with a copy of the photograph of the person wanted in the foreign jurisdiction, a comparison of the photograph with the person before the court led the officer to the conclusion that they were one and the same person, and the arrest resulted.

The advantage of calling the police officer who made the comparison and the arrest is two-fold. Firstly, as part of their training and their job experience, police officers are frequently required to identify suspects in criminal matters. Therefore, they are experienced in making identification comparisons. Secondly, the identifying police officer can be cross-examined by counsel for the person sought with respect to the basis for the conclusion that the person before the court is the person in the photograph. In this respect, calling the identifying police officer has the advantage of not involving the judge in making the comparison from the bench, since the judge, of course, cannot be cross-examined by counsel for the person sought or for the extradition partner with respect to the basis for any conclusion reached with respect to the issue of identity.

It is unclear whether s. 37(b) of the new Act involves a direction to the extradition judge to undertake a comparison of the person before the court with the person in the photograph. There is jurisprudence under the former Act that supports this approach, and the approach appears to be settled practice in British Columbia (*United States v.*

Jang (May 8, 1975), (Fed. C.A.); *United States v. Wong* (1995), 98 C.C.C. (3d) 332 (B.C. C.A.), leave to appeal to S.C.C. refused (1995), 101 C.C.C. (3d) vi (S.C.C.)). *United States v. Jang* dates from the period when the Federal Court of Appeal reviewed extradition matters. In that case, the Court held that it was acceptable practice for the judge at the extradition hearing to make the comparison between the photograph in the documents and the person before the court. In the more recent case of *United States v. Wong*, the British Columbia Court of Appeal held the extradition judge's comparison of the person before the court with the authenticated photograph was in accordance with long-established practice. In *United States v. Sanders* (March 18, 1996), Koenigsberg J. (B.C. S.C.), the British Columbia Supreme Court followed the practice endorsed in *United States v. Wong*, albeit with some reluctance. Koenigsberg J. stated that she had been invited to, and did, make the comparison with the photograph. However, she added the following comment, at p. 7 of the judgment:

> However, the seeming inappropriateness of the proceeding should not be passed by without comment. First, I agreed to the procedure on the basis solely that just such a procedure had been employed in the British Columbia Supreme Court by judges in earlier extradition hearings. For example, specifically in the *United States v. Wong*, Mr Justice Holmes performed such an examination.

Although Koenigsberg J. followed this practice, she stated, at p. 7, that she agreed with Mr Justice Holmes, the extradition judge in *United States v. Wong*, that it was a "somewhat risky method to follow."

The acceptability of this approach seems to have been settled by the Supreme Court of Canada in *R. v. Nikolovski* (1996), 111 C.C.C. (3d) 403 (S.C.C.). Although not an extradition case, the principle involved seems equally applicable to extradition matters. In that case, the Supreme Court upheld the conviction of Nikolovski for the robbery of a convenience store. The store was video-monitored and the trial judge had viewed a videotape of the robbery in progress and concluded that the accused was the perpetrator in the video. The Ontario Court of Appeal disapproved of the conduct of the judge and held that the judge should not have relied solely upon her own comparison between the appearance of the person on the videotape and the appearance of the accused in court to reach a conclusion that had no other support in the evidence. The Supreme Court reversed the Ontario Court of Appeal and approved the practice, notwithstanding that the conclusion reached by the trial judge could not be tested by cross-examination.

(B) Fingerprints

Section 37(b) of the *Extradition Act* provides that fingerprint evidence is evidence that the person before the court is the person sought. A person arrested in Canada under the authority of the *Extradition Act* is liable to be fingerprinted and photographed in the same fashion as persons arrested for indictable offences in Canada (see s. 2(1)(b) of the *Identification of Criminals Act*; note that s. 16(6) of the *Extradition*

Act extends s. 2(1)(b) to persons summonsed under s. 16 of the Act). In many cases, the person sought will have been arrested and fingerprinted by the extradition partner prior to leaving that jurisdiction. In those circumstances, the extradition partner may provide copies of the fingerprints to the authorities in Canada. This will allow for a more certain method of identification by fingerprint comparison. Like any other piece of evidence provided by the extradition partner, the fingerprints must be provided in a form admissible under the *Extradition Act* and they must be identified as the fingerprints of the wanted party. Fingerprint evidence may also be provided to establish identity as the author of the alleged crime, as in the case of fingerprints taken from a weapon used in an offence. A certificate of comparison can then be issued by a qualified Canadian fingerprint analyst to establish that the fingerprints of the person before the court match the fingerprints of the person sought by the extradition partner. Introducing the results of the comparison requires calling as witnesses the individual who took the fingerprint impressions in Canada from the person before the court and the analyst who made the comparison between the Canadian prints and the fingerprints provided by the extradition partner.

(C) Statements of the person sought

There is case law holding that, if the person sought disputes the issue of identity, the person must raise the issue, and that a lack of protest on arrest is admissible evidence of identity (*United States v. Garcia, supra*, §4.1(b)(iii)(A), at p. 5; *United States v. Kerslake* (1996), 142 Sask. R. 112 (Sask. Q.B.)). An admission by the person sought upon arrest, or subsequently, is admissible at the extradition hearing to prove identity, as would be an admission by the person that he or she committed the offence. An admission of identity in these circumstances would require a *voir dire*. Consequently, the evidence of the arresting officers could be led, in the same manner as would be done in a domestic criminal proceeding to establish voluntariness. Section 32(2) of the new Act provides that evidence gathered in Canada must satisfy the rules of evidence under Canadian law in order to be admitted.

(iv) Test for committal under s. 29(1)(a)

Having established that the person before the court is the person wanted by the extradition partner, it becomes necessary for the extradition judge to consider the sufficiency of the evidence pursuant to s. 29(1)(a) of the *Extradition Act*. This test involves determining whether evidence of conduct has been produced by the extradition partner that would justify committal for trial in Canada on the offence(s) set out in the authority to proceed. As in s. 18(1)(b) of the former Act, the applicable test is that which applies to committal for trial in Canada. This is the so-called "*Shephard* test," the name stemming from the Supreme Court of Canada decision in *United States v. Shephard* (1976), (*sub nom. United States v. Sheppard*), *supra*, §1.1.

In *Philippines (Republic) v. Pacificador* (October 5, 1992), (Ont. Gen. Div.), Watt J. provided a useful overview of the test and its antecedents. He described his function as an extradition judge and the test he was required to apply as follows:

> It is beyond controversy that the standard to which reference is made in s. 18(l)(b) of the *Act* is the selfsame standard erected by s. 548(1)(a) of the *Criminal Code*.
>
> The foundational case whereby the test imposed by present s. 548(i)(a) was given content is *United States of America v. Shephard*, [1977] 2 S.C.R. 1067, *(sub nom. R. v. Sheppard)* 30 C.C.C. (2d) 424, itself an extradition case. The standard to be applied was felicitously described by Ritchie, J. at p. 427 C.C.C. in the terms which follow:
>
>> I agree that the duty imposed upon a "justice" under s. 475(1) is the same as that which governs a trial Judge sitting with a jury in deciding whether the evidence is "sufficient" to justify him in withdrawing the case from the jury and this is to be determined according to whether or not there is *any evidence upon which a reasonable jury properly instructed could return a verdict of guilty.* The "justice", in accordance with this principle, is, in my opinion, required to commit an accused person for trial in any case in which there is *admissible evidence which could, if it were believed, result in a conviction.* [Emphasis added.]
>>
>> . . .
>
> Ritchie, J. concluded at p. 433 C.C.C.:
>
>> . . . I cannot accept the proposition that a trial Judge is ever entitled to take a case from the jury and direct an acquittal on the ground that, *in his opinion*, the evidence is "manifestly unreliable". If this were the law it would deprive the members of the jury of their function to act as the sole judges of the truth or falsity of the evidence and would thus, in my opinion, be contrary to the accepted role of the jury in our legal system. [Emphasis in original.]
>>
>> . . .
>
> In the result, as it would appear to me, it is *not* the function of a justice at preliminary inquiry, a judge at trial under domestic law upon application for a directed verdict, for the judge presiding upon an extradition hearing
>
> (i)   to *weigh* the evidence given;
> (ii) to *test the quality or reliability* of the evidence; or
> (iii) to draw or weigh *competing* inferences, or decide which inference a jury is more likely to draw.
>
> See, for example, *United States of America* v. *Shephard, supra,* at p. 430, per Ritchie J.; *Mezzo v. R.*, [1986] 1 S.C.R. 802 at 842, per McIntyre J.; *R. v. Paul*, [1977] 1 S.C.R. 181 at p. 192, per Ritchie J.; and R. v. *Monteleone* (1987), 35 C.C.C. (3d) 193 at p. 198, per McIntyre J.

The standard has not changed in the new *Extradition Act*. The standard, as is clear from the wording of s. 29(1)(a), remains that required to be met for a committal for trial in Canada. As indicated in the speech of the Parliamentary Secretary when the Bill was introduced the intention in enacting the new *Extradition Act* was that the test for committal remain the same as that in the former Act (*House of Commons Debates*, October 8, 1998, 1st Session, 36th Parliament, v. 135, pp. 9003-9004). Watt J.'s conclusions based on *Mezzo v. R.* (1986), 27 C.C.C. (3d) 97 (S.C.C.), *United States v. Shephard, supra*, §1.1, and *R. v. Monteleone* (1987), 35 C.C.C. (3d) 193 (S.C.C.), have to be considered in light of the Supreme Court of Canada decision in *R. v. Arcuri* (2001), 157 C.C.C. (3d) 21 (S.C.C.), which has now indicated that in the narrow circumstances of a case where the evidence is circumstantial there may be a limited scope for consideration of defence evidence in weighing the sufficiency of the case for committal.

(v) *Evidence which may be led at hearing regarding test for committal*

The evidence led at the extradition hearing by the Attorney General on behalf of the extradition partner to establish the sufficiency of evidence to commit will consist of one or more of the categories of evidence described in the *Extradition Act*. More specifically, under s. 32 of the Act, the following categories of evidence are admissible at the hearing: evidence that would otherwise be admissible under Canadian law, evidence submitted in conformity with an extradition treaty, and evidence contained in a record of the case.

The person sought may also present evidence at the extradition hearing under s. 32(1)(c) provided the evidence is relevant to the tests set out in s. 29(1). Two appeal level decisions — *United States v. Wagner* (1995), 104 C.C.C (3d) 66 (B.C.C.A.), *supra*, and *United States v. Adam* (1999), 120 O.A.C. 271 (Ont. C.A.), *supra* — discussed the effect of a person sought calling evidence at an extradition hearing in regard to the *prima facie* case. The cases were decided under the former *Extradition Act*. However, they may continue to be of assistance in interpreting s. 32(1)(c). In *United States v. Wagner*, the fugitive was sought for extradition on charges involving attempted burglary and rape in the state of Washington. The American evidence consisted of what the British Columbia Court of Appeal described, at p. 70, as "weak" photographic identification evidence by the complainants and fingerprint evidence. With respect to one of the charges, the court noted that the eyewitness identification was made five years after the offence. At the extradition hearing, the fugitive presented alibi evidence. The fugitive also presented the evidence of a fingerprint expert challenging the fingerprint evidence of the requesting state. The court characterized the alibi evidence as "powerful" and made the following comment, at p. 70:

> [14] Mr. Botting's argument on the 1989 charges was the same. In that case the court had only the photograph of Mr. Peters and the statement of the witness that that was the man who had perpetrated the offences against her in 1989. The rest of the

photographic montage was not placed before the extradition judge. In addition to the weak proof of identification offered by the extraditing country, Mr. Peters had presented powerful alibi evidence to support his story that he was in Victoria at the time of the 1989 offences.

In upholding the committal for surrender, the court seemed to recognize that evidence might be called on behalf of a fugitive at an extradition hearing, but that this evidence would be of no effect given the test to be applied, at pp. 75–76:

> [29] Occasionally in extradition hearings, as in preliminary inquiries, the accused person will call evidence of alibi or some other evidence. It is not incumbent on the extraditing state (or the Crown at a preliminary hearing) to cross-examine with a view to discrediting the alibi, or to call evidence in rebuttal at that stage of the proceedings.
>
> . . .
>
> [27] On the basis of the caselaw as it stands today I cannot accept Mr. Botting's arguments with respect to the quality of evidence. Mr. Botting made no argument that the evidence was not admissible; he directed his submissions entirely to the question of weight. In my view, the extradition judge was correct in determining that the extraditing state had met the requirements of the *Sheppard* test. I would dismiss this ground of appeal.

In the more recent case of *United States v. Adam, supra,* the Ontario Court of Appeal held that a fugitive did have the right to call evidence on the *prima facie* case issue. In that case, the extradition judge had refused to allow the fugitive to give evidence. The Court of Appeal stated as follows, at p. 274:

> [11] The appellant did not tell this court or the extradition judge what his evidence might be. We are only dealing with the right to speak. If his evidence, as delivered, is contrary to the principles applicable to a preliminary hearing then rulings and exclusionary orders may be made. We cannot conclude that anything he might say will only serve to contradict and thus invite a credibility issue. It may be that his evidence could complement other evidence and lead to a conclusion that there is no prima facie case for extradition. In any event, our reasoning is not based upon the facts of this case. It is directed by the simple principle that the appellant should have been permitted to give evidence — relevance and admissibility rulings to follow.

United States v. Wagner and *United States v. Adam* appear to be somewhat at odds. In the former case, the British Columbia Court of Appeal found that even powerful evidence led by the fugitive to contradict weak evidence adduced by the requesting state would have no impact on the *prima facie* case assessment. In the latter case, as quoted above, the Ontario Court of Appeal stated that the fugitive's "evidence could complement other evidence and lead to a conclusion that there is no prima facie case for extradition." In this respect, the court appeared to invite a degree of weighing of the fugitive's evidence and perhaps a drawing of certain inferences in favour of the fugitive. In the Supreme Court of Canada case of *R. v. Arcuri* (2001),

157 C.C.C. (3d) 21, the Supreme Court recognized in the domestic context at a preliminary inquiry that a limited weighing of defence evidence may be appropriate when the case against the accused is circumstantial.

(c) Matters which can be contested at extradition hearing

A person sought may contest the following issues at the extradition hearing:

* A person may contend that the requirements of the *Extradition Act* or the applicable extradition agreement have not been met regarding the introduction of documentary evidence. (See the discussion under "Rules of Evidence Governing Extradition Hearings," ss. 31–36.)

* A person may argue that the Attorney General has not established that he or she is the person sought by the extradition partner. (See §4.1(b)(ii), "Establishing identity", *supra*.)

* A person may argue that the Attorney General cannot establish that there is sufficient evidence that would result in a committal for trial in Canada for the offence set out in the authority to proceed. (See the discussion under s. 23, s. 29§3.0 and §4.1(b)(iv), "Test for committal under s. 29(1)(a).")

* A person may wish to raise *Charter* issues at the extradition hearing which are within the juridiction of the extradition hearing judge such as the constitutionality of the legislation, or the admissibility of evidence gathered in Canada, or such as post-arrest statements, intercepted communications, and searches executed at Canadian premises. The extradition judge also has jurisdiction to stay the proceedings for abuse of process (*United States v. Cobb* (2001), 152 C.C.C. (3d) 270 (S.C.C.), reconsideration refused (June 14, 2001), Docs. 26912, 27610, 27774 (S.C.C.)).

(d) Matters which cannot be contested at extradition hearing

The jurisprudence under the former Act indicated that there were a number of matters with respect to which the extradition judge ought not to be concerned. This jurisprudence will continue to be applicable as the role of the extradition hearing judge under the new *Extradition Act* continues to be narrow. Matters which will continue to be excluded from the consideration of the extradition hearing judge are: monitoring treaty compliance by the extradition partner; interpreting foreign indictments; considering treaty documentation provided for ministerial purposes; determining whether the person sought is subject to prosecution by the extradition partner; entertaining *Charter* issues within the jurisdiction of the Minister of Justice; entertaining collateral attacks on foreign orders; classifying murder; and entertaining defences.

(i) No monitoring of treaty compliance by extradition judge

The extent to which extradition judges could look to the provisions of the extradition treaties was litigated frequently under the former *Extradition Act* because of s. 3 of that Act, which provided that in the event of a conflict between the Act and the treaty, the latter prevailed. The two most frequently litigated issues in this regard were whether the offence which was the subject of the extradition request was a crime in the foreign state, and whether the foreign state had jurisdiction to prosecute the crime in question.

Ultimately, the Supreme Court of Canada held that s. 3 of the former Act did not have the effect of incorporating into the Act every provision of a treaty. It was determined that, other than those treaty provisions relating directly to the extradition hearing judge's function, the provisions of extradition treaties did not apply to the judicial stage of the extradition process. This point was made by La Forest J. in *United States v. McVey* (1992), 77 C.C.C. (3d) 1, at p. 15:

> Barring statutory provision, the task of dealing with international treaty obligations is for the political authorities, and is performed by the Ministers and departments in the course of fulfilling their appropriate mandates. The *Extradition Act*, of course, gives the Minister of Justice authority respecting the surrender of a fugitive: see ss. 20 to 22, and 25. The treaty terms are aimed at the obligations of the parties and not the internal procedures by which these are to be carried into effect.

United States v. McVey involved an extradition request from the United States with respect to eleven charges, one of conspiring to export high-technology equipment to the former U.S.S.R. and ten of having made false statements to the United States Department of Commerce and the United States Customs Service in order to carry out the exportation. The Supreme Court of Canada concluded that it was not the task of the extradition judge to determine whether the act charged was a crime under American law. Rather, this was a monitoring task of the executive to ensure that it was covered by the treaty (at p. 39):

> I have thus concluded that the evidence of foreign law in the present case should not have been admitted by the extradition judge and was irrelevant. The issue of whether the act charged was a crime under United States law was for the prosecutors in the United States to decide, and it was for them and the U.S. State Department to assess whether in their view it came within the treaty, subject to monitoring by Canada pursuant to the treaty. The monitoring task has not, for good reason, been assigned to the extradition judge, so it remains with the executive. Barring the possible exception of political offences, only one task has been assigned to the judiciary, but it is an important one — the task of assessing whether there is sufficient evidence that the alleged offence would, if committed in Canada, constitute a crime mentioned in the treaty. That is the duty conferred upon the extradition judge by the *Extradition Act*.

Similarly, the Supreme Court of Canada in *United States v. Lépine* (1994), 87 C.C.C. (3d) 385, 163 N.R. 1, held that the issue of whether the requesting state had jurisdiction to prosecute the offences for which extradition was sought was a role for the Minister of Justice when monitoring treaty compliance at the surrender stage and not for the extradition judge. At the extradition hearing stage, the extradition judge had dismissed the requesting state's application for committal on the basis that the state of Pennsylvania had no jurisdiction to prosecute a charge of conspiracy to distribute cocaine (at p. 389). The extradition judge held that there was no evidence of either an intention to produce detrimental effects in or any substantial link between the conspiracy and the foreign jurisdiction. La Forest J. held that the extradition judge had erred in considering the jurisdiction of the requesting state to prosecute the offence (at p. 391):

> The issue of the jurisdiction of the requesting state and its organs to prosecute a crime is essentially a matter governed by the law of that state. And the decision of this court in *McVey (Re)* (1992), 77 C.C.C. (3d) 1 at p. 23, 97 D.L.R. (4th) 193 at p. 215, [1992] 3 S.C.R. 475 (S.C.C.) (a case, it should be said, that had not been decided at the time of the extradition hearing in the present case) makes it clear that "the extradition judge 'is not concerned with foreign law at all'". The difficulties and delays inherent in a judge's examining issues of foreign law are fully set forth in *McVey*, at pp. 21-2 C.C.C., pp. 213-4 D.L.R., and I need not repeat them. I need only say that, if anything, the determination of the jurisdiction of a foreign state by a judge unfamiliar with the relevant law seems to me to be an even more thorny task than a determination of the substantive law of that state.

La Forest J. concluded that there was nothing in the *Extradition Act* providing the extradition judge with the authority to deal with the issues of territoriality or jurisdiction.

In *Themens v. United States* (February 12, 1996), nos. C.A. Montréal 500-10-000212-959, 500-010-000397-958, the Quebec Court of Appeal followed *United States v. Lépine*. The Court held that the extradition judge's duty under the *Extradition Act* did not include inquiring into whether the requesting state had jurisdiction to prosecute the offences charged.

MacDonald J. in *Romania (State) v. Cheng* (1997), 114 C.C.C. (3d) 289 (N.S. S.C.), distinguished the decision in *Lépine*, holding that it was concerned with the extradition judge's erroneous consideration of whether the state of Pennsylvania had jurisdiction to prosecute rather than the United States generally, and that in addition the subjects of the extradition request were not fugitives as defined in s. 2 of the former *Extradition Act* because the alleged offences had not occurred within the territory of the state of Romania. Influenced by the fact that the relevant treaty described the obligation of each party to extradite as being with respect to offences alleged to have occurred within the territory of the other party, he held that the term "jurisdiction" as contained in the term "fugitive" meant territorial jurisdiction. Therefore, notwithstanding that the Supreme Court in *McVey* and *Lépine* had determined that it was a ministerial responsibility to monitor requests to determine if they were covered by the relevant treaty, this interpretation of the domestic law gave that determination to the extradition judge. The Nova Scotia Court of Appeal ((1997), 119 C.C.C. (3d) 561) declined to deal with the merits of the appeal from the decision of MacDonald J. since the alleged fugitives had left Canada after being discharged and the appeal was rendered moot. However, Hallett J.A., speaking for the court, observed, at p. 564, that:

> MacDonald J.'s decision, to a substantial extent, turned on the provisions of Article 1 of the *1893 Treaty* with Romania.
>
> Furthermore, the principles established by the Supreme Court of Canada in *Lépine* are not overruled by MacDonald J.'s interpretation of that decision.

In contrast to the decision in *Romania (State) v. Cheng*, it was argued before Watt J. in *Germany (Federal Republic) v. Schreiber* (July 6, 2000), [2000] O.J. No. 2618, 2000 CarswellOnt. 5257 (Ont. S.C.J.), that the provisions of s. 29(1) of the new Act require the extradition judge to first determine whether the person is "a person sought for prosecution," before proceeding to determine whether sufficient evidence has been provided to justify an order of committal under s. 29(1)(a) of the Act. Watt J. rejected this submission and held that the determination of whether the person is a "person sought for prosecution" is for the Minister and not the extradition judge. He stated:

> [87] . . . It is the responsibility of the Minister to implement extradition agreements, administer the Act and deal with the requests for extradition made under either or both of them. The requests for provisional arrest or extradition are made to the Minister. It is for the Minister to review the materials offered by the extradition partner in support of the request to determine whether it is in order. This determination involves, amongst other things, a consideration of foreign law. It is the Minister who must be satisfied that the requirements of s. 3(1)(a) of the Act have been met before she or he is entitled to instruct the Attorney General to apply for a provisional warrant of arrest under s. 12 or issue an authority to the Attorney General to proceed under s. 15(1) of the Act. Section 3(1)(a) of the Act defines extraditable conduct. It also makes it clear that the *purpose* of the extradition partner in requesting extradition must be any of
>
> i. *prosecuting* the fugitive;
> ii. *imposing a sentence*; or,
> iii. *enforcing a sentence* already imposed in the foreign jurisdiction.
>
> There is nothing in the Act or treaty that entitles the extradition hearing judge to review the Minister's decision or decide, *de novo* as it were, whether the fugitive is a person sought for prosecution. I lack the authority to make any such order. [Emphasis in original.]

The new *Extradition Act* has obviated the debate over judicial involvement in monitoring treaty compliance. Section 7 of the Act establishes that the Minister is the individual responsible for monitoring treaty requests. Section 7 reads as follows:

7. The Minster is responsible for the implementation of extradition agreements, the administration of this Act and dealing with requests for extradition made under them.

The combination of s. 15 (authority to proceed) and s. 3 (extraditable conduct) of the Act requires the Minister, when considering whether to issue an authority to proceed, to have regard to the terms of a relevant extradition agreement and to be satisfied that in his or her view the request comes within the treaty. It is for the Minister to be satisfied that the particular treaty is in force (see *Thailand (Kingdom) v. Karas* (January 11, 2001), Doc. CC991269, 2001 BCSC 72 (B.C.S.C.). In addition, s. 5 of the new Act specifically indicates that territorial jurisdictional issues are not a bar to extradition. The fact that it is a discretionary ground of refusal by the Minister under s. 47(e) underscores that matters of territorial jurisdiction are not matters for the determination of the extradition judge but that of the Minister.

The new *Extradition Act* has no equivalent to s. 3 of the former Act. Section 3 of the former Act gave the treaties precedence over every provision of the Act to the extent of any inconsistency. The new Act, by contrast, specifically itemizes the instances in which the provisions of a treaty will override the provisions of the Act.

With respect to judicial functions, the following circumstances are situations when the extradition judge will be required to consider treaty provisions:

- Section 32(1)(b), which makes the contents of documents that are submitted in conformity with the terms of an extradition agreement admissible at the extradition hearing.

- The requirement of applying the s. 29(1)(a) committal test to a person who was tried and convicted without the person being present (see s. 29(5)).

- Section 39, which allows the judge who makes an order of committal to order any property seized when the person sought was arrested, to be transferred to the extradition partner.

Other than these three situations, there will be no occasion for the extradition judge to look to the extradition treaty to monitor treaty compliance.

(ii) *Extradition judge cannot interpret foreign indictment*

The *United States v. Lépine* case, *supra*, §4.1(d)(i), decided under the former *Extradition Act*, held that interpretation of a foreign indictment involved an examination of foreign law and was therefore not an inquiry that could properly be undertaken by an extradition judge. In noting in that case that the extradition judge had assessed the evidence with a view to considering whether there were sufficient links to the United States to support the charges in the foreign indictment, La Forest J. made the following observation, at p. 393:

All of these acts taken together are quite sufficient overt acts in the United States, even apart from what occurred in Allentown, to constitute a "real and substantial link" to the United States. . . . As is earlier indicated, the extradition judge would have come to the same conclusion had he not focussed wholly on the activities in Allentown, a matter related, as I have indicated earlier, more to the jurisdiction of the particular court (a matter *par excellence* of United States law) than to the territorial jurisdiction of the United States. Indeed, this amounted to an interpretation of the indictment, also a matter of United States law.

The decision in *Lépine* was not interpreted in the cases which followed it as a blanket prohibition against the extradition judge referring to the foreign indictment at a hearing. There were many instances in the jurisprudence under the former *Extradition Act* in which courts did countenance looking at the foreign indictment for a variety of purposes, although not necessarily with a view to interpreting the foreign law. For instance, in *United States v. Shulman* (1998), 128 C.C.C. (3d) 475 (reversed on other grounds (2001), 152 C.C.C. (3d) 294 (S.C.C.)), the Ontario Court of Appeal looked to the foreign indictment in order to determine whether evidence had been supplied with the request to support each of the counts upon which the fugitive would, if surrendered, be tried in the foreign state. In that case, the court determined that no evidence had been provided with respect to 51 of the 52 counts in the foreign indictment and that discharges under s. 18(2) of the former Act were warranted with respect to those counts. Similar to *Shulman* is the decision of the Quebec Court of Appeal in *United States v. Tavormina* (1996), 112 C.C.C. (3d) 563 (Que. C.A.), at p. 569, in which a fugitive was discharged on a conspiracy to import narcotics request because the evidence supplied "had nothing to do with the conduct charged" in the foreign indictment.

Tavormina was released the same day as its companion case *United States v. Manno* (1996), 112 C.C.C. (3d) 544 (Que. C.A.), leave to appeal to S.C.C. refused (1997), 221 N.R. 311 (note) (S.C.C.). In *Manno*, the Quebec Court of Appeal held that the extradition judge could assess the foreign indictment in order to orient the judge as to the facts upon which the foreign prosecution would proceed. The court found that this would assist the extradition judge in performing the analysis required under s. 18(1)(b) of the former Act. In other words, viewing the foreign indictment would assist the extradition judge in determining whether the conduct underlying the foreign charges would be an offence in this country, on the basis of which committal for trial could be ordered. The court commented as follows, at p. 558:

> Accordingly, although the purpose of the foreign accusation set out in the arrest warrant which is at the origin of the extradition judicial process is to limit the jurisdictional framework of the hearing, it is the reprehensible nature of the conduct with which the fugitive is charged which is at the centre of the preoccupations of the extradition judge. That being said, *an examination of the wording of the foreign accusation is necessary for the sole purpose of establishing the relevance of the facts on which the extradition judge will ultimately have to decide.*

It is not necessary that the internal or domestic law provide for a defined offence which corresponds on all points with the offence which is the subject of an accusation of the requesting state. It is sufficient that the criminal law of the respective states, in one form or another, consider the conduct in question as criminal in its very substance. [Emphasis in original.]

The Ontario Court of Appeal, in *United States v. Commisso* (2000), 143 C.C.C. (3d) 158 (Ont. C.A.), explicitly adopted the reasoning in *Manno*. O'Connor J.A. noted, at p. 168:

[35] The extradition judge may look to the foreign indictment, but only for the purpose of determining what conduct is to be included in the assessment under s. 18(1)(*b*). The foreign indictment enables the extradition judge to identify the conduct with which a fugitive is charged in the requesting juridiction. In referring to the foreign indictment however, the court must not be concerned with whether the conduct establishes the commission of the foreign charge nor with whether the foreign court has jurisdiction to try the charge: *Manno* at pp. 558-59.

As discussed below, this analysis has been superseded in the new Act with the introduction of the authority to proceed. As a result, there will be no reason for the extradition court to refer to the foreign indictment in proceedings under the new legislation, and it is unlikely that the foreign indictment would even be put before the court.

The "authority to proceed" is issued by the Minister of Justice under s. 15 of the Act and forms the basis of extradition proceedings. In the authority to proceed, the Minister sets out the Canadian offence(s) corresponding to the impugned conduct. There is no longer any need for the extradition court to use the foreign indictment as a way of determining the relevant evidence in support of the request. The extradition judge now will have the authority to proceed setting out, like a Canadian charging document, the Canadian offence disclosed by the impugned conduct. The evidence can then be assessed to determine if it supports the Canadian offence named in the authority to proceed, this being the exercise required under s. 29(1)(a) of the Act. Consequently, with the introduction of the authority to proceed, the approach advocated by the Quebec Court of Appeal in *United States v. Manno, supra,* and the Ontario Court of Appeal in *United States v. Commisso*, has been overtaken. As Dambrot J. observed in *United States v. Drysdale* (2000), 32 C.R. (5th) 163 (Ont. S.C.J.): "The new Act does not even require the foreign warrant or indictment to be placed before the extradition judge." (p. 189, para. 76)

(iii) Types of treaty documentation for ministerial use only

Section 32(1)(b) of the new *Extradition Act* makes the contents of documents submitted in compliance with the terms of a treaty admissible at the extradition hearing. However, this provision should not be read as making all of the documentation that may be submitted pursuant to a treaty the concern of the extradition hearing judge. A great deal of the material which is required to be provided by the provisions of extradition treaties is of concern only to the executive which, as set out above, has the responsibility for monitoring treaty compliance. Only those treaty provisions which are relevant to the conduct of the extradition hearing, such as the documentation tendered to establish identity, a sufficient case for committal, or to prove a conviction, are of concern to the extradition hearing judge. For example, in the *Canada–United States Extradition Treaty* there are certain articles that require specified documentation to accompany the request for extradition, not all of which is intended to be tendered as evidence at the extradition hearing. Article 9 is such a provision. Article 9 outlines the documentation that must accompany an extradition request by the requesting signatory. It reads as follows:

9. (1) The request for extradition shall be made through the diplomatic channel.

(2) The request shall be accompanied by a description of the person sought, a statement of the facts of the case, the text of the laws of the requesting State describing the offense and prescribing the punishment for the offense, and a statement of the law relating to the limitation of the legal proceedings.

(3) When the request relates to a person who has not yet been convicted, it must also be accompanied by a warrant of arrest issued by a judge or other judicial officer of the requesting State and by such evidence as, according to the laws of the requested State, would justify his arrest and committal for trial if the offense had been committed there, including evidence proving the person requested is the person to whom the warrant of arrest refers.

(4) When the request relates to a person already convicted, it must be accompanied by the judgment of conviction and sentence passed against him in the territory of the requesting State, by a statement showing how much of the sentence has not been served, and by evidence proving that the person requested is the person to whom the sentence refers.

Subsection (2) of Article 10 of the *Canada–United States Extradition Treaty* provides that the documentary evidence in support of a request for extradition or copies of these documents shall be admitted in evidence in the examination of the extradition request if authenticated and certified according to the terms set out in that subsection. Therefore, at an extradition hearing, the documentation mentioned in subss. (3) and (4) of Article 9 may be admitted at an extradition hearing if authenticated and certified in accordance with the terms set out in subs. (2) of Article 10.

The judgment of La Forest J. in *United States v. McVey, supra,* §2.1, implicitly confirms that the only documentation referred to in Article 9 that is relevant to the extradition hearing would be the following: in the case of a fugitive not yet convicted in the requesting state, evidence justifying committal for trial and identification evidence; in the case of a fugitive already convicted, the judgment of conviction and sentence, a statement indicating the remainder of the sentence to be served, and identification evidence.

As indicated above, subs. (2) of Article 9 of the *Canada–United States Extradition Treaty* requires that the extradition request be accompanied by the following: a description of the fugitive, a statement of facts of the case, the text of the laws of the requesting state describing the offence and the punishment for the offence, and a statement of the law relating to the limitation period for the offence in question. This is not documentation that is required to be produced at the extradition hearing since such documentation is not necessary to establish a *prima facie* case or proof of conviction. Rather, such documentation is of concern to the executive in monitoring treaty compliance during the ministerial phase of the extradition process during which the Minister of Justice must determine whether the person should be surrendered to the requesting state.

La Forest J. in *United States v. McVey, supra*, discussed how the documentation in Article 9 would be of assistance to the Minister of Justice in making the determination of whether the offence in question is an offence in the requesting state, at pp. 17–18:

> The evidence that the offence is a crime in the foreign country is determined by the executive of the requested state in considering the validity of the requisition. Article 9 of the treaty enables it to do so. That provision requires that the request for surrender be accompanied by, among other things, a statement of the facts of the case and "*the text of the laws of the requesting State describing the offense and prescribing the punishment for the offense*" (art. 9(2)). As well, in the case of an accused fugitive (the situation here), the requesting state must provide *a warrant of arrest issued by a judge or other judicial officer of the requesting state* (art. 9(3)), and in case of a convicted fugitive, *the judgment of conviction and sentence. . . .* Nowhere is the duty to consider the foreign law assigned to the extradition judge. This, as I mentioned, is a task for the political authorities at common law, now assigned by statute to the Minister of Justice. It is not unreasonable for the Minister to rely on the material supplied with the requisition as proof of foreign law, as demonstrated by the fact that it has been accepted for that purpose in both the House of Lords and this court: see *Postlethwaite, supra*, at pp. 953-4, and *Washington (State) v. Johnson, supra*. (Emphasis in original.)

In the Supreme Court of Canada case of *Washington (State) v. Johnson* (1988), 40 C.C.C. (3d) 546, at p. 560, Le Dain J. (dissenting on other issues) held that compliance with subs. (2) of Article 9 was not a condition precedent to the exercise of the extradition hearing judge's jurisdiction to issue a warrant of committal:

> In my opinion, the failure of the requesting state to comply with art. 9(2) of the treaty did not affect the jurisdiction of the extradition judge to issue a warrant for committal pursuant to s. 18(1)(*a*) of the *Extradition Act*. Article 9(2) is directed, as art. 9(1) indicates, to the request for extradition through diplomatic channels and not to the proceedings before an extradition judge. There is nothing in the relevant provisions in ss. 10 and following of the *Extradition Act* to suggest that compliance with art. 9(2) of the treaty

is a condition precedent to the exercise of the extradition judge's jurisdiction. That it is not an implication of the cases, with which I agree, in which it has been held that it is not necessary to place the request for extradition in evidence before an extradition judge: *Re Von Einem and Federal Republic of Germany* (1984), 14 C.C.C. (3d) 440 (B.C.C.A.). I am, accordingly, of the view that the failure to comply with art. 9(2) of the treaty did not render the committal invalid.

Subsection (3) of Article 9 requires that extradition requests for fugitives who have not yet been convicted be accompanied by a warrant of arrest issued by a judge or judicial officer of the requesting state. In light of the Supreme Court of Canada decision in *United States v. McVey*, it was arguable under the former Act that the existence of the foreign arrest warrant was solely a matter for the executive to monitor and was not relevant to the role of the extradition hearing judge.

At the extradition hearing before Watt J. of the Ontario Court (General Division) in *Philippines (Republic) v. Pacificador* (October 5, 1992), the fugitive argued that the foreign arrest warrant included in the documentary evidence tendered at the hearing did not comply with Article 7(2)(b)(i) of the *Canada–Philippines Extradition Treaty*. This provision requires that the extradition request be supported by "the original or a certified true copy of the warrant of arrest . . . in the Requesting state." The fugitive alleged that the arrest warrant was invalid because it did not contain the signature of the issuing officer. The decision in *United States v. McVey* was released after the conclusion of the extradition hearing. Nonetheless, Watt J. seriously questioned his jurisdiction as an extradition hearing judge to determine the validity of the foreign arrest warrant. Watt J. stated that it was not the business of the extradition judge to assume responsibility for reviewing the actions of foreign officials who prepare evidence for an extradition hearing. He further indicated that, in the absence of express statutory or treaty provisions, the sole purpose of the extradition hearing was to ensure that the evidence submitted in support of the request for extradition established a *prima facie* case that the extradition crime had been committed by the fugitive. Watt J. indicated that he was unable to find any express provisions in the Act or treaty that would make the hearing a more expansive inquiry. However, Watt J. added that it was unnecessary to finally determine the jurisdictional issue because the warrant in question complied with the treaty requirements.

The jurisdictional issue was argued before the Court of Appeal in *Philippines (Republic) v. Pacificador* (1993), 83 C.C.C. (3d) 210, leave to appeal to S.C.C. refused (1994), 87 C.C.C. (3d) vi (S.C.C.), following the release of the decision in *United States v. McVey*. The Court of Appeal found it unnecessary to deal with the issue because the Court concurred with Watt J. that the warrant in question complied with the requirements of the Act and the Treaty. However, in his judgment for the court, Doherty J.A. stated (at p. 215) that, "[t]here is much force in the tentative view of Watt J. that the extradition court cannot concern itself with the validity of the foreign warrant."

The case law discussed above was all decided under the former *Extradition Act*. However, it will be of direct relevance to any discussion of what may appropriately be considered by an extradition court with respect to documentation submitted at the extradition hearing pursuant to s. 32(1)(b) of the new Act. Dambrot J. in *United States v. Drysdale, supra*, §4.1(d)(ii), noted that the new Act did not require the extradition judge to receive either the foreign warrant or indictment. In *Germany (Federal Republic) v. Schreiber* (July 6, 2000), [2000] O.J. No. 2618 (Ont. S.C.J.), Watt J. refused to order disclosure of the warrant of arrest and supporting material provided to the Minister, noting that it was for the Minister to review these materials to determine whether they were in order, not the extradition judge (para. 87). Similarly, in *Germany (Federal Republic) v. Ebke* (2001), 2001 NWTSC 2, 2001 CarswellNWT 4 (N.W.T.S.C.), Vertes J., held that, as it is a ministerial concern, the diplomatic note, or original request for extradition, is not subject to being disclosed.

(iv) *Extradition judge cannot consider whether person is person subject to prosecution in requesting jurisdiction*

The status of a person as being subject to extradition is variously described in Canada's extradition agreements. For instance, in the treaties with Belgium (1902), India (1987), and the Netherlands (1991), the obligation to extradite is undertaken with respect to "accused" persons. In the treaties with Finland (1985), Italy (1985), France (1989), and the United States (1992), the obligation is with respect to persons who are "charged" in the requesting state. In the treaties with the Philippines (1990), Spain (1990), Korea (1995), and Switzerland (1996), the obligation concerns persons "wanted for prosecution," while the treaty with Germany (1979) speaks of persons who are "subject to prosecution." The trend since the latter part of the 1980s appears to be towards treaties being applicable to persons "wanted for prosecution." This is particularly true with respect to civil law countries, which possess an inquisitorial judicial structure and which have different charging procedures than common law jurisdictions. Section 29(1)(a) of the *Extradition Act* refers to a "person sought for prosecution." This is in contrast to s. 18(1)(b) of the former Act, which applied to "accused" persons. In this sense, s. 29(1)(a) reflects the trend in Canada's newer extradition agreements.

The terminology of the former *Extradition Act* gave rise to arguments over the issue of whether a fugitive was subject to that Act. This was because status as an accused was one aspect of the definition of a "fugitive" under s. 2 of that Act and the power to commit a fugitive for surrender under s. 18(1)(b) operated with respect to persons who were "accused" of an extradition crime. The change in the new *Extradition Act* to the broader category of "person sought for prosecution" accommodates civil law extradition partners and reflects the terminology of Canada's newer extradition agreements. The House of Lords in *Re Ismail*, [1999] 1 A.C. 320 (U.K.H.L.), discussed the meaning of the phrase "accused person" as used in the British *Extradition Act*. Counsel for Ismail contended that Ismail was not accused of an offence in the requesting state, Germany, as no decision to prosecute had been made. Counsel argued that Ismail was merely a suspect wanted for pre-trial investigations. Lord

Steyn on behalf of the House of Lords wrote that the strict meaning of "accused" according to English law should not be applied in the extradition context and that a flexible approach had to be adopted in order to facilitate the purposes of the Act. Lord Steyn stated, at pp. 326–327:

> It is common ground that mere suspicion that an individual has committed offences is insufficient to place him in the category of "accused" persons. It is also common ground that it is not enough that he is in the traditional phrase "wanted by the police to help them with their inquiries." Something more is required. What more is needed to make a suspect an "accused" person? There is no statutory definition. Given the divergent systems of law involved, and notably the differences between criminal procedures in the United Kingdom and in civil law jurisdictions, it is not surprising that the legislature has not attempted a definition. For the same reason it would be unwise for the House to attempt to define the word "accused" within the meaning of the Act of 1989. It is, however, possible to state in outline the approach to be adopted. The starting point is that "accused" in section 1 of the Act of 1989 is not a term of art. It is a question of fact in each case whether the person passes the threshold test of being an "accused" person. Next there is the reality that one is concerned with the contextual meaning of "accused" in a statute intended to serve the purpose of bringing to justice those accused of serious crimes. There is a transnational interest in the achievement of this aim. Extradition treaties, and extradition statutes, ought, therefore, to be accorded a broad and generous construction so far as the texts permits it in order to facilitate extradition: *Reg. v. Governor of Ashford Remand Centre, Ex Parte Postlethwaite* [1988] A.C., 924, 946–947. That approach has been applied by the Privy Council to the meaning of "accused" in an extradition treaty: *Rey v. Government of Switzerland* [1999] A.C. 54, 62G. It follows that it would be wrong to approach the problem of construction solely from the perspective of English criminal procedure, and in particular from the point of view of the formal acts of the laying of an information or the preferring an indictment.
>
> . . .
>
> It is not always easy for an English court to decide when in a civil law jurisdiction a suspect becomes an "accused" person. All one can say with confidence is that a purposive interpretation of "accused" ought to be adopted in order to accommodate the differences between legal systems. In other words, it is necessary for our courts to adopt a cosmopolitan approach to the question whether as a matter of substance rather than form the requirement of there being an "accused" person is satisfied.

The same argument as in *Re Ismail, supra,* was made before the Ontario Court of Appeal in *Germany (Federal Republic) v. Kretz* (May 19, 1998), 1998 CarswellOnt 1999, [1998] O.J. No. 2062 (Ont. C.A.). The Court of Appeal dismissed the appeal. In a short endorsement, the court made the following comment:

> Assuming that the extradition judge had the authority to determine whether the appellant is a person subject to prosecution in Germany, the record contains ample evidence that the appellant was so subject. We see no basis for interfering with the decision of Hoilett J. The appeal is therefore dismissed.

The court's endorsement uses the language of the *Canada–Germany Extradition Treaty*, which engages the obligation to extradite with respect to persons who are "subject to prosecution." The endorsement does not use the wording of the former Act which referred to fugitives who were "accused." This is because s. 3 of the former Act provided that treaties prevailed over the Act to the extent of any inconsistency.

In *Germany (Federal Republic) v. Kretz*, the Court of Appeal appears to have viewed the jurisdiction of the extradition judge to consider the status of the fugitive in the requesting state as an unsettled point. The endorsement indicates that the appeal was being disposed of "[a]ssuming that the extradition judge had the authority" to determine the matter. Under the new *Extradition Act*, the status of the person sought will not be an issue for the extradition judge. Section 7 of the Act provides that the Minister of Justice is responsible for the implementation of extradition agreements and the administration of the Act. The validity of an extradition request and the engagement of the obligation to extradite will be determined by the Minister of Justice before the Minister issues an authority to proceed under s. 15 of the Act. If an extradition partner were to request the extradition of a person who did not fall within the terms of the applicable extradition agreement, that would be a matter for the political authorities, specifically the Minister. Section 15 requires the Minister to be satisfied that extradition requests meet the requirements in s. 3 of the Act. Section 3 includes the determination that the request is "for the purpose of prosecuting the person or imposing a sentence on — or enforcing a sentence imposed on — the person". Therefore, under the new Act, the status of the person sought is not an issue for the extradition judge. The wording of s. 29(1)(a) suggests that the status of a person as a person sought for prosecution is a predetermined point. There is no suggestion that the judge is to make the determination. Section 29(1)(a) provides as follows:

> **29.** (1) A judge shall order the committal of the person into custody to await surrender if
>
> (a)   in the case of a person sought for prosecution, there is evidence admissible under this Act of conduct . . . .

Watt J., in *Germany (Federal Republic) v. Schreiber* (July 6, 2000), [2000] O.J. No. 2618, 2000 CarswellOnt 5257 (Ont. S.C.J.), observed that there was no authority "express or implied, which assigns jurisdiction to determine whether someone is a person 'sought for the purpose of prosecution' to the extradition hearing judge." This, Watt J. held, is the responsibility of the Minister under the Act (para. 66).

(v) *Person sought may not raise* Charter *issues that are within jurisdiction of Minister of Justice*

In *United States v. Kwok* (2001), 152 C.C.C. (3d) 225 (S.C.C.), a case decided under the former Act, the Supreme Court of Canada confirmed that the two stages of the extradition process are distinct and separate. Accordingly, matters which arise for determination at the ministerial phase such as s. 6(1) *Charter* rights, are premature and non-justiciable at the extradition hearing stage, barring exigent circumstances. The Supreme Court held that judicial review of the Minister's surrender decision by the relevant court of appeal, provides for a timely, effective and complete remedy for any *Charter* infringements which may have occurred in the process and that accordingly, there is no basis for anticipatory *Charter* breach arguments to be made at the committal stage.

In one of the early decisions under the new Act, Romilly J. in *Australia v. Ho* (January 26, 2000), Doc. Vancouver CC990288 (B.C. S.C.), indicated that the previous jurisprudence setting out the distinct roles and jurisdictions of the Minister and the extradition judge continued to apply. He observed:

> [17] In the scheme for extradition from Canada there are no areas of joint jurisdiction shared by the Minister and the extradition judge. The Minister may not review the determination of the trial [sic] judge as to the admissibility of evidence or of there being sufficient or insufficient evidence to commit. Similarly, the extradition judge may not rule on matters specifically assigned to the Minister: *United States of America v. D'Agostino* (1997) 41 C.R.R. (2d) 325 at p. 338 (Ont. Gen. Div.).
>
> [18] This division of extradition-related issues between the Minister and the extradition judge leaves to the Minister all issues surrounding whether it is fair and appropriate to surrender a fugitive to the requesting state. Therefore, any issue concerning whether a fugitive will receive a fair trial or will be dealt with fairly in the requesting state falls to the Minister to decide.

Watt J. was of the same view in *Germany (Federal Republic) v. Schreiber, supra.* In that case he refuted the assertion that he had the jurisdiction to consider an abuse of process application grounded in allegations of improper motive or bias by the Minister or her staff in approving the extradition request. He also rejected the assertion that the judge rather than the Minister had the authority to determine whether the person in this case was a "person sought for prosecution" as that phrase appears in s. 29(1)(a). He observed that review of matters within ministerial jurisdiction, including *Charter* matters, is assigned to the Court of Appeal of the province under s. 57 of the Act, and not to the extradition judge. Watt J. described the respective roles of the Minister and the extradition judge as "two . . . different solitudes":

> [72] Under the Act, the Minister and extradition judge occupy two (2) different solitudes. The Minister has a role at the beginning and the end of the extradition process. The judge discharges his or her function in the middle. Each operates independently of the other, except to the extent that the Minister's final involvement is contingent on a judicial order for committal. Neither intrudes into the other's area of responsibility. Neither reviews the other's determination or decision. The reviewing tribunal is the provincial court of appeal. Sections 49–56 govern appeals from committal or discharge and s. 57, review of the Minister's surrender decision.

223

[73] In the result, at least as it seems to me, the authority to determine whether a person whose extradition is sought is "a person sought for prosecution" is given to the Minister. It is *not* awarded to the extradition judge, either at first instance, *de novo* or by way of review. [Emphasis in original.]

See the commentary to s. 25 for a fuller discussion.

(vi) *Extradition judge cannot entertain collateral attacks on foreign orders*

In *United States v. Singh* (October 14, 1994), Doc. E-21, [1994] O.J. No. 3941 (Ont. Gen. Div.), the state of California requested the extradition of Singh on a charge of child abduction. The fugitive argued that the requesting state was required to establish at the extradition hearing that the *ex parte* custody order obtained by Singh's wife in California granting her sole custody of the abducted child "would have been granted to her by a Canadian court had the circumstances been transposed to Canadian soil." In rejecting the "mirror image" approach, Ewaschuk J. of the Ontario Court (General Division) stated as follows:

[3] The applicant concedes that the Supreme Court of Canada judgment in *United States v. Lépine* (1994), 87 C.C.C. (3d) 385, requires that an extradition judge view the factual background of the foreign offence as if it had occurred in Canada in order to determine whether the conduct establishes the commission of an offence in Canada. The offence obviously must be known to Canadian law. However, the applicant disputes that it must also establish that a court in Canada would have granted Mrs. Singh an *ex parte* order granting her sole custody of the abducted child.

[4] In reply, the respondent Singh submits that the Ontario Court of Appeal judgment in *R v. Ilcyszyn* (1988), 45 C.C.C. (3d) 91, requires that the applicant establish that the custody order was valid and subsisting.

[5] I read the latter judgment as requiring that the custody order be valid on its face and subsisting at the time that it was allegedly breached. In this case, the order is that of a superior court, and the order has yet to be set aside, and it is valid on its face.

[6] It is my view that the respondent is not allowed to collaterally attack the validity of the foreign order here in Canada, and I find no authority requiring the applicant State to establish that the order would have been granted in Canada. International comity does not require such mirrored reciprocity. Instead the doctrine of comity between foreign states requires the Canadian extradition judge to recognize the validity of a foreign superior court order valid on its face, and subsisting at the time of its alleged breach.

[7] Furthermore, the principle of transposition of facts from the requesting to the requested state requires the extradition judge to assume that the facts which occurred in the foreign jurisdiction had occurred in Canada. One of the facts which must be assumed is that a superior court judge issued a custody order. That fact is a given, and cannot be challenged at this hearing.

[8] In any event, I am satisfied that a court in Canada would have jurisdiction to have granted such an order. In the end, I rule the applicant State need not call evidence on the matter, and that the respondent cannot dispute the validity of the order at this

hearing. Thus, I find that the applicant has established a *prima facie* case of child abduction under both ss. 282 and 283 of the *Criminal Code* of Canada, and also has established a *prima facie* case of disobedience of a court order under s. 127 of the same Act.

The decision in *Singh* was followed by Chapnik J. in *United States v. Soul* (November 25, 1994), [1994] O.J. No. 2838, Chapnik J. (Ont. Gen. Div.), affirmed (February 17, 1995), Doc. CA C20236 (Ont. C.A.). In *Soul*, a charge of failing to appear in court in Tennessee was challenged on the basis that the method of releasing an accused from court on a promise to appear in Tennessee was not the same as the Canadian procedure. Because of this, it was argued that, on the facts of the case, there could not have been a warrant for failing to appear had the facts occurred in Canada. Chapnik J. did not accept this submission but instead adopted the approach taken by Ewaschuk J. in *United States v. Singh, supra*. Chapnik J. stated as follows:

> [39] In the present case, the warrant for the arrest of the fugitives constitutes proof of the court order and establishes the procedural validity of the process in the requesting state.

The Ontario Court of Appeal upheld Chapnik J.'s decision (February 17, 1995), Doc. CA C20236 (Ont. C.A.).

Under the new Act, the validity of foreign warrants is not a matter assigned to the extradition judge (see *Germany (Federal Republic) v. Schreiber* (July 6, 2000), [2000] O.J. No. 2618, 2000 Carswell 5257 (Ont. S.C.J.)).

(vii) *Classification of murder is not issue for extradition hearing judge*

In *United States v. Bounnam* (April 3, 1995), Doc. Toronto E14/94 (Ont. Gen. Div.), affirmed (1996), (*sub nom. R. v. Bounnam*) 91 O.A.C. 319 (Ont. C.A.), leave to appeal to S.C.C. refused (1997), 99 O.A.C. 79 (note) (S.C.C.), the fugitive was alleged to have participated with three other persons in a robbery-murder in which three employees of a restaurant in Tennessee were shot to death. The evidence disclosed that the fugitive was armed with a firearm during the robbery, but that he did not discharge the firearm. The other three individuals were also armed and two of these individuals actually committed the murders. The State of Tennessee sought the extradition of the fugitive for the following offences contrary to Tennessee law: three counts of premeditated or first degree murder; three counts of first degree murder during a robbery of the same victims; and four counts of assault with a deadly weapon involving the same three victims and one additional victim.

At the extradition hearing, Ewaschuk J. of the Ontario Court (General Division) committed the fugitive for surrender on all of the counts. He found that the conduct of the fugitive as disclosed by the evidence would, had it occurred in Canada, have constituted murder. However, Ewaschuk J. went a step further and classified the murder. He indicated that, if he were committing the fugitive for trial in Canada, the fugitive would only have been committed for trial on second degree murder as a secondary party to the murders. Nonetheless, Ewaschuk J. committed the fugitive for surrender on all the charges for which extradition was sought. He stated that once double criminality was satisfied, he was required to commit the fugitive on all counts requested by the foreign state and it was for the Minister of Justice to determine on which offences the fugitive would be surrendered.

On appeal, amongst other grounds, it was argued that the Minister of Justice's decision to surrender Bounnam on three counts of premeditated murder would be a violation of his rights under s. 7 of the *Charter*. The basis for this argument was that the extradition judge did not find evidence of planning and deliberation as would be required for a Canadian charge of first degree murder. Rather, the extradition judge only found sufficient evidence to constitute a Canadian charge of second degree murder. The Ontario Court of Appeal dismissed the fugitive's argument. In so doing, they found no error on the part of the Minister in surrendering the fugitive to face trial under what they described "as the rigorous Tennessee felony murder law."

The exercise in classification undertaken by the extradition judge in *United States v. Bounnam, supra*, was probably unnecessary because murder, regardless of the degree, is an extradition crime. Therefore, the classification of murder is irrelevant in the extradition context. All that the extradition judge was required to determine was whether the conduct of the fugitive as disclosed by the evidence would, had it occurred in Canada, constitute any Canadian crime and attract the penalty specified in the applicable treaty.

In *United States v. Soffitt* (1993), 36 B.C.A.C. 155, 58 W.A.C. 155 (B.C. C.A.), the British Columbia Court of Appeal was clear that the extradition judge was not required to classify murder by degree. This case was decided prior to the 1991 amendments to the *Canada–United States Extradition Treaty* which replaced the list of extradition crimes with a punishability standard. The pre-1991 list of extradition crimes in the Treaty included "murder." In *United States v. Soffitt*, the fugitive contended that he should be committed for surrender on second rather than first degree murder. The basis for this argument was that only second degree murder would be supported by the evidence as a matter of Canadian law. McEachern J.A. for the British Columbia Court of Appeal declined to distinguish between the degrees of murder, at p. 157:

> [9] In my judgment the *Treaty* and the enabling legislation, that is the *Extradition Act*, are framed in terms of offenses in the requesting country which are described in well recognized terms. One of those described offenses is murder. In Canadian law there is an offence which is easily identified by that same term, murder, and it is indeed punishable in this country. As I understand the authorities first and second degree murder in both countries fall within the rubric of murder and that distinction exists in Canada only for the purposes of sentencing. . . .

[10] . . . Our only responsibility is to satisfy ourselves that the conduct alleged is specified or described in the *Treaty* and that it is punishable in Canada. There can be no doubt that this test is satisfied.

Under the new *Extradition Act*, the determination that conduct would amount to murder in Canada is made by the Minister of Justice under ss. 3 and 15 in deciding whether to issue the authority to proceed. For the reasons set out above, it is unnecessary for the Minister of Justice to make any distinction between first and second degree murder when naming the equivalent Canadian offence in the authority to proceed. On the same reasoning, there is no basis to apply to the extradition judge under s. 23 to amend the authority to proceed to reflect a particular classification of murder to coincide with evidence adduced at the extradition hearing. In the case of *Thailand (Kingdom) v. Karas* (June 1, 2001), Doc. CC991269, 2001 BCSC 72 (B.C.S.C.), however, the extradition judge did see a distinction between murder and manslaughter and permitted an amendment to the authority to proceed to allow a committal for manslaughter rather than murder.

(viii) *Defences not to be raised at extradition hearing*

The jurisprudence under the former *Extradition Act* was clear that defences were not to be raised at the extradition hearing. This rule continues to apply under the new *Extradition Act*. The new Act is structured so as to provide a complete code for extradition. In this sense, the absence of any provision regarding the calling of defences at extradition hearings is a strong indication that raising defences at the hearing is precluded. Moreover, where the Act does provide for the calling of evidence by the person sought, as in s. 32(1)(c), it is restricted to the tests to be applied in s. 29(1).

In *R. v. Schmidt* (1987), 33 C.C.C. (3d) 193, decided under the former Act, the Supreme Court of Canada gave a clear direction that defences should not be raised at extradition hearings. The State of Ohio had requested the extradition of Schmidt to face charges of child stealing. The fugitive had previously been acquitted of a federal United States charge of kidnapping. Schmidt attempted to rely upon the defence of *autrefois acquit* in order to resist the extradition. The defence was rejected by the extradition judge, the *habeas corpus* judge, and the Ontario Court of Appeal. The case was appealed to the Supreme Court of Canada. La Forest J. rejected the appeal on the basis, amongst others, that s. 11(h) of the *Charter* had no application to extradition.

In the course of his judgment, La Forest J. stated that there was no place for the raising of defences, given the purpose of an extradition hearing, at p. 209:

It must be emphasized that this hearing is not a trial and no attempt should be made to make it one. The trial, when held, will be in the foreign country according to its laws for an alleged crime committed there, and it should require no demonstration that such a prosecution is wholly within the competence of that country. A judge at an extradition

227

hearing has no jurisdiction to deal with defences that could be raised at trial unless, of course, the Act or the treaty otherwise provides.

It should be noted that, under the new *Extradition Act*, the double jeopardy issue is addressed in the context of the ministerial discretion under s. 47(a) to refuse surrender on that basis. This is a strong indication that double jeopardy is not a matter for the extradition judge.

In the case of *Thailand (Kingdom) v. Saxena* (April 29, 1999), Doc. Vancouver CC960599, 1999 CarswellBC 922 (B.C. S.C.), decided under the former *Extradition Act*, the fugitive wished to tender documentary evidence that he contended would complete and fully detail the transactions relied upon by Thailand and would assist in the determination of the *prima facie* case issue. The extradition judge held a *voir dire* in order to fully consider the evidence which was proposed to be tendered. (In light of the provisions of s. 32(1)(c) of the new Act, which allows the person sought to adduce evidence relevant to the tests to be applied by the extradition judge under s. 29(1), the holding of a *voir dire* in similar circumstances may be an appropriate manner in which to consider the admissibility of evidence proposed to be tendered by a person sought.) The extradition judge considered that the evidence proposed was in the nature of a defence and he refused to admit it. The judge noted that it had been conceded by all counsel "that the accused is not entitled to lead evidence by way of a defence at an extradition hearing. This proposition is so well known that it requires no further comment" (at para. 12).

In *United States v. Martinez* (February 28, 2000), Doc. E24/99, 2000 CarswellOnt 561 (Ont. S.C.J.), a case under the new Act concerning the alleged abduction of three children by their father, Juriansz J. refused to permit the person sought to testify that his wife had given him permanent custody of the children and that therefore he had done nothing wrong by taking them out of the United States. Juriansz J. observed that this evidence was directed at contradicting the evidence in the record of the case and was thus a defence. As such it was not relevant to the test set out in s. 29(1) of the Act and was ruled inadmissible.

(e) Extradition judge's discretion to receive evidence for use at ministerial stage

There was an issue under the former *Extradition Act* as to the extent to which the forum of the extradition hearing could be used to receive evidence which, although not relevant to the extradition judge's function, would have been useful to the fugitive in building a record for use during the ministerial phase of the proceedings. Under the former Act, the only provision that dealt specifically with this issue was s. 15. This provision permitted evidence to be tendered at the extradition hearing to show the following: that the fugitive was accused or convicted of an offence of a political character; that the proceedings were being taken with a view to prosecuting or punishing the fugitive for an offence of a political character; or that the offence was not otherwise an extradition crime. Sections 21 and 22 of the former Act provided that the Minister of Justice could refuse surrender for reasons based upon the political offence considerations referred to in s. 15.

There is no provision in the new Act for the extradition judge to hear evidence relating to a matter solely within the jurisdiction of the Minister, not even with respect to political offences. The cases decided under the former Act which discuss this issue (referred to below) concluded that the extradition hearing judge had the discretion to admit evidence on issues which were exclusively within the Minister's determination. Two cases dealt with this issue in the context of fugitives facing the death penalty in the requesting state. At the extradition hearing in *Canada v. Ng*, Trussler J. of the Alberta Court of Queen's Bench refused to receive evidence on the death penalty issue on the ground that it pertained to the Minister of Justice's determination during the ministerial phase of the extradition process rather than to the extradition hearing judge's decision during the judicial phase of the process. The Alberta Court of Appeal upheld this decision ((1989), 97 A.R. 241).

In *Kindler v. Canada (Minister of Justice)* (1991), 67 C.C.C. (3d) 1 (S.C.C.), the fugitive argued that the extradition hearing judge erred in refusing to receive evidence concerning the death penalty given that this punishment would be imposed if the fugitive was extradited to the requesting state (Ohio, U.S.A.). The fugitive analogized the receipt of this evidence to evidence that an extradition judge was required to receive under s. 15 of the former *Extradition Act* dealing with crimes of a political character. Greenberg J. of the Quebec Superior Court rejected this argument. He held that, unlike the death penalty situation, the jurisprudence and legislation clearly showed that the extradition judge under s. 15 of the Act must receive evidence regarding the political character of the offence for the use of the Minister. The Minister may then refuse extradition under ss. 21 and 22 of the Act.

Both *Canada v. Ng* and *Kindler v. Canada (Minister of Justice)* proceeded in tandem to the Supreme Court of Canada on the basis of a review of the Minister of Justice's decision in those cases not to seek assurances from the United States under Article 6 of the *Canada–United States Extradition Treaty* that the death penalty would not be imposed. In both cases, the Supreme Court upheld the Minister's decision. The Court did not expressly deal with the record-building issue.

United States v. Bembenek (January 31, 1992), Doc. U156/91, 16 W.C.B. (2d) 112 (Ont. Gen. Div.), involved a request for extradition from Wisconsin for Lawrencia "Bambi" Bembenek. The fugitive had escaped from an American prison while serving a life sentence for murdering her husband's ex-wife. Watt J. of the Ontario Court (General Division) held that the extradition judge did have a discretion to receive evidence at the extradition hearing that, although not relevant to the extradition judge's function, could be relevant to the Minister's decision with respect to the surrender of the fugitive during the ministerial phase of the extradition process. In this case, both parties consented to the evidence being adduced for this purpose. Both the requesting state and the fugitive called experts on American law with regard to the issue of whether there was recourse to the fugitive to have her conviction reviewed in the United States.

The specific implications of this determination were discussed in the Ontario Court of Appeal's decision in *Pacificador v. Philippines (Republic), supra,* §4.1(d)(iii). At the extradition hearing in *Pacificador v. Philippines (Republic)* (July 27, 1992), (Ont. Gen. Div.), the fugitive contended that he ought to be permitted to adduce the evidence of an R.C.M.P. officer who attended the Philippines and took sworn statements from eight residents of that country. The case involved an extradition request from the Philippines for murder and other related charges allegedly arising from the death of a supporter of Corazon Aquino by a supporter of Ferdinand Marcos during an election in that country in 1986. The statements taken by the R.C.M.P. officer were contained in the documentary evidence relied upon by the requesting state at the extradition hearing. Two of the reasons advanced by the fugitive in arguing for the tendering of this evidence were as follows: Firstly, there were inconsistencies and contradictions between the sworn statements taken by the officer and previous sworn statements given by the witnesses. Therefore, the fugitive should be permitted to cross-examine the officer about the circumstances under which the officer took the statements. Secondly, it would enable the fugitive to establish an evidentiary basis for the *habeas corpus* application and ministerial proceedings. The evidence, it was argued, would assist "in establishing a case of political motivation for the treaty, as well [as] the exclusion of murder from the political offence or the political crime exception." (p. 32 of the judgment)

Watt J. of the Ontario Court (General Division) held that the evidence would have no value to him as an extradition hearing judge because weighing the evidence was beyond his jurisdiction. In addition, Watt J. indicated that it was not his function as an extradition judge "to create or facilitate the creation of an evidentiary record for future proceedings, whether in the form of an application for *habeas corpus* or representations to be made at the executive level, in the event a warrant shall issue at the conclusion of these proceedings." (p. 35 of the judgment)

Doherty J.A. of the Ontario Court of Appeal affirmed Watt J.'s decision (1993), 83 C.C.C. (3d) 210. In so doing, Doherty J.A., at p. 219, discussed the decision of the Ontario Court (General Division) in *United States v. Bembenek, supra,* and relied on the decision of the Ontario Court (General Division) in *United States v. Houslander* (1993), 13 O.R. (3d) 44 (Ont. Gen. Div.):

> Nor does the case-law fix the extradition judge with any such obligation. It goes no further than to suggest that an extradition judge has the discretion to hear evidence on issues which may ultimately be relevant on a *habeas corpus* application or to the Minister's ultimate decision with respect to the surrender of the fugitive: *Bembenek v. United States of America,* a decision of Watt J., released January 31, 1992 (Ont. Ct. (Gen. Div.)) [summarized 16 W.C.B. (2d) 112]. To the extent that such a discretion may exist, it supports the respondent's position that Watt J. was not obligated to hear such evidence in this case.
>
> I agree with the comments of Blair J. in *United States of America v. Houslander* (1993), 13 O.R. (3d) 44, 39 A.C.W.S. (3d) 617, 19 W.C.B. (2d) 264 (Ont. Ct. (Gen. Div.)), where in rejecting the same argument advanced by the appellant in this case he said at pp. 51–52:

"Building a case for another purpose" is not consistent with the nature of the extradition hearing, which is designed simply to provide a summary and expeditious determination as to whether there is sufficient evidence to commit the fugitive for surrender. A court is entitled to control its own process. It is not an effective or necessary use of judicial time to have judges sitting passively by while counsel rummage about in evidence which is admittedly completely irrelevant to their mandate at hand, albeit that such an exercise may yield useful results for the fugitive at a later stage.

The discretionary aspect of admitting record-building evidence was illustrated by the fact that the same extradition judge, Watt J. of the Ontario Court (General Division), admitted record-building evidence in *United States v. Bembenek* (although the parties consented to the admission of the evidence) and refused to receive it in *Pacificador v. Philippines (Republic)*.

The case of *United States v. Whitley* (1994), 94 C.C.C. (3d) 99 (Ont. C.A.), affirmed (1996), 104 C.C.C. (3d) 447 (S.C.C.), involved an extradition request by the State of New York for charges relating to the exportation of marijuana to Canada. The fugitive had sought to introduce evidence at the extradition hearing for the purpose of supporting an argument before the Minister of Justice regarding the "*Cotroni* issue." The *Cotroni* issue concerns whether a person sought should be surrendered to the foreign state as opposed to being prosecuted domestically when domestic prosecution for the same conduct is an option. Laskin J.A., on behalf of the Court of Appeal, upheld the extradition judge's decision to refuse to hear evidence of a Canadian police officer who headed the Canadian investigation and which was directed at the issue of why extradition was preferred to domestic prosecution. Laskin J.A. referred to the decision of Doherty J.A. for the Ontario Court of Appeal in *Pacificador v. Philippines (Republic)* (1993), 83 C.C.C. (3d) 210, and held that "the extradition judge has a discretion to hear evidence which may be relevant to the Minister's surrender decision, but is not obliged to do so," at p. 108. The Supreme Court of Canada dismissed the fugitive's appeal on this and other issues and adopted the reasons of Laskin J.A.

This line of cases culminated in the Supreme Court of Canada decision in *United States v. Kwok* (2001), 152 C.C.C. (3d) 225, decided under the terms of the former Act. In that case, Arbour J. recognized the discretionary authority of an extradition judge to receive, but not rule upon, evidence unrelated to the extradition hearing itself, but for use at a subsequent proceeding, or before the Minister. In that case it was argued that the judge ought to have received evidence related to the fugitive's s. 6(1) *Charter* rights. Arbour J. observed that it would be an authority exercised only when convenience and expediency required it. She stated, at p. 260:

[74] If s. 6 issues are premature at the committal stage, it would follow that evidence dealing with an alleged s. 6 breach would be irrelevant and therefore inadmissible at the committal hearing. However, on efficiency grounds, it has been recognized that extradition judges could have the *discretion* to hear, without deciding, evidence on alleged s. 6 *Charter* violations when the allegations hold an air of reality: *Whitley* and *Pacificador, supra.* This may indeed be an appropriate course of action, for instance when the

issues relevant to the committal are intertwined with the factual basis upon which the *Charter* challenge will subsequently be based, or when the same witnesses may conveniently be heard on both issues, but I stress that this is entirely within the discretion of the extradition judge. As the Minister may decline to surrender the fugitive committed for extradition, efficiency may equally dictate waiting for the Minister's decision before arguing *Charter* remedies, particularly if it calls for an evidentiary foundation unrelated to that presented in relation to the committal. This concern was well expressed by Blair J. in *United States of America v. Houslander* (1993), 13 O.R. (3d) 44 (Gen. Div.), at p. 51:

> "Building a case for another purpose" is not consistent with the nature of the extradition hearing, which is designed to provide a summary and expeditious determination as to whether there is sufficient evidence to commit the fugitive for surrender.

> [75] Although I would not oust altogether the discretion of the extradition judge to receive evidence related solely to s. 6 *Charter* issues, he or she should keep in mind the need for an expeditious disposition of the committal issues, the danger of confusion that may arise if irrelevant evidence is received, and the waste that will result if the Minister ultimately declines to surrender.

Although there is no express prohibition in the new Act preventing the admission of evidence at the hearing for use during the ministerial phase of the proceedings, it may be argued that this line of authority does not continue to be applicable to proceedings under the new legislation. This position is supported by the fact that the new Act is more specific than was the former Act about the manner in which the proceedings are to unfold. In particular, the new Act sets out in great detail the evidence that may be considered at the extradition hearing (ss. 32–37) and the role of the extradition judge is limited to a consideration of whether the evidence tendered supports the offence(s) set out by the Minister in the authority to proceed. In addition, the right of the person sought to call evidence, specifically addressed in s. 32(1)(c), is solely limited to the extradition judge's determination regarding the committal issue. Section 32(1)(c) does not permit evidence to be led which is directed to any of the issues within ministerial jurisdiction.

A further argument to support the position that the extradition judge no longer has discretion to receive evidence for use at the ministerial level is that recourse to the Minister with respect to the ultimate surrender issue is comprehensively dealt with in the new Act. The new Act, unlike the former Act, specifically provides for the right to make submissions to the Minister and details the discretionary and mandatory grounds of refusal for the Minister to consider when determining the surrender issue (ss. 43–47). (While the former Act did not specifically provide the right to make submissions to the Minister, it was the practice for the Minister to receive them, and the jurisprudence confirmed that it was a procedure which natural justice and fairness requirements mandated.) The strict delineation of the respective roles of the extradition hearing judge and the Minister in the new Act is supportive of the position that the forum for dealing with issues for the Minister's consideration, is not the extradition hearing, but at the ministerial submissions stage. As Romilly J. observed in *Australia v. Ho, supra,* there are no areas of overlapping jurisdiction in the new Act between the extradition judge and the Minister. (at paras. 17 and 18)

Watt J. in *Germany (Federal Republic) v. Schreiber, supra,* expressed a similar opinion. He described the respective roles of the Minister and the extradition judge as being "two . . . different solitudes" and noted that "[n]either intrudes into the other's area of responsibility." (para. 72)

(f) Advising person sought of rights subsequent to committal

In the event that an order of committal is issued by the extradition judge at the conclusion of the hearing, s. 38(2) of the *Extradition Act* requires the judge to advise the person sought that the person will not be surrendered until the expiry of 30 days and that the person has the right to appeal the order and the right to apply for judicial interim release. A failure on the part of the extradition judge to observe s. 38(2) may not be fatal to the validity of the order of committal. This was the view of the Ontario Court of Appeal in *United States v. Leon* (1995), 96 C.C.C. (3d) 568 (Ont. C.A.), affirmed (1996), 105 C.C.C. (3d) 385 (S.C.C.), with respect to the failure to observe similar procedural requirements under the former Act. Section 19.1(2) of the former Act required that the extradition judge advise a fugitive at the commencement of an extradition hearing of the right to make submissions to the Minister of Justice within 30 days of the committal order. At the conclusion of the hearing, s. 19 of the former Act required the judge to advise the fugitive that he or she would not be surrendered for 30 days and that the fugitive had a right to appeal the committal order. In *United States v. Leon,* it was argued that the proceedings were defective because the judge had failed to advise the fugitive at the commencement of the hearing of the right to make submissions to the Minister in accordance with s. 19.1(2). The Ontario Court of Appeal dismissed this argument, stating as follows, at p. 573:

> In our view, this somewhat fastidious and technical argument has little merit. Even assuming a technical breach of s. 19, the proceedings were not thereby rendered a nullity and the breach was of no consequence because the appellant eventually exercised his right to be heard by the Minister.

§4.2 Extradition Hearing When Person Sought Has Already Been Convicted (s. 29(1)(b))

(a) Disclosure

The same analysis given for s. 29(1)(a) is applicable to s. 29(1)(b). The disclosure rules for extradition hearings apply in the same manner to both accused and convicted persons.

(b) Conduct of hearing

(i) Tendering authority to proceed

Under s. 24(1) of the *Extradition Act*, it is a condition precedent to the holding of the extradition hearing that the authority to proceed, issued by the Minister of Justice under s. 15, has been filed with the court by the Attorney General. Since the authority to proceed is the condition precedent to the commencement of the hearing, it follows that the authority to proceed should be filed with the court on or before the hearing. This need not be the original as s. 15(4) is clear that copies have the same probative force as originals.

(ii) Identity

The identity analysis given for s. 29(1)(a) is applicable to s. 29(1)(b). As in the case of a person sought for trial, it will be necessary to establish that the person before the court is the person sought for extradition. The second branch of identity, for accused persons, requires *prima facie* evidence that the person sought committed the alleged offence. In the case of convicted persons, the second branch of identity requires, as Justice Watt stated in *United States v. Bembenek* (January 31, 1992), Doc. U156/91, 16 W.C.B. (2d) 112 (Ont. Gen. Div.), at p. 4, that there be proof that "the fugitive is one and the same as the person convicted of the offence alleged." (para. 3)

(iii) Evidentiary considerations

After filing the authority to proceed, the Attorney General will file the documentary material. This will be done by one of two methods: by way of a record of the case pursuant to ss. 32(1)(a) and 33(1)(b) or in conformity with the terms of the applicable extradition agreement under s. 32(1)(b). In the former case, s. 33(1)(b) requires the record of the case to include a copy of the record of conviction and a description of the conduct for which the person was convicted. An example of the treaty method is Article 9 of the *Canada–United States Extradition Treaty*. Article 9(4) requires that the request for a convicted person be accompanied by a judgment of conviction and sentence and a statement showing the amount of the sentence that is left to be served. Like the record of the case method, Article 9(2) requires that a statement of the facts of the case be provided.

Under ss. 3(3) and 15 of the new Act, the requirement of a statement showing what is left to be served on the sentence will be an issue for the Minister of Justice, rather than for the extradition judge, to determine when considering whether to issue an authority to proceed. Section 15 provides the Minister with the authority to issue an authority to proceed. The authority to proceed serves as the basis for the extradition proceedings. In the case of convicted persons sought, s. 15 requires that s. 3(3) be met as a condition precedent to the issuance of an authority to proceed. Section 3(3) provides that, subject to the terms of an applicable extradition agreement, a convicted person may not be extradited unless he or she has at least six months remaining to be served on his or her sentence.

As a practical matter, the analysis required to be undertaken pursuant to s. 29(1)(b) that the conviction was in respect of the conduct corresponding to the offence(s) set out in the authority to proceed will be on essentially the same material, whichever of the two methods is chosen.

In *United States v. Wong* (1995), 98 C.C.C. (3d) 332 (B.C.C.A.), decided under the former *Extradition Act*, the British Columbia Court of Appeal liberally construed the requirement under the *Canada–United States Extradition Treaty* that the request be accompanied by a judgment of conviction. The court held that it was sufficient that the affidavit of the American prosecutor contained the jury's verdict form which recorded the conviction and a minute-order pronouncement of judgment. This case will continue to be persuasive in situations in which the documentary material is provided pursuant to the terms of an extradition agreement under s. 32(1)(b) of the new Act. It may also be relevant to the record of the case method, given the broad wording of the requirement under s. 33(1)(b)(i) that the record of the case include "a copy of the document that records the conviction of the person." The broad description contained in s. 33(1)(b)(i) is necessary in order to accommodate different methods of recording convictions by extradition partners. Consequently, the fair and liberal interpretation principle enunciated by the Supreme Court of Canada in *R. v. Schmidt* (1987), 33 C.C.C. (3d) 193; *United States v. McVey* (1992), 77 C.C.C. (3d) 1; *Argentina (Republic) v. Mellino* (1987), 33 C.C.C. (3d) 334; and *United States v. Dynar* (1997), 115 C.C.C. (3d) 481, would appear to be applicable when considering the sufficiency of conviction documents.

The requirements for the issuance of a warrant of committal for a convicted person under the former *Extradition Act* were described by Watt J. in *United States v. Bembenek, supra*, as follows:

[3] It is common ground, that in a case such as at present, it is incumbent upon the requesting State to establish with the necessary degree of certainty,

(i)   that the fugitive is in fact the person requested by the requesting State;

(ii)   that the fugitive is one and the same as the person convicted of the offences alleged;

(iii)   that the offence alleged and of which the fugitive is proven to have been convicted is an offence listed in the Schedule to the treaty [this was before the amendment of the American treaty to the no-list but punishability standard to extradition crimes];

(iv)   that the conviction recorded and sentence imposed was entered by a court of competent jurisdiction; and

(v)   that the sentence has not yet been served.

Of the five factors listed by Watt J., only the first two are to be decided by the extradition judge under the new *Extradition Act*. Points (iii), (iv), and (v) are to be dealt with by the Minister of Justice under ss. 15 and 3(3) as part of the Minister's decision regarding whether an authority to proceed should be issued.

In addition to the identity considerations set out in points (i) and (ii) above, the extradition judge must consider the conduct underpinning the conviction. The extradition judge undertakes an inquiry, similar to that which occurs in the case of an accused person, into the conduct underlying the offence. The difference is that the accused's situation requires evidence sufficient to justify committal. In the case of a convicted person, all that is required is a synopsis sufficient to satisfy the extradition judge that the conduct for which the person was convicted by the extradition partner corresponds with the offence named in the authority to proceed.

Ewaschuk J. discussed this in *United States v. Persaud* (November 3, 1999), 1999 CarswellOnt 4263, [1999] O.J. No. 4992 (Ont. S.C.J.), at paras. 12, 13:

> [12] . . . However, I must nonetheless be satisfied that the conduct underlying the foreign convictions corresponds in a general sense to the Canadian offences set out in the authority to proceed.
>
> [13] It is the federal Minister of Justice's responsibility, pursuant to s. 15(3)(c) of the *Extradition Act*, to determine the name of the Canadian offences which correspond to the conduct in respect of which the fugitive was convicted, and to set out those offences in the authority to proceed. However, it is the extradition judge's responsibility, pursuant to s. 29(1)(b), to determine if the foreign convictions were in respect of "conduct" that corresponds to the Canadian offences set out in the authority to proceed. It is the fugitive's "conduct," not his foreign convictions, which must correspond to the Canadian offences set out in the authority to proceed. Obviously, the validity of the foreign convictions is immaterial to the judge's statutory responsibilities.

Section 29(1)(b) provides a simplified process for committing convicted persons for surrender. The appropriateness of a simplified process for committing convicted persons for surrender was acknowledged by the Supreme Court of Canada in cases decided under the former Act. In *United States v. McVey, supra*, at p. 31, La Forest J. stated as follows:

> Section 18(1)(*a*) was intended to simplify the process of proving that the offence for which a convict is sought is an extradition crime under the Act.

The continuation of the simplified process provided for in s. 29(1)(b) of the new Act was discussed by Ewaschuk J. in *Persaud, supra*:

> [14] Parenthetically, I agree with applicant counsel that Parliament intended that it be easier to extradite a fugitive already convicted of a foreign offence than to extradite one merely charged with a foreign offence. In that regard, I note that s. 29(1)(a) requires admissible evidence of the foreign conduct in respect of an offence extradition, whereas s. 29(1)(b) merely refers to conduct which has already been found to be factually true by a foreign court and which has resulted in a conviction. The latter applies in respect of conviction extraditions.

The basis upon which a simplified process is justified in the case of a convicted individual is that the convicted person has had a trial, and has received the full benefit of the protections which accrue to an accused in the foreign jurisdiction. Section 29(5) mandates that persons not present for their trial and conviction be dealt with as accused persons under s. 29(1)(a). This provision implicitly recognizes that the simplified procedure is appropriate for individuals who were convicted after trial in which they had the opportunity to avail themselves of trial protections.

(iv) *Wrongful conviction assertions not reviewable by extradition judge*

It was clear under the former *Extradition Act* that the statutory scheme of the Act with respect to convicted fugitives gave no role to the extradition judge concerning the issue of whether the foreign conviction was a just one. Once the statutory prerequisites of s. 18(1)(a) of the former Act were met, the extradition judge was required to commit the convicted fugitive for surrender. This issue was canvassed thoroughly in *United States v. Bembenek, supra, supra.* In that case, counsel for the fugitive argued that the conviction of the fugitive for the offence of first degree murder in the State of Wisconson, for which she had received a sentence of life in prison minus three days, was occasioned by a miscarriage of justice. In holding that it was not appropriate for him to review that conviction, Watt J. defined the role of the extradition judge in dealing with convicted fugitives:

> [7] The role, function and duty of an extradition judge is circumscribed by statute. The matters to be decided fall within comparatively narrow compass. It but falls for me to determine whether the requirements of the *Act* and any enabling treaty have been met. I decided no more and certainly no less. It is readily acknowledged in this case, as indeed it must, that compliance has been made with the conditions precedent to the issuance of a warrant committing the fugitive for surrender. Indeed, in the case of a convicted fugitive whose identity is not in issue and whose sentence has not expired, there would appear little factual latitude.

Watt J. was clear that his role did not include retrying a case which had already been determined by a trial court in the foreign jurisdiction:

> [8] It is as well to record, however, in light of the media attention this case has received, further the suggestion that a determination would be made here whether the fugitive pulled the trigger, thereby fired the shot that caused the death of the deceased, that neither I nor any other extradition judge retry cases determined by foreign courts of competent jurisdiction upon evidence then and there received. It is no part of my duty, nor that of any other Canadian judge, to decide who fired the shot or shots that extinguished the life of Christine Schultz, nor what gun was used to do so. I do not sit on appeal somehow to decide or determine whether the original finding and conviction was soundly based on the evidence adduced at trial. Neither do I consider whether the foreign conviction remains firmly rooted, when the evidence adduced at the trial is considered

together with or in light of further evidence adduced in concurrent immigration proceedings, and which relates to but a part of the prosecutor's case at trial. To put the
matter in another way, as an extradition judge, I do not sit to determine, in accordance
with domestic law or otherwise, whether there has here been a miscarriage of justice
occasioned this fugitive.

Watt J. went further and indicated that it would be inappropriate for the extradition
judge to comment upon the possible impact fresh evidence might have on the soundness of the conviction:

> [9] The nature and scope of my function as an extradition judge has persuaded me,
> notwithstanding Mr. Hunt's persuasive argument, that I ought not comment upon the
> soundness or otherwise of the fugitive's underlying foreign conviction. I know little of
> the prosecutor's case at the fugitive's trial. To comment upon the apparent impact of
> further evidence concerning the identity of the weapon used to fire the fatal shots in
> profound ignorance of the trial record would be, at best, imprudent.

The extradition judge did, however, allow evidence to be called concerning the
"state and federal remedies which may be available to the fugitive to put in issue the
validity of the underlying conviction in light of subsequent developments" (para. 10)
for the assistance of the Minister of Justice in making the surrender determination.

Watt J.'s comments in *United States v. Bembenek*, *supra*, regarding the role of
the extradition judge when dealing with convicted fugitives will still be applicable
under the new *Extradition Act*.

§4.3 Contents of Order of Committal (s. 29(2))

Section 29(2) specifies the required contents of the order of committal. In so
doing, this provision leaves no doubt as to what information the order should contain.
The information it sets out contains full particulars so as to assist the entities and/or
individuals who will be dealing with the person sought subsequent to the committal.

If a required item of information is omitted from the committal order, through
inadvertence or otherwise, the principles enunciated in *R. v. Schmidt* (1987), 33 C.C.C.
(3d) 193 (S.C.C.), *United States v. McVey* (1992), 77 C.C.C. (3d) 1 (S.C.C.), and
United States v. Lépine (1993), 87 C.C.C. (3d) 385, 163 N.R. 1 (S.C.C.), namely, that
a fair and liberal interpretation should be given to extradition proceedings and that
technical arguments should be minimized, would probably be applied. In his judgment
in *United States v. McVey*, at p. 40 N.R., La Forest J. set out the principle of fair and
liberal interpretation:

> What has just been said is consistent with the frequently repeated principle that the
> fine or nice distinctions of criminal law are out of place in the law of extradition. This
> court put the matter bluntly in *Mellino*, *supra*, at p. 348 C.C.C., p. 88 D.L.R.:

In assessing the issue, a court must not overlook that extradition proceedings must be approached with a view to conform with Canada's international obligations. The courts have on many occasions reiterated that the requirements and technicalities of the criminal law apply only to a limited extent in extradition proceedings.

Similarly, the Ontario Court of Appeal in *United States v. Leon* (1995), 96 C.C.C. (3d) 568 (Ont. C.A.), affirmed (1996), 105 C.C.C. (3d) 385 (S.C.C.), indicated that technical arguments on procedural points would not be favourably entertained. The information required in an order of committal is the type of matter to which the fair and liberal approach ought to apply.

§4.4 Discharge of Person Sought (s. 29(3))

See the discussion above under this section, §§2.4 and 3.4.

§4.5 Relevant Date for Committal Determination (s. 29(4))

Section 29(4) of the new *Extradition Act* provides that the relevant date for the committal determination is the date of the authority to proceed. This is in contrast to s. 34 of the former Act which required the offence for which extradition was sought to be an offence in Canada at the time it occurred in the other jurisdiction (see *United States v. Allard* (1991), 64 C.C.C. (3d) 159 (S.C.C.), reconsideration refused (July 11, 1991), Doc. 20626 (S.C.C.)). This is no longer the rule under the new *Extradition Act*. The relevant date for the s. 29(1) committal determination is the date of the authority to proceed.

Section 29(4) of the new Act now focuses the inquiry on whether the alleged conduct is an offence in Canada as of the date of the authority to proceed, a change which may in fact better promote the objectives sought to be advanced by the extradition system. For instance, in *United States v. Cotroni* (1989), 48 C.C.C. (3d) 193 (S.C.C.), the Supreme Court of Canada held that extradition was a reasonable limit on the right of a citizen under s. 6 of the *Charter* to remain in Canada. In reaching this conclusion, the Court made the following comments about the nature of international co-operation in the suppression of crime and the place of extradition in that context, at pp. 215–216:

> The objectives sought by the legislation, the parties agree, relate to concerns that are pressing and substantial. The investigation, prosecution and suppression of crime for the protection of the citizen and the maintenance of peace and public order is an important goal of all organized societies. The pursuit of that goal cannot realistically be confined within national boundaries. That has long been the case, but it is increasingly evident today. Modern communications have shrunk the world and made McLuhan's global village a reality. The only respect paid by the international criminal community to national boundaries is when these can serve as a means to frustrate the efforts of law enforcement and judicial authorities

. . .

The importance of extradition for the protection of the Canadian public against crime can scarcely be exaggerated. To afford that protection, there must be arrangements that ensure prosecution not only of those who commit crimes while they are physically in Canada and escape abroad, but also of those whose acts abroad have criminal effects in this country.

The same principles and objectives animate the new legislation.

The Canadian extradition regime can be contrasted with that prevailing in the United Kingdom, which is similar to the former Canadian regime. In *R. v. Bartle, Ex parte Pinochet Ugarte (No. 3), (sub nom. R. v. Bow Street Metropolitan Stipendiary Magistrate)*, [2000] 1 A.C. 147 (U.K. H.L.), the former Chilean head of state was sought by Spain to face charges of torture allegedly committed in Chile during Pinochet's dictatorship. The number of offences for which General Pinochet could be extradited to Spain was greatly reduced by the House of Lords from the number of offences for which he was sought. This was because Pinochet was sought for a number of crimes of torture that had allegedly been committed prior to 1988, the year in which the 1984 International Convention against Torture was implemented, and the offence of torture wherever committed worldwide made an offence under British law. The House of Lords held that Pinochet was not extraditable for the alleged acts of torture committed before the 1988 change in British law because the U.K. statute could only be satisfied in relation to conduct that was criminal in the United Kingdom on the date that it was committed. Lord Phillips, in language reminiscent of *United States v. Cotroni*, discussed the desirability of international co-operation in bringing offenders to trial, at pp. 288–289:

> My Lords, this is an area where international law is on the move and the move has been effected by express consensus recorded in or reflected by a considerable number of international instruments. Since the Second World War states have recognised that not all criminal conduct can be left to be dealt with as a domestic matter by the laws and the courts of the territories in which such conduct occurs. There are some categories of crime of such gravity that they shock the conscience of mankind and cannot be tolerated by the international community. Any individual who commits such a crime offends against international law. The nature of these crimes is such that they are likely to involve the concerted conduct of many and liable to involve the complicity of the officials of the state in which they occur, if not of the state itself. In these circumstances it is desirable that jurisdiction should exist to prosecute individuals for such conduct outside the territory in which such conduct occurs.
>
> I believe that it is still an open question whether international law recognises universal jurisdiction in respect of international crimes—that is the right, under international law, of the courts of any state to prosecute for such crimes wherever they occur. In relation to war crimes, such a jurisdiction has been asserted by the State of Israel, notably in the prosecution of Adolf Eichmann, but this assertion of jurisdiction does not

reflect any general state practice in relation to international crimes. Rather, states have tended to agree, or to attempt to agree, on the creation of international tribunals to try international crimes. They have however, on occasion, agreed by conventions, that their national courts should enjoy jurisdiction to prosecute for a particular category of international crime wherever occurring.

Notwithstanding the desirability of international cooperation recognized by the House of Lords, the result in *R. v. Bartle, Ex parte Pinochet Ugarte* was dictated by the terms of the U.K. *Extradition Act*, which require the crime alleged to have also been an offence under U.K. law at the time of its commission. The effect of this requirement on the *Pinochet* request was described by Lord Hope, at p. 238:

> What is the effect of the qualification which I have just mentioned, as to the date on which these allegations of torture and conspiracy to torture first became offences for which, at the request of Spain, Senator Pinochet could be extradited? In the circumstances of this case its effect is a profound one. It is to remove from the proceedings the entire course of such conduct in which Senator Pinochet is said to have engaged from the moment he embarked on the alleged conspiracy to torture in January 1972 until 29 September 1988. The only offences of torture and conspiracy to torture which are punishable in this country as extraterritorial offences against the law of the United Kingdom within the meaning of section 2(2) of the Act of 1989 are those offences of torture and conspiracy to torture which he is alleged to have committed on or after 29 September 1988. But almost all the offences of torture and murder, of which there are alleged to have been about 4,000 victims, were committed during the period of repression which was at its most intense in 1973 and 1974. The extradition request alleges that during the period from 1977 to 1990 only about 130 such offences were committed. Of that number only three have been identified in the extradition request as having taken place after 29 September 1988.

Had the request in *R. v. Bartle, Ex parte Pinochet Ugarte* been made to Canada under the new Canadian *Extradition Act*, the result would have been different. Under s. 29(4), the alleged conduct underlying the request need only be criminal in Canada on the date of the issuance of the authority to proceed, regardless of the status of domestic law on the date of the commission of the alleged offence(s).

While the rule against retrospective application of criminal laws which is embodied in the U.K. legislation is a basic tenet of most legal systems, including Canada's, there is justification for distinguishing it in the case of extradition as s. 29(4) of the Canadian *Extradition Act* has done. The rule that no one should be prosecuted for conduct which was not criminal when committed is really a matter for the country where the trial will be held. Countries have criminalized a wide range of activities at different times. If Canada criminalizes the conduct domestically as of the date of the issuance of the authority to proceed, then forcing Canadian criminal legislation to also match the dates of corresponding statutes in foreign countries or international tribunals would only have the effect of making extradition more difficult for what both parties agree is a crime.

Although the rule against retrospective application of criminal laws domestically is enshrined in s. 11(g) of the *Charter*, this has no direct application to extradition because the trial and any ultimate determination of guilt will not take place in this country. (Section 11(g) provides: "Any person charged with an offence has the right . . . not to be found guilty on account of any act or omission unless, at the time of the act or omission, it constituted an offence under Canadian or international law or was criminal according to the general principles of law recognized by the community of nations; . . .")

A rule requiring double criminality at the time of the alleged offence is found in certain extradition treaties to which Canada is a party. For instance, Article II of the *Canada–Mexico Extradition Treaty* provides that the contracting parties undertake to extradite for offences which were offences against the laws of both countries at the time of the commission of the offence and at the time of the request. Canada's extradition treaties with the Philippines (Article 3(5)) and Spain (Article III(4)) also contain provisions which may bear on this issue. These two treaties allow for mandatory refusal of extradition when the prosecution identified in the extradition request would be barred by lapse of time or for any other reason under the law of the requested state. Section 11(g) of the *Charter* may be considered to be such a law, barring prosecution domestically for the offence set out in the request if, at the time of the commission of the crime, it was not an offence known to Canadian law. This is not an argument for extraterritorial application of the *Charter*, of the type disapproved of in *R. v. Schmidt, supra,* §4.3 and *Argentina (Republic) v. Mellino, supra,* §4.2(b)(iii). It is not, however, a matter for the extradition judge to resolve. There is no authority provided in the Act for the extradition judge to depart from the stipulation in s. 29(4) that the relevant date is the date of the authority to proceed.

It can be argued with justification that the philosophy underlying the extradition system is not offended by the change in approach brought about by s. 29(4). The approach taken in this provision accords with the well established principle enunciated in a number of Supreme Court of Canada cases that a fair and liberal approach should be taken in extradition matters and technicalities should be minimized (see *R. v. Schmidt, supra; Argentina (Republic) v. Mellino, supra;* and *United States v. McVey, supra,* §4.3). Expanding the scope of extradition to include extradition for crimes that did not exist in Canada at the time they were committed, but that do exist at the time the request is made, does not undermine the principle enunciated by La Forest J. in *R. v. Schmidt* that the purpose of the extradition hearing is simply to ensure that persons are not extradited to foreign jurisdictions for offences which are not crimes in Canada.

So long as the crime for which the person is sought is a crime in Canada at the time of the request, it would appear that the focus of this protection is not undermined. In other words, the protection is not displaced by the timing issue.

Section 29(4) continues a trend reflected in some of Canada's more recent extradition treaties. For instance, a provison similar to s. 29(4) can be found in the *Canada–Korea Extradition Treaty*, which came into force on February 1, 1995. In particular, Article 2(6) provides as follows:

Extradition may be granted pursuant to the provisions of this Treaty in respect of an offence provided that:

(a)   it was an offence in the Requesting Party at the time of the conduct constituting the offence; and

(b)   the conduct alleged would, if it had taken place in the territory of the Requested Party at the time of the making of the request for extradition, have constituted an offence against the law in force in the territory of the Requested Party.

§4.6 Extradition When Person Sought Was Not Present for Trial and Conviction (s. 29(5))

Section 29(5) of the *Extradition Act* provides that an extradition hearing with respect to a person tried and convicted without being present is to be conducted in accordance with s. 29(1)(a). Therefore, for the purposes of the hearing, such an individual is treated as an accused person. This raises the issue of the materials needed to be put before the court in such a situation. The record of the case provisions in s. 33(1), for instance, make no separate provision for a person who was tried and convicted without being present. Therefore, it would follow logically from the application of s. 29(5) that the evidentiary requirements would be those applicable to a person who is sought for prosecution. This conclusion is supported by the fact that under certain of Canada's newer extradition treaties, such as those with Korea and Spain, it is specifically provided that the same material be supplied in the case of accused individuals and individuals tried and convicted without being present. Accordingly, all of the procedural and evidentiary considerations discussed with respect to s. 29(1)(a) above will apply to such conviction hearings.

The application of s. 29(5) is subject to the terms of an applicable extradition agreement. While many of Canada's newer extradition treaties have identical provisions, many of the older treaties do not. Some provide for convictions in contumacy to be treated as accused situations (see, for example Article 10 of the *Canada–France Extradition Treaty*, in force as of December 1, 1989). A conviction in contumacy is a conviction entered in the absence of an accused which will be set aside, and the trial itself held in the event the person is arrested or surrendered. It is therefore not a final judgment, and because a trial would ultimately be held, these treaties provided for individuals in this category to be treated as accused persons for the purpose of an extradition request.

If the terms of a treaty operate so as to require a person tried and convicted in his or her absence to be treated as any other convicted person, then s. 29(1)(b) would operate since s. 29(5) is subject to a relevant extradition agreement.

As indicated by the English cases of *R. v. Brixton Prison Governor, Ex parte Kotronis*, [1969] 3 All E.R. 304 (U.K.), and *Athanassiadis v. Greece (Government)*, [1969] 3 All E.R. 293 (U.K.), and the Canadian case of *Yugoslavia (Republic) v. Rajovic (No. 3)* (1981), 62 C.C.C. (2d) 544 (Ont. Co. Ct.), situations have arisen in

243

the past in which the regular regime applicable to convicted persons was applied to persons tried and convicted without being present. The fairness of extradition in such circumstances has been questioned. In *R. v. Brixton Prison Governor, Ex parte Kotronis*, the fugitive had been convicted in Greece of obtaining money by false pretences. The conviction had been obtained in his absence and without his knowledge, and was not a conviction in contumacy, that is, there was no automatic right to a retrial upon return to Greece. Lord Parker commented upon the situation as follows, at pp. 307–308:

> It is an unfortunate state of affairs and one would hope one which rarely occurs, and, if it is, as I think, a matter for the Secretary of State for Home Affairs, it may be that this is a case in which in his discretion he would refuse to allow the applicant to be extradited.

It may be expected that, under the structure of the new Act, the Minister of Justice would be urged to refuse surrender in the case of convictions entered when the person was not present for the trial, and which are final, on the grounds set out in s. 44(1) of the Act. That is, that it would be unjust and oppressive in the circumstances. Failing that, it may be urged that the condition of the right to a re-hearing upon return be attached to any surrender as contemplated by s. 40(4). Neither s. 40(4) nor 44(1) are subject to treaty override.

§5.0 CASE LAW

Argentina (Republic) v. Mellino (1987), 33 C.C.C. (3d) 334 (S.C.C.).
Athanassiadis v. Greece (Government), [1969] 3 All E.R. 293 (U.K.H.L.).
Australia v. Ho (January 26, 2000), Doc. Vancouver CC990288 (B.C.S.C.).
Australia v. Ho (December 11, 2000), Doc. Vancouver CC990288, [2000] B.C.J. No. 2651 (B.C.S.C.).
Canada v. Ng (1989), 97 A.R. 241 (C.A.), affirming Trussler J. (Alta. Q.B.).
Coppin, Re (1866), 2 Ch. App. 47 (U.K.).
Germany (Federal Republic) v. Ebke (2001), 2001 NWTSC 2, 2001 CarswellNWT 4 (N.W.T.S.C.).
Germany (Federal Republic) v. Krapohl (1995), 79 O.A.C. 77 (Ont. C.A.).
Germany (Federal Republic) v. Krapohl (1998), 110 O.A.C. 129 (Ont. C.A.).
Germany (Federal Republic) v. Kretz (May 19, 1998), 1998 CarswellOnt 1999, [1998] O.J. No. 2062 (Ont. C.A.).
Germany (Federal Republic) v. Schreiber (July 6, 2000), [2000] O.J. No. 2618, 2000 CarswellOnt 5257, Watt J. (Ont. S.C.J.).
Ismail, Re, [1999] 1 A.C. 320 (U.K. H.L.).
Kindler v. Canada (Minister of Justice) (1991), 67 C.C.C. (3d) 1 (S.C.C.).
Mezzo v. R., [1986] 1 S.C.R. 802.
Pacificador v. Philippines (Republic) (July 27, 1992), Watt J. (Ont. Gen. Div.).
Philippines (Republic) v. Pacificador (October 5, 1992), Watt J. (Ont. Gen. Div.).

Philippines (Republic) v. Pacificador (1993), 83 C.C.C. (3d) 210 (Ont. C.A.), leave to appeal to S.C.C. refused (1994), 87 C.C.C. (3d) vi (S.C.C.).

Puerto Rico (Commonwealth) v. Hernandez (No. 2) (1973), 15 C.C.C. (2d) 56 (Fed. C.A.).

R. v. Arcuri (2001), 157 C.C.C. (3d) 21 (S.C.C.).

R. v. Barranca (December 14, 1994), [1994] O.J. No. 3942, Keenan J. (Ont. Gen. Div.).

R. v. Brixton Prison Governor, Ex parte Kotronis, [1969] 3 All E.R. 304 (U.K.).

R. v. Governor of Pentonville Prison, [1993] 3 All E.R. 504 (Q.B.).

R. v. Monteleone (1987), 35 C.C.C. (3d) 193 (S.C.C.).

R. v. Nikolovski (1996), 111 C.C.C. (3d) 403 (S.C.C.).

R. v. Schmidt (1987), 33 C.C.C. (3d) 193 (S.C.C.).

R. v. Stinchcombe, [1991] 3 S.C.R. 326.

R. v. Turnbull, [1976] 3 All E.R. 549 (C.A.).

Romania v. Cheng (1996), 153 N.S.R. (2d) 271, 450 A.P.R. 271 (N.S. S.C. [In Chambers]).

Romania (State) v. Cheng (1997), 114 C.C.C. (3d) 289 (N.S. S.C.), dismissed as moot (1997), 119 C.C.C. (3d) 561 (N.S. C.A.).

Thailand (Kingdom) v. Karas (January 11, 2001), Doc. CC991269, 2001 BCSC 72 (B.C.S.C.).

Thailand (Kingdom) v. Saxena (April 29, 1999), Doc. Vancouver CC960599, 1999 CarswellBC 922 (B.C. S.C.).

Themens v. United States (February 12, 1996), nos. C.A. Montréal 500-10-000212-959, 500-010-000397-958 (Que. C.A.).

United States v. Adam (1999), 120 O.A.C. 271 (Ont. C.A.).

United States v. Akrami, 2000 BCSC 1438 (B.C.S.C.).

United States v. Allard (1991), 64 C.C.C. (3d) 159 (S.C.C.), reconsideration refused (July 11, 1991), Doc. 20626 (S.C.C.).

United States v. Bembenek (January 31, 1992), Doc. U156/91, 16 W.C.B. (2d) 112 (Ont. Gen. Div.).

United States v. Bonamie (October 24, 2001), Doc. Edmonton Appeal 0003-0281-A3, 2001 ABCA 267 (Alta. C.A.).

United States v. Bounnam (April 3, 1995), Doc. Toronto E14/94 (Ont. Gen. Div.), affirmed (1996), *(sub nom. R. v. Bounnam)* 91 O.A.C. 319 (Ont. C.A.), leave to appeal to S.C.C. refused (1997), 99 O.A.C. 79 (note) (S.C.C.).

United States v. Cheema (1999), 65 C.R.R. (2d) 234 (B.C.S.C.), leave to appeal to S.C.C. refused (2001), 271 N.R. 193 (note) (S.C.C.).

United States v. Cobb (2001), 152 C.C.C. (3d) 270 (S.C.C.), reconsideration refused (June 14, 2001), Docs. 26912, 27610, 27774 (S.C.C.).

United States v. Commisso (2000), 143 C.C.C. (3d) 158 (Ont. C.A.), leave to appeal to S.C.C. refused (2000), 261 N.R. 197 (note) (S.C.C.).

United States v. Cotroni (1989), 48 C.C.C. (3d) 193 (S.C.C.).

United States v. Debarros (February 9, 2000), Doc. E-9/99, LaForme J. (Ont. S.C.J.).

United States v. Drysdale (2000), 32 C.R. (5th) 163 (Ont. S.C.J.).

United States v. Dynar (1997), 115 C.C.C. (3d) 481 (S.C.C.).

United States v. Garcia (May 11, 1994), Doc. E16/92, [1994] O.J. No. 1027 (Ont. Gen. Div.), affirmed (July 18, 1996), Doc. CA C21023, 1996 CarswellOnt 2408 (Ont. C.A.), leave to appeal to S.C.C. refused (1997), 102 O.A.C. 318 (note) (S.C.C.).

United States v. Houslander (1993), 13 O.R. (3d) 44 (Ont. Gen. Div.).

United States v. Jang (May 8, 1975), (Fed. C.A.).

United States v. Kerslake (1996), 142 Sask. R. 112 (Q.B.).

United States v. Kwok (2001), 152 C.C.C. (3d) 225 (S.C.C.).

United States v. Leon (1995), 96 C.C.C. (3d) 568 (Ont. C.A.), affirmed (1996), 105 C.C.C. (3d) 385 (S.C.C.).

United States v. Lépine (1993), 87 C.C.C. (3d) 385, 163 N.R. 1 (S.C.C.).

United States v. Manno (1996), 112 C.C.C. (3d) 544 (Que. C.A.), leave to appeal to S.C.C. refused (1997), 221 N.R. 311 (note) (S.C.C.).

United States v. Martinez (February 28, 2000), Doc. E24/99, 2000 CarswellOnt 561 (Ont. S.C.J.).

United States v. McVey (1992), 77 C.C.C. (3d) 1 (S.C.C.).

United States v. Mokdad (February 12, 1999), Doc. E-25/98 (Ont. Gen. Div.).

United States v. Persaud (November 3, 1999), 1999 CarswellOnt 4263, [1999] O.J. No. 4992 (Ont. S.C.J.).

United States v. Sanders (March 18, 1996), Koenigsberg J. (B.C.S.C.).

United States v. Shephard (1976), (*sub nom. United States v. Sheppard*) 30 C.C.C. (2d) 424 (S.C.C.).

United States v. Shulman (September 13, 1995), Lyon J., [1995] O.J. No. 4497 (Ont. Gen. Div.), affirmed (1998), 128 C.C.C. (3d) 475 (Ont. C.A.), reversed (2001), 152 C.C.C. (3d) 294 (S.C.C.), reconsideration refused (June 14, 2001), Docs. 26912, 27610, 27774 (S.C.C.).

United States v. Singh (October 14, 1994), Doc. E-21, Ewaschuk J., [1994] O.J. No. 3941 (Ont. Gen. Div.).

United States v. Smith (1984), 15 C.C.C. (3d) 16 (Ont. Co. Ct.), affirmed (1984), 16 C.C.C. (3d) 10 (Ont. H.C.).

United States v. Soffitt (1993), 36 B.C.A.C. 155, 58 W.A.C. 155 (B.C. C.A.).

United States v. Soul (November 25, 1994), [1994] O.J. No. 2838, Chapnik J. (Ont. Gen. Div.), affirmed (February 17, 1995), Doc. CA C20236 (Ont. C.A.).

United States v. Tavormina (1996), 112 C.C.C. (3d) 563 (Que. C.A.).

United States v. Wagner (1995), 104 C.C.C. (3d) 66 (B.C. C.A.), leave to appeal to S.C.C. refused (1996), 106 C.C.C. (3d) vi (note) (S.C.C.).

United States v. Whitley (1994), 94 C.C.C. (3d) 99 (Ont. C.A.), affirmed (1996), 104 C.C.C. (3d) 447 (S.C.C.).

United States v. Wong (1995), 98 C.C.C. (3d) 332 (B.C. C.A.), leave to appeal to S.C.C. refused (1995), 101 C.C.C. (3d) vi (S.C.C.).

Washington (State) v. Johnson (1988), 40 C.C.C. (3d) 546 (S.C.C.).

Whipple, Re (1972), 6 C.C.C. (2d) 517 (B.C.S.C.).

Yugoslavia (Republic) v. Rajovic (No. 3) (1981), 62 C.C.C. (2d) 544 (Ont. Co. Ct.).

§6.0 RELATED SECTIONS

s. 3 — Extraditable Conduct

s. 5 — Jurisdiction

s. 7 — Responsibillities of Minister of Justice

s. 15 — Authority to Proceed

s. 23 — Substitution and Amendment of Power of Minister to Issue Authority to Proceed

s. 24 — Extradition Hearing

s. 32 — Admissibility of Evidence at Extradition Hearing

s. 33 — Record of the Case

s. 37 — Evidence of Identity

s. 38 — Judge's Report and Judge's Obligation to Inform Person Sought of Rights

s. 40(4) — Power of Minister to Subject Surrender to Assurances

s. 44 — When Surrender Order Not to be Made by Minister of Justice

Authority to Keep Person Sought in Custody Following Order of Committal and Duration of Order (s. 30)

§1.0 DESCRIPTION

Section 30 of the *Extradition Act* provides as follows:

AUTHORITY TO KEEP PERSON IN CUSTODY

30. (1) The order of committal constitutes the authority to keep the person in custody, subject to an order of judicial interim release.

DURATION OF ORDER

(2) The order of committal remains in force until the person is surrendered or discharged or until a new hearing is ordered under paragraph 54(*a*).

Section 30 provides for the detention of the person sought following the extradition judge's order of committal. Section 30(1) states that the order of committal is sufficient authority to keep the person in custody. The final clause of s. 30(1) adds that the subsection is "subject to an order of judicial interim release." Judicial interim release after committal is provided for in s. 20 of the Act. Section 20 makes the bail pending appeal provisions of s. 679 of the *Criminal Code* applicable to three situations after committal: pending appeal of the committal order, pending the Minister of

Justice's surrender decision under s. 40, or pending a judicial review of the Minister's decision under s. 40.

Subsection 30(2) provides that an order of committal remains in force until the occurrence of one of the three following events: (i) the person sought is surrendered; (ii) the person is discharged; or (iii) a new extradition hearing is ordered as the result of an appeal, as provided by s. 54(a).

§2.0 COMPARISON WITH FORMER ACT

There was no specific provision under the former *Extradition Act* dealing with the duration of committal orders. However, the effect of s. 19.5(1) of the former Act, which made applicable the provisions of s. 679 of the *Criminal Code*, contemplated committal orders being held in abeyance until the outcome of an appeal. The committal order otherwise stayed in effect until set aside by a court of appeal.

§3.0 SIGNIFICANCE OF CHANGE

Section 30 asserts what was implicit in the former system, namely, that the order of committal provides the authority for the detention of a person sought for extradition until either the person is surrendered or the committal is set aside on appeal. A judicial interim release order may apply until this final determination occurs.

§4.0 ANALYSIS

See §3.0, "Significance of Change," above.

§5.0 RELATED SECTIONS

s. 20 — Application of s. 679 of *Criminal Code* to Judicial Interim Release
s. 54(a) — Setting Aside Committal Orders on Appeal

Rules of Evidence Governing Extradition Hearings (ss. 31–36)

§1.0 DESCRIPTION

§1.1 Definition of "Document" (s. 31)

Section 31 of the *Extradition Act* provides as follows:

DEFINITION OF "DOCUMENT"

31.   For the purposes of sections 32 to 38, "document" means data recorded in any form, and includes photographs and copies of documents.

Section 31 provides a broad definition of "document" designed to avoid technical arguments over the various forms in which material may be stored. Section 31 is also a recognition of the modern technological reality that information may be stored in many forms. This recognition is also reflected in the amendments to the *Canada Evidence Act* and the *Mutual Legal Assistance in Criminal Matters Act*, which now provide for testimony for the purposes of those Acts to be given by means of video link technology.

§1.2 Admissible Evidence (s. 32)

Section 32 of the *Extradition Act* provides as follows:

EVIDENCE

32.   (1) Subject to subsection (2), evidence that would otherwise be admissible under Canadian law shall be admitted as evidence at an extradition hearing. The following shall also be admitted as evidence, even if it would not otherwise be admissible under Canadian law:

> **(a) the contents of the documents contained in the record of the case certified under subsection 33(3);**
>
> **(b) the contents of the documents that are submitted in conformity with the terms of an extradition agreement; and**
>
> **(c) evidence adduced by the person sought for extradition that is relevant to the tests set out in subsection 29(1) if the judge considers it reliable.**

EXCEPTION — CANADIAN EVIDENCE

(2) Evidence gathered in Canada must satisfy the rules of evidence under Canadian law in order to be admitted.

Under s. 32(1), there are four categories of evidence that may be admitted at an extradition hearing:

• evidence that is otherwise admissible under Canadian law (s. 32(1));

• the record of the case (s. 32(1)(a), certified in accordance with s. 33(3));

• evidence tendered in conformity with the provisions of an extradition agreement (s. 32(1)(b)); and

- evidence adduced by the person sought that is relevant to the test for committal under s. 29(1) of the Act and that is considered reliable by the extradition judge (s. 32(1)(c)).

Section 32(2) adds that evidence gathered in Canada must satisfy Canadian rules of admissibility.

§1.3 Record of the Case (s. 33)

Section 33 of the *Extradition Act* provides as follows:

RECORD OF THE CASE
>   33. (1) **The record of the case must include**

>   (a) **in the case of a person sought for the purpose of prosecution, a document summarizing the evidence available to the extradition partner for use in the prosecution; and**
>   (b) **in the case of a person sought for the imposition or enforcement of a sentence,**
>   (i) **a copy of the document that records the conviction of the person, and**
>   (ii) **a document describing the conduct for which the person was convicted.**

OTHER DOCUMENTS — RECORD OF THE CASE
>   (2) **A record of the case may include other relevant documents, including documents respecting the identification of the person sought for extradition.**

CERTIFICATION OF RECORD OF THE CASE
>   (3) **A record of the case may not be admitted unless**

>   (a) **in the case of a person sought for the purpose of prosecution, a judicial or prosecuting authority of the extradition partner certifies that the evidence summarized or contained in the record of the case is available for trial and**
>   (i) **is sufficient under the law of the extradition partner to justify prosecution, or**
>   (ii) **was gathered according to the law of the extradition partner; or**
>   (b) **in the case of a person sought for the imposition or enforcement of a sentence, a judicial, prosecuting or correctional authority of the extradition partner certifies that the documents in the record of the case are accurate.**

(4) No authentication of documents is required unless a relevant extradition agreement provides otherwise.

RECORD OF THE CASE AND SUPPLEMENTS
(5) For the purposes of this section, a record of the case includes any supplement added to it.

Section 33(1) specifies the contents of the record of the case. For persons sought for prosecution, the record of the case must contain a summary of the evidence. For convicted persons, it must include a record of conviction and a document describing the conduct upon which the person was convicted. Section 33(2) adds that, for both accused and convicted persons, the record of the case may include other relevant documents, such as those relating to the identity of the person sought.

Section 33(3) sets out the admissibility requirements for the record of the case. For persons sought for prosecution, a judge or prosecutor of the extradition partner must certify that the evidence summarized in the record of the case is available for trial and either sufficient to justify prosecution by the extradition partner or gathered in accordance with the laws of the extradition partner. For convicted persons, a judge, prosecutor, or corrections officer of the extradition partner must certify that the documents contained in the record of the case are accurate. Section 33(4) adds that no authentication of the documents is required unless a relevant extradition agreement provides otherwise. Section 33(5) provides that the record of the case can be supplemented by additional material.

§1.4 Oath or Solemn Affirmation Not Required (s. 34)

Section 34 of the *Extradition Act* provides as follows:

OATH OR SOLEMN AFFIRMATION
34. A document is admissible whether or not it is solemnly affirmed or under oath.

Section 34 statutorily eliminates the requirement for evidence to be provided under oath or solemn affirmation.

§1.5 Proof of Signature Not Required (s. 35)

Section 35 of the *Extradition Act* provides as follows:

NO PROOF OF SIGNATURE
35. A document purporting to have been signed by a judicial, prosecuting or correctional authority, or a public officer, of the extradition

partner shall be admitted without proof of the signature or official character of the person appearing to have signed it.

Section 35 provides that a document is admissible without proof of the signature or official character of the judge, prosecutor, correctional officer, or public officer who purportedly signed the document.

§1.6 Translated Documents (s. 36)

Section 36 of the *Extradition Act* provides as follows:

TRANSLATED DOCUMENTS
    36. A translation of a document into one of Canada's official languages shall be admitted without any further formality.

Section 36 provides that English or French translations of the documents in support of an extradition request are admissible at the extradition hearing.

§2.0 COMPARISON WITH FORMER ACT

Section 32(1) of the new *Extradition Act* addresses four categories of evidence that may be admitted at an extradition hearing: evidence that is otherwise admissible under Canadian law, the record of the case (providing it meets the certification requirements under s. 33(3)), evidence tendered in conformity with the provisions of an extradition agreement, and evidence adduced by the person sought that is relevant to the test for committal under s. 29(1) of the Act and that is considered reliable by the extradition judge. Section 32(2) adds that evidence gathered in Canada must satisfy Canadian rules of admissibility.

Two of the four categories dealt with in s. 32 had counterparts under the former *Extradition Act*, namely, evidence gathered in Canada and tendered according to Canadian evidentiary law and evidence submitted pursuant to an extradition treaty. These two categories had statutory authority for their introduction under s. 14 and s. 3, respectively, of the former Act. Section 14 allowed *viva voce* evidence to be called at the extradition hearing and s. 3 gave treaty terms precedence over the terms of the former Act to the extent of any inconsistencies. Within the category of evidence tendered according to a treaty, certain newer treaties have provisions for supplying evidence similar in form to the record of the case. Except with respect to evidence directed towards showing that the offence was an offence of a political character or otherwise not an extradition crime, there was neither statutory nor treaty authority under the former regime for the calling of evidence by the person sought to challenge the *prima facie* case. However, as will be discussed, there was some jurisprudence recognizing such a right and it did occur.

§2.1 Nothing Comparable in Former Act to Record of the Case (ss. 32(1)(a) and 33)

The introduction of the record of the case is one of the most significant features of the new legislation. It had no counterpart under the former Act. Conversely, ss. 16 and 17 of the former Act, which provided for the introduction of affidavit evidence at an extradition hearing, have no counterparts in the new Act. Now, affidavit evidence will only be available at an extradition hearing if a relevant extradition arrangement makes provision for it. The record of the case will be the primary method for introducing evidence under the new system. It will be the only available method other than *viva voce* testimony for those extradition partners with which Canada has no extradition treaty. In addition, the record of the case will be available even to those countries with which Canada has treaty arrangements. Significantly, the United States, the extradition partner which makes the largest number of requests to Canada, has been providing evidence by way of record of the case rather than according to the treaty provisions since the inception of the new Act.

Section 33 of the new Act specifies the contents of a record of the case. For persons sought for prosecution, the record must contain a summary of the evidence. For convicted persons, the record must include a record of conviction and a document describing the conduct upon which the person was convicted. In both situations, the record may include other relevant documents, such as those dealing with the issue of identity.

The form the record of the case will take may depend upon the legal system of the country making the extradition request. In the case of the United States the summary of the evidence will usually be provided by the investigating police officer. In the case of civil law countries it will more usually be an investigating magistrate or prosecutor in charge of the investigation.

Section 33 sets out the admissibility requirements for a record of the case. For persons sought for prosecution, a judge or prosecutor must certify that the summary of the evidence contained in the record of the case is available for trial and either sufficient to justify prosecution by the extradition partner or gathered according to the laws of the extradition partner. For convicted persons, certification regarding the accuracy of the documents contained in the record of the case is required by either a judge, prosecutor, or correctional authority.

The objectives of these new provisions were described by Dambrot J. in *United States v. Drysdale* (2000), 32 C.R. (5th) 163 (Ont. S.C.J.). He commented, at p. 175, that:

> Among the innovations contained in the *Act* are a series of provisions designed to relax and streamline the rules of evidence at an extradition hearing, in order to make the hearing more expeditious, and in order to ameliorate the difficulties arising between states when a requesting state with a legal system that differs from that of the requested state tries to prepare extradition material that will satisfy the law of evidence in the requested state.

Although there was nothing comparable in the former *Extradition Act* to the tendering of evidence by way of a record of the case, some of Canada's extradition treaties provided for the introduction of material in a similar manner. A review of Canada's more recent extradition treaties reveals instances in which evidentiary changes were effected by negotiated terms in particular extradition arrangements to allow for evidence to be provided in more summary form. Changes to the evidentiary regime could be achieved in this fashion because s. 3 of the former Act provided that if there were inconsistencies between the terms of the Act and the terms of an extradition arrangement, the arrangement prevailed. In this way, it was possible, though hardly efficient, to change the evidentiary rules for admissibility on a state-by-state basis.

By way of example, the following treaty articles make provision for the intro-duction of summaries of the evidence available in the requesting state, provided that they are certified by an authority in the requesting state as constituting evidence in accordance with the laws of that state: Article 10(2)(c) of the *Canada–France Extra-dition Treaty* (in force December 1, 1989); Article 7(2)(b)(iii) of the *Can-ada–Philippines Extradition Treaty* (in force November 12, 1990); Article 5(2)(b) of the *Canada–Switzerland Extradition Treaty* (in force March 19, 1996); Article 7(1)(b) of the *Canada–Netherlands Extradition Treaty* (in force December 1, 1991); and Article 7(2)(b)(i) of the *Canada–Korea Extradition Treaty* (in force February 1, 1995).

Under the former Act, evidence similar to a record of the case was introduced in *Philippines (Republic) v. Pacificador* (1993), 83 C.C.C. (3d) 210 (Ont. C.A.), leave to appeal to S.C.C. refused (1994), 87 C.C.C. (3d) vi (S.C.C.); *Netherlands (Kingdom) v. Clarkson* (1998), 59 C.R.R. (2d) 178 (B.C. S.C. [In Chambers]), affirmed (2000), 146 C.C.C. (3d) 482 (B.C.C.A.), leave to appeal to S.C.C. refused (2000), 2000 CarswellBC 2445 (S.C.C.); and *Germany (Federal Republic) v. Kretz* (May 19, 1998), Doc. CA C26686, 1998 CarswellOnt 1999, [1998] O.J. No. 2062 (Ont. C.A.). In *Philippines (Republic) v. Pacificador*, no challenge was made to the introduction of such evidence, although it was not specifically relied upon by the requesting state. Doherty J.A. simply noted as follows, at p. 215:

> The "Prosecutor's Resolution", the document relied on to commence proceedings in the requesting state, was included in the material placed before Watt J. Under the terms of the treaty, the Resolution was offered as evidence of the facts alleged therein.

In *Clarkson, supra*, a constitutional attack on the introduction of the evidence in this form was unsuccessful. Boyd J., at p. 186, found "no violation of s. 7 of the *Charter* since the admission and reliance on evidence, which meets the requirements of the treaty, nevertheless accords with the principles of fundamental justice." As to the argument that s. 7 was violated by the provision of the treaty allowing for the introduction of evidence "whether taken on oath or solemnly affirmed or not," Boyd J. rejected it, at p. 184, observing that there were numerous exceptions domestically to the requirement for an oath and "[m]ore particularly, in the case of extradition hearings, the courts have allowed for the admissibility of unsworn documents tendered by the requesting state, where the documents were prepared in conformity with a treaty." Boyd J.'s decision was upheld by the British Columbia Court of Appeal.

Under the new Act, in *Bourgeon v. Canada (Attorney General)* (2000), 35 C.R. (5th) 25 (Ont. S.C.J.), a similar constitutional challenge was brought against the provisions of s. 32(1)(a) and (b), concerning the introduction of evidence in the form of a record of the case. It was contended that these sections were unconstitutional insofar as they permitted the introduction of evidence which contravened Canadian rules of admissibility and which was not required to be under oath or on solemn affirmation. Ewaschuk J., at p. 38, para. 46, like Boyd J. in *Clarkson, supra*, accepted that abolition of the oath requirement was not contrary to fundamental justice in the extradition context and indeed it was frequently "a meaningless ritualistic incantation for many witnesses" in the domestic context (*per* Cory J. in *R. v. B. (K.G.)* (1993), 79 C.C.C. (3d) 257 (S.C.C.), at p. 306). However, he held at p. 41, para. 57, that it was a violation of s. 7 of the *Charter* "to permit an extradition judge to admit evidence at an extradition hearing that would not otherwise be admissible at a Canadian hearing, in the absence of a statutory safeguard against the reception of unreliable evidence." In the result, he remedied the perceived deficiency by reading in the words "if the judge considers it reliable" to the end of s. 32(1)(a) and (b) so as to allow the extradition judge to consider the reliability of the evidence contained in the record of the case or material similar to a record of the case tendered pursuant to treaty. The decision in *Bourgeon* was adopted by Boilard J. in *United States v. Palmucci* (June 4, 2001), no. 500-36-002280-009 (Que. S.C.)

However, in *Canada v. Yang* (September 25, 2000), (Ont. S.C.J.), affirmed (*sub nom. United States v. Yang*) (2001), 157 C.C.C. (3d) 225 (Ont. C.A.), Dilks J. disagreed with Ewaschuk J. and held that there is no violation of s. 7 occasioned by the application of the provisions of s. 32(1)(a) and (b) of the Act as written. Dilks J. considered that the reliability of the requesting state's evidence is adequately established by the authentication and certification provisions of the legislation itself. This was also the opinion of Vertes J. in *Germany (Federal Republic) v. Ebke*, [2001] 6 W.W.R. 517 (N.W.T.S.C.).

On appeal, the Ontario Court of Appeal in *United States v. Yang* (2001), 157 C.C.C. (3d) 225, approved the approach taken by Dilks J. in that case, and Vertes J. in *Ebke, supra*, and disapproved of the reasoning of Ewaschuk J. in *Bourgeon, supra*. The Court of Appeal held that the extradition judge has no jurisdiction to consider the reliability of the extradition partner's evidence. Rosenberg J.A. observed that the Supreme Court of Canada has repeatedly observed that the jurisdiction of an extradition judge is strictly circumscribed, and that in determining the sufficiency of the evidence for committal, the extradition judge is not to consider the quality of the evidence. He concluded, at pp. 251–252:

> [58] It follows that I do not agree with Ewaschuk J. that fairness requires that the reliability condition imposed by statute upon evidence sought to be adduced by the fugitive must also be applied to the evidence sought to be adduced by the extradition partner. As Vertes J. noted in *Ebke*, at para. 79, this fails to give effect to the reliability

requirement inherent in the certification requirements of the Act. Under s. 33(3), the judicial or prosecuting authority must certify that the evidence summarized in the record of the case is available and either would be sufficient under the law of the extradition partner to justify extradition or was gathered according to the law of the extradition partner. In short, the evidence must be available and must satisfy the legal standards of the extradition partner. I do not see why Canada should demand any greater guarantee of reliability from the extradition partner. Further, I do not see how the extradition judge would be in a position to make the reliability determination without having a detailed knowledge of the legal system of the extradition partner and then, purportedly passing on its legitimacy. Both concepts are antithetical to the extradition process. Doherty J.A. made this point in *Pacificador v. Philippines (Republic)* (1993), 83 C.C.C. (3d) 210 (Ont. C.A.), at p. 218, in considering the jurisdiction of the extradition judge to require that a Canadian police officer be produced for cross-examination to provide information about his involvement in the extradition request:

> The extradition judge could not possibly determine whether certain evidence offered at the extradition hearing is relevant to a fugitive's right to make full answer and defence at some subsequent proceeding, when the extradition judge has no knowledge of what full answer and defence means in the context of the foreign proceeding, and no knowledge of the legal matrix in which the ultimate adjudication of the merits of the charge would occur.

[59] Accordingly, in my view the decision in *Bourgeon* holding that paras. 32(1)(a) and (b) are unconstitutional and reading in a right to exclude unreliable evidence is incorrect and should not be followed.

§2.2 Evidence Otherwise Admissible Under Canadian Law (s. 32(1))

Section 14 of the former *Extradition Act* allowed the testimony of any witness "to show the truth of the charge or the fact of the conviction." Under the new Act, this method of adducing evidence is encompassed by s. 32(1), which provides that evidence "otherwise . . . admissible under Canadian law" is admissible at the extradition hearing. In this way, s. 32(1) contemplates *viva voce* evidence as a possible form of evidence at the hearing. The usual types of evidence that were led *viva voce* under the former *Extradition Act* and which it is likely will continue to be tendered in this fashion are as follows: evidence of identity, evidence from police witnesses who took post-arrest statements from the person sought in Canada, evidence obtained as a result of searches in Canada, evidence pursuant to communications intercepted under Canadian authorizations, evidence from witnesses to the crime who are located in Canada or witnesses willing to come to Canada to testify.

The case of *United States v. Leon* (1995), 96 C.C.C. (3d) 568 (Ont. C.A.), affirmed (1996), 105 C.C.C. (3d) 385 (S.C.C.), is an example of a case in which some of the evidence was obtained in Canada as a result of the execution of Canadian search warrants. The evidence concerning the results of the execution of the Canadian search warrants was led *viva voce* at the extradition hearing pursuant to s. 14 of the former Act and Canadian evidentiary standards were required to be met.

There is at least one example in which the entirety of the evidence in support of the request for extradition was led *viva voce*. In *Romania (State) v. Cheng* (1997), 114 C.C.C. (3d) 289 (N.S. S.C.), dismissed as moot (1997), 119 C.C.C. (3d) 561 (N.S. C.A.), the crew members of a container ship who allegedly observed stowaways being thrown overboard on the high seas were living in Canada at the time of the extradition hearing and were called as witnesses. There was no documentary evidence tendered to establish the sufficiency of the case for committal.

Section 32(1) of the new Act, like s. 14 of the former Act, does not just contemplate *viva voce* evidence. It may also encompass evidence admissible in Canadian proceedings pursuant to Canadian statutory authority such as affidavits tendered pursuant to the *Canada Evidence Act* (for example, a s. 30 business records affidavit). As a result of the consequential amendments made to the *Criminal Code*, the *Canada Evidence Act* and the *Mutual Legal Assistance in Criminal Matters Act*, with respect to the availability of evidence by way of video link technology, s. 32(1) could encompass the tendering of this form of evidence in appropriate circumstances at the extradition hearing.

§2.3 Evidence Tendered Pursuant to Extradition Agreement (s. 32(1)(b))

There was no specific provision in the former *Extradition Act* that provided for the tendering of documentation at an extradition hearing pursuant to an extradition agreement. Only ss. 16 and 17 of the former Act made specific provision for the introduction of documentary evidence. They provided that depositions taken on oath or solemn affirmation and authenticated in the manner specified in s. 17 could be introduced as evidence at the extradition hearing. In practice, however, treaty provisions did displace the provisions of ss. 16 and 17. This occurred by the operation of s. 3 of the former Act which provided that extradition arrangements, such as treaties, prevailed over the Act to the extent of any inconsistency between the two (see *Re Nixon* (1984), 10 C.C.C. (3d) 376 (Ont. C.A.), leave to appeal to S.C.C. refused (1984), 55 N.R. 396n (S.C.C.)).

(a) Procedure for authentication

When dealing with extradition requests from the United States in which the treaty rather than the record of the case is used, the applicable provision for tendering documentary evidence will continue to be Article 10(2) of the *Canada–United States Extradition Treaty*, which states:

> **10.** (2) The documentary evidence in support of a request for extradition or copies of these documents shall be admitted in evidence in the examination of the request for

extradition when, in the case of a request emanating from Canada, they are authenticated by an officer of the Department of Justice of Canada and are certified by the principal diplomatic or consular officer of the United States in Canada, or when, in the case of a request emanating from the United States, they are authenticated by an officer of the Department of State of the United States and are certified by the principal diplomatic or consular officer of Canada in the United States.

Individual certification and authentication of documents is not required. The usual practice is for the entire package of documentary evidence to be subject to one process of certification and authentication. In the case of material from the United States, the authenticated package will arrive bound by a ribbon run through the entire bundle of documents at the top left corner. The ribbon will be affixed to the front page of the package by a foil or wax seal. This document is the authentication certificate provided by the authentication officer of the United States Department of State. On the back of this page will appear a stamp and the signature of the certification of this material by the Canadian principal diplomatic or consular official in the United States. Sometimes the material will also include special certificates from the State Governor or other state officials. These are not required by the treaty but rather are matters internal to the United States and its procedure concerning the making of extradition requests. The material thus provided should not be unbound because the authentication of the documents will be undone as a result.

In *Re Nixon, supra*, Houlden J.A., at pp. 379–380, adopted a "fair and liberal" approach regarding authentication when considering the admissibility of documents submitted pursuant to the *Canada–United States Extradition Treaty* (see also *R. v. Schmidt* (1987), 33 C.C.C. (3d) 193 (S.C.C.); *Argentina (Republic) v. Mellino* (1987), 33 C.C.C. (3d) 334 (S.C.C.); *United States v. McVey* (1992), 77 C.C.C. (3d) 1 (S.C.C.)):

> 3. The third objection is based on the evidence that the respondents presented in support of the request for extradition. The respondents called no oral evidence; instead, they tendered two bundles of documents which were marked by the extradition judge as items A and B for the purpose of identification. Before admitting the documents into evidence, the extradition judge heard the objections of counsel for the appellant to their admissibility. Mr. O'Hara has advanced a number of the same objections on the argument of this appeal.
>
> Item A was comprised of two affidavits of Robert E. Keller, District Attorney for the Clayton Judicial Circuit, State of Georgia. Attached to the affidavits were a number of exhibits, some of which were also affidavits. Item B was a transcript of the evidence given by witnesses at the trial of the appellant's co-accused, Anthony Zolun, also known as Tony Zalum. Attached to the documents is a certificate by Annie R. Maddux, authentication officer of the Secretary of State of the United States, certifying that she has authenticated the documents annexed to it. On the back of the certificate of authentication is a certificate by the principal consular officer of Canada in the United States that the annexed papers are the documentary evidence in support of the request for extradition authenticated by Annie R. Maddux, authentication officer of the Department of State of the United States.

The authentication is rather loosely done. It would have been preferable if the authenticating and certifying officers had initialled or otherwise identified the various documents. I believe it is clear, however, that they were authenticating the entire package of documents submitted to the Secretary of State by the Governor of the State of Georgia. The extradition judge made the following finding on this point:

> I observe, and find, that each of items A and B has been authenticated by an officer under the seal of the Secretary of State of the United States of America and has been certified by the principal consular officer of Canada in the United States of America under his seal.

I agree with this finding.

In *United States v. Wong* (1995), 98 C.C.C. (3d) 332 (B.C. C.A.), leave to appeal to S.C.C. refused (1995), 101 C.C.C. (3d) vi (S.C.C.), the British Columbia Court of Appeal took a similar approach. In that case, certain exhibits were not attached to the corresponding affidavit but were in the material that had been authenticated pursuant to treaty requirements. The Court of Appeal, at p. 347, agreed with the finding of the extradition hearing judge who stated "that where affidavits have exhibits marked in the lax fashion I have noted, the authenticating authorities are ensuring that they are the proper documents originally described in the affidavit making reference to them."

(b) Contents of authenticated material

In addition to specifying the procedure for authentication, the *Canada–United States Extradition Treaty* (in paragraphs (2)–(4) of Article 9) also describes, in general terms, the documentation and information which should be provided in the authenticated materials. Some of the required material is for the purpose of establishing the sufficiency of evidence to commit at the extradition hearing. In particular, Article 9(2) and (3) require evidence sufficient to establish committal and identity. Some of the material is for the use of the Minister of Justice both in issuing the authority to proceed and at the surrender stages of the proceedings. For instance, Article 9(2) and (3) require the following: the text of the laws of the extradition partner describing the offence and prescribing the punishment for the offence; information relating to limitation periods; and, in the case of persons sought for prosecution, a warrant of arrest. In the case of convicted persons, Article 9(4) requires documents establishing the conviction, the sentence remaining to be served, and the identity of the person sought.

In the case of extradition requests from the United States, under the former Act, the documentary evidence tendered pursuant to Article 9 of the *Canada–U.S. Extradition Treaty* was generally in the form of first person affidavits. Material provided for the use of the Minister was also included in the documentary package. While affidavit evidence of this type is still admissible at an extradition hearing under s. 32(1)(b) of the new Act, in practice, since the inception of the new Act, the United States and many other countries have been submitting extradition evidence in the form of a record of the case. Under the new Act the practice has been for the extradition partner at the extradition hearing to tender a record of the case dealing only with the evidence required to obtain a committal order. The record of the case does not include any material which is only for ministerial purposes such as that relating to the text of the laws, penalties, and limitation periods, as required by Article 9 of the treaty described above.

The requirements for authentication and the specification concerning the material and form of evidence in support of an extradition will vary according to the particular treaty. Many of the newer treaties, such as those with Korea, Switzerland, and the Netherlands, specify that certain certification by public officials may be required but that authentication *per se* is not required. With respect to the form of evidence, Article XIV(4) of the *Canada–Germany Extradition Treaty*, for example, like the treaties with certain other civil law jurisdictions, provides that "[a] statement on oath or affirmation, a deposition or any other statement which satisfies the requirements of the law of the requesting state shall be admissible as evidence in extradition proceedings in the requested state." In this way the treaty allows for the form of the material to be governed by the admissibility laws of the requesting state. However, it is unlikely that recourse to Article XIV(4) or similar provisions in other treaties will be resorted to since the evidence can be presented in the form of a record of the case pursuant to the Act.

Treaties with extradition partners whose language is not an official language of Canada also generally contain a provision requiring the requesting state to provide a certified translation of the authenticated documents. Such treaties usually also state that any translation shall be admitted into evidence at the extradition hearing. Section 36 of the new *Extradition Act* also provides that a translation of a document into one of Canada's official languages is admissible without any further formality. The wording of s. 36 appears to leave open the possibility that the translation need not be provided by the requesting state. There would seem to be no impediments to Canadian authorities obtaining translations here for use at the extradition hearing in appropriate circumstances.

§2.4 Evidence Adduced by Person Sought (s. 32(1)(c))

The person sought may present evidence at the extradition hearing pursuant to s. 32(1)(c) if it is relevant to the tests set out in s. 29(1), that is, it is relevant to the issues of identity and the *prima facie* case. The former *Extradition Act* did not provide for the calling of evidence by the person sought, apart from s. 15, which allowed the fugitive to call evidence about whether the offence was an extradition crime or a political crime. However, under the former regime, there was some recognition by the courts that a fugitive may be entitled to testify at the hearing in relation to issues other than those provided for in s. 15. The extent of this right remained unclear.

In *United States v. Wagner* (1995), (*sub nom. R. v. Peters*) 104 C.C.C. (3d) 66 (B.C. C.A.), leave to appeal to S.C.C. refused (1996), 106 C.C.C. (3d) vi (note)

(S.C.C.), the fugitive was sought for extradition on charges involving attempted burglary and rape in the State of Washington. The Court of Appeal described the American evidence identifying the perpetrator of the alleged offences as "weak," and at the hearing the fugitive was permitted to testify to what the Court of Appeal described as a "powerful alibi." The Court of Appeal recognized the right of the fugitive to testify as an accused would have the right to testify at a preliminary inquiry (at p. 75). However, the Court of Appeal upheld the committal, stating that the "*Shephard*" test had been met (*United States v. Shephard* (1976), (*sub nom. United States v. Sheppard*) 30 C.C.C. (2d) 424 (S.C.C.)). Since the *Shephard* test leaves the weighing of the evidence to the ultimate trier of fact, the evidence of the fugitive could not have affected the outcome of the extradition hearing so long as there was "some evidence" presented by the requesting state to satisfy the *prima facie* case test.

In a more recent decision, *United States v. Adam* (1999), 120 O.A.C. 271 (Ont. C.A.), the Ontario Court of Appeal ordered a new hearing because the extradition judge had not allowed the fugitive to testify at his hearing. The Court of Appeal commented as follows, at p. 274:

> [11] The appellant did not tell this court or the extradition judge what his evidence might be. We are only dealing with the right to speak. If his evidence, as delivered, is contrary to the principles applicable to a preliminary hearing then rulings and exclusionary orders may be made. We cannot conclude that anything he might say will only serve to contradict and thus invite a credibility issue. It may be that his evidence could complement other evidence and lead to a conclusion that there is no prima facie case for extradition. In any event, our reasoning is not based upon the facts of this case. It is directed by the simple principle that the appellant should have been permitted to give evidence — relevance and admissibility rulings to follow.

Unlike the British Columbia Court of Appeal, the Ontario Court of Appeal appeared to be inviting some degree of weighing of the evidence. However, the *United States v. Adam* decision appears to be somewhat at odds with the decision of the same Ontario Court of Appeal in *Philippines (Republic) v. Pacificador* (1993), 83 C.C.C. (3d) 210 (Ont. C.A), leave to appeal to S.C.C. refused (1994), 87 C.C.C. (3d) vi (S.C.C.). In that case, the Court of Appeal dealt with two issues of interest to the present discussion. The first was the extradition judge's refusal to permit the fugitive to introduce into evidence affidavits from a witness recanting the statements attributed to him in the authenticated material tendered at the hearing. Watt J., the extradition judge, refused to admit the recanting affidavits. He commented that by their very nature the affidavits were inadmissible because their sole purpose was to impeach the credibility of the affiant and to diminish the weight to be attributed to his evidence, a matter beyond the jurisdiction of the extradition judge. Watt J. also noted that the requesting state was not placing any reliance upon the statements in the authenticated material to which the recanting affidavits were directed. Doherty J.A. held that Watt J. was correct in refusing to admit the recanting affidavits (at p. 215).

The second issue considered by the Court of Appeal in *Philippines (Republic) v. Pacificador* concerned the decision of the extradition judge to refuse to allow the fugitive to call a police witness, a Corporal Monroe. The fugitive's intention was to have Corporal Monroe testify and produce a wide array of documents designed to contradict evidence tendered in the requesting state's authenticated materials. Corporal Monroe had travelled to the Philippines and had conducted interviews with several witnesses. Some of the statements of these individuals were inconsistent with the affidavits they had given in the authenticated documents. Watt J. refused the defence the opportunity to call this evidence. His refusal was based on the grounds that, as in the case of the recanting affidavits, he could not weigh the evidence or resolve inconsistencies because it was irrelevant to his function as an extradition judge. The Court of Appeal upheld the decision of Watt J. to issue a warrant of committal based on the evidence tendered by the requesting state.

In *United States v. Bray* (1997), 97 O.A.C. 388 (C.A.), leave to appeal to S.C.C. refused (1997), 110 O.A.C. 399 (note) S.C.C.), the Ontario Court of Appeal upheld the refusal of an extradition judge to admit the evidence of the fugitive's mother at the hearing. Weiler and Austin JJ.A. held as follows, at p. 390:

> [5] . . . The only reason for putting such evidence before the extradition judge would be to invite that judge to weigh the evidence and draw competing inferences. Such is not the function of the judge presiding upon an extradition hearing: *Philippines (Republic) v. Pacificador* unreported decision of the Ontario Court (General Division) dated October 5, 1992 (Watt, J.); affirmed (1993), 64 O.A.C. 344; 14 O.R. (3d) 321 (C.A.), at 328-329 [O.R.]. Accordingly, the evidence of Peggy Bray was irrelevant in the extradition proceedings and was properly excluded by the extradition judge.

In *United States v. Down* (1998), 124 C.C.C. (3d) 289 (Q.B.), the Manitoba Court of Queen's Bench also considered the issue of the right of a fugitive to call evidence. The court determined that the fugitive in that case was entitled to call evidence under s. 15 of the former *Extradition Act* because the evidence related to the extradition crime determination rather than to the merits of the case presented by the requesting state. Implicitly, had the proposed evidence been directed to the issue of a *prima facie* case, Oliphant A.C.J.Q.B. would have viewed the evidence as inadmissible.

Regardless of the effect of these cases under the former *Extradition Act*, it is clear that s. 32(1)(c) of the new Act has codified the right of the person sought to adduce evidence at the extradition hearing as long as it is relevant to the sufficiency test and is considered reliable. This would appear to be a statutory recognition that defence evidence may be relevant to the issue of the sufficiency of the evidence to commit.

In the domestic preliminary inquiry context the Supreme Court of Canada in *R. v. Arcuri* (2001), 157 C.C.C. (3d) 21, recognized that in circumstantial Crown cases, evidence led by an accused could be considered by the preliminary inquiry judge in determining whether, on the whole of the evidence, there was a sufficient case for committal for trial. (For further discussion, see the commentary under s. 29, §3.1(d), "Significance of Change.")

§2.5 No Oath or Solemn Affirmation Required (s. 34)

Documentary evidence tendered at an extradition hearing in reliance on the provisions of ss. 16 and 17 of the former Act was required to be taken on oath or solemn affirmation. Certain treaties did not require evidence to be taken under oath or on solemn affirmation and because of the provisions of s. 3 of the former Act, the treaty provisions prevailed. Section 34 has now clearly resolved the issue that statements are not required to be taken under oath, even in the face of treaty requirements in that regard, since s. 34 is not subject to treaty override. For a fuller discussion, see above, §2.1, and §3.4 below.

§2.6 Proof of Signature Not Required (s. 35)

Section 35 provides that proof of the signature or official character of a judicial, prosecuting, or correctional authority or a public officer contained in documents submitted by the extradition partner is not required in order for the documents to be admitted. There was no comparable section in the former Act, which often led to arguments being made in this regard (see, for instance, *Philippines (Republic) v. Pacificador* (1993), 83 C.C.C. (3d) 210 (Ont. C.A.), *per* Watt J. and Doherty J.A. regarding the validity of the foreign warrant of arrest discussed in the commentary to s. 29, §4.1(d)(iii), "Analysis."

§2.7 Translated Documents (s. 36)

Section 36, which provides for the admissibility of documents in either the English or French languages at an extradition hearing, had no comparable provision in the former Act. Treaties with extradition partners whose language is not an official language of Canada also generally contain a provision requiring the requesting state to provide a certified translation of the authenticated documents. Such treaties usually also state that any translation shall be admitted into evidence at the extradition hearing.

The wording of s. 36 appears to leave open the possibility that the translation need not be provided by the extradition partner. There would seem to be no impediments to Canadian authorities obtaining translations here for use at the extradition hearing in an appropriate circumstance.

§3.0 SIGNIFICANCE OF CHANGE

§3.1 Record of the Case (s. 32(1)(a))

(a) Reason for introduction of record of the case

The introduction of the record of the case to the evidence sections of the new *Extradition Act* was a response to the perceived inability of many of Canada's extradition partners to meet Canadian evidentiary requirements. When the new Act was introduced in Parliament, Ms. Eleni Bakopanos, Parliamentary Secretary to the Minister of Justice, advised the House of Commons that under the former regime some countries had simply declined to request the extradition of fugitives from Canada because they could not comply with Canadian legal requirements under the former *Extradition Act* and the *Fugitive Offenders Act* for first person affidavits devoid of hearsay (*House of Commons Debates*, October 8, 1998, 1st Session, 36th Parliament, *Hansard*, v. 135, pp. 9003-9004):

> We have seen in the last few years a number of cases where Canada's extradition laws have not been sufficient to enable Canada to fulfill its international obligation and expeditiously extradite fugitives to other countries in order to face justice. The problem has been most acute in respect of countries of a different legal tradition such as those in Europe.
>
> In the case of a number of requests from countries other than the United States extradition proceedings cannot be instituted. In other instances states are so discouraged by the different hurdles imposed by our current extradition law that they do not even initiate an extradition request. The primary problem is that the current legislation mandates that the foreign states submit evidence in support of their request in a form which meets the complicated requirements of Canadian evidentiary rules.
>
> For countries which do not have a common law system, and for which concepts such as hearsay are unknown, this requirement makes the preparation of a request for extradition a tremendously difficult task, and in some instances an impossible one. Even with countries with a similar legal tradition such as the United States, we have heard on numerous occasions how difficult it is to obtain extradition from Canada. In the context of our other common law jurisdictions such as Great Britain and Australia, Canada's system is viewed as one fraught with difficulties due to the antiquity of our legislation.
>
> With global crime becoming a significant concern at home and internationally, we know that the deficiencies in our legislation will continue to be questioned. Within the G-7 P-8 forum for example, states have been requested to modernize their extradition laws in order to be responsive to the challenges of today's transnational crimes and criminals. All the fora which have considered the serious problem of transnational organized crime have identified extradition as a critical tool to combat this growing threat to world order. In the P-8, the United Nations and within the Commonwealth there have been calls for countries to put in place a comprehensive, effective and modern process for extradition.

(b) New U.K. and Australian legislation

The United Kingdom and Australia perceived the same difficulties. The 1982 committee which was set up to review the operation of extradition law and practice in the United Kingdom, reported in its Report of Interdepartmental Working Party, *A Review of the Law and Practice of Extradition in the United Kingdom* (1982) that:

> It has been apparent for some time that our extradition law and practice are not easily compatible with those of the European countries with which most of our extradition

traffic is conducted. The difficulties arise mainly from the differences between the English common law system and the system based on Roman law commonly used in continental Europe. Many countries find the requirements of our law difficult to meet. We believe that their experience of these difficulties when their applications fail (or succeed only with disproportionate effort) has on occasion discouraged some countries from applying to the United Kingdom for the return of accused persons. This may have meant in some cases that criminals have escaped justice.

A similar view was presented in the 1986 British Government White Paper (*Criminal Justice: Plans for Legislation*, Cmnd 9658), which took into account a 1985 *Green Paper on Extradition*. The report indicated that the requirements of its extradition law had made the United Kingdom one of the most difficult countries from which to secure extradition, a state of affairs which jeopardized that country's ability to fully meet its international responsibilities:

> The basic framework of United Kingdom extradition law has not, however, changed in line with the expansion of international crime. It is also clear that parts of our law and practice do not fit easily with those of many of the countries with which we have or would wish to have extradition arrangements. The United Kingdom is thus regarded as one of the most difficult countries from which to secure extradition. In the Government's view, the effectiveness of the present law does not match the gravity of the present situation. Some people believe that as a consequence of this we are not meeting our full responsibility for the maintenance of the international rule of law. The changes proposed are intended to end this unsatisfactory state of affairs while preserving adequate safeguards for individuals affected by the extradition procedure.

The British response was to eliminate the requirement for a judicial assessment of the sufficiency of evidence with respect to states party to the *1957 European Convention on Extradition*. No evidence is required from these extradition partners although other safeguards continue to exist including the requirement of double criminality, the political offences exception and the rule of specialty. This simplified approach with no sufficiency of evidence required to be demonstrated goes beyond the position adopted by Canada in the new Act.

The Australian *Extradition Act*, 1988, addressed the same perceived difficulties. Australia, like Canada, had dealt with extradition in two statutes, *Extradition (Foreign States) Act*, 1966, and the *Extradition (Commonwealth Countries) Act*, 1966. The Australian *Extradition Act*, 1988, now governs extradition to all states. Australian commentators had observed the same debate concerning the difficulties in extraditing to other states caused by the evidentiary requirements to be met (H. Woltring, "Extradition Law" (1987) 61 *Law Institute Journal* 919 at p. 920):

> [F]oreign countries, particularly civil law countries, could only succeed in securing extradition from Australia by producing a case acceptable to a legal system, and subject to evidentiary laws, totally unknown to them. The requirement had the effect of enabling fugitives to escape justice on technical, as opposed to meritorious, grounds.

The Australian response, for non-Commonwealth countries, was to dispense with the need for evidence and a determination of sufficiency. Instead, the supporting documents required are a copy of the warrant of arrest, a statement in writing setting out a description of the person, and the applicable penalty, and a statement in writing setting out the conduct constituting the offence.

(c) American approach

The American approach to extradition is also of interest because the United States not only guarantees similar constitutional protections to those set out in the Canadian *Charter of Rights and Freedoms*, but its extradition law has many similarities with the new Canadian scheme.

The rules of evidence normally observed in American criminal and civil trials are not applied to extradition hearings. This is because the role of the court in an extradition hearing is a unique one limited to determining (a) whether the relevant extradition treaty applies, and (b) whether there is sufficient evidence to commit the fugitive for trial. Absent from this inquiry is any consideration of the guilt or innocence of the individual, or any inquiry into the fairness of the foreign procedures or the treatment which may await the fugitive. (See *Glucksman v. Henkel*, 221 U.S. 508 (U.S.S.C.), at p. 512.)

The domestic rules of evidence are not applied at American extradition hearings. American jurisprudence has held that the standards and practices applicable to extradition proceedings do not violate the due process provisions of the U.S. *Constitution* (*Wacker v. Bisson*, 370 F.2d 894).

A variety of evidence may be admitted into evidence at an American extradition proceeding, including depositions, warrants, affidavits, photographs and other papers, provided the evidence is authenticated by the principal consular or diplomatic authority in the demanding state (18 U.S.C.S. 3190). Once it is authenticated, the evidence is admissible at the hearing and the following principles operate.

1. The fugitive is not allowed to present evidence that the documents would not be admissible under the law of the foreign country. [*United States v. Galanis*, 429 F. Supp. 1215 (D.C. Tex.)] Neither is the person sought for extradition permitted to adduce evidence to contradict the requesting state's evidence or to impeach the credibility of witnesses.

2. Unsworn statements [*Elias v. Ramirez*, 215 U.S. 398, 54 L.Ed. 253, 30 S. Ct. 131] and depositions [*Galanis, supra,* and *McNamara v. Henkel*, 226 U.S. 520, 57 L.Ed. 330, 33 Ct. 146] which have been certified by the consular authority as properly authenticated are admissible. Evidence which is normally excluded from civil or criminal trials as "hearsay" can be admitted. [*Artukovic v. Rison*, 784 F.2d 1354 (U.S.C.A. 9th Cir.) where unsworn hearsay statements describing war crimes constituted competent evidence in an extradition hearing] Police reports

summarizing the evidence of witnesses is good evidence. [*Zanazanian v. United States*, 729 F.2d 624 (9th Cir., 1984)]

3. Affidavits are admissible even if taken without the opportunity for defence to cross-examine. [*Bingham v. Bradley*, 241 U.S. 511 at p. 517]

4. Technical objections to authenticated documents or copies of documents are not to be given favour by the court in light of the U.S.'s obligations to foreign states. [*Neely v. Henkel (No.1)*, 180 U.S. 109, 45 L. Ed. 448, 21 S. Ct. 302 No. 387] "Form is not to be insisted upon beyond the requirements of safety and justice." [*Fernandez v. Phillips*, 268 U.S. 311 at p. 312]

(d) Issues responded to by record of the case

In addition to the difficulties perceived by civil law jurisdictions in meeting the evidentiary requirements under the former *Extradition Act* and *Fugitive Offenders Act*, there were the other following shortcomings in the former legislation, some of which were referred to in the speech of Eleni Bakopanos, *supra*, which the record of the case has sought to eliminate:

•   The affidavit requirements of the former system were difficult to comply with in complex cases in both civil and common law countries because of the volume of evidence, number of witnesses and the location of the evidence. Documentary evidence posed a problem because of the need for affidavits in Canadian form from all the record keepers, seizers or possessors of the records. If there were a large number of witnesses, including victims, everyone had to swear an affidavit. (See *United States v. Shulman* (1998), 128 C.C.C. (3d) 475 (Ont. C.A.), reversed on other grounds (2001), 152 C.C.C. (3d) 294 (S.C.C.), reconsideration refused (June 14, 2001), Docs. 26912, 27610, 27774 (S.C.C.), in which the absence of affidavits from 51 alleged victims of a fraud resulted in a discharge on 51 out of 52 counts in the indictment.

•   The former system gave rise to difficulties when the evidence was located across a number of jurisdictions particularly when it required obtaining affidavit evidence from jurisdictions unfamiliar with affidavits or with no procedure for compelling witnesses to provide affidavits.

•   The requirement for affidavit evidence may have had the effect of requiring the requesting state to reconstitute its case from the manner in which it was gathered and put it into a different form acceptable to Canadian law. This form would have excluded certain evidence such as hearsay, which might, however, have been admissible at the trial.

- There was no mechanism for extraditing to entities other than states, such as the United Nations War Crimes Tribunals for Rwanda and the former Yugoslavia (which are designated as extradition partners in the new Act). Moreover, as these tribunals operate in the civil law tradition, the materials generated by these tribunals in support of a request for extradition would in any case not have been gathered in a form admissible under the former evidentiary rules.

The new Act has not made a distinction between common law countries and others with respect to the availability of the record of the case. It is available to all extradition partners regardless of their legal system.

§3.2 Evidence Otherwise Admissible Under Canadian Law (s. 32(1))

Section 32(1) is similar to s. 14 of the former Act. Please see the discussion under §2.2 above, "Comparison with Former Act."

§3.3 Sections 32(1)(b), 32(1)(c), 35 and 36

Please see the discussion under §§2.3, 2.4, 2.6 and 2.7 above, "Comparison with Former Act."

§3.4 No Oath or Solemn Affirmation Required for Documents Tendered (s. 34)

Section 34 of the new Act states that, "[a] document is admissible whether or not it is solemnly affirmed or under oath." This section is not restricted in its application and would apply to documentary evidence tendered pursuant to an extradition agreement or by way of a record of the case. Section 34 is not overridden by treaty provisions. Therefore, even if a treaty provides for statements to be on oath or solemn affirmation, s. 34 will govern with respect to documents tendered in reliance on the provisions of the treaty. Section 34 constitutes an express statutory response to an issue that arose under Canada's former extradition regime.

Some of the treaties do require evidence to be provided under oath or solemn affirmation, but even under the former Act the courts took a liberal approach to the determination of whether the requirement had been satisfied. *Italy (Republic) v. Piperno* (1982), 66 C.C.C. (2d) 1 (S.C.C.), dealt with the *Canada–Italy Extradition Treaty*, which required evidence to be on oath. The current Treaty, which came into force in 1985, still requires evidence to be on oath or solemn affirmation. Italy provided depositions which were not under oath but which had been taken in circumstances in which the deponent was aware of the need to tell the truth and the possibility of penal consequences for failure to do so. The Supreme Court of Canada held that the depositions were admissible, and supplemented the terms of the Treaty with reference to s. 16 of the former *Extradition Act* which allowed for the admission of "[d]epositions or statements taken in a foreign state on oath, or on solemn affirmation, where affirmation is allowed by the law of that state." Since the deponents recognized the gravity and importance of telling the truth, the court treated the depositions as affirmations as contemplated by s. 16 of the former Act. In effect, a fair and liberal approach was taken in order to give effect to the treaty.

Although evidence provided according to the terms of the *Canada–United States Extradition Treaty* generally took the form of sworn or affirmed first person affidavits, it was not in fact necessary that the affidavits had been sworn or affirmed in order to be admissible pursuant to the terms of the treaty. This was the opinion of the Ontario Court of Appeal in *Re Nixon, supra*. One of the arguments made by the fugitive against introduction of a particular transcript from American court proceedings was that the transcript was not sworn. Houlden J.A. dismissed this submission, noting as follows, at p. 382:

> Article 10(2) does not require that documentary evidence be in the form of a sworn deposition or statement, but only that it be authenticated in the manner set out in the article. Since the transcript was authenticated in this manner, I am of the opinion that it was properly admitted into evidence by the extradition judge.

As an alternative finding, Houlden J.A. indicated that the transcripts contained evidence of witnesses who had taken an oath at proceedings in the United States (at p. 384).

Some treaties specify that, whether or not taken under oath, evidence will be admissible in a Canadian extradition hearing if the evidence is admissible evidence according to the law of the extradition partner. The newer treaties take this approach, which is similar to that adopted in the record of the case provisions of the new *Extradition Act* (see s. 33(3)(a)). In *Netherlands (Kingdom) v. Clarkson* (1998), 59 C.R.R. (2d) 178 (B.C. S.C. [In Chambers]), affirmed (2000), 146 C.C.C. (3d) 482 (B.C. C.A.), leave to appeal to S.C.C. refused (2000), 2000 CarswellBC 2445 (S.C.C.), the documents, statements and summaries of statements, while neither sworn nor affirmed, constituted admissible evidence according to Dutch law. Therefore, under Article 7 of the *Canada–Netherlands Extradition Treaty*, the evidence was admissible in the extradition proceedings. The person sought challenged the introduction of this evidence on the basis that it was neither sworn nor affirmed. Boyd J. held that there was no overriding requirement in Canadian law for sworn or affirmed evidence, and that the introduction of this material in accordance with the terms of the treaty did not violate the principles of fundamental justice enshrined in s. 7 of the *Charter*.

In *Bourgeon v. Canada (Attorney General)* (2000), 35 C.R. (5th) 25 (Ont. S.C.J.), a case under the new Act, Ewaschuk J. agreed with the conclusion of Boyd J. in *Clarkson, supra*, with respect to the requirements concerning oaths. Ewaschuk J. made the following observation, at pp. 37-40:

[43] . . . The frustration with the need for a solemn affirmation or oath to render evidence admissible at a Canadian extradition hearing is best exemplified by *Lind v. Sweden* (1987), 36 C.C.C. (3d) 327 (Ont. C.A.), leave to appeal to S.C.C. refused, [[1987] 2 S.C.R. viii (S.C.C.)] *loc. cit.* at *vi.* In that second application for extradition of the fugitive Lind from Canada to Sweden, the requesting state tendered a sworn statement from an interested party, even though Swedish law prohibited an interested party from testifying under solemn affirmation or oath, though the witness was otherwise permitted to testify. The Ontario Court of Appeal held that the statement of the interested witness made on oath was admissible at the Canadian extradition hearing. However, the fugitive's extradition was later quashed by a Swedish court on the ground that the extradition was based, in part, on the inadmissible evidence of the interested party, who had deposed his evidence on oath, contrary to Swedish law.

. . . .

[46] In the end, I adopt Mr. Justice Boyd's conclusion that the abolition of a solemn affirmation or oath as a precondition to the admissibility of a document at an extradition hearing does not contravene s. 7 of the *Charter* on the basis that it is the quality of evidence that is fundamentally more important than any form of intitial self-serving authentication. In that regard, it is unnecessary for Canada to impose its own form of witness authentication on foreign countries, particularly those which do not require a solemn affirmation or oath as a threshold requirement for evidence to be admissible in their country.

With the introduction of s. 34, a source of litigation under the former Act is eliminated.

Section 34 will only be of practical application to documents submitted in conformity with the terms of an extradition agreement, which normally contains depositions. However, it will also apply with respect to the record of the case when the extradition partner submits unsworn statements as part of the record.

§4.0 ANALYSIS

§4.1 Record of the Case (ss. 32(1)(a) and 33)

(a) Admissibility requirements for introduction of evidence by record of the case

While the judicial assessment of the sufficiency of the evidence has been maintained, the admissibility rules applicable to extradition hearings have been broadened by the introduction of ss. 32(1)(a) and 33 in the new Act. The new provisions regarding the record of the case provide that evidence which has been gathered according to the rules and procedures of the extradition partner is admissible in the Canadian proceedings so long as it is certified by the appropriate authorities in the requesting state and accompanied by certain assurances with respect to the availability, gathering of the evidence, or sufficiency of the evidence for the purpose of prosecution in the foreign jurisdiction.

The admissibility requirements for the record of the case are set out in s. 33(3) of the new *Extradition Act*. Section 33(3)(a), which applies to a person sought for trial, requires that the judicial authorities of the requesting state do two things:

1. Certify that the evidence summarized or contained in the record of the case is available for trial. A summary of the evidence will suffice in the case of a request for a person sought for prosecution. This is set out in s. 33(1)(a), which requires the evidence to take the form of "a document summarizing the evidence available to the extradition partner."

2. Certify either that the evidence was gathered pursuant to the law of the requesting state or that it is sufficient under the law of the requesting state to justify prosecution.

The requirements set out in point 2 are alternatives. The two options address differences in legal concepts and procedures between common law and civil law countries. The option of certifying that the evidence referred to in the record of the case is sufficient to justify prosecution is a familiar concept to most common law countries as it is a standard which is required to be met at preliminary hearings. It would be a useful requirement for countries such as the United States, England, Australia, New Zealand, and South Africa. By contrast, the inquisitorial systems of civil law countries, which engage in an ongoing investigative process, would more easily be able to comply with the second option of certifying that the evidence referred to in the record of the case was gathered according to their law. In *R. v. Zingre* (1981), 61 C.C.C. (2d) 465 (S.C.C.), at p. 478, Dickson J. (as he then was) described the prosecutorial system in civil law countries as follows:

> One should be wary of analysing the Swiss judicial system using our model. The European approach is quite different. In continental systems of criminal justice, there are three distinct stages to criminal procedure. The first is a preliminary investigation conducted by police officials and prosecution. This is followed by a judicial phase in which there is investigation by career Judges known as "examining magistrates" or "juges d'instruction". Witnesses are required to testify and documents are examined. If, following this judicial inquiry, the case is deemed by the prosecuting attorneys to be an appropriate one for trial a formal trial is held: see generally Gerhard O. W. Mueller and Fré Le Poole-Griffiths, *Comparative Criminal Procedure* (1969), c. 2.

Therefore, it is only at the final stages of the process in civil law countries that the appropriate officials are able to make the assessment of whether the evidence justifies a trial. As Dickson J. observed in *R. v. Zingre, supra*, at p. 469:

> In accordance with the order of the Chamber of Indictment, two "extraordinary investigating judges" were appointed in Thurgau. The function of these Magistrates is to examine documents and to interrogate witnesses in order to assist the authorities in determining whether the evidence justified a formal trial. At the end of the investigation

271

> a report is submitted to the State Attorney who will then make a decision as to whether or not there is sufficient evidence before him. If he thinks that a crime has been committed, he will submit the case to the competent Court and the accused will have to stand trial to face the charges brought by the State Attorney.

Therefore, evidence may be submitted in support of an extradition request before it has been submitted to the State Attorney. The officials who would be involved in the prosecution at the earlier stage would be able to comply with a requirement of certifying that the evidence gathered to date was in accordance with their law. It would not be their function to make assessments regarding justification for prosecution. By contrast, common law countries might find it difficult to certify that evidence was gathered in accordance with their law if the certifying official was a prosecutor who was not involved in the evidence-gathering process. However, the prosecutor in common law jurisdictions routinely fulfils the role of assessing the sufficiency of evidence.

Civil law jurisdictions may avail themselves of the option under s. 33(3)(a)(ii) of certifying that the evidence has been gathered in accordance with their laws. However, there is still the requirement under s. 29 of the Act that the evidence provided justifies committal for trial according to Canadian law. The evidence gathered by the civil law country would have to be sufficient to meet the s. 29 test in order for Canada to be able to proceed with the extradition process.

The legislation contemplates a generous approach to the admissibility of the record of the case. This is reinforced by s. 33(4) and (5). Section 33(4) provides that authentication is unnecessary unless otherwise required by a relevant extradition agreement. Section 33(5) provides that the record of the case may be supplemented by material added to it by the extradition partner.

The *Canada–United States Extradition Treaty* is an example of an extradition agreement that will require authentication of the record of the case as contemplated by s. 33(4). Article 10(2) of the Treaty requires that, in order for documentary evidence to be admitted, it must be authenticated as provided by the article. In such a case, it would appear that the supplementary material envisaged by s. 33(5) would also have to be authenticated in accordance with the terms of the treaty. (See also the discussion concerning authentication requirements in connection with evidence tendered pursuant to an extradition agreement, under §2.3, above.

The treaties with Spain (1990), Switzerland (1996), and Korea (1995) have provisions for certification of documents similar to the record of the case provisions set out in s. 33(3)(a). These treaties also provide that no further authentication is required. If the certification provisions of the Act differ from those of the treaty, it is the provisions of the Act which must be complied with as s. 33(3) does not indicate that the terms of a treaty are to have priority over the Act. Having complied with the certification requirements of s. 33(3), there would be no further requirement for authentication with respect to requests from Spain, Switzerland, and Korea. The authentication and certification requirements are matters for judicial determination at the hearing.

In the case of a convicted person who is sought for the imposition or enforcement of a sentence, s. 33(3)(b) provides that the correctional or judicial authorities of the extradition partner are required to certify that the documents in the record of the case are accurate. The necessary documents, as set out in s. 33(1)(b), are a copy of the document recording the conviction and a document describing the conduct for which the person was convicted.

(b) Similar record of the case provisions in newer treaties

The provisions dealing with the record of the case in the new *Extradition Act* continue a trend that was already reflected in some of Canada's newer extradition treaties. For example, the *Canada–Switzerland Extradition Treaty* (in force March 19, 1996) contains similar evidentiary stipulations to those in the new Act. Article 5(2)(b) provides that, in the case of persons sought for the purpose of prosecution and persons convicted in absentia, the request for extradition must be supported by a copy of the order of arrest and:

> (b) in the event that the law of the Requested State so requires, evidence that would justify committal for trial if the conduct had been committed in the Requested State. For this purpose a summary of the facts of the case setting out the evidence, including evidence of identity of the offender, whether or not the evidence was gathered or obtained in the Requesting State, shall be admitted in evidence as proof of the facts contained therein, whether or not this evidence would otherwise be admissible under the law of the Requested State, provided that the summary is signed by a judicial authority or a prosecutor who certifies that the evidence described in the summary was obtained in accordance with the law of the Requesting State.

The extradition treaty with the Netherlands (in force December 1, 1991) contains a similar provision. Article 7(1)(b)(ii) provides that a request for an accused person must be accompanied by a copy of the order of arrest and:

> (b)(ii) in support of requests from the Kingdom of the Netherlands, evidence that would justify a committal for trial of the person sought. For the purpose, originals or certified copies of exhibits, statements and summaries of statements, reports, or any other document, whether taken on oath or solemnly affirmed or not, and whether obtained in the Kingdom of the Netherlands or elsewhere, shall be admitted in evidence as proof of the facts contained therein, if a rechter-commissaris (investigating judge) certifies that they constitute evidence admissible under Dutch law and were the basis for the issuance of the order of arrest; ....

Article 7(2)(b)(i) of the extradition treaty with the Republic of Korea (in force February 1, 1995) stipulates that, in order to establish a *prima facie* case:

> (b)(i) ... a summary of the facts of the case setting out the evidence, including evidence of the identity of the offender shall be admitted in evidence as proof of the facts

contained therein provided that a prosecutor certifies that the evidence described in the summary was obtained in accordance with the law of the Requesting Party.

Thus, in the case of requests from the Netherlands, Switzerland, and Korea, the nature of the evidentiary package will be substantially similar whether the package is submitted pursuant to the terms of the applicable treaty under s. 32(1)(b) of the new Act or by way of a record of the case pursuant to s. 33(1)(a).

(c) Constitutional considerations

(i) *Constitutional jurisprudence under former Act concerning fundamental justice*

Jurisprudence under the former Act recognized the constitutional validity of a number of aspects of extradition proceedings which did not accord with what would have been required in domestic prosecutions.

In *United States v. Smith* (1984), 10 C.C.C. (3d) 540 (Ont. C.A.), leave to appeal to S.C.C. refused (1984), 8 C.R.R. 245n (S.C.C.), the Ontario Court of Appeal held that it was not contrary to the principles of fundamental justice that a fugitive at an extradition hearing was not given the opportunity to cross-examine on the affidavits or depositions provided in support of the extradition request.

In *Philippines (Republic) v. Pacificador* (1993), 83 C.C.C. (3d) 210 (Ont. C.A.), leave to appeal to S.C.C. refused (1994), 87 C.C.C. (3d) vi (S.C.C.), the Ontario Court of Appeal held that the evidentiary standard of s. 18(1)(b) of the former *Extradition Act*, which is the same standard as applied under s. 29(1)(a) of the new Act, met the requirements of the principles of fundamental justice. The court also held that it was not a violation of s. 7 of the *Charter* that the *Extradition Act* contained a lower standard for committal than that set out in the now-repealed *Fugitive Offenders Act*, which applied to the rendition of fugitives to commonwealth countries. Doherty J.A. found that the unique purpose of an extradition hearing dictated particular considerations, at p. 218:

> The extradition court cannot be concerned with the ultimate merits of the charge or the fairness of the adjudicative process to which the fugitive will be subject in the foreign court: *United States of America v. Allard* (1987), 33 C.C.C. (3d) 501 at p. 507, 40 D.L.R. (4th) 102, [1987] 1 S.C.R. 564. Equally, the extradition court cannot oversee a discovery process relating to some potential future proceeding in a foreign country when that proceeding will be conducted according to foreign laws and possibly to different notions of concepts such as "full answer and defence".

The recognition in the jurisprudence that the trial will take place in a foreign jurisdiction under different rules than Canada's and perhaps with different notions of full answer and defence, was cited by the Ontario Court of Appeal in *United States v. Yang* (2001), 157 C.C.C. (3d) 225 (Ont. C.A.), as a factor supporting the constitutionality of the record of the case. The Court of Appeal observed that in *R. v. Schmidt* (1987), 33 C.C.C. (3d) 193 (S.C.C.), at pp. 214–215, La Forest J. made the point as follows:

> A judicial system is not, for example, fundamentally unjust — indeed it may in its practical workings be as just as ours — because it functions on the basis of an investigatory system without a presumption of innocence or, generally, because its procedural or evidentiary safeguards have none of the rigours of our system.
>
> . . .
>
> [T]he courts must begin with the notion that the Executive must first have determined that the general system for the administration of justice in the foreign country sufficiently corresponds to our concepts of justice to warrant entering into the treaty in the first place
> . . . .

As noted above, the terms of Canada's extradition treaty with the Netherlands with respect to evidence to be supplied in support of a request from that country are substantially similar to the provisions regarding the record of the case in the new *Extradition Act*. The introduction of evidence tendered at a hearing under the former Act pursuant to the Dutch treaty was challenged in the case of *Netherlands (Kingdom) v. Clarkson, supra*, as being contrary to both ss. 7 and 11(d) of the *Charter*. The Netherlands had filed evidence consisting of documents variously titled "Statement of a Witness," "Record of an Interview," or "Official Report." Boyd J. described the evidence as follows, at pp. 180–181:

> None of the documents, reports, statements or summaries of statements are made either by a witness who is under oath or one who affirms the truth of the contents of the statements. However, the various statements and summaries of statements of witnesses are appended to the official reports of the Examining Magistrates W. Lok (dated September 12, 1997) and J. Silvis (dated February 20, 1998), which official reports declare that the appended documents "constitute admissible evidence in accordance with Dutch law, in so far as they bear the stamp and signature of the . . . examining magistrate."

Boyd J. summarily dismissed the s. 11(d) *Charter* challenge, holding that the Supreme Court of Canada decision in *R. v. Schmidt, supra*, foreclosed reliance upon this section because the fugitive was not "charged with an offence" in Canada. On the s. 7 grounds, Boyd J. dismissed the fugitive's assertions that the unsworn evidence could not be admitted in a Canadian extradition proceeding without violating the principles of fundamental justice. With respect to the latter point, s. 34 of the new *Extradition Act* eliminates the issue by expressly waiving any requirement for documents to be on oath or solemn affirmation. In any event, even prior to the statutory direction of s. 34, the courts evidenced a flexible approach to the issue.

Although not in the context of *Charter* challenges, the Ontario Court of Appeal accepted that unsworn evidence was admissible in extradition proceedings under the former *Extradition Act*. In *Re Nixon, supra*, at p. 381, Houlden J.A. noted that the *Canada–United States Extradition Treaty* did not require that statements be sworn in order for the statements to be admissible at an extradition hearing. Rather, the statements simply had to be authenticated.

(ii) Hearsay evidence, abolition of Canadian exclusionary rules and fundamental justice

The diminished importance of hearsay in extradition proceedings is apparent in a number of cases under the former Act in which hearsay was admitted. In *United States v. Dries* (November 20, 1997), Doc. CA C24507, 1997 CarswellOnt 4646 (Ont. C.A.), for instance, the Ontario Court of Appeal upheld the extradition judge's decision to rely on a title search report which was provided in the authenticated materials notwithstanding that there was no affidavit from the person who had conducted the search. The court observed, at para. 5: "What would the affidavit of the title searcher add to the credibility of these documents?" In *United States v. Bray* (1997), 97 O.A.C. 388 (Ont. C.A.), leave to appeal to S.C.C. refused (1997) 110 O.A.C. 399 (note) (S.C.C.), the Ontario Court of Appeal allowed into evidence a hearsay statement attributed to a victim of the crime and contained in the affidavit of another witness. Similarly, in *United States v. Kerslake* (1996), 142 Sask. R. 112 (Sask. Q.B.), Baynton J. stated, at p. 118:

> The nature and function of the extradition hearing, and the practical difficulties and expense facing an applicant to obtain and present direct evidence in a foreign court, lends itself to the consideration in appropriate cases of reliable secondhand evidence.

These decisions are of course consistent with developments in the domestic approach to hearsay evidence. Even in domestic trial situations where guilt and innocence are at stake, the prohibition has fallen, and has been replaced by a principled approach to the admission of evidence on the basis of reliability and necessity. In *R. v. B. (K.G.)* (1993), 79 C.C.C. (3d) 257 (S.C.C.), Lamer C.J.C. noted, at p. 280, in dealing with domestic proceedings that it was appropriate to depart from the orthodox rule because it was "necessary to keep the common law in step with the dynamic and evolving fabric of our society" (quoting Iacobucci J. in *R. v. Salituro* (1991), 68 C.C.C. (3d) 289 (S.C.C.), at p. 301). In addition, it was held that reforming the rule against hearsay did not violate the *Charter*. These comments lend support in response to any challenge to the abolition of strict hearsay or other exclusionary rules in the new *Extradition Act*.

Such a challenge to the evidentiary provisions of the new Act was heard and dismissed by the Ontario Court of Appeal in *United States v. Yang* (2001), 157 C.C.C. (3d) 225. In that case, the extradition judge, Dilks J., had upheld the constitutionality of the provisions of ss. 32, 33 and 34 of the Act as written. In so doing, he rejected the competing authority of the decision of Ewaschuk J. in *Bourgeon v. Canada (Attorney General)* (2000), 35 C.R. (5th) 25 (Ont. S.C.J.), which had held that it was a violation of s. 7 of the *Charter* to permit evidence to be admitted at an extradition hearing that would not otherwise be admissible in Canada. The Court of Appeal in

Yang noted that in addition to Dilks J. in the case under appeal, the decision of Ewaschuk J. had not been followed by Low J. in *United States v. Reid* (May 23, 2000), (Ont. S.C.J.), or Vertes J. in *Germany (Federal Republic) v. Ebke*, [2001] 6 W.W.R. 517 (N.W.T.S.C.).

The court described the ruling in *Bourgeon* as follows, at pp. 243–244:

> [37] A challenge similar to the one made in this case came before Ewaschuk J. in *Bourgeon v. Canada (Attorney General)*. He made the following findings concerning the evidentiary provisions:
>
> (i)   Abolition of the requirement of evidence on oath or by way of solemn affirmation did not contravene s. 7 of the *Charter*.
>
> (ii) Admissibility of otherwise inadmissible foreign evidence must not be determined by foreign standards, varying from country to country.
>
> (iii) Abolition of the common law exclusionary rules as they apply to foreign evidence may result in the deprivation of the fugitive's liberty in a fundamentally unjust manner since the extradition judge may base committal on unreliable evidence. It was "inexplicable" that evidence in favour of the fugitive must meet a reliability threshold under s. 32(1)(*c*), but evidence adduced by the requesting state need not. This is "fundamentally unfair".
>
> (iv) Thus, s. 32(1)(*a*) and (*b*) contravene s. 7 as it is fundamentally unjust to a fugitive to permit an extradition judge to admit evidence at an extradition hearing that would not otherwise be admissible in the absence of "a statutory safeguard against the reception of unreliable evidence". Further, this contravention was not a reasonable limit within the meaning of s. 1 of the *Charter*.
>
> (v)   However, the appropriate remedy was to "read down" the provisions by reading the provisions to authorize the admission of otherwise inadmissible evidence only "if the judge considers it reliable". As so interpreted the provision, although contravening s. 7, would constitute a reasonable limit.
>
> [38] Justice Ewaschuk's holding that s. 32 of the *Extradition Act* should be read down, authorizing the admission of otherwise inadmissible evidence at the instance of the demanding state only if the judge considers that evidence to be reliable, has been considered by other superior court judges. As indicated, Dilks J. refused to follow the decision in this case and it was not followed by Low J. in *United States of America v. Reid* (Ont. S.C.J.; May 23, 2000) or by Vertes J. in *Germany v. Ebke*, [2001] N.W.T.J. No. 13 (QL) (S.C.) [reported [2001] 6 W.W.R. 517]. Low J. made the point in *Reid* at p. 22:
>
> > [T]he extradition judge has a very limited, indeed a negligible ability to assess the reliability of the evidence, for, apart from the situation relating to evidence adduced *viva voce* at the extradition hearing, there is no opportunity to assess the quality of the potential witnesses whose evidence is summarized in the authenticated documentary evidence and the record of the case adduced under section

32 of the Act. At best, the extradition judge may be able to say that there is or is not evidence before him to indicate that such evidence may be unreliable.

[39] As I understand it, other judges of the Superior Court of Justice have been following the *Bourgeon* case and applying a reliability test to evidence tendered on behalf of the extradition partner.

The Court of Appeal in *Yang* determined that *Bourgeon* was wrongly decided and should not be followed. Rosenberg J.A. for the court held that there was no principle of fundamental justice that required evidence to be in a particular form. He disposed of the argument that the admission of evidence that would not ordinarily be admitted in Canadian proceedings rendered the extradition hearing unfair as follows, at pp. 249–250:

[51] On the argument of this appeal, much was made of the disturbing specter of a fugitive being committed for surrender based upon fifth-hand hearsay, non-expert opinion and prejudicial character evidence. For example, in *Ebke*, the record of the case from the Federal Republic of Germany is described as containing "hearsay, character evidence, unqualified opinion evidence, and other forms of evidence that would not ordinarily be admissible in domestic Canadian criminal proceedings" (at para. 13). This is disturbing only when viewed through the lens of the Canadian system and its paradigm of the jury trial. If such evidence is admissible in our extradition partners it is because their experience is that this kind of evidence can be weighed by the judicial official and will be accorded the weight it deserves. It is not for this country to assume that it alone knows how to arrive at a true verdict.

[52] It seems to me that much of the concern about the reliability of evidence from civilian states is based upon a lack of understanding of that system and a tendency to isolate certain parts of the process, such as admission of hearsay, without an appreciation that there are other safeguards in the system that protect the accused from wrongful conviction. Thus, although all manner of information goes into the dossier that is presented to the court, usually that evidence is gathered under the supervision of a legal officer, either a prosecutor or a magistrate. At all phases of the investigation and trial an expert judge has wide powers to seek out additional evidence, for example from court-appointed neutral experts, and control the investigatory process. [Footnote omitted.]

[53] Most telling against the appellant's submission are the remarks of La Forest J. for the majority of the court in *Republic of Argentina v. Mellino* (1987), 33 C.C.C. (3d) 334 at 351, 40 D.L.R. (4th) 74 (S.C.C.), that he saw "nothing offensive to fundamental justice in surrendering in accordance with our extradition procedures an accused to a foreign country for trial in accordance with its traditional judicial processes for a crime alleged to have been committed there." And, as he said at p. 353, our courts "must assume that he will be given a fair trial in the foreign country. Matters of due process generally are to be left for the courts to determine at the trial there as they would be if he were to be tried here".

However, Rosenberg J.A. recognized that the fact that evidence is admissible under ss. 32 to 34 because it has been gathered in accordance with the law of the extradition partner will not preclude an extradition judge from concluding in a particular case that evidence should be excluded. Rosenberg J.A. noted that such a juris-diction under the *Charter* had been recognized by Arbour J. in *United States v. Shulman* (2001), 152 C.C.C. (3d) 294 (S.C.C.), reconsideration refused (June 14, 2001), Docs. 26912, 27610, 27774 (S.C.C.), at p. 315, when she stated:

> [56] . . . [I]n an appropriate case, the extradition judge could exclude evidence gathered by the foreign authorities in such an abusive manner that its admission *per se* would be unfair under s. 7 of the *Charter*. . . .

He pointed out, however, that no such basis for exclusion had been advanced on behalf of Yang.

In another context, Romilly J. of the British Columbia Supreme Court also rejected a role for the extradition judge in the consideration of reliability issues. In *United States v. Akrami*, 2000 BCSC 1438, 2000 CarswellBC 1961, a disclosure application was brought before the court in order to obtain evidence which the person sought wished to lead pursuant to s. 32(1)(c) of the Act to challenge the reliability of the requesting state's evidence. Romilly J. rejected the disclosure request on the basis that reliability was not a justiciable issue. He stated:

> [26] In my view, it is to avoid the time-consuming assessment of the reliability of foreign evidence that Parliament enacted the *Extradition Act* and its exceptions to Canadian rules of evidence in extradition hearings.

In the view of Romilly J., the expedited nature of the proceedings would be compromised with the injection of reliability arguments which would have the effect of complicating and lengthening the proceedings.

§4.2 Evidence Otherwise Admissible Under Canadian Law (s. 32(1))

(a) Whether evidence gathered in Canada contained in record of the case or in documents submitted in accordance with treaty must meet Canadian evidentiary standards

The issue of whether the provisions of s. 32(2) of the Act apply to Canadian evidence which is included in a record of the case or in documents submitted pursuant to treaty is unresolved. There is no dispute that for evidence led *viva voce* at an extradition the effect of s. 32(1) and (2) is that evidence gathered in Canada and being entered in the same manner as it would be in any other Canadian proceeding will have to satisfy the ordinary rules of Canadian evidence. This is to be distinguished from evidence which may have been obtained in Canada but which is being introduced by way of a record of the case or on the basis of treaty provisions. Canadian-obtained evidence which makes its way into the hands of the requesting state and from there into a record of the case or into authenticated documents tendered pursuant to a treaty may not be subject to the stringent requirements of Canadian evidentiary law. Certainly, this was a distinction recognized in the jurisprudence under the former Act in cases such as *United States v. Miller* (1991), 66 C.C.C. (3d) 20 (Ont. C.A.), leave to appeal to S.C.C. refused (1992), 69 C.C.C. (3d) vii (S.C.C.), and *United States v. Fox* (January 29, 1987), Smith D.C.J. (Ont. Dist. Ct.), affirmed (*sub nom. R. v. Fox*) (May 20, 1987), Doc. 273/87 (Ont. C.A.), in which post-arrest statements were taken by American police officers in Canada from the fugitive and then referred to in an affidavit contained in authenticated documentary evidence submitted pursuant to the *Canada–United States Extradition Treaty*. The statements were challenged on the basis of non-compliance with Canadian law pertaining to the taking of statements. The Ontario Court of Appeal held that it was not necessary for the requesting state to satisfy the Canadian *voir dire* requirements for the admissibility of statements although it left open the possibility of an inquiry if on the face of the record there was some question as to voluntariness raised.

However, the issue of whether Canadian-obtained evidence which is admitted under s. 32(1)(a) (the record of the case), or s. 32(1)(b) (in conformity with a treaty), must also satisfy the rules of Canadian evidence as stipulated by s. 32(2) has been considered afresh in two decisions under the new Act, with conflicting results.

In *United States v. Debarros* (February 9, 2000), Doc. E-9/99, LaForme J. (Ont. S.C.J.), affidavit evidence was supplied in support of an American request for the extradition of persons sought for drug offences. The evidence was in accordance with the terms of the *Canada–United States Extradition Treaty* and was therefore admissible under the terms of s. 32(1)(b) of the new Act. Among the evidence provided by the United States were three affidavits from members of the R.C.M.P. who had gathered evidence in Canada while they were conducting an unrelated investigation into drug trafficking. When the connection was made between the Canadian investigation and the crimes upon which the United States sought extradition, the R.C.M.P. officers travelled to Buffalo, New York and swore affidavits. Included as exhibits in this affidavit material were certificates of analysis indicating that certain evidence seized in Canada had tested positive as hashish. Other evidence in the affidavits established that the hashish seized in Canada was part of the same quantity of drugs as that in the crimes alleged by the United States.

Counsel for Debarros took issue with the fact that the R.C.M.P. officers had gathered their evidence in Canada but that the evidence had been presented by way of affidavits sworn in the United States. Included in this argument was the submission that evidence of the analysis of the drugs seized in Canada had to be made *viva voce* since s. 32(1) of the Act permitted the extradition court to admit evidence that would "otherwise be admissible" under Canadian law. Certificates of analysis under the terms of the *Controlled Drugs and Substances Act*, it was submitted, were admissible only at a "prosecution for an offence," which an extradition hearing was not.

LaForme J. rejected these submissions, noting that the approach taken under the former Act still applied. He held that since the affidavits were authenticated in accordance with the treaty they were admissible under s. 32(1)(b) of the Act, notwithstanding that they referred to evidence gathered in Canada. He stated, at para. 23:

> [N]othing would be gained by an extradition court ordering that the R.C.M.P. officers attend to give their evidence as to the analysis of the substance by way of oral testimony. It would only cause delay and be contrary to the purpose and function of extradition hearings.

He held that the affidavits sworn in Buffalo were admissible in their own right, and, as such, that s. 32(2) of the Act did not govern even though the affidavits contained Canadian-derived evidence (para. 24):

> If the affidavits are admissible in their own right, even if the content of them is inconsistent with s. 32(2) of the *Extradition Act*, then so too are the Certificates of Analysis.

Juriansz J., in *United States v. Martinez* (February 28, 2000), Doc. E24/99, 2000 CarswellOnt 561, [2000] O.J. No. 647 (Ont. S.C.J.), took a different approach. In *Martinez*, the evidence in support of the extradition request was provided in a record of the case. The judge noted that "there was information in the record of case which arguably was 'gathered in Canada'." This concerned:

1. a summary of calls by American police to Martinez' father in Canada, and to the Bell Canada information line, in Ontario. The source of the information was Canada but it was recorded by an American officer who had made the calls from California;

2. a summary of surveillance observations made by a Canadian police officer in Ontario, and a summary of observations made by a Canadian immigration agent, which were communicated to an American police officer by telephone and included in the record of the case.

With respect to the summaries of calls made by the American officer, Juriansz J. held that these were admissible since the focus of s. 32(2) was the location of the gathering of the evidence, in that case the United States, and not the location of the source of the information gathered. However, the summaries of the surveillance observations he excluded as being hearsay and inadmissible by operation of s. 32(2) because the surveillance evidence was gathered in Canada.

Juriansz J. was of the opinion that as a matter of strict construction of the statute, s. 32(2) applied to evidence gathered in Canada that is contained in a record of the case. He rejected the argument that s. 32(2) applies only to the first sentence of s. 32(1), which is concerned with evidence otherwise admissible according to Canadian law, but not to the second sentence of s. 32(1), which makes other forms of evidence admissible even if they do not comply with Canadian rules of evidence. That is, he did not accept that s. 32(1) could be read disjunctively such that only evidence tendered in reliance on domestic Canadian law is subject to the limitation of s. 32(2). He stated:

> [11] Counsel for the extradition partner argued that s. 32(2) had no application to information in a certified record of the case. She pointed out that there are two sentences in s. 32(1) and she contended that the opening limiting words of the subsection, i.e., "subject to subsection (2) . . . " applied only to the first sentence and s. 32(2) had no limiting effect on the second sentence. I find such a construction tortuous. In my view the French version of s. 32(1) puts the matter beyond doubt. The French version is comprised of only one sentence and the use of "ainsi que" makes clear that subsection (1) is to be read in totality.
>
> [12] I conclude, as a matter of statutory construction, that s. 32(2) applies to evidence gathered in Canada that is contained in a record of the case that would otherwise be admissible under para. 32(1)(a).

The reasoning enunciated by Juriansz J., if correct, would amount to a departure from the often less stringent approach under the former Act to evidence obtained in Canada but introduced in the requesting state's documentary evidence. Indeed, it would also appear to be contrary to the philosophy of the new Act, which has relaxed the rules of evidence to facilitate a more expeditious extradition scheme. The fact situation in the *Debarros* case provides an apt illustration of the potential to frustrate this intention. As La Forme J. observed, had the certificates of analysis in that proceeding been required to be introduced through the *viva voce* evidence of R.C.M.P. officers, it would have meant that the evidentiary burden at the extradition hearing would have been higher than that at a domestic trial or preliminary inquiry where it would have been permissible for the certificates to be filed without the necessity of *viva voce* evidence.

The interpretation favoured by Juriansz J. would also have implications for evidence obtained through mutual legal assistance channels in Canada, if such evidence appears in the record of the case submitted by the extradition partner, or in documentary evidence tendered in reliance on the terms of an extradition agreement. Frequently, Canadian bank records, telephone tolls, business records, and witness testimony will be obtained in Canada pursuant to orders under the *Mutual Legal Assistance in Criminal Matters Act* and provided to the investigating or prosecuting authorities of the extradition partner. Evidence obtained in this way could be contained in the extradition material submitted by the extradition partner for use at the hearing. For instance, the extradition partner by way of a mutual legal assistance request may have obtained Canadian telephone records in order to demonstrate a criminal association. If such evidence can only be admitted at the Canadian extradition hearing by satisfying the Canadian rules of evidence, then it might require at the hearing, leading evidence from the telephone company which will have already provided the same information in a form suitable to the requirements of the foreign prosecution via mutual legal assistance channels.

Even if s. 32(2) does not apply to Canadian evidence in a record of the case or documents submitted pursuant to the terms of a treaty, it would probably still be open to a person who alleges that such evidence was obtained as a result of a breach of his or her *Charter* rights in Canada to bring a challenge to its admissibility. This is a different issue than admissibility *per se*, as discussed in connection with the *Martinez* and *Debarros* cases above. Those cases were concerned with the method of the introduction of evidence. It is quite a different issue to consider whether a person sought should be entitled to challenge evidence obtained in Canada such as wiretap, searches, or confessions, if it is alleged that the evidence was illegally obtained. Otherwise Canadian police would be immune from *Charter* scrutiny if their activities were not for the purpose of furthering a Canadian investigation but rather for the purpose of gathering evidence to provide to an extradition partner. (See the discussion under s. 25, §4.3, "*Charter* motions concerning evidence gathered in Canada.")

For example, with respect to statements such as those taken in Canada but tendered through the record of the case or in reliance on treaty terms such as occurred in the *Miller* and *Fox* cases discussed above, even if there is nothing on the face of the record to raise a concern about voluntariness or oppression in the taking of a statement, it may still be open to the person sought to allege that his or her statement was involuntary. In that situation, s. 32(1)(c) may allow the person sought to apply to the extradition judge for permission to call evidence about the voluntariness of the statement. If this is allowed, it would only be applicable to post-arrest statements taken in Canada. It is difficult to imagine that, if a confession were coerced from a suspect in Canada, the person would not be able to find a remedy in a Canadian court concerning the use to which that evidence has been put.

(b) Former jurisprudence regarding whether evidence gathered in Canada and submitted in documentary form in accordance with treaty must meet Canadian evidentiary standards

The jurisprudence under the former Act held that post-arrest statements gathered in Canada and then subsequently submitted by the requesting state in documentary form was not required to meet Canadian evidentiary standards at the extradition hearing unless some violation was apparent on the face of the materials.

In *United States v. Miller, supra*, and *United States v. Fox, supra*, post-arrest statements were taken from fugitives located in Canada, by American police officers who had come to Canada for that purpose. These statements were then referred to in an affidavit contained in authenticated documentary evidence submitted pursuant to the *Canada–United States Extradition Treaty*. The statements were challenged on the basis of non-compliance with Canadian law pertaining to the taking of statements. The Ontario Court of Appeal held that it was not necessary for the requesting state to satisfy the Canadian *voir dire* requirements for the admissibility of statements. Notwithstanding that the statements were obtained in Canada, the court was of the opinion that, as there was nothing in the material to suggest that the statements were involuntary, no further inquiry by the extradition judge was required. Catzman J.A., in the

United States v. Miller decision, at p. 23, quoted the following passage from the Ontario Court of Appeal's endorsement in *United States v. Fox*:

> The only issue before the court was whether the statement by the appellant to the American officers was admissible. We are satisfied that the extradition judge properly instructed herself on this issue. We agree with Campbell J. that there was cogent evidence of voluntariness contained in the statement made to the American officers on which the extradition judge relied in deciding that the statement was admissible.
>
> We also agree with the conclusion of Campbell J. that the holding of a *voir dire* was unnecessary in the circumstances of this case.

In *United States v. Ngai* (August 4, 1995), Doc. E9/95 (Ont. Gen. Div.), the fugitive was permitted, pursuant to the decision in *United States v. Miller*, to call evidence on the voluntariness issue. The fugitive testified and a videotape of the fugitive's interrogation in Canada by the United States prosecutor was viewed at the extradition hearing. The court determined that the statement was voluntary largely as a result of the admission by the fugitive in his evidence that he knew that he had the right to refuse to answer the questions. In addition, the extradition judge held that the *Miranda* rights read to the fugitive prior to the questioning were substantially in compliance with the provisions of s. 10(b) of the *Charter*. In reaching this conclusion, the court made due allowance for the principle that the technicalities of criminal law are to be kept to a minimum in extradition matters.

Implicit in the reasoning of the Court of Appeal in *Miller* is that a voluntariness *voir dire* may be required if the materials on their face raise concerns about the voluntariness of the statement. The procedure suggested in these cases would likely only pertain to documentary evidence submitted pursuant to a treaty that provides for the submission of documents in the form of affidavits, statements, or depositions. Material of this nature normally contains enough detail in order to make such an assessment about voluntariness.

Section 32(1)(a) of the new *Extradition Act*, which provides for summaries of evidence to be contained in the record of the case, militates against the holding of *voir dires* because a summary of a statement is unlikely to contain information as to how the statement was taken. However, as discussed above under §4.2(a), it would be open to a person sought to challenge a statement taken in Canada, on *Charter* grounds.

If the extradition partner under the new Act is relying on a statement made after the person's arrest in Canada, and the statement is not contained in the documentary evidence, the person will, if the voluntariness of the statement is at issue, be entitled to a *voir dire* to determine the admissibility of the statement pursuant to s. 32(1) and 32(2). The *voir dire* would be conducted by calling *viva voce* evidence in the same manner as a *voir dire* at a domestic preliminary hearing or trial.

This would also have been required under the former *Extradition Act. United States v. Leon* (1995), 96 C.C.C. (3d) 568 (Ont. C.A.), at p. 573, affirmed (1996), 105 C.C.C. (3d) 385 (S.C.C.), made it apparent that evidence sought to be tendered *viva voce* which was obtained in Canada had to comply with Canadian evidentiary requirements such as those which were applicable to search and seizure law.

The nature of cross-border co-operation between police forces is such that Canadian authorizations for the interception of private communications are often obtained in aid of American or joint Canadian-American investigations. This occurs frequently in drug investigations. Transcripts or tapes of communications intercepted in Canada are then routinely provided to the American investigators. Similar to the situation in *United States v. Leon,* where evidence from Canadian-obtained search warrants was relied upon at the hearing, intercepted communications made in Canada and which are to be tendered at the hearing must comply with Canadian admissibility requirements. This could encompass *Charter* challenges.

It was less clear in the jurisprudence under the former Act whether Canadian law could be brought to bear in an attempt to exclude evidence of communications taken in Canada but tendered through authenticated documents. In *United States v. Ahluwalia (sub nom. United States v. Ahluwalia and Sohal)* (December 1, 1995), Doc. Toronto E-15/93 (Ont. Gen. Div.), a case which involved R.C.M.P. co-operation with the American Drug Enforcement Administration, transcripts of intercepted communications were included in the documentary evidence. Counsel for the fugitives argued that, since the material did not specify where the communications were intercepted, the communications may have been intercepted in Canada, and thus were subject to *Charter* challenge in the same way as they would be in a domestic proceeding. Hoilett J. found, at p. 13, that the communications in question were intercepted in the United States through American investigations, and thus the *Charter* did not apply to these communications:

> There is no merit in the *Charter* argument advanced. All the indications are that such electronic surveillance as took place was the result of U.S.A. interceptions conducted by DEA agent/s. It would be rank speculation, in my view, to suggest that there were any unauthorized interceptions by Canadian police authorities and it is common ground that the *Charter* has no extra-territorial application, concerning which reference may usefully be made to *R. v. Schmidt* (1987), 33 C.C.C. (3d) 193 (S.C.C.).

Although the fugitive's submission on this point was dismissed, the decision left open the possibility that the extradition judge had jurisdiction to deal with *Charter* breaches in connection with communications intercepted in Canada but tendered in documentary evidence pursuant to a treaty. In *R. v. Barranca* (December 14, 1994), [1994] O.J. No. 3942 (Ont. Gen. Div.), Keenan J. supported this position. Keenan J. ruled that the fugitives could have disclosure of intercepted communications and the corresponding authorizations obtained in Canada. The affidavit evidence tendered by the United States included affidavits of F.B.I. agents involved in the investigation who gave a narration of events without specifically relying on the intercepted communications. In terms of jurisdiction, Keenan J. held that s. 9(3) of the former *Extradition Act* gave the extradition judge the power to grant *Charter* relief in appropriate cases, at p. 3. With respect to the specific point in issue, Keenan J. made the following comment, at pp. 3–4:

> The extradition judge has an obligation to examine the evidence that is submitted and pass on its sufficiency. The fugitive is entitled to be represented by counsel and is entitled to mount a challenge to the sufficiency of the evidence. It is axiomatic that the fugitive has a right to information which may assist him in challenging the validity of or the sufficiency of the evidence.
>
> In this case the evidence upon which the requesting state relies is the affidavit evidence of the FBI agents who participated in the intercepted communication. In order to successfully challenge the accuracy or the interpretation of those communications given by the author of the affidavit, the defence is entitled to examine the communication itself and to mount any challenge that there may be to its accuracy.
>
> The fact that the requesting state presents as evidence only the content that it has collected from the conversations themselves does not disable this court from examining other evidence which may be pertinent. It does not disable the fugitive or his counsel from presenting other evidence of other parts of the conversation which may tend to call into question the sufficiency of the evidence relied upon.

In a clarification issued the same day, at p. 1, Keenan J. indicated that his order only encompassed those interceptions made under authorizations granted by Ontario justices and not those obtained pursuant to orders granted in the requesting state.

§4.3 Specific Evidentiary Issues at Extradition Hearings

The cases which are discussed below were decided under the former Act but will continue to be of assistance if the issues arise under the new Act, irrespective of whether the evidence is submitted in the form of the record of the case or pursuant to treaty.

(a) Intercepted communications

In *United States v. Cotroni* (1984), 38 C.R. (3d) 299 (Que. S.C.), reversed (1986), 53 C.R. (3d) 339 (Que. C.A.), reversed (1989), 48 C.C.C. (3d) 193 (S.C.C.), Phelan J. held that a *voir dire* pertaining to communications intercepted in the requesting state was not required when the requesting state has protection of privacy laws similar to those in Canada. The documentary evidence relied upon at the extradition hearing contained transcripts of intercepted communications attached to the law enforcement officer's affidavit. In coming to this determination, Phelan J. made the following comment, at pp. 303–304:

> I am aware from the affidavit produced in Ex. R-3 that the electronic intercepts in the present case purport to be duly sanctioned by the provisions of American law. It has been suggested that I should not presume to inquire into the laws and procedures of the demanding state, but I believe I must, to a certain extent at least.

Namely, I consider it my duty, in deciding upon the admissibility of affidavit 5, to satisfy myself that the United States legal provisions respecting the securing of wiretap evidence are, in principle, equivalent to the standards prescribed in Pt. IV.1 of our Criminal Code, and that the actual method of securing the subject evidence conformed to such legal requirements of the United States.

When the *United States v. Cotroni* case was before the Supreme Court of Canada ((1989), 48 C.C.C. (3d) 193), this issue was not commented upon by the court. What the court did deal with was the form of the evidence. The issue was raised as to whether the tape recordings of the intercepted communications should be tendered at the extradition hearing, as opposed to transcripts of the recordings. La Forest J. for a majority of the court, dismissed the argument, at p. 227. Under the record of the case provisions of the new Act, even transcripts will be unnecessary. A summary of the content of the communications would be sufficient if this type of evidence is to be relied upon.

In *United States v. Ahluwalia (sub nom. United States v. Ahluwalia and Sohal)*, *supra*, counsel for Sohal argued that his client's rights under s. 8 of the *Charter* had been infringed by the use in the authenticated materials of intercepted communications which counsel alleged were unauthorized (at p. 6). Hoilett J. of the Ontario Court (General Division) found that the communications in question were intercepted in the United States through American investigations and thus the *Charter* did not apply to these communications, since pursuant to *R. v. Schmidt, supra*, "the *Charter* has no extra-territorial application" (at p. 13).

As is fully discussed above under §4.2(b), in *R. v. Barranca, supra*, Keenan J. ordered disclosure of Canadian-obtained wiretap evidence which was referred to in the documentary evidence submitted pursuant to an American extradition request. However, he made it clear that his order did not apply to interceptions made pursuant to American orders.

The decision of Phelan J. in *United States v. Cotroni* predates the *R. v. Schmidt* case which Hoilett J. relied upon in holding that the *Charter* has no extra-territorial application. More recently, in the non-extradition cases of *R. v. Terry* (1996), 106 C.C.C. (3d) 508 (S.C.C.), *Schreiber v. Canada (Attorney General)* (1998), 124 C.C.C. (3d) 129 (S.C.C.), and *R. v. Cook* (1998), 128 C.C.C. (3d) 1, the Supreme Court of Canada confirmed that evidence taken in foreign countries is not subject to Canadian *Charter* requirements absent the direct participation of Canadian officials (*R. v. Terry* and *Schreiber v. Canada (Attorney General)* are discussed in Appendix A, "Letters Rogatory").

(b) Confessions

As discussed above, post-arrest statements taken in Canada from the person sought and which are tendered through the *viva voce* evidence of witnesses at the extradition hearing, are subject to the usual rules of Canadian evidence regarding admissibility. If voluntariness is an issue then a *voir dire* may be required. As also discussed above, the Ontario Court of Appeal cases of *Miller* and *Fox*, decided under the former Act, indicate that confessions obtained in Canada and subsequently submitted in the form of documentary evidence pursuant to treaty would only require an inquiry into voluntariness if there was a question in this regard apparent on the face of the material.

In the case of *India v. Singh* (1996), 108 C.C.C. (3d) 274 (B.C. S.C.), the extradition judge, Oliver J., embarked on an inquiry into the fugitive's assertion that post-arrest statements made by five co-conspirators in India and referred to in the documentary evidence submitted pursuant to treaty, were obtained by torture. The fugitive tendered affidavits from the co-conspirators to support this contention. The requesting state countered with further affidavit materials from the alleged torturers denying four of the five claims. Oliver J. held that the burden was on the fugitive on a balance of probabilities to establish that the confessions had been obtained by torture. He held that only one of the statements was obtained as a result of torture and was therefore inadmissible by virtue of the provisions of the *Criminal Code*. The fugitive was ultimately discharged.

In *Australia v. Lau* (2001), 149 B.C.A.C. 171 (B.C.C.A.), an inculpatory statement of the fugitive taken in Australia was submitted in the evidentiary record in support of a rendition request pursuant to the *Fugitive Offenders Act*. The rendition judge had held that the fugitive had not raised a "sufficient and compelling cause that an inquiry ought to be conducted" into the voluntariness of the confession. The British Columbia Court of Appeal upheld this decision. Writing for the court, MacKenzie J.A. stated, at p. 174:

> [15] I do not think that a requesting state is required to prove that a statement of the fugitive is voluntary in a voir dire as a condition of admissibility. Section 27 of the *Fugitive Offenders Act* authorizes the receipt of deposition evidence in rendition proceedings. It would frustrate the purpose of deposition evidence to require voluntariness to be proved by viva voce evidence in every case: See *Australia (Commonwealth) v. Morgan* (1993), 81 C.C.C. (3d) 328 (Ont. C.J. Prov. Div), at pp. 227-228. This is also the position taken in extradition cases: *Re Bertholotte* (unreported) 13 August 1986, No. 500-10-000045-8541844; *United States of America and Shaw* (unreported) 10 April 1984 (Ont. Dist. Ct).

Under the new Act there are two conflicting decisions as to the scope of s. 32(2) as to whether Canadian evidentiary requirements apply to evidence obtained in Canada but submitted in either a record of the case or pursuant to treaty. In *United States v. Debarros, supra*, LaForme J. found that s. 32(2) did not apply to govern the admissibility of Canadian-gathered evidence submitted in documentary form pursuant to treaty terms. In *United States v. Martinez, supra*, Juriansz J. came to the opposite conclusion and held that s. 32(2) applied to Canadian-gathered evidence which was set out in a record of the case. Neither of these cases were dealing with post-arrest statements and it would appear that when a record of the case is involved, the summary nature of the material would not lend itself to the holding of *voir dires* because it is unlikely to contain enough information about how the statement was taken. However, a person sought may be able to challenge a statement taken in Canada on *Charter* grounds.

(c) DNA evidence

In the case of *R. v. Reid* (February 11, 1994), Corbett J. (Ont. Gen. Div.), the fugitive sought to invoke s. 8 of the *Charter* with respect to a blood sample taken pursuant to a search warrant issued in Pennsylvania. The sample was taken for the purpose of DNA testing. Relying on s. 32 of the *Charter*, Corbett J. held that the *Charter* did not apply since the evidence was obtained in the United States in accordance with apparently lawful procedures (at pp. 21–23).

(d) *Canada Evidence Act*

The applicability of the *Canada Evidence Act* under the new Act will be discussed with respect to the three categories which follow.

(i) *Records obtained in Canada and tendered at extradition hearing pursuant to rules of* Canada Evidence Act

There may be situations where records are obtained in Canada and tendered at the extradition hearing pursuant to the rules of the *Canada Evidence Act*. For example, banking records pursuant to s. 29 of the *Canada Evidence Act* or business records pursuant to s. 30 might be obtained in Canada, but not submitted by the extradition partner in its documentary material. If the extradition partner were to rely upon this material at the extradition hearing, it would be required to be submitted pursuant to the Canadian rules of evidence and consequently the requirements of the *Canada Evidence Act* would have to be complied with.

(ii) *Records obtained in Canada and submitted in record of the case (s. 32(1)(a)) or tendered pursuant to treaty (s. 32(1)(b))*

Records may be obtained in Canada and submitted in a record of the case (s. 32(1)(a)) or tendered pursuant to treaty (s. 32(1)(b)) as, for example, when Canadian business or banking records have been obtained in Canada and provided to the extradition partner, either voluntarily or pursuant to mutual legal assistance applications. Such material may, in turn, be included by the extradition partner in its documentary evidence submitted pursuant to treaty or in a record of the case for the purposes of the extradition hearing. Juriansz J. of the Superior Court of Ontario in the *Martinez* case, *supra,* has indicated that evidence submitted in this way would still be required to comply with Canadian evidentiary requirements because of s. 32(2), which provides that evidence gathered in Canada must satisfy the rules of evidence under Canadian law in order to be admitted. Juriansz J. rejected the argument that s. 32(2) applies only to evidence led pursuant to the ordinary rules of Canadian evidence and not to evidence tendered pursuant to either treaty provisions or by way of a record of the case (s. 32(1)(a) and (b)). However, LaForme J. of the Superior Court of Ontario in *Debarros, supra*, has taken a more liberal approach to the introduction of Canadian-obtained documentary material when it is submitted in accordance with an extradition agreement. In that case it was held that Canadian certificates of analysis submitted by the United States in documentary evidence tendered pursuant to treaty under s. 32(1)(b) of the Act, were admissible in their own right without the necessity of compliance with s. 32(2) of the Act. This is more in keeping with the philosophy of the new Act, which has relaxed the rules of evidence to facilitate a more expeditious scheme. It is also the interpretation that would best take account of the practical functioning of mutual legal assistance requests. Evidence already provided pursuant to a mutual legal assistance request, in a form suitable to the requirements of the foreign court, and then submitted in documentary evidence to support an extradition request, would, if s. 32(2) of the Act is applicable, have to re-comply with Canadian rules of evidence which could necessitate resorting to witnesses twice in order to provide *Canada Evidence Act* affidavits, or *viva voce* testimony.

(iii) Records obtained outside of Canada and submitted in record of the case (s. 32(1)(a)) or pursuant to a treaty (s. 32(1)(b))

The issue of whether the provisions of the *Canada Evidence Act* applied to extradition proceedings under the former *Extradition Act* when foreign business records were submitted in the authenticated documents was raised in jurisdictions across the country, but was not considered by any of the courts of appeal. The cases of *Ng, Cheng v. Hong Kong, Doan*, and *Masini*, which dealt with this issue under the former Act and which are discussed below will still be of assistance, since evidence tendered under the new Act pursuant to a treaty or by way of a record of the case, if it involves provision of a copy of the record itself, may lead to arguments about the applicability of the *Canada Evidence Act*. The case of *Quintin*, decided under the new Act, and also discussed below, has held that the *Canada Evidence Act* has no application to foreign business records provided pursuant to the terms of an extradition agreement.

The applicability of the *Canada Evidence Act* was raised before Trussler J. in *United States v. Ng* (October 17, 1988) (Alta. Q.B.). The fugitive Ng was wanted to stand trial in California for the abduction and murder 11 people. He was apprehended in Alberta. Amongst the affidavit evidence tendered at the extradition hearing were affidavits attaching certain business records. Counsel for the fugitive sought to have these records disregarded by the extradition judge. Counsel argued that they were not in compliance with s. 30 of the *Canada Evidence Act*. In particular, as required by s. 30(3), there was nothing in the affidavits to indicate that the affiant had made the copies of the records attached to the affidavit or explaining why an original record could not be produced for the court. In response to the fugitive's argument that the requesting state had failed to comply with s. 30(3), Trussler J. made the following observations:

> But the first part of subsection (3) obviously would not apply in the sense I don't think there is any reason why they have to set out why it is not possible or reasonably practicable to produce the record. I don't think there is any obligation on them—on the State of California—to produce original records in this forum.
>
> But it seems to me that where a state is requesting extradition that there is no reason why they must send their original evidence to the state from which they are requesting extradition, and that in itself is a good reason for not producing the original document.

Trussler J. also held that there was no requirement that there be an affidavit from the person who made the copies describing the source from which the copy was made and attesting to its authenticity. This was not the form of the affidavits from California.

Trussler J. ruled that the documents attached to the affidavits as submitted by the *United States* were admissible:

> Well, I am not convinced that section 30 of the *Evidence Act* even applies. The scheme of the Act allows for evidence by affidavit, that includes documents. Those documents do not have to be originals.
>
> And in this particular case I am satisfied that the documents are authentic; and on that basis I am going to allow them to be admitted into evidence.

In *Cheng v. Hong Kong* (December 17, 1992), (Ont. Gen. Div.), Wright J. made a more direct pronouncement upon the applicability of the *Canada Evidence Act*. Cheng was committed for surrender pursuant to the provisions of the now-repealed *Fugitive Offenders Act*. An appeal of the committal was brought before Wright J. Counsel for the fugitive argued that s. 30 of the *Canada Evidence Act* rendered inadmissible the affidavits of Hong Kong banking officials because original documents had not been produced and the requesting jurisdiction had not complied with the requirements of s. 30(3) with respect to the production of copies.

Wright J. rejected this submission, stating that the *Canada Evidence Act* did not apply to the proceedings:

> In my view, s. 30(3) does not apply by reason of s. 28 of the *Fugitive Offenders Act*. Depositions which include affidavits, and copies, thereof, are deemed duly authenticated by being sealed (as in this case) with the official seal of the Governor of Hong Kong.
>
> Section 28(2) provides that all courts shall take judicial notice of every seal, and shall admit in evidence without further proof of documents authenticated by it.

This reasoning is equally applicable to proceedings under the *Extradition Act*. In fact, in the case of *United States v. Doan* (April 22, 1996), (Ont. Gen. Div.), Wein J. expressly endorsed the reasoning in the *Extradition Act* context. In this case, it had been argued that printouts from the California Department of Vehicles identifying Doan as the owner of a particular vehicle were inadmissible for failure to comply with the requirements of s. 30 of the *Canada Evidence Act*. Wein J. found that the attachments in question did, in fact, comply with s. 30. However, she went further and held that admissibility in extradition proceedings was not governed by the provisions of the *Canada Evidence Act*:

> In any event, at least for the purposes of subsection (3) of section 30 of the *Canada Evidence Act*, I agree with the reasoning of the Court in *Cheng v. Hong Kong* (Ont. Gen. Div. *per* Wright J, December 17, 1992) that the authentication provisions of the relevant extradition legislation provide a sufficient basis for admissibility. The affidavit otherwise meets the terms of section 30(2) of the *Canada Evidence Act*. It is said that the printouts are the business records of the state of California and are relied upon as such by the courts of that state. In my view the exact words of the Canadian section need not be parroted by the affiant if the substance and intent of the provisions are met, as here, by the evidence in the affidavit.

By contrast, in the case of *United States v. Masini* (September 15, 1995), Doc. E12/94 (Ont. Gen. Div.), Keenan J. considered an extradition request which, among other charges, contained a count alleging a violation of United States immigration law. Masini was a Canadian citizen who had been deported from the United States. He was subsequently arrested in the United States on drug charges and, in addition to these charges, he was charged with re-entering the United States without first having obtained the permission of the United States Attorney General. Keenan J. described the evidence before him on this point as consisting of an affidavit from an agent of the U.S. Immigration and Naturalization Service to the effect that a review of the fugitive's file disclosed no evidence of an application for the consent of the Attorney General.

Keenan J. ruled that the affidavit did not provide evidence of the charge. He held that the proper way to prove the non-existence of the Attorney General's permission was by the production of the business record. In so finding, he implicitly found that the requesting jurisdiction must comply with s. 30(2) of the *Canada Evidence Act*. Section 30(2) reads as follows:

> (2) Where a record made in the usual and ordinary course of business does not contain information in respect of a matter the occurrence or existence of which might reasonably be expected to be recorded in that record, the court may on production of the record admit the record for the purpose of establishing that fact and may draw the inference that the matter did not occur or exist.

Keenan J. also strictly applied the aspect of s. 30(2), which requires a document proffered to be a "record made in the usual and ordinary course of business." He found that the failure of the affiant to so state rendered inadmissible the documents attached to his affidavit which purported to be from the immigration file of the fugitive. Keenan J. concluded that the *Canada Evidence Act* required production before the extradition court of the entire immigration file relating to Masini. Keenan J. stated, at p. 7 of the judgment:

> There is no evidence that the three documents constitute the complete "record" or that it is the only record. If one is permitted to draw an inference of non-existence from the absence of an entry in the record, it seems axiomatic that the "absence" can be established only if the entire record has been examined. Accordingly, I have to conclude that the Cookfair affidavits are ineffective as proof under s. 30(2) of the *Canada Evidence Act.*

In a case decided under the new Act, Dambrot J. in *United States v. Quintin* (2000), 4 Imm. L.R. (3d) 255 (Ont. S.C.J.), came to a different conclusion than that reached by Keenan J. with respect to the applicability of the *Canada Evidence Act.* In *Quintin*, the evidence at the extradition hearing was tendered in reliance upon the terms of the treaty with the United States. Counsel for the persons sought for extradition objected to the extradition judge taking into consideration most of the government documents, bank documents, and business records in the material on the basis of non-compliance with s. 30 of the *Canada Evidence Act*, the business record provision. Dambrot J. concluded that the documents were admissible, since they constituted a principled exception to the hearsay rules as described by the Ontario Court of Appeal in the extradition case of *United States v. Dries, supra.* However, he was also of the opinion that the *Canada Evidence Act* had no application to the introduction of these documents. He concluded, at p. 285:

> [79] Once again, I do not consider compliance with the niceties of the *Canada Evidence Act* to be decisive of admissibility in an extradition proceeding. I am fortified in this conclusion by the British Columbia Court of Appeal in *United States v. Wong* (1995), 98 C.C.C. (3d) 332 (B.C. C.A.). At p. 346 of Legg J.A.'s judgment for the Court, the following passage from LaForest's *Extradition to and from Canada*, 3rd ed., at p. 154 is adopted:
>
>> In all events, properly authenticated depositions and statements under oath or affirmation, should be received in evidence at extradition hearings in this country if they have been taken in a manner recognized as valid in the foreign country. The judge should not inquire whether formalities required by Canadian law have been complied with.
>
> [80] In my view, these documents are admissible by virtue of Article 10 of the Treaty, regardless of compliance with s. 30.

The *Extradition Act* in combination with the treaties has made specific provision for the introduction of documentary evidence in an extradition proceeding. Therefore, it is persuasive to conclude that the field has been occupied and that there is no room for the application of the *Canada Evidence Act*, which has separate and competing rules for the introduction of documentary evidence.

In particular, the summary nature of the record of the case is incompatible with requiring compliance with the *Canada Evidence Act*, since the record of the case permits a summary of the evidence to be tendered. Therefore, while s. 33(2) permits a document to be included in the record of the case, it is not compulsory and all that would be necessary would be for the contents of a business or banking record, for instance, to be summarized. The whole focus of the record of the case is to allow the evidence to be presented in a form so as to facilitate compliance by extradition partners and to avoid imposing, in the extradition context, strict domestic evidentiary rules such as those in the *Canada Evidence Act*.

(e) Collateral attacks on foreign orders

In the case of *United States v. Singh* (October 14, 1994), Doc. E-21, Ewaschuk J., [1994] O.J. No. 3941, the fugitive was alleged to have contravened an American *ex parte* custody order by removing his children from their mother. Counsel for the fugitive argued that the order which the fugitive was alleged to have contravened could not have given rise to an offence in Canada because the order could not have been granted in Canada. Ewaschuk J. dismissed this submission, stating as follows:

> [6] It is my view that the respondent is not allowed to collaterally attack the validity of the foreign order here in Canada, and I find no authority requiring the applicant state to establish that the order would have been granted in Canada. International comity does not require such mirrored reciprocity. Instead the doctrine of comity between foreign states requires the Canadian extradition judge to recognize the validity of a foreign superior court order valid on its face, and subsisting at the time of its alleged breach.
>
> [7] Furthermore, the principle of transposition of facts from the requesting state to the requested state requires the extradition judge to assume that the facts which occurred in the foreign jurisdiction had occurred in Canada. One of the facts which must be assumed is that a superior court judge issued a custody order. That fact is a given, and cannot be challenged at this hearing.

This passage was relied upon by Chapnik J. in *United States v. Soul* (November 25, 1994), Chapnik J. (Ont. Gen. Div.), affirmed (February 17, 1995), Doc. CA C20236, [1994] O.J. No. 2838 (Ont. C.A.). In this case, a charge of failing to appear in court in Tennessee was challenged on the basis that the method of releasing an accused from court on a promise to appear in Tennessee was not the same as the Canadian procedure. Therefore, it was argued that, on the facts of the case, there could not have been a warrant for failing to appear had the facts occurred in Canada. Chapnik J. did not accept this submission. She adopted the approach advocated by Ewaschuk J. in *United States v. Singh* and stated as follows:

> [39] In the present case, the warrant for the arrest of the fugitives constitutes proof of the court order and establishes the procedural validity of the process in the requesting state.

The Ontario Court of Appeal upheld Chapnik J.'s decision (February 17, 1995), Doc. CA C20236 (Ont. C.A.).

(f) Death of witness

In *United States v. Palmer* (January 23, 1996), Doc. E-20/94, Wein J. (Ont. Gen. Div.), appeal dismissed [1997] O.J. No. 608 (Ont. C.A.), an affidavit had been provided in the authenticated evidence from an important witness who had since died. The extradition hearing judge was urged on behalf of the requesting state to accept the affidavit of the deceased witness on the basis of the expanded admissibility provisions outlined by the Supreme Court of Canada in *R. v. Khan* (1990), 59 C.C.C. (3d) 92 (S.C.C.), and *R. v. Smith* (1992), 75 C.C.C. (3d) 257 (S.C.C.). The extradition judge admitted the affidavit, stating as follows, at pp. 10–11:

> In the circumstances of this case, the affidavit remains as reliable now as it was before the death of the affiant. Clearly its admissibility is not undermined by the absence of cross-examination, since there would have been no cross-examination in any event. Problems with respect to the admissibility of evidence subsequent to this hearing are not the direct concern of this court at this stage. While the issue remains troubling, it seems to me that the issue of the continuing ability of the state to effectively prosecute is properly considered at the executive level of review. Accordingly it is my view that the affidavit of Mr. Funovitz is properly considered by me.
>
> Further, even if the death were to be said to have an impact of the admissibility of the affidavit, I would hold that in the circumstances of this case the prerequisites of necessity and reliability have been met and the evidence ought to be admitted in this affidavit form.

A similar application of the *Smith/Khan* line of cases was considered by the Ontario Court of Appeal in *United States v. Bray* (1997), 97 O.A.C. 388 (Ont. C.A.), leave to appeal to S.C.C. refused (1997), 110 O.A.C. 399 (note) (S.C.C.). In that case, the extradition judge admitted into evidence a statement allegedly made by the fugitive's deceased wife (the alleged murder victim of the fugitive) to another witness, to the effect that she was being stalked by her husband and that he had threatened to kill her.

The majority of the Court of Appeal upheld the introduction of the statement. Weiler and Austin JJ.A. held as follows, at p. 390:

> [3] . . . In order to have properly admitted this statement as an exception to the hearsay rule, the extradition judge had to be satisfied that it met the requirements of necessity and reliability: *R. v. Smith (A.L.)*, [1992] 2 S.C.R. 915; 139 N.R. 323; 55 O.A.C. 321; (1992), 75 C.C.C. (3d) 257; 15 C.R. (4th) 133; 94 D.L.R. (4th) 590 (S.C.C.). The appellant conceded that the proposed evidence met the necessity requirement. However, he submitted that the evidence did not meet the test of reliability and that the extradition judge failed to consider factors which would raise the possibility that either Ernestine Goins or Audrey Bray was untruthful or mistaken.

[4] The evidence of Ernestine Goins as to the statement made to her by Audrey Bray regarding the history of violence and the threat of murder was found by the extradition judge to be reliable. We cannot say that he erred in this conclusion. Indeed, the affidavit of Mary Hall, another sister of the deceased wife is to the same effect and was also before the extradition judge.

The majority of the Court of Appeal recognized the right of the extradition judge to apply the test in a more summary fashion, adapted to the extradition context, than would be usual in domestic proceedings of the same nature. Finlayson J.A., at p. 392, dissented on this point, observing that the extradition judge had no knowledge of the procedures used to gather the evidence and did not know whether there had been any attempt to follow up on the deceased's statements. Finlayson J.A. noted, at p. 392, para. 16, that if a follow-up had been done, it would have gone a "long way in assisting him as to the reliability of the hearsay statement."

(g) Calling evidence on behalf of person sought

See discussion under §2.4, "Comparison with Former Act," above and the commentary to s. 29, §3.1(d), "Significance of Change," and §4.2(b), "Analysis."

§5.0 CASE LAW

Argentina (Republic) v. Mellino (1987), 33 C.C.C. (3d) 334 (S.C.C.).
Artukovic v. Rison, 784 F.2d 1354 (U.S.C.A. 9th Cir.).
Australia v. Lau (2001), 149 B.C.A.C. 171 (B.C.C.A.).
Bingham v. Bradley, 241 U.S. 511.
Bourgeon v. Canada (Attorney General) (2000), 35 C.R. (5th) 25 (Ont. S.C.J.).
Canada v. Yang (September 25, 2000), (Ont. S.C.J.), affirmed (*sub nom. United States v. Yang*) (2001), 157 C.C.C. (3d) 225 (Ont. C.A.).
Cheng v. Hong Kong (December 17, 1992), Wright J. (Ont. Gen. Div.).
Elias v. Ramirez, 215 U.S. 398, 54 L. Ed. 253, 30 S. Ct. 131.
Fernandez v. Phillips, 268 U.S. 311.
Germany (Federal Republic) v. Ebke, [2001] 6 W.W.R. 517 (N.W.T.S.C.).
Germany (Federal Republic) v. Kretz (May 19, 1998), Doc. CA C26686, 1998 CarswellOnt 1999, [1998] O.J. No. 2062 (Ont. C.A.).
Glucksman v. Henkel, 221 U.S. 508 (U.S.S.C.).
India v. Singh (1996), 108 C.C.C. (3d) 274 (B.C.S.C.).
Italy (Republic) v. Piperno (1982), 66 C.C.C. (2d) 1 (S.C.C.).
McNamara v. Henkel, 226 U.S. 520, 57 L. Ed. 330, 33 Ct. 146.
Neely v. Henkel (No. 1), 180 U.S. 109, 45 L. Ed. 448, 21 S. Ct. 302 No. 387.
Netherlands (Kingdom) v. Clarkson (1998), 59 C.R.R. (2d) 178 (B.C. S.C. [In Chambers]), affirmed (2000), 146 C.C.C. (3d) 482 (B.C.C.A.), leave to appeal to S.C.C. refused (2000), 2000 CarswellBC 2445 (S.C.C.).

Nixon, Re (1984), 10 C.C.C. (3d) 376 (Ont. C.A.), leave to appeal to S.C.C. refused (1984), 55 N.R. 396n (S.C.C.).

Philippines (Republic) v. Pacificador (1993), 83 C.C.C. (3d) 210 (Ont. C.A.), leave to appeal to S.C.C. refused (1994), 87 C.C.C. (3d) vi (S.C.C.).

R. v. Arcuri (2001), 157 C.C.C. (3d) 21 (S.C.C.).

R. v. B. (K.G.) (1993), 79 C.C.C. (3d) 257 (S.C.C.).

R. v. Barranca (December 14, 1994), Keenan J., [1994] O.J. No. 3942 (Ont. Gen. Div.).

R. v. Cook (1998), 128 C.C.C. (3d) 1 (S.C.C.).

R. v. Khan (1990), 59 C.C.C. (3d) 92 (S.C.C.).

R. v. Reid (February 11, 1994), Corbett J. (Ont. Gen. Div.).

R. v. Salituro (1991), 68 C.C.C. (3d) 289 (S.C.C.).

R. v. Schmidt (1987), 33 C.C.C. (3d) 193 (S.C.C.).

R. v. Smith (1992), 75 C.C.C. (3d) 257 (S.C.C.).

R. v. Terry (1996), 106 C.C.C. (3d) 508 (S.C.C.).

R. v. Zingre (1981), 61 C.C.C. (3d) 465 (S.C.C.).

Romania (State) v. Cheng (1997), 114 C.C.C. (3d) 289 (N.S. S.C.), dismissed as moot (1997), 119 C.C.C. (3d) 561 (N.S. C.A.).

Schreiber v. Canada (Attorney General) (1998), 124 C.C.C. (3d) 129 (S.C.C.).

United States v. Adam (1999), 120 O.A.C. 271 (Ont. C.A.).

United States v. Ahluwalia (*sub nom. United States v. Ahluwalia and Sohal*) (December 1, 1995), Doc. Toronto E-15/93 (Ont. Gen. Div.).

United States v. Akrami, 2000 BCSC 1438, 2000 CarswellBC 1961 (B.C.S.C.).

United States v. Bray (1997), 97 O.A.C. 388 (Ont. C.A.), leave to appeal to S.C.C. refused (1997), 110 O.A.C. 399 (note) (S.C.C.).

United States v. Cotroni (1984), 38 C.R. (3d) 299 (Que. S.C.), reversed (1986), 53 C.R. (3d) 339 (Que. C.A.), reversed (1989), 48 C.C.C. (3d) 193 (S.C.C.).

United States v. Debarros (February 9, 2000), Doc. E-9/99, LaForme J. (Ont. S.C.J.).

United States v. Doan (April 22, 1996), Wein J. (Ont. Gen. Div.).

United States v. Down (1998), 124 C.C.C. (3d) 289 (Man. Q.B.).

United States v. Dries (November 20, 1997), Doc. CA C24507, 1997 CarswellOnt 4646 (Ont. C.A.).

United States v. Drysdale (2000), 32 C.R. (5th) 163 (Ont. S.C.J.).

United States v. Fox (January 29, 1987), Smith D.C.J. (Ont. Dist. Ct.), affirmed (*sub nom. R. v. Fox*) (May 20, 1987), Doc. 273/87 (Ont. C.A.).

United States v. Galanis, 429 F. Supp. 1215 (D.C. Tex.).

United States v. Kerslake (1996), 142 Sask. R. 112 (Sask. Q.B.).

United States v. Leon (1995), 96 C.C.C. (3d) 568 (Ont. C.A.), affirmed (1996), 105 C.C.C. (3d) 385 (S.C.C.).

United States v. Martinez (February 28, 2000), Doc. E24/99, 2000 CarswellOnt 561, [2000] O.J. No. 647 (Ont. S.C.J.).

United States v. Masini (September 15, 1995), Doc. E12/94, Keenan J. (Ont. Gen. Div.)

United States v. McVey (1992), 77 C.C.C. (3d) 1 (S.C.C.).

United States v. Miller (1991), 66 C.C.C. (3d) 20 (Ont. C.A.), leave to appeal to S.C.C. refused (1992), 69 C.C.C. (3d) vii (S.C.C.).

United States v. Ng (October 17, 1988), Trussler J. (Alta. Q.B.).

United States v. Ngai (August 4, 1995), Doc. E9/95 (Ont. Gen. Div.).

United States v. Palmer (January 23, 1996), Doc. E-20/94, Wein J. (Ont. Gen. Div.), appeal dismissed [1997] O.J. No. 608 (Ont. C.A.).

United States v. Palmucci (June 4, 2001), no. 500-36-002280-009, Boilard J. (Que. S.C.).

United States v. Quintin (2000), 4 Imm. L.R. (3d) 255 (Ont. S.C.J.).

United States v. Reid (May 23, 2000), Low J. (Ont. S.C.J.).

United States v. Shephard (1976), (*sub nom. United States v. Sheppard*) 30 C.C.C. (2d) 424 (S.C.C.).

United States v. Shulman (1998), 128 C.C.C. (3d) 475 (Ont. C.A.), reversed on other grounds (2001), 152 C.C.C. (3d) 294 (S.C.C.), reconsideration refused (June 14, 2001), Docs. 26912, 27610, 27774 (S.C.C.).

United States v. Singh (October 14, 1994), Doc. E-21, Ewaschuk J., [1994] O.J. No. 3941 (Ont. Gen. Div.).

United States v. Smith (1984), 10 C.C.C. (3d) 540 (Ont. C.A.), leave to appeal to S.C.C. refused (1984), 8 C.R.R. 245n (S.C.C.).

United States v. Soul (November 25, 1994), Chapnik J. (Ont. Gen. Div.), affirmed (February 17, 1995), Doc. CA C20236, [1994] O.J. No. 2838 (Ont. C.A.).

United States v. Wagner (1995), (*sub nom. R. v. Peters*) 104 C.C.C. (3d) 66 (B.C. C.A.), leave to appeal to S.C.C. refused (1996), 106 C.C.C. (3d) vi (note) (S.C.C.).

United States v. Wong (1995), 98 C.C.C. (3d) 332 (B.C. C.A.), leave to appeal to S.C.C. refused (1995), 101 C.C.C. (3d) vi (S.C.C.).

United States v. Yang. See *Canada v. Yang.*

Wacker v. Bisson, 370 F.2d 894.

Zanazanian v. United States, 729 F.2d 624 (9th Cir., 1984).

§6.0 RELATED SECTIONS

s. 29 — Order of Committal
Canada Evidence Act, s. 30 — Business Records

Evidence of Identity (s. 37)

§1.0 DESCRIPTION

Section 37 of the *Extradition Act* provides as follows:

EVIDENCE OF IDENTITY

37. The following are evidence that the person before the court is the person referred to in the order of arrest, the document that records the conviction or any other document that is presented to support the request:

(a) the fact that the name of the person before the court is similar to the name that is in the documents submitted by the extradition partner; and

(b) the fact that the physical characteristics of the person before the court are similar to those evidenced in a photograph, fingerprint or other description of the person.

Section 37 specifies two types of evidence for the purpose of establishing that the person before the court at an extradition hearing is the person referred to in the foreign document of arrest or conviction: firstly, similarities between the name of the person before the court and the name referred to in the documents submitted by the extradition partner (s. 37(a)); secondly, similarities between the physical characteristics of the person before the court and those contained in a photograph, fingerprint, or other description of the person (s. 37(b)).

§2.0 COMPARISON WITH FORMER ACT

Under the former extradition regime, the requesting state generally provided proof of the identity of the fugitive named in the warrant by including either a photograph or fingerprints of the individual in the authenticated documents sent for use at the extradition hearing. A comparison of the person before the court could then be made against the photograph or fingerprints provided. However, identity could be established without reference to either fingerprints or photographs if, as frequently occurred, the fugitive made a statement upon arrest by Canadian law enforcement officials implicating himself or herself in the crime for which extradition was sought. To be admissible, such a statement is required to meet Canadian admissibility requirements and therefore would be subject to a voir dire.

§3.0 SIGNIFICANCE OF CHANGE

The methods of proving identity referred to in the previous section will still pertain under the new *Extradition Act*. Additionally, however, it is clear that the new Act has endorsed the use of readily available information, such as similarities between the name of the person before the court and that referred to in the documents submitted by the extradition partner and similarities between the physical characteristics of the person before the court and those contained in photographs, fingerprints, or other descriptions of the person.

§4.0 ANALYSIS

§4.1 Establishing Identity By Way of Comparison of Names (s. 37(a))

Under s. 37(a), it appears that the presiding extradition judge is entitled to take judicial notice of the similarity between the name of the person before the court and the person named in the documents submitted in support of the extradition request.

§4.2 Establishing Identity By Way of Comparison of Physical Characteristics (s. 37(b))

British Columbia and Supreme Court of Canada jurisprudence has established that it is permissible for the judge to make a comparison of physical characteristics from the bench (see *United States v. Wong* (1995), 98 C.C.C. (3d) 332 (B.C. C.A.), leave to appeal to S.C.C. refused (1995), 101 C.C.C. (3d) vi (S.C.C.) and *R. v. Nikolovski* (1996), 111 C.C.C. (3d) 403 (S.C.C.). Notwithstanding these authorities, some judges have expressed discomfort in engaging directly in a matter of evidentiary proof such as establishing identity by comparison. In *United States v. Sanders* (March 18, 1996), (B.C. S.C.), Koenigsberg J. stated that she had been invited to, and did, make the comparison with the photograph herself. However, she added the following comment:

> However, the seeming inappropriateness of the proceeding should not be passed by without comment. First, I agreed to the procedure on the basis solely that just such a procedure had been employed in the British Columbia Supreme Court by judges in earlier extradition hearings. For example, specifically in *United States v. Wong*, Mr. Justice Holmes performed such an examination.

Although Koenigsberg J. followed this practice, she stated that she agreed with Holmes J., the extradition hearing judge in *United States v. Wong*, *supra*, that it was a "somewhat risky method to follow."

Indeed, there may be instances in which it would be preferable to call a witness with respect to physical comparison of the person before the court and the description of the person sought in the documentary material. This is true, for instance, when the comparison may involve close contact with and scrutiny of the person, such as the detection of scars, moles, or other similar features which may not be readily visible from the bench. (See the s. 29 commentary under §4.1(b)(ii), "Establishing identity" and §4.1(b)(iii), "Methods of establishing identity.")

§5.0 CASE LAW

R. v. Nikolovski (1996), 111 C.C.C. (3d) 403 (S.C.C.).
United States v. Sanders (March 18, 1996), Koenigsberg J. (B.C.S.C.).
United States v. Wong (1995), 98 C.C.C. (3d) 332 (B.C.C.A.), leave to appeal to
S.C.C. refused (1995), 101 C.C.C. (3d) vi (S.C.C.).

Judge's Report (s. 38)

§1.0 DESCRIPTION

Section 38 of the *Extradition Act* provides as follows:

REPORT OF THE JUDGE
    (1) A judge who issues an order of committal of a person to await surrender shall transmit to the Minister the following documents:

    (a) a copy of the order;
    (b) a copy of the evidence adduced at the hearing that has not already been transmitted to the Minister; and
    (c) any report that the judge thinks fit.

RIGHT TO APPEAL
    (2) When the judge orders the committal of a person, the judge shall inform the person that they will not be surrendered until after the expiry of 30 days and that the person has a right to appeal the order and to apply for judicial interim release.

Section 38(1) requires that a judge who commits a person for surrender to send to the Minister of Justice a copy of the committal order; a copy of the evidence adduced at the extradition hearing that has not already been transmitted to the Minister; and any report that the judge thinks fit.

Section 38(2) adds that the judge must inform the person that they will not be surrendered for 30 days and that they have a right to appeal the committal order (under s. 49 of the Act) and to apply for judicial interim release (under s. 18 of the Act).

§2.0 COMPARISON WITH FORMER ACT

Section 19 of the former *Extradition Act* was in all significant respects the same as s. 38. Section 19 read as follows:

    19. The judge who commits a fugitive to prison shall, on the committal,

(a) inform the fugitive that the fugitive will not be surrendered until after the expiration of thirty days and has a right to appeal the committal; and

(b) transmit to the Minister of Justice a certificate of the committal, with a copy of all the evidence taken before the judge not already so transmitted, and such report on the case as the judge thinks fit.

§3.0 SIGNIFICANCE OF CHANGE

The only change between s. 38 and s. 19 of the former Act is that the judge, in addition to advising the person of his or her right to appeal, must now also indicate that the person can apply for judicial interim release.

§4.0 ANALYSIS

In addition to a copy of the committal order and a copy of evidence adduced at the extradition hearing that has not already been transmitted to the Minister of Justice, s. 38(1) permits the extradition judge to transmit to the Minister "any report that the judge thinks fit." This provision is significant because it enables the extradition judge to add any comments regarding the case that the judge believes are appropriate and relevant to the Minister's surrender decision.

§5.0 RELATED SECTIONS

s. 18 — Judicial Interim Release
s. 49 — Right of Appeal Against Committal Order

Property (s. 39)

§1.0 DESCRIPTION

Section 39 of the *Extradition Act* provides as follows:

PROPERTY SEIZED
39. (1) Subject to a relevant extradition agreement, a judge who makes an order of committal may order that any thing that was seized when the person was arrested and that may be used in the prosecution of the person for the offence for which the extradition was requested be transferred to the extradition partner at the time the person is surrendered.

CONDITIONS OF ORDER
(2) The judge may include in the order any conditions that the judge considers desirable, including conditions

(a) respecting the preservation and return to Canada of a thing; and

(b) respecting the protection of the interests of third parties.

Section 39(1) empowers the extradition judge, upon committing a person for surrender, to order that any seized property be turned over to the extradition partner. Certain criteria must be met for the judge to order the turning over of property: the property must have been seized at the time of the person's arrest and it must be potentially relevant to the prosecution of the person for the offence for which extradition was requested. The latter point appears to limit the scope of the provision to evidence, that is, the provision does not appear to extend to proceeds of crime.

Section 39(2) enables the judge to add to the order "any conditions that the judge considers desirable." In particular, paras. (a) and (b) state that the judge may add conditions respecting the following matters: the preservation and return to Canada of the property; the protection of third party interests.

§2.0 COMPARISON WITH FORMER ACT

In spirit and intent, s. 39 of the new Act is similar to s. 27 of the former Act. Section 27 provided as follows:

> Everything found in the possession of the fugitive at the time of his arrest that may be material as evidence in making proof of the crime may be delivered up with the fugitive on his surrender, subject to all rights of third persons with regard thereto.

Section 27 did not state who had the authority to order the surrender of property. In *Re Borovsky & Weinbaum, Ex parte Salaman*, [1902] 2 K.B. 312, at p. 315, the English Court of Appeal, referring to a similar provision in the English legislation, held that the extradition hearing judge had authority over this decision. This position was also supported in *United States v. Tounder* (1914), 23 C.C.C. 76 (N.S. Co. Ct.), in which the court implicitly accepted that it was the extradition judge who would make the decision regarding the surrender of the property. However, in *R. v. Lushington* (1893), [1894] 1 Q.B. 420 (Eng. Q.B.) at p. 424), the English Court of Appeal found that once the extradition hearing judge had committed the fugitive for surrender, she or he was *functus officio* and no longer had authority to order the surrender of property.

Section 39 of the new Act, while similar in intent and effect to s. 27, is more comprehensively drafted. Section 39(1) specifies that the judge who orders committal is the person with the authority to order that seized property be surrendered to the extradition partner. Section 39(2) sets out the purposes for which conditions may be attached to the surrender of the property.

§3.0 SIGNIFICANCE OF CHANGE AND ANALYSIS

Section 39 of the new Act explicitly confers on the extradition judge the power to surrender property, eliminating a source of ambiguity that existed under s. 27 of the former Act. The judge has the authority to impose any conditions that are deemed desirable including conditions relating to the return of the property to Canada and the protection of third parties.

Requests made to Canada to gather evidence for use in a foreign prosecution are most often dealt with by recourse to the *Mutual Legal Assistance in Criminal Matters Act*, which provides a wide range of measures with regard to the provision of mutual legal assistance. The *Mutual Legal Assistance in Criminal Matters Act*, however (save in the case of requests from the International Criminal Tribunals for Rwanda and the former Yugoslavia), can only be used to gather evidence on behalf of a country with which Canada has a treaty on mutual legal assistance or with which Canada has entered into a case specific administrative arrangement pursuant to s. 6 of the Act. Section 39 of the *Extradition Act* may be resorted to by extradition partners that have no treaty with Canada on mutual legal assistance, although unlike the provisions of the *Mutual Legal Assistance in Criminal Matters Act*, s. 39 is limited by its terms to property seized at the time of the person's arrest.

Many of Canada's extradition treaties contain provisions relating to the surrender of property seized from the person who is being extradited. For instance, Article 15 of the *Canada–United States Treaty* provides:

> (1) To the extent permitted under the law of the requested State and subject to the rights of third parties, which shall be duly respected, all articles acquired as a result of the offense or which may be required as evidence shall, if found, be surrendered to the requesting State if extradition is granted.

> (2) Subject to the qualifications of paragraph (1) of this Article, the above-mentioned articles shall be returned to the requesting State even if the extradition, having been agreed to, cannot be carried out owing to the death or escape of the person sought.

The provisions of s. 39 give precedence to the terms of an extradition agreement over those of the Act in regard to the surrender of seized property.

In effect, the provisions of s. 39 are akin to the sending hearing provisions of s. 15 (which deal with evidence obtained pursuant to execution of a search warrant) and s. 20 (which deals with evidence obtained pursuant to subpoena-like evidence gathering orders) of the *Mutual Legal Assistance in Criminal Matters Act*. Under those sections, evidence obtained in Canada may be authorized by the court to be sent to the requesting jurisdiction. Like s. 39, such orders can be subject to the imposition of terms for the protection of the interests of third parties or for the subsequent return of the property. The *Mutual Legal Assistance in Criminal Matters Act* contains no specific provision for the giving of notice to persons who may claim an interest in any record or thing which may be subject to an application for a sending order. Rather the giving of notice is a matter left to the discretion of the judge hearing the application (see *United Kingdom v. James and Boyden, (sub nom. United Kingdom v. Ramsden)* (1996), 108 C.C.C. (3d) 289 (Ont. C.A.)). Presumably the same discretion to give notice to third parties who may have an interest in the property would operate in the case of a judge hearing an application for a transfer of property order under s. 39 of the *Extradition Act.*

§4.0 CASE LAW

Borovsky & Weinbaum Re, Ex parte Salaman, [1902] 2 K.B. 312 (C.A.).
R. v. Lushington (1893), [1894] 1 Q.B. 420.
United Kingdom v. James and Boyden, (sub nom. United Kingdom v. Ramsden) (1996), 108 C.C.C. (3d) 289 (Ont. C.A.).
United States v. Tounder (1914), 23 C.C.C. 76 (N.S. Co. Ct.).

§5.0 RELATED SECTIONS

Canada–United States Extradition Treaty, Article 15
Mutual Legal Assistance in Criminal Matters Act, ss. 20–21

Powers of Minister (ss. 40–42) and Submissions to Minister (s. 43)

§1.0 DESCRIPTION

§1.1 General Power to Order Surrender (s. 40(1))

Section 40(1) of the *Extradition Act* provides as follows:

SURRENDER
   40. (1) The Minister may, within a period of 90 days after the date of a person's committal to await surrender, personally order that the person be surrendered to the extradition partner.

Section 40(1) sets out in general terms the discretionary power of the Minister of Justice to order the surrender of persons sought for extradition.

§1.2 Impact of Refugee Claims (s. 40(2))

Section 40(2) of the *Extradition Act* provides as follows:

WHEN REFUGEE CLAIM

(2) Before making an order under subsection (1) with respect to a person who has claimed Convention refugee status under section 44 of the *Immigration Act*, the Minister shall consult with the minister responsible for that Act.

If the person sought has claimed refugee status in Canada, s. 40(2) requires the Minister of Justice to consult with the Minister of Citizenship and Immigration before making a surrender order under s. 40(1).

§1.3 Power of Minister to Seek Assurances and Conditions (s. 40(3) and (4))

Section 40(3) and (4) of the *Extradition Act* provide as follows:

POWERS OF THE MINISTER

(3) The Minister may seek any assurances that the Minister considers appropriate from the extradition partner, or may subject the surrender to any conditions that the Minister considers appropriate, including a condition that the person not be prosecuted, nor that a sentence be imposed on or enforced against the person, in respect of any offence or conduct other than that referred to in the order of surrender.

NO SURRENDER

(4) If the Minister subjects surrender of a person to assurances or conditions, the order of surrender shall not be executed until the Minister is satisfied that the assurances are given or the conditions agreed to by the extradition partner.

Section 40(3) permits the Minister of Justice to seek assurances from the extradition partner and to make the surrender order subject to any conditions that the Minister deems appropriate. Section 40(3) makes specific reference to conditions that relate to the rule of specialty. The rule of specialty provides that a surrendered person cannot be tried or sentenced for an offence with respect to which extradition has not been ordered.

If the Minister does seek assurances or attach conditions, s. 40(4) permits the Minister to delay the surrender until the assurances have been given and the conditions agreed to by the extradition partner.

§1.4 Extension of Time for Minister's Surrender Decision (s. 40(5) and (6))

Section 40(5) and (6) of the *Extradition Act* provide as follows:

EXTENSION OF TIME

(5) If the person has made submissions to the Minister under section 43 and the Minister is of the opinion that further time is needed to act on those submissions, the Minister may extend the period referred to in subsection (1) as follows:

>   **(a) if the person is the subject of a request for surrender by the International Criminal Court, and an issue has been raised as to the admissibility of the case or the jurisdiction of that Court, for a period ending not more than 45 days after the Court's ruling on the issue; or**

>   **(b) in any other case, for one additional period that does not exceed 60 days.**

NOTICE OF EXTENSION OF TIME

(6) If an appeal has been filed under section 50 and the Minister has extended the period referred to in subsection (1), the Minister shall file with the court of appeal a notice of extension of time before the expiry of that period.

Section 40(5)(b) provides the Minister of Justice with the discretion to extend the period for making the surrender decision by an extra 60 days beyond the 90-day period provided for in s. 40(1).

Where a person is sought by the International Criminal Court and the person questions the admissibility of the case before that court or that court's jurisdiction, s. 40(5)(a) allows the Minister to await the decision of the International Criminal Court on the issue raised, and then permits the Minister a further 45 days in which to act.

If the person sought has filed a notice of appeal of the extradition judge's order of committal under s. 50 and the Minister has opted for a 60-day extension under s. 40(5), s. 40(6) provides that the Minister must file a notice of extension of time with the court of appeal before the expiry of the initial 90-day surrender period provided for in s. 40(1).

§1.5 Power of Minister to Postpone Surrender Decision Until After Appeal of Extradition Judge's Committal Order (s. 41)

Section 41 of the *Extradition Act* provides as follows:

WHEN APPEAL PENDING

41. (1) The Minister may postpone the making of the order of surrender if

>   **(a) an appeal has been filed under section 50;**

  (b) the Minister files a notice of postponement with the court of appeal before the expiry of the period referred to in subsection 40(1); and

  (c) the order is made not later than 45 days after the date of the decision of the court of appeal

No further deferral of appeal
(2) When the Minister has filed a notice of postponement with the court of appeal under paragraph (1)(b), that court may not defer the hearing of the appeal under subsection 51(2).

Section 41(1) allows the Minister of Justice to postpone the surrender decision until after a decision is rendered in an appeal of the extradition judge's committal decision. In order for the Minister to rely on this provision, the following conditions must be met: an appeal has been filed by the person sought pursuant to s. 50; the Minister has filed a notice of postponement with the court of appeal prior to the completion of the 90-day period for the Minister's surrender decision set out in s. 40(1); and the Minister makes the surrender decision no later than 45 days after the decision of the court of appeal.

Section 41(2) provides that, where the Minister of Justice has filed a notice of postponement, the court of appeal may not resort to s. 51(2). Section 51(2) allows the court of appeal to defer an appeal of an extradition judge's committal order until after the Minister has made a decision regarding surrender.

§1.6 Minister's Power to Amend Surrender Order (s. 42)

Section 42 of the *Extradition Act* provides as follows:

Amendments
42. The Minister may amend a surrender order at any time before its execution.

§1.7 Submissions to Minister (s. 43)

Section 43 of the *Extradition Act* provides as follows:

Submissions
43. (1) The person may, at any time before the expiry of 30 days after the date of the committal, make submissions to the Minister in respect of any ground that would be relevant to the Minister in making a decision in respect of the surrender of the person.

Late acceptance of submissions
(2) The Minister may accept submissions even after the expiry of those 30 days in circumstances that the Minister considers appropriate.

Section 43(1) provides the person sought with the right to make submissions to the Minister of Justice on grounds relevant to the Minister's surrender decision within the 30 days following the extradition judge's order of committal. Section 43(2) provides the Minister with the discretion to extend the 30-day time limit for making submissions.

§2.0 COMPARISON WITH FORMER ACT

§2.1 General Power to Order Surrender (s. 40(1))

The comparable provision of the former *Extradition Act* was s. 25(1), which gave the Minister the authority upon the requisition of the foreign state to order the surrender of the fugitive to named persons within 90 days of the fugitive's committal. In contrast with s. 25(1), the power of the Minister to order surrender under s. 40(1) does not refer to the requirement of a requisition from the foreign state. The time period within which the Minister may make the surrender order remains the same as in the former Act, that being 90 days, subject to extensions. Section 58(e) of the new Act specifies that the surrender order must designate the person or class of persons authorized to receive a surrendered person. The option of designating a class of persons rather than named individuals is a new feature. Section 58 sets out in detail the contents of the surrender order. The contents of the surrender order were not detailed in the former Act.

§2.2 Impact of Refugee Claims (s. 40(2))

The former *Extradition Act* did not contain a provision similar to s. 40(2) of the new Act. Nonetheless, under the former Act, it was not unusual for extradition proceedings and immigration proceedings with respect to the same person to proceed in tandem. This raised issues regarding the interaction between the two types of proceedings and concerns such as those expressed by Campbell J. of the Ontario Court (General Division) in *Bembenek v. Canada (Minister of Employment & Immigration* (1991), 69 C.C.C. (3d) 34. Bembenek had been convicted of murder in the United States and subsequently fled to Canada. Immigration proceedings were undertaken in an effort to deport her to the United States. When she unexpectedly obtained bail on the immigration matters, she was arrested pursuant to an extradition warrant. Bembenek brought a *habeas corpus* application alleging that the immigration proceedings were a sham and a disguised form of extradition. Campbell J. dismissed the *habeas corpus* application. However, in the course of his reasons, at p. 48, he expressed concern at the lack of guidance regarding the relationship and interaction between the two types of proceedings:

> It is a matter of particular concern that the government is proceeding with the immigration proceedings at the very same time it proceeds against the applicant on the

extradition proceedings. Counsel for the Minister takes the position that the deportation and extradition should both proceed at the same time. Counsel was unable to say which proceedings will go first, which proceedings will take precedence, or which proceedings would defer to the other. The position, that both would proceed simultaneously, poses obvious practical problems. It aggravates the multiplicity of proceedings when the applicant has to face two simultaneous attacks on her presence in the country by two separate branches of the government at the very same time with no hint how the two simultaneous proceedings are intended to interact and no assurance that the practical problems of multiplicity have been or will be considered.

In *Argentina (Republic) v. Mellino* (1987), 33 C.C.C. (3d) 334 (S.C.C.), although it does not appear to have been raised as an issue for argument, it was noted, at p. 342, in the reasons of La Forest J. that Mellino had claimed and been granted refugee status:

> Mellino then applied for convention refugee status under the *Immigration Act*, and was granted that status on December 1, 1983. However, from some time during the spring of 1983 up to the first half of 1984, meetings were held between officials of the Department of Justice of Canada regarding the preparation of evidence in a form admissible in a Canadian extradition hearing.

Mellino was sought to stand trial for murder in Argentina. The issue before the Supreme Court was whether the 17-month delay between Mellino's discharge on a first extradition request and the institution of proceedings as a result of a second extradition request was unreasonable and contrary to the *Charter*. The court determined that the extradition proceedings did not violate the *Charter* and could proceed. The matter of his status as a refugee claimant does not appear to have been raised as an issue before the court. However, in the reasons of the court, there is no indication that Mellino's refugee status, of which the court was clearly aware, was any impediment to the institution of the extradition proceedings.

In the more recent case of *Pacificador v. Canada (Minister of Justice)* (1999), (*Sub nom. Philippines (Republic) v. Pacificador*) 60 C.R.R. (2d) 126 (Ont. Gen. Div.), Dambrot J. had occasion to consider whether a refugee claim precluded a person's extradition. He held that it did not and stated, at p. 171:

> [I]n *Argentina v. Mellino*, supra, the fact that the respondent had been granted refugee status (see pp. 265-66 C.R.R, p. 342 C.C.C.) did not prevent the Supreme Court from allowing an appeal by Argentina and ordering an extradition judge to continue the extradition proceedings brought against the respondent.

In this case, Dambrot J. was reviewing the decision of the Minister of Justice to surrender the fugitive to the Philippines. The fugitive, a Marcos supporter, was sought for the alleged murder of an Aquino supporter during the 1986 presidential election in the Philippines. The fugitive entered Canada as a refugee claimant on October 9, 1987. He was arrested on an extradition warrant on November 12, 1991. On April

28, 1991, in a split decision, the fugitive passed the "credible basis" hearing that is required in order to be given a hearing to determine refugee status. A hearing to determine refugee status had not been held as of the time of the Minister's surrender decision.

As indicated above, Dambrot J. determined that a fugitive can be ordered surrendered even when a refugee claim is outstanding. He noted that refugee and extradition law are significantly different, pointing out that Canadian citizens, who have a constitutional right to remain in Canada, are subject to extradition. He held, at pp. 170–171, that:

> Convention refugees, whose right to remain in Canada is found in the *Immigration Act*, and not in the *Charter*: see *Singh v. Canada (Minister of Employment & Immigration)*, [1985] 1 S.C.R. 177 at 189, (1985), 14 C.R.R. 13 at p. 34 can have no greater immunity from extradition. While s. 7 of the *Charter* may preclude extradition of Convention refugees in certain circumstances, a decision made under the *Immigration Act* cannot.
>
> An examination of the pertinent provisions of the *Immigration Act* confirms that the conferring of refugee status does not preclude extradition. First, s. 2(1) of the Act excludes from the definition of Convention refugee a person who has committed a serious non-political crime outside the country of refuge prior to admission. What is more important, s. 4(2.1) of the Act explicitly provides that the right of a Convention refugee to remain in Canada is "[s]ubject to any other Act of Parliament." The *Extradition Act*, of course is another Act of Parliament.

§2.3 Power of Minister to Seek Assurances and Conditions (s. 40(3) and (4))

The former *Extradition Act* did not provide for attaching conditions or seeking assurances as a condition precedent to surrender, although treaties often did. The new Act in s. 40(3), in addition to providing the Minister with the general authority to attach conditions or require assurances, also cites the rule of specialty as an appropriate condition to attach to a surrender order. The rule of specialty provides that a surrendered person cannot be tried or sentenced for an offence with respect to which extradition has not been ordered. This provision was not addressed in the former Act.

Section 33 of the former Act applied the rule of specialty to a person returned to Canada as a result of a Canadian extradition request to another country. Canada's extradition treaties also provide for the rule of specialty to apply (see, for example, Article XV of the *Canada–Mexico Extradition Treaty* and Article 12 of the *Canada–United States Extradition Treaty*).

§2.4 Extension of Time for Minister's Surrender Decision (s. 40(5) and (6))

Section 40(5) and (6) of the new *Extradition Act* are similar in effect to s. 25(2) and (3) of the former Act. They provide for an extension of the time within which the

Minister's surrender decision is to be made and require such an extension of time to be communicated to the Court of Appeal if an appeal from committal is outstanding.

§2.5 Power of Minister to Postpone Surrender Decision Until After Appeal of Extradition Judge's Committal Order (s. 41)

Section 41 of the new *Extradition Act* is identical to s. 25.1 of the former Act.

§2.6 Minister's Power to Amend Surrender Order (s. 42)

The former *Extradition Act* did not contain a similar provision to s. 42 of the new Act.

§2.7 Submissions to Minister (s. 43)

The comparable provision in the former *Extradition Act* to s. 43 was s. 19.1. As with s. 43 of the new Act, s. 19.1 provided fugitives sought with the right to make submissions to the Minister within 30 days of the committal order or after that time period within the Minister's discretion. The only difference between the two sections was that the right to make submissions to the Minister under the former Act had to be brought to the attention of the fugitive at the extradition hearing. Under s. 19.1(2), the extradition judge was required to inform the fugitive of this right at the commencement of the hearing.

§3.0 SIGNIFICANCE OF CHANGE

§3.1 General Power to Order Surrender (s. 40(1))

The requirement in s. 25(1) of the former *Extradition Act* of a requisition from the foreign state was designed to ensure that persons would not be surrendered without a formal extradition request from the foreign state. The modes of requisition were set out in s. 20(1) of the former Act. Under the new *Extradition Act*, the extradition process is commenced through the issuance by the Minister of Justice of an authority to proceed (s. 15). The Minister can only issue an authority to proceed after an extradition request has been received from a foreign jurisdiction (s. 15). Therefore, an extradition request, or requisition, is required under the new Act prior to the commencement of extradition proceedings. This makes it unnecessary to require a requisition in s. 40(1). Although the former Act did not require an extradition request until surrender, Canada's extradition treaties generally provide that a request is to be sent through diplomatic channels and accompanied by documentation required for committal at an extradition hearing (see, for example, Article 9 of the *Canada–United States Extradition Treaty*).

§3.2 Impact of Refugee Claims (s. 40(2))

Section 40(2) of the new *Extradition Act* requires, as a condition precedent to surrender, that the Minister of Justice consult with the Minister of Citizenship and Immigration when the person sought for extradition is also a refugee claimant

Ms. Eleni Bakopanos, Parliamentary Secretary to the Minister of Justice and Attorney General of Canada, described the intention behind the modification to the *Extradition Act* (and the related amendments to the *Immigration Act*) while introducing Bill C-40 (now the *Extradition Act*) to the House of Commons on second reading (*House of Commons Debates*, October 8, 1998, 1st Session, 36th Parliament, v. 135, pp. 9004–9005):

> Finally, the proposed legislation also seeks to harmonize the extradition and refugee processes, as conflict may arise when someone subject to an extradition request makes a claim for refugee status.

> Thus, Bill C-40 modifies the *Extradition Act* and the *Immigration Act* in order to avoid duplication of decision making and to limit delay in the extradition process. The legislation also provides a means for consultation between the Minister of Justice and the Minister of Citizenship and Immigration in such matters.

> More specifically, the *Immigration Act* would be modified to provide that if extradition proceedings have been initiated for an offence punishable in Canada by a maximum of 10 years' imprisonment or more and that person has claimed refugee status, a hearing by the convention refugee determination division of the Immigration and Refugee Board shall not be commenced or shall be adjourned until a final decision on extradition is rendered.

> If the decision is made not to extradite the person, the convention refugee determination division hearing may commence or resume.

> If the person is committed for extradition by an extradition judge and ordered surrendered by the Minister of Justice, the order of surrender is deemed to be a decision by the CRDD that the person is not a convention refugee because of the evidentiary grounds presented in the extradition case of a serious non-political offence.

> This is in keeping with the exclusion on grounds of serious non-political crimes provided by article 1F(b) of the Refugee Convention to which Canada is bound.

Under the former *Extradition Act*, as indicated in *Pacificador v. Canada (Minister of Justice), supra*, there was no requirement for the Minister of Justice and the Minister of Citizenship and Immigration to consult. However, it was recognized that the refugee status of a fugitive would be a consideration that might have an impact on the Minister of Justice's surrender decision. Section 40(2) of the new Act goes further, by mandating consultation, and thereby requiring that the Minister of Justice consider the refugee status of a person sought. The *Extradition Act* gives the force of domestic law to the principles recognized by Dambrot J. in *Pacificador v. Canada (Minister of Justice)* with respect to the Minister of Justice's duty to consider refugee status. Dambrot J. made the point as follows, at p. 171:

> This is not to say that the fact that a refugee claim has been made, and the circumstances underlying the claim, are not relevant considerations when a Minister of Justice is deciding whether to surrender a fugitive. The actual conferring of refugee status, moreover, would undoubtedly be a most powerful consideration. The Convention, and the *Charter*, oblige a minister to consider the matter, and decide whether surrender would, as a result, be unacceptable. That decision, in turn, is susceptible to judicial review. This is precisely the approach adopted by the Court of Appeal in analogous circumstances in *Hurley*. Accordingly, I reject the submission that the minister was precluded from ordering surrender while the applicant's refugee claim was outstanding.

It is significant to note that section 96 of the new *Extradition Act* contains significant related amendments to the *Immigration Act*. Section 96 reads as follows:

> 96. Section 69.1 of the *Immigration Act* is amended by adding the following after subsection (11):
>
> (12) If an authority to proceed has been issued under section 15 of the *Extradition Act* with respect to a person for an offence under Canadian law that is punishable under an Act of Parliament by a maximum term of imprisonment of 10 years or more, a hearing under subsection (1) or (2) shall not be commenced with respect to the person, or if commenced, shall be adjourned, until the final decision under that Act with respect to the discharge or surrender of the person has been made.
>
> (13) If the person is finally discharged under the *Extradition Act*, the hearing may be commenced or continued, or the Refugee Division may proceed, as though there had not been any proceedings under the *Extradition Act*.
>
> (14) If the person is ordered surrendered by the Minister of Justice under the *Extradition Act* and the offence for which the person was committed by the judge under section 29 of that Act is punishable under an Act of Parliament by a maximum term of imprisonment of 10 years or more, the order of surrender is deemed to be a decision by the Refugee Division that the person is not a Convention refugee because of paragraph (b) of Section F of its Article 1, except that no appeal or judicial review of the decision shall be permitted except to the extent that a judicial review of the order of surrender is provided for under the *Extradition Act*.
>
> (15) For greater certainty, if the person has not made a claim under section 44 before the order or surrender referred to in subsection (14), the person may not do so before the surrender.

For an offence that in Canada would attract a punishment of imprisonment of ten years or more, or some greater sentence, the effect of these amendments is to prevent the commencement, or require the adjournment, of a refugee hearing until a discharge or surrender order has been made under the *Extradition Act*. A surrender order in such an instance is deemed to be a decision of the Refugee Board that the person is not a Convention refugee. This deeming provision appears to take into account the provision of the Convention that states that the Convention does not apply to a person who is considered to have committed a serious offence outside the country of refuge. A person who has not made a refugee claim before the order of surrender is precluded from doing so after the order. Given the effect that the Minister's surrender decision has upon the refugee determination process under the new *Extradition Act*, the requirement of consultation under s. 40(2) of the new Act is perhaps understandable.

For an offence that in Canada would attract a punishment of less than ten years' imprisonment, the commencement of extradition proceedings does not have the effect of holding the refugee determination process in abeyance. It would appear that the two proceedings can co-exist. Consultation between the Minister of Justice and the Minister of Citizenship and Immigration is still required and it appears that in this situation, extradition will take priority in the event that the Minister of Justice orders surrender. This position is supported by the fact that there is no specific provision in the new *Extradition Act* precluding surrender in these circumstances. Section 64 delays the effect of a surrender order when there is an outstanding domestic charge or sentence to be served, unless the Minister of Justice orders otherwise. The absence of a similar provision dealing with immigration proceedings suggests that the Minister's surrender order takes effect regardless of ongoing immigration refugee proceedings.

§3.3 Power of Minister to Seek Assurances and Conditions (s. 40(3) and (4))

The power of the Minister of Justice to make provision for the rule of specialty and to require other assurances or conditions has in the past generally been dealt with by treaty. Section 40(3) and (4) mean that this power is now part of Canada's domestic extradition law.

§3.4 Extension of Time for Minister's Surrender Decision (s. 40(5) and (6))

Section 40(5) and (6) of the new *Extradition Act* have not effected any change from the former Act. See §2.4, *supra*.

§3.5 Power of Minister to Postpone Surrender Decision Until After Appeal of Extradition Judge's Committal Order (s. 41)

The former Act did not contain a provision similar to s. 41 of the new *Extradition Act*.

§3.6 Minister's Power to Amend Surrender Order (s. 42)

The former Act did not contain a provision similar to s. 42 of the new *Extradition Act*.

§3.7 Submissions to Minister (s. 43)

Under s. 19.1(2) of the former *Extradition Act*, the failure to notify the fugitive at the commencement of the extradition hearing of the right to make submissions to the Minister of Justice was considered a technicality of no consequence. (See *United States v. Leon* (1995), 96 C.C.C. (3d) 568 (Ont. C.A.), affirmed on other issues (1996), 105 C.C.C. (3d) 385 (S.C.C.).) Under the new *Extradition Act*, notification of this right at the commencement of the extradition hearing is unnecessary.

§4.0 ANALYSIS

§4.1 General Power to Order Surrender (s. 40(1))

Under the new *Extradition Act*, just as under the former Act, the ministerial phase of the extradition process involves the exercise of executive discretion by the Minister of Justice as to whether persons sought for extradition, against whom an extradition judge has issued an order of committal during the judicial phase of the process, should be surrendered to the extradition partner. The decision in the judicial phase of the extradition process is clearly judicial in nature and warrants the application of the complete range of procedural rights. By contrast, the ministerial phase of the extradition process requires the Minister to make a decision that is largely political in nature. The Minister must weigh the representations of the person sought against Canada's international obligations. As put by La Forest J. in *R. v. Schmidt* (1987), 33 C.C.C. (3d) 193 (S.C.C.), at p. 215, the Minister's decision involves "the good faith and honour of this country in its relations with other states."

The nature of the Minister of Justice's obligations at the surrender stage of the extradition process was succinctly set out by the Ontario Court of Appeal in *United States v. Whitley* (1994), 94 C.C.C. (3d) 99 (Ont. C.A.), at p. 113, affirmed (1996), 104 C.C.C. (3d) 447 (S.C.C.):

The Minister's surrender decision is political in nature, not judicial. It lies at the legislative end of the spectrum of administrative decision-making. The Minister is obligated to ensure that a fugitive has adequate disclosure of the case against him and a reasonable opportunity to state his or her own case. The Minister, however, is not obligated to hold an oral hearing nor is he required to provide the kind of disclosure or the kind of procedural safeguards applicable in judicial proceedings. He is not bound by the record before the extradition judge but may consider other material relevant to the exercise of his discretion, and he is not even obligated to provide detailed reasons for his decision though he certainly did so in this case: *Kindler v. Canada, supra, Idziak v. Canada (Minister of Justice)* (1992), 77 C.C.C. (3d) 65, 97 D.L.R. (4th) 577, 12 C.R.R. (2d) 77 (S.C.C.).

From the above decision, it is apparent that the Minister of Justice's surrender decision must be made within the following parameters:

- The Minister is required to give the fugitive a reasonable opportunity to state his or her case.

- The Minister is required to consider submissions submitted by counsel. The submissions are usually written. Consideration of oral submissions is within the discretion of the Minister.

- The Minister is not bound by the record that was before the extradition judge. The Minister may consider other relevant material.

- The Minister is required to provide disclosure sufficient for the fugitive to know the case against him or her.

- The Minister is not required to provide the kind of disclosure that would be expected in judicial proceedings.

- The Minister is not required to give detailed reasons for his or her decision.

§4.2 Impact of Refugee Claims (s. 40(2))

It is apparent that the new *Extradition Act* envisages the communication of information between the Minister of Justice and the Minister of Citizenship and Immigration. However, the exact nature of this interchange is not clear. The new Act does not specify what input the Minister of Citizenship and Immigration is supposed to provide to the Minister of Justice. The consultation between the Ministers could include those matters within the expertise of the Minister of Citizenship and Immigration. This would presumably include the meaning of the terminology contained in the Convention refugee definition in s. 2(1)(a) of the *Immigration Act*, which involves terms such as race, religion, nationality, membership in a particular social group or political opinion. These factors, among others, are included in s. 44(1)(b) of the *Extradition Act* and provide reasons for the Minister of Justice to refuse surrender. The origin of s. 44(1)(b) was described by Ms. Eleni Bakopanos, Parliamentary Secretary to the Minister of Justice and Attorney General of Canada, while introducing Bill C-40 (now the *Extradition Act*) to the House of Commons on second reading (*House of Commons Debates*, October 8, 1998, 1st Session, 36th Parliament, v. 135, pp. 9004–9005):

> Where a person could face prosecution or punishment because of a prohibited ground of discrimination, the clause we chose was directly taken from the United Nations model treaty on extradition. The U.N. treaty provides greater protection than exists in most bilateral treaties.

When the extradition partner is the country from which the person sought is seeking refuge, the Minister of Justice may also wish to obtain from the Minister of Citizenship and Immigration information pertaining to human rights conditions in that country.

In requiring consultation with the Minister of Citizenship and Immigration, s. 40(2) recognizes that the status of the refugee claim may have an impact on the extradition proceedings or on the view the Minister of Justice takes regarding the appropriateness of surrender. The expertise of the Minister of Citizenship and Immigration may provide information that would assist the Minister of Justice in deciding whether to surrender and, if the Minister decides in favour of surrender, whether to attach conditions or seek assurances. Indeed, deciding on the possible need for assurances or conditions may be one of the prime factors to which the consultation process in s. 40(2) is directed, given its placement in the Act. The following provision, s. 40(3), provides the Minister with the authority to seek assurances or attach conditions regarding the surrender.

It is possible that the person sought will be the subject of an extradition request from a country other than the country that is the subject of the refugee claim. In that case, persons sought may seek assurances from the Minister of Justice that, upon completing a sentence in the requesting jurisdiction, they will not be returned to the country with respect to which they claim to have a well-founded fear of persecution. For example, a person might be extradited to the United States and have an ongoing refugee claim before the Immigration and Refugee Board against Iran, the person's country of nationality. Such a person may seek assurances from the Minister of Justice that, upon being surrendered to the American authorities and completing the sentence in the United States, he or she will not be turned over to Iranian officials. The structure of the Act is such that this type of assurance may be a possibility, at least with respect to offences which in Canada would not be subject to a term of imprisonment of ten years or more.

For offences carrying a term of imprisonment of ten years or more, or a more severe punishment, a surrender order under the *Extradition Act* deems the person sought not to be a refugee. With such offences, conditions concerning what happens to the person after serving any sentence in the requesting state are unlikely to be sought. This is because, insofar as Canada is concerned, the person's status as a potential Convention refugee claimant has been determined against him or her. The distinction between offences carrying more or less than ten years' imprisonment stems from section 96 of the *Extradition Act*. Section 96 made related amendments to the *Immigration Act*. One of the effects of these amendments was to oust the jurisdiction of the Immigration and Refugee Board in respect of persons whose extradition has been sought for offences that, in Canada, would be punishable by imprisonment of ten years or more, or a more severe punishment.

Section 96 may lead to substantive arguments about a conflict with the Supreme Court of Canada's decision in *Singh v. Canada (Minister of Employment & Immigration)*, [1985] 1 S.C.R. 177, and with recent pronouncements of the Supreme Court with respect to the refugee process. The Supreme Court in *Singh v. Canada (Minister of Employment & Immigration)* found need for refugee claimants to have an oral hearing for a proper determination of whether or not the person is a Convention refugee. In this regard, the Supreme Court has taken an absolutist position with respect to the principles of fundamental justice. There are comments in the recent case of *Pushpanathan v. Canada (Minister of Employment & Immigration)*, [1998] 1 S.C.R. 982 (S.C.C.), amended [1998] 1 S.C.R. 1222 (S.C.C.), which indicate that the court has not retrenched from its earlier position. Although *Pushpanathan v. Canada (Minister of Employment & Immigration)* did not deal with the issue of an oral hearing for Convention refugee claimants, several of the judges commented on the need for such a hearing, even in cases where the refugee was considered to be a danger to the security of Canada. On the other hand, in the extradition context, the answer to this may be that the principles of fundamental justice are not offended since the determination that the person is not a Convention refugee will have been taken after judicial proceedings (the extradition hearing). At the hearing, a superior court judge entertains the representations of counsel and determines whether there is *prima facie* evidence that the person has committed a serious non-political offence "outside the country of refuge." In such instances, the extradition hearing may be seen as a substitute for the oral refugee hearing.

As the Supreme Court of Canada has stated, extradition is primarily a political decision touching upon matters involving the good faith and honour of this country in its relations with other states (see *R. v. Schmidt, supra*). Therefore, s. 40(2) will possibly also involve the Minister of Citizenship and Immigration in advising the Minister of Justice as to whether a surrender would violate Canada's international obligations under the *United Nations Convention Relating to the Status of Refugees*. Extradition under the *Extradition Act* and refugee determination under the *Immigration Act* each involve international obligations undertaken by Canada. The Minister of Justice may wish to consider the effect that surrender, in compliance with one of Canada's extradition treaties, would have on Canada's international obligations concerning refugees.

The interaction between the two proceedings is underscored by s. 48(2) of the new *Extradition Act*. When the Minister of Justice discharges a person sought and the person has an outstanding refugee claim, s. 48(2) requires the Minister to send to the Minister of Citizenship and Immigration "copies of all relevant documents."

§4.3 Power of Minister to Seek Assurances and Conditions (s. 40(3) and (4))

Section 40(3) permits the Minister of Justice to seek assurances from the extradition partner and to make the surrender order subject to any conditions that the Minister deems appropriate. Section 40(3) makes specific reference to conditions that concern the rule of specialty. The rule of specialty provides that a surrendered person cannot be tried or sentenced for any offence other than that with respect to which extradition was ordered. The rule of specialty was addressed in the extradition treaties (see, for example, Article XV of the *Canada–Mexico Extradition Treaty* and Article 12 of the *Canada–United States Extradition Treaty*). The specialty provisions of s. 40(3) in the new Act will encompass those extradition partners designated by the Act who are not subject to the provisions of a treaty.

It had been argued under the former *Extradition Act* that the legislation did not give the Minister of Justice the authority to attach conditions to surrender (see *United States of Mexico v. Hurley* (1997), 116 C.C.C. (3d) 414 (Ont. C.A.); and *Gervasoni v. Canada (Minister of Justice)* (1996), 72 B.C.A.C. 141 (B.C. C.A.), leave to appeal to S.C.C. refused (1996), 84 B.C.A.C. 240 (S.C.C.). In explicitly providing for conditional surrender, the new Act puts to rest any debate as to the Minister's authority to impose conditions or seek assurances. Although not mandatory, the fact that specialty and other conditions and assurances are expressly dealt with in the legislation can be seen as an indication that the Minister will consider conditions when addressing the surrender issue. There are treaty provisions which allow for conditional surrender to be contemplated. Such treaty provisions enable the requested state to subject surrender to conditions without being accused of failing to fulfil its international obligations, in the event that surrender is refused owing to a failure on the part of the requesting state to meet the conditions, most notably in death penalty cases.

One situation where the Minister of Justice will rely on s. 40(3) in seeking assurances from an extradition partner is in death penalty cases. Section 44(2) provides that "[t]he Minister may refuse to make a surrender order if the Minister is satisfied that the conduct in respect of which the request for extradition is made is punishable by death under the laws that apply to the extradition partner." Section 44(2) is not subject to treaty override (s. 45 provides that treaty provisions override the refusal to surrender provisions in ss. 46 and 47, but not those in s. 44). Although s. 44(2) indicates that the Minister has discretion in this request, the Supreme Court of Canada case of *United States v. Burns* (2001), 151 C.C.C. (3d) 97, mandates refusal to surrender in death penalty cases if assurances that it will not be imposed are not forthcoming. Section 40(3) and (4) enable the Minister to seek assurances from the extradition partner that it will not be imposed. A number of Canada's extradition treaties already contain provisions enabling the requested state to seek such assurances (for instance, see Article 6 of the *Canada–United States Extradition Treaty*).

In some death penalty cases, the courts have considered the form, type, and sufficiency of the assurances. In *Gervasoni v. Canada (Minister of Justice), supra*, the British Columbia Court of Appeal held that the Minister of Justice could rely on communications from the American prosecutors that the death penalty would not be sought on the first degree murder charge which the fugitive was facing. The court rejected the fugitive's contention that the Minister was required to seek formal assurances under Article 6 of the Treaty. However, in *R. v. Bounnam* (1996), 91 O.A.C. 319 (Ont. C.A.), leave to appeal to S.C.C. refused (1997), 99 O.A.C. 79 (note) (S.C.C.), because it appeared at the time the appeal was argued that the only assurances from the state of Tennessee that the death penalty would not be imposed were oral assurances, the Ontario Court of Appeal directed the Minister to obtain written assurances from the state. If such a document was not forthcoming, the court urged the Minister "to require the necessary assurance under Article 6 of the Treaty."

Other types of conditions or assurances that the Minister of Justice can seek from the extradition partner are those relating to the treatment of the person sought when surrendered. For instance, in *United States of Mexico v. Hurley, supra*, the Minister ordered the surrender of the fugitive, a gay man, to stand trial for the murder of his male lover in Mexico. The Minister had accepted that there were ongoing human rights abuses in Mexico involving certain arms of the government against certain identifiable groups, including homosexuals. Nevertheless, the Minister ordered the surrender of the fugitive, albeit only after certain assurances were given by the requesting state, directed at ensuring the safety and well-being of the fugitive. The Ontario Court of Appeal found it relevant that Hurley had been surrendered on the condition that he would be treated in accordance with the Treaty and the Mexican constitution, that he would be eligible, if convicted, to serve his sentence in Canada pursuant to the *Transfer of Offenders Treaty*, and that he would be regularly visited and have his case monitored by Canadian officials in Mexico. Based upon the actual manner in which the extradition was to be conducted, the court found that the fugitive had not met the onus upon him to demonstrate that the Minister's decision to surrender was a violation of s. 7 of the *Charter*.

Kitakufe v. Canada (Minister of Justice) (1999), 135 C.C.C. (3d) 255 (Ont. C.A.), is an example of a case where the courts did not interfere with the Minister of Justice's refusal to seek assurances. The Ontario Court of Appeal held that the Minister did not err in refusing to seek assurances from the United States that the fugitive's parole ineligibility on the fraud charges for which he was surrendered would not be increased because he had failed to appear at his sentencing hearing. The court found that the matter pertained to the administration of the fugitive's sentence and was not a specialty issue since the fugitive was not charged with failing to appear. Consequently, neither the specialty provisions of the Treaty nor the *Charter* were violated.

§4.4 Extension of Time for Minister's Surrender Decision (s. 40(5) and (6))

Section 25(2) and (3) of the former *Extradition Act* were added to the Act in 1992 in order to provide the Minister with the flexibility to obtain additional time in which to make a decision on surrender. This flexibility is continued in s. 40(5) of the new Act, which provides that the Minister may extend the period of time in which to make a decision, and s. 40(6) which provides for such an extension of time to be communicated to the court of appeal in the event an appeal from committal is outstanding.

The significance of the issues which may be raised with the Minister concerning surrender requires that the Minister be provided with the ability to obtain more time if it would be necessary in order to fully canvass all of the issues. Recognizing this, in practice persons sought often waive ministerial time requirements completely.

§4.5 Power of Minister to Postpone Surrender Decision Until After Appeal of Extradition Judge's Committal Order (s. 41)

Section 41 of the new *Extradition Act* is identical to s. 25.1 of the former Act, which was added to the former Act in 1992. Section 41(1) provides flexibility in the timing of the Minister of Justice's surrender decision. It was acknowledged under the former Act that the Minister was not required to await the outcome of an appeal from committal before making a decision on surrender (see *United States v. Brisson* (1994), 23 W.C.B. (2d) 472 (Que. C.A.)). The court of appeal also had flexibility to defer a decision on an appeal from committal until the Minister had made a decision on surrender (see s. 19.4 of the former Act). This power is continued in respect to the court of appeal under s. 51(2) and allows for convenient use of court time if the person sought is also expected to bring a judicial review of the Minister's decision. Section 51(2) enables the appeal of the committal order and the surrender decision to be heard at once.

Section 41(1) addresses situations in which the Minister of Justice would prefer to await a decision from the court of appeal concerning the committal order before embarking on a consideration of the issue of surrender. When the Minister files a notice of postponement with the court of appeal, the court is required to determine the appeal from committal without awaiting the Minister's surrender decision. The Minister may find this manner of proceeding desirable when the issue to be determined in the appeal involves a question as to whether a particular matter is within the jurisdiction of the Minister or the extradition judge. It would be prudent for the Minister to await determinations of such jurisdictional concerns before embarking on a consideration of surrender issues.

§4.6 Minister's Power to Amend Surrender Order (s. 42)

The former *Extradition Act* did not contain a similar provision to s. 42 of the new Act. Section 42 adds flexibility to the surrender process, providing the Minister of Justice with the discretion to make any changes to the surrender order that may be necessary during the time period leading up to the date of surrender. Section 42 appears to be directed at non-contentious amendments to the surrender order. These might include naming the persons who have custody of the person and naming the persons who are authorized to accept custody of the person. Section 58 of the Act specifies the required contents of the surrender order. Section 58(d) and (e) require the naming of the persons who have custody of the person and the naming of the persons or class of persons who are authorized to accept custody of the person.

§4.7 Submissions to Minister (s. 43)

(a) Form of submissions

(i) *Written submissions*

As with the former *Extradition Act*, the new Act is silent on the form for submissions to the Minister of Justice. As Watt J. observed in *Germany (Federal Republic) v. Schreiber* (2001), 152 C.C.C. (3d) 499 (Ont. S.C.J.), at p. 505, quoting from the endorsement on an earlier application, in the context of denying a request to receive evidence at the hearing for use before the Minister: "There would seem little restriction on what may be placed before the Minister except that it must be relevant to the ministerial decision under s. 43(1) of the *Act*." The practice is that counsel for the person sought will usually prepare written submissions setting out the reasons why the Minister should refuse to surrender or surrender only with conditions. The submissions will usually refer to the background of the person, the pertinent facts, and the applicable law. The submissions may also be accompanied, where relevant, by documentary material, such as letters from family and friends, periodical literature, and material from experts on issues referred in §4.7(b) below, "Issues to be raised in submissions to Minister of Justice."

When making submissions that the person should not be surrendered at all, the focus of the submissions should be directed to considerations of fair trial and treatment by the extradition partner. When doing so, it is expected that reference will be made to considerations of injustice and oppression referred to in s. 44(1)(a), or the discrimination factors set out in s. 44(1)(b). In addition, if evidence can be submitted to substantiate the existence of the situations set out in s. 46(1) regarding the offence being statute-barred, or a military or political offence, this would justify the refusal by the Minister to surrender at all.

If conditions or assurances are sought, evidence should be provided to convince the Minister that the situation warrants conditions or assurances and that they would alleviate the concerns demonstrated.

As a practical matter it will not be viable to ask the Minister to reconsider the facts. The hearing judge will have already pronounced on the sufficiency of the evidence by ordering the committal and there is an avenue of appeal from that decision.

(ii) Oral submissions and oral hearing

In *Idziak v. Canada (Minister of Justice)* (1989), 53 C.C.C. (3d) 464 (Ont. H.C.), affirmed (1990), 72 O.R. (2d) 480 (Ont. C.A.), affirmed (1992), 77 C.C.C. (3d) 65 (S.C.C.), reconsideration refused (1992), 9 Admin. L.R. (2d) 1n (S.C.C.), Doherty J. (as he then was) reviewed the Minister's surrender decision on a *habeas corpus* application. Doherty J. considered whether the Minister should have held an oral hearing. He noted that there had been neither a request for an oral hearing nor a request that counsel be permitted to appear personally before the Minister to make submissions. Doherty J. commented as follows, at pp. 469–470:

> Procedural due process may require that a hearing be held, but a hearing is not a *per se* requirement of fundamental justice in any case where a liberty interest is affected: *Kindler v. Canada (Minister of Justice)*, supra, *Singh v. Canada (Minister of Employment and Immigration)*, supra, at p. 465. In deciding whether an oral hearing is required in order to provide fundamental justice, it is appropriate to consider various factors including the nature of the decision being made, the nature of the material relevant to that decision, the capacity or function of the decision-maker, plus any relevant statutory provisions. In this case there are no relevant statutory provisions which suggest that a hearing is required or anticipated as part of the decision-making process. The decision made by the Minister is in essence a policy-driven one; there were no facts in dispute and, hence, no determinations of credibility to be made. I see nothing in the nature of the decision to be made which necessitated an oral hearing in order that the Minister give fair consideration to relevant representations.

Doherty J. held that, on the facts of the case, the failure to conduct an oral hearing in the absence of a request for one did not violate any principle of fundamental justice. He stated that he was not suggesting that the Minister should never order an oral hearing. Rather, it will depend on the factual circumstances of each case as to whether an oral hearing should be held to satisfy fundamental justice requirements.

Section 43 of the new *Extradition Act*, like s. 19.1 of the former Act, does not specify the form of submissions. It follows, therefore, that the form is in the discretion of the Minister of Justice. The Minister in *Kindler v. Canada (Minister of Justice)* (1991), 67 C.C.C. (3d) 1 (S.C.C.), exercised his discretion by hearing oral submissions but refusing to entertain *viva voce* evidence in the form of an oral hearing. This was commented upon by the Supreme Court of Canada in the judgments of Cory J. (dissenting on other issues) and McLachlin J. (for the majority). Both Cory J. and McLachlin J. upheld the Minister's decision not to hold an oral hearing and indicated that the fugitive was afforded the right at the extradition hearing to call evidence and have issues of the strength of the case determined. There was no requirement for an oral hearing at the ministerial phase of the proceeding. Cory J. stated as follows, at pp. 22–23:

> In my view, these submissions are based upon a misunderstanding of the extradition process. In Canada, extradition proceeds in two steps. First, an extradition judge examines the factual basis for the charge and ensures that it is one for which extradition is available under the *Extradition Act*. The first step is complete when the extradition judge is satisfied as to both the factual basis for the charge and the availability of extradition. It is only then that the second step can be taken by the Minister of Justice. The Minister, if requested, may hear representations and exercise a discretion as to whether to surrender the fugitive. This second step obviously requires the Minister to make a decision which is largely political in nature. It involves, in the words of La Forest J. in *R. v. Schmidt* (1987), 33 C.C.C. (3d) 193 at p. 215, 39 D.L.R. (4th) 18, [1987] 1 S.C.R. 500: "the good faith and honour of this country in its relations with other states".
>
> In this two-step process any issues of credibility or claims of innocence must be addressed by the extradition judge. Kindler had ample opportunity before Pinard J. to challenge the credibility of the evidence led against him at his trial. This he did not do. It was therefore not open to him to seek to adduce fresh evidence before the Minister of Justice as to the credibility of witnesses or his innocence of the offence. The Minister was obliged neither to consider such issues, nor to hear *viva voce* evidence.

McLachlin J. commented as follows, at p. 60:

> As for the other arguments, it has not been demonstrated that the Minister erred in law or exercised his discretion upon an inadmissible basis in either case. I reject Kindler's submission that he had the right to an oral hearing before the Minister. He was afforded that right at the stage of the judicial hearing. No further oral hearing is required at the second stage of the Minister's final decision.

The Minister exercised his discretion in the *Kindler v. Canada (Minister of Justice)* case to hear the oral submissions of counsel. Oral submissions are not routinely made at this phase of the proceedings. It appears that the Minister entertained oral submissions in that case due to the seriousness of the issue involved, namely, that the fugitive was subject to the death penalty in the requesting state.

In *Kindler*, Cory J. referred to the fugitive having had the right to deal with the credibility of witnesses and claims of innocence before the extradition judge. In that case, Kindler sought to be allowed to give oral evidence on those issues before the Minister. In the subsequent cases of *United States v. McVey* (1992), 77 C.C.C. (3d) 1 (S.C.C.), and *United States v. Lépine* (1993), 87 C.C.C. (3d) 385, the Supreme Court of Canada made it clear that the role of the extradition judge is solely to determine whether there is sufficient evidence to justify committal. This would exclude from the extradition hearing considerations of the credibility of witnesses or determinations of innocence and guilt. Consequently, the pronouncements of Cory J. and McLachlin J. in *Kindler v. Canada (Minister of Justice)* appear to mean that any issues directed at challenging the sufficiency of the evidence are committal issues and should be dealt with at the extradition hearing. Section 32(1)(c) of the new *Extradition Act* specifically provides that the person sought can call evidence at the extradition hearing that is relevant to the sufficiency issue and is reliable.

In *United States v. Whitley, supra,* the fugitive was sought for extradition on drug offences by the State of New York. One of the issues raised by the fugitive during the ministerial phase was the "*Cotroni* issue," that is, that domestic prosecution for the same conduct was equally viable and therefore should be preferred to extradition. (See *United States v. Cotroni* (1989), 48 C.C.C. (3d) 193 (S.C.C.), at p. 215.) Whitley requested that the Minister of Justice hold an oral hearing to take the evidence of the Canadian police officer who headed the investigation. In the alternative, Whitley requested the production of the police and Department of Justice files pertaining to the investigation and prosecution of the fugitive. The Minister decided not to convene an oral hearing. The Minister relied upon the reasons of McLachlin J. in *Kindler v. Canada (Minister of Justice), supra,* holding that the fugitive does not have a right to an oral hearing during the ministerial phase of extradition proceedings. At the Ontario Court of Appeal level in *United States v. Whitley,* Laskin J.A. quoted from the Minister's decision in this regard at p. 111: "hearings at this juncture of the process should only be exceptionally granted and . . . this case does not come within the ambit of such exception." The Court of Appeal upheld the Minister's decision and found no denial of natural justice or any procedural unfairness.

(b) Issues to be raised in submissions to Minister of Justice

Under the new *Extradition Act,* the issues raised in the submissions to the Minister of Justice will be guided by the factors enumerated in ss. 44 and 46 to 47. These sections permit or require the Minister to refuse to make a surrender order. The circumstances in which the Minister must refuse to make a surrender order are enumerated in ss. 44(1) and 46 and encompass fair trial and treatment considerations. The circumstances when the Minister may refuse to make a surrender order are set out in ss. 44(2) and 47.

The former *Extradition Act* did not enumerate reasons for refusal, with the exception of offences of a political character (see ss. 21 and 22). However, similar considerations to those enumerated in the new Act could have resulted in the Minister's refusal to make a surrender order. For instance, the cases of *Idziak v. Canada (Minister of Justice), supra,* and *United States of Mexico v. Hurley, supra,* dealt with fair trial and treatment considerations that would now come under s. 44(1)(a), namely refusing surrender on the basis of unjust or oppressive circumstances. Accordingly, the jurisprudence decided under the former Act will continue to be relevant when examining the Minister's obligations with respect to the surrender decision.

The judicial review decision in *Idziak v. Canada (Minister of Justice)* (1989), 53 C.C.C. (3d) 464 (Ont. H.C.), affirmed (1990), 72 O.R. (2d) 480 (Ont. C.A.), affirmed (1992), 77 C.C.C. (3d) 65 (S.C.C.), reconsideration refused (1992), 9 Admin. L.R.

(2d) 1n (S.C.C.), illustrates the type of personal circumstances raised before the Minister of Justice in support of submissions against surrender. *Idziak* was sought for extradition on fraud charges by the United States. In arguing against surrender, he raised his "health and age, his wife's illness, his long-time connection to Canada, his non-involvement in the American aspect of the fraud, his good character, his prior conviction and sentence (60 days) in Canada on a factually related charge, and the delay by American authorities in instituting the extradition proceedings. The material stressed the humanitarian grounds, and made less of the prosecutorial delay and prior conviction'' (at p. 466).

The Minister's surrender decision was reviewed by Doherty J. (as he then was) on a *habeas corpus* application. The case was decided prior to the 1992 amendments to the *Extradition Act* that eliminated review by way of *habeas corpus* and enabled a direct appeal to the Court of Appeal. Doherty J. found that the humanitarian grounds evoked considerable sympathy. However, they did not come close to the type of exceptional circumstances warranting judicial intervention with the Minister's surrender decision referred to by the Supreme Court of Canada in *R. v. Schmidt, supra,* at p. 214. Doherty J. also found that the previous conviction, which was factually related but not identical to the American charge, did not amount to the kind of oppression by repeated prosecution referred to in *R. v. Schmidt.* Doherty J. held that the delay was not such that it should be taken out of the general rule pronounced by the Supreme Court of Canada in *Argentina (Republic) v. Mellino, supra,* that it should be left for the consideration of the foreign court.

United States of Mexico v. Hurley, supra, provides an example of material submitted to demonstrate a social climate in the requesting state that could be detrimental to the fugitive. The Ontario Court of Appeal was required to determine whether the Minister of Justice's decision to surrender Hurley to Mexico, in the face of documented human rights violations against homosexuals, constituted a violation of s. 7 of the *Charter.* Hurley, a homosexual, was sought to stand trial for the murder of his male lover, who had been found dead in the home that they shared in Mexico. Hurley fled Mexico during the investigation. In reviewing the Minister's surrender decision, the Court of Appeal referred to the material that the Minister had before him when making his decision. The material included reports of human rights abuses against homosexuals carried out by, or with the involvement of, certain arms of the Mexican government (police and military). The reports included statements from Amnesty International and from leading gay rights organizations and a document on the Mexican judicial system prepared by the U.S. State Department. The court held that the fugitive had not demonstrated that surrender would constitute a s. 7 violation. However, the court found it appropriate that the fugitive be surrendered with assurances regarding his well-being and safety.

In *Gwynne v. Canada (Minister of Justice)* (1998), 50 C.R.R. (2d) 250 (B.C.C.A.), leave to appeal to S.C.C. refused (1998), 52 C.R.R. (2d) 188 (note) (B.C.C.A.), an extradition request was made by the United States seeking the return of the fugitive to serve the remainder of a lengthy prison sentence in Alabama where he had been convicted of extortion. In support of his submissions to the Minister that it would breach his s. 7 rights to be returned to Alabama, Gwynne submitted an affidavit of his incarceration there which described conditions that were dangerous and degrading. He also submitted a report from an expert on prison conditions in the United States. The Minister's decision to surrender Gwynne to the United States was upheld by the British Columbia Court of Appeal. Goldie J.A. found that while the conditions described by Gwynne were shocking, it was not proper to interfere with the Minister's decision since Alabama did have safeguards in place which were working.

(c) Advice to Minister of Justice

Submissions should be forwarded to the Department of Justice's International Assistance Group (IAG) in Ottawa. During the ministerial phase of extradition proceedings, the IAG acts as the Minister of Justice's counsel. Therefore, the IAG not only forwards submissions to the Minister but gives the Minister advice on the issue of surrender. The advice takes two forms: firstly, a memorandum of legal argument that includes a recommendation on the issue; secondly, a ministerial brief that summarizes submissions of counsel for the person sought and includes information on various issues raised by counsel. Counsel for the person sought does not receive a copy of the memorandum of legal advice and recommendation to the Minister. It is deemed privileged on the basis that it is legal advice (*Idziak v. Canada (Minister of Justice)* (S.C.C.), *supra*, at p. 89). However, counsel does receive a copy of the ministerial brief and does have an opportunity to comment on the brief. The brief, counsel's comments on the brief, counsel's submissions, and the memorandum of legal advice are then forwarded to the Minister.

Counsels' comments regarding the ministerial brief usually involve suggestions that information supplied by counsel has not been adequately addressed or has been inaccurately characterized or that certain information should or should not have been included in the brief (see *United States v. Whitley* and *United States of Mexico v. Hurley*, both *supra*).

(d) Disclosure at ministerial phase

As with the judicial phase of the extradition process, the degree of disclosure required in the ministerial phase is determined by the nature of the proceedings (*United States v. Dynar* (1997), 115 C.C.C. (3d) 481 (S.C.C.); *United States v. Kwok* (2001), 152 C.C.C. (3d) 225 (S.C.C.)). During the ministerial phase, there is no case to meet. As stated by Cory J. in *Idziak v. Canada (Minister of Justice)* (S.C.C.), *supra*, at p. 87, there "is no longer a lis in existence." The decision of the Minister of Justice is administrative rather than judicial. As in other types of administrative functions, the Minister of Justice has a duty to act with fairness in reaching his or her decision on the matter of surrender. The disclosure requirements are determined according to what the duty of fairness demands in the circumstances.

The nature of the Minister of Justice's role was described by Cory J. in *Idziak v. Canada (Minister of Justice)*, *supra*, at p. 87:

> [T]he decision to issue a warrant of surrender involves completely different considerations from those reached by a court in an extradition hearing. The extradition hearing is clearly judicial in nature while the actions of the Minister of Justice in considering whether to issue a warrant of surrender are primarily political in nature. This is certainly not a case of a single official acting as both judge and prosecutor in the same case. At the judicial phase the fugitive possesses the full panoply of procedural protections available in a court of law. At the ministerial phase, there is no longer a *lis* in existence. The fugitive has by then been judicially committed for extradition. The Act simply grants to the Minister a discretion as to whether to execute the judicially approved extradition by issuing a warrant of surrender.

(i) Disclosure of advice to Minister of Justice

In *Idziak v. Canada (Minister of Justice)*, *supra*, the Supreme Court of Canada did not set out the specific disclosure requirements of the Minister of Justice. However, the Court did address the allegations that the Minister had improperly withheld certain material with respect to the surrender of the fugitive. Specifically, a memorandum had been given to the Minister that included a summary of all the proceedings involving Idziak, a summary of his counsel's representations concerning the decision, and a recommendation. Idziak did not learn of this memorandum until after the Minister's decision to surrender, and when he did, he alleged procedural unfairness on the part of the Minister. Idziak argued that the memorandum should have been disclosed so that he could have prepared his own representations with full knowledge of "the case against him." The Supreme Court dismissed this argument on two grounds: firstly, the memorandum was privileged as it had been prepared by Minister's counsel in order to provide advice to the Minister; secondly, given the nature of the proceedings before the Minister, there was no unfairness. Cory J. described the duty of fairness as follows, at pp. 89–90:

> Once again there can be no doubt that the Minister, in considering the issuance of the writ of surrender, must act fairly. What must be assessed is whether the legislative scheme of ministerial review achieves a reasonable balance between the interest of the state and that of the individual.
>
> . . .
>
> The Minister quite properly claims solicitor-client privilege for the memorandum. As a result of the nature of the proceedings before the Minister and the conclusion that s. 7 of the Charter has not been violated, very little need be said on this issue and what little will be said should be restricted in the application to the situation presented on this appeal. It is noteworthy that, apart from the recommendation, there was nothing in the document that was not known to the applicant. Further, the confidential memorandum was not evidence to be used in an adversary proceeding. Rather, it was a briefing note to the Minister from a staff member who did not have any interest in the outcome. I agree with the findings and conclusion of Doherty J. that this document was indeed

privileged. It meets the criteria outlined in *R. v. Solosky* (1979), 50 C.C.C. (2d) 495 at p. 508, 105 D.L.R. (3d) 745 at p. 758, [1980] 1 S.C.R. 821. As a result, it did not have to be disclosed to the appellant. The failure to disclose it did not constitute unfairness viewed in light of the nature of the proceedings before the Minister.

(*ii*) *Disclosure of materials regarding* Cotroni *issue*

Under s. 47(d) of the new *Extradition Act*, the Minister of Justice may refuse surrender if the conduct in respect of which the request for extradition is made is the subject of criminal proceedings in Canada against the person sought. The *Cotroni* issue involves the determination of whether domestic prosecution is to be preferred to extradition when both Canada and the extradition partner can claim jurisdiction to prosecute the criminal conduct.

There was no provision similar to s. 47(d) in the former *Extradition Act*. However, the jurisprudence decided under the former Act indicated that the surrender of fugitives had to be made with due consideration of constitutional norms (see *United States v. Cotroni, supra*; and *United States v. Whitley, supra*). This would include consideration of whether domestic prosecution should be preferred to extradition.

Arguments based on an alleged breach of the duty of fairness as a result of non-disclosure pertaining to a *Cotroni* issue arose in *United States v. Whitley* (1994), 94 C.C.C. (3d) 99 (Ont. C.A.), affirmed (1996), 104 C.C.C. (3d) 447 (S.C.C.). Whitley was charged in the United States with offences involving the exportation of marihuana from the United States to Canada. He was also charged in Ontario with *Narcotic Control Act* offences based on the same criminal enterprise. The Canadian charges were withdrawn after the United States requested Whitley's extradition. At the hearing, Whitley's counsel had sought to have the officer in charge of the Canadian investigation testify. This evidence was not requested to assist the fugitive in the extradition committal proceedings. Rather, it was sought to assist the fugitive in his argument to the Minister of Justice that he should remain in, and be prosecuted in, Canada. The extradition judge refused to receive this evidence. Counsel for the fugitive then asked the Minister of Justice to hold a hearing to take the evidence of the police officer during the ministerial phase of proceedings. Alternatively, counsel requested disclosure of the police and Department of Justice files pertaining to the Canadian investigation and prosecution. Both requests were denied. There was no oral hearing and the files were not disclosed.

There were three categories of files sought by Whitley:

1. Information in the police files concerning the Canadian charge against him;

2. Information pertaining to the plea and sentencing arrangements for his co-conspirators; and

3. Documents and notes on the decision to prefer a foreign prosecution to a domestic one.

In addition, there was a certain amount of other material that had been given to the Minister of Justice that had not been given to counsel for the fugitive, including the following:

1. A supplementary brief prepared by counsel for the Minister which included a summary of the submission made on behalf of Whitley in the original ministerial brief and "new information and clarification of previous information."

2. A memorandum from the Minister's counsel which appended memoranda from the prosecutor about the decision not to prosecute Whitley in Canada.

3. A summary of the case along with an analysis and recommendations prepared by the executive assistant to the Minister.

On appeal to the Ontario Court of Appeal, counsel for the fugitive argued that there had been a lack of procedural fairness in the circumstances. Counsel claimed that the Minister had a duty to provide the fugitive with all of the undisclosed material as it was relevant to the vindication of Whitley's constitutional rights under s. 6(1) of the *Charter*. Laskin J.A. for the Court of Appeal disagreed with counsel's argument. Laskin J.A.'s reasoning was subsequently adopted by the Supreme Court of Canada. Laskin J.A. held, as per *Idziak v. Canada (Minister of Justice)*, *supra*, that the legal memoranda which went to the Minister were privileged and not disclosable. With respect to the remaining material, the fugitive had either been provided with a copy or advised of the substance of the material that went to the Minister.

Laskin J.A. also observed that the fugitive was not entitled to disclosure of the decision to terminate the Canadian charge in favour of the U.S. prosecution. Laskin, J.A. based this finding on the decision of the Supreme Court of Canada in *R. v. Power* (1994), 89 C.C.C. (3d) 1, namely, that one cannot go behind prosecutorial discretion in the domestic context except in the clearest of cases. This principle was held to be equally applicable in the extradition context. The fugitive argued that the *Power* test had been met. He alleged that there was improper motive to prefer extradition to domestic prosecution, that being the more severe sentence in the United States. Although Laskin J.A. conceded that improper motive is a ground for judicial review of prosecutorial discretion, he added that there must be an air of reality to this contention. Laskin J.A. concluded that there was no such air of reality in this case commenting as follows, at p. 114:

> Improper motive is a ground for judicial review of prosecutorial discretion but there has to be an air of reality to the allegation before a court will require disclosure of the kind of information requested by the appellant. The only suggestion of improper motive that the appellant can point to is the evidence of higher penalties for the offences in the United States. In my view, there is no air of reality to the appellant's allegation. Therefore, I conclude that the Minister did not breach his duty of fairness to the appellant in refusing to order production of the material requested.

Laskin J.A. concluded that the Minister of Justice was not bound by the principles of disclosure that might be applicable in judicial proceedings. As a primarily political act, something less would suffice to meet the dictates of natural justice. Laskin J.A. made the point as follows, at p. 113:

> [T]he appellant received a copy of or was told the substance of all of the government's material that went to the Minister. He was given a reasonable opportunity to state his own case and to comment on the materials prepared by the Minister's staff. The appellant made detailed submissions on the application of the principles in *Cotroni, supra,* and the Minister considered those submissions in his decision. I do not think that the Minister's duty of fairness calls for anything more in this case.

The issue of disclosure at the ministerial phase was again considered by the Supreme Court of Canada in *United States v. Kwok* (2001), 152 C.C.C. (3d) 225. In that case, throughout the process of his extradition, Kwok had sought disclosure of additional materials with a view to establishing unjustified violations of his *Charter* rights. He had specifically sought disclosure of (1) documentation concerning a related Canadian investigation into his alleged involvement in drug trafficking; (2) all discussions between Canadian police and American investigative authorities; and (3) all discussions between Canadian police and both Canadian and American prosecuting authorities concerning the decision to proceed in the United States rather than in Canada. Having been denied this disclosure by the extradition judge, Kwok renewed his disclosure request before the Minister and was again refused. Arbour J. for the Supreme Court held that the decision in *Dynar* was determinative of the appeal and that the Minister was correct in denying the fugitive's disclosure request. Arbour J. stated, at p. 269:

> [108] In this case, I agree with the Court of Appeal that the materials sought by appellant were not relevant either on appeal from the judicial decision to commit, or on judicial review of the executive decision to surrender. There is nothing to suggest that the Minister failed to consider the *Cotroni* factors or the fugitive's constitutional rights. Nor is there any indication that the Minister based his decisions not to prosecute domestically and to surrender the fugitive for extradition on improper motives.
>
> [109] Bearing in mind the expedient and summary nature of the committal hearing, the discretion that attaches to the Minister's decision to surrender and the nature of extradition proceedings generally, the appellant received adequate disclosure at all stages of the extradition process.

Based on the jurisprudence, it appears that the courts are willing to give the Minister of Justice wide latitude in determining the appropriate level of disclosure during the ministerial phase of extradition proceedings. The courts are unlikely to interfere as long as the person sought is made aware of the substance of the government's material. If this is done, the Minister will be considered to have fulfilled the duty of fairness.

(iii) Disclosure of information obtained from third parties

In *United States of Mexico v. Hurley, supra,* Hurley was wanted in Mexico to stand trial for murder. Among the many issues raised on appeal, it was contended that the Minister's surrender decision had been procedurally unfair because of non-disclosure of a quantity of material to the fugitive. At issue were the following:

1. Letters to the Minister from the father of the deceased and other individuals in support of the extradition.

2. Information provided by the Department of Foreign Affairs to the effect that Canadian consular officials in Mexico were aware of no complaints from Canadians of mistreatment in Mexican jails.

3. Information from the Office of the Solicitor General advising the Minister of the number of Canadians who had applied for, and been accepted for, transfer of their sentences to Canada under the *Transfer of Offenders Treaty* with Mexico.

McMurtry C.J.O., on behalf of the Ontario Court of Appeal, held that since the substance of these communications had been described in the brief to the Minister which had been disclosed, the Minister's duty of fairness had been fulfilled. Failure to make the materials themselves available did not constitute a breach of the fugitive's disclosure rights.

(iv) Requirement for Minister of Justice to disclose material to challenge extradition hearing committal

In *United States v. Dynar, supra,* the fugitive was sought by the United States for conspiracy to money launder. Dynar was the target of an F.B.I. sting operation based in Nevada. An F.B.I. agent made a number of telephone calls to Dynar. Dynar was at all times in Canada. The F.B.I. agent offered Dynar the opportunity to launder illicit drug trafficking moneys. The calls, intercepted pursuant to the requirements of American law, formed the evidence in support of the extradition request. The authorities in Canada had been apprised of the investigation by the F.B.I. In fact, a formal cooperative arrangement was in place between the Canadian and American authorities. The fugitive only learned of the Canadian involvement in the investigation subsequent to his committal at the extradition hearing. Counsel for the fugitive, in his written submissions to the Minister of Justice, requested disclosure of the Canadian involvement. The basis for the request was that, since this information was not known at the time of the extradition hearing, its production would justify a new extradition hearing and may provide the basis for a stay of proceedings.

In dealing with this issue, the Supreme Court of Canada noted that the extent and nature of disclosure required as a principle of fundamental justice under s. 7 of the

Charter depended upon the context in which it was claimed. The court in effect held that this type of material is not disclosable in extradition proceedings because:

1. It is not appropriate to simply transplant the full range of disclosure requirements in *Stinchcombe* (*R. v. Stinchcombe*, [1991] 3 S.C.R. 326), which is applicable to domestic proceedings, to the extradition context.

2. There is no requirement under the *Extradition Act* or the *Canada–United States Extradition Treaty* to disclose information of this nature.

3. The material did not pertain to the issue of the sufficiency of evidence to commit, which is the sole disclosure concern at the extradition hearing given the limited function of the extradition judge.

The reasoning in *Dynar* was reconfirmed by the decision of the Supreme Court of Canada in *United States v. Kwok, supra.*

§5.0 CASE LAW

Argentina (Republic) v. Mellino (1987), 33 C.C.C. (3d) 334 (S.C.C.).
Bembenek v. Canada (Minister of Employment & Immigration) (1991), 69 C.C.C. (3d) 34 (Ont. Gen. Div.).
Germany (Federal Republic) v. Schreiber (2001), 152 C.C.C. (3d) 499 (Ont. S.C.J.).
Gervasoni v. Canada (Minister of Justice) (1996), 72 B.C.A.C. 141 (B.C.C.A.), leave to appeal to S.C.C. refused (1996), 84 B.C.A.C. 240 (S.C.C.).
Gwynne v. Canada (Minister of Justice) (1998), 50 C.R.R. (2d) 250 (B.C.C.A.), leave to appeal to S.C.C. refused (1998), 52 C.R.R. (2d) 188 (note) (B.C.C.A.).
Idziak v. Canada (Minister of Justice) (1989), 53 C.C.C. (3d) 464 (Ont. H.C.), affirmed (1990), 72 O.R. (2d) 480 (Ont. C.A.), affirmed (1992), 77 C.C.C. (3d) 65 (S.C.C.), reconsideration refused (1992), 9 Admin. L.R. (2d) 1n (S.C.C.).
Kindler v. Canada (Minister of Justice) (1991), 67 C.C.C. (3d) 1 (S.C.C.).
Kitakufe v. Canada (Minister of Justice) (1999), 135 C.C.C. (3d) 255 (Ont. C.A.).
Pacificador v. Canada (Minister of Justice) (1999), (*sub nom. Philippines (Republic) v. Pacificador*) 60 C.R.R. (2d) 126 (Ont. Gen. Div.).
Pushpanathan v. Canada (Minister of Employment & Immigration), [1998] 1 S.C.R. 982, amended [1998] 1 S.C.R. 1222.
R. v. Bounnam (1996), 91 O.A.C. 319 (Ont. C.A.), leave to appeal to S.C.C. refused (1997), 99 O.A.C. 79 (note) (S.C.C.).
R. v. Power (1994), 89 C.C.C. (3d) 1 (S.C.C.).
R. v. Schmidt (1987), 33 C.C.C. (3d) 193 (S.C.C.).
Singh v. Canada (Minister of Employment & Immigration), [1985] 1 S.C.R. 177.
United States v. Brisson (1994), 23 W.C.B. (2d) 472 (Que. C.A.).
United States v. Burns (2001), 151 C.C.C. (3d) 97 (S.C.C.).

United States v. Cotroni (1989), 48 C.C.C. (3d) 193 (S.C.C.).

United States v. Dynar (1997), 115 C.C.C. (3d) 481 (S.C.C.)

United States v. Kwok (2001), 152 C.C.C. (3d) 225 (S.C.C.).

United States v. Leon (1995), 96 C.C.C. (3d) 568 (Ont. C.A.), affirmed (1996), 105 C.C.C. (3d) 385 (S.C.C.).

United States v. Lépine (1993), 87 C.C.C. (3d) 385 (S.C.C.).

United States v. McVey (1992), 77 C.C.C. (3d) 1 (S.C.C.).

United States of Mexico v. Hurley (1997), 116 C.C.C. (3d) 414 (Ont. C.A.).

United States v. Whitley (1994), 94 C.C.C. (3d) 99 (Ont. C.A.), affirmed (1996), 104 C.C.C. (3d) 447 (S.C.C.).

§6.0 RELATED SECTIONS

s. 11 — Minister's Power to Receive Provisional Arrest or Extradition Requests

s. 15 — Power of Minister to Issue Authority to Proceed

ss. 44–47 — Reasons for Refusal

s. 48(2) — Consequence of Discharge by Minister When Refugee Claim Outstanding

s. 50 — Time Period for Filing of Notice of Appeal of Extradition Judge's Committal Order

s. 51(2) — Deferral of Appeal of Extradition Judge's Committal Order Until After Minister's Surrender Decision

s. 58 — Contents of Surrender Order

s. 64 — Postponement of Surrender for Canadian Offence

s. 96 — Related Amendments to *Immigration Act*

Reasons for Refusal (ss. 44–47)

§1.0 DESCRIPTION

Sections 44 to 47 of the *Extradition Act* provide as follows:

WHEN ORDER NOT TO BE MADE

44. (1) The Minister shall refuse to make a surrender order if the Minister is satisfied that

(a) the surrender would be unjust or oppressive having regard to all the relevant circumstances; or

(b) the request for extradition is made for the purpose of prosecuting or punishing the person by reason of their race, religion, nationality, ethnic origin, language, colour, political opinion, sex, sexual

335

orientation, age, mental or physical disability or status or that the person's position may be prejudiced for any of those reasons.

WHEN MINISTER MAY REFUSE TO MAKE ORDER

(2) The Minister may refuse to make a surrender order if the Minister is satisfied that the conduct in respect of which the request for extradition is made is punishable by death under the laws that apply to the extradition partner.

REFUSAL IN EXTRADITION AGREEMENT

45. (1) The reasons for the refusal of surrender contained in a relevant extradition agreement, other than a multilateral extradition agreement, or the absence of reasons for refusal in such an agreement, prevail over sections 46 and 47.

EXCEPTION—MULTILATERAL EXTRADITION AGREEMENT

(2) The reasons for the refusal of surrender contained in a relevant multilateral extradition agreement prevail over sections 46 and 47 only to the extent of any inconsistency between either of those sections and those provisions.

WHEN ORDER NOT TO BE MADE

46. (1) The Minister shall refuse to make a surrender order if the Minister is satisfied that

(a) the prosecution of a person is barred by prescription or limitation under the law that applies to the extradition partner;

(b) the conduct in respect of which extradition is sought is a military offence that is not also an offence under criminal law; or

(c) the conduct in respect of which extradition is sought is a political offence or an offence of a political character.

RESTRICTION

(2) For the purpose of subparagraph (1)(c), conduct that constitutes an offence mentioned in a multilateral extradition agreement for which Canada, as a party, is obliged to extradite the person or submit the matter to its appropriate authority for prosecution does not constitute a political offence or an offence of a political character. The following conduct also does not constitute a political offence or an offence of a political character:

(a) murder or manslaughter;

(b) inflicting serious bodily harm;

(c) sexual assault;

(d) kidnapping, abduction, hostage-taking or extortion;

(e) **using explosives, incendiaries, devices or substances in circumstances in which human life is likely to be endangered or serious bodily harm or substantial property damage is likely to be caused; and**

(f) **an attempt or conspiracy to engage in, counselling, aiding or abetting another person to engage in, or being an accessory after the fact in relation to, the conduct referred to in any of paragraphs (*a*) to (*e*).**

WHEN MINISTER MAY REFUSE TO MAKE ORDER

47. The Minister may refuse to make a surrender order if the Minister is satisfied that

(a) **the person would be entitled, if that person were tried in Canada, to be discharged under the laws of Canada because of a previous acquittal or conviction;**

(b) **the person was convicted in their absence and could not, on surrender, have the case reviewed;**

(c) **the person was under the age of 18 years at the time of the offence and the law that applies to them in the territory over which the extradition partner has jurisdiction is not consistent with the fundamental principles governing the *Young Offenders Act*;**

(d) **the conduct in respect of which the request for extradition is made is the subject of criminal proceedings in Canada against the person; or**

(e) **none of the conduct on which the extradition partner bases its request occurred in the territory over which the extradition partner has jurisdiction.**

Sections 44 to 47 of the new *Extradition Act* appear under the heading "Reasons for Refusal." These sections itemize the factors that permit or require the Minister of Justice to refuse the surrender of a person sought for extradition.

§1.1 Mandatory Grounds for Refusal (ss. 44(1) and 46)

The Minister is required to refuse the surrender of a person sought in the following circumstances:

• Surrender would be "unjust or oppressive having regard to all the relevant circumstances" (s. 44(1)(a)).

• The extradition request is made for the purpose of prosecuting or punishing the person by reason of the person's race, religion, nationality, ethnic origin, language, colour, political opinion, sex, sexual orientation, age, mental or physical

337

disability or status, or that the person's position may be prejudiced for any of these reasons (s. 44(1)(b)).

- The prosecution is statute-barred under the law of the requesting jurisdiction (s. 46(1)(a)).

- The conduct in respect of which the extradition request is made is a military offence that is not also an offence under criminal law (s. 46(1)(b)).

- The conduct in respect of which the extradition request is made is a political offence or an offence of a political character (s. 46(1)(c)). However, s. 46(2) makes two qualifications to s. 46(1)(c). Firstly, conduct that constitutes an offence mentioned in a multilateral extradition agreement for which Canada, as a party to the agreement, is obliged to extradite the person or submit the matter to its appropriate authority for prosecution does not constitute a political offence or an offence of a political character. Secondly, the following conduct does not constitute a political offence or an offence of a political character: murder, manslaughter, inflicting serious bodily harm, sexual assault, kidnapping, abduction, hostage-taking, extortion, using explosives, and attempt, conspiracy, counselling, aiding and abetting with respect to these offences.

§1.2 Discretionary Grounds for Refusal (ss. 44(2) and 47)

The Minister of Justice has the discretion to refuse surrender in the following circumstances:

- The conduct in respect of which the extradition request is made is punishable by death under the laws of the extradition partner (s. 44(2)).

- The person sought would be entitled, were he or she tried in Canada, to be discharged under Canadian law because of a previous acquittal or conviction (s. 47(a)).

- The person sought was convicted in the person's absence and could not, on surrender, have the case reviewed (s. 47(b)).

- The person sought was under the age of 18 years at the time of the offence and the law that applies to him or her in the territory over which the extradition partner has jurisdiction is not consistent with the fundamental principles governing the *Young Offenders Act* (s. 47(c)).

- The conduct in respect of which the request for extradition is made is the subject of criminal proceedings in Canada against the person sought (s. 47(d)).

• None of the conduct on which the extradition partner bases its request occurred in territory over which the extradition partner has jurisdiction (s. 47(e)).

§1.3 Effect of Extradition Agreements (s. 45)

Section 45 adds two qualifications to the mandatory and discretionary grounds of refusal set out in ss. 46 and 47 to account for extradition agreements. Section 45(1) provides that the reasons for refusing surrender contained in a relevant extradition agreement, other than a multilateral extradition agreement, or the absence of reasons for refusal in such an agreement, prevail over ss. 46 and 47. Section 45(2) provides that the reasons for refusing surrender contained in a relevant multilateral extradition agreement prevail over ss. 46 and 47 only to the extent of any inconsistency between the two.

§2.0 COMPARISON WITH FORMER ACT

Under the former *Extradition Act*, the only statutory provisions dealing with the Minister of Justice's refusal to make a surrender order were ss. 21 and 22 regarding political offences. The Minister's power to surrender under s. 25 of that Act was otherwise a process of complete discretion. This was the view of Goudge J.A. of the Ontario Court of Appeal in *Germany (Federal Republic) v. Krapohl* (1998), 110 O.A.C. 129, in which he made the following comment, at p. 131:

> The statutory language is that of full discretion. This ministerial phase in the extradition process arises only once there has been an extradition hearing resulting in a judicial decision to commit the fugitive for extradition. The Minister's task, engaging as it does both the circumstances of the individual and Canada's international obligations, has been described as primarily political not judicial.

The jurisprudence dealing with s. 25 recognized that there was an overriding requirement for the Minister of Justice to surrender when the surrender request met with treaty requirements. This primary obligation was recognized by the Supreme Court of Canada in *United States v. Cotroni* (1989), 48 C.C.C. (3d) 193 (S.C.C.), wherein La Forest J. made the following statement, at p. 226:

> Counsel for El Zein also drew attention to the executive discretion to surrender, but I do not think it is of much relevance here. In the absence of proceedings against the accused in this country, Canada is under an international obligation to surrender a person accused of having committed a crime listed in an extradition treaty if it meets the requirements of the treaty, in particular presenting sufficient evidence before a judge to satisfy the requirements of a *prima facie* case. There is, it is true, some discretion in the federal government under the treaties to refuse surrender, for example, where the crime is one of a political character. There may, as well, be cases where the government, for high political purposes or for the protection of an accused, may be prepared not to conform

with a treaty. But this executive discretion would rarely be exercised and is impossible to define in the abstract. That is scarcely surprising. The extradition process is not arbitrary, unfair or based on irrational considerations. As was noted in *Schmidt, supra,* at p. 209, the procedure is tailored with an eye to the liberty of the individual.

Nonetheless, the Minister of Justice was required to consider whether surrendering a person would violate the person's *Charter* rights. Some examples of *Charter* rights engaged by the Minister's surrender decision in cases under the former Act were the following (these rights are discussed further under §4.0, "Analysis," below):

1. Section 6, namely, surrendering Canadian citizens when domestic prosecution was equally viable (the "*Cotroni* issue" — see *United States v. Cotroni, supra*).

2. Section 7, where surrender could be considered to be "fundamentally unjust." The Supreme Court of Canada in *Kindler v. Canada (Minister of Justice)* (1991), 67 C.C.C. (3d) 1 (S.C.C.), interpreted this to mean that surrender "would shock the Canadian conscience" and be "simply unacceptable." The violation of s. 7 was raised in situations where the fugitive was facing the death penalty (*Kindler v. Canada (Minister of Justice), supra, Re Ng* (1991), 67 C.C.C. (3d) 61 (S.C.C.) and *United States v. Burns* (2001), 151 C.C.C. (3d) 97 (S.C.C.), or a minimum sentence for an offence which would not attract a minimum sentence in Canada (*United States v. Whitley* (1996), 104 C.C.C. (3d) 447 (S.C.C.), *Ross v. United States* (1996), 104 C.C.C. (3d) 446 (S.C.C.) and *United States v. Jamieson* (1996), 104 C.C.C. (3d) 575 (S.C.C.)). Section 7 was also raised where the personal circumstances of the fugitive might have put him or her at risk in the requesting state (*United States of Mexico v. Hurley* (1997), 116 C.C.C. (3d) 414 (Ont. C.A.)). As well, it was argued that the physical conditions prevailing in foreign jails could render a surrender decision in violation of s. 7 (*Gwynne v. Canada (Minister of Justice)* (1998), 50 C.R.R. (2d) 250 (B.C.C.A.)).

§3.0 SIGNIFICANCE OF CHANGE

Under the new *Extradition Act,* when making a surrender order, the Minister of Justice is required to consider the grounds for refusal enumerated in ss. 44 to 47. A number of these grounds are not novel considerations at the ministerial phase of extradition proceedings. This is because many of these grounds were included as grounds for refusal in extradition treaties entered into or negotiated by Canada in the late 1980s and 1990s. In refusing surrender for a ground enumerated in the applicable treaty, the Minister avoided being in violation of Canada's international obligations. Under the current regime, with the inclusion of many of these factors in the *Extradition Act,* the weight of domestic law is brought to bear on matters that were previously left to be determined on a treaty-by-treaty basis. The following list provides some of the parallels between ss. 44 to 47 and provisions in Canada's extradition treaties:

- Section 44(1)(b) requires the Minister to refuse surrender if the prosecution in the requesting jurisdiction is based on certain impermissible considerations, such as race, sex, religion, nationality, ethnic origin, political opinion, or status. This is similar to Article IV(b) of the *Canada–Mexico Extradition Treaty* and Article 3(2) of the *Canada–Philippines Extradition Treaty*.

- Section 44(2) provides the Minister with the discretion to refuse surrender if the conduct is punishable by death in the requesting state. This is similar to Article 6 of the *Canada–United States Extradition Treaty*, Article 6 of the *Canada–India Extradition Treaty*, Article VI of the *Canada–Mexico Extradition Treaty*, Article VI of the *Canada–Philippines Extradition Treaty*, and Article V of the *Canada–Spain Extradition Treaty*.

- Section 46(1)(a) requires the Minister to refuse surrender if the prosecution in the requesting jurisdiction is statute-barred. This is similar to Article 4(ii) of the *Canada–United States Extradition Treaty*, Article IV(e) of the *Canada–Mexico Extradition Treaty*, Article III(4) of the *Canada–Spain Extradition Treaty*, and Article 3(5) of the *Canada–Philippines Extradition Treaty*.

- Section 46(1)(b) requires the Minister to refuse surrender for military conduct that is not a domestic offence. This is similar to Article IV(c) of the *Canada–Mexico Extradition Treaty*, Article 5(2)(a) of the *Canada–India Extradition Treaty*, Article III(2) of the *Canada–Spain Extradition Treaty*, and Article 3(3) of the *Canada–Philippines Extradition Treaty*.

- Section 46(1)(c) requires the Minister to refuse surrender for political offences. This provision had its counterpart in ss. 21 and 22 of the former *Extradition Act*. However, unlike the former Act, s. 46(2) of the new Act exempts certain offences from being considered political. The exempted offences are as follows: murder, manslaughter, inflicting serious bodily harm, sexual assault, kidnapping, abduction, hostage-taking, extortion, using explosives, and attempt, conspiracy, counselling, aiding and abetting with respect to these offences. Certain of Canada's extradition treaties (the United States, the Philippines, Spain, and India) also contain an exemption list for political offences. For example, Article 4(2) of the *Canada–United States Extradition Treaty* exempts the same offences as s. 46(2) with the exception of sexual assault and extortion.

- Section 47(c) provides the Minister with the discretion to refuse surrender in certain circumstances when the person sought for extradition is under the age 18. Similar considerations for persons under 18 are provided for in Article 5 of the *Canada–United States Extradition Treaty*.

- Section 47(e) provides for refusal when none of the conduct in question occurred in a territory over which the requesting state has jurisdiction. This is similar to provisions in Canada's extradition treaties with Mexico (Article II(2)(b)) and Spain (Article IV(5)).

Under the former regime, the *Charter* required the Minister to consider whether the surrender would be fundamentally unjust or simply unacceptable according to Canadian norms and thus contrary to s. 7. Under the new *Extradition Act*, this consideration has statutory authority as well, insofar as s. 44(1)(a) requires the Minister to refuse surrender if it would be unjust or oppressive having regard to all the relevant circumstances. The jurisprudence under the former Act dealing with the *Charter* issues raised in this regard will still be applicable (see *Kindler v. Canada (Minister of Justice)*, *supra*, *United States v. Burns*, *supra*, *United States of Mexico v. Hurley*, *supra*).

Moreover, it has always been open to extradition partners to include in extradition agreements humanitarian considerations as grounds for refusal. For instance Article IV(b) of the *Canada–Mexico Extradition Treaty* allows refusal if "in the circumstances of the case, extradition would be inconsistent with the principles of fundamental justice." Article IV(2) of the *Canada–Spain Extradition Treaty* permits refusal for humanitarian reasons related to the health and age of the person sought.

In addition, under the former regime, s. 7 of the *Charter* permitted the Minister to consider situations that might give rise to the pleas of *autre fois acquit* or *convict* (see *R. v. Schmidt* (1987), 33 C.C.C. (3d) 193 (S.C.C.)). This consideration is now explicitly authorized as a ground of refusal for surrender under s. 47(a) of the new Act.

Section 47(d) allows the Minister to refuse surrender if the conduct in question is the subject of criminal proceedings in Canada. This would have been dealt with under the former regime as a s. 6(1) *Charter* issue with reference to the considerations set out in the *Cotroni* case, *supra*.

§4.0 ANALYSIS

§4.1 Mandatory Refusal of Surrender Where Surrender Would Be "unjust or oppressive having regard to all the relevant circumstances" (s. 44(1)(a))

(a) Interpreting phrase "unjust or oppressive having regard to all the relevant circumstances"

Section 44(1)(a) provides the framework for submissions on grounds not specifically enumerated in ss. 44 to 47. It is a broad "catch-all" phrase which codifies the Minister's obligation, in the exercise of his or her executive discretion to surrender, to give due regard to *Charter* considerations. While it has been recognized that the Minister has a broad discretion to surrender, the cases have also held that the Minister's discretion must be exercised in accordance with the dictates of the *Charter*. In *United*

States v. Burns (2001), 151 C.C.C. (3d) 97 (S.C.C.), the Supreme Court of Canada held, at p. 217, that the test enunciated in *Kindler, supra,* continued to be applicable and that "the *Charter* required a balancing on the facts of each case of the applicable principles of fundamental justice." The Minister's surrender decision must ultimately be in accordance with the principles of fundamental justice.

Section 44(1)(a) encompasses a broad range of possible factors for the Minister to deal with, from humanitarian considerations, to whether the person will receive a fair trial and be fairly treated by the extradition partner. Although the *Charter* does not have extraterritorial application, the courts have made it clear that the treatment a person might expect to receive in the other jurisdiction is not an irrelevant consideration. In *R. v. Schmidt* (1987), 33 C.C.C. (3d) 193 (S.C.C.), La Forest J. stated, at p. 214:

> I have no doubt either that in some circumstances the manner in which the foreign State will deal with the fugitive on surrender, whether that course of conduct is justifiable or not under the law of that country, may be such that it would violate the principles of fundamental justice to surrender an accused under those circumstances. To make the point, I need only refer to a case that arose before the European Commission on Human Rights, *Altun v. Germany* (1983), 5 E.H.R.R. 611, where it was established that prosecution in the requesting country might involve the infliction of torture. Situations falling far short of this may well arise where the nature of the criminal procedures or penalties in a foreign country sufficiently shocks the conscience as to make a decision to surrender a fugitive for trial there one that breaches the principles of fundamental justice enshrined in s. 7.

The use of the "shocks the conscience" terminology and the types of considerations which might be of concern at the ministerial phase of the extradition process were elaborated upon by the Supreme Court in *United States v. Burns, supra.* The court stated, at pp. 128-129:

> [68] Use of the "shocks the conscience" terminology was intended to convey the exceptional weight of a factor such as the youth, insanity, mental retardation or pregnancy of a fugitive which, because of its paramount importance, may control the outcome of the *Kindler* balancing test on the facts of a particular case. The terminology should not be allowed to obscure the ultimate assessment that is required: namely whether or not the extradition is in accordance with the principles of fundamental justice. The rule is *not* that departures from fundamental justice are to be tolerated unless in a particular case it shocks the conscience. An extradition that violates the principles of fundamental justice will *always* shock the conscience. The important inquiry is to determine what constitutes the applicable principles of fundamental justice in the extradition context.
>
> [69] The "shocks the conscience" language signals the possibility that even though the rights of the fugitive are to be considered in the context of other applicable principles of fundamental justice, which are normally of sufficient importance to uphold the extradition, a particular treatment or punishment may sufficiently violate our sense of fundamental justice as to tilt the balance against extradition. Examples might include stoning to death individuals taken in adultery, or lopping off the hands of a thief. The

punishment is so extreme that it becomes the controlling issue in the extradition and overwhelms the rest of the analysis.

Language similar to that of s. 44(1)(a) was found in the now repealed *Fugitive Offenders Act* which was the legislation that formerly governed the return of fugitives to Commonwealth jurisdictions recognizing the Queen as Head of State. Section 16 of the *Fugitive Offenders Act* permitted the reviewing court to discharge the fugitive if, having regard to all of the circumstances of the case, it would have been ''unjust and oppressive'' to return the fugitive. Section 16 stated:

> **16.** Whenever it appears to the court that by reason of the trivial nature of the case or by reason of the application for the return of a fugitive not being made in good faith in the interests of justice, or that, for any other reason, it would, having regard to the distance, to the facilities for communication and to all the circumstances of the case, be unjust or oppressive or too severe a punishment to return the fugitive either at all or until the expiration of a certain period, the court may
>
> (a) discharge the fugitive, either absolutely or on bail;
> (b) order that he shall not be returned until after the expiration of the period named in the order; or
> (c) make such other order in the premises as to the court seems just.

The following are some of the cases which considered ''unjust and oppressive'' circumstances under s. 16.

1. *Bennett, Ex Parte* (1974), 17 C.C.C. (2d) 274 (Ont. H.C.)

Circumstances were not considered unjust since the epilepsy suffered by the fugitive was of a mild form, the offence of drug exportation was serious, and delays in the proceedings were attributable to the fugitive.

2. *R. v. Fai* (1979), 48 C.C.C. (2d) 173 (Que. S.C.)

Surrender was found to be unjust considering that there was long, unexplained delay in the issuance of the arrest warrant by Hong Kong, the fugitive and his family in the interim had become well integrated into the community, and an acceptable restitution had been offered.

3. *Hong Kong v. Sun* (December 11, 1992) (Ont. Gen. Div.), appeal to Ont. C.A. dismissed (1996), 109 C.C.C. (3d) 383 (Ont. C.A.)

Due to the charges of the co-accused having been stayed in Hong Kong because of delay, a s. 16 application was successful with respect to an elderly fugitive from Hong Kong who faced fraud, conspiracy, and false accounting charges.

4. *Cheng v. Hong Kong* (December 17, 1992) (Ont. Gen. Div.), appeal to Ont. C.A. dismissed (1996), 109 C.C.C. (3d) 384 (Ont. C.A.)

A s. 16 application was ultimately successful considering the suicidal nature of the fugitive's wife and the effect his rendition would have on his ability to care for their 8-year-old son.

5. *Chan v. Tanguay* (1995), (*sub nom. Chan c. Maison Tanguay*) [1996] R.J.Q. 335 (Que. S.C.), affirmed (1996), 113 C.C.C. (3d) 270 (Que. C.A.), leave to appeal to S.C.C. refused (May 22, 1997), Doc. 25761 (S.C.C.)

An application under s. 16 alleging that the return of the fugitive would constitute unjust or oppressive circumstances or result in too severe a punishment was unsuccessful. One of the issues which was considered was whether the return of the fugitive to Hong Kong should be refused due to the impending transfer of Hong Kong to the People's Republic of China. The application was unsuccessful due to insufficient evidence that China would not honour its treaty with the United Kingdom to maintain the legal system in Hong Kong.

Under the new Act, the Minister's decision with respect to "unjust and oppressive" considerations will be subject to judicial review in the court of appeal and to assessment against the standards required by s. 7 of the *Charter*. The case law developed under the former Act will continue to be relevant in this area, and the "shocks the conscience" test developed in *Schmidt, supra, Kindler, supra*, and *Burns, supra*, will continue to apply.

(b) Specific situations in which it could be contended that surrender would be "unjust or oppressive"

(i) *Mental illness*

In his reasons in *Kindler v. Canada (Minister of Justice), supra*, at p. 12, La Forest J. speculated on some of the factors which may come into play in assessing the constitutionality of an extradition:

> [S]ituations could arise where an order was unconstitutional. Apart from torture, the nature of the offence, the age or mental capacity of the accused (see the *Soering* case, E.H.R.R., judgment of July 7, 1989, Series A, No. 161, at pp. 44 and 45), and other circumstances may constitutionally vitiate an order for surrender.

It would appear to be open to defence counsel to argue that mental illness would constitute unjust or oppressive circumstances under s. 44(1)(a).

In *Larabie v. R.* (1988), 42 C.C.C. (3d) 385 (Ont. H.C.), Arbour J. considered a *habeas corpus* application on behalf of a fugitive who alleged that to proceed with extradition in his particular circumstances would amount to a violation of his right not to be subjected to cruel and unusual punishment. Larabie was wanted in the United States for robberies alleged to have been perpetrated in 1980. By the time of the extradition request in 1988, the fugitive had been in and out of mental institutions, and his mental health had deteriorated substantially. The extradition judge had ordered an assessment and it had been determined that he was fit to proceed with the hearing. He was ordered committed for extradition. However, by the time of the *habeas corpus* application before Arbour J., Larabie was presenting symptoms of serious mental illness. The uncontradicted evidence of the medical experts was that the "fact of extradition itself, quite apart from the possible outcome of trial proceedings in the United States, would irretrievably damage the applicant's mental condition," and he "would relapse into a psychotic state" (at p. 388).

As a pre–*Kindler* case, Arbour J. did not have the benefit of the decision of the Supreme Court of Canada on the applicability of s. 12 of the *Charter* to extradition surrender decisions. The majority of the court in Kindler held that s. 12 of the *Charter* did not apply because s. 32 of the *Charter* expressly provides that the *Charter* applies only to the actions of the Canadian government. In the result, Arbour J. treated the application as being premature because the effects the extradition would have on the mental health of the fugitive was a matter that the Minister would have to consider. In any event, Arbour J. considered that the evidence of the fugitive fell short of establishing a *Charter* violation. She stated that extradition in itself could not be viewed as cruel and unusual. She also found that, on the evidence before her, she could not accept that a constitutional violation had been made out. She was, however, prepared to accept that, in extreme cases, the consequences for the individual might vitiate the constitutionality of surrender (at p. 390):

> [T]here may come a point where the consequences of extradition would be so extreme as to outrage the standards of decency. For example, even though fitness to stand trial is not in itself a specific constitutional guarantee, it would be open to the courts to find that to conduct a criminal trial in this country of a person who, because of his or her mental condition, is unfit to stand trial, would amount to a cruel and unusual treatment and a violation of the principles of fundamental justice. Consequently, if the evidence in this case was such as to allow the conclusion that if extradited, the accused would then become unfit to stand trial in the United States, I would be inclined to think that the decision to extradite him would outrage the standards of decency and would constitute a violation of his rights under s. 12 of the Charter.

If surrendering the fugitive were to cause him to become psychotic and unfit to stand trial, then in Arbour J.'s view it is the surrender decision itself which outrages the standards of decency, and amounts to cruel and unusual treatment contrary to s. 12 of the *Charter*. The reasoning of the Supreme Court in *Kindler v. Canada (Minister of Justice)*, *supra*, may not have completely displaced a role for s. 12 in the review of ministerial decisions, focused as it was on objectionable treatment coming about as a result of actions taken by the foreign state. Even if the *Kindler* decision has confined constitutional review of the surrender to considerations under s. 7 of the *Charter*, clearly the values emanating from s. 12 would have to be considered in any s. 7 analysis. As the Supreme Court affirmed in *United States v. Burns, supra,* ''the values underlying various sections of the *Charter,* including s. 12, form part of the balancing process engaged under s. 7.'' (p. 125) Under either approach, the effects of surrender on the mental health of the individual would be a factor to be duly considered by the Minister of Justice in deciding whether or not to surrender due to unjust or oppressive circumstances under s. 44(1)(a).

(*ii*) *Mandatory minimum jail penalties*

The cases of *Ross v. United States, supra; United States v. Jamieson, supra;* and *United States v. Whitley, supra,* brought the issue of mandatory minimum penalties before the Supreme Court of Canada. In each case, the Supreme Court upheld the surrender of fugitives on drug charges to face mandatory minimum penalties on conviction. As a result of these decisions, it will be difficult to argue that the severity of a jail sentence in the requesting state, if imposed after a trial with reasonable procedural safeguards, leads to constitutional concerns under s. 7 of the *Charter* and consequently constitutes unjust or oppressive circumstances.

In *United States v. Whitley, supra,* the fugitive faced a minimum 20-year sentence if convicted in the United States for engaging in a continuing criminal enterprise and a minimum 10-year sentence for his part in possessing and attempting to export 1,100 pounds of marihuana. The fugitive had an extensive criminal record that included convictions for drug trafficking and possession for the purpose of drug trafficking. In *Ross v. United States, supra,* it was alleged that the fugitive went to Florida to buy a kilogram of cocaine which he intended to export to Canada. He faced a mandatory minimum sentence of 15 years if convicted. In *United States v. Jamieson, supra,* the fugitive faced a 20-year minimum sentence in Michigan for allegedly trafficking 273 grams of cocaine. He had no record.

The three cases were heard in the Supreme Court of Canada together, and the court found no violation of s. 7 of the *Charter* in extraditing the fugitives to face mandatory minimum sentences in the United States. In the *Whitley* and *Ross* cases, the court adopted the reasons of the majority in the courts below, upholding the surrender of the fugitives. In the *Jamieson* case, the majority of the Quebec Court of Appeal had held that the surrender violated the fugitive's s. 7 rights and denied the surrender. The Supreme Court adopted the dissenting reasons of Baudouin J.A. ((1994), 93 C.C.C. (3d) 265) and reinstated the surrender warrant.

The penalty to be imposed could be a factor in the Minister's determination as to whether surrender would be unjust or oppressive under s. 44(1)(a). However, the penalty is only one factor. That the sentence would not be constitutionally valid in Canada does not in itself lead to the conclusion that surrender would violate the principles of fundamental justice or be simply unacceptable. Of equal importance is a consideration of Canada's international obligation to surrender persons sought to extradition partners for serious crimes, and to prevent Canada from becoming a safe haven for criminals (*Ross v. United States* (1994), 93 C.C.C. (3d) 500 (B.C. C.A.), at pp. 533-534, affirmed (1996), 104 C.C.C. (3d) 446 (S.C.C.)).

(iii) Conditions or treatment in foreign jails

The decision of the British Columbia Court of Appeal in *Gwynne v. Canada (Minister of Justice)* (1999), 50 C.R.R. (2d) 250, may be of assistance with respect to whether the conditions in foreign jails could constitute unjust or oppressive circumstances under s. 44(1)(a). Gwynne was decided under the former scheme but raised matters which could have application under the new Act. In that case, a majority of the court held that the Minister's decision to surrender the fugitive to Alabama did not breach the requirements of fundamental justice. This was notwithstanding that the fugitive would be held in conditions in the Alabama penal system that were described as "degrading, dangerous and apparently endemic within the prison system of that state." (p. 259) Goldie J.A. for the majority held that the underlying basis for judicial intervention occurs when surrender would be a breach of fundamental justice under s. 7 of the *Charter*. He found that the prison conditions in Alabama were "subjectively shocking." (p. 263). Nevertheless, he did not find that surrender would be contrary to fundamental justice.

Goldie J.A. referred to a decision of the United States Supreme Court which held that while the United States *Constitution* did not mandate comfortable prisons neither did the *Constitution* permit inhumane ones. Accepting that as true, Goldie J.A. found that the fugitive's complaint was with respect to the fugitive's rights to a safe environment within the Alabama penal system. That procedures were in place by which the fugitive could attempt to enforce his rights was seen as a factor in favour of granting the extradition. In other words, the fugitive could raise his concerns with the authorities in the United States. The fugitive's constitutional concerns were in the United States, not in Canada.

Goldie J.A. added that requiring the Minister of Justice to evaluate the conditions in foreign jails would impose too onerous a task upon the Minister. He noted that the evidence before the Minister disclosed that, by any measure of correctional standards, Alabama was deficient. He referred, at pp. 261–262, to a report which indicated that Alabama was seventh of the fifty states in terms of the volume and rate of civil rights cases flowing from the conditions of prisons and jails:

> This suggests there are six other states where conditions, measured by this particular yardstick are worse than Alabama. While I doubt the validity of any such conclusion, would a fugitive in Canada whose return to one of these six states was sought be entitled to contend that his s. 7 *Charter* rights would be violated?
>
> I have not found in the material before us that the corrections system in Alabama is, by all standards, the worst of the 50 state systems. Even if this could be demonstrated the fact remains that a decision of this court to grant the relief sought by Mr. Gwynne would almost inevitably require the minister in future cases to embark upon a compar-

ative examination of the penal systems in the United States on a state by state basis with a view to determining at what point and with what system in what state he could safely conclude the Canadian conscience would not be shocked by the surrender of the fugitive.

I am also of the view that if this court determines s. 7 of the *Charter* required an examination of the penal conditions in the United States there are features in other countries with which Canada has extradition treaty relations where the conditions might approximate those found in Alabama.

In *United States of Mexico v. Hurley* (1997), 116 C.C.C. (3d) 414 (Ont. C.A.), submissions were made on behalf of the fugitive that as a homosexual accused of murdering his same-sex partner, his life and security of the person would be at risk if he were to be incarcerated and tried in Mexico. In response to these concerns the Minister sought diplomatic assurances from Mexico in relation to the well-being of the fugitive. On review, the Ontario Court of Appeal upheld the Minister's decision and set out, at p. 430, the test to be met with respect to a claim that surrender would amount to a violation of s. 7 of the *Charter*:

> [50] In light of the existing case law, a consideration of s. 7 in the circumstances of this case requires a two-step approach. First, it is necessary to establish if the persecution to which the appellant may be subjected is such that it "sufficiently shocks the conscience" and would be "fundamentally unacceptable to our society". If it does, the second prong of the analysis requires a consideration of whether or not the appellant has demonstrated, in accordance with the applicable onus of proof, that he will, in fact, be subjected to such persecution if he is extradited to Mexico.

The court held that the applicable onus of proof was on a balance of probabilities. It may be expected that the same burden of proof will be applicable to arguments made under s. 44(1)(a) since it is a statutory embodiment of this *Charter* right.

§4.2 Mandatory Refusal Due to Impermissible Grounds (s. 44(1)(b))

Section 44(1)(b) sets out specific circumstances that would render surrender unjust:

- The request is for the purpose of prosecuting or punishing the person sought by reason of the person's race, religion, nationality, ethnic origin, language, colour, political opinion, sex, sexual orientation, age, mental or physical disability or status.

- The person's position, once surrendered, may be prejudiced by reason of the above.

349

Section 44(1)(b) appears to make applicable to extradition the types of considerations set out in the *Charter*, with particular similarity to s. 15 of the *Charter*. Section 15 reads as follows:

> **15.** (1) Every individual is equal before and under the law and has the right to the equal protection and equal benefit of the law without discrimination and, in particular, without discrimination based on race, national or ethnic origin, colour, religion, sex, age or mental or physical disability.

The reference to "political opinion" in s. 44(1)(b) of the *Extradition Act* is similar to the "freedom of thought, belief, opinion and expression" under s. 2(b) of the Charter.

Jurisprudence under the former *Extradition Act* held that discrimination by foreign authorities cannot constitute a violation of s. 15 of the *Charter* for the reason that such discrimination would be attributable to the action or inaction of the foreign authorities rather than the Canadian government. The case law found that the *Charter* cannot have extraterritorial application (see *Kindler v. Canada (Minister of Justice)*, *supra*; *R. v. Schmidt*, *supra*; *Argentina (Republic) v. Mellino* (1987), 33 C.C.C. (3d) 334 (S.C.C.); and *United States v. Allard* (1991), 64 C.C.C. (3d) 159 (S.C.C.), reconsideration refused (July 11, 1991), Doc. 20626 (S.C.C.)). Consequently, in *United States of Mexico v. Hurley*, *supra*, where it was argued that extradition should not be ordered due to potential mistreatment owing to the sexual orientation of the fugitive, the court held that s. 15 was inapplicable to a review of the Minister's decision to surrender.

With the inclusion of s. 44(1)(b) in the new *Extradition Act*, the motivations for the request and the anticipated consequences of surrender to the extradition partner are directly relevant to the Minister's decision to surrender. The factors specified in s. 44(1)(b), which are similar to domestic *Charter* protections, were considered to be of such importance that they were expressly itemized rather than left under the more general provision of s. 44(1)(a).

The latter part of s. 44(1)(b) precludes surrender if the person's position, once surrendered, may be prejudiced by reason of his or her race, religion, nationality, ethnic origin, political opinion, sex, sexual orientation, age, mental or physical disability or status, even if the extradition request itself is not motivated by any of these factors. This was the alleged situation in *Hurley*, *supra*, in which the fugitive argued that he would suffer prejudicial treatment in the requesting state due to his sexual orientation. Under the new *Extradition Act*, such an argument would be possible under s. 44(1)(b). Prior to the new Act, this argument was only possible under s. 7 of the *Charter*. This was the provision relied upon in *Hurley*.

Note that inconsistent extradition agreement provisions do not override the grounds for mandatory refusal of surrender enumerated in s. 44. Under s. 45 of the Act, extradition agreement provisions only override the reasons for refusal set out in ss. 46 and 47.

§4.3 Discretionary Refusal Due to Imposition of Death Penalty (s. 44(2))

Section 44(2) provides the Minister of Justice with the discretion to refuse surrender if the death penalty is applicable to the conduct in question under the laws of the extradition partner. This provision is similar to its treaty counterparts in that it is discretionary. Article 6 of the *Canada–United States Extradition Treaty*, which is representative of the treaties which provide for this consideration, allows for the refusal of surrender when the offence for which extradition is requested is punishable by death under the laws of the requesting state and the laws of the requested state do not permit such punishment for that offence. However, in such circumstances, Article 6 provides that extradition may nonetheless be granted if the requesting state provides the requested state with sufficient assurances that the death penalty will not be carried out.

Notwithstanding the discretionary nature of the Minister's right to refuse to order surrender under s. 44(2) of the Act and pursuant to the treaties, as a result of the decision of the Supreme Court of Canada in *United States v. Burns, supra*, it is now the case that in all but exceptional cases it will be constitutionally necessary for the Minister to seek assurances that the death penalty will not be imposed. In *Burns*, the decisions of *Kindler v. Canada (Minister of Justice), supra* and *Re Ng, supra*, which had held that the *Charter* was not violated by surrender without assurances in death penalty cases, were reconsidered. Arbour J. in *Burns* summarized the facts and the results of *Kindler* and *Ng* as follows, at pp. 126–127:

> [61] In their submissions on whether extradition without assurances is contrary to the principles of fundamental justice, the parties drew heavily on the decisions in *Kindler* and *Ng*. It may be helpful to recall the facts of those cases. Kindler was an American citizen who had escaped to Canada after being convicted in Pennsylvania for the brutal murder of an 18-year old who was scheduled to testify against him in a burglary case. The jury which convicted Kindler had recommended that he face the death penalty. Prior to being sentenced, he escaped to Canada. After seven months as a fugitive in Quebec, Kindler was captured and escaped again. After remaining at large for nearly two years, Kindler was recaptured. Judicial review of Kindler's surrender order was dismissed by this Court even though (unlike this case) the death penalty was no longer simply a possibility. It had already been recommended by the jury. Nevertheless, we held that the Minister was entitled to extradite without assurances.

> [62] In the companion appeal, the respondent Ng was a British subject born in Hong Kong and subsequently resident in the United States. He had been arrested in Calgary after shooting at two department store security guards who tried to apprehend him for shoplifting. Once his identity was established, he was extradited to the State of California to face numerous charges of murder. He has since been convicted and sentenced to death for murdering 11 people — six men, three women and two baby boys — during what one newspaper described as a "spree of sexual torture and murder in rural California". In that case, as well, the Minister was held to have the power, though not the duty, to extradite without assurances.

The Supreme Court had held in *Kindler* and *Ng* that the *Charter* required a balancing on the facts of each case of the applicable principles of fundamental justice. The court wrote that surrender would be considered to be unconstitutional, if, after a balancing of the applicable factors, it would "shock the conscience" or be "simply unacceptable" to do so. The continuing applicability of the *Kindler* and *Ng* approach was raised in *Burns*.

Burns and Rafay were wanted in the state of Washington for a crime that, like those of Kindler, was "brutal and shocking." The two were visiting the parents of Rafay in the state of Washington. During the visit, they allegedly murdered Rafay's parents and sister. They were arrested in Canada and, following their arrest, allegedly confessed to the police that they had committed the killings to benefit from life insurance and the value of the home owned by Rafay's parents. The victims were bludgeoned to death with a baseball bat. The Minister of Justice decided to surrender the fugitives without seeking assurances that capital punishment would not be imposed in the event of a conviction. The majority of the British Columbia Court of Appeal (McEachern and Donald JJ.A.) ((1997), 116 C.C.C. (3d) 524) set aside the Minister's decision and directed that the assurances described in Article 6 of the *Canada–United States Extradition Treaty* be sought as a condition of the surrender of Burns and Rafay.

The majority of the British Columbia Court of Appeal agreed that the result in *Kindler* made the provisions of ss. 7 and 12 of the *Charter* unavailable to Burns and Rafay on the facts of the case. However, they relied upon s. 6 of the *Charter*, which provides that "[e]very citizen has the right to enter, remain in and leave Canada." The argument made by the fugitives and accepted by the majority was that the fugitives' constitutional right to return to Canada would be extinguished if they were to be executed by the United States. In *United States v. Cotroni, supra*, the Supreme Court of Canada had found that extradition was a reasonable limit on the rights enshrined in s. 6 of the Charter. However, Donald J.A. noted that La Forest J. had made the following observation in that case, at p. 213:

> An accused may return to Canada following his trial and acquittal or, if he has been convicted, after he has served his sentence. The impact of extradition on the rights of a citizen to remain in Canada appears to me to be of secondary importance. In fact, so far as Canada and the United States are concerned, a person convicted may, in some cases, be permitted to serve his sentence in Canada; see *Transfer of Offenders Act*, S.C. 1977-78, c. 9.

Given that the death penalty would completely terminate the possibility of returning to Canada, Donald J.A. held that, unlike the situation in *Cotroni*, it could not be argued that extradition of a citizen to face the death penalty infringed the s. 6(1) right as little as possible.

On appeal to the Supreme Court of Canada, the Supreme Court held that while it agreed with the result reached by the majority of the British Columbia Court of Appeal, it disagreed with that court's reliance on s. 6 of the *Charter*. The Supreme Court observed that the death penalty issue was only marginally a mobility rights issue and that the issue of the death penalty should be confronted under s. 7 of the *Charter*. The court made no distinction between Canadian citizens and others who might face the death penalty if extradited.

The court in *Burns* determined that while the balancing test enunciated in *Kindler* and *Ng*, remained valid, that the "balance which tilted in favour of extradition without assurances in *Kindler* and *Ng* now tilts against the constitutionality of such an outcome." (p. 155, para. 144) The court observed, at p. 151, that:

> [131] The arguments against extradition without assurances have grown stronger since this Court decided *Kindler* and *Ng* in 1991. Canada is now abolitionist for all crimes, even those in the military field. The international trend against the death penalty has become clearer. The death penalty controversies in the requesting State — the United States — are based on pragmatic, hard-headed concerns about wrongful convictions. None of these factors is conclusive, but taken together they tilt the s. 7 balance against extradition without assurances.

While the court has left open the possibility that surrender without assurances may be possible in "exceptional cases," it declined to speculate on what might constitute exceptional circumstances.

§4.4 Interaction of Ss. 46 and 47 with Extradition Agreements (s. 45)

With respect to refusals to surrender pursuant to ss. 46 and 47 of the *Extradition Act*, s. 45(1) ensures that the Minister of Justice's power of refusal will accord with the provisions of an applicable bilateral extradition agreement. Section 45(1) accomplishes this by providing that the reasons for refusal of surrender in a bilateral agreement, or the absence of reasons for refusal in such an agreement, prevail over ss. 46 and 47.

The new Act provides for extradition without the necessity of an extradition agreement, and because it may be necessary to deal with extradition in the absence of a treaty, the Act contains many of the same provisions usually found in extradition treaties. This includes provisions concerning the grounds which would justify the refusal of a request. The inclusion of such provisions in the Act, however, was not meant to displace the bilateral arrangements already existing between Canada and other countries. Canada is under an international obligation to honour the commitments set out in its bilateral extradition treaties which represent the terms and conditions agreed to with respect to extradition between Canada and the treaty partner. For that reason, s. 45(1) provides that if a bilateral treaty with another state sets out the grounds of refusal which can operate with respect to extradition requests, then only those grounds, and not the grounds in ss. 46 and 47 the Act, will be operable with respect to requests from that state. If the extradition agreement does not provide for grounds of refusal which are in ss. 46 and 47 of the Act, the silence of the treaty will also prevail over the terms of the Act, as it is taken that the parties chose not to provide for that ground of refusal.

In the case of multilateral agreements, s. 45(2) provides that the terms of the agreement will prevail over the terms of ss. 46 and 47 of the Act only to the extent of the inconsistency. Unlike s. 45(1), s. 45(2) does not provide for the absence of reasons for refusal to take precedence. There are a number of multilateral conventions to which Canada is a signatory. These agreements deal with issues of transnational concern directed to a particular type of criminal activity and may contain provisions dealing with extradition, such as:

- International Agreement for suppression of white slave traffic (1949)

- Convention on the Prevention and Punishment of Genocide (1952)

- Convention for the suppression of the unlawful seizure of aircraft (1972)

- Convention for the suppression of unlawful acts against the safety of civil aviation (1973)

- Convention on the prevention and punishment of crimes against internationally protected persons, including diplomatic agents (1977)

- Convention against illicit traffic in Narcotic drugs and Psychotropic Substances (1988)

- Convention against Transnational Organized Crime (2000)

Multilateral agreements, since they are designed to create general obligations applicable to a number of signatories, do not usually deal with extradition in detailed fashion but rely instead upon the use of domestic extradition laws and treaties to give effect to the convention obligations. Most multilateral agreements contain limited or no reference to grounds of refusal in the expectation that domestic grounds at law, or grounds in any applicable bilateral extradition treaty, will be applied in the process. As a consequence, the Act recognizes that silence with respect to grounds of refusal in a multilateral agreement should not be the governing principle in extradition under such agreements. The multilateral agreement will prevail in the case of a direct conflict between its terms and those of the Act, but otherwise the terms of ss. 46 and 47 of the Act will govern with respect to the grounds for refusal of a request for extradition.

The effect of s. 45 in relation to ss. 46 and 47 can be summarized as follows:

1.	s. 45(1)	Bilateral extradition agreement applicable	Ss. 46 and 47 have no application
2.	s. 45(2)	Multilateral extradition agreement applicable	Ss. 46 and 47 operate to the extent not inconsistent with agreement
3.	—	No extradition agreement applicable	Ss. 46 and 47 apply fully

§4.5 Mandatory Refusal to Surrender Under S. 46

(a) Mandatory refusal to surrender for statute-barred offences (s. 46(1)(a))

Section 46(1)(a) mandates refusal to surrender in situations where the offence is statute-barred in the foreign state. As indicated previously, this provision is already contained as a basis for mandatory refusal for surrender in some of the treaties such as the American treaty (Article 4(1)(ii)); the Mexican treaty (Article IV(e)); the Spanish treaty (Article III(4)); and the Philippines treaty (Article 3(5)).

(b) Mandatory refusal to surrender for military offences (s. 46(1)(b))

Section 46(1)(b) mandates the Minister to refuse surrender in situations where the offence for which extradition is sought is a military offence which is not also an offence under domestic criminal law. Two types of extradition requests will attract the consideration of this section.

1. Military offences which would also be domestic criminal offences;

2. Military offences which have no equivalent in domestic criminal law.

The first category presents no bar to extradition. A review of Canadian military law, the *National Defence Act*, indicates a number of offences which have also counterparts in the Canadian *Criminal Code*. For example:

National Defence Act			*Criminal Code*		
S. 75	—	Offences related to security	Ss. 46–47	—	Treason
S. 75(a)	—	Improperly holding communications with or giving intelligence to the enemy	Ss. 46–47	—	Treason
S. 75(b)	—	Disclosing troop movements to the enemy	Ss. 46–47	—	Treason
S. 78	—	Offence of being a spy	Ss. 46–47	—	Treason
S. 81	—	Offences related to mutiny	S. 53	—	Inciting to mutiny
S. 82	—	Seditious offences — Advocating governmental change by force	S. 61	—	Seditious offences
S. 114	—	Stealing	Ss. 322–324	—	Theft

Consequently, if the request from extradition partners, are with respect to military offences similar to those referred to in the list above, extradition is permitted.

The second category is more problematic. By its plain terms, if the military offence does not involve conduct which constitutes an offence under Canadian criminal law the Minister is required to refuse extradition. However, this seemingly straightforward provision, as already discussed, has to be considered in conjunction with ss. 45(1) and (2). Since s. 45(1) gives precedence to treaty provisions when they conflict or are silent on a reason for refusal referred to in ss. 46 and 47, it will be necessary when the requested military offence is not also a domestic criminal offence to consider the treaty provisions or the lack of them in this regard before determining whether refusal is mandated. For instance, neither the American nor Korean treaties make any provisions for refusing to surrender for military offences. Accordingly, if a request were made for a strictly military offence which has no counterpart under Canadian criminal law, the silence of these treaties would take precedence over s. 46(1)(b). Therefore, the Minister could not refuse to surrender for the reason that the offence is a military one with no domestic criminal law counterpart.

That said, the request still has to meet the requirements of double criminality in the sense of the conduct amounting to an offence under Canadian law punishable by the penalties set out in the treaties. In the American context, Article 2(1) of the treaty provides that "[e]xtradition shall be granted for conduct which constitutes an offense punishable by the laws of both Contracting Parties by imprisonment or other form of detention for a term exceeding one year or any greater punishment."

Consequently, if the United States requested extradition for conduct in Canada which would amount to desertion under s. 88 of the Canadian *National Defence Act*, which meets the penalty criteria of the treaty (if on active service the maximum penalty is life and in any other case five years), the Minister could not resort to s. 46(1)(b) to preclude extradition.

Considering that a number of treaties specifically deal with extradition being precluded for purely military offences (Mexico, in force 1990 — Article IV(c); India, in force 1987 — Article 5(2)(a); Spain, signed 1985 and in force 1990 — Article III(2); Philippines, 1989 — Article 3(3)), the failure of other treaties to preclude purely military offences would appear to be intentional.

(c) Mandatory refusal to surrender for political offences (s. 46(1)(c))

Section 46(1)(c) makes it mandatory for the Minister to refuse surrender when "the conduct in respect of which extradition is sought is a political offence or an offence of a political character."

(i) *What is a political offence or an offence of a political character?*

The Act and the international agreements contain many exemptions specifying what may not be considered to be a political offence or offence of a political character, with the result that there is little or no room left for an offence to fall outside extradition on this basis. Virtually all crimes of violence have been excluded from being considered political offences. As well, the proliferation of international tribunals and creation of international criminal courts has weakened the justification for exempting politically motivated crimes.

The term "political character" is not defined in the *Extradition Act* or any of Canada's extradition treaties. For a definition of the term, one must look to the jurisprudence. There are two cases in particular which are of assistance: *Wisconsin (State) v. Armstrong* (1973), 10 C.C.C. (2d) 271 (Fed. C.A.), leave to appeal to S.C.C. refused (1973), 10 C.C.C. (3d) 271n (S.C.C.), and *Gil v. Canada (Minister of Employment & Immigration)* (1994), 25 Imm. L.R. (2d) 209 (Fed. C.A.). If the facts in these cases were to arise in the extradition context today, it would probably not be necessary to consider whether the conduct constituted political offences given that the Act and most of the newer treaties specifically exempt the conduct in these cases from the political offence category. Nevertheless, the analysis and tests enunciated in those cases continue to provide useful guidance on this issue.

In *Wisconsin (State) v. Armstrong, supra*, the Federal Court of Appeal had occasion to consider what amounted to an offence of a political character in its review of the decision of the extradition judge under s. 15 of the former Act. Section 15 directed the extradition judge to receive evidence tendered to show that the offence in question was of a political character. This enabled the Minister under ss. 21 and 22 of the former Act to determine whether surrender should be refused for that reason. At the extradition hearing, the judge had determined that the offences in question were not of a political character. The Court of Appeal found that the extradition judge was required under s. 15 of the former Act to receive evidence regarding the political character of the offence, but that the Act did not confer upon the judge the authority to decide the question. Nonetheless, the Court of Appeal decided to express its opinion on the issue.

The applicant Armstrong had been indicted in the State of Wisconsin on four charges of arson and one charge of first-degree murder. The charges arose out of alleged attacks on university buildings at the University of Wisconsin. Witnesses were called at the extradition hearing to show that the incidents giving rise to the charges were related to "widespread dissatisfaction and protests against the involvement of the Government of the United States and its military forces in the war in Vietnam and of the dissatisfaction of some elements of American society with the capitalist system of the United States and the alleged influence of the United States Government and of United States corporations in other parts of the world." (p. 290) The witnesses also testified that the university buildings in question were "in whole or in part used for purposes of or connected with the military forces of the United States." (p. 290)

Thurlow J.A., of the Federal Court of Appeal, found that there was no evidence regarding the purpose and motivation of the fugitive in allegedly committing the offences to be able to conclude that the activity was political and therefore the offences of a political character. Thurlow J.A. added that, "murder and arson are not *per se* or ordinarily offences of a political character and the existence of a political motive or purpose has been consistently held to be a necessary feature for the purpose of characterizing an offence as one of a political character . . . ." (p. 291) Furthermore, he noted that the activities were aimed at the university rather than the government and that the alleged offences did not occur "in the course of a political tumult or revolution." (p. 292)

In a concurring judgment, Sweet D.J. outlined specific factors that must be considered in assessing a political offence argument. Firstly, referring to the judgment of Viscount Radcliffe of the House of Lords in *Schtraks v. Government of Israel* (1962), [1964] A.C. 556 (U.K. H.L.), Sweet D.J. held at p. 301 that an individual cannot unilaterally make an offence political. Secondly, an individual who takes it upon himself or herself to use illegal means to achieve an organization's aims cannot escape the jurisdiction of the requesting state. Thirdly, a political offence argument must be particularly closely scrutinized when the act in question was made against the person or property of non-governmental parties.

In the more recent Federal Court of Appeal decision of *Gil v. Canada (Minister of Employment & Immigration)*, *supra*, the court provided several useful insights into defining the "political character" of an offence. *Gil v. Canada (Minister of Employment Immigration)* was an immigration case. The appellant was an Iranian citizen who, after the Khomeini revolution in Iran, was alleged to have joined a group of militant anti-Khomeini activists. During 1980 and 1981, the appellant was believed to have been involved in five or six incidents of bombing and arson. The acts were allegedly aimed at wealthy supporters of the Khomeini regime and consisted of placing bombs at the business premises of these persons. The premises were usually crowded at the time of the attacks and resulted in injury and death to innocent bystanders. The Board found as a fact, at p. 213, that the appellant "was personally responsible for the murder of innocent people."

After coming to Canada, the appellant had claimed Convention refugee status. The Convention Refugee Board found that the appellant had a well-founded fear of persecution in Iran. However, the Board excluded the appellant from Convention refugee status on the basis of Article 1, para. (F)(b) of the United Nations *Convention Relating to the Status of Refugees*. This paragraph denies the protection of the Convention to persons who have committed "serious non-political" crimes outside the country of refuge prior to admission to that country.

The Board's decision was appealed to the Federal Court of Appeal. Hugessen J.A. for the court found that the appellant had committed "serious non-political" offences and dismissed the appeal. In reaching this conclusion, Hugessen J.A. reviewed case law from the field of extradition, particularly U.S. and U.K. decisions, dealing with the political offences exemption. Hugessen J.A. indicated that the 1891 British case of *Re Castioni*, [1891] 1 Q.B. 149 (Eng. Q.B.), laid down what became known as the "incidence" test for determining whether an offence is of a political character (p. 217). According to this test, a fugitive is not to be surrendered to a requesting state if the extradition crime is "incidental to and formed a part of political disturbances." Hugessen J.A. noted, at p. 222, that the American courts have adapted and refined the incidence test as set out in *Castioni*. In this light, Hugessen J.A. referred to the decision of *Quinn v. Robinson*, 783 F.2d 776 (9th Cir. Cal., 1986) and quoted approvingly as follows, at p. 227:

> The incidence test has two components, designed so that the exception comports with its original justification and protects acts of the kind that inspired its inclusion in extradition treaties. First, there must be an uprising — a political disturbance related to the struggle of individuals to alter or abolish the existing government in their country. An uprising is both temporally and spatially limited. Second, the charged offense must have been committed in furtherance of the uprising; it must be related to the political struggle or be consequent to the uprising activity.

Elaborating on the second component of the test, Hugessen J.A. referred to the following passage from the 1988 United States District Court decision of *Forti v. Suarez-Mason*, 694 F. Supp. 707 (U.S. N.D. Cal., 1988), in which the court held that there must be a nexus between the uprising and the offence, at p. 228:

> American Courts appear to have taken a liberal view toward the "incidental to" requirement. See e.g., *Quinn*, 783 F.2d at 797; Garcia-Mora, *The Nature of Political Offenses: A Knotty Problem of Extradition Law*, 48 Va. L. Rev. 1226, 1244 (1962). Nevertheless, as persuasively articulated in *Extradition of Artukovic*, 628 F. Supp. 1370 (C.D. Cal. 1986), *the person seeking to invoke the exception must show a rational nexus between the uprising and the offense*:
>
> > [R]espondent cannot avail himself of the defense merely because the alleged crimes occurred at the same time as a political disturbance. A rational nexus between the alleged crimes and the prevailing turmoil must be demonstrated . . . *the focus of the inquiry is on the circumstances, and on the status of those harmed*, and not on

> whether the acts merely were committed during the disorder. [Emphasis added by Hugessen J.A.]

On the facts of the case, Hugessen J.A. held that the appellant came within the first branch of the incidence test. However, he found that the appellant did not meet the second branch of the incidence test, at pp. 232–233:

> Where the appellant's claim fails the incidence test, however, is in the second branch thereof. There is, in my view, simply no objective rational connection between injuring the commercial interests of certain wealthy supporters of the regime and any realistic goal of forcing the regime itself to fall or to change its ways or its policies. . . . Even if we accept (which the board appears not to have done) that some of the businesses targeted were owned by highly placed members of local revolutionary committees, the nexus between such businesses and the general structure of the government of Iran at the time appears far too tenuous to support or justify the kind of indiscriminate violence which the appellant admitted to.

According to Hugessen J.A., a further detrimental factor for the appellant was that the attacks were not committed against armed adversaries and were bound to injure innocent bystanders.

With no equivalent to s. 15 in the new Act, there will be no requirement for the extradition court to receive evidence regarding political offence issues for the Minister's consideration. The political offence issue including reception of evidence will be dealt with entirely at the ministerial level. However, the factors enumerated in *Wisconsin (State) v. Armstrong* and *Gil v. Canada (Minister of Employment & Immigration)* will still be useful to counsel in drafting submissions to the Minister on this issue. They will also be of assistance in any subsequent judicial review of the Minister's decision in this regard.

(ii) *Political nature of offence versus political motivation for request*

Under s. 46(1)(c), the Minister must refuse to surrender if the conduct in respect of which extradition is sought is a political offence or an offence of a political character. This is a different consideration from the Minister's requirement to refuse surrender under s. 44(1)(b). Under the latter section the Minister must refuse to surrender if the request for extradition is made for the purpose of prosecuting or punishing the person by reason of their political opinions.

There is a distinction to be made between an offence of a political character and politically motivated requests for extradition. For instance, persons sought for an ordinary *Criminal Code* offence could still have recourse under s. 44(1)(b) of the Act, alleging that the request was motivated due to their political opinions. They could not have recourse under s. 46(1)(c) since s. 46(1)(c) focuses on the political nature of the offence itself rather than the surrounding proceedings.

In order for s. 46(1)(c) to operate, the offence itself must have a political nexus. This distinction was discussed by Doherty J.A. of the Ontario Court of Appeal in

Philippines (Republic) v. Pacificador (1993), 83 C.C.C. (3d) 210 (Ont. C.A.), leave to appeal to S.C.C. refused (1994), 87 C.C.C. (3d) vi (S.C.C.). It was discussed in terms of evidence which the fugitive wished to tender at the hearing under s. 15 of the former Act, which required that the extradition judge receive evidence that an offence was of a political character. In *Philippines (Republic) v. Pacificador*, the fugitive sought to avoid extradition by, among other things, arguing that the crimes with which he was charged, murder and attempted murder, were in the circumstances, political offences. The fugitive was alleged by the Philippines to have been a party to the killing of a political opponent of the fugitive's father.

Doherty J.A. held that the extradition hearing judge had no authority under s. 15 to receive evidence related to an argument made under Article 3(2) of the extradition treaty between Canada and the Philippines. Article 3(2) precludes extradition when the request is made for the purpose of prosecuting or punishing a person for their political beliefs. Doherty J.A. found that it was not the political nature of the offence but rather the political motivation of the proceedings which was an issue (at p. 221). He concluded that the motivation for the proceedings was a matter to be addressed by the Minister and that it was not relevant to the extradition hearing. Doherty J.A. stated, at pp. 220–221:

> It is true, as the appellant contends, that Article III(2) of the treaty directs that extradition shall not be granted for any criminal offence where there are substantial grounds for believing that the request for extradition "has been made for the purpose of prosecuting or punishing a person on account of that person's race, religion, nationality, or political beliefs." The ground for refusing extradition does not, however, turn on the political nature of the offence, but rather on the purpose underlying the prosecution. Section 15 of the Act is not directed to evidence relating to the purpose behind the prosecution, but only to the nature of the offence alleged. Evidence intended to demonstrate an improper prosecutorial purpose is not rendered admissible before the extradition court pursuant to s. 15 of the Act.
>
> I am further of the view that it is for the Minister of Justice to determine whether extradition should be denied based on the motives driving the request for extradition. Evidence of those motives is not relevant in proceedings before the extradition judge.

Under the new *Extradition Act,* the distinction between politically motivated requests and offences of a political character ceases to have any meaning in terms of introducing evidence at the hearing since, as indicated previously, there is no provision under the new Act requiring the extradition judge to receive evidence on either issue or, in fact, any evidence not related to the *prima facie* case consideration. It is clear from the structure of the new Act that, as under the former Act, consideration of both of these issues is within the Minister's sole jurisdiction at the second phase of the extradition process.

In both situations the Minister's refusal is mandatory. However, as discussed above, s. 46 is subject to being overridden by the terms or silence of an applicable treaty regarding refusal to surrender, or the positive terms of relevant multilateral extradition agreements. Therefore, although s. 46(1)(c) states that the Minister must refuse to surrender for offences of a political character, it is open to the treaty partners to provide for a regime to apply other than that set out in the Act. In contrast, s. 44(1)(b) of the Act, which precludes extradition for requests made for the purpose of prosecuting or punishing the person by reason of, among other things, their political opinions, is immune from s. 45 treaty or multilateral agreement overrides.

This recognizes the flexibility accorded to treaty partners to determine which conduct they are not willing to consider as constituting an offence of a political character. It allows the parties, by negotiation, to take out of the political arena certain offences that they agree should still be considered extraditable crimes. On the other hand, the mandatory refusal for requests motivated by the political opinions of the person sought, it would appear, are not subject to treaty or multilateral extradition agreement override because it is not the crime which is at issue, but the beliefs of the person sought. A request based not on the crime but on the personal opinions of the person sought for the crime is totally at odds with the rationale of the extradition process. Persons are returned for the prosecution of crimes not for the purpose of prosecuting for reasons of their personal beliefs.

(iii) *Exemptions from category of political offences*

Section 46(2) exempts offences referred to in a multilateral extradition agreement and five specified categories of conduct from being considered political offences or offences of a political character. The five specified categories — which include attempts, conspiracies, counselling, aiding or abetting or being an accessory after the fact — are the following:

- murder or manslaughter;

- inflicting serious bodily harm;

- sexual assault;

- kidnapping, abduction, hostage-taking, or extortion; and

- using explosives, incendiaries, devices or substances in circumstances in which human life is likely to be endangered or serious bodily harm or substantial property damage is likely to be caused.

The exemption of political offences from extradition is a relatively recent development. In fact, until the latter part of the nineteenth century, extradition was used principally to extradite fugitives for political offences. This point is made by Castel and Williams in *Canadian Criminal Law: International and Transnational Aspects* (Toronto: Butterworths, 1981), at pp. 348–349:

Historically extradition has done an about face. As an instrument for international co-operation in the suppression of crime it can be traced to ancient times. However, it was not used very frequently until the end of the seventeenth century. In actual fact, in the few cases in which extradition was requested, the motive for the request was political. Thus, extradition was used to ensure political stability.

It was not until the beginning of the nineteenth century that the usefulness of the extradition process was extended to ordinary common crimes.

Consistent with this development, ss. 15 and 22 of the former *Extradition Act* were first enacted in Canada in 1877 (*Extradition Act 1877*, S.C. 1877, c. 25; see *Wisconsin (State) v. Armstrong, supra*, at p. 283; the wording of ss. 15 and 22 — then ss. 12 and 16 — had not changed significantly since 1877). Section 15 required that the extradition judge receive evidence regarding offences of a political character and s. 22 gave the Minister discretion to refuse surrender for this reason. Similarly, at the international level, it was only in 1889 that a political offences exclusion was added to the extradition arrangement then in force between Canada and the United States (see C.T.S. 1952, No. 12, at 18-22; this document contains the *Supplementary Convention Between Her Majesty and the United States of America for the Extradition of Criminals*, signed in Washington, D.C., on July 12, 1889; the political offences exclusion is contained in Article II; see *Wisconsin (State) v. Armstrong, supra*, and *Meier v. Canada (Minister of Justice)* (1983), 6 C.C.C. (3d) 563 (Fed. T.D.), at p. 568).

If the political offences exclusion is a relatively recent development, an even more recent development is the inclusion in extradition treaties of provisions expressly rendering certain offences ineligible for the political offences exclusion. Moreover, the tolerance for the political offences exclusion appears to be narrowing. For instance, it was not until 1976, when the current *Canada–United States Extradition Treaty* came into force, that the extradition treaty lifted certain offences from the ambit of ss. 15 and 22 (the history of the extradition treaty currently in force between Canada and the United States is as follows: the treaty was signed in Washington, D.C., on December 3, 1971; the treaty was amended by an Exchange of Notes on June 28 and July 9, 1974; Instruments of Ratification were exchanged and the treaty came into force on March 22, 1976; the treaty was amended by Protocol on November 26, 1991). More specifically, Article 4(2) formerly read as follows:

> (2) The provisions of subparagraph (iii) of paragraph (1) of this Article [stating that extradition shall not be granted for offences of a political character] shall not be applicable to the following:
>
> > (i) A kidnapping, murder or other assault against the life or physical integrity of a person to whom a Contracting Party has the duty according to international law to give special protection, or any attempt to commit such an offense with respect to any such person.
> >
> > (ii) When offense 23 of the annexed Schedule [aircraft hijacking], or an attempt to commit, or a conspiracy to commit, or being a party to the commission of

that offense, has been committed on board an aircraft engaged in commercial services carrying passengers.

However, the scope of this provision was fairly narrow. It only encompassed kidnapping, murder, and assault against a limited group of persons as well as the hijacking of a commercial passenger aircraft (similarly narrow provisions are contained in Canada's extradition treaties with Finland, Germany, Italy, Mexico, and the Netherlands).

The scope of Article 4(2) was broadened by an amendment to the *Canada–United States Extradition Treaty* that came into force in 1991. As amended, Article 4(2) reads as follows:

> (2) For the purpose of this Treaty, the following offenses shall be deemed not to be offenses within subparagraph (iii) of paragraph 1 of this Article:
>
> (i) An offense for which each Contracting Party has the obligation pursuant to a multilateral international agreement to extradite the person sought or to submit the case to its competent authorities for the purpose of prosecution;
> (ii) Murder, manslaughter or other culpable homicide, malicious wounding or inflicting grievous bodily harm;
> (iii) An offense involving kidnapping, abduction, or any form of unlawful detention, including taking a hostage;
> (iv) An offense involving the placing or use of explosives, incendiaries, or destructive devices or substances capable of endangering life or of causing grievous bodily harm or substantial property damage; and
> (v) An attempt or conspiracy to commit, or counselling the commission of, any of the foregoing offenses, or aiding or abetting a person who commits or attempts to commit such offenses.

As can be seen, Article 4(2) no longer restricts the named offences to those where the victim is a "person to whom a Contracting Party has the duty according to international law to give special protection." Rather, Article 4(2) now applies to the named offences regardless of the status under international law of the victim. Moreover, the number of offences excepted from the political offences exclusion is now larger, extending beyond kidnapping, murder, and assault, to manslaughter, culpable homicide, malicious wounding and inflicting grievous bodily harm, abduction or any form of unlawful detention, offences involving explosives, offences for which the parties to the treaty have an obligation to extradite under a multilateral international agreement, and attempts or conspiracies to commit these offences. In other recently negotiated extradition treaties, such as the extradition treaties with India, Korea, the Philippines, and Spain, the scope of the political offence exemption has similarly been narrowed, essentially removing from the exemption the more serious crimes such as murder. This trend towards narrowing the scope of the political offence exemption is carried on in the new Act with the inclusion of the list of exceptions in s. 46(2), which narrows the exemptions further with the additions of sexual assault and extortion to those offences that cannot be considered as political offences.

(iv) Effect of s. 45 override to exemptions

Like the other provisions under s. 46, s. 46(1)(c) is subject to being overridden by treaty pursuant to s. 45(1). Silence or positive enactment in the treaty would result in overriding this provision. As indicated previously there are similar categories of exempted offences to the list of exempted offences in s. 46(2) in many of the extradition treaties Canada has signed with other countries. When an offence contained in these categories is the subject of an extradition request it is not open to argue that they are political offences or offences of a political character. This was made clear in *Philippines (Republic) v. Pacificador, supra*, when the Court of Appeal held that murder could not be considered a political offence because it was exempted under the treaty. Doherty J.A. stated on this point, at p. 220:

> The phrase "offence of a political character" is not defined in the Act. It clearly does not encompass all crimes that have a political motive: La Forest, *Extradition To and From Canada, ibid.*, pp. 87–96. In any event, the treaty between Canada and the Philippines specifically removes murder and other crimes involving the infliction of serious bodily harm from the category of political offences . . . .
>
> Extradition is primarily a matter between sovereign countries. International relationships are established and controlled through treaties. The terms of those treaties reflect the intentions and expectations of the contracting nations: *McVey v. United States of America, supra*, pp. 6-7. Canada and the Philippines could not have made it plainer that murder and the other crimes referred to in Article III(1)(c) of the treaty were not to be considered political offences for extradition purposes. Clearly, the two countries intended that fugitives should not have to resort to the "political offence" exemption from extradition when the offence charged was one of those listed in Article III(1)(c) of the treaty.

Similarly, the new *Extradition Act* very clearly indicates the intention of Parliament to exempt the five categories of offences listed under s. 46(2) from being considered to be political offences.

In situations where the treaty provides for refusal to surrender for offences of a political character, and does not list any offences as exemptions from consideration, the exemptions listed in the Act will not be applicable, because s. 45(1) provides for treaty override.

If a treaty lists categories of offences that constitute exemptions from offences of a political character, those exemptions will replace the exemptions in s. 46(2), again by reason of the s. 45(1) treaty override.

If there are omissions from the exemption list in the treaty, surrender can be refused for those offences. For example, extortion is not exempted from being considered a political offence in the American treaty. However, it is included in the categories of offences which are exempted under s. 46(2) of the Act. Nevertheless, because of the s. 45(1) treaty override when extradition is requested by the United States with respect to extortion, extradition could be refused if it is contended that the extortion was an offence of a political character.

Section 46(2) not only exempts the five categories of offences listed from constituting a political offence or offence of a political character, it also exempts offences mentioned in a multilateral extradition agreement to which Canada is a party. By definition, therefore, an offence encompassed by a multilateral extradition agreement cannot be considered to be a political offence. As an example, under the multilateral convention for the suppression of the unlawful seizure of aircraft, the offence of seizing an aircraft in flight would not be considered a political offence. Nor, under the convention on the prevention and punishment of the crime of genocide, could genocide ever be considered to be an offence of a political character.

When Canada does not have an extradition treaty with a given country, but where the state or entity is a designated extradition partner under s. 9 of the Act and named in the Schedule to the Act, the provisions of s. 46(1)(c) and (2) regarding political offences will have full force and effect.

§4.6 Discretionary Refusal to Surrender Under S. 47

Unlike s. 46, where the Minister is mandated to refuse surrender, s. 47 permits discretionary refusal. Obviously Parliament wanted to preclude surrender in political offence situations because we would not countenance such prosecutions here (s. 46(1)(c)). With respect to the statute-barred situation in s. 46(1)(a), it seems reasonable to preclude extradition if the person could not be prosecuted by the extradition partner in any event. It also safeguards against the return of persons sought for reasons other than criminal prosecution, such as civil proceedings. The appearance of military offences in s. 46(1)(b) must reflect the view that Canada is hesitant to assist in extradition for purely military offences that have no domestic criminal law counterpart.

The discretionary situations in s. 47(a) — double jeopardy, (b) — convicted in absentia, (c) — young offenders and (e) — extraterritorial jurisdiction, raise non-routine issues which even in domestic criminal law require special consideration. In s. 47(d) the Minister is permitted to refuse surrender if there are domestic criminal proceedings based upon the same conduct as that in the extradition request. In none of these situations would surrender *per se* be necessarily unfair; however the Act requires a discretionary review of these situations by the Minister to safeguard against the possibility of injustice.

(a) Discretionary refusal to surrender for double jeopardy (s. 47(a))

Section 47(a) provides for discretionary refusal to surrender in situations that would result in a discharge in Canada due to double jeopardy. The Act when not overridden by treaty now permits refusal on this basis independent of any consideration of *Charter* s. 7 violations, which was the form of recourse for consideration of this issue prior to the enactment of this legislation. (See discussion above under §4.4, "Interaction of Ss. 46 and 47 with Extradition Agreements (s. 45)." See also s. 25, §4.2, "Specific *Charter* issues," and s. 29, §4.1(d)(viii), "Defences not to be raised at extradition hearing.").

(b) Discretionary refusal to surrender when persons convicted in their absence (s. 47(b))

Section 47(b) permits the Minister to refuse surrender when the person was convicted in his or her absence and could not on surrender have the case reviewed. This is a new provision. There is no counterpart in the former Act, although there is at least one treaty, namely, that with Germany, which contains a similar provision.

At the hearing stage, a person convicted *in absentia* is treated by virtue of s. 29(1) and (5) as a person who has been charged but not yet convicted. These sections provide that subject to an extradition agreement the judge at the hearing shall order committal after being satisfied that there is evidence admissible under the Act that would be sufficient to justify the committal of the person in Canada for the offence for which the person is sought. Persons convicted *in absentia* are treated differently than other convicted persons. Section 29(1)(b) provides a more summary method of proof for requests concerning persons already convicted that is not applicable when the conviction was *in absentia*. The domestic legislation safeguards the person who has been convicted *in absentia* by requiring the same documentation and committal for surrender test to be met at the extradition hearing as is required for a person who has not yet been convicted in the requesting state, but only charged.

The safeguards are continued at the ministerial phase by giving the Minister the discretion to refuse to order surrender if the *in absentia* conviction cannot be reviewed in the requesting jurisdiction upon the return of the person sought.

In conviction cases counsel will want to ensure that the material indicates whether or not the conviction was *in absentia*, as this determines the standard to be met at the hearing. If the conviction was *in absentia*, counsel should ensure that the material indicates whether or not there is a right of review upon return, as this is important at the ministerial phase of the proceedings. Considering that the Minister's right to refuse to surrender in this situation is discretionary, and considering that *prima facie* evidence of guilt has been established, the Minister may in certain circumstances, such as for serious crimes, decide to surrender even though no review of the conviction is available. As a practical matter, the effect of the treaty override contained in s. 45 which applies to s. 47 is that the existence of a treaty will always displace the operation of this section. Unless the treaty provisions are the same, s. 47(b) will only operate in the case of non-treaty requests. However, if the Minister were to be of the view that surrender of a person convicted *in absentia* as required pursuant to treaty would be unjust or oppressive, it would still be open to the Minister to refuse surrender on this basis pursuant to the provisions of s. 44(1)(a), which is not subject to treaty override. Section 44(1)(a) requires the Minister to refuse the surrender of a person if the surrender would be "unjust or oppressive having regard to all the relevant circumstances." It would also be open to the Minister to add conditions or require assurances pursuant to s. 40(3) regarding the matter being reviewed upon the return of the person sought.

(c) Discretionary refusal to surrender in young offender situations (s. 47(c))

Section 47(c) deals with persons who were under the age of 18 at the time of the offence and where laws of the extradition partner are not consistent with Canada's *Young Offenders Act*. The Minister is required to undertake a comparison of the applicable law in the requesting jurisdiction and Canadian domestic law concerning young offenders. The fundamental principles of the *Young Offenders Act* are set out in s. 3 of that Act, which declares the policy for Canada with respect to young offenders. In essence it sets out that young people should not in all instances be held to account for criminal actions in the same manner as would be appropriate for adults. The focus is upon the protection of society through the rehabilitation of the young offender, and upon minimal interference with the freedom of the young person.

Special considerations for young people in the extradition process have been seen in certain extradition treaties. For instance, Article 5 of the American treaty provides that the requested state, in situations where the fugitive is under 18 either at the time of the request or the offence, and is a resident of the requested state, may recommend withdrawal of the request for extradition with reasons, if it is determined that extradition would disrupt the social readjustment and rehabilitation of the young person. The treaty requires a level of justification on the part of the requested state in terms of specifying the reasons for the requested withdrawal which is not duplicated in the Act. Furthermore the treaty does not oblige the requesting state to accede to the request, and if the requesting state persisted with the request for extradition of the young person, the treaty requires the Minister to surrender in any event. The basis for refusing to surrender in this instance would be with recourse to s. 44(1)(a), which requires the Minister to refuse surrender if to do so would be unjust or oppressive. Recourse could also be made to s. 7 *Charter* principles, that is, it would shock the Canadian conscience to surrender the young person in the circumstances of the case (*Kindler v. Canada (Minister of Justice)*, *supra*, and *United States v. Burns*, *supra*). In addition, the Act does not restrict the Minister's consideration to resident young offenders as does the treaty.

Considering that s. 45 provides for treaty override with regard to reasons or absence of reasons for refusal of surrender, the fact that the American treaty does not provide for refusal to surrender because the person sought is under 18 means that the Minister cannot rely on s. 47(c) as a ground upon which to refuse the request.

Section 47(c) has gone further than the American treaty provision by ensuring that there is substantial similarity between the way the young offender will be treated in the requesting state and the way he or she would be treated here. For instance, s. 4 of the *Young Offenders Act* provides for alternative measures to be resorted to in respect of the young person instead of submitting the youth to judicial proceedings under the Act. The *Young Offenders Act* in s. 3 encourages consideration of methods other than judicial proceedings for dealing with young people who have committed offences. It may be incumbent upon the Minister to consider the availability in the requesting state of diversion or other alternative measures to court proceedings before determining whether or not to order surrender.

The high profile English case of *R. v. Secretary of State for the Home Department, Ex parte Venables* (1997), [1998] A.C. 407 at 474 (U.K. H.L.), illustrates the potential for issues of non-parity in legislative schemes to arise. In that case, two 10-year-olds were tried and convicted for the murder of another child. They were sentenced to be detained during Her Majesty's pleasure.

Canada does not try children under the age of 12. For children under 12 years of age, the definition of extraditable conduct set out in s. 3 of the *Extradition Act* would not be met because in Canada children of that age cannot be convicted of a criminal offence. As well, there is no equivalent for indeterminate sentences at Her Majesty's pleasure for young offenders: "Young person" under the *Young Offenders Act* is defined as a person between the ages of 12 and 18 and custodial sentences are for specified periods of time.

Children under 12 who commit criminal acts can only be detained or controlled under provincial child protection legislation, which works to promote the safety and best interests of the child. If a child commits a serious crime, the government's only recourse is to apply for a warrant to detain the child temporarily in a "place of safety," and then to hold a judicial hearing to determine who can best take care of the child: a parent, a guardian, the children's aid society or the Crown (see, for instance, in Ontario, the *Child and Family Services Act*, R.S.O. 1990, c. C.11).

For children over 12, the sentencing regime in the requesting jurisdiction will be of particular importance to the deliberations of the Minister under this section given the emphasis in s. 3(f) of the *Young Offenders Act* on accomplishing resolutions that will have the least interference with the freedom of the young offender. There are far-ranging dispositions available to a young person in Canada under s. 20 of the *Young Offenders Act*, ranging from discharges, to fines, to community service orders. With respect to jail terms there are limits on the maximums that may be imposed, which are far more lenient than the adult sentencing provisions under the *Criminal Code*. Similar sentencing options may not be available in the requesting state and the Minister may decide to preclude surrender for that reason. In order to submit to the Minister that surrender ought to be refused for this reason, it may be helpful to tender any legislation of the extradition partner applicable to persons under 18, or evidence of the absence of such legislation, and foreign legal expert opinion as to what proceedings will ensue, and what the disposition or sentence is likely to be.

Keeping in mind that this section confers a discretionary power of refusal upon the Minister, it might be expected that the more serious the offence for which extradition of the young person is requested, the less persuasive the argument to refuse surrender will be based on differences between the foreign scheme and the *Young Offenders Act*. Surrender with conditions or assurances under s. 40(3) would be resorted to when dealing with the surrender of young persons.

(d) Discretionary refusal to surrender when conduct subject to Canadian criminal proceedings (s. 47(d))

Section 47(d) gives discretion to the Minister to refuse to order surrender when the conduct in respect of which the request is made is the subject of criminal proceedings in Canada against the person sought. The former Act made no provision for this situation. However, this very live issue was previously dealt with in the jurisprudence, namely, in the 1989 Supreme Court of Canada case of *United States v. Cotroni* (1989), 48 C.C.C. (3d) 193, reversing (*sub nom. Cotroni c. Centre de Prévention de Montréal*) 53 C.R. (3d) 339 (Que. C.A.), and reversing (*sub nom. El Zein v. R.*) 29 C.C.C. (3d) 56 (Que. C.A.), and by the 1992 amendment to the American treaty, Article 17 bis.

(i) Cotroni *Issue*

The "*Cotroni* issue" raises the issue of whether the Minister has the authority to order the surrender of a person if the person could be prosecuted in Canada for the same offence. In other words, if the courts of both countries could prosecute, should the request for extradition be respected. The seminal cases, *United States v. Cotroni*, *supra*, and *United States v. El Zein*, *supra*, were heard by the Supreme Court of Canada at the same time since they raised the same issue. The two specific questions raised were, firstly, whether the surrender of a Canadian citizen to a foreign state constitutes a violation of s. 6(1) *Charter* rights, and secondly, whether such a violation could be saved under s. 1 of the *Charter*.

Both Cotroni and El Zein were Canadian citizens sought for extradition by the United States. While both the fugitives were sought for prosecution in the United States, all of their actions in relation to the charges for which extradition was sought took place in Canada. Cotroni was sought for extradition on the charge of conspiracy to possess and distribute heroin. His personal involvement was confined to giving instructions by telephone from Montreal to his accomplices in the United States, and one in Canada. Most of the witnesses and documentary evidence were in the United States. Delivery of the drug, and payment, appeared to have taken place in Canada.

Similarly, El Zein, who was sought for extradition on charges of importation of heroin, conspiracy to import and conspiracy to traffic, was alleged to have given two individuals a package containing heroin in Montreal. The package was to be delivered by these individuals to the United States. Although the two individuals were subsequently arrested by U.S. customs authorities at the border, El Zein's involvement took place entirely in Canada.

The arguments of Cotroni and El Zein were twofold. Firstly, that any extradition of a Canadian citizen amounted to a violation of the rights granted under s. 6 of the *Charter*, and secondly, that if this was so, that in their particular circumstances surrender could not constitute a reasonable limit under s. 1 of the *Charter* given that Canada had the jurisdiction to prosecute the offence for which the United States sought extradition.

The court made the following findings:

1. Extradition *prima facie* infringes on the right guaranteed by s. 6(1) of the *Charter* (p. 212).
2. Pursuant to s. 1 of the *Charter*, the extradition process is a reasonable limit on the s. 6 right to remain in Canada, and in the circumstances of this case extradition met the relevant requirements for the application of s. 1. La Forest J. stated, at p. 219:

   > As against this somewhat peripheral Charter infringement must be weighed the importance of the objectives sought by extradition — the investigation, prosecution, repression and punishment of both national and transnational crimes for the protection of the public. These objectives, we saw, are of pressing and substantial concern. They are, in fact, essential to the maintenance of a free and democratic society. In my view, they warrant the limited interference with the right guaranteed by s. 6(1) to remain in Canada. That right, it seems to me, is infringed as little as possible, or at the very least as little as reasonably possible.

3. Section 6 of the *Charter* imposes a duty upon the domestic prosecutorial authorities to give "due weight" to the fugitive's right to remain in Canada and "in good faith direct their minds to whether prosecution would be equally effective in Canada, given the existing domestic laws and international co-operative arrangements." (pp. 224, 225)
4. The method of deciding whether there should be domestic prosecution or extradition is by consultation between the appropriate authorities in the two countries.
5. The factors which will affect the decision are (at p. 225):

   — where was the impact of the offence felt or likely to have been felt;
   — which jurisdiction has the greater interest in prosecuting the offence;
   — which police force played the major role in the development of the case;
   — which jurisdiction has laid charges;
   — which jurisdiction has the most comprehensive case;
   — which jurisdiction is ready to proceed to trial;
   — where is the evidence located;
   — whether the evidence is mobile;
   — the number of accused involved and whether they can be gathered together in one place for trial;

  — in what jurisdiction were most of the acts in furtherance of the crime committed;
  — the nationality and residence of the accused;
  — the severity of the sentence the accused is likely to receive in each jurisdiction.

6. The locus of the wrongdoing is not in itself determinative of the issue (p. 221).
7. Absent a charge in Canada, the Minister's discretion to refuse surrender is limited (p. 226).
8. With respect to general considerations, there can be no general exceptions to extradition for a Canadian citizen who could be charged in Canada, nor is there a requirement of judicial examination of each individual case with respect to this issue.

(ii) Article 17 bis of Canada–United States Extradition Treaty

The *Cotroni* factors to be considered by the authorities in determining whether domestic prosecution should be preferred to extradition have in large part been formalized by an amendment to the *Canada–United States Extradition Treaty*. Article 17 bis, which became effective on November 26, 1991, itemizes some of these factors which the requested state is to consider in cases of dual jurisdiction. Article 17 bis provides:

> If both contracting Parties have jurisdiction to prosecute the person for the offense for which extradition is sought, the executive authority of the requested State, after consulting with the executive authority of the requesting State, shall decide whether to extradite the person or submit the case to its competent authorities for the purpose of prosecution. In making its decision, the requested State shall consider all relevant factors, including but not limited to:
>
> (i) the place where the act was committed or intended to be committed or the injury occurred or was intended to occur;
> (ii) the respective interests of the Contracting Parties;
> (iii) the nationality of the victim or the intended victim; and
> (iv) the availability and location of the evidence.

(iii) Comparison of Article 17 bis with s. 47(d) of Act

While Article 17 bis of the *Canada–United States Extradition Treaty* and s. 47(d) of the Act are similar provisions, the treaty has the additional requirement of a consultative process and requires consideration of the issue by the mere fact that both countries, the requesting and requested state, have the jurisdiction to prosecute the conduct. There is no requirement in Article 17 bis that the requested state has actually commenced a prosecution. The article states "[i]f both contracting Parties have jurisdiction to prosecute the person . . ." In contrast, s. 47(d) appears to contemplate that criminal proceedings have already commenced in the requested state. It applies when "the conduct in respect of which the request for extradition is made is the subject of criminal proceedings in Canada against the person." The Minister's inquiry under the treaty is triggered by the fact that jurisdiction to prosecute in Canada exists. The Minister's inquiry under the Act is triggered by the fact that criminal proceedings have actually commenced and not just that Canada has jurisdiction to commence such proceedings.

The treaty makes it possible for the Minister to refuse surrender on the grounds that the matter will be referred to the competent Canadian prosecutorial authorities for prosecution. There is no further requirement that the prosecutorial authorities actually undertake the prosecution. For instance, if there is an extradition request for the *Criminal Code* offence of fraud, and the Canadian federal justice minister refers the matter to the appropriate provincial attorney general for prosecution in preference to extradition, the provincial attorney general is not bound to prosecute and may decline. Once the decision to refer the matter for domestic prosecution has been made in preference to extradition, extradition cannot ensue even though the domestic prosecutorial authorities decline to prosecute. However, as a practical matter, because Article 17 bis requires the two contracting states to consult on this issue, it would be unlikely that the willingness of the provincial attorney general to initiate a prosecution would not have been canvassed in advance of the decision being made.

When the domestic prosecutorial jurisdiction is with respect to federal charges, such as drug offences, whether or not to initiate domestic prosecution will be determined by the same individual, since the federal Minister of Justice is also the Attorney General of Canada. However, the two positions as Minister of Justice and Attorney General of Canada are distinct and separate roles. In *United States v. Kwok* (2001), 152 C.C.C. (3d) 225 (S.C.C.), Arbour J. stated that "[t]he Minister can reach a conclusion as to whether or not a fugitive could be effectively prosecuted in Canada by relying on an evaluation presented to him or her by responsible Department officials, after having considered the appropriate principles and Canada's international obligations." (p. 264, para. 89)

Whether the Minister is approaching the analysis under s. 47(d) ("the conduct . . . is the subject of criminal proceedings in Canada)" or under Article 17 bis of the American treaty (that Canada has jurisdiction to prosecute), in both cases the decision will be made by following the same procedure. (It should be noted that the s. 45 treaty override results in s. 47(d) of the Act being applicable only when there is no treaty or the treaty provision is identical to s. 47(d).)

(iv) *Assessment*

Prior to the enactment of s. 47(d) of the new Act, there was a particular procedure followed in the determination of whether domestic prosecution should be preferred to extradition. It is unlikely that the enactment of s. 47(d) will change the procedure.

The extradition request, which is initially received in Ottawa by the International Assistance Group (IAG) of the Department of Justice, is forwarded to the Regional Office of the Department. The regional office will have carriage of the extradition hearing. If there is jurisdiction to prosecute the person sought domestically or if domestic criminal proceedings are already underway, the International Assistance Group will request the local prosecutor to conduct a *"Cotroni* analysis." In the case of federal charges, the local prosecutor will be a prosecutor of the Department of Justice. In the case of *Criminal Code* charges, the local prosecutor will be a provincial Crown attorney.

The analysis requires consideration of a number of factors. When the American treaty is resorted to, Article 17 bis, although not exhaustive, lists four factors relevant to the analysis. They are:

   (i) the place where the act was committed or intended to be committed or the injury occurred or was intended to occur;

  (ii) the respective interests of the Contracting Parties;

 (iii) the nationality of the victim or the intended victim; and

 (iv) the availability and location of the evidence.

Article 17 bis does not limit the analysis to consideration of the factors enumerated. Further factors enumerated in the *Cotroni* decision itself can be considered. Two of the Article 17 bis factors are listed in the *Cotroni* case, namely the availability and location of the evidence (Article 17 bis (iv)) and the place where the Act was committed (Article 17 bis (i)). The second factor of Article 17 bis, namely, the respective interests of the contracting parties is a broad factor which encompasses the majority of the factors listed in the *Cotroni* case. The third factor listed in Article 17 bis, the nationality of the victim or intended victim, is not contained in the list of factors referred to in the *United States v. Cotroni* case.

The prosecutor when canvassing these factors may find it necessary to consult the prosecuting attorneys and/or law enforcement officials in the requesting state. If the documentary evidence is in hand, it can be referred to in order to assist in the analysis. If it is not available at the time the analysis is conducted, information can be obtained from any documentation submitted in support of the arrest of the person sought on the extradition or, if necessary, by directly requesting the information or documentation from the foreign authorities. Documentation which may be of assistance in this regard includes copies of the indictment, arrest warrants, a synopsis of allegations and the sentencing provisions.

The prosecutor is involved in the analysis because the principal discretion as to whether or not to prosecute in Canada is that of the Attorney General of Canada or the province as the case may be (see *United States v. Cotroni, supra*, at p. 224). The prosecutor after conducting the analysis will usually commit the opinion to writing and provide this advice to the Minister by forwarding it to counsel in the International Assistance Group of the Department of Justice in Ottawa, who acts as the Minister's counsel in extradition matters.

(v) *Timing of assessment*

The *Cotroni* analysis can be made at any time prior to the Minister's surrender determination. The extradition partner, when aware of existing domestic charges, may request an analysis prior to formally requesting extradition or making a provisional request. The reason for this is that if Canada is inclined to prefer domestic prosecution to extradition then the extradition partner will save time and effort by being advised of this, as this will eliminate the necessity of preparing materials in support of an extradition request.

If the result of the *Cotroni* analysis is that it is recommended that prosecution take place in the requesting state in preference to domestic prosecution, the Minister must ensure that such a decision is not in violation of the person's s. 6(1) *Charter* rights (see *United States v. Kwok, supra*). Consequently, as long as the *Cotroni* analysis is completed prior to when the Minister must determine the issue of surrender, it does not matter whether it is made before, during or after the extradition hearing.

(vi) *Case law*

United States v. Whitley (1994), 94 C.C.C. (3d) 99 (Ont. C.A.), affirmed (1996), 104 C.C.C. (3d) 447 (S.C.C.), involved an extradition request for a Canadian citizen who was facing charges in the United States. The American charges alleged Whitley's involvement in a drug organization that attempted to export approximately 1,100 lbs. of marihuana for distribution in Canada. He was charged in Canada with conspiracy to import marihuana, contrary to the *Narcotic Control Act*, based on the same conduct. The Canadian charges were withdrawn in favour of extradition, prior to the request for extradition being made by the United States.

The *Cotroni* issue was raised on behalf of the fugitive before the Ontario Court of Appeal, and then in the Supreme Court of Canada. The Supreme Court upheld the decision of the Ontario Court of Appeal that the fugitive's s. 6(1) *Charter* rights were not violated by preferring extradition to domestic prosecution. Laskin J.A, for the court stated, at pp. 116–117:

> The Minister's reasons indicate that he applied the correct legal principles and that he expressly took into account several of the factors referred to in *Cotroni* and in art. 17 bis of the Treaty. Some of these factors — such as the nationality and residence of the fugitive and the police force that played the major role in the development of the case — may favour a domestic prosecution; others — such as the availability and location of the evidence and the jurisdiction that has the most comprehensive case — may favour extradition. The Minister is charged with the responsibility of weighing these factors and ultimately deciding whether prosecution in Canada would be equally effective. In this case, he decided that it would not be. In my view, there are no grounds to suggest that the Minister erred in law, disregarded relevant factors or reached a decision that was unreasonable. Therefore, there is no basis for this court to interfere with the Min-

ister's determination that extradition does not violate the appellant's rights in s. 6(1) of the Charter.

United States v. Whitley describes the kinds of materials that were submitted to the Minister at the time the surrender decision was being considered. The Minister was provided with a memorandum of legal advice from his counsel in the International Assistance Group, which had annexed to it the prosecutor's *Cotroni* analysis. The prosecutor's *Cotroni* analysis was not provided as disclosure to the fugitive's counsel. The fugitive requested a copy of this together with other material, arguing that he required this information to demonstrate that prosecution in Canada would be equally effective, and that the Minister was improperly motivated to favour extradition because of the higher penalties existing in the requesting jurisdiction (*United States v. Whitley*, *supra*, Ontario Court of Appeal decision, at p. 111). The Court of Appeal concluded, at p. 114, that although "[i]mproper motive is a ground for judicial review of prosecutorial discretion, . . . there has to be an air of reality to the allegation before a court will require disclosure of the kind of information requested by the appellant."

The case of the *United States v. Leon* (1995), 96 C.C.C. (3d) 568 (Ont. C.A.), affirmed by the Supreme Court of Canada on other issues (1996), 105 C.C.C. (3d) 385 (S.C.C.), illustrates that although an individual may face charges in both jurisdictions which involve similar factual underpinnings, a *Cotroni* situation may not arise. Leon, who was a Canadian citizen, was charged in Canada with possession of eight kilos of cocaine for the purpose of trafficking, as a result of a search and seizure at a Toronto warehouse. He was subsequently charged in the United States with drug offences allegedly arising from two separate deliveries to him of cocaine in New York State. It was alleged that the first delivery was of between eight and ten kilos of cocaine, and that a month later the second delivery of four kilos of cocaine took place. One week later, the search which resulted in the seizure of eight kilos of cocaine in Canada occurred.

Leon had been aware prior to the date set for trial on the Canadian charges that the United States was going to undertake extradition proceedings. It was alleged by the fugitive that he was told by the Canadian prosecutor that if he did not plead guilty to the Canadian indictment that the proposed extradition would proceed. On the day the Canadian charges were to proceed to trial, Leon was arrested on an extradition warrant and the Canadian charge was stayed.

The Ontario Court of Appeal, *per* Griffiths J.A., held that the facts of the case did not give rise to a *Cotroni* issue. He stated, at pp. 575–576:

> *Cotroni*, in my view, has no application to the circumstances of this case where the appellant is alleged to have been guilty of discrete and separate acts of misconduct in both jurisdictions. If the appellant had been prosecuted in Canada, his conviction or acquittal on the single count of possession for trafficking would not have been a bar to his trial on the U.S. charges which involve misconduct constituting criminal conspiracy and other drug offences actionable only in the United States. That the evidence called in either prosecution might in some way be relevant to the other prosecution is of no

significance. The appellant could only be convicted of the particular offences in the jurisdictions where the charges were laid.

This issue was not revisited by the Supreme Court of Canada. The Supreme Court dealt only with whether the allegation that the prosecutor used the threat of extradition to attempt to obtain a guilty plea constituted an abuse of process. The court held that the alleged conduct was not one of the "clearest of cases" amounting to an abuse of prosecutorial discretion.

In *United States v. Kwok, supra*, the United States sought to prosecute the fugitive, a Canadian citizen, for drug trafficking offences. He had allegedly played a role, while in Canada, of bringing together customers and suppliers for the drugs. On appeal from the Minister's surrender decision, Kwok submitted that the Minister had improperly delegated to his subordinates the decision of whether prosecution in Canada would be as effective as a prosecution in the United States. He also argued that there was no evidence that a prosecution in Canada would not be "equally effective." (pp. 263–264, para. 88)

The Supreme Court of Canada found no merit in either argument. Arbour J. speaking for the court held that the Minister is entitled to "reach a conclusion as to whether or not a fugitive could be effectively prosecuted in Canada by relying on an evaluation presented to him or her by responsible Department officials, after having considered the appropriate principles and Canada's international obligations." (p. 264, para. 89) With respect to the efficacy of a domestic prosecution and its desirability, the court held that this was simply one factor in the exercise of the Minister's broad discretion to surrender and that it was open to the Minister to "yield to the superior interest of the Requesting State, even in a case where some form of prosecution in Canada is not materially impossible or totally unlikely to succeed." (p. 264, para. 89)

(e) Discretionary refusal where no territorial jurisdiction (s. 47(e))

Section 47(e) provides that the Minister may refuse surrender when none of the conduct on which the request for extradition is based occurred in territory over which the extradition partner has jurisdiction. This is a companion section to s. 5 of the Act, which in the context of extraditable conduct indicates that a person may be extradited whether or not the conduct on which the extradition partner bases its request occurs in the territory over which it has jurisdiction and whether or not Canada could exercise jurisdiction in similar circumstances. Section 5, by making extraditable, conduct which occurred outside the territory over which the extradition partner has jurisdiction, eliminates territorial jurisdiction from being an issue for the extradition judge at the hearing, and statutorily recognizes the decision of the Supreme Court of Canada in *United States v. Lépine* (1993), 87 C.C.C. (3d) 385, with respect to jurisdiction not being a matter within the consideration of the extradition judge.

Section 47(e) of the Act does make extra-territorial jurisdiction a matter for the concern of the Minister when the conduct occurred entirely outside the extradition partner's territory. In other words, it is no impediment to extradition that the conduct occurred entirely outside the extradition partner's territory, but it becomes an issue for the Minister who may refuse surrender on this basis.

It is necessary to consider the interplay between s. 5 of the Act and s. 45 as it affects s. 47(e). Section 5 provides that Canada may extradite for conduct that occurred outside the territory of the requesting state whether or not Canada would assume jurisdiction in similar circumstances. Canada, however, is not required to extradite in these circumstances because of the discretion given to the Minister by s. 47(e). The fact that the acts occurred entirely outside the territory of the requesting state is enough to give the Minster the discretion to refuse surrender. However, s. 45 of the Act provides for the treaty to override the provisions of s. 47(e). Consequently, the Minister's discretion to refuse simply because the acts took place outside the territory of the extradition partner may be eliminated if the treaty speaks differently on the point.

The Spanish treaty is illustrative of this point. Article IV(5) of the Spanish treaty states that "when the offence was committed outside the territory of the Requesting State and the law of the Requested State does not, in corresponding circumstances, provide for the same jurisdiction" that extradition may be refused. By virtue of s. 45, this treaty provision replaces s. 47(e). Therefore, in dealings with Spain, s. 5 of the Act provides that extraterritorial conduct is no bar to extradition, but read with Article IV(5) of the treaty, Canada is not required to extradite if the conduct occurred outside the territory of the requesting state and Canadian law does not provide for the same jurisdiction in corresponding circumstances. This is a narrower discretion for the Minister than that given by s. 47(e), which does not require the Minister to consider whether Canada would have jurisdiction in similar circumstances. The Spanish treaty provision would prevail because of the treaty override specified by s. 45. This would be the same situation with the Philippines treaty.

Section 5 of the Act refers to extradition being permissible whether or not the conduct took place in a territory over which the requesting state has jurisdiction. Section 47(e) gives the Minister discretionary authority to refuse surrender when "none" of the conduct occurred in the territory of the requesting state. The Minister's discretion is this regard is limited to situations where the conduct in question is entirely extra-territorial. This is distinguishable from situations where part of the conduct takes place in the requesting state and part in other foreign states, or in the requested state. When part of the conduct takes place in the requesting state, it stands to reason that there is colour of right with respect to jurisdiction over the offence. The question of jurisdiction is clearly raised when none of the conduct takes place in the state making the request, therefore necessitating consideration of the issue.

It may be that the reason for the residual discretion in these circumstances is that political considerations may come into play if conduct occurs completely outside the requesting state's territory. Extraterritorial conduct by definition has international implications. It may be that another foreign state's interests would have to be taken into consideration in dealing with the request. Competing interests may also arise when the conduct in question takes place on the high seas.

The case of *Romania (State) v. Cheng* (1997), 114 C.C.C. (3d) 289 (N.S. S.C.), dismissed as moot (1997), 119 C.C.C. (3d) 561 (N.S. C.A.), illustrates the political ramifications of the assertion of extraterritorial jurisdiction. In that case, the extradition of the fugitives had been requested by Romania, where they were charged with the murder of three Romanian stowaways on the Taiwanese registered ship, the *MV Maersk Dubai*. The fugitives, who were nationals of Taiwan, were alleged to have caused the death of the stowaways by throwing them overboard on the high seas. The offences came to light while the ship was docked in the port of Halifax and a request was then made to Canada, by Romania, for their extradition to that country to be tried for the crime of murder. None of the conduct upon which Romania based its request took place within its territory. The crimes as alleged were committed by Taiwanese nationals aboard a Taiwanese ship, in international waters. Taiwan, supported by the fugitives, applied to intervene in the extradition hearing in order to resist the Romanian request for the surrender of the crew members and to assert the right to prosecute the matter in Taiwan. The extradition hearing judge granted the intervention application, over the objection of Romania, on the basis that Taiwan had a very real interest in investigating the alleged acts and in prosecuting the alleged perpetrators of the murders.

The extradition judge ultimately found that a *prima facie* case of murder had been made out. However, he held that he had no jurisdiction to issue a warrant of committal. He held that the crew members were not "fugitives" as defined under the former Act because the acts had not occurred within the territory of the state of Romania. He held that the term "jurisdiction" as contained in the definition of "fugitive" meant territorial jurisdiction. In coming to this conclusion MacDonald J. placed significant weight on Article 1 of the Romanian treaty which provided that the contracting parties engage to extradite those persons accused or convicted of an offence committed in the territory of the requesting party.

If the fact situation in *Romania (State) v. Cheng* occurs again, the new legislation makes it clear under s. 5 that the fact that the conduct occurred outside the territory of the requesting state does not preclude the issuance of a warrant of committal. As indicated previously, the issue of extra-territorial jurisdiction does not come within the ambit of the hearing judge's powers. Section 5 together with s. 47(e) makes it clear that the extraterritorial conduct is extraditable and any right to refuse extradition for this reason lies within the discretion of the Minister who may refuse if none of the conduct occurred within the territorial jurisdiction of the extradition partner.

§5.0 CASE LAW

Argentina (Republic) v. Mellino (1987), 33 C.C.C. (3d) 334 (S.C.C.).
Bennett, Ex Parte (1974), 17 C.C.C. (2d) 274 (Ont. H.C.).
Castioni, Re, [1891] 1 Q.B. 149 (Eng. Q.B.).

Chan v. Tanguay (1995), (*sub nom. Chan c. Maison Tanguay*) [1996] R.J.Q. 335 (Que. S.C.), affirmed (1996), 113 C.C.C. (3d) 270 (Que. C.A.), leave to appeal to S.C.C. refused (May 22, 1997), Doc. 25761 (S.C.C.).

Cheng v. Hong Kong (December 17, 1992), Wright J. (Ont. Gen. Div.), appeal to Ont. C.A. dismissed (1996), 109 C.C.C. (3d) 384 (Ont. C.A.).

Forti v. Suarez-Mason, 694 F. Supp. 707 (U.S. N.D. Cal., 1988).

Germany (Federal Republic) v. Krapohl (1998), 110 O.A.C. 129 (Ont. C.A.).

Gil v. Canada (Minister of Employment & Immigration) (1994), 25 Imm. L.R. (2d) 209 (Fed. C.A.).

Gwynne v. Canada (Minister of Justice) (1998), 50 C.R.R. (2d) 250 (B.C.C.A.).

Hong Kong v. Sun (December 11, 1992) (Ont. Gen. Div.), appeal to Ont. C.A. dismissed (1996), 109 C.C.C. (3d) 383 (Ont. C.A.).

Kindler v. Canada (Minister of Justice) (1991), 67 C.C.C. (3d) 1 (S.C.C.).

Larabie v. R. (1998), 42 C.C.C. (3d) 385 (Ont. H.C.).

Meier v. Canada (Minister of Justice) (1983), 6 C.C.C. (3d) 563 (Fed. T.D.).

Ng, Re (1991), 67 C.C.C. (3d) 61 (S.C.C.).

Philippines (Republic) v. Pacificador (1993), 83 C.C.C. (3d) 210 (Ont. C.A.), leave to appeal to S.C.C. refused (1994), 87 C.C.C. (3d) vi (S.C.C.).

Quinn v. Robinson, 783 F.2d 776 (9th Cir. Cal., 1986).

R. v. Fai (1979), 48 C.C.C. (2d) 173 (Que. S.C.).

R. v. Schmidt (1987), 33 C.C.C. (3d) 193 (S.C.C.).

R. v. Secretary of State for the Home Department, Ex parte Venables (1997), [1998] A.C. 407 at 474 (U.K. H.L.).

Romania (State) v. Cheng (1997), 114 C.C.C. (3d) 289 (N.S.S.C.), dismissed as moot (1997), 119 C.C.C. (3d) 561 (N.S.C.A.).

Ross v. United States (1996), 104 C.C.C. (3d) 446 (S.C.C.), affirming (1994), 93 C.C.C. (3d) 500 (B.C.C.A.).

Schtraks v. Government of Israel (1962), [1964] A.C. 556 (U.K. H.L.).

United States v. Allard (1991), 64 C.C.C. (3d) 159 (S.C.C.), reconsideration refused (July 11, 1991), Doc. 20626 (S.C.C.), affirming (1997), 116 C.C.C. (3d) 524 (B.C.C.A.).

United States v. Burns (2001), 151 C.C.C. (3d) 97 (S.C.C.), affirming (1997), 116 C.C.C. (3d) 524 (B.C.C.A.).

United States v. Cotroni (1989), 48 C.C.C. (3d) 193 (S.C.C.), reversing (1986), (*sub nom. Cotroni c. Centre de Prévention de Montréal*) 53 C.R. (3d) 339 (Que. C.A.) and reversing (*sub nom. El Zein v. R.*) 29 C.C.C. (3d) 56 (Que. C.A.).

United States v. Jamieson (1996), 104 C.C.C. (3d) 575 (S.C.C.), reversing (1994), 93 C.C.C. (3d) 265 (Que. C.A.).

United States v. Kwok (2001), 152 C.C.C. (3d) 225 (S.C.C.).

United States v. Leon (1995), 96 C.C.C. (3d) 568 (Ont. C.A.), affirmed (1996), 105 C.C.C. (3d) 385 (S.C.C.).

United States v. Lépine (1993), 87 C.C.C. (3d) 385 (S.C.C.).

United States v. Whitley (1994), 94 C.C.C. (3d) 99 (Ont. C.A.), affirmed (1996), 104 C.C.C. (3d) 447 (S.C.C.).

United States of Mexico v. Hurley (1997), 116 C.C.C. (3d) 414 (Ont. C.A.).
Wisconsin (State) v. Armstrong (1973), 10 C.C.C. (2d) 271 (Fed. C.A.), leave to appeal to S.C.C. refused (1973), 10 C.C.C. (3d) 271n (S.C.C.).

§6.0 RELATED SECTIONS

s. 9 — Designated States and Entities (Extradition Partners)
s. 29(4) — Date of Authority to Proceed is Relevant Date for Purposes of Committal Order
s. 40(3) — Power of Minister to Seek Assurances and Conditions
s. 40(4) — Power of Minister to Subject Surrender to Assurances
Charter of Rights and Freedoms, s. 2(b) – Freedom of Expression
Charter of Rights and Freedoms, s. 6 – Mobility Rights
Charter of Rights and Freedoms, s. 7 – Life, Liberty, and Security of the Person
Charter of Rights and Freedoms, s. 12 – Cruel and Unusual Treatment or Punishment
Charter of Rights and Freedoms, s. 15 – Equality Rights
Canada–United States Extradition Treaty, Article 17 bis

When Grounds for Refusal Do Not Apply (s. 47.1)

§1.0 DESCRIPTION

Section 47.1 of the *Extradition Act* provides as follows:

WHEN GROUNDS FOR REFUSAL DO NOT APPLY
47.1 The grounds for refusal set out in sections 44, 46 and 47 do not apply in the case of a person who is the subject of a request for surrender by the International Criminal Court.

Section 47.1, which came into force in October 2000, provides that the mandatory and discretionary grounds for refusal of surrender provided for in ss. 44, 46, and 47 of the *Extradition Act* do not apply to requests from the International Criminal Court.

§2.0 COMPARISON WITH FORMER ACT

There was no similar provision in the former Act.

§3.0 SIGNIFICANCE OF CHANGE AND ANALYSIS

Some of the grounds of refusal set out in ss. 44, 46 and 47 of the Act would simply be inapplicable because of the terms of the *Rome Statute*, which created the International Criminal Court. The International Criminal Court has no death penalty (Art. 77); there is no provision for *in absentia* trials (Art. 63); it has no jurisdiction over persons who were under 18 at the time of the offence (Art. 26); there are no limitation periods for the offences within the jurisdiction of the International Criminal Court (Art. 29); and by its very nature its jurisdiction is extraterritorial. (These grounds for refusal are set out in sections 44(2), 47(b), 47(c), 46(1)(a) and 47(e) of the *Extradition Act*.)

Mandatory refusal on the basis that surrender would be unjust or oppressive, or that the accused would face discrimination in the requesting jurisdiction, as provided for in s. 44(1)(a) and (b) of the *Extradition Act*, have been deemed unnecessary in respect of surrender to the International Criminal Court. Implicitly, the preferential treatment accorded to the International Criminal Court in this regard is a recognition that the court emerged from the crystallization of an international human rights consciousness on the part of its State Parties, rendering its prosecution of offences *ipso facto* just and fair. Moreover, as a practical matter, the *Rome Statute* provides persons sought with myriad substantive and procedural rights.

§4.0 RELATED SECTIONS

s. 2 — Interpretation
s. 6.1 — No Immunity from Request for Surrender by International Criminal Court
s. 14(2) — Discharge of Person Sought If No Proceedings Instituted — Extension of Time
s. 18 — Judicial Interim Release
s. 40 — Surrender Order by Minister of Justice
s. 76 — Unscheduled Landing

Discharge of Persons Sought By Minister of Justice (s. 48)

§1.0 DESCRIPTION

Section 48 of the *Extradition Act* provides as follows:

DISCHARGE
48. (1) If the Minister decides not to make a surrender order, the Minister shall order the discharge of the person.

WHEN REFUGEE CLAIM

(2) When the Minister orders the discharge of a person and the person has claimed Convention refugee status under section 44 of the *Immigration Act*, the Minister shall send copies of all relevant documents to the minister responsible for that Act.

Section 48(1) requires the Minister of Justice to discharge the person sought if the Minister does not order the surrender of the person.

When the Minister of Justice orders the discharge of a person sought and the person has claimed Convention refugee status, s. 48(2) requires the Minister to send copies of all relevant documents in the Minister's possession to the Minister of Citizenship and Immigration.

§2.0 COMPARISON WITH FORMER ACT

Section 48(1) of the *Extradition Act* is comparable to s. 22(2) of the former Act. Section 22(2) provided the Minister of Justice with the authority to discharge a fugitive if a surrender order was not made. No section in the former Act was comparable to s. 48(2).

§3.0 SIGNIFICANCE OF CHANGE

The new *Extradition Act* not only formalizes but also mandates cooperation between the Minister of Justice and the Minister of Citizenship and Immigration when the same person is subject to both Convention refugee and extradition proceedings (see also s. 40(2)).

§4.0 ANALYSIS

Sections 44 to 47 set out various grounds upon which the Minister of Justice may refuse the surrender of a person sought. Section 48 provides that, when the Minister has declined to surrender the person sought under any of the grounds in ss. 44 to 47, the Minister must order the discharge of the person. This authority is operative after the person sought has been committed for surrender following an extradition hearing under s. 29 of the Act. Prior to the extradition hearing, the Minister of Justice also has the power to terminate the proceedings. Section 23(3) provides the Minister with the discretion to withdraw the authority to proceed, that being the document upon which extradition proceedings are based, following which the extradition judge is required to discharge the person sought.

The inclusion of ss. 48(2) and 40(2) in the new *Extradition Act* represents an attempt to regulate the conduct of extradition and refugee proceedings when they have been proceeding simultaneously. Section 40(2) requires consultation between the Minister of Justice and the Minister of Citizenship and Immigration when the person sought has also claimed Convention refugee status. The lack of direction under the former Act gave rise to duplicated proceedings and litigation over the nature of the interaction between the two proceedings. (See *Bembenek v. Canada (Minister of Employment & Immigration)* (1991), 69 C.C.C. (3d) 34 (Ont. Gen. Div.). See also *Pacificador v. Canada (Minister of Justice)* (1999), (*sub nom. Philippines (Republic) v. Pacificador*) 60 C.R.R. (2d) 126 (Ont. Gen. Div.).) This point is discussed in the commentary to s. 40, §2.2, "Impact of Refugee Claims."

§5.0 CASE LAW

Bembenek v. Canada (Minister of Employment & Immigration), (1991), 69 C.C.C. (3d) 34 (Ont. Gen. Div.).
Pacificador v. Canada (Minister of Justice) (1999), (*sub nom. Philippines (Republic) v. Pacificador*) 60 C.R.R. 92d) 126 (Ont. Gen. Div.).

§6.0 RELATED SECTIONS

s. 23(3) — Authority of Minister of Justice to Withdraw Authority to Proceed
s. 29 — Order of Committal by Extradition Judge
s. 40(2) — Consultation Between Minister of Justice and Minister of Citizenship and Immigration When Person Sought Has Made Refugee Claim
ss. 44–47 — Reasons for Refusal of Surrender

Appeal (ss. 49–56)

§1.0 DESCRIPTION

§1.1 Section 49 — Who May Appeal, Court Having Jurisdiction, and Grounds of Appeal

Section 49 of the *Extradition Act* provides as follows:

APPEAL
    49. A person may appeal against an order of committal — or the Attorney General, on behalf of the extradition partner, may appeal the discharge of the person or a stay of proceedings — to the court of appeal of the province in which the order of committal, the order discharging the person or the order staying the proceedings was made,

(a) **on a ground of appeal that involves a question of law alone;**
(b) **on a ground of appeal that involves a question of fact or a question of mixed law and fact, with leave of the court of appeal or a judge of the court of appeal; or**

(c) on a ground of appeal not set out in paragraph (*a*) or (*b*) that appears to the court of appeal to be a sufficient ground of appeal, with leave of the court of appeal.

Section 49 of the Act sets out that a person sought may appeal a committal order and the Attorney General of Canada, on behalf of an extradition partner, may appeal an order discharging a person or staying extradition proceedings. The appeal is made to the "court of appeal of the province" in which the order was made. The term "court of appeal" is defined in s. 2 of the Act to refer to the Appeal Division of the Supreme Court (in the province of Prince Edward Island) or the Court of Appeal (in all other provinces). The grounds of appeal are set out in s. 49(a) to (c). Paragraph (a) allows for an appeal of a pure question of law as of right. Paragraph (b) allows for an appeal of a question of fact or mixed law and fact with leave of the court of appeal or a judge of the court of appeal. Paragraph (c) allows for an appeal on a ground not mentioned in para. (a) or (b) that "appears to the court of appeal to be a sufficient ground of appeal, with leave of the court of appeal."

§1.2 Section 50 — Notice of Appeal: Time Limit and Form

Section 50 of the *Extradition Act* provides as follows:

NOTICE OF APPEAL
    50. (1) An appellant who proposes to appeal to a court of appeal or to obtain the leave of that court of appeal must give notice of appeal or notice of the application for leave to appeal not later than 30 days after the decision of the judge with respect to the committal or discharge of the person, or the stay of proceedings, as the case may be, in any manner that may be directed by the rules of court.

EXTENSION OF TIME
    (2) The court of appeal or a judge of the court of appeal may, either before or after the expiry of the 30 days referred to in subsection (1), extend the time within which notice of appeal or notice of an application for leave to appeal may be given.

With respect to time limits, s. 50(1) of the Act provides that an appellant must give a notice of appeal or notice of application for leave to appeal, as the case may be, "not later than 30 days after the decision of the judge. . .". Section 50(2) adds that the court of appeal or a judge of the court of appeal may, either before or after the expiration of the 30-day time period, extend the period within which the notice of appeal or notice of application for leave to appeal may be given.

Concerning form, s. 50(1) provides that the notice of appeal or notice of application for leave to appeal must be given "in any manner that may be directed by the rules of court." Therefore, one must look to the form specified in the rules of the court of appeal in the province in which the extradition hearing was held.

§1.3 Section 51 — Hearing of Appeal and Deferral of Appeal Until Minister's Decision

Section 51 of the *Extradition Act* provides as follows:

HEARING OF APPEAL
51. (1) An appeal under this Act shall be scheduled for hearing by the court of appeal at an early date whether that date is in or out of the prescribed sessions of that court.

DEFERRAL OF APPEAL
(2) The hearing of an appeal against an order of committal may be deferred by the court of appeal until the Minister makes a decision in respect of the surrender of the person under section 40.

Section 51(1) provides that the appeal must be scheduled for hearing by the court of appeal "at an early date whether that date is in or out of the prescribed sessions of that court." Section 51(2) allows the hearing of an appeal against an order of committal to be deferred by the court of appeal until the Minister of Justice makes a decision on the surrender of the appellant under s. 40 of the Act.

§1.4 Section 52 — Applicability of *Criminal Code* and *Criminal Appeal Rules* of Each Province

Section 52 of the *Extradition Act* provides as follows:

PROVISIONS OF THE *CRIMINAL CODE* TO APPLY
(1) Sections 677, 678.1, 682 to 685 and 688 of the *Criminal Code* apply, with any modifications that the circumstances require, to appeals under this Act.

RULES
(2) Unless inconsistent with the provisions of this Act, rules made by the court of appeal under section 482 of the *Criminal Code* in relation to appeals to that court under that Act apply, with any modifications that the circumstances require, to appeals under this Act.

Section 52(1) provides that ss. 677, 678.1, 682 to 685 and 688 of the *Criminal Code* apply, "with any modifications that the circumstances require," to appeals under the *Extradition Act*. These sections establish the following:

- **s. 677**: This section requires the formal judgment of the court of appeal to specify the grounds in law on which a dissenting opinion is based, assuming one is given.

- **s. 678.1**: This section allows for substitutional service of the notice of appeal or notice of an application for leave to appeal in certain circumstances. More specifically, where the respondent cannot be found after "reasonable efforts" have been made to serve the respondent with the notice of appeal or notice of an application for leave to appeal, there may be substitutional service "in the manner and within the period directed by a judge of the court of appeal."

- **s. 682**: This provision specifies certain materials that are or may be required for the purposes of an appeal. Under s. 682(1), a judge of the court of appeal may request a report from the trial judge concerning the proceedings in that forum. Under s. 682(2), a judge of the court of appeal may dispense with the filing of portions of the trial record that are not necessary for the appeal. Section 682(3) deals with jury trial situations and would therefore be inapplicable to extradition proceedings. Under s. 682(4), a party to an appeal is entitled to receive material filed for use in the appeal on payment of any charges set by the rules of court. Under s. 682(5), the Minister of Justice is also entitled to receive any material filed in the appeal.

- **s. 683**: This section sets out some of the powers that may be exercised by the court of appeal. Under s. 683(1), the court can: (a) order the production of any writing, exhibit, etc., connected with the proceeding; (b) admit "fresh evidence" (in *Berladyn v. United States* (1992), 68 B.C.L.R. (2d) 377 (B.C.C.A.), leave to appeal to S.C.C. refused (1992), 73 B.C.L.R. (2d) xxxi (S.C.C.), a decision involving the *Extradition Act* as it stood prior to 1992, when *habeas corpus* applications were still available, Southin J.A. of the British Columbia Court of Appeal admitted fresh evidence on the appeal of a *habeas corpus* ruling); (c) refer matters to a special commission for examination; (d) act on the report of a special commissioner; and (e) amend the indictment. Section 683(2) relates to s. 683(1)(e) and thus, for the reason just mentioned, does not apply to extradition proceedings. Under s. 683(3), the court of appeal can exercise any powers it has in connection with civil matters. However, the subsection adds that no costs are to be awarded. Section 683(4) provides that any process issued by the court of appeal under this subsection may be executed anywhere in Canada. Section 683(5) and (6) deal with the court's power regarding fines, forfeiture orders, etc., and are therefore inapplicable to extradition proceedings.

- **s. 684**: Section 684(1) provides that the court of appeal or a judge of the court of appeal can appoint counsel for an accused who is without means to retain such assistance independently. Where counsel is assigned under s. 684(1) and legal aid is not granted for the accused, s. 684(2) requires the Attorney General who is a party to pay the fees and disbursements of counsel for the accused. Section 684(3) provides that, in the event of a disagreement regarding fees and disbursements under s. 684(2), the registrar of the court of appeal may tax the disputed account.

- **s. 685**: This provision sets out that an appeal may be summarily dismissed on the grounds that it is "frivolous or vexatious and can be determined without being adjourned for a full hearing." A party seeking such a dismissal must make an application to the registrar of the court. However, this section only applies where the notice of appeal refers to a question of law alone.

- **s. 688**: This section deals with the right of an appellant to be present at the hearing of the appeal. Section 688(1) provides that an appellant who is in custody is entitled to be present at the hearing. This is qualified by s. 688(2), which provides that an in-custody appellant who is represented by counsel is not entitled to be present at the hearing of an appeal that involves a question of law alone, of an application for leave to appeal, or of any proceedings that are preliminary or incidental to the appeal. However, s. 688(2) does not apply if the rules of court provide that the appellant is entitled to be present or a judge of the court of appeal gives the appellant leave to be present. Section 688(3) provides that an appellant may present his or her case in writing rather than orally. Section 688(4) deals with the sentencing powers of the appeal court and is therefore inapplicable to extradition proceedings.

Section 52(2) provides that rules made by the court of appeal under s. 482 of the *Criminal Code* regarding appeals to that court under the Code apply to appeals under the *Extradition Act*, unless inconsistent with the provisions of the *Extradition Act* and with any modifications that the circumstances require.

§1.5 Section 53 — Powers of Court of Appeal in Relation to Appeals of Committal Orders

Section 53 of the *Extradition Act* provides as follows:

POWERS OF THE COURT OF APPEAL
53. On the hearing of an appeal against an order of committal of a person, the court of appeal may

(a) allow the appeal, in respect of any offence in respect of which the person has been committed, if it is of the opinion
(i) that the order of committal should be set aside on the ground that it is unreasonable or cannot be supported by the evidence,

(ii) that the order of committal should be set aside on the ground
of a wrong decision on a question of law, or

(iii) that, on any ground, there was a miscarriage of justice; or

(b) dismiss the appeal

(i) if it does not allow the appeal on any ground referred to in
paragraph (*a*), or

(ii) even though the court of appeal is of the opinion that on the
ground referred to in subparagraph (*a*)(ii) the appeal may be
decided in favour of the appellant, if it is of the opinion that no
substantial wrong or miscarriage of justice has occurred and
the order of committal should be upheld.

Section 53 of the Act sets out the powers of the court of appeal in relation to an appeal by a person sought of an extradition judge's committal order. Section 53(a)(i) to (iii) provide that the court may allow an appeal on any of three general bases: the order of committal is unreasonable or cannot be supported by the evidence; the order is based on a wrong decision on a question of law; or a miscarriage of justice has occurred.

Section 53(b)(i) and (ii) establish that the court may dismiss an appeal on two general bases:

1. where the appeal is not allowed on any basis set out in s. 53(a);

2. where the court is of the opinion that the appeal might be decided in the appellant's favour under s. 53(a)(ii) but that no substantial wrong or miscarriage of justice has occurred.

§1.6 Section 54 — Effect of Allowing Appeal Against Committal Under S. 53(a) of Act

Section 54 of the *Extradition Act* provides as follows:

EFFECT OF ALLOWING APPEAL

54. If the court of appeal allows an appeal under paragraph 53(*a*), it shall

(a) set aside the order of committal and

(i) discharge the person, or

(ii) order a new extradition hearing; or

(b) amend the order of committal to exclude an offence in respect of
which the court is of the opinion that the person has not been
properly committed on a ground referred to in subparagraph
53(*a*)(i), (ii) or (iii).

Section 54 of the Act provides the court of appeal with the following options upon allowing a person's appeal against committal under s. 53(a). The court can set aside the order of committal and either discharge the person sought or order a new extradition hearing (see s. 54(a)(i) and (ii)). Alternatively, the court can amend the order of committal to exclude any offence in respect of which the court is of the view that the person sought has not been properly committed on a ground set out in s. 53(a)(i) to (iii).

§1.7 Section 55 — Powers of Court of Appeal in Relation to Appeals Against Discharge of Person or Against Stay of Proceedings

Section 55 of the *Extradition Act* provides as follows:

POWERS

55. (1) On the hearing of an appeal against the discharge of a person or against a stay of proceedings, the court of appeal may

(a) **allow the appeal and set aside the order of discharge or stay, if it is of the opinion**

  (i) **that the order of discharge should be set aside on the ground that it is unreasonable or cannot be supported by the evidence,**

  (ii) **that the order of discharge or the stay of proceedings should be set aside on the ground of a wrong decision on a question of law, or**

  (iii) **that, on any ground, there was a miscarriage of justice; or**

(b) **dismiss the appeal.**

ORDER FOR NEW EXTRADITION HEARING OR COMMITTAL

(2) The court of appeal may, if it sets aside a stay of proceedings, order a new extradition hearing. The court of appeal may, if it sets aside an order of discharge, order a new extradition hearing or order the committal of the person.

Section 55 sets out the powers of the court of appeal in relation to an appeal by the Attorney General on behalf of an extradition partner against the discharge of a person or against a stay of extradition proceedings. Section 55(1)(a)(i) to (iii) provide that the court of appeal may allow the appeal and set aside a discharge or stay, as the case may be, on any of three grounds:

1. with respect to discharges only, that the order "is unreasonable or cannot be supported by the evidence";

2. with regard to discharges or stays, on the basis of a wrong decision on a question of law; or

3. again with respect to discharges or stays, on the basis of a miscarriage of justice.

Section 55(1)(b) provides that the court of appeal may dismiss the appeal.

Section 55(2) adds that where the court of appeal sets aside a stay of proceedings, it has the power to order a new extradition hearing, and where it sets aside a discharge, it has the power to order a new extradition hearing or to order the committal of the person.

§1.8 Section 56 — Deferral of Appeals to Supreme Court

Section 56 of the *Extradition Act* provides as follows:

> DEFERRAL OF SUPREME COURT APPEAL
> **56. (1) The Supreme Court may defer, until the Minister makes a decision with respect to the surrender of the person under section 40, the hearing of an application for leave to appeal, or the hearing of an appeal, from a decision of the court of appeal on an appeal taken under section 49, or on any other appeal in respect of a matter arising under this Act.**
>
> DEFERRAL OF SUPREME COURT APPEAL
> **(2) The Supreme Court may also, if an application for judicial review is made under section 57 or otherwise, defer the hearing until the court of appeal makes its determination on the application.**

Section 56 allows the Supreme Court to defer, until the Minister of Justice makes a decision regarding the surrender of a person under s. 40, the hearing of an application for leave to appeal or the hearing of an appeal from a decision of the court of appeal on an appeal taken under s. 49 or on any other appeal arising under the Act.

§1.9 Judicial Interim Release Pending Appeal

Section 20 of the Act deals with the issue of judicial interim release pending the determination of an appeal. See the commentary to s. 20.

§2.0 COMPARISON WITH FORMER ACT

In all significant respects, ss. 49 to 56 of the new *Extradition Act* are the same as ss. 19.2 to 19.9 of the former Act. The only differences between the provisions stem from changes in terminology between the new and former Acts, e.g., the use of "person" and "extradition partner" in place of "fugitive" and "foreign state," respectively, and changes in the way that some of the sections are structured.

In particular, the powers of a court of appeal under s. 53 of the new Act in relation to appeals from committal are the same as the powers conferred by former s. 19.6. Section 19.6 was added to the former Act in 1992 as part of the amendments made in that year to the appeal provisions. In *United States v. St.-Gelais* (1994), 90 C.C.C. (3d) 83 (Que. C.A.), at pp. 86–92, leave to appeal to S.C.C. refused (1994), 90 C.C.C. (3d) vi (note) (S.C.C.), Chamberland J.A. of the Quebec Court of Appeal discussed the effect of the 1992 amendments in eliminating *habeas corpus* and creating new rights of appeal from committal under ss. 19.2 and 19.6. The comments of Chamberland J.A. in that case continue to be relevant given that the same powers are given to the court of appeal by the new legislation. Chamberland J.A. described the effect of the new appeal provisions as follows, at p. 89:

> Appellant argues that the combined effect of eliminating judicial review by the prerogative writ of *habeas corpus* and of creating a statutory right of appeal is to significantly expand the scope of judicial review; it places the reviewing court in a position where it can question the judgment of the extradition judge and not merely determine whether there was any basis for his or her decision. I agree.

Chamberland J.A. also determined that the role of the reviewing court was not limited to deciding whether or not there was any evidence before the extradition judge, at p. 91:

> In my opinion, the role of the reviewing court, pursuant to the enactment of ss. 19.2 and 19.6 of the *Extradition Act*, is not limited to deciding whether or not there was any evidence before the extradition judge; the court must also satisfy itself that the evidence was such that the committal order is not unreasonable in the light of the test that the extradition judge had to apply. However, the reviewing court must exercise this role bearing in mind the nature of the extradition process and the limited role to be played by the extradition judge.

In this regard, the powers of the court of appeal are not limited to the application of a narrow legal test. The court is entitled to assess the reasonableness of the extradition judge's decision to commit for extradition.

§3.0 SIGNIFICANCE OF CHANGE AND ANALYSIS

Sections 19.2 to 19.9 of the former *Extradition Act*, from which ss. 49 to 56 were derived, were added to the Act in 1992 as part of the Canadian government's effort to update and streamline the appeal and review process. Section 51(1) of the new Act — which states that "[a]n appeal under this Act shall be scheduled for hearing by the court of appeal at an early date" — continues to emphasize the importance of having extradition matters proceed with dispatch. This subsection recognizes that judicial proceedings in a foreign country are awaiting the outcome of the extradition process in Canada. Section 51(2), however, provides flexibility by permitting the court of appeal to defer the hearing of an appeal from committal until the Minister's decision on surrender has been made, thereby allowing the court to hear the appeal and any judicial review of the Minister's decision at the same time. Section 56 of the new Act gives the same power to defer to the Supreme Court of Canada. It allows the court to await a decision on surrender by the Minister before considering an appeal or a leave to appeal application from a court of appeal decision regarding a committal determination. By providing the appellate courts with the authority to defer the hearing of appeals in this fashion, the appeal provisions streamline and increase the efficiency of the extradition process. The provisions avoid the pre-1992 situation in which an appeal of the committal decision would proceed to the court of appeal and perhaps to the Supreme Court of Canada, only to be followed by a separate and subsequent appeal, this time of the Minister's surrender decision. The pre-1992 provisions created lengthy delays in reaching final determinations in extradition matters. The new procedures have given the courts the ability, in appropriate circumstances, to avoid a multiplicity of proceedings by providing for the two appeals to be dealt with at the same time. (See the comments of Arbour J. in *United States v. Kwok* (2001), 152 C.C.C. (3d) 225 (S.C.C.).)

Related to this, however, s. 41(2) provides that the Minister of Justice may, by filing a notice of postponement with the court of appeal, prevent the court from deferring consideration of an appeal from committal. This provision would be invoked in situations in which the Minister is of the view that it would be desirable to have the court's decision on the appeal from committal prior to determining the surrender issue, perhaps because the decision of the court of appeal may affect the surrender decision.

§4.0 CASE LAW

Berladyn v. United States (1992), 68 B.C.L.R. (2d) 377 (B.C.C.A), leave to appeal to S.C.C. refused (1992), 73 B.C.L.R. (2d) xxxi (S.C.C.).
United States v. Kwok (2001), 152 C.C.C. (3d) 225 (S.C.C.).
United States v. St.-Gelais (1994), 90 C.C.C. (3d) 83 (Que. C.A.), leave to appeal to S.C.C. refused (1994), 90 C.C.C.(3d) vi (S.C.C.).

§5.0 RELATED SECTIONS

s. 2 — Interpretation
s. 20 — Application of s. 679 of *Criminal Code* to Judicial Interim Release
s. 41(1) — Minister's Power to Defer Surrender Order When Appeal Pending
s. 41(2) — Minister's Power to Prevent Deferral of Appeal From Committal
Criminal Code, ss. 482, 677, 678.1, 682 to 685 and 688

Judicial Review of Minister of Justice's Surrender Order (s. 57)

§1.0 DESCRIPTION

§1.1 Review of Order (s. 57(1))

Section 57(1) of the *Extradition Act* provides as follows:

> **REVIEW OF ORDER**
> **57. (1) Despite the *Federal Court Act*, the court of appeal of the province in which the committal of the person was ordered has exclusive original jurisdiction to hear and determine applications for judicial review under this Act, made in respect of the decision of the Minister under section 40.**

Section 57(1) provides the court of appeal of the province in which the committal of the person was ordered with exclusive original jurisdiction to hear and determine applications for judicial review of the Minister's decisions. The jurisdiction of the Federal Court to review the administrative decisions of federal authorities is displaced in extradition matters.

§1.2 Application (s. 57(2))

Section 57(2) of the *Extradition Act* provides as follows:

> **APPLICATION**
> **(2) An application for judicial review may be made by the person.**

Section 57(2) provides the person sought for extradition with the right to make an application for judicial review of the Minister's surrender decision under s. 57. Section 57(2) gives no judicial review rights to the extradition partner.

§1.3 Time Limitation (s. 57(3))

Section 57(3) of the *Extradition Act* provides as follows:

> **TIME LIMITATION**
> **(3) An application for judicial review shall be made, in accordance with the rules of court of the court of appeal, within 30 days after the time the decision referred to in subsection (1) was first communicated by the Minister to the person, or within any further time that the court of appeal, either before or after the expiry of those 30 days, may fix or allow.**

Section 57(3) requires that the application for judicial review be made within 30 days of the time when the Minister of Justice's decision is first communicated to the person. The court of appeal, however, may extend the time for the making of an application.

§1.4 Section 679 of *Criminal Code* — Bail Pending Appeal (s. 57(4))

Section 57(4) of the *Extradition Act* provides as follows:

SECTION 679 of the *CRIMINAL CODE*
(4) Section 679 of the *Criminal Code* applies, with any modifications that the circumstances require, to an application for judicial review.

Section 57(4) provides that the bail pending appeal provisions of s. 679 of the *Criminal Code* apply, with any modifications required by the circumstances, to applications for judicial review under s. 57.

§1.5 Hearing of Application (s. 57(5))

Section 57(5) of the *Extradition Act* provides as follows:

HEARING OF APPLICATION
(5) An application for judicial review shall be scheduled for hearing by the court of appeal at an early date whether that date is in or out of the prescribed sessions of that court.

Section 57(5) provides that judicial review applications are to be scheduled expeditiously.

§1.6 Powers of Court of Appeal (s. 57(6))

Section 57(6) of the *Extradition Act* provides as follows:

POWERS OF COURT OF APPEAL
(6) On an application for judicial review, the court of appeal may

(a) order the Minister to do any act or thing that the Minister has unlawfully failed or refused to do or has unreasonably delayed in doing; or

(b) declare invalid or unlawful, quash, set aside, set aside and refer back for determination in accordance with any directions that it considers appropriate, prohibit or restrain the decision of the Minister referred to in subsection (1).

Section 57(6)(a) and (b) outline the powers of the court of appeal in relation to an application for judicial review of the Minister's decision.

§1.7 Grounds of Review (s. 57(7))

Section 57(7) of the *Extradition Act* provides as follows:

GROUNDS OF REVIEW

(7) The court of appeal may grant relief under this section on any of the grounds on which the Trial Division of the Federal Court of Canada may grant relief under subsection 18.1(4) of the *Federal Court Act*.

Section 57(7) provides that the grounds for review of the Minister's decision are the same as those set out in relation to decisions of the Federal Court–Trial Division in s. 18.1(4) of the *Federal Court Act*, R.S.C. 1985, c. F-7, as en. S.C. 1990, c. 8, s. 5. Section 18.1(4) reads as follows:

(4) The Trial Division may grant relief under subsection (3) if it is satisfied that the federal board, commission or other tribunal

    (a) acted without jurisdiction, acted beyond its jurisdiction or refused to exercise its jurisdiction;

    (b) failed to observe a principle of natural justice, procedural fairness or other procedure that it was required by law to observe;

    (c) erred in law in making a decision or an order, whether or not the error appears on the face of the record;

    (d) based its decision or order on an erroneous finding of fact that it made in a perverse or capricious manner or without regard for the material before it;

    (e) acted, or failed to act, by reason of fraud or perjured evidence; or

    (f) acted in any other way that was contrary to law.

§1.8 Defect in Form or Technical Irregularity (s. 57(8))

Section 57(8) of the *Extradition Act* provides as follows:

DEFECT IN FORM OR TECHNICAL IRREGULARITY

(8) If the sole ground for relief established in an application for judicial review is a defect in form or a technical irregularity, the court of appeal may

    (a) refuse the relief if it finds that no substantial wrong or miscarriage of justice has occurred; or

    (b) in the case of a defect in form or a technical irregularity in the decision, make an order validating the order, to have effect from the time and on the terms that it considers appropriate.

Under s. 57(8), the court of appeal may refuse to grant relief if the sole ground established in the application is a defect in form or a technical irregularity and there has been no substantial wrong or miscarriage of justice. The court of appeal may also validate the defective order on terms it considers appropriate.

§1.9 One Hearing by Court of Appeal (s. 57(9))

Section 57(9) of the *Extradition Act* provides as follows:

ONE HEARING BY COURT OF APPEAL
> **(9) If an appeal under section 49 or any other appeal in respect of a matter arising under this Act is pending, the court of appeal may join the hearing of that appeal with the hearing of an application for judicial review.**

Under s. 57(9), the court of appeal may make an order joining the hearing of the application for judicial review with the hearing of an appeal under s. 49 from the extradition judge's order on committal or any other appeal pending under the Act.

§1.10 Provincial Rules of Judicial Review Apply (s. 57(10))

Section 57(10) of the *Extradition Act* provides as follows:

PROVINCIAL RULES OF JUDICIAL REVIEW APPLY
> **(10) Unless inconsistent with the provisions of this Act, all laws, including rules, respecting judicial review in force in the province of the court of appeal apply, with any modifications that the circumstances require, to applications under this section.**

Section 57(10) of the Act establishes that provincial rules of judicial review apply to applications made under s. 57, unless inconsistent with the provisions of the *Extradition Act* and with any modifications that the circumstances require.

§2.0 COMPARISON WITH FORMER ACT

Section 25.2 of the former *Extradition Act* was similar in terms to s. 57 of the new Act.

§3.0 SIGNIFICANCE OF CHANGE

There is no change. See §2.0, "Comparison with Former Act," above.

§4.0 ANALYSIS

§4.1 Deference to Minister of Justice's Expertise

The Supreme Court of Canada has held that judicial deference should be accorded to the decision of the Minister of Justice in extradition matters. The Supreme Court's approach to judicial review has been influenced by its characterization of the position occupied by the Minister in the extradition process. In reviewing the Minister's decision and the process by which it was determined, the Supreme Court has recognized that the Minister's decision has political and international ramifications that fall within his or her expertise to determine. This political or legislative aspect to the making of the decision has been held to militate in favour of greater deference to the Minister's decision regarding surrender and the recognition of the need for flexibility in the process employed. In this regard, in *Idziak v. Canada (Minister of Justice)* (1992), 77 C.C.C. (3d) 65 (S.C.C.) [reconsideration refused (1992), 9 Admin. L.R. (2d) 1n (S.C.C.)], at pp. 86–87, Cory J. described the role allotted to the Minister of Justice:

> Parliament chose to give discretionary authority to the Minister of Justice. It is the Minister who must consider the good faith and honour of this country in its relations with other states. It is the Minister who has the expert knowledge of the political ramifications of an extradition decision. In administrative law terms, the Minister's review should be characterized as being at the extreme legislative end of the *continuum* of administrative decision making.
>
> . . .
>
> . . . the decision to issue a warrant of surrender involves completely different considerations from those reached by a court in an extradition hearing. The extradition hearing is clearly judicial in its nature while *the actions of the Minister of Justice in considering whether to issue a warrant of surrender are primarily political in nature.* [Emphasis added.]

A similar view was also expressed in *Kindler v. Canada (Minister of Justice)* (1991), 67 C.C.C. (3d) 1 (S.C.C.). In that case, the fugitive had been convicted of murder by a Pennsylvania jury, which had also returned a sentence of death against him. He escaped from custody and fled to Canada where, after extradition proceedings had been undertaken, he was ordered surrendered by the Minister of Justice. The Minister declined to exercise the option of asking for assurances under Article 6 of the *Canada-United States Extradition Treaty* that the death penalty would not be enforced. The Supreme Court deferred to the Minister's decision. McLachlin J. described the justification for deferring in the following terms, at p. 55:

> In recognition of the various and complex considerations which necessarily enter into the extradition process, this court has developed a more cautious approach in the

review of executive decisions in the extradition area, holding that judicial scrutiny should not be over-exacting. As the majority in *Schmidt* pointed out, the reviewing court must recognize that extradition involves interests and complexities with which judges may not be well equipped to deal (p. 215). The superior placement of the executive to assess and consider the competing interests involved in particular extradition cases suggests that courts should be especially careful before striking down provisions conferring discretion on the executive. Thus, the court must be "extremely circumspect" to avoid undue interference with an area where the executive is well placed to make these sorts of decisions.

In the subsequent case of *United States v. Burns* (2001), 151 C.C.C. (3d) 97, the Supreme Court of Canada struck down a ministerial surrender decision on the basis that surrender to face the death penalty would, in all but exceptional cases, be a violation of s. 7 of the *Charter*. The court confirmed its customary deference to the Minister when dealing with the international ramifications of extradition matters. However, the court held that the factors that had been properly weighed in *Kindler v. Canada (Minister of Justice)* (1991), 67 C.C.C. (3d) 1 (S.C.C.), and which came out against the need for assurances in that case, required a different weighing today. The decision in *Burns* now requires the Minister to seek assurances against the death penalty in almost all cases. The court stated, at p. 119:

> [37] The customary deference to the Minister's extradition decisions is rooted in the recognition of Canada's strong interest in international law enforcement activities: *Cotroni, supra*, at p. 1485, cited by McLachlin J. in *Kindler*, at pp. 843-44; *Libman v. The Queen*, [1985] 2 S.C.R. 178 at p. 214, 21 C.C.C. (3d) 206, 21 D.L.R. (4th) 174; *Idziak, supra*, at p. 662. The respondents do not quarrel with these general observations. Their argument is that despite McLachlin J.'s caution in *Kindler* that "the court must be 'extremely circumspect' to avoid undue interference with an area where the executive is well placed to make these sorts of decisions", a constitutional requirement of assurances does not undermine in any significant way the achievement of Canada's mutual assistance objectives. The executive negotiated Article 6 of the extradition treaty, the United States agreed to it, and both parties must therefore have regarded its exercise as consistent with the fulfilment of their mutual assistance obligations.
>
> [38] We affirm that it is generally for the Minister, not the Court, to assess the weight of competing considerations in extradition policy, but the availability of the death penalty, like death itself, opens up a different dimension. The difficulties and occasional miscarriages of the criminal law are located in an area of human experience that falls squarely within "the inherent domain of the judiciary as guardian of the justice system": *Re B.C. Motor Vehicle Act, supra*, at p. 503. It is from this perspective, recognizing the unique finality and irreversibility of the death penalty, that the constitutionality of the Minister's decision falls to be decided.

§4.2 Standard to Be Applied

The standard of review of the Minister of Justice's decision under s. 57(6) and (7) of the Act (formerly s. 25.2(6) and (7)) was set out by Laskin J.A. in *United States v. Whitley* (1994), 94 C.C.C. (3d) 99 (Ont. C.A.), affirmed (1996), 104 C.C.C. (3d) 447 (S.C.C.). Laskin J.A. stated comprehensively, at p. 110, that:

> if the Minister violates the fugitive's constitutional rights or otherwise errs in law, or if the Minister denies the fugitive procedural fairness, acts arbitrarily, in bad faith or for improper motives, or if the Minister's decision is plainly unreasonable, then the reviewing court is entitled to interfere; otherwise, the court should defer to the Minister's surrender decision.

While the Minister is not a court, he or she is required to make a determination as to whether surrender would constitute a violation of the person's *Charter* rights. Accordingly, judicial review may take account not only of alleged procedural failings in the Minister's process but also of the constitutional dimensions of the Minister's decision. In *Whitley*, among other things, the court was concerned with the Minister's determination that surrender would not violate the rights of the fugitive under s. 6 of the *Charter*. Laskin J.A. applied the same principles of review to the Minister's determination of this constitutional question, at p. 117:

> In my view, there are no grounds to suggest that the Minister erred in law, disregarded relevant factors or reached a decision that was unreasonable. Therefore, there is no basis for this court to interfere with the Minister's determination that extradition does not violate the appellant's rights in s. 6(1) of the Charter.

Based on this analysis, Dambrot J. in *Pacificador v. Canada (Minister of Justice)* (1999), (*sub nom. Philippines (Republic) v. Pacificador*) 60 C.R.R. (2d) 126 (Ont. Gen. Div.), a *habeas corpus* application under the pre-1992 procedure of the former *Extradition Act*, refused to admit fresh evidence, refused to compel additional disclosure requested by the fugitive, and refused to compel certain witnesses to attend for cross-examination. In Dambrot J.'s view, the reviewing court should not disregard the decision of the Minister of Justice and embark on a hearing *de novo* in order to reach its own decision about whether surrender would violate *Charter* rights.

In contrast, the British Columbia Court of Appeal has held that in considering *Charter* rights on review, the reviewing court is not required to defer to the Minister and is entitled to substitute its own view for that of the Minister. In *Canada (Minister of Justice) v. Stewart* (1998), (*sub nom. United States of America v. Stewart)* 59 C.R.R. (2d) 33 (B.C.C.A.), the fugitive argued that the Minister's decision to surrender him to face fraud charges in the United States constituted a violation of s. 7 of the *Charter* because of the disparity between the penalty for the offence in the United States and the penalty for the equivalent offence in Canada. Donald J.A. reviewed the jurisprudence, including *Whitley*, and *Kindler*, and acknowledged that "on the general question of surrender much deference ought to be accorded the minister," at p. 40. Nevertheless, he concluded that a standard of deference was not appropriate to *Charter* matters determined by the Minister for the first time at the surrender stage of the process. He held, at p. 41, that the reviewing court should examine the decisions of the Minister on *Charter* issues on a standard of correctness:

> While the present structure of the process makes it necessary for the minister to determine these matters in the first instance, it should be recognized that what the minister is really deciding is whether her executive act would violate the *Charter*. If deference were accorded her assessment of the constitutional validity of her own act then I believe that judicial review would be unacceptably attenuated. In my opinion, a person affected by an executive decision is entitled to the full measure of *Charter* scrutiny unrestricted by notions of deference. It is only at the review stage that a neutral, uninvolved examination of the decision can take place.

However, on the facts of the case, Donald J.A. found that the Minister had committed no error in determining that surrender was appropriate.

In *United States v. Gillingham* (2000), 149 C.C.C. (3d) 261, the British Columbia Court of Appeal exercised its authority to refer a matter back to the Minister to consider an issue which the court felt had not been raised with sufficient clarity by the fugitive at the time of the surrender decision, namely, whether Canadian authorities may have improperly persuaded American authorities to pursue extradition proceedings.

§5.0 CASE LAW

Canada (Minister of Justice) v. Stewart (1998), *(sub nom. United States of America v. Stewart)* 59 C.R.R. (2d) 33 (B.C.C.A.).
Idziak v. Canada (Minister of Justice) (1992), 77 C.C.C. (3d) 65 (S.C.C.), reconsideration refused (1992), 9 Admin. L.R. (2d) 1n (S.C.C.).
Kindler v. Canada (Minister of Justice) (1991), 67 C.C.C. (3d) 1 (S.C.C.).
Pacificador v. Canada (Minister of Justice) (1999), *(sub nom. Philippines (Republic) v. Pacificador)* 60 C.R.R. (2d) 126 (Ont. Gen. Div.).
United States v. Burns (2001), 151 C.C.C. (3d) 97 (S.C.C.).
United States v. Gillingham (2000), 149 C.C.C. (3d) 261 (B.C.C.A.).
United States v. Whitley (1994), 94 C.C.C. (3d) 99 (Ont. C.A.), affirmed (1996), 104 C.C.C. (3d) 447 (S.C.C.).

§6.0 RELATED SECTIONS

s. 2 — Interpretation
s. 40 — Surrender Order by Minister of Justice
s. 49 — Right of Appeal Against Committal Order
Criminal Code, s. 679 — Bail Pending Appeal
Federal Court Act, s. 18.1(4) — Grounds of Review

Contents of Surrender Order (s. 58)

§1.0 DESCRIPTION

Section 58 of the *Extradition Act* provides as follows:

CONTENTS OF THE SURRENDER ORDER
    58. An order of surrender must

- **(a)** contain the name of the person who is to be surrendered;
- **(b)** describe the offence in respect of which the extradition is requested, the offence for which the committal was ordered or the conduct for which the person is to be surrendered;
- **(c)** state the extradition partner to which the person is to be conveyed;
- **(d)** direct the person who has custody of the person to be surrendered to deliver them into the custody of the person or a member of the class of persons referred to in paragraph (*e*);
- **(e)** designate the person or class of persons authorized for the purposes of section 60;
- **(f)** set out any assurances or conditions to which the surrender is subject;
- **(g)** fix, in the case of postponement of surrender under section 64, the period of time at or before the expiry of which the person is to be surrendered; and
- **(h)** fix, in the case of a temporary surrender under section 66,
  - **(i)** the period of time at or before the expiry of which the person to be surrendered must be returned to Canada, and
  - **(ii)** the period of time at or before the expiry of which final surrender shall take place.

Section 58 sets out a detailed list of the required contents for the Minister of Justice's surrender order.

§2.0 COMPARISON WITH FORMER ACT

The former *Extradition Act* contained a precedent form for the order of the Minister of Justice for surrender (Form 3). The contents of the form had some of the same requirements as s. 58. It required the following:

- the name of the person to be surrendered;

- the crime committed;

- the jurisdiction within which the crime was committed;

- a direction to the keeper of the jail to deliver the person to an identified person for the purpose of conveyance; and

- a direction that the person be conveyed to representatives of the requesting state.

§3.0 SIGNIFICANCE OF CHANGE

Although the surrender order under the former Act contained similar requirements to those set out in s. 58(a) to (e), s. 58 is more comprehensive. Section 58 is also updated to take account of the new provisions concerning postponement of surrender and temporary surrender. Moreover, if the surrender includes assurances or conditions, s. 58 requires that it be made clear on the face of the warrant what the conditions of surrender are.

§4.0 ANALYSIS

Perhaps the most significant innovation in s. 58 is the provision in s. 58(b) which provides three different ways in which the offence in question may be described: the Minister may refer to the offence set out in the extradition request, which would be the foreign offence; the Minister may refer to the offence for which the committal was ordered, which would be the Canadian equivalent offence described in the authority to proceed; or the Minister may describe the conduct upon which surrender is ordered.

Under the former Act, the Minister generally surrendered with respect to the offence as named by the requesting state. The forms under the former Act, including Form 3 concerning the order of the Minister of Justice for surrender, contemplated reference to the crime as known in the foreign jurisdiction.

In setting out three options for describing the offence, s. 58(b) gives the Minister of Justice flexibility and in particular provides for the option of describing conduct that is common ground to both extradition partners. One extradition partner may not describe or fashion charges in a way that is easily recognized or understood by the other partner.

The option chosen by the Minister for describing the offence in the order of surrender may have an impact on the way in which specialty is considered by the extradition partner. The concept of specialty ensures that a person surrendered to a foreign jurisdiction for a particular crime will not, without the permission of the state making the surrender, be tried for any other crime previously committed. This is variously seen as either a rule of customary international law or an implied condition of surrender arising out of the proper interpretation of extradition treaties (see *R. v. Parisien* (1988), 41 C.C.C. (3d) 223 (S.C.C.), at p. 228). Extradition treaties also contain specialty provisions, for example, Article 12 of the *Canada–United States Extradition Treaty*.

The courts of the extradition partner will be required to determine on which offences the person has been surrendered in order to comply with the obligations of specialty. If the surrender order is framed in terms of the charges as described in the requesting state's extradition request (the first option under s. 58(b)), this will present no problem. Any committal on the underlying conduct described in Canadian terms in the authority to proceed should allow for surrender with confidence on the offence as described by the foreign state in the extradition request.

The second option presented by s. 58(b) would allow the Minister of Justice to describe in the order of surrender the offence for which the committal was ordered at the hearing, that is, the Canadian offence described in the authority to proceed. This may be problematic from the point of view of the application of the rule of specialty. In *United States v. McVey* (1992), 77 C.C.C. (3d) 1 (S.C.C.), the fugitives were said by the Supreme Court of Canada to have engaged in conduct amounting to a Canadian fraud. The American charges, however, were offences unknown in Canada relating to the exportation of high technology equipment to the Soviet Union. It is difficult to see what use it would be to an American court to have persons surrendered to face trial on offences described in the surrender order according to the Canadian nomenclature of fraud. In this type of situation, argument over what this entitled the extradition partner to prosecute could easily ensue. Accordingly, it might be expected that this option would be the least used.

The third option — describing the conduct for which extradition is granted — will be attractive in that it avoids confusion over the terms used by each extradition partner in the framing of charges. Each partner should be able to understand the description of the conduct for which extradition is granted without regard to the way the offence is named in either country. This option may present a preferable option when the foreign charge is unknown in Canadian law, as in the example of the *McVey* case, *supra,* or with offences such as the American RICO (Racketeering Influenced and Corrupt Organizations) and CCE (Continuing Criminal Enterprise) offences. It would also be an option when only a description of the conduct is provided with the extradition request, that is, no specific offence is set out in the request. If Canada surrenders the person sought on only a part of the conduct described in the extradition request, then the issue of specialty will be a matter to be dealt with in the foreign court in terms of fewer or different offences being tried than originally anticipated.

Section 64(1) provides that the surrender of a person shall be postponed if the person sought is accused of an offence within Canadian jurisdiction or serving a Canadian sentence. In such circumstances, the surrender order does not take effect until the person has been discharged (by acquittal, expiry of sentence, or otherwise). However, this section does not apply if the Canadian offence arises from the conduct underlying the surrender order. Moreover, the opening clause of s. 64(1) — "[u]nless the Minister orders otherwise" — provides the Minister of Justice with the discretion to override this provision. In the case of postponement under s. 64, the Minister is required by s. 58(g) to specify when the surrender will be effective. This time frame could either be when the Canadian sentence has been completely served, or prior to that time such as at the date of parole eligibility.

If the surrender is made subject to conditions or assurances, s. 58(f) requires them to be specified in the surrender order.

§5.0 CASE LAW

United States v. McVey (1992), 77 C.C.C. (3d) 1 (S.C.C.).
R. v. Parisien (1988), 41 C.C.C. (3d) 223 (S.C.C.).

§6.0 RELATED SECTIONS

s. 60 — Power to Convey Person Sought
s. 64 — Postponement of Surrender
s. 66 — Temporary Surrender
Canada–United States Extradition Treaty, Article 12 — Specialty

Surrender for Other Offences (s. 59)

§1.0 DESCRIPTION

Section 59 of the *Extradition Act* provides as follows:

SURRENDER FOR OTHER OFFENCES
   59. Subject to a relevant extradition agreement, the Minister may, if the request for extradition is based on more than one offence, order the surrender of a person for all the offences even if not all of them fulfil the requirements set out in section 3, if

   (a) the person is being surrendered for at least one offence that fulfils the requirements set out in section 3; and
   (b) all the offences relate to conduct that, had it occurred in Canada, would have constituted offences that are punishable under the laws of Canada.

This section provides the Minister of Justice with the discretion to surrender a person sought for offences which do not meet the requirements of s. 3 of the Act if the following two conditions are met: firstly, the person is being surrendered for an offence which meets the requirements of s. 3; secondly, the offence relates to conduct that, had it occurred in Canada, would constitute an offence punishable in Canada. As indicated in the opening clause of s. 59, the provision is subject to the provisions of an applicable extradition agreement.

§2.0 COMPARISON WITH FORMER ACT

The former *Extradition Act* did not contain any provision similar to s. 59 and thus extradition for the kinds of offences covered by s. 59 was not possible under the former Act. The definition of "extradition crime" in the former Act was concerned with the double criminality requirements for extradition. The types of offences which might attract the operation of s. 59 of the new Act — such as failure to appear, failure to comply, and breach of probation — would not have amounted to extradition crimes under the former system. This is because they either were not listed in the schedule to the Act or the treaty or did not meet the penalty requirements of the applicable treaty in the case of no-list treaties. As they would not have been "extradition crimes," surrender would not have been possible under the former Act.

§3.0 SIGNIFICANCE OF CHANGE

Section 59 effects a significant change in Canada's extradition scheme. It vests the Minister of Justice with the power to surrender persons sought with respect to offences for which extradition has been requested but which neither meet the penalty criteria in s. 3 of the Act nor have been judicially dealt with at the extradition hearing. The requirement in s. 59(b) that such offences would constitute an offence in Canada is left to be determined by the Minister of Justice, rather than by the extradition judge who normally deals with that issue.

§4.0 ANALYSIS

As the opening clause of the provision indicates, s. 59 is subject to the provisions of an extradition agreement. In the case of the *Canada–United States Extradition Treaty*, Article 2(1) is the governing provision. It provides as follows:

> **2.** (1) Extradition shall be granted for conduct which constitutes an offense punishable by the laws of both Contracting Parties by imprisonment or other form of detention for a term exceeding one year or any greater punishment.

Section 3 of the *Extradition Act*, by its own terms, is also subject to extradition agreements. As a result, the provisions of a treaty will govern both ss. 3 and 59. This means that, if there is an applicable treaty, extradition will only take place according to the terms of the treaty. The American treaty provides that extradition shall take place for offences that carry a penalty of imprisonment for one year or any greater punishment. If a request is made for a crime that fails to meet this requirement at the s. 3 stage, the same treaty requirement will prevent reliance on s. 59. Therefore, for extradition requests governed by treaty, s. 59 cannot be resorted to for the offences it was meant to capture, such as failure to appear, failure to comply, and breach of probation, since it is unlikely that these offences will meet the treaty penalty criteria.

Section 59 appears to be directed at minor offences, since only minor offences would be unable to meet the penalty requirements of s. 3 of the Act. It might be expected that such minor offences will be connected or related to a more significant offence for which surrender will be ordered. For example, a person sought for the offence of drug importation may be charged with failure to appear for not attending on a court date for the drug offence. However, s. 59 does not require such a connection.

Section 59 may be directed at situations where a person, in addition to being sought for extradition on an offence that meets the surrender requirements of the Act, is subject to an unserved portion of a term of incarceration that is less than the six months required by s. 3(3) of the Act. In such a case, s. 59 would permit the Minister to surrender the person for the purpose of serving the remainder of the sentence if the person was surrendered on the major offence.

Section 59 increases the Minister of Justice's discretionary authority by vesting him or her with the task of determining whether an offence which does not meet the s. 3 requirements nonetheless has underlying conduct which constitutes an offence in Canada. Under the former *Extradition Act*, this was exclusively the task of the extradition judge. By contrast, under the new Act, the Minister is required to make this determination from the very outset of the extradition proceedings when determining the Canadian equivalent offence to which the alleged conduct corresponds for the purpose of issuing an authority to proceed. This is not to say that the minor offence in question would be named in the authority to proceed. Rather, the minor offence would not be named because it would fail the s. 3 penalty criteria required under s. 15 for the issuance of an authority to proceed. The new Act dispenses with the judicial assessment of the evidence because the offence is minor and because a judicial determination is made with respect to the major offence upon which the person sought will be surrendered.

Moreover, the person sought may raise issues regarding surrender on minor offences through judicial review of the Minister's decision (s. 57).

§5.0 RELATED SECTIONS

s. 3 — Extraditable Conduct
s. 57 — Judicial Review of Minister of Justice's Surrender Decision
Canada–United States Extradition Treaty, Article 2(1) — Penalty Criteria

Power to Convey Person Sought (s. 60)

§1.0 DESCRIPTION

Section 60 of the *Extradition Act* provides as follows:

POWER TO CONVEY

60. On the execution of a surrender order, the person or persons designated under paragraph 58(*e*) shall have the authority to receive, hold in custody and convey the person into the territory over which the extradition partner has jurisdiction.

Section 58(e) provides that the surrender order must designate the person or class of persons who are authorized to convey the person sought to the extradition partner. Section 60 provides the person or class of persons named under s. 58(e) with the authority to receive, hold in custody, and convey the person sought to the extradition partner.

§2.0 COMPARISON WITH FORMER ACT

Section 26 of the former *Extradition Act* was the equivalent holding and conveying authority to s. 60 of the new Act. Section 26 provided as follows:

> **26.** *Any person to whom an order of the Minister of Justice made under section 25 is directed may deliver, and the person thereto authorized by that order may receive, hold in custody and convey, the fugitive within the jurisdiction of the foreign state*, and if the fugitive escapes out of any custody to which the fugitive is delivered, on or in pursuance of that order, the fugitive may be retaken in the same manner as any person accused or convicted of any crime against the laws of Canada may be retaken on an escape. [Emphasis added.]

Section 60 of the new Act, like s. 26 of the former Act, authorizes the escorting authority of the extradition partner to receive the person in custody and transport that person to the jurisdiction of the applicable court of the extradition partner.

In comparing s. 60 of the new Act with s. 26 of the former Act, it is important to note the reference in s. 60 to s. 58(e). Section 58(e) provides that the surrender order must designate "the person or class of persons" who are authorized to convey the person sought to the extradition partner. The use of the term "class of persons" is important because it allows for more flexibility in the surrender order. By contrast, the former Act merely referred to the "person" authorized to convey the person sought. Based on the wording of the former Act, the practice developed of naming specific individuals in surrender orders. The new Act, in employing the phrase "class of persons," avoids the necessity of naming specific persons. A surrender order can now simply refer, for instance, to the "U.S. Marshals."

§3.0 SIGNIFICANCE OF CHANGE AND ANALYSIS

See §2.0, "Comparison with Former Act," above.

§4.0 RELATED SECTIONS

s. 58 — Contents of Surrender Order
s. 61 — Escape of Person Sought While in Custody and Arrest
s. 63 — Place of Surrender

Escape of Person Sought While in Custody and Arrest (s. 61)

§1.0 DESCRIPTION

Section 61 of the *Extradition Act* provides as follows:

ESCAPE
   61. (1) If the person escapes while in custody, the law that applies with respect to a person who is accused or convicted of a crime against the laws of Canada and who escapes applies with respect to the person.

ARREST
   (2) If the person escapes while in custody, the person or member of the class of persons having custody of the person has the power to arrest them in fresh pursuit.

Section 61 deals with the escape of a person sought while in custody and the rearrest of that person. Section 61(1) provides that a person sought who escapes while in custody is subject to the same laws as if the person were accused or convicted of a crime in Canada. Section 61(2) adds that the person or class of persons having custody of the person has the power to arrest the person in fresh pursuit.
   Section 61 operates in tandem with s. 58(e) and ss. 60 and 63 of the Act. Section 58(e) provides that the surrender order must designate the person or class of persons who are authorized to convey the person sought to the extradition partner. Section 60 provides the person or class of persons named under s. 58(e) with the authority to receive, hold in custody, and convey the person sought to the extradition partner. Section 63 provides that the person sought may be transferred at any location within or outside Canada as agreed to by Canada and the extradition partner.

§2.0 COMPARISON WITH FORMER ACT

Section 26 of the former *Extradition Act* provided as follows:

   26. Any person to whom an order of the Minister of Justice made under section 25 is directed may deliver, and the person thereto authorized by that order may receive, hold in custody and convey, the fugitive within the jurisdiction of the foreign state, *and if the fugitive escapes out of any custody to which the fugitive is delivered, on or in pursuance of that order, the fugitive may be retaken in the same manner as any person accused or convicted of any crime against the laws of Canada may be retaken on an escape.* [Emphasis added.]

Section 26 bore some similarity to s. 61 of the new Act in that it allowed for the rearrest in accordance with Canadian law of a fugitive who escaped while still on Canadian soil. However, s. 26 did not provide the foreign officers authorized to convey the person with the power of arrest in Canada. Rather, s. 26 merely stated that the fugitive may be rearrested, without any mention of whether that rearrest could be effected by the conveying officers of the requesting jurisdiction. If the person was picked up by the foreign officers on Canadian territory and escaped from those officers before entering the foreign jurisdiction, s. 26 did not provide the foreign officers with the power to effect a Canadian arrest.

By contrast, s. 61 of the new Act, when read together with s. 63, clearly provides the foreign officers conveying the person sought with the authority to retake a person who escapes on Canadian territory. Section 63 allows for the surrender to take place "at any place within or outside Canada that is agreed to by Canada and the extradition partner" and, if the person sought escapes while still on Canadian territory, s. 61(2) provides the foreign officers with "the power to arrest . . . in fresh pursuit."

§3.0 SIGNIFICANCE OF CHANGE

Section 61, together with s. 63, clarifies the following aspect of the surrender process. The surrender of a person may take place within or outside Canada (s. 63). If it takes place within Canada, and the person sought escapes from that custody while still on Canadian territory, the foreign officers have the power to retake the person in fresh pursuit. The absence of such an authority under s. 26 of the former Act meant that, as a practical matter, fugitives were always conveyed to border points in the custody of Canadian law enforcement officers because it was not clear that foreign authorities had the jurisdiction to receive a fugitive or pursue an escaped fugitive within Canada.

§4.0 ANALYSIS

Section 61, together with s. 63, clarifies important practical issues in connection with the surrender of a person to foreign officers. In particular, it clarifies the power of foreign officers who take custody of a person sought on Canadian territory. Importantly, however, it should be noted that the power to rearrest the person sought by officers of the extradition partner is restricted to the context of "fresh pursuit." Therefore, if the escapee evaded immediate apprehension, the foreign officials would not be empowered to continue to pursue the person with a view to arrest. The domestic authorities would have to be involved at this point, possibly obtaining a domestic arrest warrant based on the person's escape from custody.

§5.0 RELATED SECTIONS

s. 58 — Contents of Surrender Order
s. 60 — Power to Convey Person Sought
s. 63 — Place of Surrender

Delay Before Surrender and Waiver of Time Period (s. 62)

§1.0 DESCRIPTION

Section 62 of the *Extradition Act* provides as follows:

DELAY BEFORE SURRENDER
    62. (1) No person may be surrendered

    (a) until a period of 30 days has expired after the date of the committal for surrender; or
    (b) if an appeal or a judicial review in respect of a matter arising under this Act, or any appeal from an appeal or judicial review, is pending, until after the date of the final decision of the court on the appeal or judicial review.

WAIVER OF PERIOD OF TIME
    (2) The person may waive the period referred to in paragraph (1)(*a*) if they do so in writing.

Section 62(1) provides for a statutory waiting period that must elapse before a person can be surrendered to an extradition partner. More specifically, no person may be surrendered before the expiry of 30 days from the date of the extradition judge's committal for surrender or, if an appeal or judicial review is pending under the Act, until after the court has made a final decision on the appeal or review.

§2.0 COMPARISON WITH FORMER ACT

Section 23 of the former *Extradition Act* was, in all significant respects, the same as s. 62(1). In this sense, the new Act retains the statutory waiting period that existed under s. 23 of the former Act. The 30-day waiting period permits the person to bring an appeal or judicial review application, as the case may be.

§3.0 SIGNIFICANCE OF CHANGE AND ANALYSIS

Unlike the former Act, the person who does not wish to avail himself or herself of the appeal or judicial review provisions is not required to wait for the conclusion of the 30-day period before surrender can take place. Rather, under s. 62(2), the person sought may be surrendered immediately if he or she waives the right to the waiting period in writing. This procedure introduces a degree of flexibility into the extradition process that did not exist under the former Act.

§4.0 RELATED SECTIONS

s. 71 — Consent to Surrender

Place of Surrender (s. 63)

§1.0 DESCRIPTION

Section 63 of the *Extradition Act* provides as follows:

PLACE OF SURRENDER
63. A surrender may take place at any place within or outside Canada that is agreed to by Canada and the extradition partner.

Section 63 provides that the person sought may be transferred at any location within or outside Canada as agreed to by Canada and the extradition partner.

§2.0 COMPARISON WITH FORMER ACT

Section 26 of the former *Extradition Act* provided as follows:

26. Any person to whom an order of the Minister of Justice made under section 25 is directed may deliver, and the person thereto authorized by that order *may receive, hold in custody and convey, the fugitive within the jurisdiction of the foreign state*, and if the fugitive escapes out of any custody to which the fugitive is delivered, on or in pursuance of that order, the fugitive may be retaken in the same manner as any person accused or convicted of any crime against the laws of Canada may be retaken on an escape. [Emphasis added.]

Section 26 suggested that the foreign officers to whom the person sought was surrendered only had the authority under the Act to receive that person within the territory of the requesting state. By contrast, s. 63 of the new Act explicitly provides that the surrender may take place within or outside Canada.

§3.0 SIGNIFICANCE OF CHANGE

Section 63, by permitting surrender either within or outside Canada, allows the extradition partners the flexibility to make the most convenient arrangement in any particular case. A certain degree of risk is introduced because, unlike the situation in the former Act, surrender need not necessarily be effected at a border point. The possibility of escape within Canada while the person is in the custody of officials of the extradition partner is addressed in s. 61 of the new Act. Section 61 gives the foreign officials the authority to apprehend in "fresh pursuit" a person who has escaped from their custody during the process of surrender.

§4.0 ANALYSIS

Section 63, along with the other surrender provisions, creates a more flexible and realistic surrender process. It allows surrender to take place in the location that is most convenient for the extradition partner. If this location is in Canada, then s. 63 should be considered together with s. 61, which deals with the escape of a person sought while in custody and the rearrest of that person. Section 61(1) provides that a person sought who escapes while in custody is subject to the same laws as if the person were accused or convicted of a crime in Canada. Section 61(2) adds that the person or class of persons having custody of the person has the power to arrest the person in "fresh pursuit."

§5.0 RELATED SECTIONS

s. 60 — Power to Convey Person Sought
s. 61 — Escape of Person Sought While in Custody and Arrest

Postponement of Surrender (s. 64)

§1.0 DESCRIPTION

Section 64 of the *Extradition Act* provides as follows:

POSTPONEMENT OF SURRENDER
64. (1) Unless the Minister orders otherwise, a surrender order made in respect of a person accused of an offence within Canadian jurisdiction or who is serving a sentence in Canada after a conviction for an offence, other than an offence with respect to the conduct to which the order relates does not take effect until the person has been discharged, whether by acquittal, by expiry of the sentence or otherwise.

OFFENCE BEFORE OR AFTER SURRENDER

(2) For greater certainty, the person need not have been accused of the offence within Canadian jurisdiction before the surrender order was made.

Section 64(1) provides that the surrender of a person shall be postponed if the person sought is accused of an offence within Canadian jurisdiction or serving a Canadian sentence. In such circumstances, the surrender order does not take effect until the person has been discharged (by acquittal, expiry of sentence, or otherwise). However, this section does not apply if the Canadian offence arises from the conduct underlying the surrender order. Moreover, the opening clause of s. 64(1) — "[u]nless the Minister orders otherwise" — provides the Minister of Justice with the discretion to override this provision.

Section 64(2) adds a clarification to s. 64(1), stating that the person need not have been accused of the Canadian offence prior to the ordering of the person's surrender.

§2.0 COMPARISON WITH FORMER ACT

In all significant respects, s. 25(4) and (5) of the former *Extradition Act* were the same as s. 64(1) of the new Act. However, the former Act did not contain an equivalent to s. 64(2).

§3.0 SIGNIFICANCE OF CHANGE

Section 64(2) adds a degree of clarity with respect to the timing of the Canadian offence that did not exist in the former Act.

§4.0 ANALYSIS

The opening clause of s. 64 states, "[u]nless the Minister orders otherwise." This clause has the effect of providing the Minister of Justice with complete discretion regarding whether a person ought to be extradited to a requesting state notwithstanding that the person is subject to outstanding Canadian charges or convictions.

§5.0 RELATED SECTIONS

s. 65 — Return of Surrendered Person to Canada With Unexpired Sentence
s. 66 — Temporary Surrender

Return to Canada (s. 65)

§1.0 DESCRIPTION

Section 65 of the *Extradition Act* provides as follows:

RETURN TO CANADA
65. If a person returns to Canada after surrender before the expiry of a sentence that they were serving in Canada at the time of surrender, the remaining part of the sentence must be served.

If a person returns to Canada after he or she has been surrendered to an extradition partner but prior to the expiry of a Canadian sentence, the person must serve the remainder of his or her sentence.

§2.0 COMPARISON WITH FORMER ACT

The former *Extradition Act* did not contain an equivalent to s. 65.

§3.0 SIGNIFICANCE OF CHANGE AND ANALYSIS

Section 65 anticipates a situation in which the Minster of Justice orders the surrender of a person under s. 64(1) notwithstanding that the person has an unexpired Canadian sentence and the person subsequently returns to Canada.

§4.0 RELATED SECTIONS

s. 64 — Postponement of Surrender for Canadian Offence
s. 66 — Temporary Surrender

Temporary Surrender (ss. 66–68)

§1.0 DESCRIPTION

§1.1 Applicability and Purpose of Temporary Surrender Provisions (s. 66(1))

Section 66(1) of the *Extradition Act* provides as follows:

> **TEMPORARY SURRENDER**
> **66. (1) The Minister may order the temporary surrender to an extradition partner of a person who is ordered committed under section 29 while serving a term of imprisonment in Canada so that the extradition partner may prosecute the person or to ensure the person's presence in respect of appeal proceedings that affect the person, on condition that the extradition partner give the assurances referred to in subsections (3) and (4).**

Under s. 66(1), the temporary surrender of a person to an extradition partner is possible if the person has been committed for surrender by an extradition judge under s. 29 of the Act and the person is serving a sentence in Canada. In such circumstances, s. 66(1) allows the Minister of Justice to order the temporary surrender of a person so that the extradition partner may prosecute the person or ensure the person's presence at appeal proceedings that affect the person. As a condition precedent to temporary surrender, s. 66(1) requires that the extradition partner provide the assurances set out in s. 66(3) and (4).

§1.2 Time Limits for Making of Temporary Surrender Order (s. 66(2))

Section 66(2) of the *Extradition Act* provides as follows:

> **TIME LIMITS**
> **(2) An order of temporary surrender is subject to the time limits set out in subsections 40(1) and (5) and paragraph 41(1)(c).**

Section 66(2) requires that the temporary surrender order be made within the time limits specified in s. 40(1) and (5) and s. 41(1)(c) of the Act. Section 40(1) requires that the Minister of Justice make the order within 90 days of the extradition judge's committal order. If the person sought makes submissions to the Minister, s. 40(5) permits the Minister to extend the 90-day period by a further 60 days. If an appeal has been filed against the extradition judge's committal order, s. 41(1)(c) requires that the Minister make the surrender order within the 45 days following the decision of the court of appeal.

§1.3 Assurances (s. 66(3), (4), (5))

Section 66(3), (4), and (5) of the *Extradition Act* provide as follows:

ASSURANCES

(3) The Minister may not order temporary surrender under subsection (1) unless the extradition partner gives an assurance that the person will remain in custody while temporarily surrendered to the extradition partner and

> **(a) in the case of temporary surrender for a trial, that the person will be returned within 30 days after the completion of the trial, unless a relevant extradition agreement provides for another time limit; and**

> **(b) in the case of temporary surrender for an appeal, that the person will be returned within 30 days after the completion of the proceedings for which the presence of the person was required, unless a relevant extradition agreement provides for another time limit.**

TIME LIMIT

(4) The Minister may require the extradition partner to give an assurance that the person will be returned no later than a specified date or that the person will be returned on request of the Minister.

ASSURANCES IN EXTRADITION AGREEMENTS

(5) Any assurance referred to in subsections (3) and (4) that is included in a relevant extradition agreement need not be repeated as a specific assurance.

As a condition precedent to the temporary surrender of a person sought, s. 66(3) requires that the Minister of Justice obtain the following assurances from the extradition partner:

- that the person sought will remain in custody during the duration of the temporary surrender;

- that the person sought will be returned to Canada within 30 days of the completion of the trial or appeal proceedings, as the case may be, unless the applicable extradition agreement sets out another time limit.

Section 66(4) provides that the Minister of Justice may also require the extradition partner to give an assurance that the person will be returned to Canada either by a specified date or at the request of the Minister.

Section 66(5) adds that any assurance referred to in s. 66(3) or (4) that is included in the applicable extradition agreement need not be repeated in the order as a specific assurance.

§1.4 Final Surrender After Temporary Surrender (s. 66(6)–(11))

Section 66(6) to (11) of the *Extradition Act* provide as follows:

FINAL SURRENDER AFTER TEMPORARY SURRENDER

(6) A person shall, subject to subsection (7), be surrendered to the extradition partner without a further request for extradition after the person

(a) **has been temporarily surrendered;**

(b) **has been convicted by the extradition partner and had a term of imprisonment imposed on them;**

(c) **has been returned to Canada under subsection (4); and**

(d) **has finished serving the portion of the sentence that they were serving in custody in Canada at the time of the temporary surrender, unless the Minister orders that they be surrendered earlier.**

NO FINAL SURRENDER IF CIRCUMSTANCES WARRANT

(7) The Minister may, in circumstances that the Minister considers appropriate, revoke the surrender order and order the discharge of the person.

NOTICE

(8) The authority who has custody of the person to be surrendered under subsection (6) shall give the Minister reasonable notice of the time when the portion of the person's sentence to be served in custody is to expire.

FINAL SURRENDER WHEN CANADIAN SENTENCE EXPIRES

(9) When the sentence that the person is serving in Canada expires during the period during which the person is temporarily surrendered to an extradition partner, the surrender is considered to be a final surrender.

WAIVER OF RETURN

(10) The Minister may, after consultation with the Solicitor General of Canada or the appropriate provincial minister responsible for corrections, waive the return of the person by the extradition partner.

FINAL SURRENDER DESPITE SUBSECTION 3(3)

(11) A person may be surrendered under subsection (6) even if the term of imprisonment imposed by the extradition partner, or the portion of the term remaining to be served, is less than that required by subsection 3(3).

Section 66(6) sets out the general conditions for a final surrender following a temporary surrender without the requirement of another extradition request:

• the person has been temporarily surrendered;

• the person has been convicted by an extradition partner and has had a term of imprisonment imposed on him or her;

• the person has been returned to Canada; and

• the person has completed the sentence they were serving at the time of their temporary surrender, unless the Minister of Justice orders that they be surrendered earlier.

However, s. 66(7) reserves for the Minister of Justice the discretion to revoke the surrender order and order the discharge of the person (thereby eliminating final surrender) "in circumstances that the Minister considers appropriate."

For the purpose of final surrender under s. 66(6), s. 66(8) requires the Canadian custodial authorities who have custody of the person sought to give the Minister of Justice reasonable notice of the time when the person's Canadian sentence is to expire.

If the person's Canadian sentence expires during the person's temporary surrender to the extradition partner, s. 66(9) deems the surrender to be final.

Section 66(10) provides the Minister of Justice with the discretion to waive the return of a person by an extradition partner. In exercising the discretion, this subsection requires that the Minister consult the Solicitor General of Canada or the applicable provincial minister responsible for corrections.

Section 66(11) establishes that a person may be surrendered under s. 66(6) notwithstanding that the term of imprisonment imposed by the extradition partner or remaining to be served is less than the six-month minimum required by s. 3(3) of the Act.

§1.5 Temporary Surrender Order Prevails Over Other Canadian Orders (s. 67)

Section 67 of the *Extradition Act* provides as follows:

ORDER FOR SURRENDER

67. An order of surrender prevails over a prior warrant or other order under which the person to whom it applies is otherwise detained in Canada or at liberty under terms and conditions.

Pursuant to s. 67, a temporary surrender takes precedence over any other order detaining the person in Canada or any other order pursuant to which the person is on release under terms and conditions.

§1.6 Calculation of Canadian Sentence at Time of Temporary Surrender Order (s. 68)

Section 68 of the *Extradition Act* provides as follows:

CALCULATION OF SENTENCE

68. For the purposes of calculating a sentence that a person to whom an order of temporary surrender applies is serving in Canada at the time of the temporary surrender, the person

> **(a) is credited with any time that is served in custody outside Canada under a temporary surrender order; and**
>
> **(b) remains eligible for remission in accordance with the laws of the correctional system under which the person was serving the sentence in Canada.**

Section 68 provides the following guidelines for calculating the sentence that a temporarily surrendered person is serving in Canada:

- the person is credited with any time served in custody outside of Canada under the temporary surrender order; and

- the person remains eligible for remission in accordance with the applicable Canadian correctional laws under which the person was serving his or her sentence.

§2.0 COMPARISON WITH FORMER ACT

The former *Extradition Act* did not contain any equivalent to ss. 66 to 68 of the new Act.

§3.0 SIGNIFICANCE OF CHANGE

There was nothing under the former Act that permitted a temporary surrender to the extradition partner. Sections 66 to 68 of the new legislation accommodate the extradition partner in situations in which the prosecution or appeal in the requesting state could be jeopardized by delaying the surrender of the person until the Canadian sentence has been served. These sections provide procedures and time limits for temporary surrender as well as rules regarding the return of temporarily surrendered persons to Canada.

When a person is required to serve a Canadian sentence, the Minister of Justice may make a temporary surrender order of the person to the extradition partner for the purpose of prosecuting the person or enabling the person to be present at appeal proceedings. The Minister might make a temporary surrender order when a delay in the return of the person would adversely affect a prosecution in the courts of the extradition partner. Witness availability is one such consideration that may affect the ability of the requesting jurisdiction to prosecute the matter.

The scheme of temporary surrender is tightly controlled and provides for the following safeguards: the person sought must remain in custody in the foreign jurisdiction; the person must be returned to Canada within the time period required by the Minister of Justice or on demand by the Minister or within 30 days of the completion of the proceedings in the foreign jurisdiction.

The temporary surrender rules provide that a person can be finally surrendered when the person has been temporarily surrendered, convicted, and sentenced in the requesting jurisdiction and has been returned and finished serving any sentence in Canada (s. 66(6) to (8)).

A person who has been temporarily surrendered, convicted and ultimately sentenced to a term of less than six months' imprisonment cannot, under s. 66(11), argue against a final surrender on the basis that the six-month sentence requirements of s. 3(3) have not been met.

Section 68 provides that the time spent in temporary custody in the requesting jurisdiction counts in serving the outstanding Canadian sentence. When the Canadian sentence expires while the person is in temporary custody in the requesting state, the temporary surrender is deemed by s. 66(9) to be a final surrender. The Minister, in consultation with the Solicitor General, may also waive the return of the person sought to Canada and therefore dispense with the requirement that the person sought complete the time remaining to be served on any Canadian sentence (s. 66(10)).

Section 66(7) allows the Minister of Justice to reconsider the surrender order after the person has been returned to Canada. The exercise of the Minister's discretion in this regard occurs when circumstances in the foreign state have changed to such an extent as to question the appropriateness of the original determination of the person's surrender. This subsection underscores the flexibility accorded to the Minister in the exercise of ministerial discretion regarding surrender.

Section 67 enables a temporary surrender order to have effect notwithstanding that the person to whom it applies has been detained or is subject to a judicial interim release order or to terms of parole in Canada.

§4.0 ANALYSIS

The goal of the temporary surrender provisions is to enable Canada to more effectively combat transborder criminal activity and fulfil its international extradition obligations. These points were made by Parliamentary Secretary Eleni Bakopanos, introducing Bill C-40 (now the *Extradition Act*) to the House of Commons on second reading (*House of Commons Debates*, October 8, 1998, 1st Session, 36th Parliament, v. 135):

> The extradition law, as it currently stands, does not provide for a code of procedure. If one were to consult the Extradition Act or the Fugitive Offenders Act, one would be hard pressed to understand how proceedings commence, whether the fugitive is entitled to bail, how someone is to be arrested, how one can waive proceedings, *whether temporary surrender* is possible, et cetera. In other words, there is a clear need to spell out the procedure.
>
> It is important at a time when transborder crime is becoming more prevalent to have an extradition process which is effective on a practical level. [Emphasis added.]

Sections 66 and 68 are thus designed to provide a more flexible and effective regime for surrendering persons who are serving Canadian sentences.

Section 67 contrasts with s. 64 of the Act. Section 64 provides that, in the case of a final surrender order, Canadian orders that pertain to the person take precedence unless the Minister of Justice orders otherwise. It would defeat the purpose of the temporary surrender provisions to have the s. 64 rules of priority applied to temporary surrenders. If the Minister of Justice has determined that a temporary surrender is appropriate, then it follows that the determination has been made that the surrender ought not to be delayed by the existence of Canadian orders which apply to the person. Consideration will have been given to the requirement of the presence of the person in the requesting jurisdiction at a particular time and for a particular purpose. The Canadian orders are not at risk because of the availability of assurances that the person sought will be returned within a specified time period.

§5.0 RELATED SECTIONS

s. 3(3) — Extradition of Person Who Has Been Sentenced
s. 29 — Order of Committal
s. 40(1) — 90-Day Period for Surrender Order
s. 40(5) — 60-Day Extension of Initial Period to Consider Person's Submissions to Minister

s. 41(1)(c) — If Committal Order Appealed, Surrender Order Must be Made Within 45 Days of Final Decision on Appeal
s. 64 — Postponement of Surrender for Canadian Offence
s. 65 — Return of Surrendered Person to Canada with Unexpired Sentence
Mutual Legal Assistance in Criminal Matters Act, ss. 24–29

Remedy in Case of Delay (s. 69)

§1.0 DESCRIPTION

Section 69 of the *Extradition Act* provides as follows:

REMEDY IN CASE OF DELAY
   69. A judge of the superior court of the province in which the person is detained who has the power to grant a writ of habeas corpus, may, on application made by or on behalf of the person, and on proof that reasonable notice of the intention to make the application has been given to the Minister, order the person to be discharged out of custody unless sufficient cause is shown against the discharge if

   (a) the Minister has not made an order of surrender under section 40
      (i) before the expiry of the period referred to in subsection 40(1) and any additional period referred to in subsection 40(5), or
      (ii) if a notice of postponement has been filed under paragraph 41(1)(b), before the expiry of 45 days after the date of the decision of the court of appeal referred to in paragraph 41(1)(c); or
   (b) the person is not surrendered and conveyed to the extradition partner
      (i) within 45 days after the order of surrender is made by the Minister under section 40, or
      (ii) if an appeal or judicial review in respect of any matter arising under this Act, or an appeal from such an appeal or judicial review, is pending, within 45 days after the final decision of the court is made,
   over and above, in any case referred to in subparagraph (i)or (ii), the time required to convey the person to the extradition partner.

Section 69 of the Act allows for the discharge of a person sought on the grounds of delay in surrendering the person. Such a remedy is sought by way of an application for a writ of *habeas corpus* to a judge of the superior court of the province in which the person is detained. Section 69 provides that the remedy is available if the person

423

has not been surrendered within one of four periods. The first two periods, set out in s. 69(a), apply when the Minister has delayed in making a surrender order under s. 40:

- where no appeal has been filed against the extradition judge's decision, within the 90-day (or, if an extension has been taken, 90-plus 60-day) period provided for the Minister's decision under s. 40(1) and (5) (s. 69(a)(i));

- where the Minister has postponed his or her decision until after the completion of an appeal of the extradition judge's decision, within forty-five days after the court of appeal has made its decision (s. 69(a)(ii)).

The last two time periods, set out in s. 69(b), apply where a delay has occurred following the making of a surrender order by the Minister:

- where no appeal of the extradition judge's decision or judicial review of the Minister's decision is pending, within 45 days after the Minister orders the surrender of the fugitive (s. 69(b)(i));

- where an appeal or judicial review is pending, within 45 days after the final decision of the court (s. 69(b)(ii)).

However, s. 69 contains the following caveat: "unless sufficient cause is shown against the discharge." Therefore, if the person sought demonstrates that one of the above time periods has been breached, the Minister has the opportunity to establish that a reason existed for the delay. The term "sufficient cause" has been broadly defined in the case law — see the case law section, §4.0 below.

§2.0 COMPARISON WITH FORMER ACT

Section 28 of the former *Extradition Act*, as amended in 1992, was similar in all significant respects to s. 69 of the new Act. Prior to 1992, the delay period in s. 28 was different. The pre-1992 s. 28 required that the person sought be surrendered "within two months after committal for surrender, or, if a writ of *habeas corpus* is issued, within two months after the decision of the court on that writ." Apart from that difference, the pre-1992 s. 28 was the same as current s. 69, including a clause which allowed the Minister to show "sufficient cause" why the fugitive should not be discharged.

§3.0 SIGNIFICANCE OF CHANGE AND ANALYSIS

Section 69 is intended to avoid situations where persons languish in custody while waiting for the Minister of Justice to make or execute a surrender order. The section as it existed under the former Act was rarely used by persons awaiting surrender.

§4.0 CASE LAW

In *Re Shuter (No. 2)*, [1959] 3 All E.R. 481 (Q.B.), the court considered two aspects of the English equivalent to s. 69. Firstly, the court found that a "sufficient cause" is shown if the delay is reasonable having regard to all the circumstances (p. 484). Secondly, the court held that if a sufficient cause is not shown, the judge must release the fugitive, even though the provision uses the word "may" (p. 483).

§5.0 RELATED SECTIONS

s. 40(1) — 90-Day Period for Surrender Order
s. 40(5) — 60-Day Extension of Initial Period to Consider Person's Submissions to Minister
s. 41(1) — Minister's Power to Defer Surrender Order When Appeal Pending

Consent to Committal (s. 70)

§1.0 DESCRIPTION

Section 70 of the *Extradition Act* provides as follows:

CONSENT TO COMMITTAL
    70. (1) A person may, at any time after the issuance of an authority to proceed, consent, in writing and before a judge, to committal.

JUDGE TO ORDER COMMITTAL
    (2) A judge before whom a person consents under subsection (1) shall

    (a) order the committal of the person into custody to await surrender to the extradition partner; and
    (b) transmit a copy of the consent to the Minister.

Section 70(1) provides that a person sought may consent to committal in writing before a judge any time after the issuance of the authority to proceed. This has the effect of dispensing with the extradition hearing. Section 70(2) requires the judge before whom the person consents to order the committal of the person into custody pending surrender and to send a copy of the consent to the Minister.

§2.0 COMPARISON WITH FORMER ACT

Consenting to committal was not provided for in the former *Extradition Act*. However, in practice it occurred. The consent to committal procedure took place before an extradition judge. Some of the formalities stipulated under the former Act for extradition hearings were still followed. This was because the fugitive was not waiving formal extradition, but merely consenting to committal for surrender. For this reason, the fugitive was still formally subject to the extradition process and certain statutory requirements under the former Act applicable to extradition hearings were adhered to when a fugitive consents to committal. For instance, the extradition judge was required to do the following: inform the fugitive at the commencement of the proceedings of the fugitive's right to make submissions to the Minister (s. 19.1(2)); inform the fugitive that surrender would not occur until after 30 days and that there was a right to appeal the committal order (s. 19(a)); and submit a report to the Minister (s. 19(b)). Usually, the written consent of the fugitive was filed with the court and ultimately sent to the Minister through the Department of Justice's International Assistance Group (IAG) in Ottawa with the warrant of committal and report required under s. 19.

§3.0 SIGNIFICANCE OF CHANGE

The inclusion of the consent to committal provision in the new *Extradition Act* clarifies the right and streamlines the procedure for enabling a person to dispense with the extradition hearing, while still retaining the rights afforded to an individual who has had a hearing. One such right is the right of specialty. This right provides that the person can only be prosecuted in the requesting state for the offence(s) for which the person was extradited. (This is discussed in the analysis section §4.0 below.)

§4.0 ANALYSIS

When a person sought does not wish to contest committal for surrender at the extradition hearing, but there are outstanding charges against him or her in the requesting state for which extradition has not been sought, the person may wish to consent to committal for surrender. Like waiver, discussed in the commentary to s. 72, consenting to committal has the advantage of enabling an expeditious return to the requesting state, since it dispenses with the time required for a contested extradition hearing. However, in contrast with waiver, consent to committal preserves the person's right of specialty. This right provides that a person can only be prosecuted in the requesting state for the offence(s) for which the person was extradited. When a person sought waives the extradition process, he or she does not benefit from the right of specialty (the right of specialty, particularly in the context of waiver, is discussed in the commentary to s. 72). In consenting to committal, a person sought is formally subject to the extradition process and the Minister is still required to make a surrender order under s. 40 of the Act. Section 40(3) permits the Minister to include a condition in the surrender order specifically dealing with the right of specialty: "that the person not be prosecuted, nor that a sentence be imposed on or enforced against the person, in respect of any offence or conduct other than that referred to in the order of surrender." By contrast, a person who waives extradition under s. 72 waives the formal extradition process. A surrender order is not required when extradition is waived. Thus a person who consents to committal is considered to have been "extradited" in the formal sense of the term, thereby benefiting from the right to specialty. In the context of extradition to American states, this is confirmed by Article 12(1) of the *Canada–United States Extradition Treaty*:

> A person extradited under the present treaty shall not be detained, tried, or punished in the territory of the requesting State for an offense other than that for which extradition has been granted.

The use of the term "extradited" implicitly recognizes that a person returning to the requesting state under a consent to committal benefits from the right of specialty.

In contrast with waiver of extradition under s. 72 of the Act, the person sought under s. 70 merely waives the extradition hearing rather than the entire extradition process. When the person sought consents to committal, it is implied that he or she is admitting that the extradition partner can comply with s. 29 of the Act. A person might want to avail himself or herself of this option in the following situations: in the case of an accused person, he or she is satisfied that the requesting state will be able to establish a *prima facie* case at the extradition hearing or, in the case of a convicted person, he or she is satisfied that the extradition partner can prove the conviction. The person's consent eliminates the requirement to prove what is normally required to be proved at the hearing. Therefore, it is unnecessary for the evidence to be tendered at the time the person sought consents to committal. The only documentation required for this proceeding is the written consent.

In consenting to committal, the person sought preserves his or her right to make submissions to the Minister during the ministerial phase of the extradition process, unless surrender is specifically consented to under s. 71. The person sought may wish to raise issues before the Minster that weigh against surrender. This could include the *Cotroni* issue (s. 47(d)), a death penalty situation (s. 44(2)), or other humanitarian concerns (s. 44(1)). These matters are within the jurisdiction of the Minister to consider during the ministerial phase of the extradition process, rather than being within the jurisdiction of the extradition judge to consider at the judicial phase of the process.

Section 70 provides a simplified process for consenting to committal, requiring only that the person sought consent in writing before a judge. The consent document simply needs to indicate that the person sought is accused or convicted within the jurisdiction of the extradition partner and that the person consents to the issuance of an order for committal for the offences specified in the authority to proceed. The latter document could be attached to the consent. The consent may require that the signature of the person sought be witnessed. It would be advisable for the person's signature to be witnessed by his or her counsel. This would indicate that the person obtained legal advice in this regard.

In *United States v. Wilson* (2001), 56 O.R. (3d) 157, 2001 CarswellOnt 3383 (Ont. S.C.J.), the person sought brought a motion to set aside a committal order that had previously been made with his consent. Juriansz J. held that he had no jurisdiction to set aside an order made on consent under s. 70. Juriansz J. stated at p. 160:

> [10] . . . The Act provides that after making a committal order on consent, the judge must transmit a copy of the person's consent (s. 70(2)) and a copy of the order (s. 38(1)) to the Minister; thereafter the issue of the person's surrender is within the powers granted to the Minister by ss. 40 to 48 of the Act. The Act provides no mechanism by which the court can revoke the powers the Minister has acquire[d] upon the making of a committal order. Setting aside an order made as a single stage of a larger statutory process is, in my view, different to setting aside an order that itself is enforced under the supervision of the court's own process.
>
> [11] I conclude that this court does not have jurisdiction to set aside an order made on consent under s. 70 of the *Extradition Act*, even though such an order is not made on the merits.
>
> [12] I observe that this does not leave the applicant without a remedy for any injustice he alleges. In the hypothetical situation where a subject consents to a committal order on the assurance of the requesting state or the Attorney General that committal on other outstanding matter[s] will not be sought, and subsequently a second authority to proceed is issued, the subject can seek a stay of the subsequent proceeding before the court for another order of committal. Alternatively, the subject could seek to appeal the initial and any subsequent committal order under s. 53(*a*)(iii) of the Act, which provides that the court of appeal may allow an appeal [if] "on any ground, there was a miscarriage of justice".

§5.0 CASE LAW

United States v. Wilson (2001), 56 O.R. (3d) 157, 2001 CarswellOnt 3383 (Ont. S.C.J.).

§6.0 RELATED SECTIONS

s. 29 — Order of Committal
s. 40(1) — 90-Day Period for Surrender Order
s. 40(3)— Order of Surrender with Specialty Conditions
s. 71 — Consent to Surrender
s. 72 — Waiver of Extradition
Canada–United States Extradition Treaty, Article 12 — Specialty

Consent to Surrender (s. 71)

§1.0 DESCRIPTION

Section 71 of the *Extradition Act* provides as follows:

CONSENT TO SURRENDER
 71. (1) A person may, at any time after arrest or appearance, consent, in writing and before a judge, to being surrendered.

JUDGE TO ORDER SURRENDER
 (2) A judge before whom a person consents to being surrendered shall

 (a) order the committal of the person into custody to await surrender to the extradition partner; and
 (b) transmit a copy of the consent to the Minister.

WHEN MINISTER RECEIVES CONSENT
 (3) The Minister may, as soon as is feasible after receiving a consent to surrender, personally order that the person be surrendered to the extradition partner.

SECTIONS NOT APPLICABLE
 (4) When a person consents to being surrendered to the extradition partner, the following sections do not apply:

 (a) section 43 (submissions to the Minister);
 (b) section 44 (reasons for refusal);
 (c) section 48 (discharge of person);
 (d) section 57 (judicial review of Minister's decision); and
 (e) paragraph 62 (1)(a) (delay before surrender).

Section 71 provides that a person sought may consent to surrender in writing before a judge any time after arrest or appearance. The judge is mandated to order committal of the person into custody to await surrender and to send a copy of the consent to the Minister.

Section 71(4) provides that, in consenting to surrender, the person dispenses with his or her rights under ss. 43, 44, 48, 57, and 62(1)(a) of the Act. These provisions include the right to make submissions to the Minister regarding surrender, the right to judicial review of the Minister's surrender decision, and the 30-day period following the committal order during which the person may not be surrendered.

§2.0 COMPARISON WITH FORMER ACT

As in the case of consent to committal (s. 70), the consent to surrender procedure was not referred to in the former *Extradition Act*. However, it occurred informally that sometimes a written consent to surrender was executed in court at the time the fugitive consented to committal and then was filed with the consent to committal in court for transmission to the Minister.

§3.0 SIGNIFICANCE OF CHANGE

As with consent to committal under s. 70, the consent to surrender provision clarifies the existence of the right and provides for an expedited surrender procedure.

§4.0 ANALYSIS

After a person has been committed for surrender, either on consent under s. 70 or following an extradition hearing, the person is taken into custody until the Minister of Justice signs the surrender order pursuant to s. 40 of the Act and the foreign authorities arrive for the purpose of returning the person to the extradition partner. Section 20(b) provides that the person sought can apply for bail after being committed for surrender pending the Minister's surrender decision under s. 40. Section 62(1)(a) of the Act indicates that the person cannot be surrendered until 30 days after committal. This is the amount of time provided for making submissions to the Minister (s. 43) or launching an appeal of the committal order (s. 49). If the person sought does not intend to make submissions or launch an appeal of the committal order (an appeal would be unlikely when the person sought consented to the committal order), the person sought may waive his or her right to these proceedings and consent to surrender.

Waiving these rights may reduce the time the person spends in Canada, and perhaps in custody in Canada if bail was not granted, before being returned to the extradition partner. However, it could still take some time in Canada before the Minister signs the order of surrender, depending on the Minister's other commitments. As well, even in consent to committal situations where the person does not make submissions to the Minister, the Minister may still decide to review the matter, which will require further time. Moreover, after the order of surrender has been signed, a short period of time could still elapse before the foreign authorities arrive to return the person sought to the extradition partner. Nonetheless, a person who consents to surrender and thereby waives his or her submission and judicial review rights will be returned to the extradition partner in less time than a person who does not consent to surrender.

A person who has been committed for surrender, either on consent under s. 70 or following an extradition hearing, benefits from the right of specialty (this point is discussed in the commentary to s. 70, §4.0, "Analysis"). This right provides that the extradition partner may only try the person for the extradited offences. As long as the person has been committed for surrender, the person sought will still be afforded specialty protection if surrender is consented to afterwards. A person who consents to committal under s. 70 and surrender under s. 71 does not waive the formal extradition process. Therefore, the person benefits from all the protections associated with the extradition process.

The consent to surrender document need simply reflect that the person sought consents to his or her surrender by the Minister of Justice to the extradition partner for the offences set out in the authority to proceed.

§5.0 RELATED SECTIONS

s. 43 — Submissions to Minister
s. 44 — Reasons for Refusal of Surrender
s. 48 — Discharge of Person Sought by Minister of Justice
s. 57 — Judicial Review of Minister of Justice's Surrender Order
s. 58 — Contents of Surrender Order
s. 62(1)(a) — Delay Before Surrender
s. 70 — Consent to Committal
s. 72 — Waiver of Extradition

Waiver of Extradition (s. 72)

§1.0 DESCRIPTION

Section 72 of the *Extradition Act* provides as follows:

WAIVING EXTRADITION
72. (1) A person may, at any time after arrest or appearance, waive extradition in writing and before a judge.

JUDGE TO INFORM PERSON
(2) A judge before whom a person gives a waiver under subsection (1) must inform the person

(a) of the consequences of the waiver including the consequences of waiving the protection of specialty; and
(b) that they will be conveyed without delay to the extradition partner.

JUDGE TO ORDER CONVEYANCE
(3) The judge shall

(a) order the conveyance in custody of the person to the extradition partner; and

(b) transmit a copy of the waiver and the order to the Minister.

CONVEYANCE ORDER
   (4) The conveyance order must

(a) contain the name of the person who is to be conveyed; and
(b) state the extradition partner to which the person is to be conveyed.

Section 72 enables a person sought to waive the extradition process by signing a written waiver before the extradition judge. This may be done at any time after arrest or appearance. The judge is required to advise the person of the consequences of waiving, including waiving the protection of specialty. Specialty means that a person can only be prosecuted in the requesting state for the offence(s) for which the person was extradited. The judge must also advise the person that he or she will be conveyed without delay to the extradition partner. The judge's conveyance order and the written waiver are to be sent to the Minister.

§2.0 COMPARISON WITH FORMER ACT

Waiver was not provided for in the former *Extradition Act*. Once the judicial phase of the extradition process had been commenced by the issuance of the warrant of apprehension for the fugitive's arrest under s. 10 of the former Act if the fugitive subsequently wished to waive further extradition proceedings, the court's order to deliver the fugitive to the foreign authorities was based on the inherent jurisdiction of the extradition judge.The procedure that had developed in Ontario for waiving extradition was that the fugitive signed a "Waiver and Consent" form before the extradition judge. The fugitive's signature was usually witnessed by the fugitive's lawyer. The document usually indicated that the fugitive freely and voluntarily waived his or her rights under the *Extradition Act* and consented to being returned to the requesting state without formal extradition proceedings. The Waiver and Consent was then filed with the extradition judge, who signed and dated the document.

After the Waiver and Consent had been completed, the extradition judge signed an Order to Convey. The order usually indicated that the fugitive had waived his or her rights under the *Extradition Act*, including the rights to an extradition hearing and to be further dealt with in accordance with the laws of Canada. The order also indicated the fugitive's willingness to be surrendered to the requesting state to be dealt with according to law. The Order to Convey ordered Canadian authorities to deliver the fugitive to a detention centre and, subsequently, to the custody of foreign authorities at a port of entry. The waiver procedure did not require the Minister to make a surrender order under s. 25 of the former Act.

§3.0 SIGNIFICANCE OF CHANGE

Section 72 of the new *Extradition Act* codifies a procedure that was already in place. Section 72(2)(a) ensures that the judge will advise the person sought of the significance of waiving extradition, particularly that the specialty protection will be relinquished. Section 72(2)(b) requires that the judge advise the person that he or she will be conveyed to the extradition partner "without delay." The latter provision indicates that the waiver procedure and the surrender of the person sought should be conducted with dispatch.

§4.0 ANALYSIS

§4.1 When Would a Person Choose to Waive Extradition

The person sought may wish to consider waiving extradition in any of the following situations:

- When the right of specialty is not a consideration. In waiving extradition, the person waives his or her right of specialty, which is the right not to be prosecuted or sentenced for offences or conduct other than those which are the basis of the extradition request. Therefore, if there are no other charges, or no potential for other charges to be laid pertaining to prior conduct in the requesting state, the right of specialty would not be a concern to the person sought.

- The person wishes to return to the requesting state quickly.

- The person has no basis upon which to contest the extradition request.

§4.2 Waiver in Canada's Extradition Treaties

Some of Canada's extradition treaties provide for waiver (see the following treaties: India, Article 16; Korea, Article 11; Mexico, Article XI; Philippines, Article 10; and Spain, Article XI). These provisions provide that extradition may be granted on the basis that a person has consented to an order for extradition being made. In such cases, there will be no need to consider whether other treaty requirements have been met.

§4.3 Legal Consequences of Waiver

By waiving extradition, a person agrees to his or her return to the extradition partner. The person thereby waives his or her legal rights to all further proceedings in the judicial and executive phases of the extradition process. Accordingly, by waiving extradition, the person sought waives any protections which he or she is afforded under the *Extradition Act* or applicable treaty as well as under the Canadian *Charter*.

The most significant protection relinquished by the person when waiving extradition is the right of "specialty." This term refers to the person's right to be tried by the extradition partner only for those charges for which the person's extradition has been requested. For instance, if the extradition of a person is requested by the State of Pennsylvania for charges of murder, robbery, and assault, and the person is committed for surrender at an extradition hearing on these charges, the person can only be surrendered by the Canadian Minister of Justice and tried in Pennsylvania on these charges. Pennsylvania is precluded from trying the person for any offence or conduct committed prior to his or her return in that state, such as failure to appear. Moreover, any other jurisdiction, for example, Texas, is precluded from trying the person on other outstanding charges since the person was not extradited on those charges. Such charges would have to have been the subject of a separate extradition request and proceedings.

The right of specialty is provided for in most extradition treaties. For example, Article 12(1) of the *Canada–United States Extradition Treaty* reads as follows:

> **12.** (1) A person extradited under the present Treaty shall not be detained, tried or punished in the territory of the requesting State for an offense other than that for which extradition has been granted nor be extradited by that State to a third State unless:
>
> (i) He has left the territory of the requesting State after his extradition and has voluntarily returned to it;
> (ii) He has not left the territory of the requesting State within thirty days after being free to do so; or
> (iii) The requested State has consented to his detention, trial, punishment for an offense other than that for which extradition was granted or to his extradition to a third State, provided such other offense is covered by Article 2.

This right would likely exist even in the absence of an express treaty provision. This point was made by La Forest J. in *R. v. Parisien* (1988), 41 C.C.C. (3d) 223 (S.C.C.), at pp. 227–228:

> As an adjunct to the practice of restricting extradition to listed crimes, most treaties also provide that the requesting state shall not try or punish the fugitive for any crime committed before the extradition other than that for which the surrender took place. This, I suggest, would be the result in any event. When a state surrenders a fugitive in respect of a particular crime, that surrender must necessarily be subject to an implied condition that the requesting state will not try the fugitive for any other crime previously committed without the permission of the surrendering state. [Citations omitted.]

(See also the decision of the United States Supreme Court in *United States v. Rauscher* (1886), 119 U.S. 407 (U.S. N.Y.) at pp. 418–422, and the judgment of La Forest J.

on behalf of a majority of the Supreme Court of Canada in *United States v. McVey* (1992), 77 C.C.C. (3d) 1 (S.C.C.), at p. 21.)

A person who waives extradition does not benefit from the right of specialty. Rather, a person who waives extradition may be tried in the requesting state for any offence (see *R. v. Flannery* (1923), 40 C.C.C. 263 (Alta. C.A.), at p. 268 and *R. v. Liberty* (1929), 102 C.C.C. 370 (Alta. C.A.), at p. 372). A number of extradition treaties expressly provide that a person sought who waives extradition does not benefit from the right of specialty. For example, Article XI of the *Canada–Mexico Extradition Treaty* provides as follows:

> The Requested Party may surrender the person sought to the Requesting Party without formal extradition proceedings, provided the person sought consents to such surrender before a judicial authority after having been informed that the rule of specialty set out in Article XV and the prohibition of re-extradition as set out in Article XVI do not apply to such surrender.

§4.4 Advantage of Waiver: Expeditious Procedure

The advantage of waiver is that it affords the most expeditious procedure for the return of the person sought to the extradition partner. Time is saved since both phases of the usual extradition process are eliminated; there is no need for an extradition hearing to be held, and there is no ministerial involvement in surrender since the court, not the Minister, orders the person to be conveyed to the extradition partner.

The waiver procedure can be contrasted with the procedures set out in ss. 70 and 71 of the *Extradition Act*, which provide for the person to be able to consent to committal and to surrender, and which require a surrender order to be signed by the Minister before conveyance to the extradition partner can take place. While recourse to the provisions of ss. 70 and 71 will provide the person with the protection of the rule of specialty, the Minister's involvement occasioned by these sections will necessarily require more time than if extradition were waived entirely. Also there can be an additional delay between the time the Minister signs the order of surrender and the time the foreign authorities arrive in Canada to escort the person back to the extradition partner. The time lags involved with ss. 70 and 71 are reduced if the person waives extradition. Indeed, s. 72(2)(b) directs the judge before whom the person sought provides the written waiver to inform the person that he or she will be conveyed "without delay" to the extradition partner.

Under the informal waiver procedures of the former regime, persons on bail who wished to waive further proceedings without spending time in custody in Canada awaiting the arrival of the foreign conveying officers sometimes sought to make advance arrangements with counsel for the requesting state so that the conveying officers would be present in Canada to take custody of the person on the same day he or she went into custody, pursuant to the court's order to convey. This may continue to be proposed in the context of the waiver provisions of the new Act. However, foreign authorities may be reluctant to commit in advance to attend in Canada on a specified day since advance commitments entail flight and travel arrangements which would result in a wasted expense if the person subsequently changed his or her mind about waiving the extradition.

The *bona fides* of the intention to waive would be strengthened if the waiver and consent were signed and filed with the court prior to the date arranged for the arrival of the foreign authorities. The court could then be requested to delay making effective the formal order to convey until the date scheduled for the arrival of the foreign authorities. This would enable the person sought to remain at liberty from the time the waiver and consent is filed, until the order to convey is effected on a subsequent court date.

The Waiver and Consent form need only indicate that the person sought voluntarily waives his or her rights under the Act and consents to being returned to the extradition partner. The rights waived include the right to an extradition hearing, the right to make submissions to the Minister, the right to appeal the committal order and seek judicial review of the surrender order, and the right of specialty. The document should be witnessed by counsel for the person sought and signed by the judge.

§5.0 CASE LAW

R. v. Flannery (1923), 40 C.C.C. 263 (Alta. C.A.).
R. v. Liberty (1929), 102 C.C.C. 370 (Alta. C.A.).
R. v. Parisien (1988), 41 C.C.C. (3d) 223 (S.C.C.).
United States v. McVey (1992), 77 C.C.C. (3d) 1 (S.C.C.).
United States v. Rauscher (1886), 119 U.S. 407 (U.S.N.Y.).

§6.0 RELATED SECTIONS

70 — Consent to Committal
71 — Consent to Surrender
Canada–United States Extradition Treaty, Article 12
Extradition Treaty between the Government of Canada and the Government of India, Article 16
Treaty of Extradition Between the Government of Canada and the Government of the United Mexican States, Article XI
Treaty on Extradition Between Canada and Spain, Article XI
Treaty on Extradition Between Canada and the Republic of Korea, Article 11
Treaty on Extradition Between Canada and the Republic of the Philippines, Article 10

Escape While in Custody for Conveyance and Arrest (s. 73)

§1.0 DESCRIPTION

Section 73 of the *Extradition Act* provides as follows:

ESCAPE

73. (1) If the person escapes while in custody for conveyance, the law that applies with respect to a person who is accused or convicted of a crime against the laws of Canada and who escapes applies with respect to the person.

ARREST

(2) If the person escapes while in custody for conveyance, the person in whose custody the person is has the power to arrest them in fresh pursuit.

Within the context of a waiver of extradition (waiver is dealt with in s. 72 of the Act), s. 73 deals with the escape of a person sought while in custody for conveyance and the rearrest of that person. Section 73(1) provides that a person who escapes while in custody for conveyance is subject to the same laws as if the person were accused or convicted of a crime in Canada. Subs. 73(2) adds that the person having custody of the person sought has the power to arrest the person sought in fresh pursuit.

Section 61 of the Act sets out the same points in the context of a person being formally surrendered as opposed to a person who has waived the extradition process.

§2.0 COMPARISON WITH FORMER ACT

The former *Extradition Act* did not deal with waiver.

§3.0 ANALYSIS

Section 73 of the *Extradition Act* applies the same rules to a person conveyed after waiver of extradition as pertain to the escape and reapprehension under s. 61 of a person who is being formally surrendered (for a more detailed discussion of the background and nature of this provision, see the commentary to s. 61).

§4.0 RELATED SECTIONS

s. 61 — Escape of Person Sought While in Custody and Arrest (formal surrender)
s. 72 — Waiver of Extradition

Transit (ss. 74–76)

§1.0 DESCRIPTION

§1.1 Applicability of Transit Provisions (s. 74(1))

Section 74(1) of the *Extradition Act* provides as follows:

> **TRANSIT**
> **74. (1) The Minister may consent to the transit in Canada of a person surrendered by one State or entity to another, subject to any terms and conditions that the Minister considers appropriate.**

Section 74(1) provides the Minister of Justice with the authority to consent to the transit in Canada of a person surrendered by one state or entity to another state or entity. This subsection also allows the Minister to attach to the consent any conditions that the Minister considers appropriate.

§1.2 General Character and Parameters of Consent to Transit (s. 74(2)-(3))

Section 74(2) and (3) of the *Extradition Act* provide as follows:

> **CONSENT TO TRANSIT**
> **(2) A consent to transit constitutes authority to the officer of the surrendering State or entity or the receiving State or entity to keep the person in custody while in Canada.**

> **SECTIONS TO APPLY**
> **(3) Sections 58 (contents of surrender order), 60 (power to convey), 61 (escape) and 69 (remedy in case of delay) apply, with any modifications that the circumstances require, in respect of the consent to transit.**

Section 74(2) describes the general character of a consent to transit, namely, that it constitutes an authority to an officer of the surrendering state or entity or the receiving state or entity to keep the person in custody while in Canada.

Section 74(3) adds specific parameters to the consent to transit, providing that ss. 58, 60, 61, and 69 apply to the consent with any modifications that the circumstances require. Section 58 sets out the required contents of a surrender order. Section 60 provides the person or class of persons named under s. 58(e) with the authority to receive, hold in custody, and convey the person sought to the extradition partner. Section 61 deals with the escape of a person sought while in custody and the rearrest of that person. Section 61(1) provides that a person sought who escapes while in custody is subject to the same laws as if the person were accused or convicted of a crime in Canada. Section 61(2) adds that the person or class of persons having custody of the person have the power to arrest the person in fresh pursuit. Section 69 of the Act allows for the discharge of a person sought on the grounds of delay in surrendering the person.

§1.3 Authorizations for Persons Inadmissible Under S. 19 of the *Immigration Act* (s. 75)

Section 75 of the *Extradition Act* provides as follows:

SPECIAL AUTHORIZATION

75. (1) The Minister may, in order to give effect to a request for consent to transit, authorize a person in a State or entity who is a member of an inadmissible class of persons described in section 19 of the *Immigration Act* to come into Canada at a place designated by the Minister and to go to and remain in a place in Canada so designated for the period specified by the Minister. The Minister may make the authorization subject to any conditions that the Minister considers desirable.

VARIATION OF AUTHORIZATION

(2) The Minister may vary the terms of an authorization granted under subsection (1) and, in particular, may extend the period of time during which the person is authorized to remain in a place in Canada.

NON-COMPLIANCE WITH CONDITIONS OF AUTHORIZATION

(3) A person in respect of whom an authorization is granted under subsection (1) and who is found in a place in Canada other than the place designated in the authorization or in any place in Canada after the expiry of the period of time specified in the authorization or who fails to comply with some other condition of the authorization is, for the purposes of the Immigration Act, deemed to be a person who entered Canada as a visitor and remains in Canada after they have ceased to be a visitor.

For the purposes of giving effect to a consent to transit, s. 75(1) provides the Minister of Justice with the authority to authorize the entry into Canada of a person who is a member of an inadmissible class of persons under s. 19 of the *Immigration Act*. The subsection allows the Minister to designate a place and period of time for the person's transit in Canada. The subsection also enables the Minister to attach any conditions that the Minister deems desirable.

Section 75(2) allows the Minister of Justice to vary the authorization and, in particular, extend the period of time during which the person is authorized to remain in Canada.

Under s. 75(3), a person who fails to comply with any condition of the authorization is deemed for the purposes of the *Immigration Act* to be a person who entered Canada as a visitor and who remains in Canada after they have ceased to be a visitor.

§1.4 Unscheduled Landings (s. 76)

Section 76 of the *Extradition Act* provides as follows:

UNSCHEDULED LANDING
76. If a person being extradited or surrendered from one State or entity to another arrives in Canada without prior consent to transit, a peace officer may, at the request of a public officer who has custody of the person while the person is being conveyed,

> **(a) if the person is being surrendered to the International Criminal Court, hold the person in custody for a maximum period of 96 hours pending receipt by the Minister of a request for a consent to transit from that Court; or**
> **(b) in any other case, hold the person in custody for a maximum period of 24 hours pending receipt by the Minister of a request for a consent to transit from the requesting State or entity.**

Section 76 (amended in October 2000 to make provision for the International Criminal Court) addresses the unscheduled transit through Canada of persons being extradited between other jurisdictions. The requesting jurisdiction in such cases will have 24 hours in which to regularize the situation by transmitting to the Minister a request for permission that the person sought be allowed to pass through Canada. However, where the International Criminal Court is the requesting entity, the person may be held for up to 96 hours pending receipt by the Minister of a request for a consent to transit from the Court.

§2.0 COMPARISON WITH FORMER ACT

The former *Extradition Act* did not contain any equivalent to ss. 74 to 76 of the new Act.

§3.0 SIGNIFICANCE OF CHANGE

Sections 74 to 76 of the *Extradition Act* give domestic authority and procedural structure to obligations that have been undertaken in some of Canada's more recent extradition treaties. For example, Article 16 of the *Canada–United States Extradition Treaty* provides as follows:

> **16.** (1) The right to transport through the territory of one of the Contracting Parties a person surrendered to the other Contracting Party by a third State shall be granted on request made through the diplomatic channel, provided that conditions are present which would warrant extradition of such person by the State of transit and reasons of public order are not opposed to the transit.
>
> (2) The Party to which the person has been extradited shall reimburse the Party through whose territory such person is transported for any expenses incurred by the latter in connection with such transportation.

§4.0 ANALYSIS

The essential aspects of the new provisions are as follows:

1. The Minister of Justice is given the authority to consent to such a transit, subject to any terms and conditions that the Minister deems appropriate. (s. 74(1)).

2. The foreign escorting officials are provided with domestic authority to be legally in possession of the person while in Canada (s. 74(2)).

3. The Minister of Justice is given the authority to override the provisions of the *Immigration Act* in situations where the person sought would otherwise be ineligible for entry into Canada, subject to any conditions that the Minister considers desirable (s. 75(1)).

4. The provisions limit the effect of an authorization under s. 75(1) by subjecting the person sought to normal *Immigration Act* provisions if the person is found anywhere in Canada other than the place designated by the Minister of Justice in the authorization (s. 75(3)).

5. In circumstances in which a person's presence in Canada occurs unexpectedly, the provisions give domestic police the authority to take custody of the person in transit for a maximum period of 96 hours if the person is being surrendered to the International Criminal Court, or 24 hours in all other cases, pending receipt by the Minister of a request for transit from the requesting state or authority (s. 76).

Sections 74 to 76 allow Canada to coordinate more effectively with other states and entities regarding the movement of persons who are subject to extradition.

§5.0 RELATED SECTIONS

s. 58 — Contents of Surrender Order
s. 60 — Power to Convey Person Sought
s. 61 — Escape of Person Sought While in Custody and Arrest
s. 69 — Remedy in Case of Delay

Extradition to Canada (ss. 77–83)

§1.0 DESCRIPTION

§1.1 Definition of "competent authority" (s. 77)

Section 77 of the *Extradition Act* provides as follows:

DEFINITION OF "COMPETENT AUTHORITY"
   77. In this Part, "competent authority" means

   (a) in respect of a prosecution or imposition of a sentence – or of a disposition under the *Young Offenders Act* – the Attorney General, or the Attorney General of a province who is responsible for the prosecution of the case; and
   (b) in respect of the enforcement of a sentence or a disposition under the *Young Offenders Act*,
      (i) the Solicitor General of Canada, if the person would serve the sentence in a penitentiary, or
      (ii) the appropriate provincial minister responsible for corrections, in any other case.

Section 77 specifies the entities that have the authority to request that the Minister of Justice seek the extradition of an individual to Canada. More specifically, s. 77 provides that:

- For a prosecution or an imposition of sentence, including the imposition of a disposition under the *Young Offenders Act*, the competent authority is the Attorney General of Canada or the Attorney General of the province responsible for the prosecution of the offence.

- For the enforcement of a sentence, or the enforcement of a disposition under the *Young Offenders Act*, the competent authority is the Solicitor General of Canada, if the person would serve the sentence in a penitentiary, or the applicable provincial minister responsible for corrections, in any other case.

§1.2 Initiation and Scope of Extradition to Canada (s. 78)

Section 78 of the *Extradition Act* provides as follows:

REQUEST BY CANADA FOR EXTRADITION
78. (1) The Minister, at the request of a competent authority, may make a request to a State or entity for the extradition of a person for the purpose of prosecuting the person for – or imposing or enforcing a sentence, or making or enforcing a disposition under the *Young Offenders Act*, in respect of – an offence over which Canada has jurisdiction.

REQUEST FOR PROVISIONAL ARREST
(2) The Minister, at the request of a competent authority, may make a request to a State or entity for the provisional arrest of the person.

Under s. 78, requests for an extradition to Canada or for the provisional arrest of a person are made by the Minister of Justice acting upon a request from a "competent authority" (this term is defined in s. 77). Requests for extradition to Canada may be made to any "State or entity." This term is defined in s. 2 to include: a state other than Canada (including any subdivision of that state or territory falling under the jurisdiction of that state); an international tribunal; or a territory. Section 78 does not limit requests to jurisdictions with which Canada has entered an extradition agreement (in contrast to s. 30 of the former *Extradition Act*, discussed in the following section).

Section 78 provides that the extradition request may be for the following purposes: to prosecute a person for an offence over which Canada has jurisdiction; to impose or enforce a sentence for an offence over which Canada has jurisdiction; or to impose or enforce a disposition under the *Young Offenders Act* for an offence over which Canada has jurisdiction.

§1.3 Evidence Orders in Connection With Extradition Requests (s. 79)

Section 79 of the *Extradition Act* provides as follows:

ORDER IN RESPECT OF EVIDENCE
79. (1) A judge may, for the purposes of acquiring evidence for a request for extradition, on the ex parte application of a competent authority, make any order that is necessary to

(a) secure the attendance of a witness at any place designated by the judge;
(b) secure the production as evidence of data that is recorded in any form;

(c) **receive and record the evidence; and**

(d) **certify or authenticate the evidence in a manner and form that is required by the requested State or entity.**

PART XXII OF THE *CRIMINAL CODE* TO APPLY
(2) Part XXII of the *Criminal Code* applies, with any modifications that the circumstances require, to orders under subsection (1).

Section 79(1) provides that a "judge" (defined in s. 2 of the Act as a judge of the superior court of the province) may, for the purpose of acquiring evidence in connection with a request for extradition, make "any order" that is necessary to do the following: secure the attendance of a witness at any place designated by the judge; secure the production as evidence of data that is recorded in any form; receive and record the evidence; and certify or authenticate the evidence in a manner and form that is required by the requested state or entity. The trigger mechanism for a s. 79 order is an *ex parte* application by a "competent authority" (defined in s. 77).

Section 79(2) adds that Part XXII of the *Criminal Code* applies, with any modifications that the circumstances require, to orders made under s. 79. Part XXII of the Code deals with procuring the attendance of witnesses.

§1.4 Right of Specialty (s. 80)

Section 80 of the *Extradition Act* provides as follows:

80. Subject to a relevant extradition agreement, a person who has been extradited to Canada by a requested State or entity shall not, unless the person has voluntarily left Canada after surrender or has had a reasonable opportunity of leaving Canada,

(a) **be detained or prosecuted, or have a sentence imposed or executed, or a disposition made or executed under the *Young Offenders Act*, in Canada in respect of an offence that is alleged to have been committed, or was committed, before surrender other than**

　　(i) **the offence in respect of which the person was surrendered or an included offence,**

　　(ii) **another offence in respect of which the requested State or entity consents to the person being detained or prosecuted, or**

　　(iii) **another offence in respect of which the person consents to being detained or prosecuted; or**

(b) **be detained in Canada for the purpose of being surrendered to another State or entity for prosecution or for imposition or execution of a sentence in respect of an offence that is alleged to have been committed, or was committed, before surrender to Canada, unless the requested State or entity consents.**

Section 80 provides that the right of specialty applies to persons who are extradited to Canada. More specifically, s. 80(a) and (b) provide that the extradited person shall not be subject to the following in Canada:

- Detention or prosecution, imposition or execution of a sentence, or imposition or execution of a disposition under the *Young Offenders Act* for an offence committed, or alleged to have been committed, before the person's surrender other than the following: the offence in respect of which the person was surrendered or an included offence; another offence in respect of which the requested jurisdiction consents to the person being detained or prosecuted; or another offence in respect of which the person consents to being detained or prosecuted (s. 80(a)).

- Detention for the purpose of being surrendered to another jurisdiction for prosecution or for imposition or execution of a sentence in respect of an offence that is alleged to have been committed, or was committed, before surrender to Canada, unless the requested jurisdiction consents (s. 80(b)).

The opening sentence of s. 80 adds two qualifications to the section: firstly, s. 80 is subject to the terms of the relevant extradition agreement; secondly, s. 80 does not apply to a person who has voluntarily left, or has had a reasonable opportunity to leave, Canada after being surrendered.

§1.5 Conveyance of Surrendered Person (s. 81)

Section 81 of the *Extradition Act* provides as follows:

CONVEYANCE OF SURRENDERED PERSON
81. (1) A person who is surrendered to Canada by a requested State or entity may be brought into Canada by an agent of the requested State or entity if the Minister so authorizes and be delivered to an appropriate authority to be dealt with according to law.

POWER TO CONVEY
(2) On the execution of a surrender order, the authorized agent of the requested State or entity shall have the authority to hold the person in custody in Canada until delivery under subsection (1).

ESCAPE
(3) If the person escapes while in custody, the law that applies with respect to a person who is accused or convicted of a crime against the laws of Canada and who escapes applies with respect to the person.

ARREST
(4) If the person escapes, the authorized agent of the requested State or entity has the power to arrest them in fresh pursuit.

Section 81(1) provides that a person who is surrendered to Canada by a requested jurisdiction may be brought into Canada by an agent of that jurisdiction if the Minister of Justice makes such an authorization and may be delivered to an appropriate authority to be dealt with according to law. Section 81(2) adds that in executing the surrender order the authorized agent of the requested jurisdiction has the authority to hold the surrendered person in custody in Canada until delivery has been made under s. 81(1). Paralleling ss. 61 and 73 of the Act (escape of a person sought while being conveyed to another jurisdiction), s. 81(3) and (4) deal with the escape and rearrest of the surrendered person. Section 81(3) states that a person who escapes while in custody is subject to the same law that applies with respect to a person who is accused or convicted of a crime against the laws of Canada and who escapes. Section 81(4) adds that the authorized agent of the requested jurisdiction has the power to arrest the escaped person "in fresh pursuit."

§1.6 Temporary Surrender to Canada (s. 82)

Section 82 of the *Extradition Act* provides as follows:

ORDER OF DETENTION FOR TEMPORARY SURRENDER
82. (1) Subject to subsection (2), a judge shall, on application of the competent authority made at any time before the temporary surrender, order the detention in custody of a person who is serving a term of imprisonment or has otherwise lawfully been deprived of their liberty in a requested State or entity and whose temporary surrender Canada has requested for the purpose of prosecution or appeal.

TIME LIMIT
(2) The order must contain a provision that the person will not be detained in custody after

(a) a date specified in the order;
(b) in the case of surrender for a trial, 45 days after the completion of the trial; or
(c) in the case of surrender for an appeal, 30 days after the completion of the proceedings for which the presence of the person was required.

ORDER OF DETENTION TO PREVAIL
(3) An order made under subsection (1) prevails over an order made by a Canadian court, a judge of a Canadian court, a Canadian justice of

the peace or any other person who has power in Canada to compel the appearance of a person, in respect of anything that occurred before the person is transferred to Canada.

VARIATION OF DETENTION ORDER

(4) **The judge who made the detention order or another judge may vary its terms and conditions and, in particular, may extend the duration of the detention.**

RETURN

(5) **Subject to subsection (6), the person shall be returned to the requested State or entity on completion of the proceedings in Canada for which the person was temporarily surrendered or on the expiry of the period set out in the order, whichever is sooner.**

RETURN IF RIGHT OF APPEAL

(6) **The person shall not be returned to the requested State or entity**

(a) **if the person has been convicted in Canada, before 30 days after the conviction, unless the person or the competent authority declares that there will be no appeal; and**

(b) **if the person has been acquitted, before 30 days after the acquittal, unless the competent authority declares that there will be no appeal.**

RETURN FOR APPEAL

(7) **The court of appeal may, on application, recommend that the Minister request another temporary surrender of a person who has been returned to the requested State or entity after trial, if the court of appeal is satisfied that the interests of justice require their presence for the appeal.**

Section 82 sets out rules for the temporary surrender of persons to Canada (ss. 66 to 68 of the Act deal with temporary surrender from Canada). Section 82(1) provides for the detention of persons whose temporary surrender has been requested by Canada. It states that, upon an application by a "competent authority" made at any time prior to the temporary surrender, a "judge" shall order the detention in custody of a person who is serving a term of imprisonment (or who has otherwise lawfully been deprived of his or her liberty) in the requested jurisdiction and whose temporary surrender Canada has requested for the purpose of prosecution or appeal. The term "competent authority" is defined in s. 77 (see above). The term "judge" is defined in s. 2 of the Act as a judge of the superior court of the province.

Section 82(2) requires that the order contain a time limit for the detention of the person in Canada. The subsection sets out three possible time limits: a date specified in the order, 45 days after the completion of the trial (in the case of surrender for a trial), or 30 days after the completion of the appeal proceedings (in the case of surrender for an appeal).

Section 82(3) establishes that the detention order shall prevail over "an order made by a Canadian court, a judge of a Canadian court, a Canadian justice of the peace or any other person who has power in Canada to compel the appearance of a person, in respect of anything that occurred before the person is transferred to Canada."

Section 82(4) allows the judge who made the order or another judge to vary the terms and conditions of the order, including extending the duration of the detention.

Sections 82(5) and (6) set the parameters for the return of a temporarily surrendered person to the requested jurisdiction. Section 82(5) provides that the person shall be returned to the requested jurisdiction upon the earlier of the completion of the Canadian proceedings for which the person was temporarily surrendered or the expiry of the period set out in the order. However, s. 82(5) is subject to s. 82(6), which addresses rights of appeal following a Canadian trial. Section 82(6) provides that the person shall not be returned to the requested jurisdiction:

- In the case of a conviction, before 30 days after the conviction, unless the person or the competent authority declares that there will be no appeal;

- in the case of an acquittal, before 30 days after the acquittal, unless the competent authority declares that there will be no appeal.

Section 82(7) provides a mechanism for a subsequent temporary surrender in the event that the person's presence is required for appeal proceedings. The subsection enables the court of appeal, on application, to recommend that the Minister request a temporary surrender of a person who has been returned to a requested jurisdiction after a trial "if the court of appeal is satisfied that the interests of justice require their presence for the appeal."

§1.7 Commencement of Canadian Sentence (s. 83)

Section 83 of the *Extradition Act* provides as follows:

COMMENCEMENT OF SENTENCE OR DISPOSITION
83. (1) Subject to subsection (3), the sentence or disposition of a person who has been temporarily surrendered and who has been convicted and sentenced in Canada, or in respect of whom a disposition has been made under the *Young Offenders Act*, does not commence until their final extradition to Canada.

WARRANT OF COMMITTAL
(2) The warrant of committal issued under the *Criminal Code* in respect of the person must state that the person is to be committed to custody

to serve the sentence or disposition immediately on their final extradition to Canada.

IF CONCURRENT SENTENCES ORDERED

(3) The sentencing judge may order that the person's sentence, or the disposition under the *Young Offenders Act*, be executed concurrently with the sentence they are serving in the requested State or entity, in which case the warrant of committal or order of disposition shall state that the person is to be committed to custody under subsection (2) only for any portion of the sentence remaining at the time of their final extradition to Canada or that the young person's disposition is to begin only on their final extradition to Canada.

Section 83(1) provides that, subject to s. 83(3), the Canadian sentence or disposition of a person who is temporarily surrendered to Canada and who is convicted and sentenced (or against whom a disposition is been made under the *Young Offenders Act*) does not commence until the person's final extradition to Canada. Section 83(2) states that the warrant of committal issued under the *Criminal Code* must state that the person is to be committed to custody to serve the sentence or disposition immediately on his or her final extradition to Canada. Section 83(3) allows the sentencing judge to order that the sentence or disposition be served concurrently with the sentence the person is serving in the requested jurisdiction. In such a case, s. 83(3) requires that the order state that the person is to be committed to custody under s. 83(2) only for any portion of the sentence or disposition remaining at the time of their final extradition to Canada.

§2.0 COMPARISON WITH FORMER ACT

Extradition to Canada was addressed in ss. 30 to 33 of the former *Extradition Act* under the heading "Extradition from a Foreign State." Section 30 of the former Act governed the scope of extradition to Canada. It limited extradition to Canada to a "foreign state with which there is an extradition arrangement." Section 78 of the new Act is broader in two respects. Firstly, it applies to any "State or entity," which is broadly defined in s. 2 of the Act to include any state other than Canada (including any subdivision of that state or territory falling under the jurisdiction of that state), an international tribunal, or a territory. The latter two components of the definition were not included in the definition of "foreign state" in s. 2 of the former Act. Secondly, s. 78 of the new Act does not limit requests to jurisdictions with which Canada has entered an extradition agreement.

Section 30 also set out the authority for and manner of making Canadian extradition requests to foreign states. The request was to be made by the Canadian Minister of Justice, and the request could be made in three ways. Firstly, to a consular officer of the requested state resident in Ottawa. Secondly, to a minister of the requested state through a diplomatic representative of Canada located in the requested state. Thirdly, if neither of these modes was convenient, the requisition could be made "in such other mode as is settled by arrangement," that is, the parties were free to make their own arrangements.

The new Act is different in two respects. Firstly, the Canadian Minister of Justice retains the authority to make extradition requests to foreign jurisdictions. However, ss. 77 and 78 are more specific on the procedure leading up to the request. Section 77 defines the term "competent authority," i.e., either the Attorney General of Canada, the applicable provincial attorney general, the Solicitor General of Canada, or the applicable provincial corrections minister. Section 78 then specifies that the competent authority must first make an extradition request to the Minister of Justice, who will then make a request to the foreign jurisdiction. Secondly, the new Act does not list the specific ways in which the request may be made to the foreign state or entity, leaving such matters to be determined according to the convenience of the parties.

In comparing s. 30 of the former Act with ss. 77 and 78 of the new Act, it should be noted that the new Act, at s. 78(2), enables the Minister, again at the request of a competent authority, to request the provisional arrest of a person. The former Act did not contain any similar provision.

Section 31 of the former Act provided for the summoning of witnesses, the enforcement of subpoenas, and the taking of depositions in Canada for use in the requested state. Section 79 of the new Act also provides for the taking of evidence in Canada in support of an extradition request to a foreign jurisdiction. The new provision is more complete and up-to-date procedurally. It incorporates the *Criminal Code* provisions relating to procuring the attendance of witnesses and specifies (unlike the former section) that the application may be made *ex parte*. Significantly, s. 79(d) now provides that evidence received under the section may be certified or authenticated by the presiding judge in the manner and form required by the requested jurisdiction.

Section 32 of the former Act provided that the foreign surrender order was the authority for the person to be brought into Canada and delivered to the proper authorities. It was silent, however, as to who had the authority to deliver the person. Section 81 of the new Act enables the foreign authorities to bring the person into Canada if so authorized by the Minister of Justice, thus enabling the parties to make the most expeditious arrangements for the person's return. Moreover, whereas the former Act was silent on this point, s. 81 expressly permits authorized officers to hold the person in custody in Canada and, in the event of an escape, arrest the person "in fresh pursuit."

Section 33 of the former Act, like s. 80 of the new Act, specified that the right of specialty applied to a person surrendered to Canada (the case law dealing with the right of specialty for persons returned to Canada is discussed in the Analysis section, §4.0 below). More specifically, as a general rule, the surrendered person could only be detained and prosecuted in Canada for the offence for which the extradition request was granted. Both provisions provide that this is subject to the provisions of any applicable extradition agreement. Both also state that the right of specialty does not apply to a person who has had the opportunity to leave Canada following their surrender to Canada. However, s. 80 is clearer on the specific scope of the rule of specialty. Section 80(a) sets out that the surrendered person may be detained and prosecuted for the following: the offence for which the surrender was granted and included offences; another offence that the requested jurisdiction consents to the person being detained and prosecuted; or another offence in respect of which the surrendered person consents to being detained or prosecuted. In addition, s. 80(b) provides that a person may be detained in Canada for the purpose of being surrendered to another jurisdiction for prosecution or for imposition or execution of a sentence in respect of an offence that is alleged to have been committed, or was committed, before surrender to Canada if the requested jurisdiction consents.

Finally, the new Act has added sections providing for the temporary surrender of individuals to Canada and establishing rules for the calculation of the Canadian sentences of temporarily surrendered persons who are convicted in Canada (ss. 82 and 83).

§3.0 SIGNIFICANCE OF CHANGE

As can be seen from the foregoing section, the new Act has significantly revamped the provisions governing extradition to Canada. From both a substantive and a procedural standpoint, the new Act provides more flexible, more complete, and clearer guidelines. Substantively, the new Act widens the scope for extradition to Canada (s. 78), clarifies the right of specialty (s. 80), specifies the powers of foreign officers conveying a person to Canada (s. 81), and allows for temporary surrender (ss. 82–83). Procedurally, the new Act establishes the authority and means by which the "competent authority" makes an application for extradition to the Minister (ss. 77–78), anticipates applications for provisional arrest (s. 78(2)), and clarifies the procedure governing evidence-gathering orders (s. 79).

Section 78 of the Act authorizes the Minister of Justice to make a request for extradition to the extradition partner. Surrender is encompassed as part of the extradition process. Section 82 introduces a new procedural scheme for the receipt and detention of a person who has been surrendered to Canada on a temporary basis, for the purpose of prosecution or appeal. Section 82 applies in the case of a person who is in detention in the requested state and who is required by the requested state to be returned. Prior to the temporary surrender of the person, the competent authority in Canada may apply to a judge to make provision for the length of the detention of the person in Canada.

An order under s. 82 allows Canada to comply with the temporary surrender arrangements by making provision for the person to be kept in custody (s. 82(2)) and by providing that the person cannot be compelled to appear in Canadian proceedings with respect to matters arising before the person's transfer (s. 82(3)). In this way, and by the setting of time limits (s. 82(2), (4) and (5)), it can be ensured that the surrender of the person will indeed be temporary.

A further request for temporary surrender may be made pursuant to the provisions of s. 82(7). Section 82(7) provides that the Court of Appeal may on application recommend that the Minister make a further request for the temporary surrender of a person who has been returned to the requested state after trial, if the Court is of the opinion that the interests of justice require the presence of the person at the hearing of the appeal.

§4.0 ANALYSIS

§4.1 Right of Specialty (s. 80)

Section 33 of the former *Extradition Act*, like s. 80 of the new Act, specified that the right of specialty applied to a person surrendered to Canada. The right of specialty for persons returned to Canada under the former Act was the subject of jurisprudential interpretation. The case law sets out the following principles, which will remain useful in interpreting s. 80 of the new Act.

(a) Extradited person may only be tried in Canada for specific offence for which extradition was granted (and related principles)

In *R. v. Buck* (1917), 29 C.C.C. 45 (S.C.C.), Buck was extradited to Canada from the United States on a charge of fraud by instigating the publication in a newspaper, the *News-Telegram*, of a false statement that oil had been struck at a well in which Buck held an interest. Buck was subsequently convicted in Canada of the offence of fraud for concurring in the publication of the same false statement in another newspaper, the *Albertan*, no mention of which was made before the extradition judge who committed Buck for surrender to Canada. Buck appealed on the basis that his conviction was for an offence other than that for which he had been extradited.

A majority of the Supreme Court of Canada allowed the appeal. The reasoning of the majority is well-summarized in the following passage from the judgment of Anglin J. at p. 55:

> It is, in my opinion, incontrovertible that "the offence for which (the accused) was surrendered" means the specific offence with the commission of which he was charged before the Extradition Commissioner and in respect of which that official held that a *prima facie* case had been established and ordered his extradition, and not another offence or crime, though of identical legal character and committed about the same time and under similar circumstances. The Supreme Court of the United States so held in *Re Rauscher*, 119 U.S.R. 407. In delivering the judgment of the Court Mr. Justice Miller said, at p. 424:—
>
>> That right (of an extradited person), as we understand it, is that he shall be tried for only the offence with which he is charged in the extradition proceedings and for which he was delivered up.

I do not entertain the slightest doubt that this is a correct statement of the law under the present treaty and the Canadian statute, the former of which, in terms restricts the right of trying an extradited person to "the offence for which he was surrendered" while the latter prohibits his prosecution or punishment in Canada, "in contravention of any of the terms of the (extradition) arrangement. . . for any other offence" than the extradition crime of which he was accused or convicted and in respect of which he was surrendered.

In *R. v. Kelly* (1916), 27 C.C.C. 94 (Man. K.B.), affirmed (1916), 27 C.C.C. 140 (Man. C.A.), affirmed (1916), 27 C.C.C. 282 (S.C.C.), the Manitoba Court of King's Bench held that, "[t]he onus lies upon the accused to shew that the offences charged in the indictment are not offences for which he was extradited."

The case law predating the new *Extradition Act* held that a person could not be prosecuted for a lesser offence than that for which extradition was granted unless the lesser offence was itself extraditable: see *R. v. Flannery* (1923), 40 C.C.C. 263 (Alta. S.C.), at p. 268. Section 80 of the new Act expressly provides that a person who is surrendered to Canada may be prosecuted for the "offence in respect of which the person was surrendered or an included offence."

Prior to the introduction of the new *Extradition Act*, the case law suggested that, with the consent of the requested state, a person could be prosecuted in Canada for offences other than that for which the extradition was granted: see *R. v. Crux* (1971), 2 C.C.C. (2d) 427 (B.C.C.A.), leave to appeal to S.C.C. refused (1971), 2 C.C.C. (2d) 433n; (S.C.C.), *Macdonald v. Canada*, [1987] 3 F.C. 95 (T.D.). Under s. 80 of the new Act, it is clear that a person who is surrendered to Canada may be prosecuted for "another offence in respect of which the requested State or entity consents to the person being detained or prosecuted."

(b) Person who waives extradition to Canada does not benefit from right of specialty

In *R. v. Gagnon* (1956), 117 C.C.C. 61 (Que. C.S.P.), it was decided that a person who waives extradition to Canada does not benefit from the right of specialty. The issue in that case was whether Gagnon had, in fact, waived extradition. On reviewing the facts, the court made the following findings:

- While in custody in the United States, Gagnon signed a deposition indicating that he wanted to return to Canada voluntarily at his own expense.

- Gagnon subsequently gave two waivers of extradition before two separate American judges.

- The Canadian authorities never requisitioned the surrender of Gagnon under s. 30 of the *Extradition Act*.

Based on these findings, the court held that Gagnon had waived extradition and therefore he was not entitled to specialty protection under s. 33 of the former *Extradition Act*, at p. 70:

> Therefore, s. 33 of our *Extradition Act*, which reads as follows: "Where any person accused or convicted of an extradition crime is surrendered by a foreign state, in pursuance of any extradition arrangement, he is not, until after he has been restored or has had an opportunity of returning to the foreign state within the meaning of the arrangement, subject, in contravention of any of the terms of the arrangement, to prosecution or punishment in Canada for any other offence committed prior to his surrender, for which he should not, under the arrangement, be prosecuted", does not apply.
>
> The principle enunciated in s. 33, which has been adopted by every nation having conventions or treaties of extradition, dates back to the English *Extradition Act* of 1870 [c. 52]. It is herein provided, as already seen, that a surrendered criminal shall not be tried for any but the crime for which he is extradited. But, before s. 33 can be applied, the extradition must be made in pursuance of an extradition arrangement. That appears to be also a condition *sine qua non*. I would conclude, therefore, that Gagnon not having been brought back to Canada in pursuance of any extradition arrangement between Canada and the United States, cannot avail himself of the privileges of s. 33.

(c) Person extradited to Canada loses protection of specialty if remaining in Canada after reasonable opportunity to leave country

In *R. v. Parisien* (1988), 41 C.C.C. (3d) 223 (S.C.C), at pp. 227–228, the Supreme Court of Canada held that a person who is extradited to Canada loses the protection of specialty if he or she remains in Canada after having had a reasonable opportunity to leave the country. In that case, a person was extradited from Brazil to Canada under a special arrangement entered into between the two countries pursuant to Part II of the former *Extradition Act* (Part II permitted extradition in specific cases with countries with which Canada did not have a treaty. Part II has been replaced by the "specific agreement" provisions (see ss. 2 and 10) of the new *Extradition Act*). The person was a Canadian citizen. At the preliminary hearing in Canada, the person pleaded guilty to the offences that had been agreed upon in the extradition arrangement between Canada and Brazil. The person was sentenced to eighteen months' imprisonment. At the hearing, Crown counsel notified the person that with Brazil's consent before the expiry of sentence or without Brazil's consent following the sentence the Crown would proceed with additional charges dating from before the extradition. Brazil's consent was never obtained. Brazil required, as a condition precedent to its consenting, that the person consent, and the person's consent was not obtained. A few months after the expiry of his sentence, the accused traveled to Portugal. He then voluntarily returned to Canada within a month. A short time later, a new information was sworn charging him with the outstanding offences. The person objected on the basis that

Canada was prohibited from prosecuting him for offences other than those for which he had been extradited from Brazil.

The Supreme Court of Canada dismissed the appeal. La Forest J., in his judgment for the court, made the following general comment on the right of specialty, at pp. 227–228:

> As an adjunct to the practice of restricting extradition to listed crimes, most treaties also provide that the requesting state shall not try or punish the fugitive for any crime committed before the extradition other than that for which the surrender took place. This, I suggest, would be the result in any event. When a state surrenders a fugitive in respect of a particular crime, that surrender must necessarily be subject to an implied condition that the requesting state will not try the fugitive for any other crime previously committed without the permission of the surrendering state. [Citations omitted.]
>
> Canada expressly provides that a fugitive shall not be tried or punished for a crime committed before his surrender unless he has been restored or given an opportunity to return to the state that surrendered him. Section 33 of the *Extradition Act* reads as follows:

> > 33. Where any person accused or convicted of an extradition crime is surrendered by a foreign state, in pursuance of any extradition arrangement, he is not, until after he has been restored or has had an opportunity of returning to the foreign state within the meaning of the arrangement, subject, in contravention of any of the terms of the arrangement, to a prosecution or punishment in Canada for any other offence committed prior to his surrender, for which he should not, under the arrangement, be prosecuted.

Based on the facts of the case, La Forest J. decided that Canada's arrangement with Brazil did not give the person immunity after the person has had a reasonable opportunity to return to Brazil, at pp. 229–230:

> Does Canada's undertaking, then, give the appellant immunity even after he has had a reasonable opportunity to return to Brazil? In interpreting this undertaking, it must, as in the case of other terms in international agreements, be read in context and in light of its object and purpose as well as in light of the general principles of international law: see art. 31 of the Vienna Convention on the Law of Treaties, May 23, 1969, U.N. Doc. A/Conf. 39/27; (1969), 63 A.J.I.L. 875. When the arrangement was entered into, the appellant was in Brazil to which he owed local allegiance, and Brazil in turn owed him the correlative duty of protection. In surrendering a person under its protection, Brazil would have an interest in seeing that the surrender was not used for a purpose other than that for which it was made. In short, the undertaking was related to the surrender. The appellant, however, remains in this country no longer as a result of the surrender, but because he chooses to live here. This is not surprising; he is a Canadian citizen. As such, he is entitled to the protection of our laws, but both as a citizen and a resident, he owes allegiance to Canada and is subject to its laws. Brazil exercised its duty of protection by securing the appellant against prosecutions for crimes other than those for which he was surrendered. But once the appellant is no longer here because of the surrender but rather because he seeks of his own accord to live in Canada and to enjoy the protection of our

455

laws, he owes a duty of allegiance to Canada and is subject to those laws. There can be no doubt, of course, that the appellant in this case chose to stay in Canada. He was actually out of the country for a time and returned here despite the earlier warning that he would be prosecuted for the offences for which he is now charged.

. . .

In the light of the foregoing, I have no difficulty in concluding that the undertaking made to Brazil is related to prosecutions which can take place by reason of the surrender of a fugitive to the requesting state, not to cases where prosecution becomes possible because the accused decides to stay in the requesting state following such prosecution. It would require clear terms to persuade me otherwise, for the view proposed by the appellant would lead to absurd results. The approach I am taking, I might add, is consistent with all the cases from different nations that have been brought to our attention: see *United States v. Rauscher, supra*, (United States); *Re Dilasser, supra*, (Venezuela); *Novic v. Public Prosecutor of the Canton of Basel-Stadt* (1955), 22 Int. Law Rep. 515 (Switzerland); *Hungary and Austria (Extradition) Case* (1929), 5 Ann. Dig. Pub. Int. Law. 275 (Hungary); see also Hackworth, *Digest of International Law*, vol. IV, pp. 232 *et seq.*, especially at pp. 235–6 (Germany).

§5.0 CASE LAW

Macdonald v. Canada, [1987] 3 F.C. 95 (T.D.).
R. v. Buck (1917), 29 C.C.C. 45 (S.C.C.).
R. v. Crux (1971), 2 C.C.C. (2d) 427 (B.C.C.A.), leave to appeal to S.C.C. refused (1971), 2 C.C.C. (2d) 433n (S.C.C.).
R. v. Flannery (1923), 40 C.C.C. 263 (Alta. S.C.).
R. v. Gagnon (1956), 117 C.C.C. 61 (Que. C.S.P.).
R. v. Kelly (1916) 27 C.C.C. 94 (Man. K.B.), affirmed (1916), 27 C.C.C. 140 (Man. C.A.), affirmed (1916), 27 C.C.C. 282 (S.C.C.).
R. v. Parisien (1988), 41 C.C.C. (3d) 223 (S.C.C.).

§6.0 RELATED SECTIONS

s. 2 — Interpretation
s. 61 — Escape of Person sought While in Custody and Arrest (following contested extradition hearing)
ss. 66, 68 — Temporary Surrender from Canada
s. 73 — Escape While in Custody and Arrest (in context of consent to committal)
Criminal Code, Part XXII — Procuring Attendance of Witnesses

Transitional Provisions (ss. 84–85)

§1.0 DESCRIPTION

Sections 84 and 85 of the *Extradition Act* provide as follows:

CASES PENDING—FORMER *EXTRADITION ACT*
84. The *Extradition Act* repealed by section 129 of this Act applies to a matter respecting the extradition of a person as though it had not been repealed, if the hearing in respect of the extradition had already begun on the day on which this Act comes into force.

CASES PENDING — *FUGITIVE OFFENDERS ACT*
85. The *Fugitive Offenders Act* repealed by section 130 of this Act applies to a matter respecting the return under that Act of a person as though it had not been repealed, if the hearing before the provincial court judge in respect of the return had already begun on the day on which this Act comes into force.

Sections 84 and 85 are transitional provisions, providing that the former *Extradition Act* and the former *Fugitive Offenders Act* (repealed by ss. 129 and 130 of the new Act, respectively) continue to apply to matters in respect of which an extradition hearing began prior to the coming into force of the Act.

§2.0 ANALYSIS

Sections 84 and 85 give rise to the issue of when an extradition hearing can be considered to have commenced. The legislation that amended the *Extradition Act* in 1992 (*An Act to amend the Extradition Act*, S.C. 1992, c. 13) contained a similar transitional provision (s. 7):

> 7. *Any matter in respect of which an extradition hearing has commenced before a judge referred to in section 13 of the* Extradition Act *on the day on which this section comes into force*, any proceeding on *habeas corpus* from such a matter, any decision of the Minister of Justice on such a matter, any proceeding on *habeas corpus* from such a decision and any appeal from such a matter, decision or *habeas corpus* proceeding *shall be heard and disposed of as though this Act had not been enacted.* [Emphasis added.]

Two cases dealing with s. 7 of the 1992 amending legislation addressed the issue of when an extradition hearing could be considered to have commenced for the purpose of determining whether the pre or post-1992 *Extradition Act* provisions applied to the case. In *United States v. Vanasse* (1993), 67 O.A.C. 370 (Ont. C.A.), at p. 371, in somewhat unusual circumstances, the Ontario Court of Appeal dealt with the issue of when an extradition hearing can be considered to have commenced. The person sought in that case was arrested on an extradition warrant in October of 1991. On October 17, 1991, the person was brought before Houston J., at which time his counsel raised the issue of his fitness to stand trial. Both parties subsequently filed written materials concerning this issue and on November 13, 1991, some medical testimony was heard. Ultimately, on July 23, 1992, Houston J. ruled that the person was fit to have an extradition hearing. December 14, 1992, was set as the date for the hearing and then on December 18, 1992, Houston J. committed the person for surrender.

Finlayson J.A. for the Ontario Court of Appeal found that the fitness hearing was part of the extradition hearing and therefore the hearing commenced prior to December 1, 1992, when the new appeal procedures came into force (pp. 371–373). Finlayson J.A. agreed with the submission of counsel for the fugitive that the fitness issue was integral to the extradition hearing in the sense that there would have been no extradition hearing at all had Houston J. found the person unfit to participate in such a hearing (pp. 371–372). Finlayson J.A. also concurred with the submission of counsel for the fugitive that the fitness issue remained live throughout the entire extradition process (pp. 371–372 and 373). Finlayson J.A. also agreed with the view of the *habeas corpus* judge, Rutherford J., that the determination as to the date on which the extradition hearing commenced will vary according to the circumstances of the particular case (p. 372).

In *United States v. Wong* (1995), 98 C.C.C. (3d) 332 (B.C.C.A.), leave to appeal to S.C.C. refused (1995), 101 C.C.C. (3d) vi (S.C.C.), the British Columbia Court of Appeal was called upon to determine whether the pre or post-1992 extradition appeal rules applied to the case. Prior to the date on which the 1992 appeal rules came into force (December 1, 1992), the fugitive's bail hearing had been held. There had also been some set date appearances as well as two adjournments of extradition hearing dates that had been set to commence prior to December 1, 1992. No evidence was heard prior to the transition date. The extradition hearing ultimately commenced in the latter part of 1993.

Legg J.A. for the court held that the post-1992 appeal rules applied to the case. He found that the term "extradition hearing" used in s. 7 of the amending legislation, "refers to that portion of the proceedings which begin with the presentation of evidence in the committal or discharge phase of the process," at p. 10. Legg J.A. distinguished the decision of the Ontario Court of Appeal in *United States v. Vanasse* on the basis that, in that case, prior to December 1, 1992, "Houston J. heard some medical evidence and ruled that the fitness of the appellant was a live issue and that he would receive evidence and argument as to how he should dispose of it . . . By contrast, in the case under appeal, no 'live' issue was raised in the extradition proceedings prior to December 1st, 1992, when the *New Act* came into force" (at p. 15).

§3.0 CASE LAW

United States v. Vanasse (1993), 67 O.A.C. 370 (Ont. C.A.).
United States v. Wong (1995), 98 C.C.C. (3d) 332 (B.C.C.A.), leave to appeal to
S.C.C. refused (1995), 101 C.C.C. (3d) vi (S.C.C.).

§4.0 RELATED SECTIONS

s. 129 — Repeal of *Extradition Act*
s. 130 — Repeal of *Fugitive Offenders Act*
Interpretation Act, s. 44 — Repeal and Substitution

APPENDIX A
LETTERS ROGATORY

§1.0 GENERAL PRINCIPLES

Letters rogatory (or letters of request) are a medium whereby a judge or court of one state makes a request to a judge or court of another state asking for the examination of a witness by commission and/or the production of documents in the requested state (see *United States District Court, Middle District of Florida v. Royal American Shows Inc.* (1979), 49 C.C.C. (2d) 276 (Alta. Q.B.), at p. 283, reversed on other grounds (1981), 58 C.C.C. (2d) 274 (Alta. C.A.), judgment restored, the court not dealing with this point (1982), 66 C.C.C. (2d) 125 (S.C.C.); and *A-Dec Inc. v. Dentech Products Ltd.* (1988), 32 C.P.C. (2d) 290 (B.C.S.C.), at p. 294). A letters rogatory request does not require that there be a treaty or other arrangement between the requesting and the requested state. Rather, cooperation by the court or judge of the requested state is based upon the comity of nations (see the following decisions: *R. v. Zingre* (1981), 61 C.C.C. (2d) 465 (S.C.C.), at p. 472; *United States District Court, Middle District of Florida v. Royal American Shows Inc.* (S.C.C.), *supra*, at p. 130; *France (Republic) v. De Havilland Aircraft of Canada Ltd.* (1991), 65 C.C.C. (3d) 449 (Ont. C.A.), at p. 458; and *Germany (Federal Republic) v. Kretz* (1997), (*sub nom. Germany (Federal Republic) v. C.I.B.C.*) 31 O.R. (3d) 684 (Ont. Gen. Div.), at p. 695, affirmed (May 19, 1998), Doc. CA C26652 (Ont. C.A.). The principle of comity dictates that a liberal approach be taken to requests for judicial assistance (see *R. v. Zingre*, *supra*; *United States District Court, Middle District of Florida v. Royal American Shows Inc.*, *supra*; *France (Republic) v. De Havilland Aircraft of Canada Ltd.*, *supra*, at pp. 460-461; and *Germany (Federal Republic) v. Kretz*, *supra*, at p. 695). However, judicial assistance may be denied where it would violate the public policy or impinge upon the sovereignty of the requested state (see *R. v. Zingre*, *supra*, at p. 472; *Uszinska v. France (Republic)* (1980), 52 C.C.C. (2d) 39 (Ont. H.C.), at. p. 42; *France (Republic) v. De Havilland Aircraft of Canada Ltd.*, *supra*, at p. 463; and *Germany (Federal Republic) v. Kretz*, *supra*, at p. 695). These general principles were framed by Dickson J. (as he then was) on behalf of a unanimous Supreme Court of Canada in *R. v. Zingre*, *supra*, at p. 472):

> It is upon the comity of nations that international legal assistance rests. Thus the Courts of one jurisdiction will give effect to the laws and judicial decisions of another jurisdiction, not as a matter of obligation but out of mutual deference and respect. A foreign request is given full force and effect unless it be contrary to the public policy of the jurisdiction to which the request is directed . . . or otherwise prejudicial to the sovereignty or citizens of the latter jurisdiction.

§2.0 HISTORY AND OVERVIEW OF LEGISLATION GOVERNING REQUESTS

As stated in the previous section, letters rogatory involve a court in one state making a request to a court of another state for the examination of a witness by commission and/or the production of documents in the requested state. Letters rogatory requests by foreign courts to Canadian courts in connection with foreign criminal matters are governed by Part II of the *Canada Evidence Act* (ss. 43–51) (see Bradley J. Freedman and Gregory N. Harney, "Obtaining Evidence From Canada: The Enforcement of Letters Rogatory By Canadian Courts" (1987) 21 U.B.C. L. Rev. 351–387 at p. 356, and *Germany (Federal Republic) v. Kretz, supra*, at p. 693).

The precursor to the *Canada Evidence Act* letters rogatory provisions was the British *Act to provide for taking Evidence in Her Majesty's Dominions in relation to Civil and Commercial Matters before Foreign Tribunals*, 1856 (U.K.), c. 113, 19 & 20 Vict. In 1868, following the British example, the Canadian Parliament enacted the *Act to provide for taking Evidence in Canada in relation to civil and commercial matters pending before Courts of Justice in any other of Her Majesty's Dominions or before Foreign Tribunals*, S.C. 1868, c. 76. The Canadian legislation was for the most part identical to the British Act on which it was based. Moreover, the Canadian legislation has remained largely unchanged since that time. In 1886 (R.S.C. 1886, c. 140), definitions were added to the 1868 Act and letters rogatory requests were expanded to criminal matters. In 1906 (R.S.C. 1906, c. 145), the letters rogatory legislation was incorporated as a separate part of the *Canada Evidence Act* (ss. 38–46), but the provisions themselves underwent only small changes. In 1984 (S.C. 1984, c. 40, s. 27), the definitions of "court" and "judge" were amended to remove the Supreme Court of Canada and judges of the Supreme Court of Canada, respectively, from the definition of each of these terms.

The current *Canada Evidence Act* letters rogatory provisions largely mirror the 1906 version of the legislation, although certain amendments, subsequently described, were effected with the coming into force of the new *Extradition Act* on June 17, 1999.

Turning to a review of the letters rogatory provisions in Part II of the *Canada Evidence Act*, ss. 43 to 45 set out the scope of Part II as well as definitions. Section 43 states that, "[t]his Part applies to the taking of evidence relating to proceedings in courts out of Canada." Section 44 provides definitions of certain terms for the purposes of Part II. The term "cause" is defined to include "a proceeding against a criminal." The terms "court" and "judge" are defined, respectively, as "any superior court in any province" and "any judge of any superior court in any province." Accordingly, a letters rogatory request by a foreign court cannot be made to a provincial court. Finally, the term "oath" is defined to include "a solemn affirmation in cases in which, by the law of Canada, or of a province, as the case may be, a solemn affirmation is allowed instead of an oath." Section 45 provides that, "[t]his Part shall not be so construed as to interfere with the right of legislation of the legislature of any province requisite or desirable for the carrying out of the objects hereof."

The most important component of Part II is s. 46(1), which sets out when a letters rogatory request by a foreign court will be granted by a Canadian court. The section is framed in very broad terms (*R. v. Zingre, supra*, at p. 475, referring to what was then s. 43). Section 46(1), as re-enacted by S.C. 1999, c. 18, s. 89, reads as follows:

> **46.** (1) If, on an application for that purpose, it is made to appear to any court or judge that any court or tribunal outside Canada, before which any civil, commercial or criminal matter is pending, is desirous of obtaining the testimony in relation to that matter of a party or witness within the jurisdiction of the first mentioned court, of the court to which the judge belongs or of the judge, the court or judge may, in its or their discretion, order the examination on oath on interrogatories, or otherwise, before any person or persons named in the order, of that party or witness accordingly, and by the same or any subsequent order may command the attendance of that party or witness for the purpose of being examined, and for the production of any writings or other documents mentioned in the order and of any other writings or documents relating to the matter in question that are in the possession or power of that party or witness.

In s. 46 (changed by the amendments to s. 46(1)), the phrase "any court or tribunal of competent jurisdiction in the Commonwealth and Dependent Territories or in any foreign country" was replaced by the wording "any court or tribunal outside Canada" (*Extradition Act*, S.C. 1999, c. 18, s. 89, effective June 17, 1999).

Given the definition of the terms "court" and "judge" in s. 44, an order under s. 46(1) can only be made by a superior court of a province or a judge of such a court. Section 46(1) involves four conditions precedent to the issuance of an order for examination. This approach to s. 46(1) is set out by Doherty J.A. in his judgment on behalf of the Ontario Court of Appeal in *France (Republic) v. De Havilland Aircraft of Canada Ltd., supra*, at p. 454. An analysis of the four conditions is provided later in this chapter under heading §3.0, dealing with the issuance of orders under s. 46(1):

1. it must appear that a foreign court is desirous of obtaining the evidence in question;

2. the person whose evidence is sought must be within the jurisdiction of the court which, or judge who, is asked to make the order;

3. the evidence sought must be in relation to a civil, commercial, or criminal matter pending before the foreign court; and

4. the foreign court must be a court of competent jurisdiction.

If these conditions are met, "the court or judge may, in its or their discretion," make the order.

Section 46(2), which was added to the letters rogatory provisions by the *Extradition Act* (S.C. 1999, c. 18, s. 89), provides a new dimension to s. 46(1) orders. Section 46(2) reads as follows:

(2) For greater certainty, testimony for the purposes of subsection (1) may be given by means of technology that permits the virtual presence of the party or witness before the court or tribunal outside Canada or that permits that court or tribunal, and the parties, to hear and examine the party or witness.

Section 46(2) allows for the giving of testimony in Canada to the foreign court via video link and other technology permitting the virtual presence of a witness before the foreign court. Accordingly, s. 46(2) broadens the scope of letters rogatory requests to virtual testimony. Section 46(2) is a modernizing provision, which adapts the scope of mutual legal assistance to take advantage of technological advances. This point was made by Ms. Eleni Bakopanos, Parliamentary Secretary to the Minister of Justice and Attorney General of Canada, while introducing Bill C-40 (now the *Extradition Act*) to the House of Commons on second reading (*House of Commons Debates*, October 8, 1998, 1st Session, 36th Parliament, v. 135, at p. 9006):

> I cannot end my overview of Bill C-40 without mentioning the important modifications to the *Criminal Code*, the *Mutual Legal Assistance in Criminal Matters Act* and the *Canada Evidence Act* which allow for the use of video and audio-link technology to gather evidence and provide testimony from witnesses in Canada or abroad.
>
> Although these modifications will contribute to a more efficient extradition process in specific cases, their aim is much broader as they will allow the use of such technology in criminal and other proceedings as well.
>
> In an age of amazing technological development it is critical that our laws and justice system are flexible enough to permit the use of that technology where possible, appropriate and beneficial to proceedings.
>
> When globalization of new technologies is expanding the reach of organized crime we must ensure that our justice system also uses new technologies to capture and prosecute criminals. Where witnesses cannot be brought before the court because they are outside Canada or they are in another part of Canada and circumstances preclude their attendance, the use of video or audio-link technology is a much better alternative than the written statement or the taking of evidence by a foreign court.

Section 47 provides for the enforcement of the s. 46 order:

> **47.** On the service on the party or witness of an order referred to in section 46, and of an appointment of a time and place for the examination of the party or witness signed by the person named in the order for taking the examination, or, if more than one person is named, by one of the persons named, and on payment or tender of the like conduct money as is properly payable on attendance at a trial, the order may be enforced in like manner as an order made by the court or judge in a cause pending in that court or before that judge.

Section 47 is structured such that — once certain conditions are met — an order made under s. 46 may be enforced in the same manner as an order made by the court or judge in a cause pending in that court or before that judge. The conditions set out in s. 47 are as follows:

1.   the order must be served on the party or witness to whom it applies;

2.   a notice of hearing must specify the time and place for the examination;

3.   a notice of hearing must be signed by at least one of the persons named in the order for taking the examination; and

4.   there must be payment or tender of the conduct money.

Weiler J. (as she then was) of the Ontario Supreme Court in *Switzerland v. Tedball* (July 28, 1989), noted that the order "is analogous to a subpoena to a witness" (at p. 2). This comment was made in the context of a discussion concerning whether Canadian rules regarding claims of solicitor-client privilege applied to proceedings before a commissioner under s. 46. (The issue of the applicability of Canadian law to proceedings before a commissioner under s. 46 is discussed more fully later in this chapter; see §5.0 below). On this point, Weiler J. concluded as follows, at p. 2:

> After counsel for the applicant had reviewed the relevant case law I raised the question as to whether Messrs. Brogden and Spisani might claim solicitor-client privilege. Counsel responded that, since Canadian law applied (*United States v. Pressey* (Ont. C.A.) (unreported, March 16, 1988) [since reported (1988), 51 D.L.R. (4th) 152], the order should nevertheless issue and if counsel wished to claim privilege the claim should be made before the Commisioner. The order, it is argued, is analogous to a subpoena to a witness. Once the witness attends in court a claim for privilege may be made but the witness is still ordered to attend.

Section 48 deals with expenses and conduct money, providing that, "[e]very person whose attendance is required in the manner described in section 47 is entitled to the like conduct money and payment for expenses and loss of time as on attendance at a trial." The rules of court of the particular province should be referred to for the applicable witness fees.

Section 49 deals with administering the oath:

> **49.** On any examination of parties or witnesses, under the authority of any order made in pursuance of this Part, the oath shall be administered by the person authorized to take the examination, or, if more than one person is authorized, by one of those persons.

Accordingly, s. 49 requires that the oath be administered to persons who are required to attend examinations under s. 46, and the oath is to be administered by any of the persons authorized to take the examinations. For the purposes of the letters rogatory provisions, the term oath is defined in s. 44 to include solemn affirmations where such affirmations would be allowed by the law of Canada or of a province.

Section 50(1) and (2) provide persons ordered under s. 46 to attend examinations with the right to refuse to answer certain questions or produce certain documents.

Section 50(1) establishes that examinees have the same right to refuse to answer self-incriminating questions as they would have in any cause pending before the court or judge making the order:

> **50.** (1) Any person examined under any order made under this Part has the like right to refuse to answer questions tending to criminate himself, or other questions, as a party or witness, as the case may be, would have in any cause pending in the court by which, or by a judge whereof, the order is made.

The *Extradition Act*, S.C. 1999, c. 18, s. 90, added s. 50(1.1) and (1.2) to the letters rogatory provisions. These subsections provide guidelines for the giving of evidence via video or audio-link under s. 46(2). Section 50(1.1) establishes that such evidence shall be given as though the party or witness were physically before the foreign court or tribunal, with the exception that the Canadian law of non-disclosure of information and privilege applies to the proceeding:

> (1.1) Despite subsection (1), when a party or witness gives evidence under subsection 46(2), the evidence shall be given as though they were physically before the court or tribunal outside Canada, for the purposes of the laws relating to evidence and procedure but only to the extent that giving the evidence would not disclose information otherwise protected by the Canadian law of non-disclosure of information or privilege.

Section 50(1.2) provides that the Canadian law of contempt shall apply to evidence given under s. 46(2):

> (1.2) When a party or witness gives evidence under subsection 46(2), the Canadian law relating to contempt of court applies with respect to a refusal by the party or witness to answer a question or to produce a writing or document referred to in subsection 46(1), as ordered under that subsection by the court or judge.

Section 50(2) provides that examinees may refuse to produce any writing or other document that they "could not be compelled to produce at a trial of such a cause":

> (2) No person shall be compelled to produce, under any order referred to in subsection (1), any writing or other document that he could not be compelled to produce at a trial of such a cause.

Section 51 deals with the rules of court that apply to applications for the examination of witnesses under the letters rogatory provisions. Section 51(1) provides the court with authority to implement rules and orders in relation to the procedure to be applied and the evidence to be produced in support of applications under Part II:

> **51.** (1) The court may frame rules and orders in relation to procedure and to the evidence to be produced in support of the application for an order for examination of parties and witnesses under this Part, and generally for carrying this Part into effect.

Section 51(2) adds:

> (2) In the absence of any order in relation to the evidence to be produced in support of the application referred to in subsection (1), letters rogatory from a court or tribunal outside Canada in which the civil, commercial or criminal matter is pending, are deemed and taken to be sufficient evidence in support of the application.

In s. 51(2), the phrase "letters rogatory from any court of justice in the Commonwealth and Dependent Territories, or from any foreign tribunal" was replaced by "letters rogatory from a court or tribunal outside Canada," by the *Extradition Act*, S.C. 1999, c. 18, s. 91, effective June 17, 1999.

§3.0 ISSUANCE OF ORDERS UNDER S. 46 OF *CANADA EVIDENCE ACT*

§3.1 Prerequisites

As with any application, the onus of proving that the prerequisites set out in s. 46 of the *Canada Evidence Act* are met and that the court or judge should exercise the discretion under that section in favour of granting the order rests upon the party seeking the order.

Doherty J.A., in *France (Republic) v. De Havilland Aircraft of Canada Ltd.*, *supra*, §1.0, set out the basic approach to be followed by the court or judge under s. 46 of the *Canada Evidence Act*, *supra*, at p. 454:

> The section does two things. First, it requires that certain conditions precedent be established before a court can make an order directing the taking of commission evidence. Secondly, it provides that if those conditions precedent are established, the court may "in its . . . discretion" make the order.

The same basic approach was outlined by Dickson J. in *R. v. Zingre, supra*, §1.0, at pp. 475–476. This approach was followed by Lax J. of the Ontario Court (General Division) in *Germany (Federal Republic) v. Kretz, supra*, §1.0, at p. 689.

Doherty J.A. in *France (Republic) v. De Havilland Aircraft of Canada Ltd.*, *supra*, listed four prerequisites to the issuance of an order for the examination of a witness under s. 46, at p. 455:

> The prerequisites to the exercise of the discretion created by s. 46 may be summarized as follows:
>
> (i)   It must appear that a foreign court is desirous of obtaining the evidence.
>
> (ii)   The witness whose evidence is sought must be within the jurisdiction of the court which is asked to make the order.
>
> (iii) The evidence sought must be in relation to a civil, commercial or criminal matter pending before the foreign court.

(iv)   The foreign court must be a court of competent jurisdiction.

(a) It appears that foreign court is desirous of obtaining evidence in question

The first prerequisite to the issuance of an order for the examination of a witness under s. 46 of the *Canada Evidence Act* is that it must appear that a foreign court is desirous of obtaining the evidence in question. This prerequisite was discussed by the Supreme Court of Canada in *R. v. Zingre, supra*, at pp. 478–479. That case dealt with the right of a Manitoba court to issue a commission authorizing two Swiss "extraordinary investigating judges" to take testimony in Canada in respect of the prosecution in Switzerland of three Swiss nationals for crimes allegedly committed in Manitoba. The investigating judges were appointed by an order of the "Chamber of Indictment" of a Swiss Canton. The function of the investigating judges was to examine documents and interrogate witnesses in order to assist authorities in determining whether the evidence justified a formal trial. Dickson J. held that the role played by examining magistrates in the Swiss system was akin to that of the Canadian preliminary inquiry and that this prerequisite was met.

(b) Examinee must be within jurisdiction of court being asked to make the order

The second prerequisite to the issuance of an order for the examination of a witness under s. 46 is that the person whose evidence is sought must be within the jurisdiction of the court which, or judge who, is asked to make the order. This prerequisite has not been discussed in the case law and does not appear to have posed any interpretation problems.

(c) Evidence sought must be in relation to civil, commercial or criminal matter pending before foreign court

The third prerequisite is that the evidence sought must be in relation to a civil, commercial, or criminal matter pending before the foreign court. This prerequisite has been discussed in the jurisprudence. In particular, the case law has addressed when it can be said for the purposes of s. 46 that there is a criminal matter "pending" before the foreign court. In *France (Republic) v. De Havilland Aircraft of Canada Ltd., supra*, Doherty J.A. concluded that the third criteria does not require that a criminal charge has been laid against the accused in the foreign court, at p. 455:

> With respect, McRae J. [the first instance judge] erred in holding that s. 46 requires that there be a "criminal charge" pending in the foreign court. The section speaks of a pending "criminal matter" not a pending "criminal charge". The former is broader than the latter.

Dickson J. earlier had reached the same conclusion in *R. v. Zingre, supra*, at pp. 477–478. Doherty J.A. found, at p. 455, that the proceeding at issue — being analogous to a Canadian preliminary inquiry — had the characteristics of a criminal proceeding:

> The proceeding in the French court has the *indicia* of a criminal proceeding. It is being conducted by a judicial officer and is based on a formal written complaint which alleges criminal conduct by Mr. Byron-Exarcos. Magistrate Renard is charged with the responsibility of assessing the evidence led at this proceeding in order to determine whether Mr. Byron-Exarcos should stand trial on any of the charges made against him. Furthermore, the material filed on this application on behalf of Mr. Byron-Exarcos demonstrates that he is represented in the proceedings in France and is participating in those proceedings. In *Zingre, Wuest and Reiser v. The Queen*, . . . Dickson J. described proceedings like those being conducted by Magistrate Renard as "similar to the preliminary inquiry in Canadian criminal procedure". No one would suggest that a justice conducting a preliminary inquiry in this country is not a court before which a criminal matter is pending.

As alluded to in the above passage, Dickson J. in *R. v. Zingre, supra*, at p. 474, found that a criminal matter could extend to the pre-trial stages of the process:

> In general, our Courts will only order an examination for the purpose of gathering evidence to be used at a trial, but that is not to say that an order will never be made at the pre-trial stage. Section 43 does not make a distinction between pre-trial and trial proceedings. It merely speaks of the foreign Court or tribunal "desiring" the testimony of an individual "in relation to" a matter pending before it. I do not think it would be wise to lay down an inflexible rule that admits of no exceptions. The granting of an order for examination, being discretionary, will depend on the facts and particular circumstances of the individual case. The Court or Judge must balance the possible infringement of Canadian sovereignty with the natural desire to assist the Courts of justice of a foreign land. It may well be that, depending on the circumstances, a Court would be prepared to order an examination even if the evidence were to be used for pre-trial proceedings.

However, the Supreme Court noted that an order under s. 46 will not be granted if the main purpose of the examination is to allow the examiner to go on a "fishing expedition."

The decision of the Ontario Court of Appeal in *Fecht v. Deloitte & Touche* (1997), 32 O.R. (3d) 417 (Ont. C.A.), further developed the principle that s. 46 is not to be used for "fishing expeditions." In connection with a request under the Ontario equivalent to s. 46 (i.e., s. 60 of the Ontario *Evidence Act*, R.S.O. 1990, c. E.23), the court upheld the decision of the superior court refusing a letters rogatory request on the basis that it had not been shown that the evidence sought was any more than "potentially relevant," at p. 420:

> A fair reading of his reasons in their entirety indicates that Blair J. was not satisfied that the evidence sought was necessary to do justice in the foreign litigation. In so concluding,

Blair J. applied the tests prescribed in *Zingre* and *France, supra*, and determined that the appellants had not demonstrated that the evidence sought was any more than "potentially relevant", the precise description ascribed to it by the American judge issuing the letters rogatory. Blair J. was particularly conscious of the fact that many senior witnesses from Northern Telecom who had already been deposed were not even asked about the information they might have exchanged with Deloitte & Touche on the specific areas of questioning sought to be pursued with Deloitte & Touche through this request. Had this been done, it might have demonstrated that the evidence sought was necessary to do justice in the foreign proceeding. In the circumstances, Blair J. determined that there was simply not a *sufficiently substantial link* to the foreign litigation to conclude that justice required the ordering of commission evidence. We have not been persuaded that he erred in so concluding. [Emphasis in original.]

In *Germany (Federal Republic) v. Kretz, supra*, §1.0, a letters rogatory request was made by the Local Court of Stuttgart in Germany. Evidence was sought in aid of a criminal investigation against Rudolph Kretz. Kretz was alleged to have engaged in a fraudulent scheme in Germany that caused considerable losses to German investors. Kretz emigrated to Canada and acquired landed immigrant status. The Local Court of Stuttgart issued an international warrant of arrest. Mr. Kretz was subsequently arrested by Canadian authorities on immigration and extradition warrants. At the time of the letters rogatory request, Kretz was in custody awaiting the outcome of the extradition proceedings. Charges were not yet pending in the Stuttgart court. After referring to *France (Republic) v. De Havilland Aircraft of Canada Ltd., supra*, and *R. v. Zingre, supra*, Lax J. of the Ontario Court (General Division) found that the prerequisite of there being a criminal matter pending was satisfied (at pp. 691–692). In particular, Lax J. found that, "the investigation has the *indicia* of a criminal proceeding which is consistent with German criminal procedure. I conclude that there is a pending criminal matter before the German court as required by s. 46" (at p. 692).

(d) Foreign court must be court of competent jurisdiction

The fourth prerequisite is that the foreign court must be a court of competent jurisdiction. This prerequisite has also been dealt with in the jurisprudence. In *R. v. Zingre, supra*, the appellant argued that the request for legal assistance did not emanate from a Swiss court because it had been transmitted by a Swiss government department through diplomatic channels in compliance with the extradition treaty then in force between Canada and Switzerland (at p. 476). Dickson J. dismissed the appellant's argument. He concluded that as long as the source of the request is a court of competent jurisdiction, the actual making of the request can be in accordance with the extradition arrangement between the requesting and the requested state:

> I do not think this objection can be sustained, having regard to the legal proceedings conducted to date in Switzerland and the terms of the Treaty and of s. 43 of the *Canada Evidence Act*. Section 43 simply requires that there be "an application" and on that

application, it be "made to appear" that a Court or tribunal is "desirous" of obtaining testimony. The section does not speak of a specific application or request from a tribunal. I would interpret s. 43 in light of Article I of the 1880 Treaty, which recites that the commissions of examination shall be transmitted through the "proper Diplomatic channel". I consider that the Federal Office for Police Matters of the Federal Department of Justice and Police is the "proper Diplomatic channel", in light of the fact that the Swiss Chief of Federal Police was one of the signatories of the 1880 Treaty. Since the request complied with the Treaty, I would consider it sufficient for the purposes of s. 43 of the *Act*. In any event, the primary source of the letters rogatory was a "tribunal of competent jurisdiction" desirous of obtaining the testimony of witnesses within the jurisdiction of the Court of Queen's Bench in Manitoba.

In *France (Republic) v. De Havilland Aircraft of Canada Ltd.*, *supra*, the applicant also argued that the requesting court — the High Court of Grasse — was not a court of competent jurisdiction for the purposes of s. 46. The applicant contended that a foreign court is only a court of competent jurisdiction under s. 46 if it has authority to do three things: conduct the inquiry for which the evidence is requested, make the request for commission evidence, and respond in kind to a similar request for assistance from a Canadian court. The applicant conceded the first two points, but argued that the High Court of Grasse did not have authority to respond in kind to a similar request for assistance from a Canadian court (at p. 456). Doherty J.A. dismissed this argument (at pp. 456-460). In his view, a lack of authority on the part of the requesting tribunal to reciprocate the request is relevant to the exercise of the discretion conferred upon the requested court by s. 46 of the *Canada Evidence Act*. However, it does not have any bearing on the requesting court's jurisdictional competence. In the following passage, Doherty J.A. explained why judicial reciprocity is relevant to the exercise of the discretion under s. 46 (at p. 458):

> I agree with Aylesworth J.A. that the ability of the requesting tribunal to effectively reciprocate is relevant to the exercise of the discretion created by s. 46 of the *Canada Evidence Act*. International comity between friendly nations is the rationale for the existence of the power to order the taking of commission evidence. Reciprocity is a manifestation of that comity. In my view, where it is shown that a Canadian court could not look to the requesting tribunal or some other authority within that foreign country for similar assistance, the underlying rationale which supports the making of an order for commission evidence is far less compelling than in a case where that foreign country stands ready to render similar assistance.

Doherty J.A. then provided three reasons why judicial reciprocity is not relevant to the consideration under s. 46 of the court's jurisdictional competence. Firstly, the determination of jurisdictional competence necessarily precedes the consideration of reciprocity. As put by Doherty J.A., "[i]f the requesting court is not a court of competent jurisdiction, I fail to see how it could ever be appropriate to accede to a request for assistance from that court" (at p. 458). Accordingly, only after it is determined that the requesting court is a "court of competent jurisdiction" (and that the other three prerequisites are met) does the issue of reciprocity arise as part of the exercise under s. 46 of the court's discretion. Secondly, considering reciprocity as part of jurisdictional competence misplaces the significance of reciprocity. Reciprocity is a relevant consideration under s. 46 not because it has a bearing on the competence of the requesting tribunal. Rather, as indicated in the above passage, it is pertinent because it is a reflection of international comity between Canada and the requesting state. As put by Doherty J.A., at pp. 458–459:

> Reciprocity is a reflection of a relationship between nations, not a feature of the authority of a particular court or tribunal. It is inappropriate to limit considerations of reciprocity to the powers of a particular court or tribunal. Rather, the question must be, is there a mechanism in place within the foreign jurisdiction which could respond favourably to a Canadian request by way of letters rogatory?

Thirdly, Doherty J.A. held that the problems inherent in the assessment of reciprocity weighed against assessing reciprocity in connection with the requesting court's jurisdictional competence, at p. 459:

> In many cases, the presence or absence of judicial reciprocity will not admit of any absolute determination, but will depend on the particular circumstances. If judicial reciprocity is a component of the foreign court's jurisdictional competence, then a Canadian court must determine what degree of reciprocity brings that foreign court within the rubric "court or tribunal of competent jurisdiction". The language of s. 46 offers no guidance. To require absolute reciprocity as a condition precedent to jurisdictional competence would potentially limit the reach of the section and undermine the goals of international co-operation which underlie the power to order the taking of commission evidence, even in situations where the foreign country, if not the actual requesting court, stands ready to provide similar assistance to a Canadian court.

Doherty J.A.'s reasoning in this regard was followed by Lax J. of the Ontario Court (General Division) in *Germany (Federal Republic) v. Kretz, supra*, at pp. 692–693.

§3.2 Exercising Discretion

(a) Comity between nations, public policy and Canadian sovereignty

If the four prerequisites discussed in the previous sections are met, s. 46 provides that the court or judge "may, in its or their discretion," make an order under that section. As a general rule, the principle of comity of nations requires that a liberal approach should be taken to requests for judicial assistance (see the following decisions: *R. v. Zingre, supra*, at p. 472; *United States District Court, Middle District of Florida v. Royal American Shows Inc., supra*, at p. 130; *France (Republic) v. De Havilland Aircraft of Canada Ltd., supra*, at pp. 460-461; and *Germany (Federal Republic) v. Kretz, supra*, at p. 695.

In *R. v. Zingre*, Dickson J. added, at p. 479, that, where there is a treaty between the requesting and the requested state imposing a duty on the latter to give effect to requests for legal assistance, s. 46 must be given a fair and liberal interpretation with a view to fulfilling Canada's international obligations. Note, however, that letters rogatory requests do not require that an international arrangement governing such requests be in place between the requesting and the requested states.

A Canadian court may exercise its discretion against granting judicial assistance where to grant the assistance would violate Canadian public policy or impinge upon Canadian sovereignty (see *R. v. Zingre*, *supra*, at p. 472; *Uszinska v. France (Republic)*, *supra*, §1.0, at p. 42; *France (Republic) v. De Havilland Aircraft of Canada Ltd.*, *supra*, at p. 463; and *Germany (Federal Republic) v. Kretz*, *supra*, at p. 695).

In *France (Republic) v. De Havilland Aircraft of Canada*, *supra*, Doherty J.A. elaborated on the meaning of "Canadian sovereignty" in this context, at p. 463:

> The considerations encompassed by the phrase "Canadian sovereignty" are well summarized by Freedman and Harney, *supra*, at pp. 371-8, and include an assessment of whether the request would give extra-territorial authority to foreign laws which violate relevant Canadian or provincial laws, *e.g.*, see *Re Westinghouse Electric Corp. and Duquesne Light Co.* (1977), 78 D.L.R. (3d) 3, 31 C.P.R. (2d) 164, 16 O.R. (2d) 273 (H.C.); whether granting the request would infringe on recognized Canadian moral or legal principles, *e.g.*, see *Re Westinghouse Electric Corp. and Duquesne Light Co.*, *supra*, at p. 21, and whether the request would impose an undue burden on, or do prejudice to the individual whose evidence is requested.

In this case, at first instance, an order was made under s. 46 by a judge of the Ontario Supreme Court appointing a provincial court judge as a commissioner to take evidence from a representative of a corporation pursuant to a letters rogatory request issued by an examining magistrate of the High Court in France. The request was in relation to a complaint filed with the High Court alleging that a named individual had misappropriated commissions payable from a Canadian company to his personal use. The complaint accused the person of theft and breach of trust and possession of stolen property. At the time the order was made it was unopposed by the Canadian corporation and was without notice to the potential defendant (at the time of the order, the person had not yet been charged with any criminal offence).

In light of the general principles he enunciated in the above passage, Doherty J.A. upheld the order of the Ontario Supreme Court judge (at p. 463). Firstly, he found that the request did not infringe upon any recognized Canadian legal or moral principles. The applicant had argued that the production of certain documents under the order violated s. 1 of the Ontario *Business Records Protection Act* (R.S.O. 1980, c. 56), which placed certain restrictions on the sending of Ontario business records outside of Ontario. Doherty J.A. held that the Act likely did not apply to the order and, even if the Act did apply, this was an issue to be determined by the commissioner (the same argument was raised in *Germany (Federal Republic) v. Kretz*, *supra*, at p. 699; Lax J. of the Ontario Court (General Division) dismissed the argument on the basis of Doherty J.A.'s holding on the same point in *France (Republic) v. De Havilland Aircraft of Canada Ltd.*, that is, that the section does not apply to s. 46 of the *Canada Evidence Act*). Secondly, Doherty J.A. concluded that the order requested by the Republic of France did not impose an undue burden on, or prejudice to, the examinee. The information sought from the examinee was clearly set out in the request and was readily available to the examinee. Finally, he found that the interests of justice required the making of the order. If it were not made, the evidence — which was found to be material to the matter before the French court — would be unavailable (at pp. 463-464).

(b) No examination of accused for use against accused

In *Uszinska v. France (Republic), supra*, Robins J. of the Ontario High Court of Justice concluded that an order for the taking of commission evidence under s. 46 will not be granted if, as in that case, the prospective examinee is an accused in pending criminal proceedings in the requesting court and the testimony sought is for the purpose of such proceedings (at p. 42). Granting the request in these circumstances would violate the person's right against self-incrimination. As put by Robins J., at p. 42:

> In my view, since the order required to enforce the letters rogatory in those circumstances would be in conflict with basic notions of justice in Canada, the request of the foreign Court should be denied. The law in this country, unlike apparently the law in France, does not permit a prosecutor to compel the examination of an accused.

(c) Scope of order

Jones J. of the New Brunswick Court of Queen's Bench in *Seminole Electric Coop Inc. v. BBC Brown Boveri, Inc.* (1987), 35 D.L.R. (4th) 102 (N.B.Q.B.), at pp. 109-110, and Craig J. for the Ontario High Court of Justice in *Scholnick v. Bank of Nova Scotia* (1987), 59 O.R. (2d) 538 (Ont. H.C.), at p. 543, refused to order the production of documents under s. 46 where the requests were too broad or vague. In both cases, the judges found that there was no power in the court to limit or read down the requests.

However, more recent case law indicates that the courts may have the authority to limit requests. In *Fecht v. Deloitte & Touche, supra*, at p. 419, the Ontario Court of Appeal made the following comment:

> In his reasons for judgment, Blair J. asserted that courts in Ontario have no power to attempt to narrow the request contained in letters rogatory to relevant documentation and if the requested documentation or any part of it is not relevant (which he found to be the case here), the letters rogatory should be denied in their entirety. Counsel for the respondents acknowledged, and we agree, that Blair J. erred in this regard: see *Acton v. Merle Norman Cosmetics Inc.*, [1992] O.J. No. 43 (C.A.). However, we find this error

to be of little significance since any attempt by Blair J. to fashion an order narrowing the request before the court would have been virtually impossible.

Notwithstanding the principle of comity between nations, the court or judge is only to consider the request specified in the letters rogatory. The court or judge is not to go beyond the request (see *Northbrook Insurance Co. v. Marsh & McLennan Ltd.*, [1980] 2 W.W.R. 271 (B.C.S.C.), affirmed in part, [1980] 6 W.W.R. 8 (B.C.C.A.), *Douglas v. Small* (1983), 43 B.C.L.R. 21 (B.C.S.C.), at p. 22, and Freedman and Harney, *supra*, at p. 382). Moreover, the only persons who can be affected by an order made under s. 46 of the *Canada Evidence Act* are those persons named in the letters rogatory (see *Medical Ancillary Services v. Sperry Rand Corp.* (1979), 95 D.L.R. (3d) 735 (Ont. H.C.), at p. 736, *Northbrook Insurance Co. v. Marsh & McLennan Ltd.*, *supra*, and Freedman and Harney, *supra*).

(d) No order for corroboration of available evidence

In *Seminole Electric Co-op Inc. v. BBC Brown Boveri, Inc. supra*, at p. 108, Jones J. of the New Brunswick Court of Queen's Bench held that an application for letters rogatory will be refused where the evidence sought is to provide a basis for corroboration of evidence that is already available to the foreign court. The same principle was affirmed in *Westinghouse Electric Corp.* (1977), 78 D.L.R. (3d) 3 (Ont. H.C.), at p. 16, and in *Ehrman v. Ehrman*, [1896] 2 Ch. 611 (Eng. C.A.), at pp. 614-615.

(e) Order may be granted for production of documents alone

Laskin C.J.C., on behalf of the Supreme Court of Canada in *United States District Court, Middle District of Florida v. Royal American Shows Inc.*, *supra*, at pp. 130-131, held that a court may grant a request under s. 46 (then s. 43) for the production of documents alone. Moreover, it is not necessary for such a request to be ancillary to an order for examination of a specific witness.

(f) Orders in relation to government documents

The case law has dealt with two aspects of letters rogatory requests for government documents. At the first instance level in *United States District Court, Middle District of Florida v. Royal American Shows Inc.*, *supra*, Miller J. of the Alberta Court of Queen's Bench held that letters rogatory may be enforced by the court of one province with respect to documents then held by an employee of a federal department in another province, at pp. 296-297 (reversed by the Alberta Court of Appeal on other grounds, *supra*, judgment restored by the Supreme Court of Canada, the court not dealing with this point, *supra*).

In *Gulf Oil Corp. v. Gulf Canada Ltd.*, [1980] 2 S.C.R. 39, at p. 53, Laskin C.J.C. refused to exercise the discretion of the court in favour of enforcing letters rogatory from the United States. The refusal was based on federal government policy, the *Uranium Information Security Regulations*, that prohibited disclosure of the documents sought by the United States. (This case was unusual in that the letters rogatory application was made to the Supreme Court of Canada. Laskin C.J.C. acknowledged, at pp. 53-54, that it would generally be appropriate for such applications to be made to the provincial superior court. However, he decided to assume jurisdiction over the matter because the Supreme Court of Canada (prior to 1984) did have jurisdiction under Part II of the *Canada Evidence Act* and the merits of the application had been fully argued before the court.) Thus, a court faced with a letters rogatory request for government documents should be alert to any governmental policy concerning the disclosure of the documents. This reasoning would appear to be applicable to provincial as well as federal government documents.

§4.0 STANDING OF ACCUSED OR POTENTIAL ACCUSED TO CHALLENGE S. 46 ORDER

In *France (Republic) v. De Havilland Aircraft of Canada Ltd.* (1989), 50 C.C.C. (3d) 167 (Ont. H.C.), at p. 169, McRae J. recognized the standing of the potential accused (even though he was not the prospective examinee) to challenge the issuance of an order under s. 46 of the *Canada Evidence Act*:

> The party moving before me, Alexandre Byron-Exarcos, clearly has an interest in the subject-matter of the proceedings and he may be adversely affected by the judgment. As the subject of criminal proceedings, for which the evidence is requested, no one has a greater interest than he.

McRae J. was reversed by the Ontario Court of Appeal, but without reference to this point ((1991), 3 O.R. (3d) 705). However, the subsequent decision of the Ontario Court of Appeal in *United Kingdom v. Ramsden* (1996), 108 C.C.C. (3d) 289, in the mutual legal assistance context, indicates that the target of an investigation has no automatic standing to challenge investigative orders of this nature. Charron J.A. explained as follows, at p. 304:

> Nothing in the [*Mutual Legal Assistance in Criminal Matters Act*] could be interpreted as giving the target of an investigation automatic standing in any of the proceedings. In fact, the adoption of such a principle would arguably run contrary to the stated objective of the mutual legal assistance scheme to provide the widest measure of mutual legal assistance in criminal matters in a prompt and efficient manner. . . .
>
> It has never been recognized in this jurisdiction in other related contexts that automatic standing be granted to the target of a criminal investigation: see for example *R. v. Model Power* (1981), 21 C.R. (3d) 195 (Ont. C.A.); *R. v. Pugliese* (1992), 71 C.C.C. (3d) 295 (Ont. C.A.); *R. v. Edwards* (1996), 192 N.R. 81, 104 C.C.C. (3d) 136 (S.C.C.).

§5.0 APPLICABILITY OF CANADIAN LAW TO PROCEEDINGS UNDER S. 46 OF *CANADA EVIDENCE ACT*

In *United States v. Pressey* (1988), 51 D.L.R. (4th) 152 (Ont. C.A.), leave to appeal to S.C.C. refused (1989), 57 D.L.R. (4th) viii (S.C.C.), the Ontario Court of Appeal was faced with the issue of what law applies to proceedings before a commissioner under s. 46 of the *Canada Evidence Act*. In that case, the United States had made an application to O'Leary J. of the Ontario Court (General Division) under s. 43 (now s. 46) for assistance in obtaining the testimony of Mr. Pressey. The application was granted and the order was made for the examination under oath of Mr. Pressey. Mr. Pressey attended with counsel before the commissioner named in the order (a provincial court judge). However, after being sworn, Mr. Pressey's counsel indicated that Mr. Pressey was claiming the protection of s. 47 of the *Canada Evidence Act* (now s. 50) and the Fifth Amendment of the U.S. *Constitution*. Section 50(1) and (2) of the *Canada Evidence Act* currently provides as follows:

> **50.** (1) Any person examined under any order made under this Part has the like right to refuse to answer questions tending to criminate himself, or other questions, as a party or witness, as the case may be, would have in any cause pending in the court by which, or by a judge whereof, the order is made.

> (2) No person shall be compelled to produce, under any order referred to in subsection (1), any writing or other document that he could not be compelled to produce at a trial of such a cause.

In response to Mr. Pressey's request, counsel for the United States filed with the commissioner an order from the United States District Court described as an immunity order. The order provided that the testimony of Mr. Pressey, and any derivative evidence, would not be used against him in any matter in the United States. However, Mr. Pressey nonetheless persisted in his refusal to answer questions put to him.

The matter was then adjourned and a second application was brought before O'Leary J. by counsel for the United States for an order compelling Mr. Pressey to attend before the commissioner and answer questions put to him by counsel for the United States. Counsel for the United States argued that Mr. Pressey was entitled to the benefit of s. 47, but that the "like right to refuse to answer" in that section only included the right under s. 5 of the *Canada Evidence Act* (and now entrenched in a somewhat different form in s. 13 of the *Charter*) not to have evidence tending to incriminate the witness used against him or her. In other words, Mr. Pressey would have to answer the questions, but his answers could not be used against him. Counsel for Mr. Pressey argued that his client was entitled to the protection of the Fifth Amendment, excusing him from answering the questions at all. O'Leary J. concluded that the U.S. *Constitution* did not apply to evidence given before a commissioner and that the *Canada Evidence Act* and *Charter* did not excuse Mr. Pressey from answering the questions.

Zuber J.A. on behalf of the Ontario Court of Appeal upheld the decision of O'Leary J. In so doing, he affirmed the principle that proceedings before a commissioner pursuant to what is now s. 46 of the *Canada Evidence Act* are governed by Canadian law, at p. 154:

> Despite the fact that the process is initiated by a foreign court, ss. 43 to 48 [now ss. 46-51] make it clear that the examination is controlled by and rests on the authority of a Canadian court. The legal process that takes place in this country is not a mere extension of the requesting court, but is an independent process conducted to assist the requesting court. Therefore, the forum in which Mr. Pressey is examined retains its character as a Canadian forum and the ordinary rule that evidentiary matters are governed by the law of the forum should apply.

Zuber J.A. added that the law of the requesting state will only be considered in connection with technical rules of evidence, at p. 155:

> In my respectful view, however, this willingness to accommodate the evidentiary rules of the requesting court extends only to what might be described as the technical rules of evidence. For example, if a foreign jurisdiction regards hearsay as admissible then there would be little point in excluding such evidence in an examination taking place in this country. Certainly the witness would have little or no interest in whether or not he recounted hearsay.
>
> However, different considerations must apply when more fundamental values are involved and where the rights of the witness are at stake.

Zuber J.A. noted that this view was implicitly recognized by Robins J. of the Ontario High Court of Justice in *Uszinska v. France (Republic)*, *supra*. In that case, the person whose evidence was sought was the subject of criminal proceedings in France. In the latter country, the person would have been a compellable witness. In Canada, by contrast, as an accused, the person would have an absolute right to refuse to testify. Robins J. refused to make the order on the following basis, at pp. 42–43:

> In a situation of this nature, it would be wrong, in my opinion, to make an order exposing the respondent to a questioning not authorized by our law or denying her the full protection of our criminal process. A person in Ontario ought not to be subjected to a form of interrogation in respect to a foreign prosecution to which he could not be subjected if the prosecution against him was being conducted here.

After referring to this passage, Zuber J.A. made the following comment, at p. 156:

> In effect, Robins J. refused to accept the French law with respect to compellability and preserved the right of the person in question to refuse to testify.

In the case at hand the position is reversed. It is the witness who claims the applicability of the foreign law on the grounds that it affords a greater protection than does our own. In my view, however, the principle remains the same. In fundamental matters, it is the law of this country which applies to examinations authorized by s. 43 [now s. 46].

In issuing an order for the examination of witnesses in *Switzerland v. Tedball* (July 28, 1989), Weiler J. of the Ontario Supreme Court relied on the Ontario Court of Appeal's decision in *United States v. Pressey, supra,* in concluding that the Canadian rules regarding claims of solicitor-client privilege applied to proceedings before a commissioner under s. 46. Weiler J. stated, at p. 2:

After counsel for the applicant had reviewed the relevant case law I raised the question as to whether Messrs. Brogden and Spisani might claim solicitor-client privilege. Counsel responded that, since Canadian law applied (*United States v. Pressey* (Ont. C.A.) (unreported, March 16, 1988) [since reported (1988), 51 D.L.R. (4th) 152], the order should nevertheless issue and if counsel wished to claim privilege the claim should be made before the Commissioner. The order, it is argued, is analogous to a subpoena to a witness. Once the witness attends in court a claim for privilege may be made but the witness is still ordered to attend.

§6.0 PROCEDURE AND MATERIALS IN SUPPORT OF APPLICATION

The letters rogatory provisions in the *Canada Evidence Act* do not specify the procedure by which a letters rogatory request made by a foreign jurisdiction to Canada is initiated and executed. Section 46 indicates that the request is made by a "court or tribunal" in the requesting jurisdiction to a "court or judge" in Canada. The terms "court" and "judge," on the Canadian side of the request, are defined in s. 44 as a superior court of a province or a judge of that court. Accordingly, the only guidance provided by the Act is that the process involves a request from a foreign court to a superior court of a Canadian province.

Typically, a foreign court or tribunal making a letters rogatory request will submit the request to the Canadian Department of Justice. The International Assistance Group (IAG), a special department of the Department of Justice's Criminal Law Branch in Ottawa, which co-ordinates extradition and mutual legal assistance requests, will receive the request. If the request appears to be in order, the request and the supporting materials will then be sent to the appropriate regional office of the Department of Justice. Counsel from that office will be assigned to ensure the execution of the request. In some provinces, the provincial Crown will take charge of the matter when the subject matter of the request would, in this country, be prosecuted under provincial jurisdiction.

However, the initiation and execution of the request need not proceed via a government channel. As mentioned, the legislation merely indicates that the request is to be made by a foreign court to a Canadian court. There is no requirement that counsel from the Canadian government handle the request. Rather, in some instances, the requesting court may retain private counsel to handle the request. For example, in the case of *Germany (Federal Republic) v. Kretz, supra*, the requesting court (the Local Court of Stuttgart), through the German consulate in Toronto, retained a private law firm to handle the letters rogatory request.

The usual practice in Ontario, when the matter is handled by the Department of Justice, is as follows:

1.   An application is brought before a judge of the superior court of the province to obtain an order that the registrar of the court prepare and issue a commission.

2.   Section 51(2) of the *Canada Evidence Act* deems that the letters rogatory from the foreign court is sufficient evidence to support the application, in the absence of any order to the contrary. While there is no requirement for an affidavit, the notice of application will nevertheless frequently be supported by one, often sworn by a member of a law enforcement agency, or by a paralegal who is assisting counsel who has carriage of the matter.

3.   Such an affidavit will summarize the request, including the alleged foreign offences and the supporting facts. If information obtained in Canada is relevant to the application, it may be included as well, such as the location of the witnesses sought to be examined or of the requested materials.

4.   Since the application is analogous to the issuance of a subpoena, notice to the witnesses is not required for the application (*Switzerland v. Tedball, supra*). However, applications may be made in open court or on notice, particularly when there are no concerns regarding potential evasion of service or destruction of evidence, as in the case of institutional witnesses such as banks and telephone companies.

5.   The order designates a commissioner. In Ontario, the order has often appointed the senior regional judge of the provincial court, or such other judge of that court as the senior regional judge may appoint, as the commissioner. However, the commissioner need not be a provincial court judge. For example, the order may appoint as the commissioner another counsel in the same office as counsel making the application. There is nothing to preclude a person who is not legally trained from being appointed as the commissioner. The appointment of the commissioner is within the discretion of the issuing Canadian court.

6.   Any requests for foreign officials to attend the examination and/or question the witnesses may be given effect in the order.

7.   The order directs the registrar of the Superior Court to issue a commission directed to the named commissioner and frames the terms by which the commission is to be conducted. The order will identify the witnesses to be examined and the documents to be produced.

8.   After the order is granted, the commission will be taken out with the registrar of the Superior Court. Section 51 of the *Canada Evidence Act* provides that the court may frame rules and orders in relation to the procedure to be followed. For example, in Ontario, the usual practice is that the issuing court will set out, in the commission document, that the procedure to be followed for the examination be in accordance with the Ontario *Rules of Civil Procedure* for examinations out of court (Rules 34 to 36 dealing with the procedure on oral examinations). The commission document may contain other instructions such as the oath to be administered and instructions to ensure that the transcript of the evidence and the exhibits be delivered to the court office.

9.   A copy of the order and the commission will be delivered to the commissioner. The commissioner signs the notice of hearing as required by s. 47 of the *Canada Evidence Act*.

10.   A date is selected that is convenient to the commissioner and counsel (and the witnesses if they are co-operative). The witnesses will be served with the order (s. 47 of the *Canada Evidence Act*), the commission, the notice of examination, and conduct money (ss. 47 and 48 of the *Canada Evidence Act*). In Ontario, because of Rule 34 of the *Rules of Civil Procedure*, the notice of examination is signed by counsel handling the request.

§7.0 EXAMINATION OF WITNESSES AND PRODUCTION OF DOCUMENTS UNDER S. 46 OF *CANADA EVIDENCE ACT*

When an order under s. 46 of the *Canada Evidence Act* requires that a witness be examined, the witness will be required to attend at the location set out in the applicable notice of attendance. The location may be a court, if the examination is to be held before a judge, or it may be the Department of Justice or some other law office, or any other location specified in the notice. The commissioner will preside over the proceedings. There is nothing to preclude the witness from being accompanied by counsel. The other persons in attendance will be the counsel appearing on behalf of the requesting foreign state, who may, as indicated above, be from either the Department of Justice or a private law firm. If counsel from the Department of Justice is handling the matter on behalf of the requesting state, they may have recruited the assistance of local police officers with respect to locating and serving the witness and acting as affiant on the application itself. The order may provide for the local police officers to be in attendance to assist counsel. The order may also provide for the attendance of foreign investigating officers or foreign counsel for the purpose of assisting counsel and/or questioning the witnesses.

The proceedings will be recorded by a reporter since the requesting state usually, for their purposes, will require a transcript. The commissioner will administer the oath or affirmation of the witnesses as required by s. 49 of the *Canada Evidence Act*. The pertinent documentation may be filed on the record. This includes the commission, the order under s. 46, and any other documentation counsel deems appropriate, such as proof of service of the witnesses and payment of conduct money in case of non-attendance (ss. 47 and 48 *Canada Evidence Act*).

The witness will be questioned. If documentation is produced, it may be expected to be identified and recorded by way of an exhibit stamp and number.

The Ontario commission documents refer to conducting the examination in accordance with the *Rules of Civil Procedure* for the examination of witnesses for discovery. Counsel for the witness may instruct his or her client not to answer certain questions. Any objections to questions which cannot be resolved at the examination, or any refusals to answer questions, will be dealt with pursuant to rule 34.12 which requires that the court make a ruling on the propriety of the question. If the superior court judge orders that questions be answered, any subsequent refusal by the witness would necessitate a contempt application to be brought before the superior court (see rule 34.15; see also *United States v. Pressey* (September 6, 1988), Doc. CA 409/88, [1988] O.J. No. 1494 (Ont. C.A.), where a contempt order issued by the superior court for a refusal to testify was upheld by the Ontario Court of Appeal).

Similarly, contempt applications for non-attendance would have to be brought before the superior court pursuant to rule 34.15. Section 47 of the *Canada Evidence Act* also provides for the court to enforce the commission orders:

> **47.** On the service on the party or witness of an order referred to in section 46, and of an appointment of a time and place for the examination of the party or witness signed by the person named in the order for taking the examination, or, if more than one person is named, by one of the persons named, and on payment or tender of the like conduct money as is properly payable on attendance at a trial, the order may be enforced in like manner as an order made by the court or judge in a cause pending in that court or before that judge.

The conduct of the examination may vary depending upon what is required for the foreign proceeding. For instance, if the foreign state intends to use the evidence for their domestic trial purposes, it may want counsel for the accused person to be in attendance or be allowed to examine the witness. If this is the case, it would be advisable to have this included as a provision in the order issued under s. 46.

If all that the foreign state requires is the production of documents without the necessity of *viva voce* evidence, then the documents may be submitted in whichever way the foreign state requires them for the purposes of their proceedings. It may be that an affidavit describing and attaching the documents and sworn by an affiant who has custody of and/or familiarity with the documents will suffice. This is similar to what would be permissible in Canada for the introduction of documents pursuant to ss. 29 and 30 of the *Canada Evidence Act*. Alternatively, the documents may be submitted alone, without an accompanying affidavit. In either case, the documents would normally contain an indication that they were submitted to the commissioner in accordance with the order.

With respect to transmission of the evidence to the foreign court, once the evidence and documentation is submitted by the commissioner to the registrar following the conclusion of the examination, the material will be released to counsel handling the matter on behalf of the foreign state.

§8.0 CONSIDERATIONS WITH RESPECT TO CANADIAN REQUESTS FOR INVESTIGATIVE ASSISTANCE ABROAD

The *Charter* does not govern the actions of foreign police acting pursuant to a Canadian request for legal assistance. This was established by the Supreme Court of Canada in *R. v. Terry*, 106 C.C.C. (3d) 508, [1996] 2 S.C.R. 207, and *R. v. Harrer*, 101 C.C.C. (3d) 193, [1995] 3 S.C.R. 562.

In *Terry*, the accused had been arrested in the United States as a result of a Canadian extradition request. He had been charged in Canada with a fatal stabbing. Subsequent to the arrest, the Canadian police made an informal request (that is, their request was not made through a formal mechanism, such as a request under s. 46 of the *Canada Evidence Act* or under a mutual legal assistance treaty) to the U.S. police to obtain a statement from the accused. The U.S. police acted on this request and in so doing, complied with the American legal requirements for taking a statement. At his subsequent trial in Canada, the accused argued that his statement was inadmissible under s. 24(2) of the *Charter* because the conduct of the U.S. police did not comply with the Canadian *Charter* requirements applicable to post-arrest statements.

The Supreme Court of Canada refused to give effect to this assertion, and held that the practice of cooperation between police forces did not make the law of one country applicable to the other. The *Charter*, the court held, could not govern the conduct of foreign police cooperating informally with Canadian police. McLachlin J. commented, at p. 217 S.C.R.:

> The personal decision of a foreign officer or agency to assist the Canadian police cannot dilute the exclusivity of the foreign state's sovereignty within its territory, where its law alone governs the process of enforcement. The gathering of evidence by these foreign officers or agency is subject to the rules of that country and none other.

McLachlin J. pointed out however that any potential unfairness to the accused at the latter's trial in Canada could be addressed under s. 11(d) and s. 7 of the *Charter*, at pp. 218-219 S.C.R.:

The *Charter* guarantees the accused a fair trial: s. 11(d). More specifically, the *Charter* provides that the accused's liberty cannot be limited except in accordance with the principles of fundamental justice: s. 7. To admit evidence gathered in an abusive fashion may well violate the principles of fundamental justice. . . . The accused may use these and other principles of fundamental justice to obtain redress for abuses abroad in gathering evidence subsequently tendered against him or her.

In *R. v. Harrer, supra,* the accused also challenged the admissibility at her trial in Canada of a statement obtained in the United States by American authorities carrying out their duties under American law. Harrer had been arrested by immigration authorities in the United States. The immigration officials had been accompanied by American police who suspected that Harrer had assisted her boyfriend to escape from jail in Canada where he had been in custody on an American extradition request. Questioning by the American officers led to a statement which was used against her at her trial in Canada for assisting in this escape. The issue was whether the interrogation infringed s. 10(*b*) of the *Charter* and whether it should be excluded under s. 24(2).

La Forest J., writing one of the two judgments for a unanimous Supreme Court, held that the *Charter* did not apply where the acts in question were wholly those of American authorities, at p. 571 S.C.R.:

> What I think is determinative against the argument that the *Charter* applied to the interrogation in the present case is the simple fact that the United States immigration officials and the Marshals were not acting on behalf of any of the governments of Canada, the provinces or the territories, the state actors to which, by virtue of s. 32(1) the application of the *Charter* is confined; see *RWDSU* v. *Dolphin Delivery Ltd.*, [1986] 2 S.C.R. 573. It follows that the *Charter* simply has no direct application to the interrogations in the United States because the governments mentioned in s. 32(1) were not implicated in these activities.

However, in *R. v. Cook*, [1998] 2 S.C.R. 597, the majority of the Supreme Court of Canada determined that Canadian officers who were in the United States investigating a suspect in a Canadian offence were subject to Canadian *Charter* standards. Thus, the court held that a statement taken from Cook by two Canadian officers who interviewed him in a United States prison was governed by Canadian procedural *Charter* requirements and was subject to exclusion under s. 24(2) of the *Charter* at the Canadian trial, for failure to advise him properly of his s. 10(*b*) rights.

§8.1 Non-Applicability of *Charter* to Preparation of Letter of Request in Canada by Canadian Officials

In *Schreiber v. Canada (Attorney General)* (1998), 124 C.C.C. (3d) 129, [1998] 1 S.C.R. 841, a majority of the Supreme Court of Canada held that the *Charter* does not apply to the preparation of the letter of request in Canada by Canadian authorities. In this case, Canada sent a letter of request to Switzerland seeking assistance in the investigation of an alleged criminal offence. In response to the letter of request the Swiss authorities issued an order which resulted in the seizure of the respondent's banking documents and records from accounts held in Switzerland. (At the time of the request, September 29, 1995, Canada and Switzerland had not yet entered into a mutual legal assistance treaty. On November 17, 1995, these two countries did enter such a treaty.)

L'Heureux-Dubé J. on behalf of herself and three other judges of the court held that the actions of the Swiss authorities, which were undertaken according to Swiss law, were not subject to *Charter* scrutiny. Furthermore, the letter of request itself did not engage s. 8 of the *Charter*, and prior judicial authorization to send it was held not to be a requirement. L'Heureux-Dubé J. noted, at p. 860 S.C.R.:

> By itself, the letter of request does not engage s. 8 of the *Charter*. All of those actions which rely on state compulsion in order to interfere with the respondent's privacy interests were undertaken in Switzerland by Swiss authorities. Neither the actions of the Swiss authorities, nor the laws which authorized their actions, are subject to *Charter* scrutiny: *R. v. Terry*, [1996] 2 S.C.R. 207, at p. 217. The *Charter* does not protect everyone against unreasonable search and seizure in the abstract. Rather, the *Charter* guarantees everyone the right to be secure against unreasonable search and seizure by, *inter alia*, the government of Canada. [Emphasis in original.]

L'Heureux-Dubé J. acknowledged that s. 8 of the *Charter* protects people rather than places or things. However, she pointed out that it only protects people against actions of the Canadian government that interfere with a person's privacy interest through an unreasonable search or seizure. L'Heureux-Dubé J. thus concluded, at p. 861 S.C.R.:

> Therefore, it *does* matter where the search or seizure took place, if it took place outside Canada by persons not under the authority of the government of Canada. Clearly, the government of Canada did not undertake any search or seizure. Canadian officials merely requested that a search or seizure be undertaken. Because those actions that are properly subjected to *Charter* review under s. 8 were undertaken by foreign officials, the respondent instead has sought to implicate those actions undertaken in Canada which requested the search and seizure in Switzerland. But as Stone J.A. [in the Federal Court of Appeal] stated at p. 207:
>
> > To conclude that section 8 is engaged because Canadian authorities sent the request to Switzerland even though they could not and did not conduct any search and seizure there would be to contort the language of this important protection and to give it application where no governmental action of the kind envisaged by the section is involved.

Lamer C.J.C. also allowed the appeal, but on the basis that the respondent Schreiber did not have a reasonable expectation of privacy in his banking records and thus he could not benefit from s. 8 protection. He stated, at p. 857 S.C.R.:

On the facts of this case, therefore, a search carried out by foreign authorities, in a foreign country, in accordance with foreign law does not infringe a person's reasonable expectation of privacy, as he or she cannot reasonably expect more privacy than he or she is entitled to under that foreign law. In the case at bar, there is no evidence that the respondent's records were seized illegally in Switzerland.

The Supreme Court of Canada has clearly curtailed the applicability of the *Charter* with respect to Canadian applications for foreign assistance.

APPENDIX B
THE *MUTUAL LEGAL ASSISTANCE IN CRIMINAL MATTERS ACT* AND MUTUAL LEGAL ASSISTANCE AGREEMENTS

§1.0 OVERVIEW

§1.1 Purpose of Act and Agreements

In 1988, Parliament enacted the *Mutual Legal Assistance in Criminal Matters Act* (the "Act"), R.S.C. 1985, c. 30 (4th Supp.). The Act came into force on October 1, 1988 (SI/88-199, *Canada Gazette*, Part II, vol. 122:22). The purpose of the Act is to implement bilateral and multilateral agreements relating to the provision of legal assistance in criminal matters by Canada to foreign states and entities (see *R. v. Filonov* (1993), 82 C.C.C. (3d) 516 (Ont. Gen. Div.), at pp. 525–526; *United Kingdom v. Ramsden* (1996), 108 C.C.C. (3d) 289 (Ont. C.A.), at pp. 294–295; and *United Kingdom v. Hrynyk* (1996), 107 C.C.C. (3d) 104 (Ont. Gen. Div.), at p. 107).

Charron J.A. in *United Kingdom v. Ramsden, supra*, at p. 294, described the purpose of the Act with reference to the speech of the Minister of Justice at the time the bill was introduced:

> At the time that the bill was introduced in Parliament for second reading, the Minister of Justice summed up the purpose of the bill as follows:
>
> > It has long been recognized that no nation can exist in isolation. Indeed, states have always regarded international co-operation as being essential to their good relations. In criminal matters, such co-operation has traditionally taken the following forms: extradition, commissioned evidence, service of documents issued by a foreign court and informal co-operation between police forces.
> >
> > These types of assistance, although still useful and necessary, were developed at a time when crimes were not normally committed beyond the boundaries of any one country. Because of the spectacular increase in means of communication and transportation, criminals are no longer inhibited by territorial boundaries. Quite the contrary, criminals take advantage of the traditional notion of territorial jurisdiction to escape detection and prosecution.
> >
> > Crime is no longer a local or national affair. It is now transnational. A transnational crime can be described as a crime whose planning or execution has taken place in two or more countries. Obvious examples of such crimes would include drug

trafficking, crimes associated with terrorism, tax evasion, money laundering, fraud or organized crime.

Transnational crime has become an international problem which requires a solution at an international level. Hence, the purpose of mutual legal assistance in criminal matters.

Subsequently, in the case of *Russian Federation v. Pokidyshev* (1999), 138 C.C.C. (3d) 321 (Ont. C.A.), Doherty J.A. commented on the purpose of the Act in the following terms, at pp. 327–328:

> [15] The purpose of this *Act* is clear. By 1988, when the *Act* was proclaimed, international crime had become a major problem. Criminals, especially sophisticated ones, used the limits imposed on police and prosecutors by national borders to facilitate their criminal schemes and avoid detection: *United Kingdom v. Ramsden* (1996), 108 C.C.C. (3d) 289 (Ont. C.A.) at 294–95, *sub nom. United Kingdom v. James and Boyden*, leave to appeal to S.C.C. refused May 1, 1997 [reported 114 C.C.C. (3d) vi]. In 1988, Canada had international obligations under various treaties and conventions to assist other states in the investigation and detection of crime, but had no domestic legislation in place to provide the necessary assistance and cooperation. The *Act* filled that void and must be read with that purpose in mind.
>
> [16] The *Act* addresses various kinds of help that Canada and foreign states can provide to each other in their efforts to combat international crime.

The following bilateral mutual legal assistance treaties are currently in force:

Canada/Austria (December 1, 1997)	1997 *Canada Gazette* Part I, p. 3889 (Vol. 131, No. 52)
Canada/Australia (March 14, 1990)	1990 *Canada Gazette* Part I, p. 1582
Canada/Bahamas (July 10, 1990)	1990 *Canada Gazette* Part I, p. 3074
Canada/China (July 1, 1995)	1995 *Canada Gazette* Part I, p. 2866
Canada/Czech Republic (November 1, 2000)	2000 *Canada Gazette* Part I, p. 3641 (Vol. 134, No. 50)
Canada/France (May 1, 1991)	1991 *Canada Gazette* Part I, p. 1840
Canada/Hellenic Republic (January 28, 2000)	2000 *Canada Gazette* Part I, p. 686 (Vol. 134, No. 10)
Canada/Hungary (September 1, 1996)	1996 *Canada Gazette* Part I, p. 2925 (Vol. 130, No. 41)
Canada/India (October 25, 1995)	1995 *Canada Gazette* Part I, p. 4028
Canada/Israel (March 16, 2000)	2000 *Canada Gazette* Part I, p. 1066 (Vol. 134, No. 15)
Canada/Italy (December 1, 1995)	1996 *Canada Gazette* Part I, p. 159 (Vol. 130, No. 30)
Canada/Korea (February 1, 1995)	1995 *Canada Gazette* Part I, p. 442 (Vol. 129, No. 12)
Canada/Mexico (October 21, 1990)	1990 *Canada Gazette* Part I, p. 4319

Canada/Netherlands (May 1, 1992)	1992 *Canada Gazette* Part I, p. 1477
Canada/Norway (January 14, 1999)	1999 *Canada Gazette* Part I, p. 293 (Vol. 133, No. 6)
Canada/Peru (January 25, 2000)	2000 *Canada Gazette* Part I, p. 1058 (Vol. 134, No. 15)
Canada/Poland (July 1, 1997)	1997 *Canada Gazette* Part I, p. 2060 (Vol. 131, No. 29)
Canada/Portugal (May 1, 2000)	2000 *Canada Gazette* Part I, p. 2378 (Vol. 134, No. 31)
Canada/Romania (June 30, 1999)	2000 *Canada Gazette* Part I, p. 679 (Vol. 134, No. 10)
Canada/Russia (December 18, 2000)	2000 *Canada Gazette* Part I, p. 227 (Vol. 135, No. 4)
Canada/South Africa (November 12, 1999)	2001 *Canada Gazette* Part I, p. 2209 (Vol. 135, No. 25)
Canada/Spain (March 3, 1995)	1995 *Canada Gazette* Part I, p. 848 (Vol. 129, No. 12)
Canada/Switzerland (November 17, 1995)	1995 *Canada Gazette* Part I, p. 4183
Canada/Thailand (October 3, 1994)	1994 *Canada Gazette* Part I, p. 4260 (Vol. 128, No. 43)
Canada/Ukraine (March 1, 1999)	1999 *Canada Gazette* Part I, p. 762 (Vol. 133, No. 12)
Canada/United Kingdom (September 17, 1993)	1993 *Canada Gazette* Part I, p. 3458 (Vol. 127, No. 46)
Canada/United States (January 24, 1990)	1990 *Canada Gazette* Part I, p. 953

The following multilateral agreements are in force:

InterAmerican Convention on Mutual Legal Assistance in Criminal Matters (July 3, 1996)	1996 *Canada Gazette* Part I (Vol. 130, No. 35)
United Nations Convention Against Illicit Traffic in Narcotic Drugs and Psychotropic Substances (December 19, 1988)	1991 *Canada Gazette* Part I (Vol. 125, No. 1)

The following bilateral mutual legal assistance treaties are signed but not yet in force:

Canada/Argentina (January 12, 2000)
Canada/Belgium (January 11, 1996)
Canada/Brazil (January 27, 1995)
Canada/Hong Kong (February 16, 2001)

Canada/Jamaica (June 3, 1999)
Canada/Sweden (February 15, 2000)
Canada/Trinidad & Tobago (September 4, 1997)
Canada/Uruguay (July 11, 1996)

The act of making a legal assistance request in itself does not depend on or require specific legislation. Rather, the making of a request is a matter of executive decision. Requests may be made pursuant to obligations undertaken by treaty with respect to mutual legal assistance. However, requests for mutual legal assistance may also be made in the absence of a mutual legal assistance agreement (see the discussion of letters rogatory requests in Appendix A above. See also *Schreiber v. Canada (Attorney General)* (1998), 124 C.C.C. (3d) 129 (S.C.C.)).

The above points were set out by Dilks J. in *R. v. Filonov, supra*. Counsel for one of the accused in that case had argued, among other things, that a fatal flaw in the Act and the *Treaty Between the Government of Canada and the Government of the United States of America on Mutual Legal Assistance in Criminal Matters* (hereinafter *Canada–United States Mutual Legal Assistance in Criminal Matters Treaty*) was that the Act did not contain provisions governing the requirements for the making of a request by Canadian authorities to the American authorities to obtain material for use in Canadian proceedings. In dismissing this argument, Dilks J. made the following comment, at p. 526:

> Again, this argument fails to realize the purpose of the Canadian legislation, which is to implement the treaty with respect to the provision of assistance by Canada to the United States. Comparable United States legislation would do the same thing there. The sending of a request by Canada does not require special Canadian legislation. It is simply and wholly a matter of executive decision. Its ultimate authority, if authority there need be, is in the treaty itself.

In 1999, a number of changes and adjustments were made to the Act by ss. 97 to 128 of the new *Extradition Act*. Two of these changes are particularly noteworthy. Firstly, the scope of the Act was extended to include international criminal tribunals, specifically the two tribunals dealing with violations of international law in Rwanda and the former Yugoslavia (ss. 97(3) and 128 of the *Extradition Act*). Secondly, the Act was amended to allow for the taking of "virtual" testimony via the use of video and audio link technology (s. 113 of the *Extradition Act*). The Act was also amended in 2000 by the *Crimes Against Humanity and War Crimes Act*, S.C. 2000, c. 24, ss. 56 to 69.

§1.2 Statutory Scheme

Doherty J.A. in *Russian Federation v. Pokidychev, supra*, summarized the statutory scheme of Part I of the Act, which provides for assistance to foreign investigations, as follows, at pp. 328–329:

[16] . . . This appeal is concerned with Part I of the *Act* which provides various means by which a foreign state can obtain information from sources in Canada to assist that foreign state in its investigation of criminal activity.

[17] The overall scheme of Part I of the *Act* may be described in these terms. The foreign state seeking Canada's assistance must have a treaty with Canada as defined in the *Act* (s. 2). Alternatively, the Minister of Foreign Affairs for Canada must have entered into an administrative arrangement with the foreign state providing for assistance in the particular investigation being conducted by the foreign state (s. 6). If a treaty or administrative arrangement is in place, the foreign state may request the assistance of the Canadian authorities. Requests for assistance made by foreign states under the *Act* must be approved by the Minister of Justice (s. 11(1), s. 17(1)). If the Minister approves the request, a competent Canadian authority (in this case the Attorney General for Ontario) shall, where the request requires a court order for its implementation, make the necessary application to a superior court (s. 11(2), s. 17(2)). If the court grants the order and further orders the material sent to the foreign state, the material can only be sent if the Minister of Justice is satisfied that the foreign state will comply with the terms of the order (s. 16, s. 21).

[18] Under the *Act*, the Minister of Justice serves as the guardian of Canadian sovereignty interests. She effectively controls both ends of the process. No request goes forward without her approval and no sending order is implemented without her approval. The central role of the Minister of Justice in the process reflects the essentially political nature of decisions involving international relations. These decisions properly rest with the executive arm of the federal government which is responsible for the conduct of Canada's foreign relations: *Republic of Argentina v. Mellino* (1987), 33 C.C.C. (3d) 334 at p. 349, 40 D.L.R. (4th) 74 (S.C.C.).

[19] The judiciary also plays a role under Part I of the *Act*. In the request for assistance, the competent authority may seek the issuance of a search warrant (s. 11, s. 12), the examination of persons under oath in Canada (s. 17, s. 18), or the production of documents located in Canada (s. 17, s. 18). These compulsory measures can be invoked only where a judge of the Superior Court of the province so orders (s. 12, s. 18). In making the order, the judge must be satisfied that the statutory conditions precedent to the order have been met. Any information obtained under these orders can be sent to the foreign jurisdiction only if the court so orders (s. 15, s. 20). In exercising its jurisdiction to order information sent to the foreign jurisdiction, the court may place terms and conditions on the sending order (s. 15(1)(*b*), s. 20(2)). In deciding what terms, if any, to impose, the court must consider both the interests of parties affected by the order and the need to give effect to the request made by the foreign state.

Since this decision, the Act has been amended to provide for the designation in Part I of the Act for the United Nations Tribunals for Rwanda and the former Yugoslavia as entities entitled to make mutual legal assistance requests to Canada.

Part II of the Act (ss. 36–39) addresses the admissibility in Canada of evidence obtained in a foreign state under a mutual legal assistance treaty.

Part III of the Act (ss. 40–44) sets out rules in the following areas in connection with Canadian requests for legal assistance: the entry into Canada of persons who are inadmissible under s. 19 of the *Immigration Act* (s. 40); the safe conduct of persons who are in Canada pursuant to a request to give evidence or assistance in a proceeding or investigation (s. 41); the detention in Canada of persons who are in detention in a foreign jurisdiction and who are transferred to Canada pursuant to a mutual legal assistance request (s. 42); the powers of a judge under the Act to determine the validity of a refusal by a person in a foreign jurisdiction to answer a question or produce a document pursuant to a Canadian legal assistance request (s. 43); and the maintenance of privilege for documents sent to the Minister of Justice by a foreign jurisdiction pursuant to a Canadian request (s. 44). The provisions of the Act are discussed in more detail later in the chapter.

The scheme of the legislation does not detract from any informal arrangements between the authorities of different states regarding international cooperation. Section 3(2) of the Act confirms this point. The provision reads as follows:

> (2) Nothing in this Act or an agreement shall be construed so as to abrogate or derogate from an arrangement or practice respecting cooperation between a Canadian competent authority and a foreign or international authority or organization.

§2.0 THE ACT

§2.1 Interpretation and Application (ss. 2–7)

(a) Definitions

(i) *"Competent authority," "central authority"* and *"Minister"*

A "competent authority" is defined in s. 2 of the Act as follows:

> "competent authority" means the Attorney General of Canada, the attorney general of a province or any person or authority with responsibility in Canada for the investigation or prosecution of offences; . . .

In general, the competent authority has two roles. Firstly, the competent authority carries out foreign requests for legal assistance. For instance, the competent authority applies for search warrants under s. 11 of the Act or for evidence-gathering orders under s. 17. Secondly, the competent authority drafts Canadian requests for assistance from foreign jurisdictions.

The manner in which requests for assistance are to be communicated is established by the treaties themselves. For instance, Article I of the *Canada–United States Mutual Legal Assistance in Criminal Matters Treaty* provides as follows:

> "Central Authority" means
>
> (a)   for Canada, the Minister of Justice or officials designated by him;
> (b)   for the United States of America, the Attorney General or officials designated by him; . . .

Article VI of the American Treaty provides that requests must be made by the central authority of the requesting state to the central authority of the requested state. In Canada the central authority is the International Assistance Group of the Department of Justice in Ottawa. In the United States it is the Office of International Affairs in Washington, D.C. Other mutual legal assistance treaties also provide that requests must be made through central authorities (see, for example, Articles V and VI of the *Treaty Between the Government of Canada and the Government of the United Kingdom of Great Britain and Northern Ireland on Mutual Assistance in Criminal Matters*).

While the Act does not define "central authority," its provisions achieve the same result as the treaties. Section 2 defines the term "Minister" as the Minister of Justice. Section 7 lists the two general functions of the Minister under the Act. Firstly, under s. 7(1), "[t]he Minister is responsible for the implementation of every agreement and the administration of this Act." Secondly, under s. 7(2), where a request is presented to the Minister by a foreign jurisdiction or a Canadian competent authority, "the Minister shall deal with the request in accordance with the relevant agreement and this Act." Accordingly, without using the term "central authority," the Act, like the treaties, contemplates that the Minister and Department of Justice will be the central body in Canada responsible for approving requests for assistance made pursuant to mutual legal assistance treaties.

(ii) *"Offence"*

Unlike extradition, as a general rule there is no requirement of dual criminality in the mutual legal assistance context unless a treaty specifically makes provision for it. An "offence" is defined in s. 2 as "an offence within the meaning of the relevant agreement." Thus one must look to the applicable treaty to ascertain the ambit of the term "offence." For instance, when Canada is the requested state, Article I of the *Canada–United States Mutual Legal Assistance in Criminal Matters Treaty* limits the application of the Treaty to indictable offences created by Acts of Parliament and provincial offences falling within any of four categories specified in the Annex to the Treaty, namely, securities, wildlife protection, environmental protection, and consumer protection.

In *Re Dragon Pacific Marketing Inc.* (1998), 127 C.C.C. (3d) 292 (B.C.S.C.), Fraser J. held that there was no requirement for double criminality to be established in order to give effect to an American request for assistance. Similarly, in *Re Stuckey* (2000), (*sub nom. United States of America v. Stuckey*) 151 C.C.C. (3d) 312, the British Columbia Court of Appeal noted that the treaty with the United States specifically states that double criminality is not required. However, the argument in that case was that notwithstanding the terms of the treaty, the *Mutual Legal Assistance in Criminal Matters Act* "must have, to pass constitutional muster, a requirement of double criminality. . . ." The court declined to answer the constitutional question, holding that as the U.S. offences did have their Canadian counterparts, the issue did not arise on the facts (at p. 320, para. 11).

It is possible for Canada to provide assistance on an *ad hoc* basis to a state with which Canada has no treaty. Pursuant to s. 6(1) of the Act, however, one of the prerequisites to entering into such an arrangement to provide assistance is that the foreign investigation must "relat[e] to an act that, if committed in Canada, would be an indictable offence."

(iii) "Agreement"

The term "agreement" is defined broadly in s. 2 of the Act to include bilateral and multilateral agreements dealing at least in part with mutual legal assistance:

> "agreement" means a treaty, convention or other international agreement that is in force, to which Canada is a party and that contains a provision respecting mutual legal assistance in criminal matters; . . .

In the case of *R. v. Filonov*, *supra*, counsel for one of the accused argued that the words "is in force" in s. 2(1) mean that the relevant mutual legal assistance treaty (in that case, the *Canada–United States Mutual Legal Assistance in Criminal Matters Treaty*), to be effective, must have been in force prior to the coming into force of the Act. The Act came into force on October 1, 1988. The Treaty came into force on January 24, 1990. Dilks J. of the Ontario Court (General Division) dismissed this argument. His conclusion was based on the fact that the *Mutual Legal Assistance in Criminal Matters Act* is not enabling but implementing in character, at pp. 525–526:

> Apart from the fact that the *Interpretation Act*, R.S.C. 1985, c. I-21, s. 10, is clearly to the contrary, this might have been an attractive argument except that it also overlooks the fact that the Act is not enabling but implementing in character. Despite Professor Hogg's statement (*Constitutional Law of Canada*, 3rd ed., vol. 1, p. 11-5) that a treaty is not recognized as part of the internal law of Canada, and that therefore any treaty which requires a change in the domestic law of Canada can only be implemented by the enactment of a statute which makes the required change, many treaties, as Professor Hogg also points out, do not require any such change. The only provisions of the treaty which had to be addressed in new Canadian legislation were those that dealt with the procedure whereby assistance was to be given in Canada by Canadian authorities to their counterparts in the United States. The implementation of the treaty and the procedures for extending aid in the United States to Canadian authorities would surely be dealt with in comparable United States legislation, the insufficiency of which has not been argued before me.

(iv) "State or entity" and "requests"

Section 2 provides an expansive definition of a "state or entity," including all subdivisions, possessions, dependencies, and the like, of a state as well as international criminal tribunals designated in the schedule to the Act. The definition reads as follows:

"state or entity" means

(a) a state, a province, state or political subdivision of the state, or a colony, dependency, possession, protectorate, condominium, trust territory or any territory falling under the jurisdiction of the state, that is a party to an agreement with Canada, or

(b) an international criminal court or tribunal, the name of which appears in the schedule; . . .

Section 4 elaborates on the inclusion of international criminal tribunals within the scheme of the Act. Section 4(1) of the Act provides that "[t]he names of international criminal courts and tribunals that appear in the schedule are designated as states or entities for the purpose of this Act." Section 4(2) adds that "[t]he Minister of Foreign Affairs may, with the agreement of the Minister, by order, add to or delete from the schedule the names of international criminal courts and tribunals." Pursuant to s. 128 of the 1999 *Extradition Act*, two tribunals were included in the schedule: those dealing with violations of international law in Rwanda and the former Yugoslavia.

Section 2 defines the term "request" as "a request for assistance presented pursuant to an agreement."

(v) *"Judge"*

Under s. 2, the term "judge" is defined to refer to judges of the superior court of the province.

(vi) *"Data" and "record"*

Section 2 provides definitions of two terms related to the subject-matter of requests. The term "data" is defined as "representations, in any form, of information or concepts." The term "record" is defined as "any material on which data are recorded or marked and which is capable of being read or understood by a person or a computer system or other device; . . . ."

(vii) *"International Criminal Court"*

Pursuant to the amendment to the Act effective October 23, 2000, the International Criminal Court was added to s. 2(1) of the Act and means the International Criminal Court as defined in s. 2(1) of the *Crimes Against Humanity and War Crimes Act*.

(b) Inconsistency between Acts and maintenance of cooperative arrangements

Section 3(1) provides that the Act shall prevail over other Acts of Parliament to the extent of any inconsistency between the two. However, the subsection adds an exception. If the inconsistent provision of the other Act involves a prohibition on the disclosure of information, the latter shall prevail over the Act.

Section 3(2) provides that the Act does not derogate from any cooperative arrangements or practices between a Canadian competent authority and a foreign or international authority or organization.

In *MacFarlane v. Canada (Attorney General)* (May 8, 1995), Doc. RE 4923/95, [1995] O.J. No. 4619 (Ont. Gen. Div.), the United States made a mutual legal assistance request to have material already seized in Canada for Canadian purposes sent to the United States. In opposing the production of the seized material, the applicant raised the following issue: the applicant alleged that American authorities were provided with a list of items seized and were allowed to review requested documentation prior to the Canadian Minister of Justice approving the U.S. mutual legal assistance request. Relying on s. 3 of the Act as well as the general aim of the Act of fostering cooperation between countries, Mandel J. of the Ontario Court (General Division) found nothing wrong with the disclosure, noting at pp. 15–16 of the judgment:

> [35] First, the applicant states that the authorities forwarded a list of items seized under the search warrant to the American authorities prior to the Minister approving the request for obtaining such material, and allowed an American authority to view some of those documents. In that regard, the applicant has not referred me to any prohibition in any statute, treaty or law to such an action. The Canadian authorities must obtain an order to obtain the articles and to send the articles seized to the Requesting State, but that is a far cry from the remedy of prohibiting the sending of a list of such documents. As for allowing the American authorities to review some of the articles as hereinbefore recounted, there is no evidence before me as to which articles were reviewed. However, assuming that all of the articles were reviewed, there is, as I have stated, no prohibition against this. The Act in question and the Treaty are meant to foster co-operation and assistance between countries in the investigation, prosecution and suppression of crime. The Act, by s. 3(1) and 3(2), clearly contemplates disclosure except where prohibited by another Act.
>
> [36] There is no provision in the Act prohibiting disclosure, and no other Act of Parliament was brought to my attention by any of the parties, prohibiting the disclosure of the articles in question.

(c) Publication of treaties

Section 5 of the Act requires that a mutual legal assistance agreement, or the provisions of a multilateral agreement dealing with mutual legal assistance, be published in either the *Canada Gazette* or the *Canada Treaty Series* no later than 60 days after the agreement comes into force. Once published in accordance with this section, a mutual legal assistance agreement (or the mutual legal assistance provisions of a multilateral agreement) shall be judicially noticed.

(d) Mutual legal assistance in absence of agreement (administrative arrangements)

Section 6 of the Act allows for mutual legal assistance in the absence of an agreement. Section 6(1) provides that, "[i]f there is no agreement between Canada and a state or entity, or the state's or entity's name does not appear in the schedule, the Minister of Foreign Affairs may, with the agreement of the Minister, enter into an administrative arrangement with the state or entity providing for legal assistance with respect to an investigation specified in the arrangement relating to an act that, if committed in Canada, would be an indictable offence."

Section 6(2) allows for an administrative arrangement to be entered into with a treaty partner in order to provide assistance with an investigation into conduct which does not constitute an offence as defined by the terms of the treaty. To do so, s. 6(2) further stipulates that the mutual legal sssistance agreement in question must expressly provide that legal assistance may be provided in relation to acts "that do not constitute an offence within the meaning of the agreement." For instance, Article III(2) of the *Canada–United States Mutual Legal Assistance in Criminal Matters Treaty* provides that, "[t]he Central Authorities may agree, in exceptional circumstances, to provide assistance pursuant to this Treaty in respect of illegal acts that do not constitute an offence within the definition of offence in Article I." If the agreement meets this condition, the Minister of Foreign Affairs "may, in exceptional circumstances and with the agreement of the Minister," enter an administrative arrangement with the foreign jurisdiction. The arrangement must specify the investigation to which the arrangement relates and the investigation must be in connection with "an act that, if committed in Canada, would be a contravention of an Act of Parliament or of the legislature of a province." There is no requirement that the contravention would constitute an indictable offence. As is evident from the foregoing, such arrangements are only available in "exceptional circumstances."

Section 6(3), (4), and (5) of the Act add certain specifications regarding the implementation and scope of administrative arrangements entered into under s. 6(1) and (2). Section 6(3) provides that arrangements entered into under s. 6(1) and 6(2) may be implemented by the Minister of Justice "in the same manner as an agreement." Emphasizing the restrictiveness of such arrangements, s. 6(4) adds that administrative arrangements entered into under s. 6(1) and (2) remain in force "only for such period not exceeding six months as is specified therein and with respect to the type of legal assistance that is specified therein." Section 6(5) provides that ss. 4 and 5 of the Act — relating to amendments to the schedule and publication of mutual legal assistance agreements — do not apply to administrative arrangements entered into under s. 6(1) and (2).

Section 6(6) of the Act provides that an administrative arrangement entered into under s. 6(1) and (2) and "purporting" to be signed by the Minister of Foreign Affairs or by a person designated by the Minister "is admissible in evidence without proof of the signature or official character of the person appearing to have signed it and proof that it is what it purports to be."

In *Russian Federation v. Pokidyshev* (1999), 138 C.C.C. (3d) 321 (Ont. C.A.), the Ontario Court of Appeal had occasion to consider what constitutes an administrative arrangement under this section of the Act. Russia was investigating offences relating to the sale of stable nuclear isotopes which it was alleged had been stolen from Russia and illegally transported to Canada for sale through Canadian corporate entities on the world market. The Russian information in that regard led to a parallel RCMP investigation in relation to the commission of offences in Canada. For the purposes of the domestic investigation a number of Canadian *Criminal Code* search warrants were executed, including a warrant on the business premises of the appellant in this case.

Russia had originally sought access to the fruits of the Canadian investigation by way of a letters rogatory request, but this was replaced by an agreement constituting an administrative arrangement under s. 6(1) of the *Mutual Legal Assistance in Criminal Matters Act*, which was comprised of a letter from the Russian ambassador requesting assistance and attaching letters rogatory setting out the details of the investigation in Russia. It was described by Doherty J.A. as follows, at p. 329:

> [21] On January 19, 1996, the Russian ambassador to Canada wrote to the Minister of Foreign Affairs requesting Canada's assistance in respect of an ongoing investigation by the Russian authorities in conjunction with the R.C.M.P. The investigation was said to relate to the offences of bribery, the payment and acceptance of secret commissions and the theft of stable nuclear isotopes from the Russian Federation. The details of that investigation were set out in Letters Rogatory which were incorporated by reference in the ambassador's letter and attached to that letter. The Letters Rogatory made it clear that the Russian authorities were investigating the possible misappropriation of the isotopes, the payment of bribes to a Russian official and the abuse of power by that official. The Letters Rogatory requested information concerning certain bank accounts and also asked that certain persons be questioned by the Canadian authorities.

In response, the Minister of Foreign Affairs for Canada wrote back to the ambassador saying that the ambassador's letter and this letter in response from the Minister of Foreign Affairs constituted an administrative arrangement approving the request for assistance under s. 6(1) of the Act. The response indicated that the approval of the Minister of Justice had also been obtained.

On appeal, among the positions advanced by the appellant was the argument that there was no validly constituted arrangement as contemplated by s. 6(1) of the Act. Doherty J.A. rejected this stating, at p. 334:

> [45] I doubt that a judge acting under s. 18 or s. 20 of the *Act* can review the terms of an administrative arrangement to determine whether these terms conform with the

Act. Nothing in either section suggests that a judge should look behind the application and the request to satisfy herself that the Canadian and foreign authorities have properly established the necessary diplomatic channels for the making of the request.

[46] In any event, I need not come to any final conclusion as to whether a judge acting under s. 18 or s. 20 can consider the validity of the administrative arrangement. I am satisfied that the letters exchanged between the ambassador and the Secretary of State considered along with the appended documents made the nature of the requested assistance clear.

§2.2 Assisting Foreign Investigations (Part I of Act)

(a) Implementation of Part I (s. 8)

Section 8(1) of the Act deals with mutual legal assistance requests made under agreements. This section will govern requests other than those made by an international criminal tribunal named in the schedule, with respect to which an agreement is not required (see definition of "state or entity"). Section 8(1) provides that Part I may not be used to give effect to a request for assistance unless the agreement between Canada and the requesting jurisdiction provides for assistance with respect to the subject-matter of the request.

Section 8(2) deals with mutual legal assistance requests made by states or entities listed in the schedule. These are the international criminal tribunals dealing with violations of international law in Rwanda and the former Yugoslavia. Section 8(2) provides that Part I may be used to provide mutual legal assistance to the tribunals with respect to any subject-matter.

(b) Fine collection (s. 9)

Section 9(1) permits the Minister to approve a foreign state's request to enforce the payment of a fine imposed by a criminal court in the foreign jurisdiction. Once approved by the Minister, the requesting state may institute civil proceedings in a Canadian court to enforce payment of the fine. Proceedings undertaken pursuant to s. 9(1) must be instituted within five years after the fine was imposed (s. 9(2)).

Amendments to the Act effective October 23, 2000 added sections 9.1 and 9.2. Section 9.1 permits steps to be taken in Canada to enforce an International Criminal Court order for the restraint or the seizure of proceeds of crime. Section 9.2 deals similarly with the mechanism for the enforcement of International Criminal Court orders imposing fines, reparation, or forfeiture.

Both ss. 9.1 and 9.2 would allow for International Criminal Court orders to be enforced by counsel for the Attorney General of Canada upon the authorization of the Minister of Justice. Once filed and registered with the superior court of criminal jurisdiction in the relevant province the orders would be enforceable as if they were orders made by the Canadian court.

Orders of reparation, or forfeiture, or fines enforced pursuant to s. 9.2 are to be paid into the Crimes Against Humanities Fund established under s. 30 of the *Crimes Against Humanity and War Crimes Act*. Section 9.2(7) provides for the Canadian court to provide notice to third parties who might have a valid interest in property subject to such an order.

The Nova Scotia Court of Appeal in *United States v. Zscheingner* (2001), 154 C.C.C. (3d) 547, adopted a liberal approach to the definition of "fine" in s. 9. In that case, Zscheingner had been convicted in the United States of pollution offences contrary to the *Clean Water Act*. In addition to 16 months' imprisonment he was ordered to pay $650,000 to the Environmental Protection Agency as restitution for the costs associated with the clean-up. The United States made a mutual legal assistance request to Canada, seeking the sale of land owned by Zscheingner in Nova Scotia in order to satisfy the restitution order. The Nova Scotia Court of Appeal held that although s. 9 of the Act does not make reference to the enforcement of foreign restitution orders, it was appropriate to interpret the statute in a fair and liberal manner in order to give effect to Canada's international obligations. In the result, the court held that the s. 9 definition of a "fine" was broad enough to include the restitution orders made in this case.

(c)   Search and seizure (ss. 10–16)

(*i*) *Application of* Criminal Code

Section 10 of the Act establishes that the provisions of the Canadian *Criminal Code* apply to searches and seizures executed under the Act "with any modifications that the circumstances require." Section 10 adds that in the event of an inconsistency between the Act and the Code, the provisions of the former prevail.

Prior to the amendments to the Act effective October 23, 2000, s. 10 excluded the application of s. 487.1 of the *Criminal Code* dealing with telewarrants. The amendment removed that prohibition.

(*ii*) *Application for search warrant*

Section 11 provides as follows:

> **11.** (1) When the Minister approves a request of a state or entity to have a search or a seizure, or the use of any device or investigative technique or other procedure or the doing of any other thing to be described in a warrant, carried out regarding an offence, the Minister shall provide a competent authority with any documents or information necessary to apply for a search warrant or other warrant.

> (2) The competent authority who is provided with the documents or information shall apply *ex parte* for a search warrant or other warrant to a judge of the province in which the competent authority believes that evidence may be found.

Prior to the amendments to the Act effective October 23, 2000, s. 11(1) provided that "[w]hen the Minister approves a request of a state or entity to have a search or a seizure carried out in Canada regarding an offence with respect to which the state or entity has jurisdiction, the Minister shall provide a competent authority with any documents or information necessary to apply for a search warrant." The amendment to s. 11 has now broadened the authorizing power of the Minister to include the power to authorize application for "the use of any device or investigative technique or other procedure or the doing of any other thing to be described in a warrant." All *Criminal Code* warrants are now available under the *Mutual Legal Assistance in Criminal Matters Act.*

(iii) *Issuance of search warrants*

Section 12(1) is the central provision regarding the issuance of search warrants:

12. (1) A judge of a province to whom an application is made under subsection 11(2) may issue a search warrant authorizing a peace officer named therein to execute it anywhere in the province, where the judge is satisfied by statements under oath that there are reasonable grounds to believe that

    (a) an offence has been committed;

    (b) evidence of the commission of the offence or information that may reveal the whereabouts of a person who is suspected of having committed the offence will be found in a building, receptacle or place in the province; and

    (c) it would not, in the circumstances, be appropriate to make an order under subsection 18(1).

(Prior to the amendment of the Act effective October 23, 2000, s. 12(1)(a) required that the judge considering an application for a search warrant had to be satisfied that there were reasonable grounds to believe that an offence had been committed *over which the requesting state or entity has jurisdiction*. The amendment has removed from the judge's consideration the jurisdiction of the requesting state over the offence. The judge is now only required to be satisfied that an offence has been committed. It would appear that the assertion of jurisdiction by a requesting state will not be challenged, perhaps as a matter of international comity.)

Section 12(2) to (4) set out various rules regarding the issuance and content of search warrants obtained under the Act. Section 12(2) provides that a judge issuing a warrant under s. 12(1) "may subject the execution of the warrant to any conditions that the judge considers desirable, including conditions relating to the time or manner of its execution." Section 12(3) requires the issuing judge to "fix a time and place for a hearing to consider the execution of the warrant as well as the report of the peace officer concerning its execution." Section 12(4) provides that the warrant "may be in Form 5 in Part XXVIII of the *Criminal Code*, varied to suit the case." Section 12(4) requires that the warrant contain the following information:

1. the time and place for the hearing referred to in s. 12(3);

2. a statement that, at that hearing, an order will be sought to send to the requesting state or entity the records or things seized in execution of the warrant; and

3. a statement that every person from whom a record or thing is seized in execution of the warrant and any person who claims to have an interest in a record or thing so seized has the right to make representations at the hearing before any order is made concerning the record or thing.

In *R. v. Rutherford Ltd.* (1995), 101 C.C.C. (3d) 260 (B.C.S.C.), an application was brought to quash search warrants issued pursuant to an *ex parte* application by the Crown on behalf of the United Kingdom. The applicants alleged that s. 12(1)(c) of the Act had not been met, that is, that there did not exist reasonable grounds to believe that, in the circumstances, it would be inappropriate to make an order under s. 18(1) of the Act. Section 18(1) provides a judge with the authority to issue an order for the gathering of evidence by compelling the examination of witnesses and the production of documents. The applicants claimed that the warrants had been issued without full and frank disclosure by the Crown on its *ex parte* application of information that went to the issue of whether it was appropriate, in the circumstances, to make an order under s. 18(1) of the Act. The information that was withheld from the court was the fact that, in the four months leading up to the issuance of the warrants, the police officer authorized to conduct the search had been conducting negotiations with the applicants' counsel concerning the information sought by the United Kingdom police. In particular, during the negotiation, one of the applicants apparently indicated a willingness to provide statements to the police in exchange for a letter of immunity from the prosecution.

Hutchison J. of the British Columbia Supreme Court dismissed the application. Hutchison J. found that the information that had been withheld actually confirmed that an order under s. 18 of the Act would not have been sufficient for the purposes of the requesting state (at pp. 268-269):

> [21] While it is true the affidavit of Detective Sergeant Johnstone sworn June 7, 1995, failed to reveal to the court the existence of Mr. John Green's retainer and the arrangements attempted to be made between him and the London Metropolitan Police, I cannot conclude that it was relevant to any issue save whether in the circumstances it would not be appropriate to make an order under s. 18(1) of the Act. By not revealing to the court previously that Mr. Tarantino was prepared to give statements to the police, providing that they gave him a letter of immunity from prosecution, how could that information do anything but strengthen the argument that an order under s. 18(1) of the Act was unlikely to reveal all the information that could be obtained were the search warrants issued?

In *Alberta (Attorney General) v. Dawson* (1999), (*sub nom. R. v. Dawson*) 248 A.R. 82 (Alta. Q.B.), leave to appeal to Alta. C.A. refused (1999), 250 A.R. 165 (Alta.

C.A.), leave to appeal to S.C.C. refused (2000), 261 A.R. 339 (note) (S.C.C.), Smith J. in commenting on the nature of the evidence required in support of an application for a search warrant under the Act, held that while the information to obtain the search warrant has to be sworn, the material provided by the requesting state in support of the request is not required to be either first hand or under oath. In that case the Canadian officer swearing the information based his grounds for belief on two letters from the Director and Acting Director, respectively, of the Office of International Affairs, in Washington, D.C. The writers of the letters had little personal knowledge of the investigation but rather were lawyers to whom the information regarding the investigation had been provided for the purpose of making the request to Canada. Smith J. held that the Canadian affiant was entitled to rest his belief on the contents of the letters and was not required to independently corroborate what was stated in them. However, with respect to evidence collected in Canada in order to support the American request for a search warrant, Smith J. stated as follows, at p. 94:

> [45] . . . . Because this evidence was collected in Canada, in my view, the Canadian tests on whether it ought to be admissible are applicable. In other words, if our authorities intend to conduct an investigation here in Canada to support the one done by the foreign authority, it makes sense to hold the Canadian police to the level of corroboration required in Canada. Presumably if the Canadian police can conduct the investigation, they can get the corroboration.

In *R. c. Future Électronique Inc.* (2000), 42 C.R. (5th) 132 (Que. C.A.), leave to appeal to S.C.C. granted, 2001 CarswellQue 1215 (S.C.C.), the Quebec Court of Appeal rendered a decision quashing a search warrant issued under the Act and ordering the return of the documents which had been seized in aid of an American investigation. The information in support of the search warrant had been submitted by the Canadian police officer assigned to the case who had repeated in his affidavit the information he had received from the U.S. authorities, including information provided by informants to the U.S. authorities. The Quebec Court of Appeal held that the warrant did not meet the requirements of s. 8 of the *Charter* as it was issued on information provided by third parties whose reliability had not been demonstrated by the Canadian officer who had received it. In the view of the court, it was insufficient for the Canadian affiant to simply repeat, uncorroborated, or without providing grounds addressing reliability, the statements of the U.S. authorities.

(iv) *Procedure for obtaining search warrant*

The following are the procedural steps involved in obtaining a search warrant under ss. 11 and 12 of the Act:

1. The mutual legal assistance request is forwarded from the International Assistance Group (IAG) in Ottawa to the appropriate regional office of the competent authority (i.e., the Attorney General of Canada or of a province).

2. Counsel from the regional office is assigned to the matter.

3. The evidence must be under oath and will usually be in the form of an affidavit. The affiant will often be a member of a police force assigned to assist with the preparation of the request. An application will be prepared indicating that the competent authority is applying for the warrant.

4. The Minister of Justice's approval to proceed with the request could be attached to the affidavit as an exhibit, but it would not appear to be necessary as ministerial approval is not a matter for the judge's consideration under s. 12.

5. The document or information supplied by the requesting jurisdiction will be set out in the affidavit.

6. The affidavit should address the three preconditions set out in s. 12(1) for the issuance of a search warrant (see §2.2(c)(iii) above).

7. The application is made *ex parte*.

(v) *Execution of search warrants*

Sections 12(5) and (6), 13 and 14 of the Act govern the execution of search warrants issued under the Act. Section 12(5) requires a peace officer who executes a search warrant, "before entering the place or premises to be searched or as soon as practicable thereafter, to give a copy of the warrant to any person who is present and appears to be in charge of the place or premises." Section 12(6) provides that a peace officer who executes a search warrant issued under s. 12(1) in an unoccupied place or premises must cause a copy of the warrant to be affixed in a prominent place within the place or premises. This must be done "on entering the place or premises or as soon as practicable thereafter."

Section 13 sets out that a peace officer who executes a warrant issued under s. 12 may, in addition to seizing the items specified in the warrant, "seize any thing that he believes on reasonable grounds will afford evidence of, has been obtained by or used in or is intended to be used in, the commission of an offence against an Act of Parliament." This section therefore provides authority for the seizure of evidence of domestic offences discovered in the course of the execution of a mutual legal assistance search warrant. When evidence of a domestic offence is obtained in such circumstances, s. 13 specifies that the domestic procedures set out in ss. 489.1 to 492 of the *Criminal Code* then apply in respect of any such item seized. (Section 489.1 deals with the disposition of property that has been seized by a peace officer under a warrant. Section 490 provides a procedure for dealing with seized items that are brought before a justice. Section 491 provides rules for the forfeiture of weapons and ammunition. Section 491.1 deals with the disposition of property obtained by crime.

Section 491.2 provides rules for the photographing of seized evidence prior to the disposition of such evidence. Finally, s. 492 sets out special provisions for seizing and disposing of explosives.). Section 13.1 allows the judge, in addition to search warrants under s. 12 of the Act, to issue warrants for the use of other investigative techniques and devices provided for by the *Criminal Code.*

Section 14(1) requires a peace officer who executes a warrant issued under s. 12 to file with the court of which the issuing judge is a member a written report concerning the execution of the warrant and including a general description of the records or things seized, other than things seized under s. 13. The report must be filed at least five days before the hearing held under s. 12(3) to consider the execution of the warrant. Section 14(2) provides that the peace officer must send a copy of the report to the Minister "forthwith after its filing."

In *R. v. Rutherford Ltd., supra*, an application was brought to quash search warrants issued pursuant to an *ex parte* application by the Crown on behalf of the United Kingdom. The applicants argued, among other things, that the searches were invalid because members of the police force from the requesting state were present during the searches. Hutchison J. of the British Columbia Supreme Court responded (at p. 270) that: "I find no merit in the submissions as the searches were under the direct supervision of Detective Sergeant Johnstone [of the Victoria City Police Department] who was the officer authorized under the warrants."

In *R. v. Gladwin* (1997), 116 C.C.C. (3d) 471 (Ont. C.A.), leave to appeal to S.C.C. refused (*sub nom. Euro-Can-Am Trading Inc. v. Ontario (Attorney General)*) 224 N.R. 393 (note) (S.C.C.), the search warrant failed to name the peace officer authorized to execute the warrant as required by s. 12(1) of the Act. Finlayson J.A. for the court held that the defect was not fatal, and did not render the search warrant void. The court noted that the deficiencies in the warrant were of diminished importance in light of the consideration that "[h]ad the objects seized been ordered returned, there would have been nothing to prevent the R.C.M.P. from seizing them again with a proper warrant." (p. 476, para. 12)

It was also argued in *Gladwin* that the warrant was defective for not stating the "nature of the offence committed, suspected of having been committed or intended to be committed." (p. 476, para. 13) Finlayson J.A. dismissed this complaint noting that particulars of the offence in the United States were set out in the information to obtain the warrant or its appendices and there was no suggestion that the alleged lack of particularity in the warrant had prejudiced the parties named, or their solicitors.

Also at issue in the *Gladwin* appeal was the fact that the R.C.M.P. videotaped the search of the premises as it occurred, without prior authorization. The Court of Appeal found no merit in this ground of complaint. Finlayson J.A. stated, at p. 476:

> [15] Similarly, with respect to the complaint that the police officers made a videotape recording during the course of the executing of the warrant, O'Driscoll J. was satisfied that they were entitled to do so as an adjunct to the search. In our opinion the audio/videotape was nothing more than a record of the search and seizure that would be admissible if required to show how and where the search was conducted. The videotaping

was not covert nor was it directed to obtaining inculpatory evidence relating to the predicate offences underlying the warrant. As such, it is distinguishable from cases where covert police video surveillance in circumstances where there is an expectation of privacy have been held to be unlawful: see *R. v. Wong* (1990), 60 C.C.C. (3d) 460 (S.C.C.).

(vi) *Sending evidence abroad following search and seizure*

Sections 15 and 16 of the Act set out the manner in which seized evidence is to be dealt with. Section 15(1) is the key provision. The first part of s. 15(1) indicates that representations may be made to the judge at the hearing held under s. 12(3) by the Minister, by the competent authority, by the person from whom a record or thing was seized, and by any person who claims to have an interest in the record or thing. (The issue of standing to make representations under s. 15(1) was addressed in *United Kingdom v. Ramsden, supra*, §1.1. The issue of standing is discussed below under §2.2(f).) Section 15(1)(a) sets out the circumstances in which the thing seized may be returned to the person from whom it was seized or to the lawful owner. Section 15(1)(b) describes when and subject to what conditions the seized item may be sent to the requesting state or entity:

> **15.** (1) At the hearing to consider the execution of a warrant issued under section 12, after having considered any representations of the Minister, the competent authority, the person from whom a record or thing was seized in execution of the warrant and any person who claims to have an interest in the record or thing so seized, the judge who issued the warrant or another judge of the same court may
>
> (a) where the judge is not satisfied that the warrant was executed according to its terms and conditions or where the judge is satisfied that an order should not be made under paragraph (b), order that a record or thing seized in execution of the warrant be returned to
> > (i) the person from whom it was seized, if possession of it by that person is lawful, or
> > (ii) the lawful owner or the person who is lawfully entitled to its possession, if the owner or that person is known and possession of the record or thing by the person from whom it was seized is unlawful; or
> (b) in any other case, order that a record or thing seized in execution of the warrant be sent to the state or entity mentioned in subsection 11(1) and include in the order any terms and conditions that the judge considers desirable, including terms and conditions
> > (i) necessary to give effect to the request mentioned in that subsection,
> > (ii) with respect to the preservation and return to Canada of any record or thing seized, and
> > (iii) with respect to the protection of the interests of third parties.

Section 15(2) adds that, at the hearing referred to in s. 15(1), the judge may require that a record or thing seized in execution of the warrant be brought before him or her.

The requirements imposed upon a judge by the operation of s. 15(1) was described by Finlayson J.A. for the Ontario Court of Appeal in *Gladwin, supra*, at pp. 474-475:

> [8] In my opinion, despite the awkward language of this section, couched as it is in negatives and coupled with the disjunctive "or" instead of the conjunctive "and", this section imposes a double burden upon the judge called upon to make an order under s. 15(1)(*b*) of the *Act* sending the material seized to the foreign state. He or she is obliged under s. 15(1)(*a*) to review what has transpired to the date of the return of the application. Before he can order that the record or thing seized be sent to the foreign state, the reviewing judge must be satisfied, first, that the warrant was executed according to its terms and conditions and, second, that he is satisfied that there is no reason why the order should not be made. The respondent submits, and I agree, that the inherent nature of this second condition necessarily bestows discretion on the reviewing judge to consider all relevant factors bearing on the application.
>
> [9] In both of these instances, the reviewing judge is exercising a jurisdiction akin to that of a trial judge considering the admissibility into evidence of the things seized pursuant to a search warrant. In the case in appeal, the reviewing judge had to consider the conduct of the police in the execution of the warrant and whether the search warrant was facially valid.

In *Canada (Attorney General) v. Ross* (1994), 44 B.C.A.C. 228 (B.C.C.A.), at p. 239, the British Columbia Court of Appeal held that it was not a condition precedent to a sending order under s. 15 that the material be shown to be admissible in evidence at the trial in the requesting jurisdiction. Nor was it found to be necessary for the judge to examine each item to ascertain whether it would probably assist in the prosecution of the crime.

In *Germany (Federal Republic) v. Ebke* (2001), 158 C.C.C. (3d) 253, 2001 NWTSC 52 (N.W.T.S.C.), a sending order was refused because the judge was not satisfied that the search warrant had been executed according to its terms. In that case, the warrant had been directed, as required by the provisions of s. 12(1), to a named police officer to execute it. However, it was not the named officer, but another, who supervised the search. In addition, the warrant permitted the attendance, as an observer to the search, of a German investigator. The judge determined that the German police officer had participated in the search beyond the role of observer as specified in the warrant. In the result, the judge found that there had been a disregard for the terms and conditions of the warrant which the court could not countenance by allowing the material seized to be sent overseas.

Section 16 provides that no record or seized item that has been ordered under s. 15 to be sent to the requesting state or entity shall be sent until the Minister is satisfied that the state or entity has agreed to comply with any terms or conditions imposed in respect of the sending abroad of the record or thing.

(vii) *Procedure for obtaining sending order*

In order to obtain an order under s. 15 to have seized evidence sent to the requesting jurisdiction, it will be necessary to prepare an application for the sending order. Pursuant to s. 14, the officer who executed the search must file a report with the court at least five days before the hearing of the sending application.

There are no strict rules on notice. It will depend on the circumstances. It is within the discretion of the judge to order that notice be given to particular parties (see *United Kingdom v. Ramsden, supra*, at p. 296).

(d) Gathering evidence for use by requesting state or entity (ss. 17–23)

(i) *Application for issuance of evidence-gathering order*

Section 17(1) of the Act provides that "[w]hen the Minister approves a request of a state or entity to obtain, by means of an order of a judge, evidence regarding an offence, the Minister shall provide a competent authority with any documents or information necessary to apply for the order." Section 2 defines a "competent authority" as the Attorney General of Canada or the attorney general of a province or any person in Canada with responsibility for the investigation and prosecution of offences. Section 17(2) requires the competent authority who is provided with the documents or information to "apply *ex parte* for an order for the gathering of evidence to a judge of the province in which the competent authority believes part or all of the evidence may be found." Section 2 defines a "judge" as a judge of the superior court of the province.

Section 17(1) was amended effective October 23, 2000, so that the jurisdiction of the requesting state or entity over the offence in respect of which an evidence-gathering order is sought would no longer be a consideration for the Minister in the authorization of an evidence-gathering application.

The standard for granting an order is set out in s. 18(1) of the Act. That subsection provides that the judge to whom the application is made "may" make an order for the gathering of evidence where there are reasonable grounds to believe that (a) an offence has been committed, and (b) evidence of the commission of the offence or information that may reveal the whereabouts of a person who is suspected of having committed the offence will be found in Canada. The use of the term "may" suggests that the judge has a residual discretion to refuse the granting of the order notwithstanding that the requirements of s. 18(1) are met. As in the case of the recent amendment to s. 12(1)(a) regarding the issuance of search warrants referred to above, s. 18(1)(a) was similarly amended to remove from the judge's consideration the jurisdiction of the requesting state over the offence.

The constitutional requirements for the issuance of an evidence-gathering order were commented upon by the British Columbia Court of Appeal in *Re Stuckey, supra*, §2.1(a)(ii). Southin J.A. for the court observed, at p. 319:

> [6] We have heard a great deal about Canadian constitutional standards for search and seizure. In my opinion, s. 18 does not engage those standards because it requires a judge, not some person of lesser constitutional dignity, to be satisfied that there are reasonable grounds and so forth as set out in the section.

Section 18(2) governs the substance of the order. Firstly, it provides that the order "must provide for the manner in which the evidence is to be obtained." Secondly, in s. 18(2)(a) to (c), it mentions three other things that "may" be set out in the order. Section 18(2)(a) empowers the issuing judge to order that a party appear for examination, subject to the conditions mentioned in the paragraph. The judge may:

> (a) order the examination, on oath or otherwise, of a person named therein, order the person to attend at the place fixed by the person designated under paragraph (c) for the examination and to remain in attendance until he is excused by the person so designated, order the person so named, where appropriate, to make a copy of a record or to make a record from data and to bring the copy or record with him, and order the person so named to bring with him any record or thing in his possession or control, in order to produce them to the person before whom the examination takes place . . . .

Section 18(2)(b) enables the issuing judge to order the production of documents alone, that is, an order for the production of documents need not be ancillary to an order for examination. It provides that the judge may:

> (b) order a person named therein to make a copy of a record or to make a record from data and to produce the copy or record to the person designated under paragraph (c), order the person to produce any record or thing in his possession or control to the person so designated and provide, where appropriate, for any affidavit or certificate that, pursuant to the request, is to accompany any copy, record or thing so produced . . . .

Section 18(2)(c) permits the issuing judge to designate an examiner. The judge may:

> (c) designate a person before whom the examination referred to in paragraph (a) is to take place or to whom the copies, records, things, affidavits and certificates mentioned in paragraph (b) are to be produced.

For the purposes of s. 18(2)(c), s. 18(3) allows the issuing judge to designate "himself or another person, including another judge."

Under s. 18(4) of the Act, the evidence-gathering order is effective throughout Canada.

Section 18(5) provides that the order may include "any terms or conditions that the judge considers desirable, including those relating to the protection of the interests of the person named therein and of third parties." Section 18(6) stipulates that the issuing judge or another judge of the same court may vary the terms and conditions of the order. The target of an investigation is not by that fact alone "an interested third party" within the meaning of s. 18(5) and so has no standing to seek a variance of an evidence-gathering order under s. 18(6). (See *United Kingdom v. Ramsden*, *supra*, §1.1, pp. 308-309.)

In *MacFarlane v. Canada (Attorney General)*, *supra*, §2.1(b), an application was brought alleging, among other things, that ss. 17 and 18 of the Act were contrary to fundamental justice and not reasonably justifiable in a free and democratic society and thus infringe s. 7 of the *Charter* (at p. 30). The applicant framed his argument as follows, at pp. 30-31, para. 56):

> 78. It is respectfully submitted that additional safeguards contained in section 12 of the Act inform the principles of justice whenever an individual is deprived of his or her Charter rights in the context of a seizure in furtherance of a foreign criminal investigation. Sections 11 and 12 encompass the production of documents and therefore ss. 17–18 are unnecessary for the purpose of effecting a seizure of documents.
>
> 79. It is respectfully submitted that, to the extent that ss. 17–18 of the Act authorize a seizure, i.e., a court-ordered production of evidence, in a manner inconsistent with ss. 11–12 of the Act, ss. 17–18 are contrary to the principles of fundamental justice.

This argument pertained to an order of Wren J. of the Ontario Court (General Division) for the gathering of certain evidence pursuant to s. 18 of the Act.

In distinguishing between search warrants and evidence-gathering orders under the Act, and quoting from the decision of the Supreme Court of Canada in *Thomson Newspapers Ltd. v. Canada (Director of Investigation & Research)* (1990), 54 C.C.C. (3d) 417 (S.C.C.), at pp. 554–555, Mandel J. of the Ontario Court (General Division) dismissed the applicant's argument, at pp. 31-32:

> [57] I do not accept such submissions. The procedure contemplated by ss. 11 and 12 of the Act are intrusive, namely, a search and seizure. The procedure contemplated by ss. 17 and 18 is a demand for production, a less intrusive procedure, and "impairs considerably less on a corporation or on an individual's privacy than the actual entry into and search of its place of business or home." And the more intrusive the procedure, the more stringent is the test of reasonableness. In that regard, see *Thompson Newspapers*, hereinbefore referred to, at pages 544 and 546. Furthermore, the Act provides, by section 12(1)(c), that a Judge may issue a search warrant if he is satisfied that there are reasonable grounds to believe that it would not in the circumstances be appropriate to make an order under section 18(1).

Mandel J. also pointed to the numerous safeguards under both the search warrant and the evidence-gathering procedures. Firstly, under both procedures, the Minister must approve the request (at p. 32, para. 59). Secondly, again under both procedures, the judge must be satisfied that certain preconditions have been met (p. 32, para. 59). The difference between the two procedures is that it is only under the search warrant procedure that the judge must be satisfied based upon evidence under oath. However, Mandel J. found that this difference was justifiable, at pp. 32–33:

> [59] . . . [T]his is not unreasonable having regard to the fact that it is a Superior Court Justice that is to be satisfied and that there is little intrusion in a s. 18 order in that the persons from whom the documents are to be taken can object to the delivery up of the documents, as was done in the matter of the order of Mr. Justice Wren, whereas under s. 12, the peace officer searches and takes away.

Mandel J. referred to a third safeguard of the evidence-gathering procedure under s. 18, at p. 33:

> [60] . . . [T]he terms and conditions of such order may be varied by such judge or another judge of the same court. As well, the judge may include terms and conditions on the sending of the articles to the Requesting State after having considered any representations of the Minister, the person who produced the record, and any person who claims to have an interest in any record produced. This is exactly what is happening with respect to the order of Mr. Justice Wren.

In *United States v. Ross* (1995), 100 C.C.C. (3d) 320, the Quebec Court of Appeal considered the validity of judicial orders made pursuant to ss. 17 and 18 of the Act. It was argued that the orders made under these sections violated the respondents' constitutionally protected right to silence. Fish J.A. found no violation. In the course of his reasons Fish J.A. discussed the jurisprudence concerning the right to silence and referred to the decisions of the Supreme Court of Canada in a number of cases, including *R. v. S. (R.J.)* (1995), 96 C.C.C. (3d) 1 (S.C.C.); *British Columbia (Securities Commission) v. Branch* (1995), 97 C.C.C. (3d) 505 (S.C.C.); *R. v. Jobin* (1995), 97 C.C.C. (3d) 97 (S.C.C.); *R. v. Crawford* (1995), 96 C.C.C. (3d) 481 (S.C.C.); and *R. v. Primeau* (1995), 97 C.C.C. (3d) 1 (S.C.C.). He stated:

> These cases deal with testimonial compulsion within and without the criminal justice system, both at trial and prior to trial. Read together, they establish that:
>
> 1. The right to silence has become constitutionally entrenched in Canada. This right, however, is not absolute.
> 2. The right to silence derives in large measure from the principle against self-incrimination, which is a principle of fundamental justice within the meaning of s. 7 of the Charter.
> 3. Any statute that compels a person to testify diminishes that person's liberty and must therefore comply with the principles of fundamental justice.
> 4. The principles of fundamental justice are not hierarchical and none may be considered subordinate or impervious to the others.

5. The structure of the Charter reveals the intention of its framers to enact in consti-tutional form the same structural protection against self-incrimination for witnesses that existed historically.
6. This structure is founded upon the Crown's obligation to make a case, but it also assumes a general rule of compellability coupled with evidentiary immunity.
7. The principles of fundamental justice sometimes compete with one another. This is true of the privilege against self-incrimination and the principle that all relevant evidence should be accessible to triers of fact.
8. The principle against self-incrimination requires that persons compelled to testify be granted "derivative-use immunity" in addition to the "use immunity" guaranteed by s. 13 of the Charter.
9. In addition, courts may exempt witnesses from testifying where they are satisfied that the predominant purpose for compelling those witnesses to testify is to obtain incriminating evidence against them rather than some legitimate public purpose.
10. To qualify as a valid public purpose, compelled testimony in a criminal or penal prosecution must be for the purpose of obtaining evidence in furtherance of that prosecution.

Applying these principles to the present case, I am satisfied that compelling the respondents to give evidence pursuant to the order made by Piché J., at least in its amended form, does not violate their constitutionally protected right to silence.

The order strikes a commendable balance in safeguarding individual rights and the public interest.

It respects, for respondents' benefit, the principle against self-incrimination by assuring evidentiary immunity in accordance with the precepts I have outlined.

At the same time, it permits Canada to fulfill its treaty obligations entered into to promote international co-operation in the investigation, prosecution and suppression of serious criminal offences. The examination of respondents clearly has this as its predom-inant and valid purpose.

There is no suggestion whatever that respondents are being compelled to testify in order to obtain incriminating evidence *against them*.

In short, the compelled testimony here in question is: (1) authorized by law; (2) solicited by the authorities in a context of international co-operation in the administration of justice; (3) ordered by a judge acting on reasonable grounds; (4) subject throughout to judicial control; and (5) consistent with the general rule of compellability coupled with full evidentiary immunity.

United Kingdom v. Hrynyk (1996), 107 C.C.C. (3d) 104 (Ont. Gen. Div.), con-cerned a similar constitutional challenge to the evidence-gathering provisions of the *Mutual Legal Assistance in Criminal Matters Act* (ss. 17 and 18 of the Act). The applicants were subject to an order issued pursuant to s. 18 of the Act, requiring their examination under oath and the production of documents concerning certain financial and business transactions involving one Terence Ramsden who was the subject of an investigation by the Serious Fraud Office of the United Kingdom. This investigation concerned allegations that Ramsden had committed serious offences of bankruptcy fraud in the amount of approximately $200,000,000. It was contended on behalf of the proposed witness, Hrynyk, that it was a violation of s. 7 of the *Charter* to compel him to cooperate in this way. He asserted that because officers in a domestic criminal investigation would not have the power to require, or seek judicial authorization to compel, a witness in a Canadian investigation to cooperate, that such a power could not be constitutionally accorded to foreign authorities investigating a foreign crime in Canada.

MacPherson J. (as he then was) held that ss. 17 and 18 of the Act did not violate the principles of fundamental justice and were not contrary to s. 7 of the *Charter*. He noted that there was no absolute right to silence in Canada and that in this case Hrynyk was not a target of the United Kingdom investigation, but a witness. MacPherson J. held that it was proper to balance the interests of the witness with the interests of the state, and observed that in this case the order under s. 18 of the Act granted Hrynyk both use and derivative use immunity with respect to his testimony and did not violate a constitutionally protected right to silence.

In undertaking the balancing of interests between those of the witness and those of the state, MacPherson J. commented as follows, at pp. 116–117, with respect to the witness's interests:

> On the witness side of the balance, I observe that ss. 17 and 18 and other provisions of the Act provide very substantial safeguards for persons compelled to give evidence and produce documents. The safeguards include the following:
>
> (1) The request from the foreign state must be approved by the Minister.
> (2) The evidence-gathering order must be made by a superior court judge.
> (3) The judge *may* make an order (*i.e.*, it is discretionary) only if he is satisfied that there are reasonable grounds to believe that:
>   (a) an offence has been committed;
>   (b) with respect to which the foreign state has jurisdiction; and
>   (c) that evidence of the commission of the offence or information that may reveal the whereabouts of a person who is suspected of having committed the offence *will* be found in Canada.
> (4) The judge may designate a person to preside over such evidence-gathering proceedings as may be ordered. In the present case the superior court judge designated an experienced Provincial Court judge, Mary Hogan, to take the evidence.
> (5) The judge may include in the order any terms or conditions that the judge considers desirable, including those relating to the protection of the interests of the persons named therein and of third parties. In the present case, the order was amended, on Mr. Hrynyk's application, to provide him with both use and derivative use immunity and to exclude an R.C.M.P. officer from the evidence-gathering hearing.
> (6) The judge who made the order, or another judge of the same court, may vary its terms and conditions. As described in (5), that happened in this case.
> (7) Persons named in the order may refuse to answer questions or to produce records or things on the basis of specific questions of law and privilege.
> (8) The person presiding over the evidence-gathering proceedings *shall* make a report to the judge. The required contents of the report are specified in detail.
> (9) Upon receipt of the report the judge *may* order that the report and things seized be sent to the foreign state (*i.e.*, again it is discretionary).

(10) The judge may include terms and conditions on the sending of the report and things to the foreign state "after having considered any representations of the Minister, the competent authority, the person who produced any record or thing . . . , and any person who claims to have an interest in any record or thing so produced" (s. 20(2)).

(11) No record or thing shall be sent until the Minister is satisfied that the foreign state has agreed to comply with any terms and conditions imposed by the judge (s. 21).

(12) An appeal lies from any of the above-mentioned orders (s. 35).

In my view, these safeguards indicate that when Parliament enacted the *Mutual Legal Assistance in Criminal Matters Act*, it considered very carefully both sides of the equation — the rights of individuals, including potential witnesses, in a criminal investigation context *and* the desirability of co-operating with foreign states in the detection and suppression of crime. The safeguards in the Act speak to the "rights" side of the equation. [Emphasis in original.]

With respect to the state interest, MacPherson J. noted, at pp. 117–118:

> On the public interest side of the balance, I observe that the Act as a whole responds to the legitimate goal of crime detection in difficult and complex situations: see *Thomson Newspapers, supra*. It also responds to the important value of international comity in matters that cut across national boundaries: see *Republic of Argentina v. Mellino* (1987), 33 C.C.C. (3d) 334, 40 D.L.R. (4th) 74, [1987] 1 S.C.R. 536; *Schmidt v. The Queen* (1987), 33 C.C.C. (3d) 193, 39 D.L.R. (4th) 18, [1987] 1 S.C.R. 500; *France (Republic) v. De Havilland Aircraft of Canada Ltd.* (1991), 65 C.C.C. (3d) 449, 1 C.P.C. (3d) 76, 3 O.R. (3d) 705 (C.A.); and *Pacificador v. Philippines (Republic of)* (1993), 83 C.C.C. (3d) 210, 23 C.R. (4th) 171, 14 O.R. (3d) 321 (C.A.).
>
> My conclusion is the same as Fish J.A.'s in *Ross, supra*. Sections 17 and 18 of the Act strike "a commendable balance in safeguarding individual rights and the public interest". The judicial orders in the present case, made pursuant to these sections, strike a similar commendable balance.

This case was referred to with approval by Doherty J.A. of the Ontario Court of Appeal in *Russian Federation v. Pokidyshev* (1999), 138 C.C.C. (3d) 321, at p. 329, when he stated in his discussion of the statutory scheme of Part I of the Act:

> [20] . . .The judge must ensure compliance with the statutory conditions precedent to the making of the order requested and the judge must craft an order which balances the legitimate state and individual interests at stake: *United Kingdom v. Hrynyk* (1996), 107 C.C.C. (3d) 104 at 117, 135 D.L.R. (4th) 693 (Ont. Ct. (Gen. Div.)). The terms of the order will depend, to a large extent, on the nature of the order made and the individual interests affected by the order. For example, where the order involves the taking of evidence from a person, it may well be necessary to impose terms which will protect that person's right not to incriminate herself. *e.g.* see *United States of America v. Ross* (1995), 100 C.C.C. (3d) 320 (Que. C.A.), leave to appeal to S.C.C. refused February 8, 1996 [reported 103 C.C.C. (3d) vi]; *United Kingdom v. Hrynyk, supra*.

In *United States v. Beach* (1999), 136 Man. R. (2d) 276, Oliphant A.C.J.Q.B. of the Manitoba Court of Queen's Bench observed that while the latitude granted by his order compelling the testimony of witnesses in Canada to assist an investigation in Oklahoma would never be available to Canadian law enforcement officers, it was "exactly what is provided for in the treaty and the Act." The order in that case also granted the witnesses immunity from criminal prosecution except for perjury, on the basis of anything said by them in the course of giving evidence upon the investigation. (p. 281)

When making an application for an evidence-gathering order, it is not necessary that a requesting state disclose the entirety of its investigation. It is sufficient to disclose enough information to provide reasonable grounds for the issuance of the order. This was the opinion of Twaddle J.A. in *United States v. Beach* (1999), 132 C.C.C. (3d) 156 (Man. C.A.). He stated, at pp. 161-162:

> [19] Whatever information may be passed between the States pursuant to the *Treaty's* protocol, s. 18 of the *Mutual Assistance Act* does not require disclosure of all of it to the court. All that need be disclosed to the court is sufficient information to show that there are reasonable grounds to believe that
>
> > (a) a serious crime over which the requesting State has jurisdiction has been committed; and
> > (b) evidence of its commission will be found in Canada.
>
> [20] The standard of "reasonable grounds" does not require disclosure of the requesting State's entire case. For the purpose of this proceeding, it would have been sufficient to prove that there was a death in circumstances which make foul play reasonably probable and that the respondents have a connection to the crime or the suspect which makes it reasonably probable that they have knowledge of facts which, if the subject of testimony, could aid the investigation or prosecution of the crime.

(ii) *Procedure for obtaining evidence-gathering order*

The following are the procedural steps involved in obtaining an evidence-gathering order under ss. 17 and 18 of the Act:

1. The mutual legal assistance request is approved and forwarded from the International Assistance Group (IAG) in Ottawa to the appropriate regional office of the competent authority (i.e., the Attorney General of Canada or of a province).

2. Counsel from the regional office is assigned to the matter.

3. The evidence will usually be in the form of an affidavit. The affiant will often be a member of a police force assigned to assist with the preparation of the

request. An application will be prepared indicating that the competent authority is applying for the order.

4.   The Minister of Justice's approval to proceed with the request could be attached to the affidavit as an exhibit, but it would not appear to be necessary as ministerial approval is not a matter for the judge's consideration under s. 18.

5.   The document or information supplied by the requesting jurisdiction will be set out in the affidavit. It is not necessary to attach the foreign letter of request itself as long as sufficient information to meet the requirements of s. 18 is provided in the affidavit (see *United States v. Beach* (1999), 132 C.C.C. (3d) 156 (Man. C.A.)).

6.   The affidavit should address the two preconditions discussed above in §2.2(d)(i), as set out in s. 18(1), for the issuance of an evidence-gathering order.

7.   The application is made *ex parte*.

(iii) Refusals to answer, report to judge, and assessment of refusals to answer based on Canadian law

The current versions of s. 18(7) to (9) of the Act were effected by amendments made by the passage of the *Crimes Against Humanity and War Crimes Act*, S.C. 2000, c. 24, s. 63(2):

(7) A person named in an order under subsection (1) shall answer questions and produce records or things to the person designated under paragraph (2)(*c*) in accordance with the laws of evidence and procedure in the state or entity that presented the request, but may refuse if answering the questions or producing the records or things would disclose information that is protected by the Canadian law of non-disclosure of information or privilege.

(8) If a person refuses to answer a question or to produce a record or thing, the person designated under paragraph (2)(*c*)

(a)   may, if he or she is a judge of a Canadian or foreign court, make immediate rulings on any objections or issues within his or her jurisdiction; or

(b)   shall, in any other case, continue the examination and ask any other question or request the production of any other record or thing mentioned in the order.

(9) A person named in an order made under subsection (1) who, under subsection (7), refuses to answer one or more questions or to produce certain records or things shall, within seven days, give to the person designated under paragraph (2)(*c*), unless that person has already ruled on the objection under paragraph (8)(*a*), a detailed statement in writing of the reasons on which the person bases the refusal to answer each question

that the person refuses to answer or produce each record or thing that the person refuses to produce.

These sections address the manner in which refusals to answer or to produce evidence in the course of an examination will be resolved. Under the previous provisions of the Act, s. 18(7) to (9) also dealt with refusals by examinees to answer questions or produce evidence. Under former s. 18(7)(a) to (c), a person named in an evidence-gathering order could refuse to answer one or more questions or to produce certain records or things if any of three situations existed. That is, (a) if the refusal was based on a law in force in Canada; or (b) if to require the person to answer the questions or to produce the records or things would have constituted a breach of a privilege recognized by a law in force in the state or entity that presented the request mentioned in s. 17(1); or (c) if to answer the questions or to produce the records or things would have constituted the commission by the person of an offence against a law in force in the state or entity that presented the request mentioned in s. 17(1).

Notwithstanding the refusal, the former s. 18(8) required the person designated under s. 18(2)(c) to continue with the examination. Under former s. 18(9), persons who refused to answer questions or to produce certain records or things were required within seven days to give to the person designated under s. 18(2)(c) a detailed statement in writing of all of the reasons on which the person based the refusal. The person designated then included this in the report to the judge who ordered the examination, or another judge of the same court as required by s. 19(1), and the validity of the refusal was determined by the court.

The addition of current s. 18(7) to (9) changed the Act in two significant ways. First, current s. 18(7) narrowed the former right to refuse to answer based on "a law in force in Canada," to a more restricted right to refuse if compliance "would disclose information that is protected by the Canadian law of non-disclosure of information or privilege." Otherwise the examination is to be governed in accordance with the laws of the state or entity making the request, and not the procedural and evidentiary laws of Canada.

Secondly, unlike the former version of the Act, s. 18(8) now provides authority for the designated person conducting the examination to make an immediate ruling on the validity of any refusals if the designated person is a Canadian judge or a judge of the requesting state or entity and the law upon which the refusal is based is within that judge's competence. If the designated person does not have the jurisdiction to rule on a particular refusal, then s. 18(9) requires, as before, that the witness provide a detailed statement in writing within seven days, setting out the grounds upon which the refusal to answer or to produce evidence, is based.

Section 18(10) of the Act provides that a person named in an order made under s. 18(1) is entitled to be paid the travel and living expenses to which the person would be entitled if the person were required to attend as a witness before the judge who made the order.

Section 19(1) requires the examiner appointed under s. 18(2)(c) to make a report to the judge who made the order or another judge of the same court. Section 19(1)(a) to (c) require that the report be accompanied by three things:

(a)   a transcript of every examination held pursuant to the order;
(b)   a general description of every record or thing produced to the person pursuant to the order and, if the judge so requires, a record or thing itself; and
(c)   a copy of every statement given under subsection 18(9) of the reasons for a refusal to answer any question or to produce any record or thing.

Section 19(2) requires the examiner to send a copy of the report to the Minister as soon as possible after it is made.

Section 19(3) of the Act was amended effective October 23, 2000 to provide as follows:

19. (3) If any reasons contained in a statement given under subsection 18(9) are based on the Canadian law of non-disclosure of information or privilege, a judge to whom a report is made shall determine whether those reasons are well-founded, and, if the judge determines that they are, that determination shall be mentioned in any order that the judge makes under section 20, but if the judge determines that they are not, the judge shall order that the person named in the order made under subsection 18(1) answer the questions or produce the records or things.

In the event that a refusal to answer or to produce evidence is based upon Canadian law of non-disclosure or privilege and the designated person was not competent to rule on the issue, then the judge to whom the report under s. 18(9) is made shall rule with respect to whether the reason for such refusal is well founded. If it is determined that the reason for refusal is not well founded the judge has the authority to compel the witness to answer the questions or produce the record or things.

Under s. 19(4), a copy of every refusal statement given under s. 18(9) containing reasons that purport to be based on the law of the requesting state or entity must be appended to any order that the judge makes under s. 20.

In *United States v. Ross*, *supra*, as indicated above under §2.2(d)(i), the United States made a request to Canada under the Act for the examination of certain persons in connection with the prosecution of three other persons in Florida for murder. The request was granted by the Minister and an evidence-gathering order was issued. The order included a condition that, during the examination of the witness, only those questions relating to the prosecution of three named individuals for the particular alleged murder were permitted, and that any statements given as a result of those questions could only be used in that prosecution, and could not be used either in Canada or the United States to incriminate the person giving the statement except in a prosecution for perjury.

The examinees refused to answer all questions put to them pursuant to the evidence-gathering order. The examinees advanced two grounds for their refusal. Firstly, that the Act does not provide for, and the requesting state did not seek, the kind of compelled "exploratory and police interrogation" to which they allegedly were subjected by the order (p. 324). Fish J.A., on behalf of the Quebec Court of Appeal, rejected this argument, relying on the principle of fair and liberal interpretation, at p. 324:

> The wording used by the demanding state [the United States of America] in its request for assistance must be read in the context of the treaty and statute under which it was made. Courts must construe both the treaty and the statute in a fair and liberal manner so as to favour the fulfilment by Canada of its international obligations and the accomplishment by Parliament of its legislative objectives.

In reaching this conclusion, Fish J.A. relied on two decisions made in connection with letters rogatory requests — *R. v. Zingre* (1981), 61 C.C.C. (2d) 465 (S.C.C.), and *France (Republic) v. De Havilland Aircraft of Canada Ltd.* (1991), 65 C.C.C. (3d) 449 (Ont. C.A.) — as well as s. 12 of the *Interpretation Act*, R.S.C. 1985, c. I-21, which reads as follows:

> **12.** Every enactment is deemed remedial, and shall be given such fair, large and liberal construction and interpretation as best ensures the attainment of its objects.

In light of this principle, Fish J.A. found that the American request provided an adequate basis for the Minister's application for an evidence-gathering order. Fish J.A. concluded that "the order made against [the] respondents seems to be consistent with the request made, supported by the application filed, and authorized by the governing statute." (p. 324)

The second ground advanced by the examinees in support of their blanket refusal to answer questions was that the order violated their right to silence. The only provision under which this objection could be made within this particular proceeding was former s. 18(7)(a), that is, a Canadian judge under the scheme of the Act only has jurisdiction to assess refusals based on "a law in force in Canada." Fish J.A., at pp. 325-329, dismissed the argument. He found that the only Canadian law that serves as a source for a right to silence is s. 7 of the *Charter*. Fish J.A. held that the right to silence is not absolute and that compelling the respondents to give evidence pursuant to the order would not violate their constitutionally protected right to silence. The order respected the principle against self-incrimination by ensuring evidentiary immunity. At the same time, it permitted Canada to fulfil its treaty obligations entered into to promote international co-operation in the investigation, prosecution, and suppression of serious criminal offences.

The same issue was raised in *United Kingdom v. Hrynyk, supra*. In that case, a request was made under the Act by the United Kingdom for assistance in an investigation of suspected fraud offences allegedly committed by a third party. Pursuant to this request, a Canadian citizen was ordered to attend and be examined under oath and produce copies of various documents. The original order was varied to provide use and derivative-use immunity to the witness and to delete a provision permitting the attendance of a Canadian police officer at the proceeding. Counsel for the witness filed a statement of refusals as required by s. 18(9) of the Act setting out reasons for the witness's refusal to answer the questions asked. These reasons included an assertion that the order, and the legislation underpinning the order, infringed the witness's right to silence and thereby breached the principles of fundamental justice under s. 7 of the *Charter* (at p. 110). In particular, it was alleged that the balancing of the individual's right to silence and the interests of the state only applies after charges have been laid, and that the right to silence at the investigative stage is absolute (at p. 113).

MacPherson J. of the Ontario Court (General Division) dismissed this argument. He found that the witness's liberty was infringed by the order, given that the witness was being compelled to do something that he did not want to do (at p. 111). However, he concluded that the deprivation of liberty was in accordance with the principles of fundamental justice (see discussion under §2.2(d)(i) above).

(iv) *Sending evidence to requesting jurisdictions and assessment of refusals to answer based on foreign law*

Sections 20 and 21 of the Act govern the sending of evidence gathered pursuant to ss. 17 and 18 to requesting jurisdictions. Section 20(1) provides that the judge to whom a report is made under s. 19(1) may order that any of the following be sent to the foreign state or entity:

- the report;

- any record or thing produced;

- a copy of the order accompanied by a copy of any statement given under s. 18(9) that contains reasons that purport to be based on a law in force in the foreign state or entity; and

- any determination of the judge made under s. 19(3) that the reasons (based on Canadian law) contained in a statement given under s. 18(9) are well-founded.

Section 20(2) provides that "[a]n order made under subsection (1) may include any terms or conditions that the judge considers desirable . . . ." According to this subsection, the judge may only attach terms and conditions "after having considered any representations of the Minister, the competent authority, the person who produced any record or thing to the person designated under paragraph 18(2)(c) and any person who claims to have an interest in any record or thing so produced . . . ." Section 20(2)(a) to (c) specify the types of terms and conditions that the judge may include:

1. those necessary to give effect to the request to obtain evidence under s.17(1);

2. those ensuring the preservation and return to Canada of any record or thing so produced; and

3. those safeguarding the interests of third parties.

Section 21 adds that "[n]o record or thing that has been ordered under section 20 to be sent to the state or entity mentioned in subsection 17(1) shall be so sent until the Minister is satisfied that the state or entity has agreed to comply with any terms or conditions imposed in respect of the sending abroad of the record or thing."

Under s. 20(3), with respect to matters not already ruled on pursuant to s. 18(8)(a), if a court of the requesting state or entity or person designated by the state or entity determines that a refusal by an examinee, by reason of a law in force in that jurisdiction, to answer one or more questions or to produce certain records or things was not well-founded under the law of that jurisdiction and the foreign jurisdiction so advises the Minister, the examination may be continued (if an examinee persists in refusing to answer, he or she may be held in contempt of court under s. 22 of the Act — see §2.2(d)(vi) below). Under s. 20(4), the examinee at the continued examination may not refuse to answer the same question or refuse to produce the same record or thing as at the original examination, except with the permission of the judge who made the ruling on the objection or another judge of the same court.

The general functions of a judge under s. 20 of the Act were discussed by Doherty J.A. for the Ontario Court of Appeal in *Russian Federation v. Pokidyshev, supra*. He stated, at pp. 332–333:

> [38] Before turning to the specific grounds of appeal, I will address in more general terms the function of the judge under s. 20 of the *Act*. Section 20(1) provides that a judge *may* order the produced material sent to the foreign jurisdiction and s. 20(2) states that a judge *may* impose terms and conditions on that order. Both subsections give the judge a discretion. Neither require, as s. 15 does when the material gathered was seized by a search warrant, that the judge satisfy herself that the material was gathered in accordance with the gathering order. Nor must the judge acting under s. 20 be satisfied that the material will afford evidence of the commission of an offence in a foreign jurisdiction. I do not regard s. 20 as providing either an appeal from or a review of the gathering order under s. 18.
>
> [39] The discretion vested in a judge by s. 20(1) and s. 20(2) is framed broadly so that the judge may consider the specific issues raised in a particular application made for an order to send material to the foreign jurisdiction. Those issues will involve a consideration of a number of factors, including the nature of the material which the applicant seeks to have sent to the foreign jurisdiction and the representations made by the applicant or any other party appearing on the application for the sending order. For example, where a party with an interest in the material contends that it has no connection to the investigation of any crime within the foreign state's jurisdiction, the judge will consider that submission and any evidence relevant thereto in deciding what order, if any, to make under s. 20. Similarly, if an interested party contends that the s. 18 order was based on false or inaccurate information or offers additional information which is

relevant to the basis upon which the gathering order was obtained, the s. 20 judge can hear evidence and any factual findings she makes can be factored into both her decision to make the order and her decision as to the terms, if any, to be included in the order. The factors to be considered by the s. 20 judge will depend on the circumstances of each application.

[40] There are, however, limits on the discretion vested in the s. 20 judge. These limits flow from the nature of the judicial role in the process contemplated by the *Act*. In my view, a judge under s. 20 is not concerned with the advisability of assisting the foreign jurisdiction or whether the foreign jurisdiction will comply with any order the judge might make. Those matters must be addressed by the Minister of Justice. Similarly, I do not think that a judge on a s. 20 application can be concerned with either the ultimate evidentiary value of the requested material to the foreign jurisdiction or with the conduct of any proceedings in the foreign jurisdiction: *United States of America v. Ross* (1994), 44 B.C.A.C. 228 (B.C.C.A.), *per* Southin J.A. (in Chambers).

One of the issues in *Russian Federation v. Pokidyshev* was whether documents could be made the subject of a sending order if they were not specifically the subject of the request made by the foreign state. In that case certain bank documents which had been made the subject of an evidence-gathering order had not been specifically identified in the Russian request, although the affidavit of the Canadian officer sworn in support of the application for the evidence-gathering order did set out reasonable grounds to believe that these documents could afford evidence of the commission of the Russian offences. Doherty J.A. held that these materials could properly be subject to a sending order, at pp. 335–336:

[49] The appellant acknowledges that the documents were relevant to the investigation, but submits that as they were not specifically identified in the request for assistance, they could not be included in the gathering order. It follows, the appellant contends, that if they were not properly the subject of a gathering order, German J. should not have ordered them sent to the Russian Federation. This submission relates to five of the hundreds of documents that are subject to the gathering and sending orders.

[50] This submission is without merit. Nothing in the *Act* suggests that the request from the foreign state must comply with the statutory prerequisites to a gathering order set out in s. 18(1). The section refers by incorporation to the application being made by the "competent authority". In this case, the application contains the affidavit of Corporal Hillyard and the attachments to that affidavit including the request. Ferguson J. was entitled to look at all of the information filed on the application in determining what documents should be included in the gathering order. Corporal Hillyard's affidavit clearly establishes the basis for including the copies of the documents related to Pokidyshev's bank account.

In considering whether documents should be made the subject of a sending order, the court in *Russian Federation* indicated that the judge determining the application under s. 20 ought to take a generous approach to the issue of relevance, particularly in the context of complex commercial investigations. Doherty J.A. observed that "relevance in this context means helpful to the authorities in discovering, understanding and proving the complex events underlying the allegations . . . " (p. 338).

(v) *Procedure for obtaining sending order*

The following are the procedural steps involved in obtaining an order under s. 20 to have evidence gathered under ss. 17 and 18 sent to the requesting jurisdiction:

1. Prepare an application for the sending order.

2. Attach the report, prepared pursuant to s. 19, of the person before whom the examinations took place.

3. The report must be accompanied by the following:

   • A transcript of the examination of the witnesses;
   • A description of the records produced at the examination;
   • A copy of the original order.

4. Prepare a draft sending order (the composition of the order may change depending on the submissions of interested parties and the ruling of the judge).

There are no strict rules regarding notice. It will depend on the circumstances. It is within the discretion of the judge to order that notice be given to particular parties (see *United Kingdom v. Ramsden, supra,* §1.1, at p. 296).

(vi) *Contempt of court*

Section 22 of the Act as amended effective October 23, 2000 provides that an examinee may be guilty of contempt of court in the following circumstances:

> **22.** (1) A person named in an order made under subsection 18(1) commits a contempt of court if the person refuses to answer a question or to produce a record or thing to the person designated under paragraph 18(2)(*c*) after a judge has ruled against the objection under paragraph 18(8)(*a*).
>
> (2) If no ruling has been made under paragraph 18(8)(*a*), a person named in an order made under subsection 18(1) commits a contempt of court if the person refuses to answer a question or to produce a record or thing to the person designated under paragraph 18(2)(*c*)
>
> (a) without giving the detailed statement required by subsection 18(9); or
> (b) the person so named was already asked the same question or requested to produce the same record or thing and if the reasons on which that person based the earlier refusal were determined not to be well-founded by

(i) a judge, if the reasons were based on the Canadian law of non-disclosure of information or privilege, or

(ii) a court of the state or entity or by a person designated by the state or entity, if the reasons were based on a law that applies to the state or entity.

It is a contempt of court for a witness to refuse to provide the reasons for a refusal to answer questions or produce evidence as required by s. 18(9), or to continue to refuse to answer or to produce the evidence after such a refusal has been determined not to be well-founded.

(vii) Virtual testimony

Sections 22.1 to 22.4 provide for the giving of "virtual testimony" to a foreign state or entity via video and audio-link technology. These provisions enable a foreign state or entity to obtain the evidence of a witness who is physically located in Canada by means of technology that permits the virtual presence of the witness in the foreign state or entity. Sections 22.1 to 22.4 were added to the Act by the 1999 amendments contained in the *Extradition Act*, S.C. 1999, c. 18, s. 113.

Section 22.1(1) provides that the Minister of Justice must first approve a foreign state or entity's virtual testimony request. Once the request is approved, the Minister must provide a "competent authority" with any documents or information necessary to apply for the virtual testimony order. The term "competent authority" is defined in s. 2 of the Act as the Attorney General of Canada, the attorney general of a province, or any person in Canada with responsibility for the investigation and prosecution of offences. Section 22.1(1) reads as follows:

> **22.1** (1) If the Minister approves a request of a state or entity to compel a person to provide evidence or a statement regarding an offence by means of technology that permits the virtual presence of the person in the territory over which the state or entity has jurisdiction, or that permits the parties and the court to hear and examine the witness, the Minister shall provide a competent authority with any documents or information necessary to apply for the order.

(This section was amended effective October 23, 2000 to remove from the Minister's consideration the jurisdiction of the requesting state over the matter with respect to which a request for video link evidence has been made.)

Section 22.1(2) provides for an *ex parte* application by the competent authority to a superior court judge of the province in which the witness is located:

> (2) The competent authority who is provided with the documents or information shall apply *ex parte* to a judge of the province in which the person may be found for an order for the taking of the evidence or statement from the person under subsection (1).

Section 22.2(1) provides that the judge "may" make the order if there "are reasonable grounds to believe" that an offence has been committed over which the state or entity has jurisdiction and that the state or entity believes that the person's evidence would be relevant to the investigation or prosecution of the offence:

> **22.2** (1) The judge may make the order if satisfied that there are reasonable grounds to believe that
>
> (a)   an offence has been committed; and
> (b)   the state or entity believes that the person's evidence or statement would be relevant to the investigation or prosecution of the offence.

The use of the word "may" suggests that the judge has a residual discretion to refuse the order even if there are reasonable grounds to believe that the two grounds are present.

Section 22.2(2) sets out the contents of the judge's order:

> (2) An order made under subsection (1) shall order the person
>
> (a)   to attend at the place fixed by the judge for the taking of the evidence or statement by means of the technology and to remain in attendance until the person is excused by the authorities of the state or entity;
> (b)   to answer any questions put to the person by the authorities of the state or entity or by any person authorized by those authorities, in accordance with the law that applies to the state or entity;
> (c)   to make a copy of a record or to make a record from data and to bring the copy or record, when appropriate; and
> (d)   to bring any record or thing in his or her possession or control, when appropriate, in order to show it to the authorities by means of the technology.

Section 22.2(3) adds that the order "may be executed anywhere in Canada." Section 22.2(4) provides that the order "may include any terms or conditions that the judge considers desirable, including those relating to the protection of the interests of the person named in it and of third parties." Section 22.2(5) allows the judge who made the order or another judge of the same court to vary the terms and conditions of the order. Section 22.2(6) deals with conduct money, providing that "[a] person named in an order made under subsection (1) is entitled to be paid the travel and living expenses to which the person would be entitled if the person were required to attend as a witness before the judge who made the order."

Section 22.3 establishes that the laws of evidence and procedure of the foreign state or entity apply to the giving of evidence under s. 22.2, but only to the extent that such evidence would not disclose information otherwise protected by the Canadian law of non-disclosure of information or privilege:

> **22.3** For greater certainty, when a witness gives evidence or a statement pursuant to an order made under section 22.2, the evidence or statement shall be given as though the witness were physically before the court or tribunal outside Canada, for the purposes

of the laws relating to evidence and procedure but only to the extent that giving the evidence would not disclose information otherwise protected by the Canadian law of non-disclosure of information or privilege.

Section 22.4 adds that the Canadian law of contempt of court applies when a witness giving evidence under s. 22.2 refuses to answer a question or produce a record or thing:

> **22.4** When a witness gives evidence under section 22.2, the Canadian law relating to contempt of court applies with respect to a refusal by the person to answer a question or to produce a record or thing as ordered by the judge under that section.

(viii)   Arrest Warrants

Section 23 of the Act allows for the issuance of an arrest warrant against examinees. Section 23(1) sets out the criteria for issuing the warrant:

> **23.** (1) The judge who made the order under subsection 18(1) or section 22.2 or another judge of the same court may issue a warrant for the arrest of the person named in the order where the judge is satisfied, on an information in writing and under oath, that
>
> (a)   the person did not attend or remain in attendance as required by the order or is about to abscond;
>
> (b)   the order was personally served on the person; and
>
> (c)   in the case of an order made under subsection 18(1), the person is likely to give material evidence and, in the case of an order under section 22.2, the state or entity believes that the testimony of the person would be relevant to the prosecution of the offence.

Accordingly, a sworn information must be presented to the judge who ordered the gathering of the evidence or another judge of the same court demonstrating the three points listed in s. 23(1)(a) to (c). Section 23(2) stipulates that the warrant is effective throughout Canada. Section 23(3) requires that the peace officer who executes the warrant have the examinee brought before the judge who issued the warrant or another judge of the same court. Section 23(3) allows the judge before whom the person is brought to order that the person be detained in custody or released on recognizance, with or without sureties, to ensure compliance with the evidence-gathering order. Section 23(4) provides that, upon request, a person who is arrested in execution of a warrant issued under s. 23(1) is entitled to receive a copy of the information on which the warrant was issued.

(ix) *Examination of place or site*

Section 23.1 was added effective October 23, 2000:

> **23.1** (1) When the Minister approves a request of a state or entity to examine a place or site in Canada regarding an offence, including by means of the exhumation and examination of a grave, the Minister shall provide a competent authority with any documents or information necesary to apply for an order.
>
> (2) The competent authority that is provided with the documents or information shall apply *ex parte* for an order for the examination of a place or site to a judge of the province in which the place or site is located.
>
> (3) An order may include any terms or conditions that the judge considers desirable, including those relating to the time and manner of its execution, and a requirement for notice.

The Minister may approve an *ex parte* application for the examination of a place or site in Canada, including the exhumation and examination of gravesites.

(e) **Transfer of detained persons**

Sections 24 and 25 of the Act deals with the transfer of persons detained in Canada to foreign jurisdictions. Section 24 governs the approval of transfer requests by the Minister of Justice and the application for transfer orders by a "competent authority" (defined in s. 2 of the Act as the Attorney General of Canada or of the applicable province). Section 24(1) provides that, once the Minister of Justice has approved a transfer request, the Minister must provide the competent authority with any documents or information necessary to apply for a transfer order:

> **24.** (1) When the Minister approves a request of a state or entity to have a detained person who is serving a term of imprisonment in Canada transferred to the state or entity, the Minister shall provide a competent authority with any documents or information necessary to apply for a transfer order.

Section 24(2) requires the competent authority to apply for the transfer order in the province in which the person is detained:

> (2) The competent authority who is provided with the documents or information shall apply for a transfer order to a judge of the province in which the person is detained.

Section 24(3) specifies the required contents of the transfer application:

> (3) An application made under subsection (2) must

    (a) state the name of the detained person;

    (b) state the place of confinement of the detained person;

    (c) designate a person or class of persons into whose custody the detained person is sought to be delivered;

    (d) state the place to which the detained person is sought to be transferred;

    (e) state the reasons why the detained person is sought to be transferred; and

    (f) specify a period of time at or before the expiration of which the detained person is to be returned.

Section 25 deals with the making of transfer orders by a "judge" (defined in s. 2 of the Act as a judge of the superior court of the province). Section 25(1) sets out the basis upon which a judge may order the transfer of a person:

> **25.** (1) If the judge to whom an application is made under subsection 24(2) is satisfied, having considered, among other things, any documents filed or information given in support of the application, that the detained person consents to the transfer and that the state or entity has requested the transfer for a fixed period, the judge may make a transfer order.

Section 25(2) permits the judge to order that the detained person be brought before him or her so that that person may be examined with respect to the transfer:

> (2) A judge to whom an application is made under subsection 24(2) may order that the detained person be brought before him so that that person may be examined with respect to the transfer.

Section 25(3) sets out the required contents of the transfer order:

> (3) A transfer order made under subsection (1) must
>
>   (a) set out the name of the detained person and his place of confinement;
>
>   (b) order the person who has custody of the detained person to deliver him into the custody of a person who is designated in the order or who is a member of a class of persons so designated;
>
>   (c) order the person receiving the detained person into custody under paragraph (*b*) to take him or her to the state or entity and, on the return of the detained person to Canada, to return that person to the place of confinement where he or she was when the order was made;
>
>   (d) state the reasons for the transfer; and
>
>   (e) fix the period of time at or before the expiration of which the detained person must be returned.

Section 25(4) provides that the transfer order may include any terms and conditions that the judge deems desirable:

(4) A transfer order made under subsection (1) may include any terms or conditions that the judge making it considers desirable, including those relating to the protection of the interests of the detained person.

(f) Standing in proceedings under Part I of Act

In *United Kingdom v. Ramsden, supra,* the United Kingdom requested the assistance of the Government of Canada under the Act. The request concerned an investigation into the activities of a British citizen named Terence Ramsden. Ramsden had been petitioned into bankruptcy in the United Kingdom and was alleged to have failed to disclose assets to the trustee in bankruptcy. As a result, Ramsden was charged in the United Kingdom with bankruptcy fraud. Pursuant to the request for assistance, four search warrants and an evidence-gathering order were issued under the Act. In subsequent proceedings including an application under s. 15 to send the documents seized to the requesting state, and an application under s. 20(1) to send evidence obtained pursuant to an evidence-gathering order to the requesting state, Ramsden asserted that he was a "person who claims to have an interest in any record or thing" seized or produced, as referred to in ss. 15(1) and 20(2) respectively. On this basis he sought access to the material seized under s. 12 and produced under s. 18, and standing to make representations to the court on the issue of whether this material should be sent to the United Kingdom.

The Ontario Court of Appeal found that Ramsden did not have standing to become involved in the sending proceedings or to request access to the material. The court observed a distinction between a person who is "interested" in proceedings because of his status as the target of the investigation, and a person who has "an interest in any record or thing" seized or produced under the terms of the Act. Being the target alone confers no standing in any proceedings under the Act. Charron J.A. for the court stated, at pp. 303-304:

> Mr. Ramsden is the target of the investigation in the United Kingdom which led to the requests for assistance in this country. As such, he is undoubtedly interested in the proceedings and centrally connected to the whole process. Although in first instance Mr. Ramsden relied, at least in part, upon the fact that he was the target of the investigation as a basis for obtaining standing in relation to some of the proceedings, he concedes before this Court that this fact, in and of itself, would not serve to give him standing with respect to any of the proceedings in question. In my view, this concession is a wise one.
>
> Nothing in the Act could be interpreted as giving the target of an investigation automatic standing in any of the proceedings. In fact, the adoption of such a principle would arguably run contrary to the stated objective of the mutual legal assistance scheme to provide the widest measure of mutual legal assistance in criminal matters in a prompt and efficient manner.

Accordingly, Charron J.A. concluded that Ramsden would have to bring himself within the purview of the Act "on some other basis" than that of target of the investigation. (p. 304)

The "other basis" advanced by Ramsden was that he was both a "person claiming an interest" in the records or things seized or produced within the meaning of ss. 15(1) and 20(2) of the Act and a "third party" the protection of whose interests may be the subject-matter of terms and conditions attached to orders made under ss. 15(1), 18(5) and 20(2) of the Act. Charron J.A. considered two possible types of interest that Ramsden might have in the proceedings. The first was a proprietary or possessory interest. Charron J.A. found that a proprietary or possessory interest in material seized or produced would bring an individual within the ambit of the Act (at p. 305): "It is conceded, and rightly so, that a proprietary interest, or even a mere possessory interest, in the material seized or produced would bring Mr. Ramsden within the purview of the Act." However, Charron J.A. found that the material before the court was "incapable of supporting Mr. Ramsden's claim to a proprietary or possessory interest in the material seized or produced pursuant to the search warrants and the evidence-gathering order." (p. 305)

Ramsden advanced a second type of interest, that being his relationship with some of the individuals named in the search warrants and the evidence-gathering order. One individual was a stockbroker who had dealings with Ramsden. The other persons were solicitors who had either personally or through their firms rendered legal assistance to Ramsden, to a trust of which Ramsden was alleged to be the beneficiary, and to companies with which Ramsden was allegedly associated. Ramsden argued that by the very nature of these relationships any information communicated by him to these persons was subject either to privilege or to a right of confidentiality having regard to the limited purpose for which the information was imparted. Ramsden claimed that he had a right to ensure that these rights were respected, and thus he had a legal interest in the information imparted by these persons. He argued that this interest brought him within the purview of the Act. Charron J.A. found that the evidence before the court did not support the existence of any legal interest arising out of the relationships alleged (at pp. 306–307):

> In my view, the material before the court cannot support a finding of any legally recognized interest arising out of the "relationships" as alleged. While solicitor-client privilege and a right to confidentiality of information are legally recognized interests in certain circumstances, more is required to found such a claim than the bare allegation of the existence of "a relationship." Nowhere in the material is there even an assertion that Mr. Ramsden in fact imparted information to any given individual nor is there any assertion that such information was imparted in circumstances giving rise to the claims asserted. Lastly, there is nothing in the material linking the interest as asserted to the particular evidence seized or produced.

Similarly, in *Russian Federation, supra*, Doherty J.A. held that there was no basis upon which the appellant corporation, which had been made the subject of an evidence-gathering order under s. 18 of the Act, could challenge an application for a sending order related to bank documents obtained under separate order from the account of the target. He stated, at p. 336:

> [52] There is a second reason why this submission must be rejected. It relates to copies of documents that had been seized from Pokidyshev's bank account. The appellant has no connection to or interests in those documents. There is nothing in the material which provides any basis upon which the appellant could have standing to challenge the application for an order sending these documents to the Russian Federation: *United Kingdom v. Ramsden, supra*, at pp. 303-306.

In contrast, the authorities of Taiwan received standing to participate in a s. 15 hearing in the case of *Romania v. Cheng* (1996), 32 W.C.B. (2d) 291 (N.S.S.C.). In that case Romania had made an extradition request to Canada for the surrender of Cheng and other officers of a Taiwanese-registered ship based on allegations that they had murdered Romanian stowaways at sea by throwing them overboard. In aid of the request for extradition, a mutual legal assistance request was effected when the ship docked in the port of Halifax, and a search of the ship pursuant to a warrant issued under s. 12 of the Act took place. In granting standing to Taiwan to participate at the s. 15 sending hearing, Cacchione J. of the Nova Scotia Supreme Court held that Taiwan was a third party with respect to whose interests a judge may include terms and conditions in a sending order under s. 15. The decision is noteworthy because it was not a possessory or proprietary interest which was recognized by the court but rather the interest of Taiwan in its governmental capacity, in the investigation and prosecution of offences allegedly committed by its nationals on a ship flying its flag. Leave to appeal this decision was granted by the Nova Scotia Court of Appeal, *per* Chipman J.A. in *Canada (Attorney General) v. China (Republic)* (1996), 113 C.C.C. (3d) 470 (N.S.C.A. [In Chambers]). The appeal did not go forward as a result of the ultimate discharge of the fugitives at the extradition hearing.

(g) Appeals

Section 35 of the Act, which is located within Part I of the Act, provides for appeals to the "court of appeal," but only in connection with questions of law and with leave of the court of appeal:

> **35.** An appeal lies, with leave on a question of law alone, to the court of appeal, within the meaning of section 2 of the *Criminal Code*, from any order or decision of a judge or a court in Canada made under this Act, if the application for leave to appeal is made to a judge of the court of appeal within fifteen days after the order or decision.

The term "court of appeal" is defined in s. 2 of the *Criminal Code* as the court of appeal of the province.

In *Canada (Attorney General) v. Ross, supra,* the applicant applied for leave to appeal under s. 35 of the Act from a judgment of the British Columbia Supreme Court ordering the transmission to the United States of materials seized and gathered under ss. 12 and 18 of the Act. The applicant was facing a charge of murder in the United States. To assist the prosecution, the United States had obtained a search warrant under s. 12 of the Act for the person's Canadian residence and evidence-gathering orders under s. 18 to obtain telephone and health records. The documents in question were ordered to be transmitted to the United States after a hearing held under ss. 15 and 20 of the Act. In seeking leave to appeal the transmission order, the applicant advanced three grounds of appeal: (1) that the transmitting judge erred in interpreting the phrase "evidence of commission of the offence" in ss. 12 and 18; (2) that the transmitting judge erred in failing to examine each document in order to determine whether it constituted evidence; (3) that the transmitting judge erred in limiting his jurisdiction in the course of the review (at pp. 230-231). Southin J.A. of the British Columbia Court of Appeal dismissed the leave application.

Southin J.A. set out four criteria for the s. 35 leave determination, at p. 237:

[33] Applying to this Act the test developed on analogous provisions, I consider the criteria are:

1.   Is the question raised not settled by authority?
2.   Is it of importance generally and, if not of importance generally, is it nonetheless of great importance to a person with serious interests, such as his liberty, at stake?
3.   Does the proposition of law put forward have any merit or, to put it another way, does it appear to the judge not to be frivolous?
4.   Are there other discretionary considerations, such as prejudice to either the applicant or the requesting state which require to be taken into account?

In determining that leave to appeal ought to be refused, Southin J.A. relied on the fourth criteria, given the prejudice that could be caused to the American prosecution if the transmission of the documents was delayed, at pp. 237-238:

[34] In the case at bar, I consider the answer to both the first and second questions to be clearly yes.

[35] If it were not for the fourth consideration, I would grant leave on the simple footing that it is not right that a serious question should be determined, in effect, by one judge of this court. I might think that an argument was without merit which one of my brethren might think to be of great merit. But the fourth of the tests prevents my disposing of this matter in such an easy way.

[36] There may well be, on the evidence, serious prejudice to the United States of America if I grant leave. The trial is, as I have said, set for the 12th July. This court cannot, I think, in the light of its present caseload, hear this appeal and deliver considered reasons by the end of May. The United States authorities need these records and things sufficiently before the trial to prepare for the trial and the end of May is, I think, too late for that purpose.

This passage suggests the criteria are conjunctive rather than disjunctive. In deciding a leave application under s. 35, the judge must consider all four criteria.

As for the third criteria, Southin J.A. found that the applicant had failed to demonstrate a breach under ss. 15 and 20 by the transmitting judge. Rather, Southin J.A. appeared to accept the respondent's position that, in the absence of a direct attack on the validity of the warrant or order, the judge under ss. 15 and 20 is only required to confirm that the items seized or gathered are accurately described in the report prepared under ss. 14 and 19 of the Act. With respect to the review by the judge under s. 15, Southin J.A. made the following comment, at p. 238:

> [42] To all this, Mr. Owens says that it is enough when [no] direct attack is made on the validity of the warrant, and none was made here, for the reviewing judge to determine if the records or things seized meet the description of the warrant. He says that if they meet the description, they are "seized in execution of the warrant." The judge may, at least when the things and records are adequately described in the report, decide whether to transmit simply by looking at the description. Here, everything in the report meets the description in the warrant. Once a thing is so seized, whether it should be transmitted is a matter of discretion. The judge has no duty to exercise the power conferred by s. 15(2).

With respect to the review by the judge under s. 20, Southin J.A. made the following finding, at p. 239:

> [46] . . . Parliament cannot have intended by this statute that a Canadian judge should go into questions of admissibility under the foreign law in contradistinction to questions of relevance which are not essentially questions of law, but mostly of common sense.
> [47] . . . If no attack is made on the accuracy or completeness of a report, and none was made here, the judge may, I think, take it at face value.

In *Heafey v. Canada (Procureur général)* (12 juin 1995), no C.A. Montréal 500-10-000189-959 (Qué. C.A.), the applicants sought leave to appeal from a judgment of the Superior Court of Quebec confirming that warrants issued under s. 12 of the Act were valid and ordering that evidence seized under the warrants be sent to the requesting state (the United States). Baudouin J.A. of the Quebec Court of Appeal dismissed the leave application. In so doing, Baudouin J.A. considered the requirement under s. 35 of the Act that an appeal be "on a question of law alone." He first made the general observation that the phrase "on a question of law alone" renders the appeal right under s. 35 narrow (at p. 5 — in reaching this conclusion, Baudouin J.A. relied on, among other decisions, the judgment of Southin J.A. in *Canada (Attorney General) v. Ross, supra*):

> However, I wish first to draw attention to the extremely limited nature of the right of appeal under the Act. Parliament has allowed an appeal "*on a question of law alone*". This particular expression is not confined to this particular Act; the same expression can

be found in the *Criminal Code* and other statutes. The few judgments on the matter I was able to consult indicate that the judge or Court that grants leave to appeal must be convinced that what is involved is a strict problem of law (for example, a misconstruing of the statute) and not a mistaken interpretation of the evidence or the circumstances, let alone some doubtful exercise of judicial discretion in the enforcement of legislation . . . .

Baudouin J.A. then considered the specific bases advanced by the applicants in support of the leave application. Firstly, it was argued that the judge mistakenly interpreted the tests concerning the reliability and identity of the sources in support of the affiant's allegations. Baudouin J.A. did not determine whether this was a question of law alone, concluding rather that this argument was without foundation.

Secondly, it was argued that the judge who issued the warrant failed to consider, as required by s. 12(1)(c) of the Act, whether in the circumstances it would be appropriate to make an evidence-gathering order instead of issuing a search warrant. Baudouin J.A. concluded that this was a question of fact or mixed law and fact, at p. 6:

> In my opinion, it is hard to argue that this is an issue of "*law alone*". Rather, it would seem to me to pertain to a question of fact or at least a question of mixed law and fact. Parliament wished to open up some room for judicial discretion and enable the judge to verify the appropriateness of proceeding in accordance with one of the models provided for by the statute. Thus, unless this discretion was not exercised judicially, I do not think this is a ground of appeal that Parliament intended to make available to the Court of Appeal or to one of its judges. In this case I have not been shown any reason to intervene concerning the judicial exercise of this discretion and I am therefore of the opinion that this argument must be set aside.

Thirdly, it was argued that the sending judge failed to ascertain the specific conditions in which the seized records would be preserved and the methods by which they could eventually be returned to Canada. However, Baudouin J.A. reviewed the conditions that had been imposed on the sending of the seized records and concluded that "I have some difficulty therefore in seeing how the judge could have been more specific and more explicit."

Finally, it was argued that the sending judge insufficiently protected the interests of third parties in the items seized as required by s. 15(1)(b)(iii) of the Act. Baudouin J.A. found that the protection was adequate and, in any event, that this was at best a question of mixed law and fact, at pp. 8–9:

> Here again, with all due respect for the contrary opinion, the sending of the originals, necessitated by allegations that some are forged, will certainly cause some prejudice to the applicants and perhaps to some third parties (for example, to the subscribers of promissory notes and mortgagees). However, copies were made of these records and, in the circumstances, if there is prejudice related to the relinquishment of the originals, it may be compensated by other means. Again, this fourth argument cannot in my view be relied on in support of the motion since, viewed from the perspective that is most

favourable to the applicant, it would at most constitute only a mixed question of law and fact.

Baudouin J.A. concluded that "the motion as drafted fails to demonstrate to me any ground of '*law alone*' that could enable me to grant the requested leave." (p. 8)

In *Canada (Attorney General) v. China (Republic)* (1996), 113 C.C.C. (3d) 470 (N.S.C.A. [In Chambers]), the Attorney General of Canada on behalf of the State of Romania applied for leave to appeal under s. 35 of the Act from an order of the Nova Scotia Supreme Court allowing the Republic of China (Taiwan) to intervene in a hearing held under s. 15 of the Act. The case originated with a Romanian extradition request to Canada for the surrender of seven officers of a Taiwanese-registered ship on allegations that they had murdered Romanian stowaways at sea by throwing them overboard. A mutual legal assistance request was made by Romania while the ship was docked in the port of Halifax, and as a result of a search warrant issued under s. 12 of the Act a number of items were seized. An application by Taiwan for leave to intervene in the hearing under s. 15 of the Act was granted on the basis that Taiwan had an "interest" in the investigation and prosecution by Romania of offences alleged to have been committed by Taiwanese nationals on a Taiwanese ship. The judge also adjourned the transmission hearing *sine die* pending the outcome of the extradition hearing.

The Attorney General of Canada on behalf of Romania sought leave to appeal on the basis that a proprietary or possessory interest in the things seized was required in order to come within the terms of s. 15 with respect to standing, and that the statute was not satisfied only on the basis that the fugitives were Taiwanese and the ship registered in Taiwan. Chipman J.A. of the Nova Scotia Court of Appeal [In Chambers] granted the application for leave to appeal. Chipman J.A. referred to the passage from the judgment of Baudouin J.A. of the Quebec Court of Appeal in *Heafey v. Canada (Procureur général), supra*, which held that the scope of s. 35 is confined to "a question of law alone." Chipman J.A. then reviewed Southin J.A.'s judgment in *Canada (Attorney General) v. Ross, supra*, and adopted the four criteria approach to assessing leave applications under s. 35 (at p. 474). Chipman J.A. then used the criteria to assess the two grounds advanced by the applicant. He first dealt with the ground that Taiwan was not a person with an interest in the things seized within the meaning of s. 15 of the Act. With respect to the first criteria, Chipman J.A. found that the issue was not settled by authority. In particular, he reviewed the decision of the Ontario Court of Appeal in *United Kingdom v. Ramsden* and found that that case did not settle the issue (at p. 476):

> In my opinion the Ontario Court of Appeal does not answer the question whether the interest claimed by a person within the meaning of s. [15] must be a proprietary or possessory interest although it comes tantalizingly close to doing so. Its key findings were that Mr. Ramsden did not have such an interest, and that the material before the Court could not support the finding of any legally recognized interest arising out of the relationships as alleged.

I therefore conclude that the issue raised by the applicant is not settled by authority.

Chipman J.A. also found that the ground was of importance to the applicant and not frivolous and thus it passed the second and third criteria (p. 477). Finally, with respect to the fourth criteria, contrasting this case with *Canada (Attorney General) v. Ross, supra*, Chipman J.A. concluded that the hearing of the appeal would not cause any prejudice to the parties (p. 478):

> The hearing of the applicant's appeal before this Court will not work any prejudice such as was the case in *Canada (Attorney General) v. Ross, supra*. Such appeal will, in all probability, be heard within a few months. Nobody has suggested that the extradition hearing, including any possible appeals, will be concluded before then.

In *R. v. Vonk Dairy Products B.V.* (1998), 110 O.A.C. 151, Charron J.A., of the Ontario Court of Appeal [In Chambers], denied leave to appeal a decision of the lower court which had refused standing to the applicants to make representations at a s. 15 hearing. Charron J.A. observed that the application did not raise a question of law alone and was an attempt to seek a rehearing of the issue of whether the applicants had a reasonable expectation of privacy which could support their claim to have an interest in the material seized.

(h) Transfer of persons to Canada

Section 40(1) allows the Minister of Justice, in order to give effect to a request of a Canadian competent authority, to authorize the entry into Canada of persons who are members of an inadmissible class of persons under s. 19 of the *Immigration Act*. The Minister may specify the place to which the person is to go and remain in Canada as well as the period of time during which the person may remain in Canada. The Minister may also make the authorization subject to any conditions that the Minister deems appropriate. Section 40(1) reads as follows:

> **40.** (1) The Minister may, in order to give effect to a request of a Canadian competent authority, authorize a person in a state or entity who is a member of an inadmissible class of persons described in section 19 of the *Immigration Act* to come into Canada at a place designated by the Minister and to go to and remain in a place in Canada so designated for the period of time specified by the Minister, and the Minister may make the authorization subject to any conditions that the Minister considers desirable.

Section 40(2) allows the Minister of Justice to vary an authorization given under s. 40(1), including extending the time period of the authorization:

> (2) The Minister may vary the terms of an authorization granted under subsection (1) and, in particular, may extend the period of time during which the person is authorized to remain in a place in Canada.

Section 40(3) sets out the consequences of non-compliance with an authorization made under s. 40(1). More specifically, a person who breaches the authorization is deemed, for the purposes of the *Immigration Act*, to be a person who entered Canada as a visitor and remains in Canada after he or she has ceased to be a visitor:

> (3) A person to whom an authorization is granted under subsection (1) who is found in a place in Canada other than the place designated in the authorization or in any place in Canada after the expiration of the period of time specified in the authorization or who fails to comply with some other condition of the authorization shall, for the purposes of the *Immigration Act*, be deemed to be a person who entered Canada as a visitor and remains therein after he has ceased to be a visitor.

Where the Minister of Justice authorizes the transfer to Canada of a person for the purpose of giving effect to a request of a Canadian competent authority, s. 42 enables a judge to order the detention of the person. Section 42(1) sets out the power of a judge to make the order:

> **42.** (1) When the Minister, in order to give effect to a request of a Canadian competent authority, authorizes a person who is detained in a state or entity to be transferred to Canada for a period of time specified by the Minister, a judge of the province to which the person is to be transferred may make an order for the detention of the person anywhere in Canada and for the return of the person to the state or entity.

Section 42(2) provides that an order made under s. 42(1) is paramount to any other Canadian order concerning anything that occurred before the person was transferred to Canada:

> (2) An order made under subsection (1) is paramount to any order made, in respect of anything that occurred before the person is transferred to Canada, by a Canadian court, a judge of a Canadian court, a Canadian justice of the peace or any other person who has power in Canada to compel the appearance of another person.

Section 42(3) enables a judge who makes an order under s. 42(1) or any other judge of the same court, to vary the order:

> (3) The judge who made the detention order or another judge of the same court may vary its terms and conditions and, in particular, may extend the duration of the detention.

§2.3 Admissibility in Canada of Evidence Obtained Abroad Pursuant to Agreement (Part II of Act)

Part II of the Act (ss. 36–39) deals with the admissibility in Canada of evidence obtained abroad pursuant to a mutual legal assistance agreement. Section 36 deals with records obtained by Canada from a foreign state or entity pursuant to an mutual legal assistance request. Section 36(1) states that "[i]n a proceeding with respect to which Parliament has jurisdiction, a record or a copy of the record and any affidavit, certificate or other statement pertaining to the record made by a person who has custody or knowledge of the record, sent to the Minister by a state or entity in accordance with a Canadian request, is not inadmissible in evidence by reason only that a statement contained in the record, copy, affidavit, certificate or other statement is hearsay or a statement of opinion."

Section 36(2) addresses the determination of the probative value of a foreign record admitted into evidence under the Act:

> (2) For the purpose of determining the probative value of a record or a copy of a record admitted in evidence under this Act, the trier of fact may examine the record or copy, receive evidence orally or by affidavit, or by a certificate or other statement pertaining to the record in which a person attests that the certificate or statement is made in conformity with the laws that apply to a state or entity, whether or not the certificate or statement is in the form of an affidavit attested to before an official of the state or entity, including evidence as to the circumstances in which the information contained in the record or copy was written, stored or reproduced, and draw any reasonable inference from the form or content of the record or copy.

Section 37 of the Act provides that "things" obtained pursuant to a Canadian mutual legal assistance request as well as affidavits, statements, or certificates relating to the thing are admissible in evidence notwithstanding that the affidavit, statement, or certificate contains hearsay or opinion evidence:

> **37.** In proceeding with respect to which Parliament has jurisdiction, a thing and any affidavit, certificate or other statement pertaining to the thing made by a person in a state or entity as to the identity and possession of the thing from the time it was obtained until its sending to a competent authority in Canada by the state or entity in accordance with a Canadian request, are not inadmissible in evidence by reason only that the affidavit, certificate or other statement contains hearsay or a statement of opinion.

Section 38(1) of the Act provides for the admissibility of statements contained in affidavits, certificates, or other statements referred to in ss. 36 or 37:

> **38.** (1) An affidavit, certificate or other statement mentioned in section 36 or 37 is, in the absence of evidence to the contrary, proof of the statements contained therein without proof of the signature or official character of the person appearing to have signed the affidavit, certificate or other statement.

Section 38(2) of the Act sets out a minimum seven-day notice requirement for evidence that a party intends to adduce under ss. 36 and 37:

> (2) Unless the court decides otherwise, in a proceeding with respect to which Parliament has jurisdiction, no record or copy thereof, no thing and no affidavit, certif-

icate or other statement mentioned in section 36 or 37 shall be received in evidence unless the party intending to produce it has given to the party against whom it is intended to be produced seven days notice, excluding holidays, of that intention, accompanied by a copy of the record, copy, affidavit, certificate or other statement and unless, in the case of a thing, the party intending to produce it has made it available for inspection by the party against whom it is intended to be produced during the five days following a request by that party that it be made so available.

Finally, s. 39 of the Act provides that, "[t]he service of a document in the territory over which the state or entity has jurisdiction may be proved by affidavit of the person who served it."

§3.0 The *Charter* and Extraterritorial Application

The conduct of foreign authorities in carrying out a Canadian mutual legal assistance request need not comply with Canadian legal standards, although the issue of unfairness may be raised under ss. 11(d) and 7 of the *Charter* at a subsequent Canadian trial. Secondly, the preauthorization requirements for search and seizure under s. 8 of the *Charter* do not apply to the preparation of a mutual legal assistance request seeking the seizure of documents by a foreign jurisdiction.

§3.1 Non-Applicability of *Charter* to Conduct of Foreign Authorities in Carrying Out Canadian Mutual Legal Assistance Request

In *R. v. Terry*, [1996] 2 S.C.R. 207, and *R. v. Harrer*, [1995] 3 S.C.R. 562, the Supreme Court of Canada affirmed the principle that the conduct of foreign authorities in carrying out a Canadian legal assistance request is not subject to *Charter* review, although the issue of unfairness may be raised under ss. 11(d) and 7 of the *Charter* at a subsequent Canadian trial. In *R. v. Terry*, the accused was charged in Canada with a fatal stabbing. He was arrested in the United States on a warrant issued in response to a request from Canada for his extradition. The Canadian police then made an informal request (that is, their request was not made through a formal mechanism, such as a mutual legal assistance treaty) to the U.S. police to interview the accused. The U.S. police complied with this request. In so doing, the U.S. police adhered to the American legal requirements for taking a statement. However, the taking of the statement would not have met the standards required under the Canadian *Charter* had the statement been taken in Canada. Subsequently, the accused argued that his state-ment was inadmissible under s. 24(2) of the *Charter* because the conduct of the U.S. police did not comply with the Canadian *Charter* rights of an accused upon arrest.

McLachlin J. in her judgment for the Supreme Court of Canada concluded that foreign police cooperating on an informal basis with Canadian police are not required to conform to the requirements of the *Charter*. Relying on *R. v. Filonov*, *supra*, she made the following comment, at pp. 216-217:

[18] The practice of cooperation between police of different countries does not make the law of one country applicable in the other country. Bilateral mutual legal assistance treaties negotiated under the authority of the *Mutual Legal Assistance in Criminal Matters Act*, R.S.C., 1985, c. 30 (4th Supp.), stipulate that the actions requested of the assisting state shall be undertaken in accordance with its own laws, not those of the requesting state: see, for example, the *Treaty Between the Government of Canada and the Government of the United States on Mutual Legal Assistance in Criminal Matters*, Can. T.S. 1990 No. 19, Art. VII, s. 2. As Dilks J. noted in *R. v. Filonov* (1993), 82 C.C.C. (3d) 516 (Ont. Ct. (Gen. Div.)), at p. 520, "[t]he sovereign authority of Canada ends with the sending of the request" for assistance. Thus, if Santa Rosa police in this case had been responding to a treaty request, they would not have been governed by the *Charter*.

[19] Still less can the *Charter* govern the conduct of foreign police cooperating with Canadian police on an informal basis. The personal decision of a foreign officer or agency to assist the Canadian police cannot dilute the exclusivity of the foreign state's sovereignty within its territory, where its law alone governs the process of enforcement. The gathering of evidence by these foreign officers or agency is subject to the rules of that country and none other. Consequently, any cooperative investigation involving law enforcement agencies of Canada and the United States will be governed by the laws of the jurisdiction in which the activity is undertaken: see Williams and Castel, *Canadian Criminal Law: International and Transnational Aspects* (1981), at p. 320.

McLachlin J. noted that the rule against the extraterritorial application of domestic law is not absolute, at p. 215:

[15] The principle that a state's law applies only within its boundaries is not absolute: *The Case of the SS. "Lotus"* (1927), P.C.I.J. Ser. A, No. 10, at p. 20. States may invoke a jurisdiction to prescribe offences committed elsewhere to deal with special problems, such as those provisions of the *Criminal Code*, R.S.C., 1985, c. C-46, pertaining to offences on aircraft (s. 7(1), (2)) and war crimes and other crimes against humanity (s. 7(3.71)). A state may likewise formally consent to permit Canada and other states to enforce their laws within its territory for limited purposes. In such cases, the *Charter* may find limited application abroad.

McLachlin J. added that, "these exceptions, none of which is asserted in the case at bar, do not negate the general rule that a state's laws apply only within its own territory" (p. 215).

McLachlin J. further pointed out, at pp. 218–219, that any potential unfairness to the accused at the latter's trial in Canada could be addressed under ss. 11(d) and 7 of the *Charter*:

[25] . . . . The *Charter* guarantees the accused a fair trial: s. 11(*d*). More generally, the *Charter* provides that the accused's liberty cannot be limited except in accordance with the principles of fundamental justice: s. 7. To admit evidence gathered in an abusive fashion may well violate the principles of fundamental justice . . . . The accused may use these and other principles of fundamental justice to obtain redress for abuses abroad in gathering evidence subsequently tendered against him or her.

Similarly, in *R. v. Harrer, supra*, the accused challenged the admissibility at her trial in Canada of a statement obtained in the United States by American authorities carrying out their duties under American law. Harrer was arrested by immigration authorities in the United States. The authorities had reason to believe that Harrer was illegally in the United States. The immigration authorities who arrested Harrer were accompanied by American police who suspected that Harrer had assisted her boyfriend Hagerman in escaping custody in Canada while he was being held for extradition to the United States. The questioning of Harrer was conducted in accordance with American procedural safeguards. However, these safeguards fell short of those required under the Canadian *Charter*. The information gathered by the American authorities was used by the Canadian government against Harrer in the latter's trial in Canada for assisting in Hagerman's escape. The issue was whether the interrogation infringed s. 10(b) of the *Charter* and whether it should be excluded under s. 24(2).

La Forest J., writing one of the two judgments for a unanimous Supreme Court, held that the *Charter* did not apply where the acts in question were wholly those of American authorities, at p. 571:

[12] What I think is determinative against the argument that the *Charter* applied to the interrogation in the present case is the simple fact that the United States immigration officials and the Marshals were not acting on behalf of any of the governments of Canada, the provinces or the territories, the state actors to which, by virtue of s. 32(1) the application of the *Charter* is confined; see *RWDSU* v. *Dolphin Delivery Ltd.*, [1986] 2 S.C.R. 573. It follows that the *Charter* simply has no direct application to the interrogations in the United States because the governments mentioned in s. 32(1) were not implicated in these activities.

Consistent with McLachlin J. in *R. v. Terry*, La Forest J. noted that the rule against the extraterritorial application of domestic laws is not absolute, at pp. 570–571:

[10] . . . I would not wish my remarks to be interpreted as giving credence to the view that the ambit of the *Charter* is automatically limited to Canadian territory. This is in no way inconsistent with the extradition cases decided in this Court or *Spencer* v. *The Queen*, [1985] 2 S.C.R. 278. All these cases were concerned either with the application of the *Charter* to foreign law, or to the activities of agents of a foreign state in performing their functions in their own countries. To apply our law in such situations would truly be giving the *Charter* impermissible extraterritorial application as I observed in *Canada* v. *Schmidt*, [1987] 1 S.C.R. 500. . . .

[11] Subject to whatever argument may be made to the contrary, it strikes me that the automatic exclusion of *Charter* application outside Canada might unduly restrict the protection Canadians have a right to expect against the interference with their rights by our governments or their agents. Consequently, had the interrogation about a Canadian offence been made by Canadian peace officers in the United States in circumstances that would constitute a violation of the *Charter* had the interrogation taken place in Canada, an entirely different issue would arise. A different issue would also arise if the United States policemen and immigration authorities had been acting as agents of the Canadian

police in furthering a criminal prosecution in Canada. These issues do not arise and I shall say no more about them.

In *R. v. Cook*, [1998] 2 S.C.R. 597, the majority of the Supreme Court held that the *Charter* did govern the conduct of Canadian investigators conducting an interrogation abroad. In that case, a statement was taken in the United States by Canadian police who were gathering evidence concerning a Canadian murder offence for use in a prosecution which was to take place in Canada. Cook, who was in custody in the United States as a result of a Canadian extradition request, was interviewed in prison by two Canadian detectives. Twenty minutes into the interview and after having asked Cook about whether he had committed the crime, Cook was advised of his s. 10(b) rights to counsel, his rights to legal aid, and that he did not have to speak to the detectives. In Canada it was argued on Cook's behalf that the taking of the statement was in violation of his *Charter* rights and that pursuant to s. 24(2) ought to have been excluded at his trial.

Cory and Iacobucci JJ. writing for the majority of the Supreme Court of Canada agreed and held that the principles enunciated in *R. v. Terry* and *R. v. Harrer*, which prevent the imposition of Canadian procedural requirements to foreign law enforcement officials acting on their own soil, did not apply so as to prevent the application of the *Charter* to Canadian law enforcement officers undertaking a Canadian investigation abroad. Cory and Iacobucci JJ. stated, at pp. 616, 627–628:

> [25] In our view, the *Charter* applies to the actions of the Vancouver detectives in interviewing the appellant in New Orleans. Two factors are critical to this conclusion and provide helpful guidelines for recognizing those rare circumstances where the *Charter* may apply outside of Canada: (1) the impugned act falls within s. 32(1) of the *Charter*; and (2) the application of the *Charter* to the actions of the Canadian detectives in the United States does not, in this particular case, interfere with the sovereign authority of the foreign state and thereby generate an objectionable extraterritorial effect.
>
> . . . .
>
> [49] In accordance with the principles discussed above, we conclude that the *Charter* applies to the actions of the Vancouver detectives in New Orleans in the present case. First, both the appellant's arrest and detention and subsequent interrogation were actions initiated and carried out by Canadian law enforcement officials. The arrest warrant had been granted in response to an extradition request made by Canada. The interrogation was conducted by Canadian detectives, as opposed to foreign officials, in accordance with their powers of investigation as derived from Canadian law. Thus, the impugned action falls within the purview of s. 32(1) of the *Charter* and the first criterion is satisfied.
>
> [50] Second, in the particular circumstances of this case, the application of the *Charter* on the jurisdictional basis of nationality to the actions of the Canadian detectives abroad does not result in an interference with the territorial jurisdiction of the foreign state. In reaching this conclusion, we are relying in particular on the following factual elements: although the physical arrest was executed by a U.S. official pursuant to U.S. law, the arrest and the interrogation were initiated by a Canadian extradition request and

related exclusively to an offence committed in Canada and to be prosecuted in Canada; the trial judge concluded at para. 15 that the United States Marshal "took great care not to become involved in the Vancouver investigation and impair it in any way [and that h]e had no intention of questioning the accused or advising him in any way"; and the interview was conducted solely by Canadian officers deriving their investigatory powers from Canadian legislation. In these circumstances, Canadian criminal law standards are not being imposed on foreign officials. Further, the application of the *Charter* in the circumstances to the simple questioning of the appellant by Canadian authorities does not implicate or interfere with any criminal procedures engaged by or involving U.S. authorities.

§3.2 The *Charter* and Preparation of Mutual Legal Assistance Requests to Other Countries

The sending of a request for assistance to another country does not by itself engage the s. 8 *Charter* rights of the person who is the subject-matter of the request. In *Schreiber v. Canada (Attorney General)*, [1998] 1 S.C.R. 841, a letter of request was sent by Canada to Switzerland seeking assistance in the investigation of an alleged criminal offence. At the time of the request, September 29, 1995, Canada and Switzerland had not yet entered into a mutual legal assistance treaty. On November 17, 1995, these two countries did enter such a treaty. Even though the case involves a letters rogatory request, the logic applies equally in the mutual legal assistance context. There is no legislation or treaty specifying an authorization process for Canadian mutual legal assistance or letters rogatory requests. The Act specifies the manner in which Canadian authorities are to execute foreign mutual legal assistance requests. However, it does not set out an authorization process for mutual legal assistance requests by Canada to foreign states.

The question in *Schreiber* was whether the Canadian standard for the issuance of a search warrant should have been satisfied before the Minister of Justice and the Attorney General of Canada submitted a letter of request asking Swiss authorities to search for and seize the respondent Schreiber's banking documents and records. Wetston J. of the Federal Court—Trial Division ((1996), 108 C.C.C. (3d) 208) found that s. 8 of the *Charter* did apply to a request for banking information located in Switzerland and that the request initiated a seizure which had an impact upon the respondent's reasonable expectation of privacy. This was upheld by the majority of the Federal Court of Appeal ((1997), 114 C.C.C. (3d) 97). An appeal from the decision of the Federal Court of Appeal was allowed by the Supreme Court of Canada.

L'Heureux-Dubé J. writing for herself and three members of the court held that the Canadian Government's action in sending a letter of request to Switzerland was not proscribed by s. 8 of the *Charter* (at p. 858). L'Heureux-Dubé J. made the analogy to interjurisdictional police cooperation within Canada between provinces, at pp. 859-860:

[30] . . . It is useful first to consider the issue of interjurisdictional co-operation wholly within the domestic Canadian context, in order to appreciate that the letter of request did not intrude upon the respondent's privacy, and therefore did not engage s. 8 of the *Charter*. If the police in one Canadian jurisdiction want to investigate, for instance, bank records in another Canadian jurisdiction, the investigating authorities would ask the authorities in that other jurisdiction to undertake a search or a seizure. The request itself would not be subject to *Charter* scrutiny. No prior judicial authorization would be obtained until the request had been received, at which time the authorities would secure a warrant in order to undertake the search or seizure. In the event that the search or seizure was challenged, it would be the warrant, and the actions taken pursuant to that warrant, which would be subjected to *Charter* review. The original investigator's action in making the request to the authorities in another province would not be challengeable, because it is not an action which invades anyone's right to be secure against unreasonable search and seizure.

Based on this reasoning and relying on the Supreme Court of Canada's decision in *R. v. Terry*, L'Heureux-Dubé J. emphasized that all of the actions in this case that could be said to have interfered with the respondent's privacy were undertaken in Switzerland by Swiss authorities, and thus did not fall within the purview of s. 8 protection, at p. 860:

[31] This reasoning is apposite to the present appeal. By itself, the letter of request does not engage s. 8 of the *Charter*. All of those actions which rely on state compulsion in order to interfere with the respondent's privacy interests were undertaken in Switzerland by Swiss authorities. Neither the actions of the Swiss authorities, nor the laws which authorized their actions, are subject to *Charter* scrutiny: *R. v. Terry*, [1996] 2 S.C.R. 207, at p. 217. The *Charter* does not protect everyone against unreasonable search and seizure in the abstract. Rather, the *Charter* guarantees everyone the right to be secure against unreasonable search and seizure by, *inter alia*, the government of Canada.

L'Heureux-Dubé J. approved of the decision of Dilks J. for the Ontario Court (General Division) in *R. v. Filonov* (1993), 82 C.C.C. (3d) 516 (Ont. Gen. Div.), where, in an analogous factual situation, Dilks J. had held that s. 8 of the *Charter* did not extend to a request for legal assistance. As described by L'Heureux-Dubé J., at pp. 861–862:

[33] . . . . In *Filonov*, Dilks J. considered whether the actions of U.S. authorities in conducting a search and seizure pursuant to a Canadian treaty request implicated s. 8 of the *Charter*. On facts analogous to this case, Dilks J. made two distinct findings which inform the analysis of the applicability of s. 8 of the *Charter*, and which are relevant to this appeal. First, at p. 520, he held that, "[t]he sovereign authority of Canada ends with the sending of the request" for assistance. Second, at pp. 522-23 he found that:

. . . the United States' part of the process was a discrete procedure carried out by authorities who were in no way controlled by or answerable to any Canadian authorities. The fact that the process was initiated by the latter did nothing to make their United States counterparts agents of the Canadian government. Even if they could be so considered, their conduct would not be governed by the Charter unless the Charter expressly said as much.

The implications of Dilks J.'s reasons are that s. 8 of the *Charter* did not apply to the sending of the request, and that those actions which might otherwise have been reviewable under s. 8 were not so reviewable on the facts of the case, because they were undertaken by the U.S. authorities.

L'Heureux-Dubé J., at p. 862, added that her judgment was consistent with the Supreme Court jurisprudence on Canada's international cooperation in criminal investigations and prosecutions, namely: *R. v. Schmidt, supra, Argentina (Republic) v. Mellino, supra*, and *Kindler v. Canada (Minister of Justice), supra*.

Finally, L'Heureux-Dubé J., at p. 863, noted that, in the event of a criminal trial in Canada, s. 7 of the *Charter* may serve as a basis for the exclusion of evidence obtained abroad through foreign officials where excluding the evidence was necessary to preserve the fairness of the trial.

Lamer C.J.C. also allowed the appeal, but on the basis that the respondent did not have a reasonable expectation of privacy in his banking records and thus he could not benefit from s. 8 protection, at p. 853.

The principal reason given by Lamer C.J.C. for the lack of a privacy interest in this case was that the banking records were located in Switzerland and obtained in a manner consistent with the law of that country, at pp. 856-857:

[22] . . . Of critical importance to this case is the fact that the records were located in Switzerland, and obtained in a manner consistent with Swiss law.

[23] In *Terry, supra*, McLachlin J. stated that "[p]eople should reasonably expect to be governed by the laws of the state in which they currently abide, not those of the state in which they formerly resided or continue to maintain a principal residence" (para. 24). This rule means that a Canadian residing in a foreign country should expect his or her privacy to be governed by the laws of that country and, as such, a reasonable expectation of privacy will generally correspond to the degree of protection those laws provide. This, if anything, is more true for the person who decides to conduct financial affairs and keep records in a foreign state. It may be fairly assumed that such a person has made an informed choice about where to conduct business, and thereby to create corresponding records, particularly banking records. The state of the prevailing bank secrecy laws in foreign countries is among the considerations a reasonably prudent bank client will take into account in deciding where to conduct his or her affairs. Accordingly, such a client, in my view, cannot reasonably expect greater privacy protection than is provided under the very laws he or she has expressly decided to have applied to his or her financial affairs and create the corresponding records. In short, having sought the benefit of foreign laws in choosing to place his or her funds under the jurisdiction of a foreign state, the client must also accept the burden.

Lamer C.J.C. concluded as follows, at pp. 857-858:

[25] On the facts of this case, therefore, a search carried out by foreign authorities, in a foreign country, in accordance with foreign law does not infringe a person's reasonable expectation of privacy, as he or she cannot reasonably expect more privacy than he or she is entitled to under that foreign law. In the case at bar, there is no evidence that the respondent's records were seized illegally in Switzerland.

Accordingly, the sending of a mutual legal assistance request abroad is not subject to the s. 8 *Charter* requirements of a domestic search warrant application.

INDEX